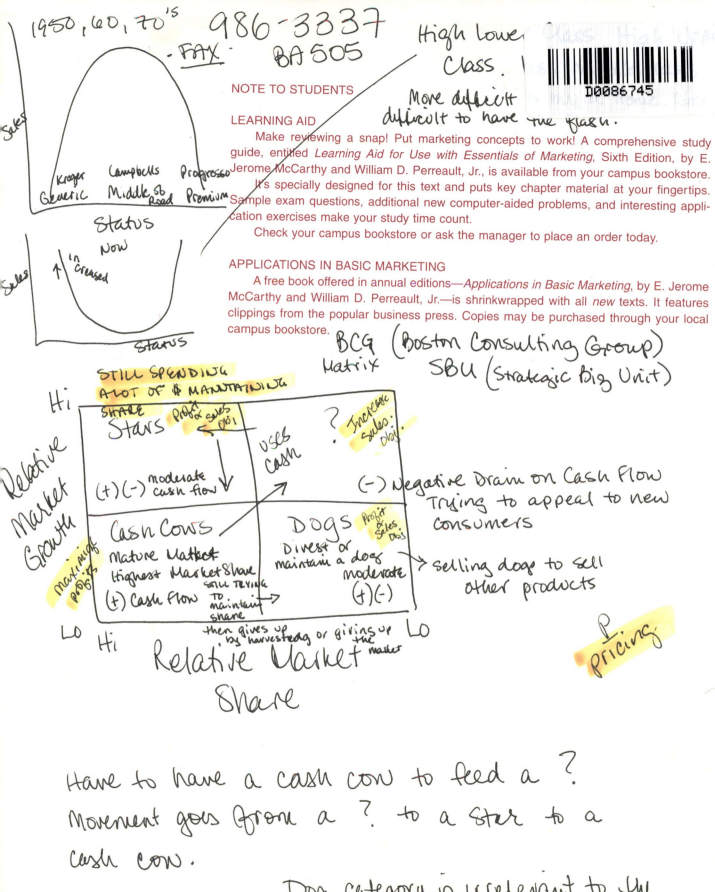

1950, 60, 70's 986-3337
- FAX - BA 505

High Lower Class.

More difficult difficult to have the flash.

D0086745

Sales

Kroger Campbells Progresso
Generic Middle of Premium
        Road
Status
Now

Sales
↑ increased
Status

NOTE TO STUDENTS

LEARNING AID

Make reviewing a snap! Put marketing concepts to work! A comprehensive study guide, entitled *Learning Aid for Use with Essentials of Marketing*, Sixth Edition, by E. Jerome McCarthy and William D. Perreault, Jr., is available from your campus bookstore. It's specially designed for this text and puts key chapter material at your fingertips. Sample exam questions, additional new computer-aided problems, and interesting application exercises make your study time count.

Check your campus bookstore or ask the manager to place an order today.

APPLICATIONS IN BASIC MARKETING

A free book offered in annual editions—*Applications in Basic Marketing*, by E. Jerome McCarthy and William D. Perreault, Jr.—is shrinkwrapped with all *new* texts. It features clippings from the popular business press. Copies may be purchased through your local campus bookstore.

BCG (Boston Consulting Group)
Matrix   SBU (Strategic Big Unit)

STILL SPENDING ALOT OF $ MAINTAINING SHARE

Hi

Relative Market Growth

Stars   Profit or sales - Obi?

? Increase sales - Obi.

(+)(−) moderate cash flow

Uses cash

(−) Negative Drain on Cash Flow Trying to appeal to new consumers

Cash Cows
Mature Market
Highest Market Share
(+) Cash Flow   STILL TRYING TO maintain share

maximize profits

DOGS   Profit or sales Obi.
Divest or maintain a dog
moderate
(+)(−)

→ selling dogs to sell other products

then gives up by harvesting or giving up the market

LO Hi

Relative Market Share

LO

pricing

Have to have a cash cow to feed a ?
Movement goes from a ? to a Star to a cash cow.

Dog category is irrelevant to the success sequence.

Product Positioning - Where consumers place the product in their mind relative to competitors products. Big K vs. Coke

Market Segmentation - people view differently so marketing is different.

Product Positioning Map - Generated thru similarities data. 20 index cards of different brands. Which are most alike. Which one is next. All the way through. Gives you the most distant brands.

Axis are unlabled to begin with.
Then labled based on values.

X = high sugar content to low left to right
Y = sugar content low to high up to down

Circles stand for markets and size of markets based on consumer research

To move to a market, change the product or the products image. Change one of the 4 P's.

Promotion

People that buy are different in the different stages.

The person that paid $1500 for a CD player were is different from a person who bought for $500

Innovators - The first + eager to try a new product or idea. Risk takers. Well educated. Smalle percent of the market.

Early Adopters - or Opinion leaders. well respected by peers. The most important group to sell to. Well read about particular products. They are the informers. A small group of people.

Early Majority - Avoid buying new products. Wait to see what the O.P.L. buys. More deliberate about their purchases.

Late Majority

Laggards - The very last group. Prefer to do things as they always have. Why change.

Sales of adoption

Market Intro

Market Growth

Market Maturity

Market Decline

TIME

Essentials of Marketing
A Global-Managerial Approach

Firm sends Ad
to consumers

by way of
Opinion Leaders

Sends to masses

Two Step Flow
& Communication or Multi Flow

This is why the opinion
leaders are such an
important group to
sell to.

Much less a

The non adopters

encoding (pictures, sound,
smells, endorsers)
M. Jordan

Sender → Media → Receiver

Communication
Model /
Process

decoding

① Problem   Feed back / messag channel
Receiver + Sender
have different perceptions
+ sometimes the signal
is misinterpreted

② Noise detracts
~~dist~~ the messag
from getting to the
receiver. Channel surfing.

THE IRWIN SERIES IN MARKETING

Gilbert A. Churchill, Jr., Consulting Editor
University of Wisconsin, Madison

About the Authors

of Essentials of Marketing, Sixth Edition

E. Jerome McCarthy received his Ph.D. from the University of Minnesota in 1958. Since then he has taught at the Universities of Oregon, Notre Dame, and Michigan State. He has been deeply involved in teaching and developing new teaching materials. Besides writing various articles and monographs, he is the author of textbooks on data processing and social issues in marketing.

Dr. McCarthy is active in making presentations to academic conferences and business meetings. He has worked with groups of teachers throughout the country and has addressed international conferences in South America, Africa, and India.

Dr. McCarthy received the American Marketing Association's Trailblazer Award in 1987, and he was voted one of the "top five" leaders in Marketing Thought by marketing educators. He was also a Ford Foundation Fellow in 1963–64, studying the role of marketing in global economic development. In 1959–60 he was a Ford Foundation Fellow at the Harvard Business School working on mathematical methods in marketing.

Besides his academic interests, Dr. McCarthy is involved in consulting for, and guiding the growth of, several businesses. He has worked with top managers from Steelcase, Dow Chemical, Dow-Corning, 3M, Bemis, Grupo Industrial Alfa, and many smaller companies. He is director of several organizations. His primary interests, however, are in (1) "converting" students to marketing and marketing strategy planning and (2) preparing teaching materials to help others do the same. This is why he has continued to spend a large part of his time revising and improving marketing texts. This is a continuing process, and this edition incorporates the latest thinking in the field.

William D. Perreault, Jr., received his Ph.D. from the University of North Carolina at Chapel Hill in 1973. He has taught at the University of Georgia and Stanford University. He is currently Kenan Professor at the University of North Carolina Kenan-Flagler Business School. At UNC, he has twice received awards for teaching excellence. In 1987, the Decision Sciences Institute recognized him for innovations in marketing education, and *Ad Week* magazine recently profiled him as one of the "10 best young marketing professors in America."

Dr. Perreault is a well-known author and his ideas about marketing management, marketing research, and marketing education have been published in many journals. He is a past editor of the *Journal of Marketing Research* and has served on the review board of the *Journal of Marketing* and other publications. In 1985, the American Marketing Association recognized his long-run contributions to marketing research with the prestigious William O'Dell Award.

Dr. Perreault has served as vice president and on the board of directors of the AMA, and as chairman of an advisory Committee to the U.S. Bureau of the Census, and he is now a trustee of the Marketing Science Institute. He has worked as a marketing consultant to many organizations, including IBM, Libby-Owens-Ford, Whirlpool, Owens Corning Fiberglas, the Federal Trade Commission, and a variety of wholesale and retail firms. He has served as an advisor evaluating educational programs for the U.S. Department of Education, Venezuelan Ministry of Education, Andenberg Foundation, and American Assembly of Collegiate Schools of Business.

Essentials of Marketing

A Global-Managerial Approach

E. Jerome McCarthy, Ph.D.
Michigan State University

William D. Perreault, Jr., Ph.D.
University of North Carolina

IRWIN

Burr Ridge, Illinois
Boston, Massachusetts
Sydney, Australia

© E. Jerome McCarthy and Associates, Inc., 1979, 1982, 1985, 1988, 1991, and 1994

All rights reserved. No part of this publication may be reproduced, stored in a retrieval system, or transmitted, in any form or by any means, electronic, mechanical, photocopying, recording, or otherwise, without the prior written permission of the copyright holder.

Senior sponsoring editor: Stephen M. Patterson
Coordinating editor: Linda G. Davis
Senior developmental editor: Nancy J. Barbour
Marketing manager: Jim Lewis
Project editor: Ethel Shiell
Senior manager, production: Bob Lange
Interior designer: Maureen McCutcheon
Cover designer: Maureen McCutcheon/Keith J. McPherson
Cover illustration: Greg Ragland
Art coordinator: Mark Malloy
Photo researcher: Michael J. Hruby
Photo research coordinator: Patricia A. Seefelt
Compositor: Carlisle Communications, Ltd.
Typeface: 9/12 Helvetica
Printer: Von Hoffmann Press

Library of Congress Cataloging–in–Publication Data

McCarthy, E. Jerome (Edmund Jerome)
    Essentials of marketing : a global-managerial approach / E. Jerome
McCarthy, William D. Perreault.—6th ed.
        p.   cm. — (Irwin series in marketing)
    Includes bibliographical references and indexes.
    ISBN 0-256-12746-8
    1. Marketing.   I. Perreault, William D.   II. Title.   III. Series
    HF5415.M378 1994   93–29973
    658.8—dc20

Printed in the United States of America

1 2 3 4 5 6 7 8 9 0 VH 0 9 8 7 6 5 4 3

Preface

We're excited about the 6th edition of *Essentials of Marketing*, and we hope you will be as well. This edition introduces a number of important innovations, while simultaneously building on the traditional strengths of the text and all of the supporting materials that accompany it. We planned this revision based on *the most extensive and detailed user feedback we've ever had*. That feedback gave us hundreds of ideas for big and small additions, changes, and improvements. We'll highlight some of those changes in this preface, but first it's useful to put this newest edition in a longer-term perspective.

A shorter text— for flexibility and a crisp pace

Essentials of Marketing is a shortened version of our *Basic Marketing*, the most widely used text in the field. Our basic objectives in preparing a shorter text have always been

- to make it easy, interesting, and fast for students to grasp the *essential* concepts of marketing;
- to provide a flexible text and choices from comprehensive support materials so that instructors can accomplish their objectives for their students even though the time available for the course is limited.

Accessibility is a key goal. In the whole text—and all of the supplements, ranging from the exciting new multimedia laser disk to the Hypertext reference disk—we spent much time and effort carefully defining terms and finding the right words, illustrations, and examples to speed understanding and motivate learning.

Building on pioneering strengths

Basic Marketing and *Essentials of Marketing* pioneered an innovative structure—using the four Ps with a managerial approach—for the introductory marketing course. It has been 34 years since publication of the first edition of *Basic Marketing,* and 15 years since the publication of the first edition of *Essentials of Marketing*. During that time marketing management changed constantly. Some changes were dramatic, others subtle. Throughout all these changes, *Basic Marketing* and *Essentials of Marketing*—and the supporting materials to accompany them—were more widely used than any other teaching materials for introductory marketing. And the four Ps proved to be an organizing structure that worked well for millions of students and teachers.

Continuous innovation and improvement

Of course, this position of leadership is not the result of a single strength—or one long-lasting innovation. With each new edition of *Essentials of Marketing*, we seized the opportunity to introduce innovations—and to better meet the needs of students and faculty. For example, included with the other innovations for this new edition are:

- completely integrated coverage of international issues and marketing ethics—throughout every chapter;

- laser disk technology to support multimedia teaching and learning;
- our Hypertext reference disk.

Further, our belief that attention to continuous quality improvement in every aspect of the text and support materials *does make a difference* is consistently reaffirmed by the enthusiastic response of students and teachers alike.

Critically revised, updated, and rewritten

We believe that the 6th edition of *Essentials of Marketing* is the highest quality teaching and learning resource ever available for the introductory course. The whole text and all of the supporting materials were critically revised, updated, and rewritten. As in past editions, clear and interesting communication was a priority. Careful explanations provide a crisp focus on the important "essentials" of marketing strategy planning. At the same time, we thoroughly:

- researched and introduced new concepts, and
- integrated hundreds of new examples that bring the concepts alive.

Clear focus on changes in today's dynamic markets

The 6th edition focuses special attention on changes taking place in today's dynamic markets. **Throughout every chapter of the text,** we have integrated discussion and examples of

- international perspectives, and
- ethical issues.

Similarly, we also integrated new material on such fast changing topics as

- the expanding role of information technologies in strategy planning,
- total quality management (with special emphasis on customer service quality),
- environmental concerns,
- the increasing channel power of large retail chains,
- just-in-time relationships,
- competitor analysis, and
- direct marketing,

to name but a sampling.

Throughout the 6th edition we continued our thrust from the 5th edition of focusing more attention on the importance of competitive advantage in strategy planning. You'll learn about the changing relationships among marketing partners—ranging from coordination of logistics efforts among firms to the new relationships between firms and their ad agencies. You'll see how intense competition—both in the United States and around the world—is affecting marketing strategy planning. You'll see why rapid response in new product development is so critical.

Some other marketing texts attempted to describe such changes. But what sets *Essentials of Marketing* apart is that the explanations and examples not only highlight the changes taking place today, but also equip students to see *why* these changes are taking place—and what changes to expect in the future. That is an important distinction—because marketing is dynamic. Our objective is to equip students to analyze marketing situations and develop workable marketing strategies—not just recite some list of terms or ideas.

A fresh design—to make important concepts even clearer

Along with the new content, we gave the text a fresh design. The changes range from the new cover to all-new artwork and illustrations. By using the latest advances in computer-aided design, we were able to research and evaluate hundreds of combinations of design elements—to arrive at an overall redesign that makes important concepts and points even clearer to students.

The aim of all this revising, refining, editing, and illustrating was to make sure that each student really does get a good feel for a market-directed system and how he or she can help it—and some company—run better. We believe marketing is important and interesting—and we want every student who reads *Essentials of Marketing* to share our enthusiasm.

18 chapters—with an emphasis on marketing strategy planning

The emphasis of *Essentials of Marketing* is on marketing strategy planning. Eighteen chapters introduce the important concepts in marketing management and help the student see marketing through the eyes of the marketing manager. The organization of the chapters and topics was carefully planned. But we took special care in writing so that it is possible to rearrange and use the chapters in many different sequences—to fit different needs.

The first two chapters deal with the nature of marketing—focusing both on its macro role in a global society and its micro role in businesses and other organizations. The first chapter stresses that the effectiveness of our macro-marketing system depends on the decisions of many producers and consumers. That sets the stage for the second chapter—and the rest of the book—which focuses on how businesspeople and, in particular, marketing managers develop marketing strategies to satisfy specific target markets.

Chapter 3 introduces a strategic planning view of how managers can find new market opportunities. The emphasis is on identifying target markets with market segmentation and positioning approaches. This strategic view alerts students to the importance of evaluating opportunities in the external environments affecting marketing—and these are discussed in Chapter 4. Chapter 5 is a contemporary view of getting information—from marketing information systems and marketing research—for marketing management planning.

The next two chapters take a closer look at customers so students will better understand how to segment markets and satisfy target market needs. Chapter 6 introduces the behavior dimensions of the consumer market, and Chapter 7 explains how business and organizational customers—like manufacturers, channel members, and government purchasers—are similar to and different from final consumers.

The next group of chapters—Chapters 8 to 17—is concerned with developing a marketing mix out of the four Ps: Product, Place (involving channels of distribution, logistics, and distribution customer service), Promotion, and Price. These chapters are concerned with developing the "right" Product and making it available at the "right" Place with the "right" Promotion and the "right" Price—to satisfy target customers and still meet the objectives of the business. These chapters are presented in an integrated, analytical way so students' thinking about planning marketing strategies develops logically.

The final chapter considers how efficient the marketing process is. Here we evaluate the effectiveness of both micro- and macro-marketing—and consider the competitive, quality management, ethical, and social challenges facing marketing managers now and in the future. After this chapter, the student might want to look at Appendix C—which is about career opportunities in marketing.

Careful integration of special topics

Some textbooks treat "special" topics—like environmental concerns, services marketing, marketing for nonprofit organizations, international marketing, marketing ethics, and business to business marketing—in separate chapters. We have not done this because we are convinced that treating such topics separately leads to an unfortunate compartmentalization of ideas. We think they are **too important to be isolated in that way.** Instead, they are interwoven and illustrated throughout the text to emphasize that marketing thinking is crucial in all aspects of our society and economy. Instructor examination copies of the new edition are packaged with a grid that shows, in detail, how and where specific topics are integrated throughout the text.

Students get how-to-do-it skill and confidence

Really understanding marketing and how to plan marketing strategies can build self-confidence—and it can help prepare a student to take an active part in the business world. To move students in this direction, we deliberately include a variety of frameworks, models, classification systems, and how-to-do-it techniques that should speed the development of marketing sense—and enable the student to analyze marketing situations in a confident and meaningful way. Taken seriously, they are practical and they work. In addition, because they are interesting and understandable, they equip students to see marketing as the challenging and rewarding area it is.

Essentials motivates real learning

So students will see what is coming in each *Essentials of Marketing* chapter, behavioral objectives are included on the first page of each chapter. And to speed student understanding, important new terms are shown in red and defined immediately. Further, a glossary of these terms is presented at the end of the book. Within chapters, major section headings and second-level headings (placed in the margin for clarity) immediately show how the material is organized *and* summarize key points in the text. Further, we placed annotated photos and ads near the concepts they illustrate to provide a visual reminder of the ideas—and to show vividly how they apply in the business world. All of these aids help the student understand important concepts—and speed review before exams. End-of-chapter questions and problems offer additional opportunities and encourage students to investigate the marketing process and develop their own ways of thinking about it. They can be used for independent study or as a basis for written assignments or class discussion.

Varied types of cases

Understanding of the text material can be deepened by analysis and discussion of specific cases. *Essentials of Marketing* features several different types of cases. Each chapter starts with an in-depth case study developed specifically to highlight that chapter's teaching objectives. In addition, each chapter features a special case report in a highlighted box. Each case illustrates how a particular company developed its marketing strategy—with emphasis on a topic covered in that chapter. All of these cases provide an excellent basis for critical evaluation and discussion.

In addition, there are several suggested cases at the end of each chapter. These cases focus on problem solving. They encourage students to apply—and really get involved with—the concepts developed in the text. Each chapter also features a computer-aided problem. These case-based exercises stimulate a problem-solving approach to marketing strategy planning—and give students hands-on experience that shows how logical analysis of alternative strategies can lead to improved decision making. For the convenience of students and faculty alike, with this edition the computer-aided problems are incorporated in the book itself. Further, the award-winning software we developed specifically for use with these problems is provided free to instructors.

Some professors and students want to follow up on text readings. Each chapter is supplemented with detailed references—to both classic articles and current readings in business publications. These can guide more detailed study of the topics covered in a chapter.

Instructor creates a system—with our P.L.U.S.

Essentials of Marketing can be studied and used in many ways—the *Essentials of Marketing* text material is only the central component of a *Professional Learning Units Systems* (our P.L.U.S.) for students and teachers. Instructors can select from our units to develop their own personalized systems. Many combinations of units are possible—

depending on course objectives. As a quick overview, in addition to the *Essentials of Marketing* text, the P.L.U.S. package includes:

- *Learning Aid for use with Essentials of Marketing*
- *Essentials of Marketing Hypertext Reference Disks*
- *Essentials of Marketing Laser Disk*
- *Color Acetates to accompany Essentials of Marketing* (225)
- *Overhead Masters to accompany Essentials of Marketing* (240)
- *Computer-Aided Problems* software
- *Lecture Guide to accompany Essentials of Marketing* and accompanying disk
- *Instructor's Manual to accompany Essentials of Marketing*
- *Manual of Tests to accompany Essentials of Marketing*
- *Computest III* test-generator system (and Teletest)
- *Teaching Videos to accompany Essentials of Marketing,* 20 new (and Instructor's Manual)
- *The Marketing Game!* (and Instructor's Manual)
- *Applications in Essentials of Marketing,* an annually updated set of marketing clippings from the popular press, free and shrinkwrapped with the text.

Hypertext—a marketing knowledge navigator

With this edition of *Essentials of Marketing* we introduce an innovative new teaching/learning unit: the *Essentials of Marketing Hypertext Reference Disks*. This easy-to-use software puts almost all of the key concepts from *Essentials of Marketing* at your fingertips. It features hyperlinks, which means that when you are reading about a concept on screen you can instantly jump to more detail on any topic. You simply highlight the concept or topic and click with a mouse or press the enter key. Books assemble information in some specific order—but hypertext allows you to integrate thinking on any topic or combination of topics, regardless of where it is treated in the text. The software can also be used to review topics in "book order"—starting with learning objectives and then "paging" through each set of ideas. We are convinced that this newest addition to the P.L.U.S. package is a step toward reshaping how people learn about and use marketing concepts. It brings new technology to making the concepts in *Essentials of Marketing* even more accessible.

Free applications book—updated each year

It is a sign of the commitment of our publisher to the introductory marketing course that it will publish a new edition of *Applications in Basic Marketing* every year, and provide it free of charge shrinkwrapped with each new copy of the 6th edition of *Essentials of Marketing! This annually updated collection of marketing clippings—from publications such as The Wall Street Journal, Fortune,* and *Business Week*—provides convenient access to short, interesting, and current discussions of marketing issues. The 1993–1994 edition features over more than 100 new articles. There are a variety of short clippings related to each chapter in *Essentials of Marketing*. In addition, because we revise this collection *each year,* it can include timely material that is available in no other text.

Learning Aid—deepens understanding

There are more components to *P.L.U.S.* A separate *Learning Aid* provides several more units and offers further opportunities to obtain a deeper understanding of the material. The *Learning Aid* can be used by the student alone or with teacher direction. Portions of the *Learning Aid* help students to review what they have studied. For example, there is a brief introduction to each chapter, a list of the important new terms (with page numbers for easy reference), true-false questions (with answers and page numbers) that cover *all* the important terms and concepts, and multiple-choice questions (with answers) illustrating the kinds of questions that may appear in examinations. In addition, the *Learning Aid* has cases, exercises, and problems—with clear instructions and worksheets for the student to complete. The *Learning Aid* also features computer-aided problems that build on the computer-aided cases in the text. The *Learning Aid* exercises can be used as classwork or homework—to drill on certain topics and to deepen understanding of others by motivating application and then discussion. In fact, reading *Essentials of Marketing* and working with the *Learning Aid* can be the basic activity of the course.

Compete and learn—with *The Marketing Game!*

Another element is *The Marketing Game! The Marketing Game!* is a microcomputer-based competitive simulation. It was developed specifically to reinforce the target marketing and marketing strategy planning ideas discussed in *Essentials of Marketing*. Students make marketing management decisions—blending the four Ps to compete for the business of different possible target markets. The innovative design of *The Marketing Game!* allows the instructor to increase the number of decision areas involved as students learn more about marketing. In fact, many instructors use the advanced levels of the game as the basis for a second course.

Support for in-class lectures and discussion

Essentials of Marketing—and all of our accompanying materials—were developed to promote student learning and get students involved in the excitement and challenges of marketing management. Additional elements of *P.L.U.S.* were specifically developed to help an instructor offer a truly professional course that meets the objectives he or she sets for students. Complete Instructor's Manuals accompany all of the P.L.U.S. components. A separate *Lecture Guide to Accompany Essentials of Marketing*—newly revised and updated for this edition—offers a rich selection of lecture material and ideas. Lecture outlines and other key material from the *Lecture Guide* are also available on computer disk—to make it easier for instructors to incorporate their own materials.

In addition, the *Lecture Guide* is accompanied by a high-quality selection of overhead masters and color transparencies—over 470 in all. The *Lecture Guide* provides detailed suggestions about ways to use them.

Exciting new videos—created by marketing experts

The newly revised and expanded *Essentials of Marketing Videos* are also available to all schools that adopt *Essentials of Marketing*. Ten video modules are completely new—based on scripts written by expert scholars and carefully linked to key topics in the text. In addition, 10 of the most popular video modules from the previous edition—the ones you said you most wanted to keep—were thoroughly revised and updated. The new videos are really great, but it doesn't stop there!

Laser disks—for multimedia teaching and learning

New with this edition, we are also introducing *Essentials of Marketing Laser Disks*, which provide exciting new opportunities for marketing faculty and students alike to take advantage of the latest advances in multimedia teaching and learning. Our laser disk system provides easy and instantaneous access not only to the video modules but also to hundreds of full-color illustrations, charts, graphs, and exhibits.

Testing that works for faculty and students

In addition, thousands of objective test questions—written by the authors to really work with the text—give instructors a high-quality resource. The Computest III program for microcomputers allows the instructor to select from any of these questions, change them as desired, or add new questions—and quickly print out a finished test customized to the instructor's course.

The responsibilities of leadership

In closing, we return to a point raised at the beginning of this preface. *Essentials of Marketing* has been a leading textbook in marketing since its first edition. We take the responsibilities of that leadership seriously. We know that you want and deserve the very best teaching and learning materials possible. It is our commitment to bring you those materials—today with this edition and in the future with subsequent editions. We recognize that fulfilling this commitment requires a process of continuous improvement. Improvements, changes, and development of new elements must be ongoing—because needs change. You are an important part of this evolution, of this leadership. We encourage your feedback. Thoughtful criticisms and suggestions from students and teachers alike helped to make *Essentials of Marketing* what it is. We hope that you will help make it what it will be in the future.

E. Jerome McCarthy
William D. Perreault, Jr.

Acknowledgments

Planning and preparing this revision of *Essentials of Marketing* has been a consuming, three-year effort. The resulting text—and all of the teaching and learning materials that accompany it—represents a blending of our career-long experiences, influenced and improved by the contributions of more people than it is possible to list.

We are especially grateful to our many students who have criticized and made comments about materials in *Essentials of Marketing*. Indeed, in many ways, our students have been our best teachers.

Many improvements in the current edition were stimulated by feedback from a number of colleagues around the country. Feedback took many forms. We received valuable insights—and hundreds of detailed suggestions—from professors who kept class-by-class diaries while teaching from *Essentials of Marketing* or *Basic Marketing*. Participants in focus group interviews shared their in-depth ideas about ways to improve teaching and materials used in the first marketing course. Professors who provided comprehensive comparative reviews helped us see ways to build on our strengths and identify where improvements would be most helpful to students and faculty. And responses to detailed surveys gave us ideas and insights for ways to update and improve not only the text but also the whole set of teaching and learning materials that accompany it. For all of these suggestions and criticisms we are most appreciative. In particular, we would like to recognize the helpful contributions of:

James J. Alling, Augusta Technical Institute

Raj Arora, University of Missouri—Kansas City

Ramon A. Avila, Ball State University

Thomas J. Babb, West Liberty State College

Angelos C. Ballas, West Chester University

Jeffrey Baum, SUNY Oneonta

Dan Bello, Georgia State University

Neil C. Bennett, Commonwealth College

Marcell Berard, Community College of Rhode Island

John Bladel, Florida Community College—Kent Campus

Betsy Boze, University of Alaska—Anchorage

Carl S. Bozman, Gonzaga University

Monica Breidenbach, DeVry Institute—Kansas City

Carter Broach, University of Delaware

Jim Burley, Central Michigan University

Lawrence J. Chase, Tompkins Cortland Community College

Pravat K. Choudhury, Howard University

Gene Conyers, North Georgia College

Robert L. Cook, Central Michigan University

Susan Cremins, Iona College

Hugh Daubek, Purdue University Calumet

Linda M. Delene, Western Michigan University

Vincent Deni, Oakland Community College

Ann Devine, Alverno College

John R. Doneth, Ferris State University

Larry Downs, Nichols College

Gary Ernst, North Central College

P. Everett Fergenson, Iona College

Charles W. Ford, Arkansas State University

Frank Franzak, Virginia Commonwealth University

David W. Glascoff, East Carolina University

Marc H. Goldberg, Portland State University

Edward Golden, Central Washington University

James S. Gould, Pace University

Matthew Gross, Moraine Valley Community College

Robert F. Gwinner, Arizona State University

Larry A. Haase, Central Missouri State University

Rolf Hackmann, Western Illinois University

Robert Harmon, Portland State University

Susan E. Heckler, University of Arizona

Thomas J. Hickey, SUNY Oswego

William Hickman, Utica College

Thomas Hitzelberger, Southern Oregon State College

George Hruby, University of Akron—Wayne College

William Johnson, Northeast Wisconsin Technical College

Vaughan C. Judd, Auburn University at Montgomery

L. Lynn Judd, California State University—San Bernardino

Chris Kanolis, Indiana Vocational Technical College—Hammond

Joan Kaufman, Metropolitan Business College

Jerry Kirkpatrick, California State Polytechnic University—Pomona

Brenda Konrad, University of San Diego

Pradeep Korgaonkar, Florida Atlantic University

Kathleen A. Krentner, San Diego State University

William F. Krumske, Jr., Illinois Institute of Technology

J. Ford Laumer, Jr., Auburn University

John Lavin, Waukesha County Technical College

Deborah H. Lester, Kennesaw State College

Frank M. Marion, Christian Brothers University

Kimball P. Marshall, Aurora University

Ed J. Mayo, Western Michigan University

H. B. McIntire, Mesa State College

Sandra L. McKee, DeVry Institute of Technology—Decatur

Eliseo Melendez, SUNY Maritime

John Milewicz, Jacksonville State University

M. Alan Miller, Tennessee State University

Thomas A. Myers, Piedmont Virginia Community College

Margaret C. Nelson, SUNY Albany

Esther S. Page-Wood, Western Michigan University

Eric R. Pratt, New Mexico State University

Paul D. Ricker, Broward Community College—North

Gary Rieman, City College of San Francisco

Phillip Schary, Oregon State University

Greg Schneider, Waukesha County Technical College

John A. Schibrowsky, University of Nevada—Las Vegas

Jack Schoenfelder, Indiana Vocational Technical College—Valparaiso

Jack Sheeks, Broward
   Community College
   Central
Vernon Stauble,
   California State
   Polytechnic
   University—Pomona
Jack L. Taylor,
   Portland State
   University
Hale N. Tongren,
   George Mason
   University

Gary Walk, Lima
   Technical College
Kathy Walton, Salt
   Lake Community
   College
Don Weinrauch,
   Tennessee Tech
   University
D. Joel Whalen,
   De Paul University
William F. Whitbeck,
   Old Dominion
   University

Tim Wilson, Clarion
   University
Linda Withrow, St.
   Ambrose University
William Wynd, Eastern
   Washington
   University
Curtis Youngman, Salt
   Lake Community
   College

Paul Rizzo's insights on the challenges of international marketing and on business ethics had a profound effect on the integration of these topics throughout the text. Similarly, Kent Pinney's detailed, chapter-by-chapter suggestions on international issues were a valuable aid. Thought-provoking reviews of a previous edition provided by William R. George and Barbara A. McCuen have had an ongoing influence in shaping this edition.

Faculty and students at our current and past academic institutions—Michigan State University, University of North Carolina, Notre Dame, University of Georgia, Northwestern University, University of Oregon, University of Minnesota, and Stanford University—have significantly shaped the book. Faculty at Notre Dame had a profound effect when the first editions of the book were developed. Professor Yusaku Furuhashi had a continuing impact on the multinational emphasis over many editions. Similarly, Professor Andrew A. Brogowicz of Western Michigan University contributed many fine ideas. Charlotte Mason and Nicholas Didow have provided a constant flow of helpful suggestions.

The designers, artists, editors, and production people at Richard D. Irwin, Inc., who worked with us on this edition warrant special recognition. All of them have shared our commitment to excellence and brought their own individual creativity to the project. Charlie Hess's can-do leadership and creative problem-solving skills bring a new standard to rapid-response production and manufacturing—which is what it takes to be certain that teachers and students get the most current information possible. Ethel Shiell's good nature and command of all the details involved in assembling the whole project make a zero-defects goal achievable. Bob Lange and Jane Lightell added value at every step of the production and editing process. Keith McPherson, Kim Meriwether, and Maureen McCutcheon contributed creative new art and design. Similarly, Mike Hruby tracked down permissions for photos and ads we wanted to illustrate important ideas. Jeff Sund, Bill Setten, and John Black consistently found time in their busy executive schedules to share their publishing insights and experience—and also gave us crucial top-management support for our objective of continuous improvement. Rob Zwettler and Jerry Saykes provided good-natured prods and great advice (along with occasional therapy!). Nancy Barbour's contributions as developmental editor have been exemplary—and her warm support and friendship have made all the work fun. Steve Patterson's energy, vision, and dedication redefine the role of senior sponsoring editor. He's a tough task-master and at the same time a role model in caring about the quality of every decision that might affect how well the book and supporting materials work for students and teachers alike.

We owe a special debt of gratitude to Linda G. Davis. As with previous editions, she made contributions in every aspect of the text and package. She provided valuable help in researching photos and case histories, and she critiqued thousands of manuscript pages through countless revisions of the text and all the accompanying materials. Her hard work and dedication to quality throughout the whole process is without match. She also demonstrated her wizardry with desktop publishing in preparing camera-ready copy on all of the supplements. We could not have done it without her, nor could we have asked for better support.

Our families have been patient and consistent supporters through all phases in developing *Essentials of Marketing*. The support has been direct and substantive. Joanne McCarthy and Pam Perreault provided invaluable editorial assistance—and many fresh ideas through each draft and revision. The quality of their inputs is matched only by their energy and enthusiasm about the book. Carol McCarthy helped research and reorient the "Career Planning in Marketing" appendix—reflecting her needs and experiences as a college student looking for a career in advertising. Young kids make some special sacrifices when parents are working on a project of this scope, but through it all Suzanne and Will Perreault were great supporters; in fact, the revision of the last element of the package was nearly complete when they stopped accepting candy from their Dad!

We are indebted to all the firms that allowed us to reproduce their proprietary materials here. Similarly, we are grateful to associates from our business experiences who have shared their perspectives and feedback, and enhanced our sensitivity to the key challenges of marketing management.

A textbook must capsulize existing knowledge while bringing new perspectives and organization to enhance it. Our thinking has been shaped by the writings of literally thousands of marketing scholars and practitioners. In some cases it is impossible to give unique credit for a particular idea or concept because so many people have played important roles in anticipating, suggesting, shaping, and developing it. We gratefully acknowledge these contributors—from the early thought-leaders to contemporary authors—who have shared their creative ideas. We respect their impact on the development of marketing and more specifically this book.

To all of these persons—and to the many publishers who graciously granted permission to use their materials—we are deeply grateful. Responsibilities for any errors or omissions is certainly ours, but the book would not have been possible without the assistance of many others. Our sincere appreciation goes to everyone who helped in their own special way.

E. J. M.
W. D. P.

Contents

Essentials of Marketing

A Global-Managerial Approach

Marketing's Role in the Global Economy

When You Finish This Chapter, You Should

❶

Know what marketing is and why you should learn about it.

❷

Understand the difference between micro-marketing and macro-marketing.

❸

Know why and how macro-marketing systems develop.

❹

Understand why marketing is crucial to economic development and our global economy.

❺

Know why marketing specialists—including middlemen and facilitators—develop.

❻

Know the marketing functions and who performs them.

❼

Understand the important new terms (shown in red).

Marketing — Any activity resulting in which results in an exchange of goods and services.

When it's time to roll out of bed in the morning, does your General Electric alarm wake you with a buzzer—or by playing your favorite radio station? Is the station playing rock, classical, or country music—or perhaps a Red Cross ad asking you to contribute blood? Will you slip into your Levi jeans, your shirt from L. L. Bean, and your Nikes, or does the day call for your Brooks Brothers suit? Will breakfast be Lender's Bagels with cream cheese or Post Raisin Bran cereal—made with grain from America's heartland—or some extra large eggs and Oscar Mayer bacon cooked in a Panasonic microwave imported from Japan? Will you drink decaffeinated Maxwell House coffee—grown in Colombia—or some Tang instant juice? Maybe you're late and an Egg McMuffin from the McDonald's drive-thru would be convenient. When you leave home, will it be in a Honda car, on a Huffy bike, or on the bus that the city bought from General Motors?

When you think about it, you can't get very far into a day without bumping into marketing—and what the whole marketing system does for you. It affects every aspect of our lives—often in ways we don't even consider.

In other parts of the world people wake up each day to different kinds of experiences. A family in China may have little choice about what food they will eat or where their clothing will come from. A farmer in the mountains of Jamaica may awake in a barren hut with little more than the hope of raising enough to survive. A person in a large city like Tokyo may have many choices but not be familiar with products that have names like Maxwell House, General Motors, and Oscar Mayer.

What explains these differences, and what do they have to do with marketing? In this chapter, we'll answer questions like these. You'll see what marketing is all about and why it's important to you. We'll also explore how marketing affects the quality of life in different societies, and why it is so crucial to economic development and our global economy.

MARKETING—WHAT'S IT ALL ABOUT?

Marketing is more than selling or advertising

If forced to define marketing, most people, including some business managers, say that marketing means "selling" or "advertising." It's true that these are parts of marketing. But *marketing is much more than selling and advertising.*

How did all those tennis rackets get here?

To illustrate some of the other important things that are included in marketing, think about all the tennis rackets being swung with varying degrees of accuracy by tennis players around the world. Most of us weren't born with a tennis racket in our hands. Nor do we make our own tennis rackets. Instead, they are made by firms like Wilson, Dunlop, Kennex, Head, and Yonex.

Most tennis rackets are intended to do the same thing—hit the ball over the net. But a tennis player can choose from a wide assortment of rackets. There are different shapes, materials, weights, handle sizes, and types of strings. You can buy a prestrung racket for less than $15. Or you can spend more than $250 just for a frame!

This variety in sizes and materials complicates the production and sale of tennis rackets. The following list shows some of the many things a firm should do before and after it decides to produce tennis rackets.

1. Analyze the needs of people who play tennis and decide if consumers want more or different tennis rackets.
2. Predict what types of rackets—handle sizes, shapes, weights, and materials—different players will want and decide which of these people the firm will try to satisfy.
3. Estimate how many of these people will want to buy tennis rackets, and when.
4. Determine where in the world these tennis players will be—and how to get the firm's rackets to them.
5. Estimate what price they are willing to pay for their rackets—and if the firm can make a profit selling at that price.

All tennis rackets can hit the ball over the net—but there are many variations to meet the needs of different people.

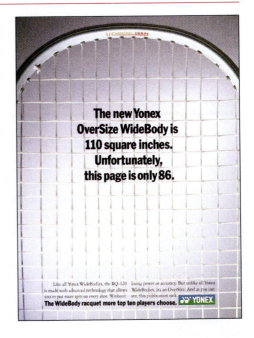

6. Decide which kinds of promotion should be used to tell potential customers about the firm's tennis rackets.

7. Estimate how many competing companies will be making tennis rackets, how many rackets they'll produce, what kind, and at what prices.

The above activities are not part of **production**—actually making goods or performing services. Rather, they are part of a larger process—called *marketing*—that provides needed direction for production and helps make sure that the right goods and services are produced and find their way to consumers.

Our tennis racket example shows that marketing includes much more than selling or advertising. We'll describe marketing activities in the next chapter. And you'll learn much more about them before you finish this book. For now, it's enough to see that marketing plays an essential role in providing consumers with need-satisfying goods and services.

HOW MARKETING RELATES TO PRODUCTION

Production is a very important economic activity. Most people don't make most of the products they use. Picture yourself, for example, building a 10-speed bicycle or a digital watch—starting from scratch! We also turn to others to produce services—like health care, air transportation, and entertainment. Clearly, the high standard of living that most people in advanced economies enjoy is made possible by specialized production.

Tennis rackets, like mousetraps, don't sell themselves

Although production is a necessary economic activity, some people overrate its importance in relation to marketing. Their attitude is reflected in the old saying: "Make a better mousetrap and the world will beat a path to your door." In other words, they think that if you just have a good product, your business will be a success.

The "better mousetrap" idea probably wasn't true in Grandpa's time, and it certainly isn't true today. In modern economies, the grass grows high on the path to the Better Mousetrap Factory if the new mousetrap is not properly marketed.

Production and marketing are *both* important parts of a total business system aimed at providing consumers with need-satisfying goods and services. Together, production and marketing supply five kinds of economic utility—form, task, time, place, and possession utility—that are needed to provide consumer satisfaction. Here, **utility** means the power to satisfy human needs. See Exhibit 1–1.

Exhibit 1–1   Types of Utility and How They Are Provided

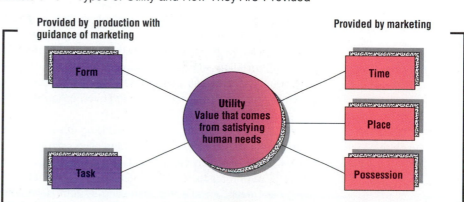

Tennis rackets do not automatically provide utility

Form utility is provided when someone produces something tangible—for instance, a tennis racket. **Task utility** is provided when someone performs a task for someone else—for instance, when a bank handles financial transactions. But just producing tennis rackets or handling bank accounts doesn't result in consumer satisfaction. The product must be something that consumers want, or there is no need to be satisfied—and no utility.

This is how marketing thinking guides the production side of business. Marketing decisions focus on the customer and include decisions about what goods and services to produce. It doesn't make sense to provide goods and services consumers don't want when there are so many things they do want. Marketing is concerned with what customers want—and it should guide what is produced and offered. This is an important idea that we will develop more completely later.

Even when marketing and production combine to provide form or task utility, consumers won't be satisfied until possession, time, and place utility are also provided. **Possession utility** means obtaining a good or service and having the right to use or consume it. Customers usually exchange money or something else of value for possession utility. **Time utility** means having the product available *when* the customer wants it. And **place utility** means having the product available *where* the customer wants it. Tennis rackets that stay at a factory don't do anyone any good. Time and place utility are very important for services too. For example, neighborhood emergency-care health clinics have recently become very popular. People just walk in as soon as they feel sick, not a day later when their doctor can schedule an appointment.

Later in this chapter we'll look at *how* marketing provides utility. First, we want to discuss why you should study marketing, and then we'll define marketing.

MARKETING IS IMPORTANT TO YOU

Marketing is important to every consumer

As a consumer, you pay for the cost of marketing activities. In advanced economies, marketing costs about 50 cents of each consumer dollar. For some goods and services, the percentage is much higher.

Marketing affects almost every aspect of your daily life. All the goods and services you buy, the stores where you shop, and the radio and TV programs paid for by advertising are there because of marketing. Even your job résumé is part of a marketing campaign to sell yourself to some employer! Some courses are interesting when you take them but never relevant again once they're over. Not so with marketing—you'll be a consumer dealing with marketing for the rest of your life.

Marketing will be important to your job

Still another reason for studying marketing is that there are many exciting and rewarding career opportunities in marketing. Throughout this book you will find information about opportunities in different areas of marketing. And Appendix C is all about career planning in marketing. Even if you're aiming for a nonmarketing job, knowing about marketing will help you do your own job better. Marketing is important to the success of every organization—including nonprofit organizations. The same basic marketing principles that firms use are also used to sell ideas, politicians, mass transportation, health-care services, conservation, museums, and even colleges.[1]

Marketing affects economic growth

An even more basic reason for studying marketing is that marketing plays a big part in economic growth and development. Marketing stimulates research and new ideas—resulting in new goods and services. Marketing gives customers a choice among products. If these products satisfy customers, fuller employment, higher incomes, and a higher standard of living can result. An effective marketing system is important to the future of all nations.[2]

Marketing stimulates product improvement and gives customers a choice.

HOW SHOULD WE DEFINE MARKETING?

Micro- or macro-marketing?

In our tennis racket example, we saw that a producer of tennis rackets has to perform many customer-related activities besides just making rackets. The same is true for an insurance company, an art museum, or a family-service agency. This supports the idea of marketing as a set of activities done by individual organizations.

On the other hand, people can't live on tennis rackets and art museums alone! In advanced economies, it takes thousands of goods and services to satisfy the many needs of society. A society needs some sort of marketing system to organize the efforts of all the producers and middlemen needed to satisfy the varied needs of all its citizens. So marketing is also an important social process.

Marketing is both a set of activities performed by organizations and a social process. In other words, marketing exists at both the micro and macro levels. Therefore, we will use two definitions of marketing—one for micro-marketing and another for macro-marketing. The first looks at customers and the organizations that serve them. The second takes a broad view of our whole production-distribution system.

MICRO-MARKETING DEFINED

Micro-marketing is the performance of activities that seek to accomplish an organization's objectives by anticipating customer or client needs and directing a flow of need-satisfying goods and services from producer to customer or client.

Let's look at this definition.[3]

Applies to profit and nonprofit organizations

To begin with, this definition applies to both profit and nonprofit organizations. Profit is the objective for most business firms. But other types of organizations may seek more members—or acceptance of an idea. Customers or clients may be individual consumers, business firms, nonprofit organizations, government agencies, or even foreign nations.

The aim of marketing is to identify customers' needs—and to meet these needs so well that the product almost sells itself.

While most customers and clients pay for the goods and services they receive, others may receive them free of charge or at a reduced cost through private or government support.

Begins with customer needs

Marketing should begin with potential customer needs—not with the production process. Marketing should try to anticipate needs. And then marketing, rather than production, should determine what goods and services are to be developed—including decisions about product design and packaging; prices or fees; credit and collection policies; use of middlemen; transporting and storing policies; advertising and sales policies; and, after the sale, installation, customer service, warranty, and perhaps even disposal policies.

Marketing does not do it alone

This does not mean that marketing should try to take over production, accounting, and financial activities. Rather, it means that marketing—by interpreting customers' needs—should provide direction for these activities and try to coordinate them.

THE FOCUS OF THIS TEXT—MANAGEMENT-ORIENTED MICRO-MARKETING

Since most of you are preparing for a career in management, the main focus of this text will be on micro-marketing. We will see marketing through the eyes of the marketing manager.

The micro-marketing decision areas we will be discussing throughout this text apply to a wide variety of situations. They are important not only for large and small business firms but also for all types of public sector and nonprofit organizations. They are useful in domestic markets and international markets, and regardless of whether the organization focuses on marketing physical goods, services, or an idea or cause. They are equally critical whether the relevant customers or clients are individual consumers, businesses, or some other type of organization. In short, every organization needs to think about its markets and how effectively it meets its customers' or clients' needs. For editorial convenience, we will sometimes use the term *firm* as a shorthand way of referring to any type of organization, whether it is a political party, a religious organization, a government agency, or the like. However, to reinforce the point that the ideas apply to all types of organizations, throughout the book we will illustrate marketing management concepts with examples that represent a wide variety of marketing situations.

Consumers in Moscow wait in a three-hour line to buy a rare delicacy—a Chiquita banana. Things are easier for most consumers in the United States, Canada, and Western Europe.

Although micro-marketing is the primary focus of the text, marketing managers must remember that their organizations are just small parts of a larger macro-marketing system. Therefore, the rest of this chapter will look at the macro-view of marketing. Let's begin by defining macro-marketing and reviewing some basic ideas.

MACRO-MARKETING DEFINED

Macro-marketing is a social process that directs an economy's flow of goods and services from producers to consumers in a way that effectively matches supply and demand and accomplishes the objectives of society.

Emphasis is on the whole production-distribution system

Like micro-marketing, macro-marketing is concerned with the flow of need-satisfying goods and services from producer to consumer. However, the emphasis with macro-marketing is not on the activities of individual organizations. Instead, the emphasis is on *how the whole marketing system works*. This includes looking at how marketing affects society, and vice versa.

Every society needs a macro-marketing system. The basic role of a macro-marketing system is to effectively match heterogeneous supply and demand *and* at the same time accomplish society's objectives.[4]

Every society needs an economic system

All societies must provide for the needs of their members. Therefore, every society needs some sort of **economic system**—the way an economy organizes to use scarce resources to produce goods and services and distribute them for consumption by various people and groups in the society.

How an economic system operates depends on a society's objectives and the nature of its political institutions.[5] But regardless of what form these take, all economic systems must develop some method—along with appropriate economic institutions—to decide what and how much is to be produced and distributed, by whom, when, to whom, and why. How these decisions are made may vary from nation to nation. But the macro-level objectives are basically similar: to create goods and services and make them available when and where they are needed—to maintain or improve each nation's standard of living or other socially defined objective.

HOW ECONOMIC DECISIONS ARE MADE

There are two basic kinds of economic systems: planned systems and market-directed systems. Actually, no economy is entirely planned or market-directed. Most are a mixture of the two extremes.

Government planners may make the decisions

In a **planned economic system**, government planners decide what and how much is to be produced and distributed, by whom, when, to whom, and why. Producers generally have little choice about what goods and services to produce. Their main task is to meet their assigned production quotas. Prices are set by government planners and tend to be very rigid—not changing according to supply and demand. Consumers usually have some freedom of choice—it's impossible to control every single detail! But the assortment of goods and services may be quite limited. Activities such as market research, branding, and advertising usually are neglected. Sometimes they aren't done at all.

Government planning may work fairly well as long as an economy is simple and the variety of goods and services is small. It may even be necessary under certain conditions— during wartime, for example. However, as economies become more complex, government planning breaks down. Planners may be overwhelmed by too many complex decisions. And consumers may lose patience if the planners don't respond to their needs. The collapse of communism in Eastern Europe dramatically illustrates this. Citizens of what was the Soviet Union were not satisfied with the government's plan because products consumers wanted were not available. That brought on a revolution—one that is leading to the development of market-directed economies in the new, independent republics of Eastern Europe.[6]

A market-directed economy adjusts itself

In a **market-directed economic system**, the individual decisions of the many producers and consumers make the macro-level decisions for the whole economy. In a pure market-directed economy, consumers make a society's production decisions when they make their choices in the marketplace. They decide what is to be produced and by whom— through their dollar "votes."

Price is a measure of value

Prices in the marketplace are a rough measure of how society values particular goods and services. If consumers are willing to pay the market prices, then apparently they feel they are getting at least their money's worth. Similarly, the cost of labor and materials is a rough measure of the value of the resources used in the production of goods and services to meet these needs. New consumer needs that can be served profitably—not just the needs of the majority—will probably be met by some profit-minded businesses. Over time, the result is a balance of supply and demand and the coordination of the economic activity of many individuals and institutions.

Greatest freedom of choice

Consumers in a market-directed economy enjoy great freedom of choice. They are not forced to buy any goods or services, except those that must be provided for the good of society—things such as national defense, schools, police and fire protection, highway systems, and public-health services. These are provided by the community—and the citizens are taxed to pay for them.

Similarly, producers are free to do whatever they wish—provided that they stay within the rules of the game set by government *and* receive enough dollar votes from consumers.

Many consumers want convenient packaging, but it can be an environmental problem. International Paper and McDonald's have started recycling programs that both satisfy consumers and meet social needs.

©1992 by Marianne Barcellona.

If they do their job well, they earn a profit and stay in business. But profit, survival, and growth are not guaranteed.

Conflicts can result

most laws are passed after a grass roots movement started by consumers who lobby their Congress people.

Producers and consumers making free choices can cause conflicts and difficulties. This is called the **micro-macro dilemma**: what is good for some producers and consumers may not be good for society as a whole.

For example, many consumers want the convenience of disposable products and products in easy-to-use, small-serving packages. But these same convenient products and packages often lead to pollution of the environment and inefficient use of natural resources. Should future generations be left to pay the consequences of pollution that is the result of free choice by today's consumers?

Questions like these are not easy to answer. The basic reason is that many different people may have a stake in the outcomes—and social consequences—of the choices made by individual managers *and* consumers in a market-directed system. As you read this book and learn more about marketing, you will also learn more about social responsibility in marketing—and why it must be taken seriously.

Kennedy Adminis. Consumer Bill of Rights Appr. 1962.

The role of government

The American economy and most other western economies are mainly market-directed—but not completely. Society assigns supervision of the system to the government. For example, besides setting and enforcing the "rules of the game," government agencies control interest rates and the supply of money. They sometimes set import and export rules that affect international competition. Government also tries to be sure that property is protected, contracts are enforced, individuals are not exploited, no group unfairly monopolizes markets, and producers deliver the kinds and quality of goods and services they claim to be offering.

Warranty Laws
Labeling
Consumer Products Safety Division
Opened the door to litigation

You can see that we need some of these government activities to make sure the economy runs smoothly. However, some people worry that too much government guidance threatens the survival of a market-directed system—and the economic and political freedom that goes with it.[7]

ALL ECONOMIES NEED MACRO-MARKETING SYSTEMS

At this point, you may be saying to yourself: all this sounds like economics—where does marketing fit in? Studying a macro-marketing system is a lot like studying an economic system except we give more detailed attention to the marketing components of the system—including consumers and other customers, middlemen, and marketing specialists. We focus on the activities they perform—and how they impact the effectiveness and fairness of a particular system.

In general, we can say that no economic system—whether centrally planned or market-directed—can achieve its objectives without an effective macro-marketing system. To see why this is true, we will look at the role of marketing in primitive economies. Then we will see how macro-marketing tends to become more and more complex in advanced economic systems.

Marketing involves exchange

In a **pure subsistence economy**, each family unit produces everything it consumes. There is no need to exchange goods and services. Each producer-consumer unit is totally self-sufficient, although usually its standard of living is relatively low. No marketing takes place because *marketing doesn't occur unless two or more parties are willing to exchange something for something else.*

What is a market?

The term *marketing* comes from the word **market**, which is a group of potential customers with similar needs who are willing to exchange something of value with sellers offering various goods and/or services—that is, ways of satisfying those needs. Of course, some negotiation may be needed. This can be done face-to-face at some physical location (for example, a farmers' market). Or it can be done indirectly—through a complex network of middlemen who link buyers and sellers living far apart.

In primitive economies, exchanges tend to occur in central markets. **Central markets** are convenient places where buyers and sellers can meet face-to-face to exchange goods and services. We can understand macro-marketing better by seeing how and why central markets develop.

Central markets help exchange

Imagine a small village of five families—each with a special skill for producing some need-satisfying product. After meeting basic needs, each family decides to specialize. It's easier for one family to make two pots and another to make two baskets than for each one to make one pot and one basket. Specialization makes labor more efficient and more productive. It can increase the total amount of form utility created. Specialization also can increase the task utility in producing services, but for the moment we'll focus on products that are physical goods.

If these five families each specialize in one product, they will have to trade with each other. As Exhibit 1–2A shows, it will take the five families 10 separate exchanges to obtain some of each of the products. If the families live near each other, the exchange process is relatively simple. But if they are far apart, travel back and forth will take time. Who will do the traveling—and when?

Faced with this problem, the families may agree to come to a central market and trade on a certain day. Then each family makes only one trip to the market to trade with all the others. This reduces the total number of trips to five, which makes exchange easier, leaves more time for producing and consuming, and also provides for social gatherings.

Money system speeds trading

While a central meeting place simplifies exchange, the individual bartering transactions still take a lot of time. Bartering only works when someone else wants what you have, and vice versa. Each trader must find others who have products of about equal value. After trading with one group, a family may find itself with extra baskets, knives, and pots. Then it has to find others willing to trade for these products.

A money system changes all this. A seller only has to find a buyer who wants the seller's products and agrees on the price. Then the seller is free to spend this income to

Exhibit 1–2

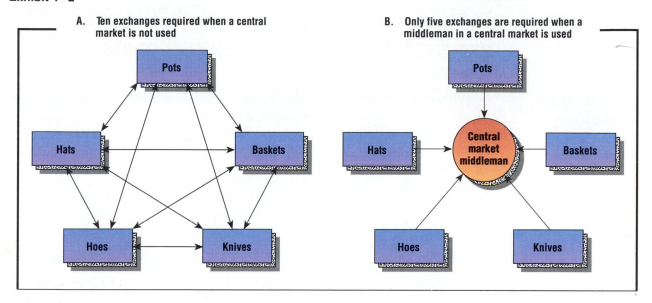

A. Ten exchanges required when a central market is not used

Pots · Hats · Baskets · Hoes · Knives

B. Only five exchanges are required when a middleman in a central market is used

Pots · Hats · Central market middleman · Baskets · Hoes · Knives

buy whatever he or she wants. (Note that if some buyers and sellers use *different* money systems—some use dollars and others use yen—they must also agree on the rate at which the money will be exchanged.)

Middlemen help exchange even more

The development of a central market and a money system simplifies the exchange process among the five families in our imaginary village. But they still need to make 10 separate transactions. So it still takes a lot of time and effort for the five families to exchange goods.

This clumsy exchange process is made much simpler by the appearance of a **middleman**—someone who specializes in trade rather than production. A middleman is willing to buy each family's goods and then sell each family whatever it needs. The middleman charges for these services, of course. But this charge may be more than offset by savings in time and effort.

In our simple example, using a middleman at a central market reduces the necessary number of exchanges for all five families from 10 to 5. See Exhibit 1–2B. Each family has more time for production, consumption, and leisure. Also, each family can specialize in producing what it produces best—creating more form and task utility. Meanwhile, by specializing in trade, the middleman provides additional time, place, and possession utility. In total, all the villagers may enjoy greater economic utility—and greater consumer satisfaction—by using a middleman in the central market.

Note that the reduction in transactions that results from using a middleman in a central market becomes more important as the number of families increases. For example, if the population of our imaginary village increases from 5 to 10 families, 45 transactions are needed without a middleman. Using a middleman requires only one transaction for each family.

Today such middlemen—offering permanent trading facilities—are known as *wholesalers* and *retailers.* The advantages of working with middlemen increase with increases in the number of producers and consumers, their distance from each other, and the number and variety of competing products. That is why there are so many wholesalers and retailers in modern economies.

THE ROLE OF MARKETING IN ECONOMIC DEVELOPMENT

Effective marketing system is necessary

Although it is tempting to conclude that more-effective macro-marketing systems are the result of greater economic development, just the opposite is true. *An effective macro-marketing system is necessary for economic development.* Improved marketing is often the key to growth in less-developed nations.

Breaking the vicious circle of poverty

Without an effective macro-marketing system, the less-developed nations may not be able to escape the vicious circle of poverty. Many people in these nations can't leave their subsistence way of life to produce for the market because there are no buyers for what they produce. And there are no buyers because everyone else is producing for their own needs. As a result, distribution systems and middlemen do not develop.

Breaking this vicious circle of poverty may require major changes in the inefficient micro- and macro-marketing systems that are typical in less-developed nations. At the least, more market-oriented middlemen are needed to move surplus output to markets—including foreign markets—where there is more demand.[8] You can see how this works, and why links between the macro-marketing systems of different countries are so important, by considering the differences in markets that are typical at different stages of economic development.

STAGES OF ECONOMIC DEVELOPMENT

Some markets are more advanced and/or growing more rapidly than others. And some countries—or parts of a country—are at different stages of economic development. This means their demands—and their marketing systems—vary.

To get some idea of the many possible differences in potential markets, we'll discuss six stages of economic development. These stages are helpful, but different parts of the same country may be at different stages of development—so it isn't always possible to identify a single country or region with only one stage. And, some countries skip one or two stages due to investments by foreign firms or investments by their own eager governments.

Stage 1—Self-supporting agriculture

In the first stage, most people are subsistence farmers. A simple marketing system may exist, but most of the people are not part of a money economy. Some parts of Africa and New Guinea are in this stage. In a practical sense, these people are not a market because they have no money to buy products.

Stage 2—Preindustrial or commercial

Some countries in sub-Saharan Africa and the Middle East are in this second stage. During this stage, we see more market-oriented activity. Raw materials such as oil, tin, and copper are extracted and exported. Agricultural and forest crops such as sugar, rubber, and timber are grown and exported. Often this is done with the help of foreign technical skills and capital. A commercial economy may develop along with—but unrelated to—the subsistence economy. These activities may require the beginnings of a transportation system to tie the extracting or growing areas to shipping points. A money economy operates in this stage.

Such countries import industrial machinery and equipment—and component materials and supplies for huge construction projects. They also need imports—including luxury products—to meet the living standards of people who benefit from this new business activity. A small, middle-income class may form, but most of the population has no money. For practical purposes, they are not in the market. The total market in Stage 2 may be so small that local importers can easily handle the demand. There is little reason for local producers to even try.

Stage 3—Primary manufacturing

In this third stage, a country may do some processing of metal ores or agricultural products it once exported in raw form. Sugar and rubber, for example, are both produced and processed in Indonesia. Companies based elsewhere in the world may set up factories to take advantage of low-cost labor. Most of the output from these factories is exported, but the income earned by the workers and managers stimulates economic development.

Even though the local market expands in this third stage, a large part of the population continues to be almost entirely outside the money economy. Local producers are likely to have trouble finding enough demand to stay in business.

Stage 4—Nondurable and semidurable consumer products manufacturing

At this stage, production of some consumer products begins—especially products that need only a small investment to get started. Often, growth starts with the small firms that supplied the processors dominating the last stage. For example, plants making explosives for extracting minerals might expand into soap manufacturing. Multinational firms may speed development of countries in this stage by investing in promising opportunities.

Paint, drug, food and beverage, and textile industries usually develop in this stage. Because clothing is a necessity, the textile industry is usually one of the first to develop. This early emphasis on the textile industry in developing nations is one reason the world textile market is so competitive.

As the middle- or even upper-income class expands, local businesses begin to see enough volume to operate profitably. So there is less need for imports to supply nondurable and semidurable products. But most consumer durables and capital equipment are still imported.

Stage 5—Capital equipment and consumer durable products manufacturing

In this stage, local production of capital equipment and consumer durable products begins. This includes cars, refrigerators, and machinery for local industries. Such manufacturing creates other demands—raw materials for the local factories, and food and clothing for the rural population entering the industrial labor force.

In this stage, industrialization begins, but the economy still depends heavily on exports of raw materials. Further, the country may still have to import special heavy machinery and equipment. Imported consumer durables may still compete with local products.

Stage 6—Exporting manufactured products

Countries that haven't gone beyond the fifth stage are mainly exporters of raw materials. They import manufactured products to build their industrial base. In the sixth stage, countries begin exporting manufactured products. Countries often specialize in certain types of manufactured products—such as iron and steel, watches, cameras, electronic equipment, and processed food.

These countries have grown richer. They have needs—and the purchasing power—for a wide variety of products. In fact, countries in this stage often carry on a great deal of trade with each other. Each trades those products in which it has production advantages. In this stage, almost all consumers are in the money economy. And there may be a large middle-income class. The United States, most of the Western European countries, and Japan are at this last stage.[9]

NATIONS' MACRO-MARKETING SYSTEMS ARE CONNECTED

As a nation grows, its international trade grows

All countries trade to some extent—we live in an interdependent world. We saw above how trade expands as a country develops and industrializes. In fact, the largest changes in world trade are usually seen in rapidly developing economies. Over the last decade, for example, exports from Hong Kong, Taiwan, and Singapore have risen dramatically.

Even so, the largest traders are highly developed nations. For example, the United States exports about 20 percent of all its manufactured goods and 40 percent of all agricultural output. In addition, the United States imports about 18 percent of the goods traded among countries.[10]

Because trade among nations is important in economic development, most countries are eager to be able to sell their goods and services in foreign markets. Yet at the same time they often don't want their local customers to spend cash on foreign-made products. They want the money—and the opportunities for jobs and economic growth—to stay in the local economy.

Tariffs and quotas may reduce marketing opportunities

Taxes and restrictions at national or regional borders greatly reduce the free flow of goods and services between the macro-marketing systems of different countries. **Tariffs**—taxes on imported products—vary, depending on whether a country is trying to raise revenue or limit trade. Restrictive tariffs often block all movement. But even revenue-producing tariffs cause red tape, discourage free movement of products, and increase the prices consumers pay.

Quotas act like restrictive tariffs. **Quotas** set the specific quantities of products that can move into or out of a country. Great market opportunities may exist in the markets of a unified Europe, for example, but import quotas (or export controls applied against a specific country) may discourage outsiders from entering.

The impact of such restrictions can be seen in South Korea. When Ford Motor Co. introduced the Mercury Sable, Korean trade restrictions blocked Ford from selling the Sable there. In late 1987, Korea lifted the restrictions. In their place, however, the Korean government imposed special taxes and tariffs. As a result, a 1988 Sable that sold for $14,800 in the United States cost $44,400 in Korea—and very few Korean consumers were willing or able to pay that much. It's easy to see why trade restrictions can be a potential source of conflict between nations.[11]

Markets may rely on international countertrade

To overcome the problems of trade restrictions, many firms have turned to **countertrade**—a special type of bartering in which products from one country are traded for products from another country. For example, soft-drink bottlers in Mexico trade locally grown broccoli for Pepsi concentrate. Then PepsiCo finds a market for the broccoli in the United States or other countries. Pepsi is not alone in using countertrade. About 6 percent of all U.S. exports rely on countertrade.[12]

CAN MASS PRODUCTION SATISFY A SOCIETY'S CONSUMPTION NEEDS?

Most people depend on others to produce most of the goods and services they need to satisfy their basic needs. Also, in advanced economies, many consumers have higher discretionary incomes. They can afford to satisfy higher-level needs as well. A modern economy faces a real challenge to satisfy all these needs.

Economies of scale mean lower cost

Fortunately, advanced economies can often take advantage of mass production with its **economies of scale**—which means that as a company produces larger numbers of a particular product, the cost for each of these products goes down.

Of course, even in advanced societies, not all goods and services can be produced by mass production—or with economies of scale. Consider medical care. It's difficult to get productivity gains in labor-intensive medical services—like brain surgery. Nevertheless, from a macro-marketing perspective, it is clear that we are able to devote resources to meeting these quality-of-life needs because we are achieving efficiency in other areas.

Thus, modern production skills can help provide great quantities of goods and services to satisfy large numbers of consumers. But mass production alone does not solve the problem of satisfying consumers' needs. We also need effective marketing.

Effective marketing is needed to link producers and consumers

Effective marketing means delivering the goods and services that consumers want and need. It means getting products to them at the right time, in the right place, and at a price they're willing to pay. That's not an easy job—especially if you think about the variety of goods and services a highly developed economy can produce and the many kinds of goods and services consumers want.

Effective marketing in an advanced economy is more difficult because producers and consumers are separated in several ways. As Exhibit 1–3 shows, exchange between producers and consumers is hampered by spatial separation, separation in time, separation in information and values, and separation of ownership. Discrepancies of quantity and discrepancies of assortment further complicate exchange between producers and consumers. That is, each producer specializes in producing and selling large amounts of a narrow assortment of goods and services, but each consumer wants only small quantities of a wide assortment of goods and services.[13]

Marketing functions help narrow the gap

The purpose of a macro-marketing system is to overcome these separations and discrepancies. The universal functions of marketing help do this.

The **universal functions of marketing** are buying, selling, transporting, storing, standardization and grading, financing, risk taking, and market information. They must be performed in all macro-marketing systems. *How* these functions are performed—and *by*

Exhibit 1–3   Marketing Facilitates Production and Consumption

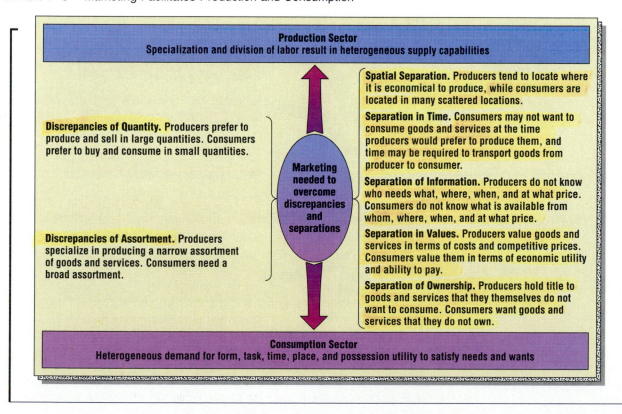

whom—may differ among nations and economic systems. But they are needed in any macro-marketing system. Let's take a closer look at them now.

Exchange usually involves buying and selling. The **buying function** means looking for and evaluating goods and services. The **selling function** involves promoting the product. It includes the use of personal selling, advertising, and other mass selling methods. This is probably the most visible function of marketing.

The **transporting function** means the movement of goods from one place to another. The **storing function** involves holding goods until customers need them.

Standardization and grading involve sorting products according to size and quality. This makes buying and selling easier because it reduces the need for inspection and sampling. **Financing** provides the necessary cash and credit to produce, transport, store, promote, sell, and buy products. **Risk taking** involves bearing the uncertainties that are part of the marketing process. A firm can never be sure that customers will want to buy its products. Products can also be damaged, stolen, or outdated. The **market information function** involves the collection, analysis, and distribution of all the information needed to plan, carry out, and control marketing activities, whether in the firm's own neighborhood or in a market overseas.

WHO PERFORMS MARKETING FUNCTIONS?

Producers, consumers, and marketing specialists

From a macro-level viewpoint, these marketing functions are all part of the marketing process—and must be done by someone. None of them can be eliminated. In a planned economy, some of the functions may be performed by government agencies. Others may be left to individual producers and consumers. In a market-directed system, marketing

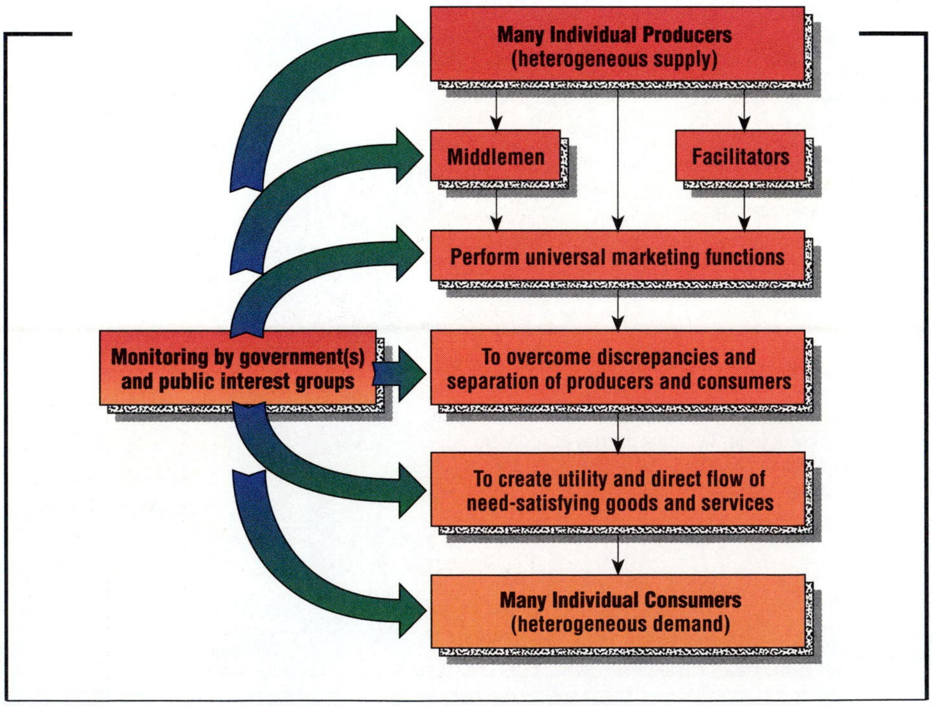

Exhibit 1–4   Model of a Market-Directed Macro-Marketing System

functions are performed by producers, consumers, and a variety of marketing specialists (see Exhibit 1–4). Keep in mind that the macro-marketing systems for different nations may interact. For example, producers based in one nation may serve consumers in another country, perhaps with help from middlemen and other specialists from both countries.

Specialists perform some functions

Some marketing functions may be performed by a variety of **facilitators**—firms that provide one or more of the marketing functions other than buying or selling. These include advertising agencies, marketing research firms, independent product-testing laboratories, public warehouses, transporting firms, communications companies, and financial institutions (including banks). Through specialization or economies of scale, marketing middlemen and facilitators are often able to perform the marketing functions better—and at a lower cost—than producers or consumers can. This allows producers and consumers to spend more time on production and consumption.

Functions can be shifted and shared

From a macro viewpoint, all of the marketing functions must be performed by someone. But *from a micro viewpoint, not every firm must perform all of the functions. Further, not all goods and services require all the functions at every level of their production.* Pure services—like a plane ride—don't need storing, for example. But storing is required in the production of the plane and while the plane is not in service.

Some marketing specialists perform all the functions. Others specialize in only one or two. Marketing research firms, for example, specialize only in the market information function. The important point to remember is this: *responsibility for performing the marketing functions can be shifted and shared in a variety of ways, but no function can be completely eliminated.*

Facilitators—including transportation firms and advertising specialists—may help a marketing manager with one or more of the marketing functions.

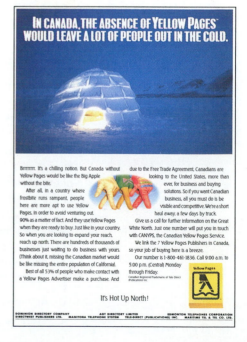

THE CHANGING MACRO-MARKETING SYSTEM IN EASTERN EUROPE

Prior to the fall of the Berlin Wall, consumers in East Germany often had to wait in long lines to make purchases at government-controlled stores. There were frequent shortages of the products consumers wanted and needed—including basic foods. The Berlin Wall was more than just a symbol of political differences between East and West. Trade with the market-directed economy of the West was very limited, and the macro-marketing system in the East was not effective in meeting consumer needs. The failure of the economic system prompted political change.

With the reunification of Germany, the political limits on trade were gone. Yet there were still problems. Even in a market-directed economy, it takes time for new middlemen and facilitators to develop. For example, eastern Germany had no efficient wholesalers to supply the chain of 170 Konsum retail stores, which were previously state-owned. And it was expensive for producers in the West who wanted to reach the market in the East to do it without help.

However, the Tegut grocery chain in the West saw the opportunity and quickly did something about it. Tegut established an automated warehouse in the East to supply the Konsum stores. The warehouse made it economical to assemble needed assortments of products from many different producers. Even so, information about which Konsum stores needed what products was bad because telecommunications systems in the East were so poor. With the help of Tandem computer company, Tegut set up a computer network to link the stores to the new warehouse. The computer system provided for timely reordering from the warehouse, online management of inventories and distribution, and even payment control.

With the help of middlemen like Tegut, both local and foreign producers are better able to meet consumer needs.[14]

HOW WELL DOES OUR MACRO-MARKETING SYSTEM WORK?

It connects remote producers and consumers

A macro-marketing system does more than just deliver goods and services to consumers—it allows mass production, with its economies of scale. Also, mass communication and mass transportation allow products to be shipped where they're needed. Oranges from California are found in Minnesota stores—even in December—and electronic parts made in Taiwan are used in making products all over the world.[15]

It encourages growth and new ideas

In addition to making mass production possible, a market-directed macro-marketing system encourages innovation—the development and spread of new ideas and products. Competition for consumers' money forces firms to think of new and better ways of satisfying consumer needs.

It has its critics

In explaining marketing's role in society, we described some of the benefits of a market-directed macro-marketing system. We can see this in the macro-marketing system of the United States. It provides—at least in material terms—one of the highest standards of living in the world. It seems to be effective and fair in many ways.

We must admit, however, that marketing—as it exists in the United States and other developed societies—has many critics. Marketing activity is especially open to criticism because it is the part of business most visible to the public. There is nothing like a pocketbook issue for getting consumers excited!

Typical complaints about marketing include:

Advertising is too often annoying, misleading, and wasteful.

Products are not safe—or the quality is poor.

Marketing makes people too materialistic—it motivates them toward things instead of social needs.

Easy consumer credit makes people buy things they don't need and really can't afford.

Packaging and labeling are often confusing and deceptive.

Middlemen add to the cost of distribution—and raise prices without providing anything in return.

Marketing creates interest in products that pollute the environment.

Too many unnecessary products are offered.

Marketing serves the rich and exploits the poor.

Such complaints cannot and should not be taken lightly. They show that many people aren't happy with some parts of the marketing system. Certainly, the strong public support for consumer protection laws proves that not all consumers feel they are being treated like royalty.

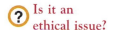 **Is it an ethical issue?**

Certainly some complaints about marketing arise because some individual firm or manager was intentionally unethical and cheated the market. But at other times problems and criticism may arise because a manager did not fully consider the ethical implications of a decision. In either case, there is no excuse for sloppiness when it comes to **marketing ethics**—the moral standards that guide marketing decisions and actions. Each individual develops moral standards based on his or her own values. That helps explain why opinions about what is right or wrong often vary from one person to another, from one society to another, and among different groups within a society. It is sometimes difficult to say whose opinions are correct. Even so, such opinions may have a very real influence on whether an individual's (or a firm's) marketing decisions and actions are accepted or rejected. So marketing ethics are not only a philosophical issue, but also a pragmatic concern. Throughout the text we will be discussing the types of ethical issues individual marketing managers face. In fact, these issues are so important that we will highlight them with the special symbol used in the heading for this section. But we won't be moralizing and trying to tell you how you should think on any given issue. Rather, by the end of the course we hope that *you* will have some firm personal opinions about what is and is not ethical in micro-marketing activities.

Keep in mind, however, that not all criticisms of marketing focus on ethical issues; fortunately, the prevailing practice of most businesspeople is to be fair and honest. Moreover, not all criticisms are specific to the micro-marketing activities of individual firms. Some of the complaints about marketing really focus on the basic idea of a market-directed macro-marketing system. These criticisms often occur because people don't understand what marketing is—or how it works. As you go through this book, we'll discuss some of these criticisms. Then in our final chapter, we will return to a more complete appraisal of marketing in our consumer-oriented society.

CONCLUSION

In this chapter, we defined two levels of marketing: micro-marketing and macro-marketing. Macro-marketing is concerned with the way the whole global economy works. Micro-marketing focuses on the activities of individual firms. We discussed the role of marketing in economic development—and the functions of marketing and who performs them. We ended by raising some of the criticisms of marketing—both of the whole macro system and of the way individual firms work.

We emphasized macro-marketing in this chapter, but the major thrust of this book is on micro-marketing. By learning more about market-oriented decision making, you will be able to make more efficient and socially responsible decisions. This will help improve the performance of individual firms and organizations (your employers). And eventually, it will help our macro-marketing system work better.

We'll see marketing through the eyes of the marketing manager—maybe *you* in the near future. And we will show how you can contribute to the marketing process. Along the way, we'll discuss the impact of micro-level decisions on society, and the ethical issues that marketing managers face. Then in Chapter 18—after you have had time to understand how and why producers and consumers think and behave the way they do—we will evaluate how well both micro-marketing and macro-marketing perform in a market-directed economic system.

QUESTIONS AND PROBLEMS

1. List your activities for the first two hours after you woke up this morning. Briefly indicate how marketing affected your activities.

2. It is fairly easy to see why people do not beat a path to a mousetrap manufacturer's door, but would they be similarly indifferent if some food processor developed a revolutionary new food product that would provide all necessary nutrients in small pills for about $100 per year per person?

3. Distinguish between macro- and micro-marketing. Then explain how they are interrelated, if they are.

4. Distinguish between how economic decisions are made in a planned economic system and how they are made in a market-directed economy.

5. A committee of the American Marketing Association defined marketing as "the process of planning and executing the conception, pricing, promotion, and distribution of ideas, goods, and services to create exchanges that satisfy individual and organizational objectives." Does this definition consider macro-marketing? Explain your answer.

6. Identify a "central market" in your city and explain how it facilitates exchange.

7. Explain why tariffs and quotas affect international marketing opportunities.

8. Discuss the prospects for a group of Latin American entrepreneurs who are considering building a factory to produce machines that make cans for the food industry. Their country is in Stage 4—the nondurable and semidurable consumer products manufacturing stage. The country's population is approximately 20 million, and there is some possibility of establishing sales contacts in a few nearby countries.

9. Discuss the nature of marketing in a socialist economy. Would the functions that must be provided and the development of wholesaling and retailing systems be any different than in a market-directed economy?

10. Discuss how the micro-macro dilemma relates to each of the following products: air bags in cars, nuclear power, bank credit cards, and pesticides that improve farm production.

11. Describe a recent purchase you made and indicate why that particular product was available at a store and, in particular, at the store where you bought it.

12. Refer to Exhibit 1–3, and give an example of a purchase you recently made that involved separation of information and separation in time between you and the producer. Briefly explain how these separations were overcome.

13. Define the functions of marketing in your own words. Using an example, explain how they can be shifted and shared.

14. Explain, in your own words, why this text emphasizes micro-marketing.

15. Explain why a small producer might want a marketing research firm to take over some of its information-gathering activities.

16. Explain why a market-directed macro-marketing system encourages innovation. Give an example.

SUGGESTED CASES

1. McDonald's "Seniors" Restaurant

4. Jim's Service, Inc.

COMPUTER-AIDED PROBLEM

1. Revenue, Cost, and Profit Relationships

This problem introduces you to the computer-aided problem software—the PLUS computer program—and gets you started with the use of spreadsheet analysis for marketing decision making. This problem is simple. In fact, you could work it without the PLUS software. But by starting with a simple problem, you will learn how to use the program more quickly and see how it will help you with more complicated problems. Complete instructions for the PLUS software are available at the end of this text. However, while you are working with the software, you can press the H key to get help on-screen whenever you need it.

Sue Cline, the business manager at Magna University Student Bookstore, is developing plans for the next academic year. The bookstore is one of the university's nonprofit activities, but any surplus (profit) it earns is used to support the student activities center.

Two popular products at the bookstore are the student academic calendar and notebooks with the school name. Sue Cline thinks that she can sell calendars to 90 percent of Magna's 3,000 students, so she has had 2,700 printed. The total cost, including art work and printing, is $11,500. Last year the calendar sold for $5.00, but Sue is considering changing the price this year.

Sue thinks that the bookstore will be able to sell 6,000 notebooks if they are priced right. But she knows that many students will buy similar notebooks (without the school name) from stores in town if the bookstore price is too high.

Sue has entered the information about selling price, quantity, and costs for calendars and notebooks in the spreadsheet program so that it is easy to evaluate the effect of different decisions. The spreadsheet is also set up to calculate revenue and profit, based on

Revenue = (Selling price) × (Quantity sold), and
Profit = (Revenue) − (Total cost).

Use the program to answer the questions below. Remember, you can press the H key to get help whenever you need it. Record your answers on a separate sheet of paper.

a. From the Spreadsheet Screen, how much revenue does Sue expect from calendars? How much revenue from notebooks? How much profit will the store earn from calendars? And from notebooks?

b. If Sue increases the price of her calendars to $6.00 and still sells the same quantity, what is the expected revenue? The expected profit? (Note: change the price from $5.00 to $6.00 on the spreadsheet and the program will recompute revenue and profit.) On your sheet of paper, show the calculations that confirm that the program has given you the correct values.

c. Sue is interested in getting an overview of how a change in the price of notebooks would affect revenue and profit, assuming that she sells all 6,000 notebooks she is thinking of ordering. Prepare a table—on your sheet of paper—with column headings for three variables: selling price, revenue, and profit. Show the value for revenue and profit for different possible selling prices for a notebook—starting at a minimum price of $1.60 and adding 8 cents to the price until you reach a maximum of $2.40. At what price will selling 6,000 notebooks contribute $5,400.00 to profit? At what price would notebook sales contribute only $1,080.00? (Hint: Use the What If analysis to compute the new values. Start by selecting "selling price" for notebooks as the value to change, with a minimum value of $1.60 and a maximum value of $2.40. Select the revenue and profit for notebooks as the values to display.)

For additional questions related to this problem, see Exercise 1–5 in the *Learning Aid for use with Essentials of Marketing,* 6th edition.

Marketing's Role within the Firm or Nonprofit Organization

Chapter  **2**

When You Finish This Chapter, You Should

❶
Know what the marketing concept is—and how it should affect strategy planning in a firm or nonprofit organization.

❷
Understand what a marketing manager does.

❸
Know what marketing strategy planning is—and why it will be the focus of this book.

❹
Understand target marketing.

❺
Be familiar with the four Ps in a marketing mix.

❻
Know the difference between a marketing strategy, a marketing plan, and a marketing program.

❼
Understand the important new terms (shown in red).

To get a better understanding of marketing strategy planning, we are going to look at things from the viewpoint of the marketing manager—the one who makes an organization's important marketing decisions. To start you thinking about the ideas we will be developing in this chapter and the rest of the book, let's consider a few decisions recently made by marketing managers.

In the winter of 1992, marketing managers in the power tool division at Black and Decker (B&D) were looking forward to improved profits because of a new marketing plan they had developed. Black and Decker tools were well known among consumers and dominated the do-it-yourself market. However, they were getting only about 10 percent of the sales to professionals who bought power tools for commercial work. There was a good opportunity for profitable growth with these customers, but B&D needed a special marketing effort targeted at their needs. Makita (a Japanese producer) already had a strong reputation with these customers. And other competitors—including Sears (with its Craftsman brand), Snap-On, and producers from Japan and Germany—were likely to join the battle for this business. To come out on top in these "saw wars," B&D's managers had to make many decisions.

B&D marketing managers spent three months visiting more than 200 tool stores and job sites to get feedback from professionals about their interests and needs. Some of the details were simple but useful: "Paint it yellow to make it easy to see and to signify safety." Other concerns also surfaced. For example, the Black and Decker brand name did not have as favorable an image with these professionals as it did with consumers. The professionals thought of it as a good "consumer brand" that had no particular advantage for their needs. They wanted very reliable tools—ones that would stand up to their demanding applications.

Working with people in research and development and manufacturing, B&D marketing managers developed a special line of 33 new tools for this target market. Tests showed that all but two of the tools would satisfy professional customers better than competing products from Makita. The two that didn't were redesigned. Going even further to meet the target customers' reliability needs, B&D set up 117 service centers and offered a 48-hour repair guarantee. B&D even promised a free loaner tool during the repair. Marketing managers also decided that it would be better to use the firm's less widely known DeWalt brand name rather than try to change the target customers' beliefs about the Black and Decker brand. Marketing research showed that the professional target market already respected the DeWalt name.

Marketing managers also had to decide the best way to reach the target market. Should they start in some introductory regions or distribute the new products in as many countries as possible all at once? Should they focus on middlemen who had sold their other products in the past? Or should they put special emphasis on working closely with middlemen, like the Home Depot chain, who already had a strong relationship with the professional target market?

B&D also had to decide how to promote the new line of DeWalt tools. Marketing managers had to decide how many salespeople would be needed to work with middlemen. They also had to develop plans for advertising to the target customers—including deciding on an advertising theme and determining how much to spend and where to spend it.

They had other decisions to make. The price on their consumer products had been set low to attract price-sensitive buyers. Should they stick with a low beat-the-competition price on the DeWalt line, or would a premium price be more profitable with professionals who were more concerned about long-term reliability? Should they offer introductory price rebates to help attract customers from Makita and other brands? Should they offer middlemen special discounts for large orders?

Black and Decker managers did a good job with all of these decisions. Their marketing plan is so promising that they hope to achieve $180 million in sales by 1996. Of course, they can't afford to be complacent as they implement the plan and check progress against their objectives. Competitors will also be making changes. Ultimately, if Black and Decker is to come out on top, it must continue to do the best job of satisfying customers.[1]

We've mentioned only a few of many decisions Black and Decker marketing managers had to make, but you can see that each of these decisions affects the others. Making marketing decisions is never easy. But knowing what basic decision areas have to be considered helps you to plan a better, more-successful strategy. This chapter will get you started by giving you a framework for thinking about all the marketing management decision areas—which is what the rest of this book is all about.

MARKETING'S ROLE HAS CHANGED A LOT OVER THE YEARS

From our Black and Decker example, it's clear that marketing decisions are very important to a firm's success. But marketing hasn't always been so complicated.

We will discuss four stages in the evolution to modern marketing: (1) the production era, (2) the sales era, (3) the marketing department era, and (4) the marketing company era. We'll talk about these eras as if they applied generally to all firms—but keep in mind that *some managers still have not made it to the final stages.* They are stuck in the past with old ways of thinking.

From the production to the sales era

Cheaper faster more efficient

From the later Industrial Revolution (about a hundred years ago) until the 1920s, most companies were in the production era. The **production era** is a time when a company focuses on production of a few specific products—perhaps because few of these products are available in the market. "If we can make it, it will sell" is management thinking characteristic of the production era. Because of product shortages, many nations—including many of the newly independent republics of Eastern Europe—continue to operate with production era thinking.

By about 1930, most companies in the industrialized western nations had more production capability than ever before. Now the problem wasn't just to produce—but to beat the competition and win customers. This led many firms to enter the sales era. The **sales era** is a time when a company emphasizes selling because of increased competition.

In 1896, a firm could easily sell all the typewriters it could produce because there were few available in the market.

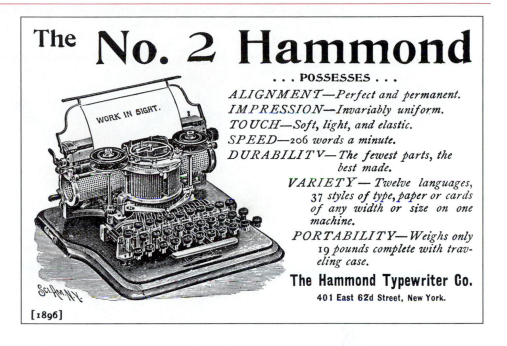

The **No. 2 Hammond**

... POSSESSES ...

ALIGNMENT—*Perfect and permanent.*
IMPRESSION—*Invariably uniform.*
TOUCH—*Soft, light, and elastic.*
SPEED—*206 words a minute.*
DURABILITY—*The fewest parts, the best made.*
VARIETY—*Twelve languages, 37 styles of type, paper or cards of any width or size on one machine.*
PORTABILITY—*Weighs only 19 pounds complete with traveling case.*

The Hammond Typewriter Co.
401 East 62d Street, New York.

[1896]

WORK IN SIGHT.

To the marketing department era

For most firms in advanced economies, the sales era continued until at least 1950. By then, sales were growing rapidly in most areas of the economy. The problem was deciding where to put the company's effort. Someone was needed to tie together the efforts of research, purchasing, production, shipping, and sales. As this situation became more common, the sales era was replaced by the marketing department era. The **marketing department era** is a time when all marketing activities are brought under the control of one department to improve short-run policy planning and to try to integrate the firm's activities.

To the marketing company era

Since 1960, most firms have developed at least some staff with a marketing management outlook. Many of these firms have even graduated from the marketing department era into the marketing company era. The **marketing company era** is a time when, in addition to short-run marketing planning, marketing people develop long-range plans—sometimes 10 or more years ahead—and the whole company effort is guided by the marketing concept.

Every department responsible for satisfying customer needs

WHAT DOES THE MARKETING CONCEPT MEAN?

Kimberly Clark
Proctor & Gamble

The **marketing concept** means that an organization aims *all* its efforts at satisfying its customers—at a profit. The marketing concept is a simple but very important idea. See Exhibit 2–1.

It is not really a new idea—it's been around for a long time. But some managers show little interest in customers' needs. These managers still have a **production orientation**—making whatever products are easy to produce and *then* trying to sell them. They think of customers as existing to buy the firm's output rather than of firms as existing to serve customers and—more broadly—the needs of society.

Well-managed firms have replaced this production orientation with a marketing orientation. A **marketing orientation** means trying to carry out the marketing concept. Instead of just trying to get customers to buy what the firm has produced, a marketing-oriented firm tries to produce what customers need.

Exhibit 2−1 Organizations with a Marketing Orientation Carry Out the Marketing Concept

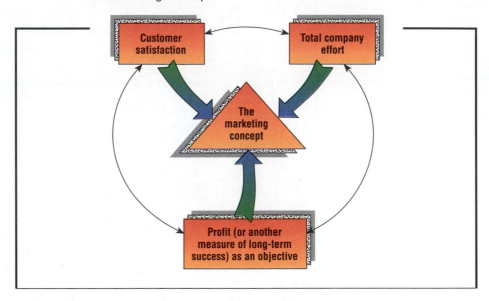

Three basic ideas are included in the definition of the marketing concept: (1) customer satisfaction, (2) a total company effort, and (3) profit—not just sales—as an objective. These ideas deserve more discussion.

Customer satisfaction guides the whole system

"Give the customers what they need" seems so obvious that it may be hard for you to see why the marketing concept requires special attention. However, people don't always do the logical and obvious—especially when it means changing what they've done in the past. In a typical company 30 years ago, production managers thought mainly about getting out the product. Accountants were interested only in balancing the books. Financial people looked after the company's cash position. And salespeople were mainly concerned with getting orders. Each department thought of its own activity as the center of the business—with others working around the edges. No one was concerned with the whole system. As long as the company made a profit, each department went merrily on—doing its own thing. Unfortunately, this is still true in many companies today.

Managers work together to do a better job

Ideally, all managers should work together because the output from one department may be the input to another. But some managers tend to build "fences" around their own departments. There may be meetings to try to get them to work together—but they come and go from the meetings worried only about protecting their own turf.

We use the term *production orientation* as a shorthand way to refer to this kind of narrow thinking—and lack of a central focus—in a business firm. But keep in mind that this problem may be seen in sales-oriented sales representatives, advertising-oriented agency people, finance-oriented finance people, directors of nonprofit organizations, and so on. It is not just a criticism of people who manage production. They aren't necessarily any more guilty of narrow thinking than anyone else.

The fences come down in an organization that has accepted the marketing concept. There are still departments, of course, because specialization makes sense. But the total system's effort is guided by what customers want—instead of what each department would like to do.

Many service industries have begun to apply the marketing concept.

"I got a loan for a loft conversion. Now everybody wants one."

Lloyds Bank

THE THOROUGHBRED BANK.

Survival and success require a profit

Firms must satisfy customers, or the customers won't continue to vote for the firm's survival and success with their money. But managers must also keep in mind that it may cost more to satisfy some needs than any customers are willing to pay. So profit—the difference between a firm's revenue and its total costs—is the bottom-line measure of the firm's success and ability to survive. It is the balancing point that helps the firm determine what needs it will try to satisfy with its total (sometimes costly!) effort.

ADOPTION OF THE MARKETING CONCEPT HAS NOT BEEN EASY OR UNIVERSAL

The marketing concept seems so logical that you would think most firms would quickly adopt it. But this isn't the case. Many firms are still production oriented. In fact, the majority are either production oriented—or regularly slip back that way—and must consciously refocus their planning on customers' interests.

The marketing concept was first accepted by consumer products companies such as General Electric and Procter & Gamble. Competition was intense in some of their markets—and trying to satisfy customers' needs more fully was a way to win in this competition. Widespread publicity about the success of the marketing concept at these companies helped spread the message to other firms.[2]

Producers of industrial commodities—steel, coal, paper, glass, chemicals—have accepted the marketing concept slowly if at all. Similarly, many retailers have been slow to accept the marketing concept.

Service industries are catching up

Service industries—including airlines, banks, investment firms, lawyers, physicians, accountants, and insurance companies—were slow to adopt the marketing concept too. But this has changed dramatically in the last decade, partly due to government regulation changes that forced many of these businesses to be more competitive.[3]

Banks used to be open for limited hours that were convenient for bankers—not customers. Many closed during lunch hour! But now financial services are less regulated, and banks compete with companies like Merrill Lynch for checking accounts and retirement investments. Banks stay open longer, often during evenings and on Saturdays. They also offer more services for their customers—automatic banking machines that take credit cards or a personal banker to give financial advice. Most banks now aggressively advertise their special services and even interest rates so customers can compare bank offerings.

Exhibit 2–2 Some Differences in Outlook between Adopters of the Marketing Concept and the Typical Production-Oriented Managers

Topic	Marketing Orientation	Production Orientation
Attitudes toward customers	Customer needs determine company plans	They should be glad we exist, trying to cut costs and bringing out better products
Product offering	Company makes what it can sell	Company sells what it can make
Role of marketing research	To determine customer needs and how well company is satisfying them	To determine customer reaction, if used at all
Interest in innovation	Focus on locating new opportunities	Focus is on technology and cost cutting
Importance of profit	A critical objective	A residual, what's left after all costs are covered
Role of customer credit	Seen as a customer service	Seen as a necessary evil
Role of packaging	Designed for customer convenience and as a selling tool	Seen merely as protection for the product
Inventory levels	Set with customer requirements and costs in mind	Set to make production more convenient
Transportation arrangements	Seen as a customer service	Seen as an extension of production and storage activities, with emphasis on cost minimization
Focus of advertising	Need-satisfying benefits of products and services	Product features and how products are made
Role of sales force	Help the customer to buy if the product fits his or her needs, while coordinating with rest of firm	Sell the customer, don't worry about coordination with other promotion efforts or rest of firm

It's easy to slip into a production orientation

The marketing concept may seem obvious, but it's very easy to slip into a production-oriented way of thinking. For example, a retailer might prefer only weekday hours—avoiding nights, Saturdays, and Sundays when many customers would prefer to shop. Or a company might rush to produce a clever new product developed in its lab—without first finding if it will fill an unsatisfied need. Many firms in high-technology businesses fall into this trap. They think that technology is the source of their success, rather than realizing that technology is only a means to meet customer needs.

Take a look at Exhibit 2–2. It shows some differences in outlook between adopters of the marketing concept and typical production-oriented managers. As the exhibit suggests, the marketing concept—if taken seriously—is really very powerful. It forces the company to think through what it is doing—and why. And it motivates the company to develop plans for accomplishing its objectives.

Where does competition fit?

Some critics say that the marketing concept doesn't go far enough in today's highly competitive markets. They think of marketing as warfare for customers—and argue that a marketing manager should focus on competitors, not customers. That viewpoint, however, misses the point. Often the best way to beat the competition is to be first to find and satisfy a need that others have not even considered. The competition between Pepsi and Coke illustrates this.

Coke and Pepsi were spending millions of dollars on promotion—fighting head-to-head for the same cola customers. They put so much emphasis on the competitor that they missed opportunities. Then Pepsi recognized consumer interest in a potential new product idea: a soft drink based on fruit juice. Pepsi's Slice brand soft drink was first on the market, and that helped Slice win loyal customers and space on retailers' shelves.

Marketing is being more widely accepted by nonprofit organizations.

THE MARKETING CONCEPT APPLIES IN NONPROFIT ORGANIZATIONS

Newcomers to marketing thinking

The marketing concept is as important for nonprofit organizations as it is for business firms. However, prior to 1970 few people paid attention to the role of marketing in nonprofits. Now all sorts of public and private nonprofit organizations—ranging from government agencies, health-care organizations, schools, and religious groups to charities, political parties, and fine arts organizations—recognize the value of marketing thinking.

Some nonprofit organizations operate just like a business. For example, there may be no practical difference between the gift shop at a museum and a for-profit shop located across the street. On the other hand, some nonprofits differ from business firms in a variety of ways.

Support may not come from satisfied "customers"

As with any business firm, a nonprofit organization needs resources and support to survive and achieve its objectives. Yet support often does not come directly from those who receive the benefits the organization produces. For example, the World Wildlife Fund protects animals. If supporters of the World Wildlife Fund are not satisfied with its efforts—don't think the benefits are worth what it costs to provide them—they will, and should, put their time and money elsewhere.

Just as most firms face competition for customers, most nonprofits face competition for the resources and support they need. A sorority will falter if potential members join other organizations. A shelter for the homeless may fail if supporters decide to focus on some other cause, such as AIDS education.

What is the bottom line

As with a business, a nonprofit must take in as much money as it spends or it won't survive. However, a nonprofit organization does not measure profit in the same way as a firm. And its key measures of long-term success are also different. The YMCA, colleges, symphony orchestras, and the post office, for example, all seek to achieve different objectives—and need different measures of success.

Profit guides business decisions because it reflects both the costs and benefits of different activities. In a nonprofit organization, it is sometimes more difficult to be objective in evaluating the benefits of different activities relative to what they cost. However, if everyone in an organization agrees to *some* measure of long-run success, it helps serve as a guide to where the organization should focus its efforts.

May not be organized for marketing

Some nonprofits face other challenges in organizing to adopt the marketing concept. Often no one has overall responsibility for marketing activities. A treasurer or accountant may keep the books, and someone may be in charge of operations—but marketing may somehow seem less crucial, especially if no one understands what marketing is all about. Even when some leaders do the marketing thinking, they may have trouble getting unpaid volunteers with many different interests to all agree with the marketing strategy. Volunteers tend to do what they feel like doing!

The marketing concept provides focus

We have been discussing some of the differences between nonprofit and business organizations. However, the marketing concept is helpful in *any* type of organization. Success is unlikely if everyone doesn't pull together to strive for common objectives that can be achieved with the available resources. Adopting the marketing concept helps to bring this kind of focus. After all, each organization is trying to satisfy some group of consumers in some way.[4]

THE MARKETING CONCEPT, SOCIAL RESPONSIBILITY, AND MARKETING ETHICS

Society's needs must be considered

The marketing concept is so logical that it's hard to argue with it. Yet when a firm focuses its efforts on satisfying some consumers—to achieve its objectives—there may be negative effects on society. (Remember that we discussed this micro-macro dilemma in Chapter 1.) This means that marketing managers should be concerned with social responsibility—a firm's obligation to improve its positive effects on society and reduce its negative effects. Being socially responsible sometimes requires difficult trade-offs.

Consider, for example, the environmental problems created by CFCs, chemicals used in hundreds of critical products, including fire extinguishers, refrigerators, cooling systems, insulation, and electronic circuit boards. We now know that CFCs deplete the earth's ozone layer. Yet it is not possible to immediately stop producing and using all CFCs. For many products critical to society, there is no feasible short-term substitute for CFCs. Du Pont and other producers of CFCs are working hard to balance these conflicting demands. Yet you can see that there are no easy answers for how these conflicts should be resolved.[5]

The issue of social responsibility in marketing also raises other important questions—for which there are no easy answers.

Should all consumer needs be satisfied?

Some consumers want products that may not be safe or good for them in the long run. Some critics argue that businesses should not offer high-heeled shoes, alcoholic beverages, sugar-coated cereals, soft drinks, and many processed foods because they aren't good for consumers in the long run.

Similarly, bicycles are one of the most dangerous products identified by the Consumer Product Safety Commission. Should Schwinn stop production? What about skis, mopeds, and scuba equipment? Who should decide if these products will be offered to consumers? Is this a micro-marketing issue or a macro-marketing issue?

What if it cuts into profits?

Being more socially conscious often seems to lead to positive customer response. For example, Gerber had great success when it improved the nutritional quality of its baby food. And many consumers have been eager to buy products that are friendly to the environment (even at a higher price).

Yet as the examples above show, there are times when being socially responsible conflicts with a firm's profit objective. The concerns prompt some critics to raise the basic question: Is the marketing concept really desirable?

Many socially conscious marketing managers are trying to resolve this problem. Their definition of customer satisfaction includes long-range effects—as well as immediate customer satisfaction. They try to balance consumer, company, *and* social interests.

You too will have to make choices that balance these social concerns—either in your role as a consumer or as a manager in a business firm. So throughout the text we will be discussing many of the social issues faced by marketing managers.

The marketing concept guides marketing ethics

Organizations that have adopted the marketing concept are concerned about marketing ethics as well as broader issues of social responsibility. It is simply not possible for a firm to be truly consumer-oriented and at the same time intentionally unethical.

Individual managers in an organization may have different values. As a result, problems may arise when someone does not share the same marketing ethics as others in the organization. One person operating alone can damage a firm's reputation and even survival. The marketing concept helps to avoid such problems because it involves a companywide focus, it is a foundation for marketing ethics common to everyone in a firm.

To be certain that standards for marketing ethics are as clear as possible, many organizations have developed their own written codes of ethics. Consistent with the marketing concept, these codes usually state—at least at a general level—the ethical standards that everyone in the firm should follow in dealing with customers and other people. Many professional societies have also adopted such codes. For example, the American Marketing Association's code of ethics—see Exhibit 2–3—sets specific ethical standards for many aspects of the management job in marketing.[6]

THE MANAGEMENT JOB IN MARKETING

Now that you know about the marketing concept—a philosophy to guide the whole firm—let's look more closely at how a marketing manager helps a firm to achieve its objectives. The marketing manager is a manager, so let's look at the marketing management process.

The **marketing management process** is the process of (1) *planning* marketing activities, (2) directing the *implementation* of the plans, and (3) *controlling* these plans. Planning, implementation, and control are basic jobs of all managers—but here we will emphasize what they mean to marketing managers.

Exhibit 2–4 shows the relationships among the three jobs in the marketing management process. The jobs are all connected to show that the marketing management process is continuous. In the planning job, managers set guidelines for the implementing job—and specify expected results. They use these expected results in the control job—to determine if everything has worked out as planned. The link from the control job to the planning job is especially important. This feedback often leads to changes in the plans—or to new plans.

Marketing managers should seek new opportunities

Marketing managers cannot be satisfied just planning present activities. Markets are dynamic. Consumers' needs, competitors, and the environment keep changing.

Consider Parker Brothers, a company that seemed to have a "Monopoly" in family games. While it continued selling board games, firms like Atari and Nintendo zoomed in with video game competition. Of course, not every opportunity is good for every company. Really attractive opportunities are those that fit with what the whole company wants—and is able to do.

Strategic management planning concerns the whole firm

The job of planning strategies to guide a whole company is called **strategic (management) planning**—the managerial process of developing and maintaining a match between an organization's resources and its market opportunities. This is a top management job that includes planning not only for marketing activities but also for production, research and development, and other functional areas.

Exhibit 2–3 Code of Ethics, American Marketing Association

CODE OF ETHICS

Members of the American Marketing Association (AMA) are committed to ethical professional conduct. They have joined together in subscribing to this Code of Ethics embracing the following topics:

Responsibilities of the Marketer

Marketers must accept responsibility for the consequences of their activities and make every effort to ensure that their decisions, recommendations, and actions function to identify, serve, and satisfy all relevant publics: customers, organizations and society.

Marketers' professional conduct must be guided by:

1. The basic rule of professional ethics: not knowingly to do harm;
2. The adherence to all applicable laws and regulations;
3. The accurate representation of their education, training and experience; and
4. The active support, practice and promotion of this Code of Ethics.

Honesty and Fairness

Marketers shall uphold and advance the integrity, honor, and dignity of the marketing profession by:

1. Being honest in serving consumers, clients, employees, suppliers, distributors and the public;
2. Not knowingly participating in conflict of interest without prior notice to all parties involved; and
3. Establishing equitable fee schedules including the payment or receipt of usual, customary and/or legal compensation for marketing exchanges.

Rights and Duties of Parties in the Marketing Exchange Process

Participants in the marketing exchange process should be able to expect that:

1. Products and services offered are safe and fit for their intended uses;
2. Communications about offered products and services are not deceptive;
3. All parties intend to discharge their obligations, financial and otherwise, in good faith; and
4. Appropriate internal methods exist for equitable adjustment and/or redress of grievances concerning purchases.

It is understood that the above would include, *but is not limited to,* the following responsibilities of the marketer:

In the area of product development and management,
- disclosure of all substantial risks associated with product or service usage;
- identification of any product component substitution that might materially change the product or impact on the buyer's purchase decision;
- identification of extra-cost added features.

In the area of promotions,
- avoidance of false and misleading advertising;
- rejection of high pressure manipulations, or misleading sales tactics;
- avoidance of sales promotions that use deception or manipulation.

In the area of distribution,
- not manipulating the availability of a product for purpose of exploitation;
- not using coercion in the marketing channel;
- not exerting undue influence over the reseller's choice to handle a product.

In the area of pricing,
- not engaging in price fixing;
- not practicing predatory pricing;
- disclosing the full price associated with any purchase.

In the area of marketing research,
- prohibiting selling or fund raising under the guise of conducting research;
- maintaining research integrity by avoiding misrepresentation and omission of pertinent research data;
- treating outside clients and suppliers fairly.

Organizational Relationships

Marketers should be aware of how their behavior may influence or impact on the behavior of others in organizational relationships. They should not demand, encourage or apply coercion to obtain unethical behavior in their relationships with others, such as employees, suppliers or customers.

1. Apply confidentiality and anonymity in professional relationships with regard to privileged information;
2. Meet their obligations and responsibilities in contracts and mutual agreements in a timely manner;
3. Avoid taking the work of others, in whole, or in part, and represent this work as their own or directly benefit from it without compensation or consent of the originator or owner;
4. Avoid manipulation to take advantage of situations to maximize personal welfare in a way that unfairly deprives or damages the organization or others.

Any AMA members found to be in violation of any provision of this Code of Ethics may have his or her Association membership suspended or revoked.

We won't discuss whole-company planning in this text, but you need to understand that marketing department plans are not whole-company plans. On the other hand, company plans should be market-oriented. And the marketing manager's plans can set the tone and direction for the whole company. So we will use *strategy planning* and *marketing strategy planning* to mean the same thing.[7]

Exhibit 2–4   The Marketing Management Process

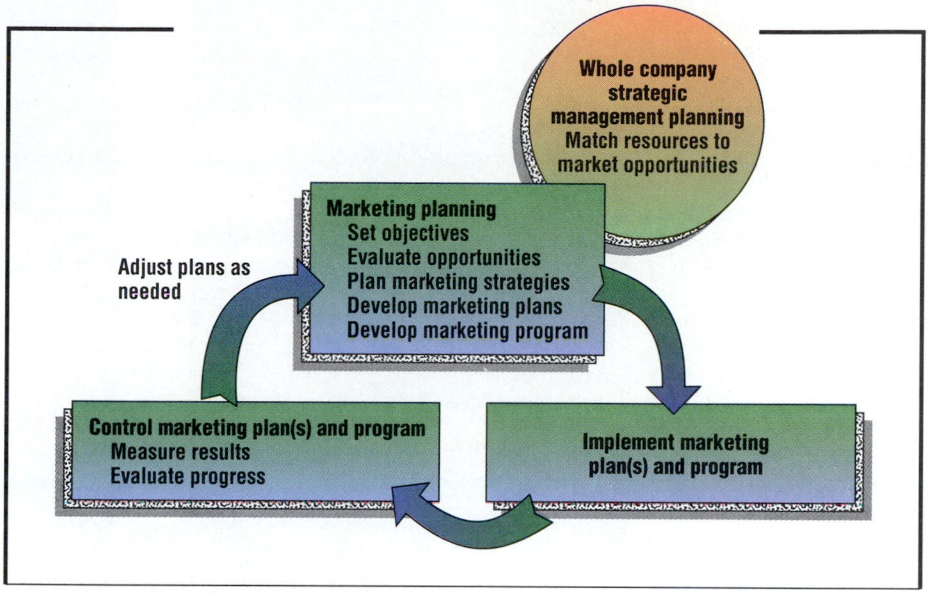

Whole company strategic management planning
Match resources to market opportunities

Marketing planning
Set objectives
Evaluate opportunities
Plan marketing strategies
Develop marketing plans
Develop marketing program

Adjust plans as needed

Control marketing plan(s) and program
Measure results
Evaluate progress

Implement marketing plan(s) and program

WHAT IS MARKETING STRATEGY PLANNING?

Marketing strategy planning means finding attractive opportunities and developing profitable marketing strategies. But what is a marketing strategy? We have used these words rather casually so far. Now let's see what they really mean.

What is a marketing strategy?

A **marketing strategy** specifies a target market and a related marketing mix. It is a big picture of what a firm will do in some market. Two interrelated parts are needed:

1. A **target market**—a fairly homogeneous (similar) group of customers to whom a company wishes to appeal.
2. A **marketing mix**—the controllable variables the company puts together to satisfy this target group.

Exhibit 2–5
A Marketing Strategy

The importance of target customers in this process can be seen in Exhibit 2–5, where the customer—the C—is at the center of the diagram. The customer is surrounded by the controllable variables that we call the "marketing mix." A typical marketing mix includes some product, offered at a price, with some promotion to tell potential customers about the product, and a way to reach the customer's place.

L. L. Bean's marketing strategy aims at target customers who are interested in enjoying the outdoors. Bean's strategy calls for quality products that are well suited to a wide variety of outdoor needs—whether it's clothing or equipment for fishing, hiking, or camping. Bean field-tests every product it plans to sell—to be certain that products live up to the firm's "100% satisfaction" guarantee. Although Bean operates a retail store in Freeport, Maine, it uses direct-mail catalog promotion to reach customers all over the world. To make ordering convenient, customers can call toll-free 24 hours a day—and they get whatever advice they need because all of the salespeople are real experts on what they sell. To ensure that orders reach the customer's place fast, Bean uses UPS to ship most items directly from its own warehouse. Bean's pricing is basically competitive with other outdoor sporting specialty stores, but the quality and convenience of dealing with Bean gives it a competitive advantage with its loyal target customers.[8]

L. L. Bean tailors its marketing mix to the needs of a specific target market.

SELECTING A MARKET-ORIENTED STRATEGY IS TARGET MARKETING

Target marketing is not mass marketing

Note that a marketing strategy specifies some *particular* target customers. This approach is called target marketing to distinguish it from mass marketing. **Target marketing** says that a marketing mix is tailored to fit some specific target customers. In contrast, **mass marketing**—the typical production-oriented approach—vaguely aims at "everyone" with the same marketing mix. Mass marketing assumes that everyone is the same—and considers everyone a potential customer.

Mass marketers may do target marketing

Commonly used terms can be confusing here. The terms *mass marketing* and *mass marketers* do not mean the same thing. Far from it! *Mass marketing* means trying to sell to everyone, as we explained above. *Mass marketers* like General Foods and Wal-Mart are aiming at clearly defined target markets. The confusion with mass marketing occurs because their target markets usually are large and spread out.

Target marketing can mean big markets and profits

Target marketing is not limited to small market segments—only to fairly homogeneous ones. A very large market—even what is sometimes called the mass market—may be fairly homogeneous, and a target marketer will deliberately aim at it. For example, a very large group of parents of young children are homogeneous on many dimensions—including their attitudes about changing baby diapers. In the United States alone, this group spends about $3.5 billion a year on disposable diapers—so it should be no surprise that it is a major target market for companies like Kimberly-Clark (Huggies) and Procter & Gamble (Pampers). These days, so many customers in this target market buy disposable diapers that the challenge isn't just offering them a product they want, but in finding an ecologically sound way to dispose of it!

The basic reason for a marketing manager to focus on some specific target customers is to gain a competitive advantage—by developing a more-satisfying marketing mix that should also be more profitable for the firm. Toshiba, for example, established a competitive advantage with traveling business computer users by being first to offer a powerful laptop computer. Tianguis, a three-store grocery chain in Southern California, attracts Hispanic customers with special product lines and Spanish-speaking employees. Charles Schwab, the discount stock

BALDOR ELECTRIC POWERS PAST WORLDWIDE COMPETITION

Baldor Electric Company manufactures and markets a variety of electric motors. A decade ago Baldor faced a real threat. There was a big slump in the demand for electric motors. Even worse, producers in Japan, South Korea, and Taiwan began pumping out low-cost commodity-type motors from automated factories. Some big U.S. firms, including Westinghouse (which had originally developed the electric motor), left the business altogether. Others, like General Electric and Emerson Electric, tried to compete by moving production offshore to reduce costs.

This tough situation prompted marketing managers at Baldor to rethink their marketing strategies. Rather than trying to compete with motors that were like those available from many other suppliers, they focused on specific target markets and their special needs. For example, Baldor developed special motors to run heart pumps in hospitals, lint-proof motors for textile plants, and even a 500-horsepower unit for rolling steel. None of these motors is a big seller. Baldor adjusts so much of its production to suit special demands that on average it only produces 50 units of any given motor. However, in combination they now give Baldor more than 10 percent of the $1 billion annual U.S. sales of industrial motors—and Baldor is expanding its distribution and market share in 40 other countries as well. Because Baldor's marketing mix offers target customers something special, they are already interested when the Baldor salesperson calls—and Baldor can command a premium price. The whole marketing program has led to record-breaking profits.[9]

brokerage firm, targets knowledgeable investors who want a convenient, low-cost way to buy and sell stocks by phone without a lot of advice (or pressure) from a salesperson.

DEVELOPING MARKETING MIXES FOR TARGET MARKETS

There are many marketing mix decisions

There are many possible ways to satisfy the needs of target customers. A product can have many different features and quality levels. Service levels can be adjusted. The package can be of various sizes, colors, or materials. The brand name and warranty can be changed. Various advertising media—newspapers, magazines, radio, television, billboards—may be used. A company's own sales force or other sales specialists can be used. Different prices can be charged. Price discounts may be given, and so on. With so many possible variables, is there any way to help organize all these decisions and simplify the selection of marketing mixes? The answer is yes.

The four "Ps" make up a marketing mix

It is useful to reduce all the variables in the marketing mix to four basic ones:

Product.   Promotion.

Place.   Price.

Exhibit 2–6
A Marketing Strategy—Showing the Four Ps of a Marketing Mix

It helps to think of the four major parts of a marketing mix as the "four Ps". Exhibit 2–6 emphasizes their relationship and their common focus on the customer—C.

Customer is not part of the marketing mix

The customer is shown surrounded by the four Ps in Exhibit 2–6. Some students assume that the customer is part of the marketing mix—but this is not so. The customer should be the *target* of all marketing efforts. The customer is placed in the center of the diagram to show this. The C stands for some specific customers—the target market.

Exhibit 2–7 shows some of the strategy decision variables organized by the four Ps. These will be discussed in later chapters. For now, let's just describe each P briefly.

Exhibit 2–7   Strategy Decision Areas Organized by the Four Ps

Product	Place	Promotion	Price
Physical good	Objectives	Objectives	Objectives
Service	Channel type	Promotion blend	Flexibility
Features	Market exposure	Salespeople	Level over
Quality level	Kinds of	Kind	product life
Accessories	middlemen	Number	cycle
Installation	Kinds and	Selection	Geographic terms
Instructions	locations of	Training	Discounts
Warranty	stores	Motivation	Allowances
Product lines	How to handle	Advertising	
Packaging	transporting	Targets	
Branding	and storing	Kinds of ads	
	Service levels	Media type	
	Recruiting	Copy thrust	
	middlemen	Prepared by	
	Managing	whom	
	channels	Sales promotion	
		Publicity	

Product—the good or service for the target's needs

The Product decision area is concerned with developing the right product for the target market. This offering may involve a physical good, a service, or a blend of both. Keep in mind that Product is not limited to physical goods. For example, the product of H & R Block is a completed tax form. The product of a political party is the set of causes it will work to achieve. The important thing to remember is that your good and/or service should satisfy some customers' needs.

Along with other Product-area decisions, we will talk about developing and managing new products and whole product lines. We'll also discuss the characteristics of various kinds of products so that you will be able to make generalizations about product classes. This will help you to develop whole marketing mixes more quickly.

Place—reaching the target

Place is concerned with all the decisions involved in getting the right product to the target market's Place. A product isn't much good to a customer if it isn't available when and where it's wanted.

A product reaches customers through a channel of distribution. A **channel of distribution** is any series of firms (or individuals) from producer to final user or consumer.

Sometimes a channel system is quite short. It may run directly from a producer to a final user or consumer. This is especially common in business markets and in the marketing of services. Often the system is more complex—involving many different kinds of middlemen and specialists. And if a marketing manager has several different target markets, several different channels of distribution might be needed.

We will also see how physical distribution service levels and decisions concerning logistics (transporting and storing) relate to the other Place decisions and the rest of the marketing mix.

Promotion—telling and selling the customer

The third P—Promotion—is concerned with telling the target market about the right product. Promotion includes personal selling, mass selling, and sales promotion. It is the marketing manager's job to blend these methods.

Personal selling involves direct communication between sellers and potential customers. Personal selling usually happens face-to-face, but sometimes the communication occurs over the telephone. Personal selling lets the salesperson adapt the firm's marketing

A firm's product may involve a physical good (like cereal), or a service (like a stay in a hotel), or a combination of both.

mix to each potential customer. But this individual attention comes at a price; personal selling can be very expensive. Often this personal effort has to be blended with mass selling and sales promotion.

Mass selling is communicating with large numbers of customers at the same time. The main form of mass selling is **advertising**—any *paid* form of nonpersonal presentation of ideas, goods, or services by an identified sponsor. **Publicity**—any *unpaid* form of nonpersonal presentation of ideas, goods, or services—is another important form of mass selling.

Sales promotion refers to those promotion activities—other than advertising, publicity, and personal selling—that stimulate interest, trial, or purchase by final customers or others in the channel. This can involve use of coupons, point-of-purchase materials, samples, signs, catalogs, novelties, and circulars.

Price—making it right

In addition to developing the right Product, Place, and Promotion, marketing managers must also decide the right Price. In setting a price, they must consider the kind of competition in the target market—and the cost of the whole marketing mix. They must also try to estimate customer reaction to possible prices. Besides this, they also must know current practices as to markups, discounts, and other terms of sale.

Each of the four Ps contributes to the whole

All four Ps are needed in a marketing mix. In fact, they should all be tied together. But is any one more important than the others? Generally speaking, the answer is no—all contribute to one whole. When a marketing mix is being developed, all (final) decisions about the Ps should be made at the same time.

Let's sum up our discussion of marketing mix planning thus far. We develop a *Product* to satisfy the target customers. We find a way to reach our target customers' *Place*. We use *Promotion* to tell the target customers (and middlemen) about the product that has been designed for them. And we set a *Price* after estimating expected customer reaction to the total offering and the costs of getting it to them.

Both jobs must be done together

It is important to stress—it cannot be overemphasized—that selecting a target market *and* developing a marketing mix are interrelated. Both parts of a marketing strategy must be decided together. It is *strategies* that must be evaluated against the company's objectives—not alternative target markets or alternative marketing mixes.

THE MARKETING PLAN IS A GUIDE TO IMPLEMENTATION AND CONTROL

Now that the key ideas of marketing strategy planning have been introduced, we can return to our overview of the marketing management process. You will see how a marketing strategy leads to a marketing plan and ultimately to implementation and control (see Exhibit 2–4).

Marketing plan fills out marketing strategy

A marketing strategy sets a target market and a marketing mix. It is a big picture of what a firm will do in some market. A marketing plan goes farther. A **marketing plan** is a written statement of a marketing strategy *and* the time-related details for carrying out the strategy. It should spell out the following in detail: (1) what marketing mix will be offered, to whom (that is, the target market), and for how long; (2) what company resources (shown as costs) will be needed at what rate (month by month, perhaps); and (3) what results are expected (sales and profits, perhaps monthly or quarterly). The plan should also include some control procedures—so that whoever is to carry out the plan will know if things are going wrong. This might be something as simple as comparing actual sales against expected sales—with a warning flag to be raised whenever total sales fall below a certain level.

Implementation puts plans into operation

After a marketing plan is developed, a marketing manager knows *what* needs to be done. Then the manager is concerned with **implementation**—putting marketing plans into operation.

Our focus has been—and will continue to be—on developing marketing strategies. But it is also important to see that eventually marketing managers must develop and implement marketing plans. We discuss this more fully in Chapter 18.[10]

Several plans make a whole marketing program

Most companies implement more than one marketing strategy—and related marketing plan—at the same time. They may have several products—some of them quite different—that are aimed at different target markets. The other elements of the marketing mix may vary too. Gillette's Right Guard deodorant, its Atra Plus razor blades, and its Liquid Paper correction fluid all have different marketing mixes. Yet the strategies for each must be implemented at the same time.[11]

A **marketing program** blends all of the firm's marketing plans into one big plan. See Exhibit 2–8. This program, then, is the responsibility of the whole company. Typically, the whole *marketing program* is an integrated part of the whole-company strategic plan we discussed earlier.

Ultimately, marketing managers plan and implement a whole marketing program. In this text, however, we will emphasize planning one marketing strategy at a time, rather than planning—or implementing—a whole marketing program. This is practical because it is important to plan each strategy carefully. Too many marketing managers fall into sloppy thinking. They try to develop too many strategies all at once—and don't develop any very carefully. Good plans are the building blocks of marketing management.

Control is analyzing and correcting what you've done

The control job provides the feedback that leads managers to modify their marketing strategies. To maintain control, a marketing manager uses a number of tools—like computer sales analysis, marketing research surveys, and accounting analysis of expenses and profits. As we talk about each of the marketing decision areas, we will discuss some of the

Exhibit 2–8   Elements of a Firm's Marketing Program

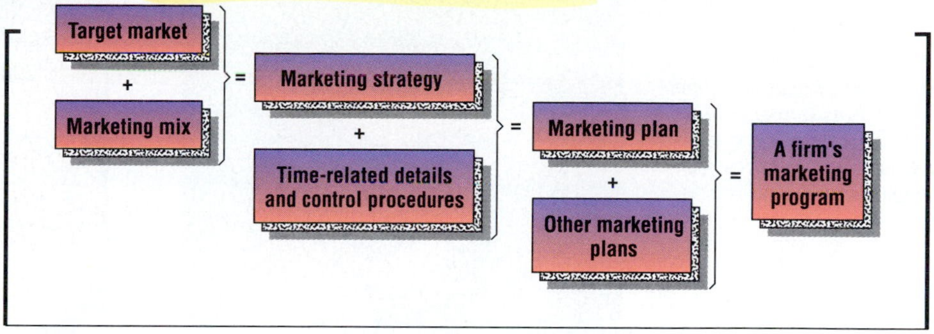

control problems. This will help you understand how control keeps the firm on course—or shows the need to plan a new course.

THE IMPORTANCE OF MARKETING STRATEGY PLANNING

We emphasize the planning part of the marketing manager's job for a good reason. The "one-time" strategy decisions—the decisions that decide what business the company is in and the strategies it will follow—usually determine success—or failure. An extremely good plan might be carried out badly and still be profitable, while a poor but well-implemented plan can lose money. The case history that follows shows the importance of planning—and why we emphasize marketing strategy planning throughout this text.

Time for new strategies in the watch industry

The conventional watch makers—both domestic and foreign—had always aimed at customers who thought of watches as high-priced, high-quality symbols to mark special events—like graduations or retirement. Advertising was concentrated around Christmas and graduation time and stressed a watch's symbolic appeal. Expensive jewelry stores were the main retail outlets.

This commonly accepted strategy of the major watch companies ignored people in the target market that just wanted to tell the time—and were interested in a reliable, low-priced watch. So the U.S. Time Company developed a successful strategy around its Timex watches—and became the world's largest watch company. Timex completely upset the watch industry—both foreign and domestic—not only by offering a good product (with a one-year repair or replace guarantee) at a lower price, but also by using new, lower-cost channels of distribution. Its watches were widely available in drugstores, discount houses, and nearly any other retail stores that would carry them.

Marketing managers at Timex soon faced a new challenge. Texas Instruments, a new competitor in the watch market, took the industry by storm with its low-cost but very accurate electronic watches—using the same channels Timex had originally developed. But other firms quickly developed a watch that used a more-stylish liquid crystal display for the digital readout. Texas Instruments could not change quickly enough to keep up, and the other companies took away its customers. The competition became so intense that Texas Instruments stopped marketing watches altogether.

While Timex and others were focusing on lower-priced watches, Japan's Seiko captured a commanding share of the high-priced gift market for its stylish and accurate quartz watches by obtaining strong distribution. All of this forced many traditional watch makers—like some of the once-famous Swiss brands—to close their factories.

In 1983 Switzerland's Swatch launched its colorful, affordable plastic watches—and changed what consumers see when they look at their watches. Swatch promoted its

Timex developed a watch with large numbers to meet the needs of older consumers. Tissot developed its Woodwatch to appeal to upscale European consumers interested in distinctive design.

watches as fashion accessories and set them apart from those of other firms, whose ads squabbled about whose watches were most accurate and dependable. Swatch was also able to attract new middlemen by focusing its distribution on upscale fashion and department stores. The marketing mix Swatch developed around its fashion watch idea was so successful it didn't just increase Swatch's share of the market. The total size of the watch market increased because many consumers bought several watches to match different fashions.

Swatch's success prompted Timex, Seiko, and others to pay more attention to consumer fashion preferences. For example, Timex developed its fashionable Watercolors line targeted at teens. Timex has also emphasized better styling to compete in the higher-priced market—and broadened its offering to defend its position in the low- to mid-priced segment.

The economic downturn in the early 1990s brought more changes. Sales of fashion watches leveled off, so Swatch is now targeting segments with other needs. For example, in 1990 it introduced a $45 scuba watch guaranteed to keep ticking at depths of 600 feet. Consumers have become more cost conscious—and less interested in expensive watches like those made by Rolex that were the in status symbol a few years earlier. The reemergence of value-seeking customers prompted Timex to return to its famous advertising tagline of the 1960s: "It takes a licking and keeps on ticking." Its position as the inexpensive-but-durable choice has helped it strengthen its distribution in department stores, sporting goods stores, and other channels.[12]

Creative strategy planning needed for survival

Dramatic shifts in strategy—like those described above—may surprise conventional, production-oriented managers. But such changes are becoming much more common—and should be expected. Industries or firms that have accepted the marketing concept realize that they cannot define their line of business in terms of the products they currently produce or sell. Rather they have to think about the basic consumer needs they serve—and how those needs may change in the future. If they are too nearsighted, they may fail to see what's coming until too late.

Exhibit 2–9   Marketing Manager's Framework

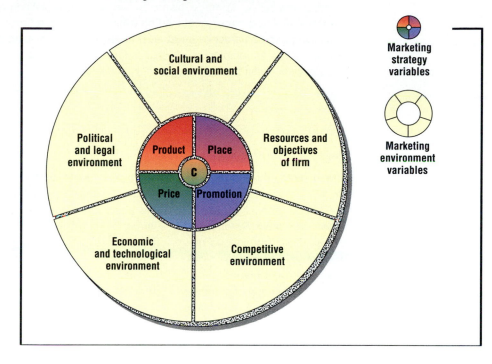

Creative strategy planning is becoming even more important because firms can no longer win profits just by spending more money on plant and equipment. Moreover, domestic and foreign competition threatens those who can't create more satisfying goods and services. New markets, new customers, and new ways of doing things must be found if companies are to operate profitably in the future—and contribute to the macro-marketing system.

STRATEGY PLANNING DOESN'T TAKE PLACE IN A VACUUM

Strategy planning takes place within a framework

Our examples show that a marketing manager's strategy planning cannot take place in a vacuum. Instead, the manager works with controllable variables within a framework involving many variables that must be considered even though the manager can't control them. Exhibit 2–9 illustrates this framework and shows that the typical marketing manager must be concerned about the competitive environment, economic and technological environment, political and legal environment, cultural and social environment, and the firm's resources and objectives. We discuss these marketing environment variables in more detail in the next two chapters. But clearly, the environment in which the marketing manager operates affects strategy planning.

MARKET-ORIENTED STRATEGY PLANNING HELPS NONMARKETING PEOPLE TOO

While market-oriented strategy planning is helpful to marketers, it is also needed by accountants, production and personnel people, and all other specialists. A market-oriented plan lets everybody in the firm know what ballpark they are playing in—and what they are trying to accomplish. In other words, it gives direction to the whole business effort. An accountant can't set budgets without a plan, except perhaps by mechanically projecting last year's budget. Similarly, a financial manager can't project cash needs without some idea of expected sales to target customers—and the costs of satisfying them.

We will use the term *marketing manager* for editorial convenience, but when we talk about marketing strategy planning, we are really talking about the planning that a market-oriented manager should do when developing a firm's strategic plans. This kind of thinking should be done—or at least understood—by everyone in the organization who is responsible for planning. And this means even the entry-level salesperson, production supervisor, retail buyer, or personnel counselor.

CONCLUSION

Marketing's role within a marketing-oriented firm is to provide direction for a firm. The marketing concept stresses that the company's efforts should focus on satisfying some target customers—at a profit. Production-oriented firms tend to forget this. Often the various departments within a production-oriented firm let their natural conflicts of interest lead them to building fences.

The job of marketing management is one of continuous planning, implementing, and control. The marketing manager must constantly study the environment—seeking attractive opportunities and planning new strategies. Possible target markets must be matched with marketing mixes the firm can offer. Then attractive strategies—really, whole marketing plans—are chosen for implementation. Controls are needed to be sure that the plans are carried out successfully. If anything goes wrong along the way, continual feedback should cause the process to be started over again—with the marketing manager planning more attractive marketing strategies.

A marketing mix has four variables: the four Ps—Product, Place, Promotion, and Price. Most of this text is concerned with developing profitable marketing mixes for clearly defined target markets. So after several chapters on analyzing target markets, we will discuss each of the four Ps in greater detail.

QUESTIONS AND PROBLEMS

1. Define the marketing concept in your own words and then explain why the notion of profit is usually included in this definition.

2. Define the marketing concept in your own words and then suggest how acceptance of this concept might affect the organization and operation of your college.

3. Distinguish between production orientation and marketing orientation, illustrating with local examples.

4. Explain why a firm should view its internal activities as part of a total system. Illustrate your answer for (*a*) a large grocery products producer, (*b*) a plumbing wholesaler, and (*c*) a department store chain.

5. Does the acceptance of the marketing concept almost require that a firm view itself as a total system?

6. Distinguish clearly between a marketing strategy and a marketing mix. Use an example.

7. Distinguish clearly between mass marketing and target marketing. Use an example.

8. Why is the customer placed in the center of the four Ps in the text diagram of a marketing strategy (Exhibit 2–6)? Explain, using a specific example from your own experience.

9. Explain, in your own words, what each of the four Ps involves.

10. Distinguish between a strategy, a marketing plan, and a marketing program, illustrating for a local retailer.

11. Outline a marketing strategy for each of the following new products: (*a*) a radically new design for a toothbrush, (*b*) a new fishing reel, (*c*) a new wonder drug, and (*d*) a new industrial stapling machine.

12. Provide a specific illustration of why marketing strategy planning is important for all businesspeople, not just for those in the marketing department.

SUGGESTED CASES

2. Nutra, Inc.

5. General Chemical Company

27. KASTORS, Inc.

COMPUTER-AIDED PROBLEM

2. Target Marketing

T-Bar, Inc., has developed a new T-shaped ski-boot carrier. T-Bar's marketing managers are comparing the potential profitability of using a target marketing strategy with a mass marketing "strategy."

The target marketing strategy would focus on buyers of new ski-boots. People who buy new boots are often interested in carriers because they keep the boots from being scratched. The plan calls for producing the T-Bar carriers in different colors—to match different boot colors. This would increase production costs slightly over making them all the same color. But T-Bar's marketing managers think the color-matched carriers will attract a larger share of the market—and command a higher price.

Alternatively, T-Bar's mass marketing effort would be directed to all skiers—a much larger number of people. But a smaller percentage of the consumers in this group will actually buy this product. Some skiers rent their equipment and won't buy any type of carrier; others already have carriers or are just not interested. Some people who are interested in buying will want a lower-priced carrier made by a competing firm. With the mass marketing approach, T-Bar would not offer different colors. While that might make the carriers less attractive to some customers, it would reduce production costs and make it possible to sell the carriers at a lower price.

Trying to reach the mass market will take more promotion and require more middlemen in more locations—so promotion costs and distribution costs are higher with that approach. In addition, handling the larger unit volume of business is expected to require more overhead expense.

The spreadsheet gives more detail about both approaches. In the spreadsheet, quantity sold (by T-Bar) is equal to the number of skiers who will actually buy any type of ski-boot carrier multiplied by the share of those purchases won by T-Bar's marketing mix. Thus, a change in the number of people in the market, the percent of people who will buy, or the firm's percent (share) will affect quantity sold. And a change in quantity sold will affect total revenue, total cost, and profit.

a. On a piece of paper, show the calculations that prove that the spreadsheet "total profit" value for the target marketing strategy is correct. (Hint: remember to multiply unit production cost and unit distribution cost by the quantity sold.) Which approach seems better—target marketing or mass marketing? Why?

b. In the targeting strategy, if T-Bar could find a way to reduce distribution cost per unit to $0.80, how much would profit increase?

c. If, in addition to reducing distribution to $0.80 per unit, T-Bar is able to fine-tune its marketing mix decisions to increase its share of purchases from 50 percent to 55 percent—without increasing costs—what would happen to total profit? What does this analysis suggest about the importance of a marketing manager knowing enough about target markets to be an effective target marketer?

For additional questions related to this problem, see Exercise 2–4 in the *Learning Aid for use with Essentials of Marketing,* 6th edition.

Economics Fundamentals

Appendix **A**

When You Finish This Appendix, You Should

❶

Understand the law of diminishing demand.

❷

Understand demand and supply curves—and how they set the size of a market and its price level.

❸

Know about elasticity of demand and supply.

❹

Know why demand elasticity can be affected by availability of substitutes.

❺

Know the different kinds of competitive situations and understand why they are important to marketing managers.

❻

Recognize the important new terms (shown in red).

A good marketing manager should be an expert on markets—and the nature of competition in markets. The economist's traditional analysis of demand and supply is a useful tool for analyzing markets. In particular, you should master the concepts of a demand curve and demand elasticity. A firm's demand curve shows how the target customers view the firm's Product—really its whole marketing mix. And the interaction of demand and supply curves helps set the size of a market—and the market price. The interaction of supply and demand also determines the nature of the competitive environment, which has an important effect on strategy planning. These ideas are discussed more fully in the following sections.

PRODUCTS AND MARKETS AS SEEN BY CUSTOMERS AND POTENTIAL CUSTOMERS

Economists provide useful insights

How potential customers (not the firm) see a firm's product (marketing mix) affects how much they are willing to pay for it, where it should be made available, and how eager they are for it—if they want it at all. In other words, their view has a very direct bearing on marketing strategy planning.

Economists have been concerned with market behavior for years. Their analytical tools can be quite helpful in summarizing how customers view products and how markets behave.

Economists see individual customers choosing among alternatives

Economics is sometimes called the dismal science—because it says that most customers have a limited income and simply cannot buy everything they want. They must balance their needs and the prices of various products.

Economists usually assume that customers have a fairly definite set of preferences—and that they evaluate alternatives in terms of whether the alternatives will make them feel better (or worse) or in some way improve (or change) their situation.

But what exactly is the nature of a customer's desire for a particular product?

Usually economists answer this question in terms of the extra utility the customer can obtain by buying more of a particular product—or how much utility would be lost if the customer had less of the product. (Students who wish further discussion of this approach should refer to indifference-curve analysis in any standard economics text.)

It is easier to understand the idea of utility if we look at what happens when the price of one of the customer's usual purchases changes.

The law of diminishing demand

Suppose that consumers buy potatoes in 10-pound bags at the same time they buy other foods such as bread and rice. If the consumers are mainly interested in buying a certain amount of food and the price of the potatoes drops, it seems reasonable to expect that they will switch some of their food money to potatoes and away from some other foods. But if the price of potatoes rises, you expect our consumers to buy fewer potatoes and more of other foods.

The general relationship between price and quantity demanded illustrated by this food example is called the **law of diminishing demand**—which says that if the price of a product is raised, a smaller quantity will be demanded and if the price of a product is lowered, a greater quantity will be demanded.

The relationship between price and quantity demanded in a market is what economists call a demand schedule. An example is shown in Exhibit A–1. For each row in the table, Column 2 shows the quantity consumers will want (demand) if they have to pay the price given in Column 1. The third column shows that the total revenue (sales) in the potato market is equal to the quantity demanded at a given price times that price. Note that as prices drop, the total *unit* quantity increases, yet the total *revenue* decreases. Fill in the blank lines in the third column and observe the behavior of total revenue—an important

Exhibit A–1   Demand Schedule for Potatoes (10-pound bags)

Point	(1) Price of Potatoes per Bag (P)	(2) Quantity Demanded (bags per month) (Q)	(3) Total Revenue per Month (P × Q = TR)
A	$1.60	8,000,000	$12,800,000
B	1.30	9,000,000	_____
C	1.00	11,000,000	11,000,000
D	0.70	14,000,000	_____
E	0.40	19,000,000	_____

number for the marketing manager. We will explain what you should have noticed—and why—a little later.

The demand curve—usually down-sloping

If your only interest is seeing at which price the company will earn the greatest total revenue, the demand schedule may be adequate. But a demand curve shows more. A **demand curve** is a graph of the relationship between price and quantity demanded in a market—assuming that all other things stay the same. Exhibit A–2 shows the demand curve for potatoes—really just a plotting of the demand schedule in Exhibit A–1. It shows how many potatoes potential customers will demand at various possible prices. This is a down-sloping demand curve.

Most demand curves are down-sloping. This just means that if prices are decreased, the quantity customers demand will increase.

Demand curves always show the price on the vertical axis and the quantity demanded on the horizontal axis. In Exhibit A–2, we have shown the price in dollars. For consistency, we will use dollars in other examples. However, keep in mind that these same ideas hold regardless of what money unit (dollars, yen, francs, pounds, etc.) is used to represent price. Even at this early point, you should keep in mind that markets are not necessarily limited by national boundaries—or by one type of money.

Note that the demand curve only shows how customers will react to various possible prices. In a market, we see only one price at a time—not all of these prices. The curve, however, shows what quantities will be demanded—depending on what price is set.

Exhibit A–2   Demand Curve for Potatoes (10-pound bags)

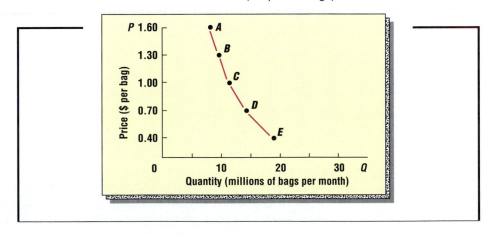

Exhibit A–3   Demand Schedule for 1-Cubic-Foot Microwave Ovens

Point	(1) Price per Microwave Oven (P)	(2) Quantity Demanded per Year (Q)	(3) Total Revenue (TR) per Year (P × Q = TR)
A	$300	20,000	$ 6,000,000
B	250	70,000	15,500,000
C	200	130,000	26,000,000
D	150	210,000	31,500,000
E	100	310,000	31,000,000

You probably think that most businesspeople would like to set a price that would result in a large sales revenue. Before discussing this, however, we should consider the demand schedule and curve for another product to get a more complete picture of demand-curve analysis.

Microwave oven demand curve looks different

A different demand schedule is the one for standard 1-cubic-foot microwave ovens shown in Exhibit A–3. Column 3 shows the total revenue that will be obtained at various possible prices and quantities. Again, as the price goes down, the quantity demanded goes up. But here, unlike the potato example, total revenue increases as prices go down—at least until the price drops to $150.

Every market has a demand curve—for some time period

These general demand relationships are typical for all products. But each product has its own demand schedule and curve in each potential market—no matter how small the market. In other words, a particular demand curve has meaning only for a particular market. We can think of demand curves for individuals, groups of individuals who form a target market, regions, and even countries. And the time period covered really should be specified—although this is often neglected because we usually think of monthly or yearly periods.

The difference between elastic and inelastic

The demand curve for microwave ovens (see Exhibit A–4) is down-sloping—but note that it is flatter than the curve for potatoes. It is important to understand what this flatness means.

We will consider the flatness in terms of total revenue—since this is what interests business managers.*

When you filled in the total revenue column for potatoes, you should have noticed that total revenue drops continually if the price is reduced. This looks undesirable for sellers—and illustrates inelastic demand. **Inelastic demand** means that although the quantity demanded increases if the price is decreased, the quantity demanded will not "stretch" enough—that is, it is not elastic enough—to avoid a decrease in total revenue.

In contrast, **elastic demand** means that if prices are dropped, the quantity demanded will stretch (increase) enough to increase total revenue. The upper part of the microwave oven demand curve is an example of elastic demand.

But note that if the microwave oven price is dropped from $150 to $100, total revenue will decrease. We can say, therefore, that between $150 and $100, demand is inelastic—that is, total revenue will decrease if price is lowered from $150 to $100.

---

*Strictly speaking, two curves should not be compared for flatness if the graph scales are different, but for our purposes now, we will do so to illustrate the idea of elasticity of demand. Actually, it would be more correct to compare two curves for one product—on the same graph. Then both the shape of the demand curve and its position on the graph would be important.

Exhibit A–4   Demand Curve for 1-Cubic-Foot Microwave Ovens

Thus, elasticity can be defined in terms of changes in total revenue. *If total revenue will increase if price is lowered, then demand is elastic. If total revenue will decrease if price is lowered, then demand is inelastic.* (Note: A special case, known as unitary elasticity of demand, occurs if total revenue stays the same when prices change.)

Total revenue may increase if price is raised

A point often missed in discussions of demand is what happens when prices are raised instead of lowered. With elastic demand, total revenue will *decrease* if the price is *raised*. With inelastic demand, however, total revenue will *increase* if the price is *raised*.

The possibility of raising price and increasing dollar sales (total revenue) at the same time is attractive to managers. This only occurs if the demand curve is inelastic. Here total revenue will increase if price is raised, but total costs probably will not increase—and may actually go down—with smaller quantities. Keep in mind that profit is equal to total revenue minus total costs. So—when demand is inelastic—profit will increase as price is increased!

The ways total revenue changes as prices are raised are shown in Exhibit A–5. Here total revenue is the rectangular area formed by a price and its related quantity. The larger the rectangular area, the greater the total revenue.

P_1 is the original price here, and the total potential revenue with this original price is shown by the area with blue shading. The area with red shading shows the total revenue with the new price, P_2. There is some overlap in the total revenue areas, so the important areas are those with only one color. Note that in the left-hand figure—where demand is elastic—the revenue added (the red-only area) when the price is increased is less than the revenue lost (the blue-only area). Now, let's contrast this to the right-hand figure, where demand is inelastic. Only a small blue revenue area is given up for a much larger (red) one when price is raised.

An entire curve is not elastic or inelastic

It is important to see that it is *wrong to refer to a whole demand curve as elastic or inelastic.* Rather, elasticity for a particular demand curve refers to the change in total revenue between two points on the curve—not along the whole curve. You saw the change from elastic to inelastic in the microwave oven example. Generally, however, nearby points are either elastic or inelastic—so it is common to refer to a whole curve by the degree of elasticity in the price range that normally is of interest—the *relevant range*.

Exhibit A–5 Changes in Total Revenue as Prices Increase

Elastic demand

Original total revenue
= $7 x 50 = $350

New total revenue
= $9 x 20 = $180

Inelastic demand

Original total revenue
= $7 x 50 = $350

New total revenue
= $9 x 47 = $423

Demand elasticities
affected by availability of
substitutes and urgency
of need

At first, it may be difficult to see why one product has an elastic demand and another an inelastic demand. Many factors affect elasticity—such as the availability of substitutes, the importance of the item in the customer's budget, and the urgency of the customer's need and its relation to other needs. By looking more closely at one of these factors—the availability of substitutes—you will better understand why demand elasticities vary.

Substitutes are products that offer the buyer a choice. For example, many consumers see grapefruit as a substitute for oranges and hot dogs as a substitute for hamburgers. The greater the number of good substitutes available, the greater will be the elasticity of demand. From the consumer's perspective, products are good substitutes if they are very similar (homogeneous). If consumers see products as extremely different—or heterogeneous—then a particular need cannot easily be satisfied by substitutes. And the demand for the most satisfactory product may be quite inelastic.

As an example, if the price of hamburger is lowered (and other prices stay the same), the quantity demanded will increase a lot—as will total revenue. The reason is that not only will regular hamburger users buy more hamburger, but some consumers who formerly bought hot dogs or steaks probably will buy hamburger too. But if the price of hamburger is raised, the quantity demanded will decrease—perhaps sharply. Still, consumers will buy some hamburger—depending on how much the price has risen, their individual tastes, and what their guests expect (see Exhibit A–6).

In contrast to a product with many substitutes—such as hamburger—consider a product with few or no substitutes. Its demand curve will tend to be inelastic. Motor oil is a good example. Motor oil is needed to keep cars running. Yet no one person or family uses great quantities of motor oil. So it is not likely that the quantity of motor oil purchased will change much as long as price changes are *within a reasonable range.* Of course, if the

Exhibit A–6 Demand Curve for Hamburger (a product with many substitutes)

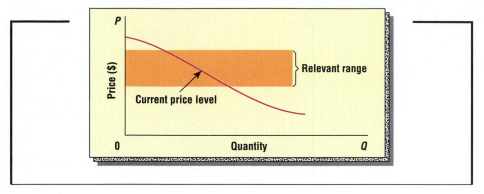

price is raised to a staggering figure, many people will buy less oil (change their oil less frequently). If the price is dropped to an extremely low level, manufacturers may buy more—say, as a lower-cost substitute for other chemicals typically used in making plastic (Exhibit A–7). But these extremes are outside the relevant range.

Demand curves are introduced here because the degree of elasticity of demand shows how potential customers feel about a product—and especially whether they see substitutes for the product. But to get a better understanding of markets, we must extend this economic analysis.

MARKETS AS SEEN BY SUPPLIERS

Customers may want some product—but if suppliers are not willing to supply it, then there is no market. So we'll study the economist's analysis of supply. And then we'll bring supply and demand together for a more complete understanding of markets.

Economists often use the kind of analysis we are discussing here to explain pricing in the marketplace. But that is not our intention. Here we are interested in how and why markets work—and the interaction of customers and potential suppliers. Later in this appendix we will review how competition affects prices, but our full discussion of how individual firms set prices—or should set prices—will come in Chapters 16 and 17.

Supply curves reflect supplier thinking

Generally speaking, suppliers' costs affect the quantity of products they are willing to offer in a market during any period. In other words, their costs affect their supply schedules and supply curves. While a demand curve shows the quantity of products customers will be willing to buy at various prices, a **supply curve** shows the quantity of products that will be supplied at various possible prices. Eventually, only one quantity will be offered and purchased. So a supply curve is really a hypothetical (what-if) description of what will be offered at various prices. It is, however, a very important curve. Together with a demand curve, it summarizes the attitudes and probable behavior of buyers and sellers about a particular product in a particular market—that is, in a product-market.

Some supply curves are vertical

We usually assume that supply curves tend to slope upward—that is, suppliers will be willing to offer greater quantities at higher prices. If a product's market price is very high, it seems only reasonable that producers will be anxious to produce more of the product—and even put workers on overtime or perhaps hire more workers to increase the quantity they

Exhibit A–7 Demand Curve for Motor Oil (a product with few substitutes)

can offer. Going further, it seems likely that producers of other products will switch their resources (farms, factories, labor, or retail facilities) to the product that is in great demand.

On the other hand, if consumers are only willing to pay a very low price for a particular product, it's reasonable to expect that producers will switch to other products—thus reducing supply. A supply schedule (Exhibit A–8) and a supply curve (Exhibit A–9) for potatoes illustrate these ideas. This supply curve shows how many potatoes would be produced and offered for sale at each possible market price in a given month.

In the very short run (say, over a few hours, a day, or a week), a supplier may not be able to change the supply at all. In this situation, we would see a vertical supply curve. This situation is often relevant in the market for fresh produce. Fresh strawberries, for example, continue to ripen, and a supplier wants to sell them quickly—preferably at a higher price—but in any case, they must be sold.

If the product is a service, it may not be easy to expand the supply in the short run. Additional barbers or medical doctors are not quickly trained and licensed, and they have only so much time to give each day. Further, the prospect of much higher prices in the near future cannot easily expand the supply of many services. For example, a hit play or an in restaurant or nightclub is limited in the amount of product it can offer at a particular time.

Elasticity of supply

The term *elasticity* also is used to describe supply curves. An extremely steep or almost vertical supply curve—often found in the short run—is called **inelastic supply** because the quantity supplied does not stretch much (if at all) if the price is raised. A flatter curve is called **elastic supply** because the quantity supplied does stretch more if the price

Exhibit A–8 Supply Schedule for Potatoes (10-pound bags)

Point	Possible Market Price per 10-lb. Bag	Number of Bags Sellers Will Supply per Month at Each Possible Market Price
A	$1.60	17,000,000
B	1.30	14,000,000
C	1.00	11,000,000
D	0.70	8,000,000
E	0.40	3,000,000

Note: This supply curve is for a month to emphasize that farmers might have some control over when they deliver their potatoes. There would be a different curve for each month.

Exhibit A–9   Supply Curve for Potatoes (10-pound bags)

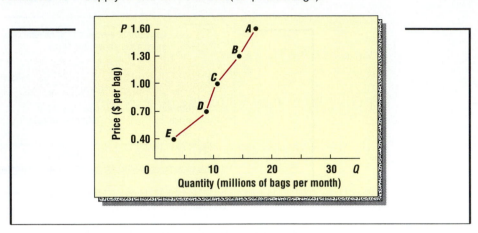

is raised. A slightly up-sloping supply curve is typical in longer-run market situations. Given more time, suppliers have a chance to adjust their offerings, and competitors may enter or leave the market.

DEMAND AND SUPPLY INTERACT TO DETERMINE THE SIZE OF THE MARKET AND PRICE LEVEL

We have treated market demand and supply forces separately. Now we must bring them together to show their interaction. The *intersection* of these two forces determines the size of the market and the market price—at which point (price and quantity) the market is said to be in *equilibrium.*

The intersection of demand and supply is shown for the potato data discussed above. In Exhibit A–10, the demand curve for potatoes is now graphed against the supply curve in Exhibit A–9.

In this potato market, demand is inelastic—the total revenue of all the potato producers would be greater at higher prices. But the market price is at the **equilibrium point**—where the quantity and the price sellers are willing to offer are equal to the quantity and price that buyers are willing to accept. The $1.00 equilibrium price for potatoes yields a smaller *total revenue* to potato producers than a higher price would. This lower equilibrium price comes about because the many producers are willing to supply enough potatoes at the lower price. *Demand is not the only determiner of price level. Cost also must be considered—via the supply curve.*

Some consumers get a surplus

Presumably, a sale takes place only if both buyer and seller feel they will be better off after the sale. But sometimes the price a consumer pays in a sales transaction is less than what he or she would be willing to pay.

The reason for this is that demand curves are typically down-sloping, and some of the demand curve is above the equilibrium price. This is simply another way of showing that some customers would have been willing to pay more than the equilibrium price—if they had to. In effect, some of them are getting a bargain by being able to buy at the equilibrium price. Economists have traditionally called these bargains the **consumer**

Exhibit A–10   Equilibrium of Supply and Demand for Potatoes (10-pound bags)

surplus—that is, the difference to consumers between the value of a purchase and the price they pay.

Some business critics assume that consumers do badly in any business transaction. In fact, sales take place only if consumers feel they are at least getting their money's worth. As we can see here, some are willing to pay much more than the market price.

DEMAND AND SUPPLY HELP US UNDERSTAND THE NATURE OF COMPETITION

The elasticity of demand and supply curves—and their interaction—help predict the nature of competition a marketing manager is likely to face. For example, an extremely inelastic demand curve means that the manager will have much choice in strategy planning—and especially price setting. Apparently customers like the product and see few substitutes. They are willing to pay higher prices before cutting back much on their purchases.

Clearly, the elasticity of a firm's demand curves makes a big difference in strategy planning, but other factors also affect the nature of competition. Among these are the number and size of competitors and the uniqueness of each firm's marketing mix. Understanding these market situations is important because the freedom of a marketing manager—especially control over price—is greatly reduced in some situations.

A marketing manager operates in one of four kinds of market situations. We'll discuss three kinds: pure competition, oligopoly, and monopolistic competition. The fourth kind, monopoly, isn't found very often and is like monopolistic competition. The important dimensions of these situations are shown in Exhibit A–11.

When competition is pure

Many competitors offer about the same thing

Pure competition is a market situation that develops when a market has:

1. Homogeneous (similar) products.
2. Many buyers and sellers who have full knowledge of the market.
3. Ease of entry for buyers and sellers; that is, new firms have little difficulty starting in business—and new customers can easily come into the market.

Exhibit A–11   Some Important Dimensions regarding Market Situations

Important dimensions	Types of situations			
	Pure competition	Oligopoly	Monopolistic competition	Monopoly
Uniqueness of each firm's product	None	None	Some	Unique
Number of competitors	Many	Few	Few to many	None
Size of competitors (compared to size of market)	Small	Large	Large to small	None
Elasticity of demand facing firm	Completely elastic	Kinked demand curve (elastic and inelastic)	Either	Either
Elasticity of industry demand	Either	Inelastic	Either	Either
Control of price by firm	None	Some (with care)	Some	Complete

More or less pure competition is found in many agricultural markets. In the potato market, for example, there are thousands of small producers—and they are in pure competition. Let's look more closely at these producers.

Although the potato market as a whole has a down-sloping demand curve, each of the many small producers in the industry is in pure competition, and each of them faces a flat demand curve at the equilibrium price. This is shown in Exhibit A–12.

As shown at the right of Exhibit A–12, individual producers can sell as many bags of potatoes as they choose at $1—the market equilibrium price. The equilibrium price is determined by the quantity that all producers choose to sell given the demand curve they face.

But a small producer has little effect on overall supply (or on the equilibrium price). If this individual farmer raises 1/10,000th of the quantity offered in the market, for example, you can see that there will be little effect if the farmer goes out of business—or doubles production.

The reason an individual producer's demand curve is flat is that the farmer probably couldn't sell any potatoes above the market price. And there is no point in selling below the market price! So, in effect, the individual producer has no control over price.

Markets tend to become more competitive

Not many markets are *purely* competitive. But many are close enough so we can talk about almost pure competition situations—those in which the marketing manager has to accept the going price.

Such highly competitive situations aren't limited to agriculture. Wherever *many* competitors sell *homogeneous* products—such as textiles, lumber, coal, printing, and laundry services—the demand curve seen by *each producer* tends to be flat.

Markets tend to become more competitive, moving toward pure competition (except in oligopolies—see below). On the way to pure competition, prices and profits are pushed down until some competitors are forced out of business. Eventually, in long-run equilibrium, the price level is only high enough to keep the survivors in business. No one makes any profit—they just cover costs. It's tough to be a marketing manager in this situation!

Exhibit A–12 Interaction of Demand and Supply in the Potato Industry and the Resulting Demand Curve Facing Individual Potato Producers

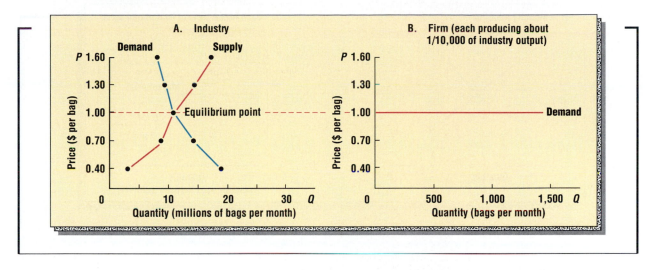

When competition is oligopolistic

A few competitors offer similar things

Not all markets move toward pure competition. Some become oligopolies. **Oligopoly** situations are special market situations that develop when a market has:

1. Essentially homogeneous products—such as basic industrial chemicals or gasoline.
2. Relatively few sellers—or a few large firms and many smaller ones who follow the lead of the larger ones.
3. Fairly inelastic industry demand curves.

The demand curve facing each firm is unusual in an oligopoly situation. Although the industry demand curve is inelastic throughout the relevant range, the demand curve facing each competitor looks "kinked." See Exhibit A–13. The current market price is at the kink.

There is a market price because the competing firms watch each other carefully—and know it's wise to be at the kink. Each firm must expect that raising its own price above the market price will cause a big loss in sales. Few, if any, competitors will follow the price increase. So the firm's demand curve is relatively flat above the market price. If the firm lowers its price, it must expect competitors to follow. Given inelastic industry demand, the firm's own demand curve is inelastic at lower prices—assuming it keeps "its share" of this market at lower prices. Since lowering prices along such a curve will drop total revenue, the firm should leave its price at the kink—the market price.

Actually, however, there are price fluctuations in oligopolistic markets. Sometimes this is caused by firms that don't understand the market situation and cut their prices to get business. In other cases, big increases in demand or supply change the basic nature of the situation and lead to price cutting. Price cuts can be drastic—such as Du Pont's price cut of 25 percent for Dacron. This happened when Du Pont decided that industry production capacity already exceeded demand, and more plants were due to start production.

Oligopoly situations don't just apply to whole industries and national markets. Competitors who are focusing on the same local target market often face oligopoly situations. A suburban community might have several gas stations—all of which provide essentially the same product. In this case, the "industry" consists of the gas stations competing with each other in the local product-market.

Exhibit A–13   Oligopoly—Kinked Demand Curve—Situation

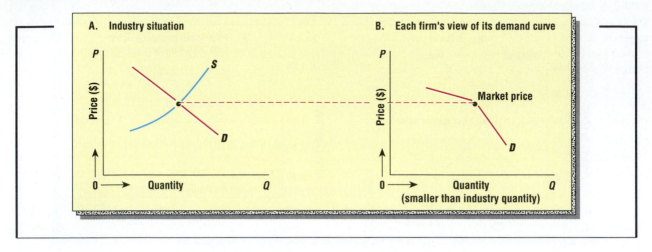

As in pure competition, oligopolists face a long-run trend toward an equilibrium level—with profits driven toward zero. This may not happen immediately—and a marketing manager may try to delay price competition by relying more on other elements in the marketing mix.

When competition is monopolistic

A price must be set

You can see why marketing managers want to avoid pure competition or oligopoly situations. They prefer a market in which they have more control. **Monopolistic competition** is a market situation that develops when a market has:

1. Different (heterogeneous) products—in the eyes of some customers.
2. Sellers who feel they do have some competition in this market.

The word *monopolistic* means that each firm is trying to get control in its own little market. But the word *competition* means that there are still substitutes. The vigorous competition of a purely competitive market is reduced. Each firm has its own down-sloping demand curve. But the shape of the curve depends on the similarity of competitors' products and marketing mixes. Each monopolistic competitor has freedom—but not complete freedom—in its own market.

Judging elasticity will help set the price

Since a firm in monopolistic competition has its own down-sloping demand curve, it must make a decision about price level as part of its marketing strategy planning. Here, estimating the elasticity of the firm's own demand curve is helpful. If it is highly inelastic, the firm may decide to raise prices to increase total revenue. But if demand is highly elastic, this may mean many competitors with acceptable substitutes. Then the price may have to be set near that of the competition. And the marketing manager probably should try to develop a better marketing mix.

CONCLUSION

The economist's traditional demand and supply analysis provides a useful tool for analyzing the nature of demand and competition. It is especially important that

you master the concepts of a demand curve and demand elasticity. How demand and supply interact helps determine the size of a market—and its price level. The interaction of supply and demand also helps explain the nature of competition in different market situations. We discuss three competitive situations: pure competition, oligopoly, and monopolistic competition. The fourth kind, monopoly, isn't found very often and is like monopolistic competition.

The nature of supply and demand—and competition— is very important in marketing strategy planning. We will return to these topics in Chapters 3 and 4— and then build on them throughout the text. So careful study of this appendix will build a good foundation for later work.

QUESTIONS AND PROBLEMS

1. Explain in your own words how economists look at markets and arrive at the law of diminishing demand.

2. Explain what a demand curve is and why it is usually down-sloping. Then give an example of a product for which the demand curve might not be down-sloping over some possible price ranges. Explain the reason for your choice.

3. What is the length of life of the typical demand curve? Illustrate your answer.

4. If the general market demand for men's shoes is fairly elastic, how does the demand for men's dress shoes compare to it? How does the demand curve for women's shoes compare to the demand curve for men's shoes?

5. If the demand for perfume is inelastic above and below the present price, should the price be raised? Why or why not?

6. If the demand for shrimp is highly elastic below the present price, should the price be lowered?

7. Discuss what factors lead to inelastic demand and supply curves. Are they likely to be found together in the same situation?

8. Why would a marketing manager prefer to sell a product that has no close substitutes? Are high profits almost guaranteed?

9. If a manufacturer's well-known product is sold at the same price by many retailers in the same community, is this an example of pure competition? When a community has many small grocery stores, are they in pure competition? What characteristics are needed to have a purely competitive market?

10. List three products that are sold in purely competitive markets and three that are sold in monopolistically competitive markets. Do any of these products have anything in common? Can any generalizations be made about competitive situations and marketing mix planning?

11. Cite a local example of an oligopoly—explaining why it is an oligopoly.

Finding Target Market Opportunities with Market Segmentation

Chapter

When You Finish This Chapter, You Should

❶
Understand how to find marketing opportunities.

❷
Know about the different kinds of marketing opportunties.

❸
Understand why opportunities in international markets should be considered.

❹
Know about defining generic markets and product-markets.

❺
Know what market segmentation is and how to segment product-markets into submarkets.

❻
Know three approaches to market-oriented strategy planning.

❼
Know dimensions that may be useful for segmenting markets.

❽
Know what positioning is—and why it is useful.

❾
Understand the important new terms (shown in red).

Illinois Tool Works (ITW) produces and sells a large array of products—ranging from nuts, bolts, screws, nails, and plastic fasteners to sophisticated equipment. You've probably never heard of ITW, but its fasteners are hidden inside or attached to appliances, cars, and many other products you buy. A key to ITW's success is that it is fast and creative in identifying target markets with specific needs, and then developing products—actually whole marketing mixes—to meet those needs.

Some competing firms make the mistake of defining their markets in terms of the products they've always produced (for example, the "screw market" or the "bolt market"). By contrast, ITW defines markets in terms of customer needs. And often ITW finds that what a customer needs is not a screw or a bolt, but something entirely new.

For example, a firm that produces life jackets needed a better way to fasten them. ITW developed just the right product for this customer—a durable, safety-rated plastic buckle. Then ITW targeted marketing mixes at other firms with similar needs. Today, millions of ITW buckles are used not only on life jackets but also on backpacks, luggage, bicycle helmets, and many types of leisure clothing.

ITW has developed many other innovative products and marketing mixes focused on the needs of specific market segments. For example, ITW makes Kiwi-Lok, a nylon fastener that New Zealand farmers use to secure their kiwi plants. It's not a fluke that ITW saw this unusual fastening need. As one ITW executive put it, "We try to sell where our competitors aren't"—one reason why ITW now serves customers from operations in 33 countries.[1]

Exhibit 3–1 Finding and Evaluating Marketing Opportunities

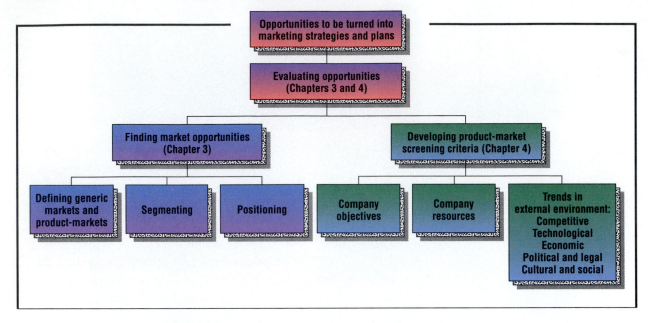

WHAT ARE ATTRACTIVE OPPORTUNITIES?

This book focuses primarily on marketing strategy planning—an important part of which involves finding attractive target markets. In this chapter and the next, you will learn how to find possible market opportunities and choose the ones to turn into strategies and plans. We will look first at how to identify attractive target markets. Exhibit 3–1 overviews the key topics we will be considering.

Attractive opportunities for a particular firm are those that the firm has some chance of doing something about—given its resources and objectives. Marketing strategy planning tries to match opportunities to the firm's resources (what it can do) and its objectives (what it wants to do).

Breakthrough opportunities are best

Throughout this book, we will emphasize finding breakthrough opportunities—opportunities that help innovators develop hard-to-copy marketing strategies that will be very profitable for a long time. Finding breakthrough opportunities is important because imitators are always waiting to "share" the profits—if they can.

Competitive advantage is needed—at least

Even if a firm can't find a breakthrough opportunity, it should try to obtain a competitive advantage to increase its chances for profit or survival. Competitive advantage means that a firm has a marketing mix that the target market sees as better than a competitor's mix.

Sometimes a firm can achieve breakthrough opportunities and competitive advantage by simply fine-tuning its marketing mix(es). Sometimes it may need new facilities, new people in new parts of the world, and totally new ways of solving problems. But every firm needs some competitive advantage—so the promotion people have something unique to sell and success doesn't just hinge on low prices.[2]

Exhibit 3–2   Four Basic Types of Opportunities

	Present products	New products
Present markets	Market penetration	Product development
New markets	Market development	Diversification

TYPES OF OPPORTUNITIES TO PURSUE

Most people have unsatisfied needs—and alert marketers who see these needs find opportunities all around them. Exhibit 3–2 shows the four broad kinds of opportunities: market penetration, market development, product development, and diversification. We will look at these separately, but some firms may pursue more than one type of opportunity at the same time.

Market penetration

Market penetration means trying to increase sales of a firm's present products in its present markets—probably through a more aggressive marketing mix. The firm may try to increase the customers' rate of use or attract competitors' customers or current nonusers. For example, Visa increased advertising to encourage customers to use its credit card when they travel—and to switch from using American Express.

New promotion appeals alone may not be effective. A firm may need to add more stores in present areas for greater convenience or cut prices to appeal to more people.

Market development

Market development means trying to increase sales by selling present products in new markets. Firms may try advertising in different media to reach new target customers. Or they may add channels of distribution or new stores in new areas, including overseas. For example, to reach new customers, McDonald's opens outlets in airports, office buildings, zoos, casinos, hospitals, and military bases. And it's rapidly expanding into international markets with outlets in places like Russia, Brazil, Hong Kong, Mexico, and Australia.

Market development may also involve searching for new uses for a product, as when Lipton provides recipes showing how to use its dry soup mixes for chip dip.

Product development

Product development means offering new or improved products for present markets. By knowing the present market's needs, a firm may see totally new ways to better satisfy customers. Computer software firms like Microsoft boost sales by introducing new versions of popular programs. Microsoft also develops other types of new products, including computer books for its customers.

Diversification

Diversification means moving into totally different lines of business—perhaps entirely unfamiliar products, markets, or even levels in the production-marketing system. Until

Attractive opportunities are often fairly close to markets the firm already knows.

recently, Japan's Sony produced electronic equipment. With its purchase of U.S.-based CBS records, Sony expanded into producing music—and it is considering other moves that will take it even further from its traditional business.

Which opportunities come first?

Usually firms find attractive opportunities fairly close to markets they already know. This may allow them to capitalize on changes in their present markets—or more basic changes in the external environment.

Most firms think first of greater market penetration. They want to increase profits where they already have experience and strengths.[3]

INTERNATIONAL OPPORTUNITIES SHOULD BE CONSIDERED

It's easy to fall into the trap of forgetting about international markets, especially when the firm's domestic market is prosperous. Why go to the trouble of looking elsewhere for opportunities?

The world is getting smaller

Advances in communications and transportation are making it easier and cheaper for even small firms to reach international customers. Around the world, potential customers have needs and money to spend. The real question is whether a firm can effectively use its resources to meet these customers' needs at a profit.

Develop a competitive advantage at home and abroad

If customers in other countries are interested in the products a firm offers—or could offer—serving them may result in economies of scale. Lower costs (and prices) may give a firm a competitive advantage both in its home markets *and* abroad. Marketing managers who are only interested in the "convenient" customers in their own backyards may be rudely surprised to find that an aggressive, low-cost foreign producer is willing to pursue those customers—even if doing so is not convenient. Many companies that

Many firms find attractive opportunities in foreign markets.

thought they could avoid the struggles of international competition have learned this lesson the hard way.

Get an early start in a new market

Different countries are at different stages of development, and their consumers have different needs at different times. For example, prior to the unification of Germany, appliance producers in East Germany found their best market opportunities in other countries, where consumers had more money.

A company facing tough competition, thin profit margins, and slow sales growth at home may get a fresh start in another country where demand for its product is just beginning to grow. A marketing manager may be able to "transfer" marketing know-how the firm has already developed.

Find better trends in variables

Unfavorable trends in the marketing environment at home—or favorable trends in other countries—may make international marketing particularly attractive. For example, population growth in the United States has slowed and income is leveling off. In other places in the world, population and income are increasing rapidly. Marketing managers for U.S. firms can no longer rely on the constant growth that once increased domestic sales. For many firms, growth—and perhaps even survival—will come only by aiming at more distant customers. So it doesn't make sense to casually assume that all of the best opportunities are "at home."

SEARCH FOR OPPORTUNITIES CAN BEGIN BY UNDERSTANDING MARKETS

Breakthrough opportunities from understanding target markets

When marketing managers really understand their target markets, they may see breakthrough opportunities. But a target market's real needs—and the breakthrough opportunities that can come from identifying and serving those needs—are not always obvious. So let's look at some ways to better understand a company's target markets.

CYBEX STAYS FIT WITH OVERSEAS MARKET DEVELOPMENT

(T)he rapid growth of the fitness market in the United States created many opportunities for companies as varied as Reebok, Schwinn, Nautilus, and General Nutrition Corporation. Now that growth in the U.S. fitness market has slowed, many marketing managers who had been competing for consumers' fitness dollars are pursuing other opportunities for profitable growth.

Many of those opportunities occur in other countries—where interest in health and fitness started later. That's not news to Cybex, a company that sells Nautilus-like exercise equipment, including some high-tech units that hook up to computers to analyze back muscle injuries. During the 1980s, Cybex realized that growing demand in overseas markets offered a good opportunity for market development.

To develop these new markets, Cybex added a director of international marketing and its own international salespeople (who speak a variety of languages). With help from middlemen who specialize in international trade, they sold Cybex's specialized $40,000 products in markets like Japan where customers have never before paid more than $3,000 for fitness equipment. Export sales of equipment—to 30 foreign markets—has been an important factor in Cybex's success.

Cybex is but one of about 10,000 smaller U.S. firms whose sales are growing rapidly because they are pursuing overseas market development through exporting. In other countries, like Germany, export sales by both large and small firms have long been the key to profits and, at the macro-level, strong economic development.[4]

What is a company's market?

Identifying a company's market is an important but sticky issue. In general, a **market** is a group of potential customers with similar needs who are willing to exchange something of value with sellers offering various goods and/or services—that is, ways of satisfying those needs.

Market-oriented managers develop marketing mixes for *specific* target markets. Getting the firm to focus on specific target markets is vital. As shown in Exhibit 3–3, target marketing requires a "narrowing-down" process—to get beyond production-oriented mass market thinking. But firms often misunderstand this narrowing-down process.

Don't just focus on the product

Some production-oriented managers ignore the tough part of defining markets. To make the narrowing-down process easier, they just describe their markets in terms of the *products* they sell. But thinking about markets only in terms of products is likely to result in missed opportunities. For example, firms that focused only on the "typewriter market" saw their sales disappear as customers switched to computers and printers. Now, rather than using letters, many businesspeople communicate with electronic mail, faxes, and telephone calls. Today's market is concerned with "thought processing and transmitting." Market-oriented strategy planners try to avoid surprises that result from such tunnel vision. Firms looking for new opportunities should focus on needs satisfied by products, *not* product characteristics themselves. They may find new ways of satisfying a need—ways that completely surprise and upset producers of current products—if they don't define the market too narrowly.

From generic markets to product-markets

It's useful to think of two basic types of markets. A **generic market** is a market with *broadly* similar needs and sellers offering various—*often diverse*—ways of satisfying those needs. In contrast, a **product-market** is a market with *very* similar needs and sellers offering various *close substitute* ways of satisfying those needs.[5]

Exhibit 3–3 Narrowing Down to Target Markets

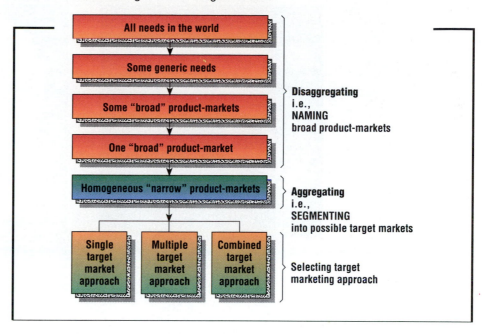

A generic market description looks at markets broadly and from a customer's viewpoint. Status-seekers, for example, have several very different ways to satisfy status needs. A status-seeker might buy a new Mercedes, a Lindblad tour, or fashions from a French designer. Any one of these *very different* products may satisfy this status need. Sellers in this generic status-seeker market have to focus on the need(s) the customers want satisfied—not on how one seller's product (car, vacation, or designer label) is better than another's.

It is sometimes hard to understand and define generic markets because *quite different product types may compete with each other.* But if customers see all these products as substitutes—as competitors in the same generic market—then marketers must deal with this complication.

Suppose, however, that one of our status-seekers decides to satisfy this status need with a new, expensive car. Then—in this product-market—Mercedes, Cadillac, and Lexus may compete with each other for the status-seeker's dollars. In the *product*-market concerned with cars *and* status (not just transportation!), consumers compare similar products to satisfy their status need.

Broaden market definitions to find opportunities

Broader market definitions—including both generic market definitions and product-market definitions—can help firms find opportunities. But deciding *how* broad to go isn't easy. Too narrow a definition limits a firm's opportunities—but too broad a definition makes the company's efforts and resources seem insignificant.

Our strategy planning process helps define relevant markets. Here we try to match opportunities to a firm's resources and objectives. So the *relevant market for finding opportunities* should be bigger than the firm's present product-market—but not so big that the firm couldn't expand and be an important competitor. A small manufacturer of screwdrivers in Mexico, for example, shouldn't define its market as broadly as "the worldwide tool users market" or as narrowly as "our present screwdriver customers." But it

Different fax companies may compete with each other in the same product-market— and with overnight carriers in a broader generic market.

may have the production and/or marketing potential to consider "the handyman's hand-tool market in North America." <mark>Carefully naming your product-market can help you see possible opportunities.</mark>

<mark>NAMING PRODUCT-MARKETS AND GENERIC MARKETS</mark>

Product-related terms do not—by themselves—adequately describe a market. A complete product-market definition includes a four-part description.

What:	1.	Product type (type of good and/or type of service).
To meet what:	2.	Customer (user) needs.
For whom:	3.	Customer types.
Where:	4.	Geographic area.

We refer to these four-part descriptions as product-market "names" because most managers label their markets when they think, write, or talk about them. Such a four-part definition can be clumsy, however, so we often use a nickname. And the nickname should refer to people—not products—because, as we emphasize, people make markets!

Product type should meet customer needs

Product type describes the goods and/or services that customers want. Sometimes the product type is strictly a physical good or strictly a service. But marketing managers who ignore the possibility that *both* are important can miss opportunities.

Customer (user) needs refer to the needs the product type satisfies for the customer. At a very basic level, product types usually provide functional benefits such as nourishing, protecting, warming, cooling, transporting, cleaning, holding, saving time, and so forth. Although we identify such basic needs first, in advanced economies, we usually go on to emotional needs—for fun, excitement, or status. Correctly defining the need(s) relevant to a market requires a good understanding of customers. We discuss these topics more fully in Chapters 6 and 7.

Exhibit 3–4   Relationship between Generic and Product-Market Definitions

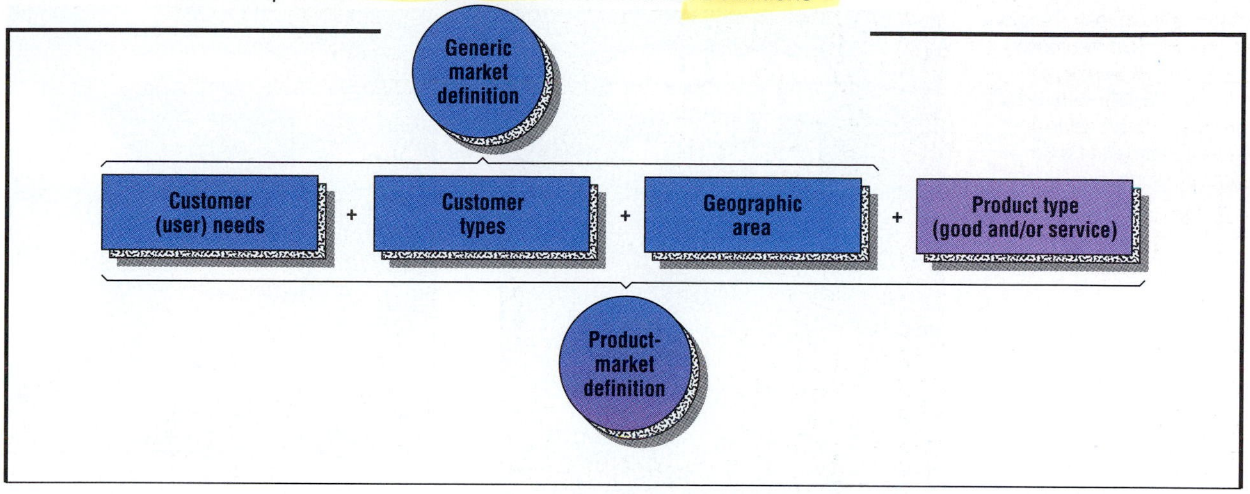

Customer type refers to the final consumer or user of a product type. Here we want to choose a name that describes all present (possible) types of customers. To define customer type, marketers should identify the final consumer or user of the product type rather than the buyer—if they are different. For instance, marketers should avoid treating middlemen as a customer type—unless middlemen actually use the product in their own business.

The *geographic area* is where a firm competes—or plans to compete—for customers. Naming the geographic area may seem trivial, but understanding geographic boundaries of a market can suggest new opportunities. Supermarkets in London, or Los Angeles, or Toronto don't cater to all consumers in these areas—there may be opportunities to serve unsatisfied customers in the same areas. Similarly, a firm aiming only at the U.S. market may want to expand into world markets.

No product type in generic market names

A generic market description *doesn't include any product-type terms.* It consists of only three parts of the product-market definition—without the product type. This emphasizes that very different product types can satisfy the customer's needs and compete in a generic market. Exhibit 3–4 shows the relationship between generic market and product-market definitions.

Later we'll study the many possible dimensions of markets. But for now you should see that defining markets only in terms of current products is not the best way to find new opportunities—or plan marketing strategies.

MARKET SEGMENTATION DEFINES POSSIBLE TARGET MARKETS

Market segmentation is a two-step process

Market segmentation is a two-step process of (1) *naming* broad product-markets and (2) *segmenting* these broad product-markets in order to select target markets and develop suitable marketing mixes.

This two-step process isn't well understood. First-time market segmentation efforts often fail because beginners start with the whole mass market and try to find one or two demographic characteristics to segment this market. Customer behavior is usually too complex to be explained in terms of just one or two demographic characteristics. For

Sony's new filmless camera may compete in the same broad product-market as Yashica's 35-mm autofocus camera—but appeal to a different submarket with different needs.

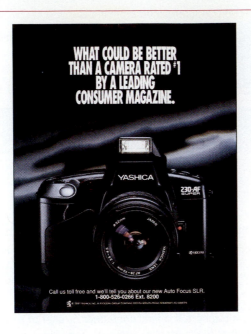

example, not all elderly men buy the same products or brands. Other dimensions usually must be considered—starting with customer needs.

Naming broad product-markets is disaggregating

The first step in effective market segmentation involves naming a broad product-market of interest to the firm. Marketers must break apart—disaggregate—all possible needs into some generic markets and broad product-markets in which the firm may be able to operate profitably. See Exhibit 3–3. No one firm can satisfy everyone's needs. So the naming—disaggregating—step involves brainstorming about very different solutions to various generic needs and selecting some broad areas—broad product-markets—where the firm has some resources and experience. This means that a car manufacturer would probably ignore all the possible opportunities in food and clothing markets and focus on the generic market "transporting people in the world" and probably on the broad product-market "cars and trucks for transporting people in the world."

Disaggregating, a practical rough-and-ready approach, narrows down the marketing focus to a product-market where the firm is more likely to have a competitive advantage— or even to find breakthrough opportunities.

Market grid is a visual aid to market segmentation

A market grid is a good way to help visualize a broad product-market and its narrow product-markets. Draw the market grid as a rectangle with boxes inside representing smaller, more homogeneous segments. Think of the whole rectangle as representing the broad product-market with its name on top. Now think of each of the boxes as narrow product-markets. Since the markets within a broad product-market usually require very different dimensions, don't try to use the same two dimensions to name the markets—or to label the sides of the market grid boxes. Rather, just think of the grid as showing the relative sizes of product-market segments. Then label each segment with its nickname.

Exhibit 3–5, for example, represents the broad product-market of bicycle riders. The boxes show different submarkets. One submarket might focus on people who want basic transportation, another on people who want exercise, and so on. Alternatively, in the

Exhibit 3–5 A Market Grid Diagram with Submarkets

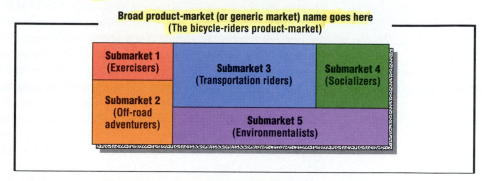

generic "transporting market" discussed above, we might see different (broader) product-markets of customers for bicycles, motorcycles, cars, airplanes, ships, buses, and "others."

Segmenting is an aggregating process

Marketing-oriented managers think of **segmenting** as an aggregating process—clustering people with similar needs into a "market segment." A **market segment** is a (relatively) homogeneous group of customers who will respond to a marketing mix in a similar way.

This part of the market segmentation process (see Exhibit 3–3) takes a different approach than the naming part. Here we look for similarities rather than basic differences in needs. Segmenters start with the idea that each person is one of a kind but that it may be possible to aggregate some similar people into a product-market.

Segmenters see each of these one-of-a-kind people as having a unique set of dimensions. Consider a product-market in which customers' needs differ on two important segmenting dimensions: need for status and need for dependability. In Exhibit 3–6A, each dot shows a person's position on the two dimensions. While each person's position is unique, many of them are similar in terms of how much status and dependability they want. So a segmenter may aggregate these people into three (an arbitrary number) relatively homogeneous submarkets—A, B, and C. Group A might be called "status oriented" and Group C "dependability oriented." Members of Group B want both and might be called the "demanders."

Exhibit 3–6 Every Individual Has His or Her Own Unique Position in a Market—Those with Similar Positions Can Be Aggregated into Potential Target Markets

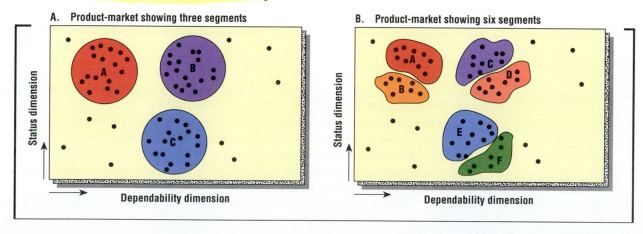

How far should the aggregating go?

The segmenter wants to aggregate individual customers into some workable number of relatively homogeneous target markets—and then treat each target market differently.

Look again at Exhibit 3–6A. Remember we talked about three segments. But this was an arbitrary number. As Exhibit 3–6B shows, there may really be six segments. What do you think—does this broad product-market consist of three segments or six?

Another difficulty with segmenting is that some potential customers just don't fit neatly into market segments. For example, not everyone in Exhibit 3–6B was put into one of the groups. Forcing them into one of the groups would have made these segments more heterogeneous—and harder to please. Further, forming additional segments for them probably wouldn't be profitable. They are too few and not very similar in terms of the two dimensions. These people are simply too unique to be catered to and may have to be ignored—unless they are willing to pay a high price for special treatment.

The number of segments that should be formed depends more on judgment than on some scientific rule. But the following guidelines can help.

Criteria for segmenting a broad product-market

Ideally, good market segments meet the following criteria:

1. *Homogeneous (similar) within*—the customers in a market segment should be as similar as possible with respect to their likely responses to marketing mix variables *and* their segmenting dimensions.
2. *Heterogeneous (different) between*—the customers in different segments should be as different as possible with respect to their likely responses to marketing mix variables *and* their segmenting dimensions.
3. *Substantial*—the segment should be big enough to be profitable.
4. *Operational*—the segmenting dimensions should be useful for identifying customers and deciding on marketing mix variables.

It is especially important that segments be *operational.* This leads marketers to include demographic dimensions such as age, income, location, and family size. In fact, it is difficult to make some Place and Promotion decisions without such information.

Avoid segmenting dimensions that have no practical operational use. For example, you may find a personality trait such as moodiness among the traits of heavy buyers of a product, but how could you use this fact? Salespeople can't give a personality test to each buyer. Similarly, advertising couldn't make much use of this information. So although moodiness might be related in some way to previous purchases, it would not be a useful dimension for segmenting.

Target marketers aim at specific targets

Once you accept the idea that broad product-markets may have submarkets, you can see that target marketers usually have a choice among many possible target markets.

There are three basic ways to develop market-oriented strategies in a broad product-market.

1. The **single target market approach**—segmenting the market and picking one of the homogeneous segments as the firm's target market.
2. The **multiple target market approach**—segmenting the market and choosing two or more segments, then treating each as a separate target market needing a different marketing mix.
3. The **combined target market approach**—combining two or more submarkets into one larger target market as a basis for one strategy.

Exhibit 3–7   Target Marketers Have Specific Aims

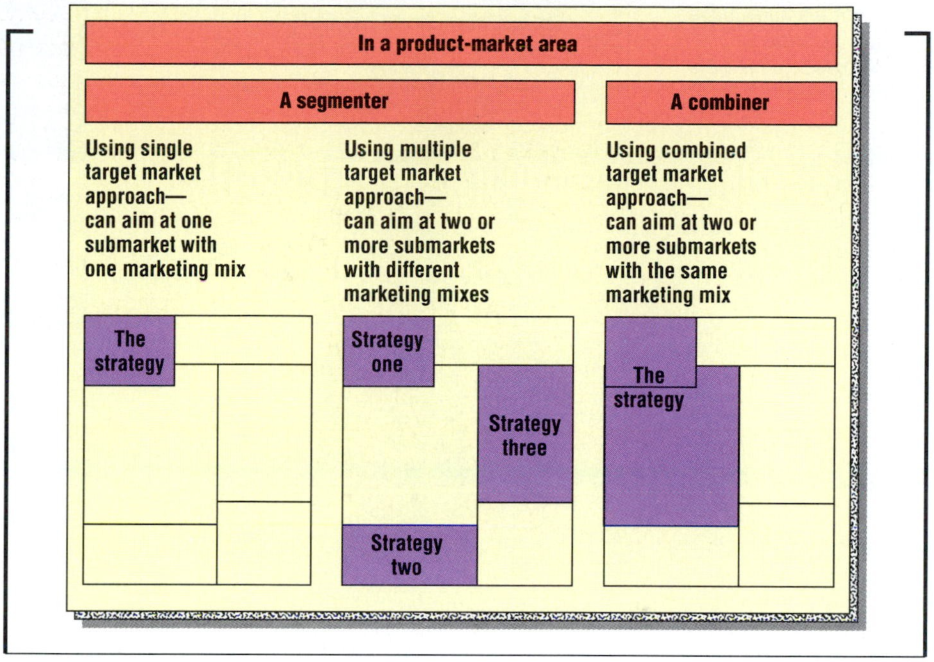

Note that all three approaches involve target marketing. They all aim at specific, clearly defined target markets. See Exhibit 3–7. For convenience, we call people who follow the first two approaches the "segmenters" and the people who use the third approach "combiners."

Combiners try to satisfy "pretty well"

Combiners try to increase the size of their target markets by combining two or more segments. Combiners look at various submarkets for similarities rather than differences. Then they try to extend or modify their basic offering to appeal to these "combined" customers with just one marketing mix. See Exhibit 3–7. For example, combiners may try a new package, more service, a new brand, or new flavors. But even if they make product or other marketing mix changes, they don't try to satisfy unique smaller submarkets. Instead, combiners try to improve the general appeal of their marketing mix to appeal to a bigger combined target market.

A combined target market approach may help achieve some economies of scale. It may also require less investment than developing different marketing mixes for different segments—making it especially attractive for firms with limited resources.

Too much combining is risky

It is tempting to aim at larger combined markets instead of using different marketing mixes for smaller segmented markets. But combiners must be careful not to aggregate too far. As they enlarge the target market, individual differences within the target market may begin to outweigh the similarities. This makes it harder to develop a marketing mix that can satisfy all the different customers. So a combiner faces the risk of innovative segmenters chipping away at the various segments of the combined target market—by offering marketing mixes that are more attractive to people in each submarket.

Segmenters try to satisfy very well

Segmenters aim at one or more homogeneous segments and try to develop a different marketing mix for each segment. Segmenters usually adjust their marketing mixes

Heinz's multiple target market approach treats consumers and hotels as separate segments needing different marketing mixes.

for each target market—perhaps making basic changes in the product itself—because they want to satisfy each segment very well.

Segmenters believe that aiming at one—or some—of these submarkets will satisfy the target customers better and provide greater profit potential for the firm.

Segmenting may produce bigger sales

Note that segmenters are not settling for a smaller sales potential. Instead, they hope to increase sales by getting a much larger share of the business in the market(s) they target. A segmenter who satisfies the target market well enough may have no real competition.

AFG Industries had a small market share when it was trying to sell glass in the big construction market. Then AFG's marketing managers focused on the special needs of firms that used tempered and colored glass in their own production. Customers in these "niche" segments didn't get attention from the bigger producers. Now, AFG sells 70 percent of the glass for microwave oven doors and 75 percent of the glass for shower enclosures and patio tabletops.[6]

Profit is the balancing point

In practice, cost considerations usually encourage more combining—to obtain economies of scale—while demand considerations suggest more segmenting—to satisfy needs more exactly. So which approach should a firm use?

In general, it's usually safer to be a segmenter—that is, to try to satisfy some customers *very* well instead of many just *fairly* well. That's why many firms use the single or multiple target market approach instead of the combined target market approach.[7]

But profit is the balancing point. It determines how unique a marketing mix the firm can afford to offer to a particular group.

WHAT DIMENSIONS ARE USED TO SEGMENT MARKETS?

Segmenting dimensions guide marketing mix planning

Market segmentation forces a marketing manager to decide which product-market dimensions might be useful for planning marketing strategies. The dimensions should help guide marketing mix planning. Exhibit 3–8 shows the basic kinds of dimensions we'll be talking about in Chapters 6 and 7—and their probable effect on the four Ps. Ideally, we

Exhibit 3–8   Relation of Potential Target Market Dimensions to Marketing Strategy Decision Areas

Potential Target Market Dimensions	Effects on Strategy Decision Areas
1. Behavioral needs, attitudes, and how present and potential goods and services fit into customers' consumption patterns.	Affects *Product* (features, packaging, product line assortment, branding) and *Promotion* (what potential customers need and want to know about the firm's offering, and what appeals should be used).
2. Urgency to get need satisfied and desire and willingness to seek information, compare, and shop.	Affects *Place* (how directly products are distributed from producer to customer, how extensively they are made available, and the level of service needed) and *Price* (how much potential customers are willing to pay).
3. Geographic location and other demographic characteristics of potential customers.	Affects size of *Target Markets* (economic potential) and *Place* (where products should be made available) and *Promotion* (where and to whom to target advertising and personal selling).

want to describe any potential product-market in terms of all three types of customer-related dimensions—plus a product type description—because these dimensions help us develop better marketing mixes.

Customers can be described by many specific dimensions. Exhibit 3–9 shows some dimensions useful for segmenting consumer markets. A few are behavioral dimensions, others are geographic and demographic. Exhibit 3–10 shows some additional dimensions for segmenting markets when the customers are businesses, government agencies, or other types of organizations. Regardless of whether customers are final consumers or organizations, segmenting a broad product-market may require using several different dimensions at the same time.[8]

With so many possible segmenting dimensions—and knowing that several dimensions may be needed to show what is really important in specific product-markets—how should we proceed?

What are the qualifying and determining dimensions?

To select the important segmenting dimensions, think about two different types of dimensions. Qualifying dimensions are those relevant to including a customer type in a product-market. Determining dimensions are those that actually affect the customer's purchase of a specific product or brand in a product-market.

A prospective car buyer, for example, has to have enough money—or credit—to buy a car and insure it. Our buyer also needs a driver's license. This still doesn't guarantee a purchase. He or she must have a real need—like a job that requires "wheels" or kids that have to be carpooled. This need may motivate the purchase of *some* car. But these qualifying dimensions don't determine what specific brand or model car the person might buy. That depends on more specific interests—such as the kind of safety, performance, or appearance the customer wants. Determining dimensions related to these needs affect the specific car the customer purchases.

Determining dimensions may be very specific

How specific the determining dimensions are depends on whether you are concerned with a general product type or a specific brand. See Exhibit 3–11. The more specific you want to be, the more particular the determining dimensions may be. In a particular case, the determining dimensions may seem minor. But they are important because they *are* the determining dimensions.

Exhibit 3–9 Possible Segmenting Dimensions and Typical Breakdowns for Consumer Markets

Behavioral

Needs	Economic, functional, physiological, psychological, social, and more detailed needs.
Benefits sought	Situation specific, but to satisfy specific or general needs.
Thoughts	Favorable or unfavorable attitudes, interests, opinions, beliefs.
Rate of use	Heavy, medium, light, nonusers.
Purchase frequency	Never, infrequent, frequent.
Brand familiarity	Insistence, preference, recognition, nonrecognition, rejection.
Kind of shopping	Convenience, comparison shopping, specialty, none (unsought product).
Type of problem solving	Routinized response, limited, extensive.
Information required	Low, medium, high.

Geographic

Region of world, country	North America (United States, Canada), Europe (France, Italy, Germany), and so on.
Region in country	(Examples in United States): Pacific, Mountain, West North Central, West South Central, East North Central, East South Central, South Atlantic, Middle Atlantic, New England.
Size of city	No city; population under 5,000; 5,000–19,999; 20,000–49,999; 50,000–99,999; 100,000–249,999; 250,000–499,999; 500,000–999,999; 1,000,000–3,999,999; 4,000,000 or over.

Demographic

Income	Under $5,000; $5,000–$9,999; $10,000–$14,999; $15,000–$19,999; $20,000–$29,999; $30,000–$39,999; $40,000–$59,999; $60,000 and over.
Sex	Male, female.
Age	Infant, under 6; 6–11; 12–17; 18–24; 25–34; 35–49; 50–64; 65 or over.
Family size	1, 2, 3–4, 5 or more.
Family life cycle	Young, single; young, married, no children; young, married, youngest child under 6; young, married, youngest child over 6; older, married, with children; older, married, no children under 18; older, single; other variations for single parents, divorced, etc.
Occupation	Professional and technical; managers, officials, and proprietors; clerical sales; craftsmen, foremen; operatives; farmers; retired; students; housewives; unemployed.
Education	Grade school or less, some high school, high school graduate, some college, college graduate.
Race	White, Black, Oriental, etc.
Social class	Lower-lower, upper-lower, lower-middle, upper-middle, lower-upper, upper-upper.

Note: terms used in this table are explained in detail later in the text.

Different dimensions needed for different submarkets

Note that each different submarket within a broad product-market may be motivated by a different set of dimensions. In the snack food market, for example, health food eaters are interested in nutrition, dieters worry about calories, and budget shoppers with lots of kids may want volume to fill them up. The related submarkets might be called health-conscious snack food market, dieters' snack food market, and kids' snack food market. They would be in different boxes in a market grid diagram for snack food customers.

Ethical issues in selecting segmenting dimensions

Marketing managers sometimes face ethical decisions when selecting segmenting dimensions. Problems may arise if a firm targets customers who are somehow at a disadvantage in dealing with the firm or who are unlikely to see the negative effects of their own choices. For example, some people criticize shoe companies for targeting poor, inner-city kids who see expensive athletic shoes as an important status symbol. Many firms, including producers of infant formula, have been criticized for targeting consumers in less-developed nations. Encyclopedia publishers have been criticized for aggressive selling to less-educated parents; they want their children to have better opportunities but don't realize that the "pennies a day" credit terms add up to more than they can afford. Some nutritionists criticize firms that market soft drinks, candy, and snack foods to children.

Exhibit 3–10 Possible Segmenting Dimensions for Business/Organizational Markets

Type of customer	Manufacturer, service producer, government agency, military, nonprofit, wholesaler or retailer (when end-user), etc.
Demographics	Geographic location (region of world, country, region within country, urban → rural) Size (number of employees, sales volume) Primary business or industry (Standard Industrial Classification) Number of facilities
How customer will use product	Installations, components, accessories, raw materials, supplies, professional services
Type of buying situation	Decentralized → centralized Buyer → multiple buying influence Straight rebuy → modified rebuy → new-task buying
Kind of relationship	Weak loyalty → strong loyalty to vendor Single source → multiple vendors Arm's length dealings → close partnership No reciprocity → complete reciprocity
Purchasing methods	Vendor analysis, inspection buying, sampling buying, specification buying, competitive bids, negotiated contracts, long-term contracts

Note: terms used in this table are explained in detail later in the text.

Sometimes a marketing manager must decide whether a firm should serve customers it really doesn't want to serve. For example, banks sometimes offer marketing mixes that are attractive to wealthy customers but basically drive off low-income consumers.

People often differ about what segmenting dimensions are ethical in a given situation. A marketing manager needs to consider not only his or her own views but also the views of other groups in society. Even when there is no clear right answer, negative publicity may be very damaging.[9]

Exhibit 3–11 Finding the Relevant Segmenting Dimensions

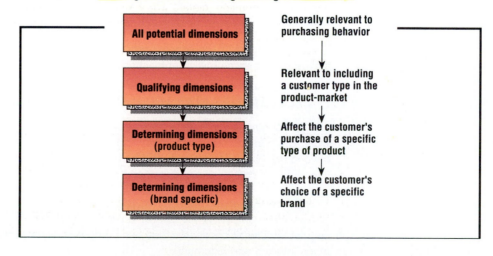

Segmenting dimensions should be useful for identifying customers and deciding on marketing mix variables.

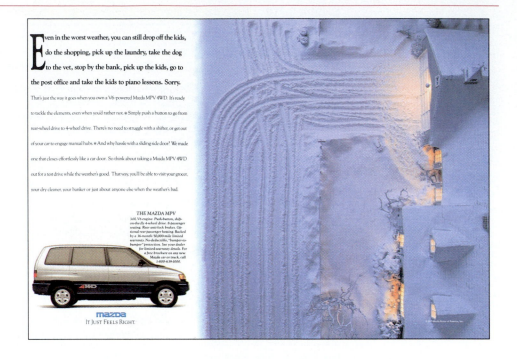

INTERNATIONAL MARKETING REQUIRES EVEN MORE SEGMENTING

Success in international marketing requires even more attention to segmenting. There are over 140 nations with their own unique cultures! And they differ greatly in language, customs (including business ethics), beliefs, religions, race, and income distribution patterns. (We'll discuss some of these differences in Chapter 6.) These additional differences can complicate the segmenting process. Even worse, critical data is often less available—and less dependable—as firms move into international markets. The number of variables increases, but the quantity and quality of data decrease. This is one reason why some firms insist that local operations and decisions be handled by natives. They, at least, have a feel for their markets.

There are more dimensions—but there is a way

Segmenting international markets may require more dimensions. But one practical method adds just one step to the approaches discussed above. First, marketers segment by country or region—looking at demographic, cultural, and other characteristics, including stage of economic development. This may help them find reasonably similar submarkets. Then—depending on whether the firm is aiming at final consumers or business markets—they apply the same basic approaches discussed earlier.

MORE-SOPHISTICATED TECHNIQUES MAY HELP IN SEGMENTING

The segmentation approaches we've been discussing are logical, practical—*and they work.* But computer-aided methods can help too. A detailed review of the possibilities is beyond the scope of this book. But a brief discussion of some approaches will give you a flavor of how computer-aided methods work.

Clustering usually requires a computer

Clustering techniques try to find similar patterns within sets of data. Clustering groups customers who are similar on their segmenting dimensions into homogeneous segments. Clustering approaches use computers to do what previously was done with much intuition and judgment.

Firms often use promotion to help "position" how a product meets a target market's specific needs.

The data to be clustered might include such dimensions as demographic characteristics, the importance of different needs, attitudes toward the product, and past buying behavior. The computer searches all the data for homogeneous groups of people. When it finds them, marketers study the dimensions of the people in the groups to see why the computer clustered them together. The results sometimes suggest new, or at least better, marketing strategies.[10]

A cluster analysis of the toothpaste market, for example, might show that some people buy toothpaste because it tastes good (the sensory segment), while others are concerned with the effect of clean teeth and fresh breath on their social image (the sociables). Still others worry about decay or tartar (the worriers), and some are just interested in the best value for their money (the value seekers). Each of these market segments calls for a different marketing mix—although some of the four Ps may be similar.

Positioning

Positioning, another important approach, shows how customers locate proposed and/or present brands in a market. It requires some formal marketing research but may be helpful when competitive offerings are quite similar. The results are usually plotted on graphs to help show where the products are positioned in relation to competing products. Usually, the products' positions are related to two or three product features that are important to the target customers.

Assuming the picture is reasonably accurate, managers then decide whether they want to leave their product (and marketing mix) alone or reposition it. This may mean *physical changes* in the product or simply *image changes based on promotion*. For example, most beer drinkers can't pick out their favorite brand in a blind test—so physical changes might not be necessary (and might not even work) to reposition a beer brand.

Managers make the graphs for positioning decisions by asking product users to make judgments about different brands—including their "ideal" brand—and then use computer programs to summarize the ratings and plot the results. The details of positioning techniques—sometimes called "perceptual mapping"—are beyond the scope of this text. But Exhibit 3–12 shows the possibilities.[11]

Exhibit 3–12 "Product Space" Representing Consumers' Perceptions for Different Brands of Bar Soap

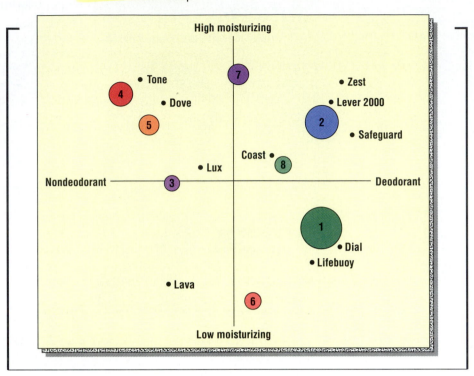

Exhibit 3–12 shows the "product space" for different brands of bar soap using two dimensions—the extent to which consumers think the soaps moisturize and deodorize their skin. For example, consumers see Dial as quite low on moisturizing but high on deodorizing. Lifebuoy and Dial are close together—implying that consumers think of them as similar on these characteristics. Dove is viewed as different and is further away on the graph. Remember that positioning maps are based on *customers' perceptions*—the actual characteristics of the products (as determined by a chemical test) might be different!

The circles on Exhibit 3–12 show different sets (submarkets) of consumers clustered near their ideal soap preferences. Groups of respondents with a similar ideal product are circled to show apparent customer concentrations. In this graph, the size of the circles suggests the size of the segments for the different ideals.

Ideal clusters 1 and 2 are the largest and are close to two popular brands—Dial and Lever 2000. It appears that customers in cluster 1 want more moisturizing than they see in Dial and Lifebuoy. However, exactly what these brands should do about this isn't clear. Perhaps both of these brands should leave their physical products alone—but emphasize moisturizing more in their promotion to make a stronger appeal to those who want moisturizers. A marketing manager talking about this approach might simply refer to it as "positioning the brand as a good moisturizer."

Note that ideal cluster 7 is not near any of the present brands. This may suggest an opportunity for introducing a new product—a strong moisturizer with some deodorizers. A firm that chooses to follow this approach would be making a segmenting effort.

Positioning analysis may lead a firm to combining—rather than segmenting—if managers think they can make several general appeals to different parts of a combined market. For example, by varying its promotion, Coast might try to appeal to clusters 8, 1, and 2 with one product.

Positioning as part of broader analysis

Positioning helps managers understand how customers see their market. As part of a broader analysis of target markets, it can be very useful. The first time such an analysis is done, managers may be shocked to see how much customers' perceptions of a market differ from their own. For this reason alone, positioning is useful.

Premature emphasis on product features is dangerous, however. And it's easy to do if you start with a product-oriented definition of a market—as in the bar soap example. Positioning bar soaps against bar soaps can make a firm miss more basic shifts in markets. For example, bars might be losing popularity to liquid soaps. Or other products, like bath oils or facial cleansers, may be part of the relevant competition. Managers wouldn't see these shifts if they looked only at alternative bar soap brands—the focus is just too narrow.

CONCLUSION

Firms need creative strategy planning to survive in our increasingly competitive markets. In this chapter, we discussed how to find attractive target market opportunities. We started by considering four basic types of opportunities—market penetration, market development, product development, and diversification—with special emphasis on opportunities in international markets. We also saw that carefully defining generic markets and product-markets can help find new opportunities. We stressed the shortcomings of a too narrow product-oriented view of markets.

We also discussed market segmentation—the process of naming and then segmenting broad product-markets to find potentially attractive target markets. Some people try to segment markets by starting with the mass market and then dividing it into smaller submarkets based on a few dimensions. But this can lead to poor results. Instead, market segmentation should first focus on a broad product-market and then group similar customers into homogeneous submarkets. The more similar the potential customers are, the larger the submarkets can be. Four criteria for evaluating possible product-market segments were presented.

Once a broad product-market is segmented, marketing managers can use one of three approaches to market-oriented strategy planning: (1) the single target market approach, (2) the multiple target market approach, and (3) the combined target market approach. In general, we encouraged marketers to be segmenters rather than combiners.

We also discussed some computer-aided segmenting approaches—clustering techniques and positioning.

In summary, good marketers should be experts on markets and likely segmenting dimensions. By creatively segmenting markets, they may spot opportunities—even breakthrough opportunities—and help their firms succeed against aggressive competitors offering similar products. Segmenting is basic to target marketing. And the more you practice segmenting, the more meaningful market segments you will see.

QUESTIONS AND PROBLEMS

1. Distinguish between an attractive opportunity and a breakthrough opportunity. Give an example.

2. Explain how new opportunities may be seen by defining a firm's markets more precisely. Illustrate for a situation where you feel there is an opportunity—namely, an unsatisfied market segment—even if it is not very large.

3. Distinguish between a generic market and a product-market. Illustrate your answer.

4. Explain the major differences among the four basic types of opportunities discussed in the text and cite examples for two of these types of opportunities.

5. Explain why a firm may want to pursue a market penetration opportunity before pursuing one involving product development or diversification.

6. In your own words, explain several reasons why marketing managers should consider international markets when evaluating possible opportunities.

7. Give an example of a foreign-made product (other than an automobile) that you personally have purchased. Give some reasons why you purchased that product. Do you think that there was a good opportunity for a domestic firm to get your business? Explain why or why not.

8. Explain what market segmentation is.

9. List the types of potential segmenting dimensions and explain which you would try to apply first, second, and third in a particular situation. If the nature of the situation would affect your answer, explain how.

10. Explain why segmentation efforts based on attempts to divide the mass market using a few demographic dimensions may be very disappointing.

11. Illustrate the concept that segmenting is an aggregating process by referring to the admissions policies of your own college and a nearby college or university.

12. Review the types of segmenting dimensions listed in Exhibits 3–9 and 3–10, and select the ones you think should be combined to fully explain the market segment you personally would be in if you were planning to buy a new watch today. List several dimensions and try to develop a short-hand name, like "fashion-oriented," to describe your own personal market segment. Then try to estimate what proportion of the total watch market would be accounted for by your market segment. Next, explain if there are any offerings that come close to meeting the needs of your market. If there aren't any, what sort of a marketing mix is needed? Would it be economically attractive for anyone to try to satisfy your market segment? Why or why not?

13. Identify the determining dimension or dimensions that explain why you bought the specific brand you did in your most recent purchase of a (a) soft drink, (b) shampoo, (c) shirt or blouse, and (d) larger, more expensive item, such as a bicycle, camera, boat, and so on. Try to express the determining dimension(s) in terms of your own personal characteristics rather than the product's characteristics. Estimate what share of the market would probably be motivated by the same determining dimension(s).

14. Consider the market for off-campus apartments in your city. Identify some submarkets that have different needs and determining dimensions. Then evaluate how well the needs in these market segments are being met in your geographic area. Is there an obvious breakthrough opportunity waiting for someone?

15. Explain how positioning can help a marketing manager identify target market opportunities.

SUGGESTED CASES

3. Gerber Products Company
7. Pillsbury's Häagen-Dazs

27. KASTORS, Inc.

COMPUTER-AIDED PROBLEM

3. Segmenting Customers

The marketing manager for Micro Software Company is seeking new market opportunities. He has analyzed needs in the broad wordprocessing market and narrowed down to three segments: the Fearful Typists, the Power Users, and the Specialists. The Fearful Typists don't know much about computers—they just want a fast way to type letters and simple reports without errors. They don't need a lot of special features. They want simple instructions and a program that's easy to learn. The Power Users know a lot about computers, use them often, and want a word processing program with many special features. All computer programs seem easy to them—so they aren't worried about learning to use the various features. The Specialists have jobs that require a lot of writing. They don't know much about computers but are willing to learn. They want special features needed for their work—but only if they aren't too hard to learn and use.

The marketing manager prepared a table summarizing the importance of each of three key needs in the three segments.

		Importance of Need 1 = Not Important, 10 = Very Important		
Segment	Features		Easy to Use	Easy to Learn
Fearful Typists	3		8	9
Power Users	9		2	2
Specialists	7		5	6

Micro's sales staff conducted interviews with seven potential customers who were asked to rate how important each of these three needs were in their work. The manager prepared a spreadsheet to help him cluster (aggregate) each person into one of the segments—along with other similar people. Each person's ratings are entered in the spreadsheet, and the clustering procedure computes a similarity score that indicates how similar (a low score) or dissimilar (a high score) the person is to the typical person in each of the segments. The manager can then aggregate potential customers into the segment that is most similar (that is, the one with the *lowest* similarity score).

a. The ratings for a potential customer appear on the first spreadsheet. Into which segment would you aggregate this person?

b. The responses for seven potential customers who were interviewed are listed in the table below. Enter the ratings for a customer in the spreadsheet and then write down the similarity score for each segment.

		Importance of Need 1 = Not important, 10 = Very important		
Customer	Computer Used	Features	Easy to Use	Easy to Learn
A	Dell	8	3	1
B	IBM	5	6	5
C	Macintosh	4	6	8
D	Macintosh	2	6	7
E	IBM	6	6	5
F	Dell	8	1	2
G	Macintosh	4	9	8

Repeat the process for each customer. Based on your analysis, indicate the segment into which you would aggregate each customer. Indicate the size (number of customers) of each segment.

c. In the interview, each potential customer was also asked what type of computer he or she would be using. The responses are shown in the table along with the ratings. Group the responses based on the customer's segment. If you were targeting the Power Users segment, what type of computer would you focus on when developing your software?

d. Based on your analysis, which customer would you say is least like any of the segments? Briefly explain the reason for your choice.

For additional questions related to this problem, see Exercise 3–4 in the *Learning Aid for use with Essentials of Marketing,* 6th edition.

Evaluating Opportunties in the Changing Marketing Environment

Chapter

4

When You Finish This Chapter, You Should

❶
Know the variables that shape the environment of marketing strategy planning.

❷
Understand why company objectives are important in guiding marketing strategy planning.

❸
See how a firm's resources affect the search for opportunities.

❹
Know how the economic and technological evnironment can affect strategy planning.

❺
Understand how the economic and technological environment can affect strategy planning.

❻
Know why you can go to prison by ignoring the political and legal environment.

❼
Know about the cultural and social environment and key population and income trends that affect it.

❽
Understand how to screen and evaluate marketing strategy opportunities.

❾
Understand the important new terms (shown in red).

Marketing managers do not plan strategies in a vacuum. When choosing target markets and developing the four Ps, they must work with many variables in the broader marketing environment. Marketing planning at Rubbermaid shows why this is important.

Top executives at Rubbermaid set ambitious objectives for the firm. They wanted to continue the growth in sales and profits the company had achieved every year for a decade—since the early 1980s.

Rubbermaid's marketing managers had built a respected brand name in plastic kitchenware—but they knew that just working harder at their current strategy for kitchenware would not be enough to achieve the firm's objectives. Rubbermaid's marketing environment was changing. The target market for kitchenware was no longer growing in the United States, so sales growth was slipping. A sluggish economy in 1992 made the problem worse. Rubbermaid had to cut prices to retailers to stimulate in-store promotions and sales, but the lower prices reduced Rubbermaid's profit margin. Competition was also becoming more intense.

These changes did not take Rubbermaid's marketing managers by surprise. They had been studying the changing environment to find new opportunities. Five years earlier they saw an opportunity to develop a new marketing mix for consumers interested in plastic toys. Rubbermaid had the money to move quickly. It acquired Little Tikes Co.—a small firm that was already producing sturdy plastic toys—and immediately expanded its product assortment. Marketing managers also took advantage of Rubbermaid's strong relationships with retailers to get scarce shelf space for the new toys—and they developed new ads to stimulate consumer interest. Unlike many toy companies, Rubbermaid was sensitive to parents' concerns about TV ads targeted at children. It aimed its cost-effective print ads at parents. This approach helped to speed Rubbermaid's entry in the market—and Little Tikes toys proved to be very profitable. However, production capacity limited additional short-term growth from that line so marketing managers looked for other opportunities as well.

For example, responding to increased environmental concerns in U.S. and Canadian markets, Rubbermaid developed a very successful "litterless" school lunch box. Designed

To achieve its objectives in a changing environment, Rubbermaid is developing new marketing strategies.

to eliminate disposable drink boxes, aluminum foil, and plastic wrap, the box had reusable sandwich holders and drink bottles.

Marketing managers also saw opportunities for growth in the newly unified European markets. But Rubbermaid was less well known in Europe; it did not have strong relationships with retailers, and the political, legal, and cultural environment was very different. So Rubbermaid formed a partnership with a Dutch firm that knew the European market, and it worked with wholesalers who could help build strong new distribution channels. By adapting its strategies, Rubbermaid already earns 10 percent of its profits from European sales—and more growth is expected.[1]

THE MARKETING ENVIRONMENT

You saw in the last chapter that finding target market opportunities takes a real understanding of what makes customers tick. The Rubbermaid case shows that understanding the marketing environment is also important in planning marketing strategy and evaluating opportunities. Exhibit 3–1 shows how Chapters 3 and 4 fit together.

A marketing manager controls the choice of marketing strategy variables within the framework of the broader marketing environment and how it is changing (see Exhibit 2–9). The marketing environment falls into five basic areas:

1. Objectives and resources of the firm.
2. Competitive environment.
3. Economic and technological environment.
4. Political and legal environment.
5. Cultural and social environment.

OBJECTIVES SHOULD SET FIRM'S COURSE

A company must decide where it's going, or it may fall into the trap expressed so well by the quotation "Having lost sight of our objective, we redoubled our efforts." Company objectives should shape the direction of the whole business.

It is difficult to set objectives that really guide the present and future development of a company. The process forces top management to look at the whole business, relate its present objectives and resources to the external environment, and then decide what the firm wants to accomplish in the future.

Three basic objectives provide guidelines

The following three objectives provide a useful starting point for setting a firm's objectives. A business should:

1. Engage in specific activities that will perform a socially and economically useful function.
2. Develop an organization to carry on the business and implement its strategies.
3. Earn enough profit to survive.[2]

Objectives should be specific

Our three general objectives provide guidelines, but a firm has to develop its own *specific* objectives. In spite of their importance, a firm seldom states its objectives explicitly. Too often it does so after the fact! If objectives aren't clear and specific from the start, different managers may hold unspoken and conflicting objectives—a common problem in large companies and in nonprofit organizations.

Objectives should be compatible

Objectives chosen by top management should be compatible—or frustrations and even failure may result. For example, top management may set a 25 percent annual return on investment as one objective, while at the same time specifying that current plant and equipment be used as fully as possible. In such a case, competition may make it impossible to use resources fully *and* achieve the target return.

Some top managements want a large sales volume or a large market share because they feel this assures greater profitability. But many large firms with big market shares have gone bankrupt. Eastern Airlines went under, and so did International Harvester. These firms sought large market shares—but earned little profit. Increasingly, companies are shifting their objectives toward *profitable* sales growth rather than just larger market share—as they realize that the two don't necessarily go together.[3]

Company objectives should lead to marketing objectives

You can see why the marketing manager should be involved in setting company objectives. Company objectives guide managers as they search for and evaluate opportunities—and later plan marketing strategies. Particular *marketing* objectives should be set within the framework of larger, company objectives. As shown in Exhibit 4–1, firms need a hierarchy of objectives—moving from company objectives to marketing department objectives. For each marketing strategy, firms also need objectives for each of the four Ps—as well as more detailed objectives. For example, in the Promotion area, we need objectives for advertising, sales promotion, *and* personal selling.

Both company objectives and marketing objectives should be realistic. Ambitious objectives are useless if the firm lacks the resources to achieve them.

COMPANY RESOURCES MAY LIMIT SEARCH FOR OPPORTUNITIES

Every firm has some resources—hopefully some unique ones—that set it apart from other firms. Breakthrough opportunities—or at least some competitive advantage—come from making use of these strengths while avoiding direct competition with firms having similar strengths.

To find its strengths, a firm must evaluate its functional areas (production, research and engineering, marketing, general management, and finance) as well as its present products and markets. By analyzing successes or failures in relation to the firm's resources, management can discover why the firm was successful—or why it failed—in the past.

Exhibit 4–1   A Hierarchy of Objectives

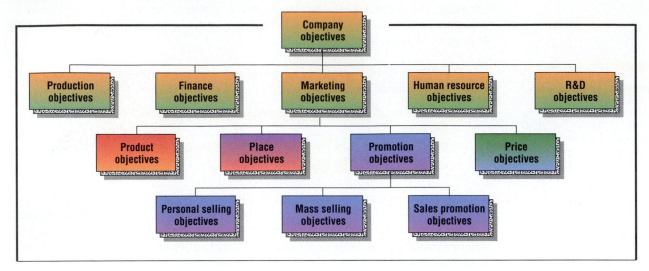

Harley-Davidson's motorcycle business was on the ropes, and it was losing customers to Japanese competitors. However, studying the Japanese firms helped Harley identify ways to reduce costs and improve quality. With these resource-use problems resolved, Harley was again on the road to achieving its objectives.[4]

The pressure of competition focused Harley's attention on manufacturing resources. Other resources that should be considered—as part of an evaluation of strengths and weaknesses—are discussed in the following sections.

Financial strength

Some opportunities require large amounts of capital just to get started. Money may be required for R&D, production facilities, marketing research, or advertising—before a firm makes its first sale. And even a really good opportunity may not be profitable for years. So lack of financial strength is often a barrier to entry into an otherwise attractive market.

Producing capability and flexibility

In many businesses, the cost of producing each unit decreases as the quantity produced increases. Therefore, smaller producers can be at a great cost disadvantage if they try to win business from larger competitors.

On the other hand, new—or smaller—firms sometimes have the advantage of flexibility. They are not handicapped with large, special-purpose facilities that are obsolete or poorly located. U.S. Steel (USX), Bethlehem, and other large steel producers once enjoyed economies of scale. But today they have trouble competing with producers using smaller, more flexible plants. Similarly, poorly located or obsolete retail or wholesale facilities can severely limit marketing strategy planning.

Firms that own or have assured sources of supply have an important advantage—especially in times of short supply. Big firms often control their own sources of supply. Companies that don't have guaranteed supply sources may have difficulty meeting demand—or even staying in business.

Marketing managers for the Lincoln Continental recently had to deal with this problem. They had developed a strategy that focused on special safety features, including dual air bags. Advertising touted these advantages and helped to attract buyers. However, Lincoln had to change the whole strategy after a fire at its air bag supplier's factory made it impossible to equip every car with dual air bags.[5]

A familiar brand—and other marketing strengths—can be an advantage in seeking new opportunities.

Marketing strengths

Our marketing strategy framework helps in analyzing current marketing resources. In the product area, for example, a familiar brand can be a big strength or a new idea or process may be protected by a *patent.* A patent owner has a 17-year monopoly to develop and use its new product, process, or material. If one firm has a strong patent, competitors may be limited to second-rate offerings—and their efforts may be doomed to failure.

Good relations with established middlemen—or control of good locations—can be an important resource. When Bic decided to compete with Gillette by selling disposable razors, Bic's other products had already proved profitable. So retailers were willing to give Bic shelf space.

Promotion and price resources must be considered too. Westinghouse already has a skilled sales force. Marketing managers know these sales reps can handle new products and customers. And low-cost facilities may enable a firm to undercut competitors' prices.

Finally, thorough understanding of a target market can give a company an edge. Many companies fail in new product-markets because they don't really understand the needs of the new customers—or the new competitive environment.

THE COMPETITIVE ENVIRONMENT

Choose opportunities that avoid head-on competition

The **competitive environment** affects the number and types of competitors the marketing manager must face—and how they may behave. Although marketing managers usually can't control these factors, they can choose strategies that avoid head-on competition. And, where competition is inevitable, they can plan for it.

Economists describe four basic kinds of market (competitive) situations: pure competition, oligopoly, monopolistic competition, and monopoly. Understanding the differences among these market situations is helpful in analyzing the competitive environment, and our discussion assumes some familiarity with these concepts. (For a review, see Exhibit A–11 and the related discussion in Appendix A, which follows Chapter 2).

Most product-markets move toward pure competition—or oligopoly—over the long-run. In these situations, competitors offer very similar products and customers see them as close substitutes. So the firms must compete with lower and lower prices, and their profit margins shrink. Avoiding pure competition is sensible—and certainly fits with our emphasis on target marketing.

Hammermill wants to avoid head-on competition from other paper producers, a difficult goal if potential customers view the products as essentially similar.

Monopolistic competition is typical—and a challenge

In monopolistic competition, a number of different firms offer marketing mixes that at least some customers see as different. Each competitor tries to get control (a monopoly) in its own target market. But competition still exists because some customers see the various alternatives as substitutes. Most marketing managers in developed economies face monopolistic competition.

In monopolistic competition, marketing managers sometimes try to differentiate very similar products by relying on other elements of the marketing mix. For example, Clorox bleach uses the same basic chemicals as other bleaches. But marketing managers for Clorox may help to set it apart from other bleaches by offering an improved pouring spout, by producing ads that demonstrate its stain-killing power, or by getting it better shelf positions in supermarkets. Yet such approaches may not work, especially if competitors can easily imitate the new ideas.

Analyze competitors to find a competitive advantage

The best way for a marketing manager to avoid head-on competition is to find new or better ways to satisfy customers' needs. The search for a breakthrough opportunity—or some sort of competitive advantage—requires an understanding not only of customers but also of competitors. That's why marketing managers turn to **competitor analysis**—an organized approach for evaluating the strengths and weaknesses of current or potential competitors' marketing strategies. A complete discussion of competitor analysis is beyond the scope of the first marketing course. But we will briefly cover one approach that works well. It is a logical extension of our marketing strategy planning framework.

The basic idea is simple. You compare your current (or planned) target market and marketing mix with what competitors are currently doing or are likely to do in response to your strategy. As Exhibit 4–2 shows, you also consider **competitive barriers**—the conditions that may make it difficult, or even impossible, for a firm to compete in a market. Such barriers may limit your own plans or, alternatively, block competitors' responses to an innovative strategy. For example, NutraSweet's patent on its low-calorie sweetener effectively limited direct competitors from quickly entering the market.

The initial step in competitor analysis is to identify potential competitors. It's useful to start broadly—and from the viewpoint of target customers. Companies may offer quite

Exhibit 4–2   A Framework for Competitor Analysis

	Firm's Current or Planned Strategy	Competitor 1's Strengths and Weaknesses	Competitor 2's Strengths and Weaknesses
Target Market			
Product			
Place			
Promotion			
Price			
Competitive Barriers			
Likely Response(s)			

different products to meet the same needs, but they are competitors if customers see them as offering close substitutes. For example, Dow ZipLock bags, Reynold's aluminum foil, Saran Wrap, and Tupperware containers compete in the same generic market for food storage needs. Identifying a broad set of potential competitors helps marketing managers understand the different ways customers are currently meeting needs—and sometimes points to new opportunities. Usually, however, marketing managers quickly narrow the focus of a competitor analysis to the set of rival firms who will be the closest competitors.

Rivals offering similar products are usually easy to identify. However, with a really new and different product concept, there may not be a current competitor with a similar product. In that case, the closest competitor may be a firm that is currently serving similar needs with a different product. Such firms are likely to fight back—if new offerings start to take away customers.

Anticipate competition that will come

Marketing managers must consider how long it might take for competitors to appear. It's easy to make the mistake of assuming that there won't be competition in the future—or of discounting how aggressive competition may become. But a successful strategy attracts others who are eager to jump in for a share of the profit.

Finding a sustainable competitive advantage requires special attention to competitor strengths and weaknesses. For example, it is very difficult to dislodge a competitor who is already a market leader simply by attacking with a strategy that has similar strengths. An established leader can usually defend its position by quickly copying the best parts of what a new competitor is trying to do. On the other hand, an established competitor may not be able to respond quickly if attacked where it is weak. For example, Right Guard deodorant built its strong position with an aerosol spray dispenser. But many consumers don't like the messy aerosol cloud—or the effect of aerosols on the environment. That weakness prompted Old Spice to introduce a pump dispenser. Right Guard did not respond quickly with its own pump because the company thought a pump dispenser would hurt sales of its established product.[6]

Seek information about competitors

A marketing manager should actively seek information about current or potential competitors. Although most firms try to keep the specifics of their plans secret, much public information may be available. Sources of competitor information include trade publications, alert sales reps, middlemen, and other industry experts. In business markets, customers may be quick to explain what competing suppliers are offering.

Ethical issues may arise

The search for information about competitors sometimes raises ethical issues. For example, it's not unusual for people to change jobs and move to a competing firm in the same industry. Such people may have a great deal of information about the competitor, but is it ethical for them to use it? Similarly, some firms have been criticized for going too far—like waiting at a landfill for competitors' trash to find copies of confidential company reports.

Beyond the moral issues, spying on competitors to obtain trade secrets is illegal, and damage awards can be huge. For example, the courts ordered Frito-Lay to pay Procter & Gamble millions in damages for stealing secrets about its Duncan Hines soft cookies. A Frito-Lay employee had posed as a potential customer to attend a confidential sales presentation.[7]

The competition may vary from country to country

A firm that faces very stiff competition may find that the competitive environment—and the opportunities—are much better in another region or country.

Twenty years ago, marketing managers at H. B. Fuller Co. saw international markets as an opportunity—and a matter of survival. It was hard for their small firm, a producer of paints and industrial coatings, to compete against giant suppliers like Du Pont and Dow Chemical for a larger share of the U.S. market. Fuller's marketing managers didn't want to diversify into some other business, so they decided to go where the competition wasn't. Fuller's move to overseas markets has been worth the effort. Foreign business now accounts for half of its profit.[8]

Direct competition cannot always be avoided

Despite the desire to avoid highly competitive situations, a firm may find that it can't. Some firms are already in an industry before it becomes intensely competitive. Then as competitors fail, new firms enter the market, possibly because they don't have more attractive alternatives and can at least earn a living. In less-developed economies, this is a common pattern with small retailers and wholesalers. New entrants may not even know how competitive the market is—but they stick it out until they run out of money. Production-oriented firms are more likely to make such a mistake.

THE ECONOMIC ENVIRONMENT

The **economic and technological environment** affects the way firms—and the whole economy—use resources. We will treat the economic and technological environments separately to emphasize that the technological environment provides a *base* for the economic environment. Technical skills and equipment affect the way companies convert an economy's resources into output. The economic environment, on the other hand, is affected by the way all of the parts of a macro-economic system interact. This then affects such things as national income, economic growth, and inflation. The economic environment may vary from one country to another, but economies around the world are linked.

Economic conditions change rapidly

The economic environment can—and does—change quite rapidly. The effects can be far reaching—and require changes in marketing strategy.

Interest rates and inflation affect buying

Changes in the economy are often accompanied by changes in the interest rate—the charge for borrowing money. Interest rates directly affect the total price borrowers must pay for products. So the interest rate affects when—and if—they will buy. This is an especially important factor in some business markets. But it also affects consumer purchases of homes, cars, furniture, and other items usually bought on credit.

Interest rates usually increase during periods of inflation, and inflation is a fact of life in many economies. In some Latin American countries, inflation has exceeded 400 percent a year in recent years. In contrast, recent U.S. levels—5 to 20 percent—seem low. Still, when costs are rising, a marketing manager may have to increase prices. But the decisions of individual marketing managers to raise prices add to macro-level inflation. That can lead to government policies that reduce income, employment, *and* consumer spending.

World economies are connected

In the past, marketing managers often focused their attention on the economy of their home country. It's no longer that simple. The economies of the world are connected. Changes in one economy affect others. One reason for this is that the amount of international trade is increasing—and it is affected by changes in and between economies.

Many companies find themselves helpless during such economic change. In fact, a country's whole economic system can change as the balance of imports and exports shifts—affecting jobs, consumer income, and national productivity.

A marketing manager must watch the economic environment carefully. In contrast to the cultural and social environment, economic conditions can change rapidly—requiring immediate strategy changes.[9]

THE TECHNOLOGICAL ENVIRONMENT

The technological base affects opportunities

Underlying any economic environment is its **technological base**—the technical skills and equipment that affect the way an economy's resources are converted to output. Technological developments affect marketing in two basic ways: with new products and with new processes (ways of doing things). Many argue, for example, that we are moving from an industrial society to an information society. Advances in electronic communications make it possible for people in different parts of the world to communicate face to face with satellite video-conferencing and to transmit faxes—including complex design drawings—by regular telephone lines. Computers allow more sophisticated planning and control. These

Rapid changes in information technology create many new market opportunities.

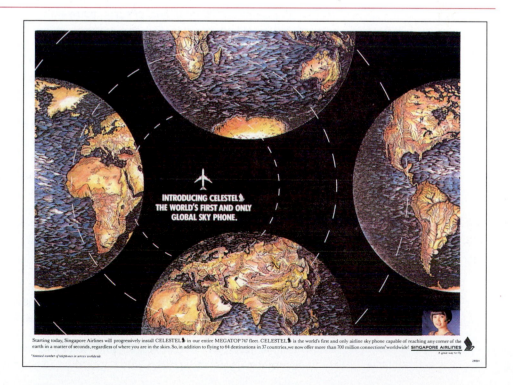

ZOOMING IN ON NEW MARKET OPPORTUNITIES

While he was in college, Frank Manning designed an automatic telephone dialer so that he could break through busy signals to get reservations for crowded tennis courts. With a bit more tinkering, his Demon Dialer became the first hit product for his company, Zoom Telephonics. Three years later, sales shot up to $6 million.

Within a year, however, sales nearly disappeared. Government regulators changed the way long-distance telephone customers reached carriers like MCI. The change eliminated the need to dial a long string of digits before each call—and that eliminated the need for the Demon Dialer. Small firms with a single product are very vulnerable to a change in the marketing environment—especially fast-changing technology markets. As Manning puts it, you "have to be able to see new openings and dash through them before they close."

And that is what he did at Zoom Telephonics. He switched to producing modems, a device people use so their computers can communicate over telephone lines. In 1991, Zoom's modem sales grew to about $20 million a year. But by then about 20 competitors had entered the market with similar devices. Worse, many computer makers began building modems into their computers. So Manning refocused his resources on developing a new voice synthesizer that links personal computers to corporate phone mail systems.

Zoom Telephonics is very successful—in spite of challenging changes in regulation, technology, and competition. But success isn't automatic. Manning looked for new opportunities to help him reinvent his firm. In his fast-changing market environment, he will probably have to do it again in the future.[10]

process changes are accompanied by an exciting explosion of high-tech products—from robots in factories to skin patches that dispense medicines to home refrigerators that "talk."

New technologies have created important markets that didn't even exist a few years ago. In 1981 Microsoft was a tiny software company. Now it's worth more than General Motors. With such big opportunities at stake, there is rapid transfer of technology from one part of the world to another. But this transfer is not automatic. Someone—perhaps you—has to see the opportunity.

Many of the big advances in business come from early recognition of new ways to do things. Marketers should help their firms see such opportunities by trying to understand the why of present markets—and possible uses of new technologies.

Technology and ethical issues

Marketers must also help their firms decide what technical developments are ethically acceptable. For example, some attractive technological developments may be rejected because of their long-run effects on the environment. Aseptic drink boxes are very convenient but difficult to recycle. In a case like this, what's good for the firm and some customers may not be good for the cultural and social environment—or acceptable in the political and legal environment. Being close to the market should give marketers a better feel for current trends—and help firms avoid serious mistakes.[11]

THE POLITICAL ENVIRONMENT

The attitudes and reactions of people, social critics, and governments all affect the political environment. Consumers in the same country usually share a common political environment, but the political environment can also have a dramatic effect on opportunities at a local or international level.

Exhibit 4–3 Current and Potential Member Countries of the European Community

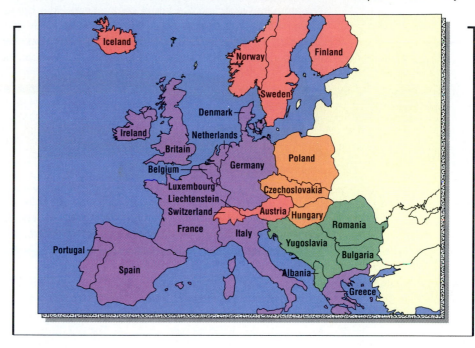

Nationalism can be limiting in international markets

Strong sentiments of **nationalism**—an emphasis on a country's interests before everything else—affect how macro-marketing systems work. And they can affect how marketing managers work as well. Nationalistic feelings can reduce sales—or even block all marketing activity—in some international markets. For many years, Japan made it difficult for outside firms to do business there—in spite of the fact that Japanese producers of cars, color TVs, VCRs, and other products established profitable markets in the United States, Europe, and other parts of the world.

The "Buy American" policy in many government contracts and business purchases reflects this same attitude in the United States—as does support for protecting U.S. producers from foreign competition—especially producers of footwear, textiles, production machinery, and cars.[12]

Regional groupings are becoming more important

Important dimensions of the political environment are likely to be similar among nations that band together to have common regional economic boundaries. An outstanding example of this sort of regional grouping is the movement toward economic unification of Europe.

The unification effort began when the 12 countries (shown in purple in Exhibit 4–3) that form the European Community (EC) dared to abandon old squabbles in favor of cooperative efforts to reduce taxes and other barriers to European trade.

Now the individual countries are reshaping into a unified economic superpower—what some have called the United States of Europe. The changes are by no means complete. By the year 2000 the EC may expand to include at least 25 countries and 450 million people. Of course, removal of some economic and political barriers will not eliminate the need to adjust strategies to reach submarkets of European consumers. Centuries of cultural differences will not disappear overnight—they may never disappear.[13]

Five years ago few people could have predicted the changes in the political environment—including the fall of communism—that brought about massive changes in these markets. Clearly, the political environment usually doesn't change as dramatically or as rapidly as it has in Europe. Some important political changes—both within and across nations—evolve more gradually. The development of consumerism is a good example.

Consumerism is here—and basic

Consumerism is a social movement that seeks to increase the rights and powers of consumers. In the last 30 years, consumerism emerged as a major political force. Although the consumer movement spread to many different countries, it was born in America.

The basic goals of modern consumerism haven't changed much since 1962 when President Kennedy's "Consumer Bill of Rights" affirmed consumers' rights to safety, to be informed, to choose, and to be heard.

Twenty-five years ago, U.S. consumerism was much more visible. Consumers staged frequent boycotts and protest marches, and attracted much media attention. Today, consumer groups provide information and work on special projects like product safety standards. Publications like *Consumer Reports* provide product comparisons and information on other consumer concerns.

Business is responding to public expectations

Many companies responded to the spirit of consumerism. For example, Chrysler adopted a consumer bill of rights, and Ford set up a consumer board to help resolve customer complaints. Clearly, top management—and marketing managers—must continue to pay attention to consumer concerns. The old, production-oriented ways of doing things are no longer acceptable.[14]

THE LEGAL ENVIRONMENT

Changes in the political environment often lead to changes in the legal environment—and in the way existing laws are enforced. The legal environment sets the basic rules for how a business can operate in society. To illustrate the effects of the legal environment, we will discuss how it evolved in the United States. However, keep in mind that laws often vary from one geographic market to another—especially in different countries.

Trying to encourage competition

American economic and legislative thinking is based on the idea that competition among many small firms helps the economy. Therefore, attempts by business to limit competition are considered contrary to the public interest.

Starting in 1890, Congress passed a series of antimonopoly laws. Exhibit 4–4 shows the names and dates of these laws. Although the specific focus of each law is different, in general they are all intended to encourage competition.

Antimonopoly law and marketing mix planning

In later chapters we will specifically apply antimonopoly law to the four Ps. For now you should know what kind of proof the government must have to get a conviction under each of the major laws. You should also know which of the four Ps are most affected by each law. Exhibit 4–4 provides such a summary—with a phrase following each law to show what the government must prove to get a conviction.

Prosecution is serious—you can go to jail

Businesses and *business managers* are subject to both criminal and civil laws. Penalties for breaking civil laws are limited to blocking or forcing certain actions—along with fines. Where criminal law applies, jail sentences can be imposed. For example, several managers at Beech-Nut Nutrition Company were recently fined $100,000 each and sentenced to a year in jail. In spite of unfair ads claiming that Beech-Nut's apple juice was 100 percent natural, they tried to bolster profits by secretly using low-cost artificial juices.[15]

Exhibit 4–4   Focus (mostly prohibitions) of Federal Antimonopoly Laws on the Four Ps

Law	Product	Place	Promotion	Price
Sherman Act (1890) Monopoly or conspiracy in restraint of trade	Monopoly or conspiracy to control a product	Monopoly or conspiracy to control distribution channels		Monopoly or conspiracy to fix or control prices
Clayton Act (1914) Substantially lessens competition	Forcing sale of some products with others—tying contracts	Exclusive dealing contracts (limiting buyers' sources of supply)		Price discrimination by manufacturers
Federal Trade Commission Act (1914) Unfair methods of competition		Unfair policies	Deceptive ads or selling practices	Deceptive pricing
Robinson-Patman Act (1936) Tends to injure competition		Prohibits paying allowances to direct buyers in lieu of middlemen costs (brokerage charges)	Prohibits fake advertising allowances or discrimination in help offered	Prohibits price discrimination on goods of like grade and quality without cost justification, and limits quantity discounts
Wheeler-Lea Amendment (1938) Unfair or deceptive practices	Deceptive packaging or branding		Deceptive ads or selling claims	Deceptive pricing
Antimerger Act (1950) Lessens competition	Buying competitors	Buying producers or distributors		
Magnuson-Moss Act (1975) Unreasonable practices	Product warranties			

Consumer protection laws are not new

Although antimonopoly laws focus on protecting competition, the wording of the laws in Exhibit 4–4 has, over time, moved toward protecting consumers. Some consumer protections are also built into the English and U.S. common law system. A seller has to tell the truth (if asked a direct question), meet contracts, and stand behind the firm's product (to some reasonable extent). Beyond this, it is expected that vigorous competition in the marketplace will protect consumers—*so long as they are careful.*

Yet focusing only on competition didn't protect consumers very well in some areas. So the government found it necessary to pass other laws. For example, various laws regulate packaging and labels, credit practices, and environmental issues. Usually, however, the laws focus on specific types of products.

Foods and drugs are controlled

Consumer protection laws in the United States go back to 1906 when Congress passed the Pure Food and Drug Act. Unsanitary meat-packing practices in the Chicago stockyards stirred consumer support for this act. This was a major victory for consumer protection. Before the law, it was assumed that common law and the old warning "let the buyer beware" would take care of consumers.

Later acts corrected some loopholes in the law. The law now bans the shipment of unsanitary and poisonous products and requires much testing of drugs. The Food and Drug Administration (FDA) attempts to control manufacturers of these products. It can seize products that violate its rules—including regulations on branding and labeling.

Product safety is controlled

The Consumer Product Safety Act (of 1972), another important consumer protection law, set up the Consumer Product Safety Commission. This group has broad power to set safety standards and can impose penalties for failure to meet these standards. Again, there is some question as to how much safety consumers really want—the commission found the bicycle the most hazardous product under its control!

But given that the commission has the power to *force* a product off the market—or require expensive recalls to correct problems—it is obvious that safety must be considered in product design. And safety must be treated seriously by marketing managers.[16]

State and local laws vary

Besides federal legislation—which affects interstate commerce—marketers must be aware of state and local laws. There are state and city laws regulating minimum prices and the setting of prices, regulations for starting up a business (licenses, examinations, and even tax payments), and in some communities, regulations prohibiting certain activities—such as door-to-door selling or selling on Sundays or during evenings.

Consumerists and the law say "Let the seller beware"

The old rule about buyer-seller relations—*let the buyer beware*—has changed to *let the seller beware.* The current shift to proconsumer laws and court decisions suggests that lawmakers are more interested in protecting consumers. This may upset production-oriented managers. But times have changed—and managers must adapt to this new political and legal environment. After all, it is consumers—through their government representatives—who determine the kind of society they want.[17]

The government regulates marketing of many goods and services.

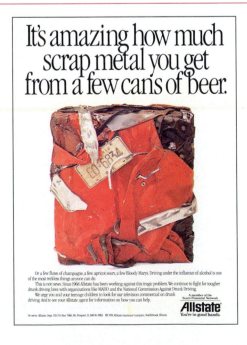

THE CULTURAL AND SOCIAL ENVIRONMENT

The **cultural and social environment** affects how and why people live and behave as they do—which affects customer buying behavior and eventually the economic, political, and legal environment. Many variables make up the cultural and social environment. Some examples are the languages people speak, the type of education they have, their religious beliefs, what type of food they eat, the style of clothing and housing they have, and how they view marriage and family.

Changes in a society and in its basic cultural values usually come slowly. An individual firm can't hope to encourage big changes in the short run. Instead, it should identify current attitudes and work within these constraints. At the same time, a marketing manager must watch for signs of the longer-run shifts. Even small shifts may lead to new needs—and new market opportunities.

Demographic data and trends tell us a lot about a society and its culture. Understanding the demographic dimensions is also important for marketing strategy planning—because markets consist of people with money to spend. So it makes sense to start with a broad view of population, income, and other key demographic dimensions.

Where people are around the world

Exhibit 4–5 summarizes current data for representative countries from different regions around the world. With a population of about 250 million, the United States is among the largest countries. Even so, it makes up less than 5 percent of the total world population—which is over 5.3 billion.[18]

Exhibit 4–5   Demographic Dimensions for Representative Countries

Country	1990 Population (000s)	Years for Population to Double	Percent of Population- Urban Areas	1990 GNP (millions of $U.S.)	Percent Annual GNP Growth	1990 GNP per Capita	Literacy Percent
Afghanistan	15,166	30	17.7%	3,307	2.4%	218	12%
Australia	16,649	58	85.7	211,456	1.7	12,638	100
Brazil	153,765	35	73.8	348,210	2.9	2,245	79
Canada	26,521	87	76.5	474,079	4.1	17,309	96
China	1,130,096	44	20.6	439,231	11.0	356	73
Egypt	56,202	27	45.2	33,583	0.5	610	45
France	56,162	231	73.4	940,485	2.3	16,419	99
Germany	77,546	n/a	90.4	1,415,946	3.3	17,659	99
India	850,090	35	25.8	277,994	1.2	330	41
Indonesia	191,216	37	26.2	81,843	3.8	420	74
Iraq	18,761	19	68.0	40,000	0.0	2,213	46
Israel	4,445	41	88.9	39,213	1.0	8,882	92
Japan	123,836	139	76.7	2,829,825	4.8	21,914	99
Kenya	25,369	17	19.7	9,127	4.8	358	59
Mexico	88,266	32	66.3	156,152	1.4	1,783	90
Mozambique	14,532	39	19.4	1,676	4.0	113	17
Singapore	2,703	63	100.0	29,529	10.9	9,958	83
South Korea	43,911	54	69.9	188,499	12.0	3,883	93
South Africa	38,509	n/a	55.9	81,814	2.6	2,071	79
Switzerland	6,651	116	60.5	187,842	2.6	27,693	99
Taiwan	20,456	63	70.6	99,464	7.2	4,355	91
United Kingdom	57,142	347	89.6	646,255	3.8	10,917	99
United States	250,465	77	73.7	4,961,434	1.0	19,789	96
Venezuela	19,745	28	83.2	64,484	4.2	3,213	90

Although the size of a market is important, the population trend is also important. The world's population is growing fast and is expected to nearly double in the next 20 years—but population growth varies dramatically from country to country. In general, less-developed countries are growing the fastest. The populations of Kenya, India, and Egypt are expected to double in 35 years or less. It will take more than twice as long for the populations of Japan, the European countries, Canada, and the United States to double. In fact, many U.S. marketers who enjoyed rapid and profitable growth know that the domestic picnic is over. They now turn to international markets where population—and sales revenues—continue to grow.[19]

The graying of America

Because the U.S. population is growing slowly, the average age is rising. In 1970, the average age of the population was 28—but by the year 2000 the average age will jump to about 37.

Stated another way, the percentage of the population in different age groups is changing. Exhibit 4–6 shows the number of people in different age groups in 1980 and 1990—and how the size of these groups will look in 2000. Note the big increases in the 25–44 age group from 1980 to 1990—and how that growth will carry over to the 45–64 age groups from 1990 until 2000.

The major reason for the changing age distribution is that the post–World War II baby boom produced about one fourth of the present U.S. population. Some of the effects of this big market are very apparent. For example, recording industry sales exploded—to the beat of rock and roll music and the Beatles—as the baby boom group moved into their record-buying teens. Soon after, colleges added facilities and faculty to handle the

Exhibit 4–6 U.S. Population Distribution by Age Groups for the Years 1980, 1990, and 2000

Age Group:	Under 5	5–17	18–24	25–44	45–64	65 or over
Year 2000		48,815	25,231	81,060	61,381	34,882
Population estimate (000)	16,898					
Percent of population in this age group	6.3%	18.2%	9.4%	30.2%	22.9%	13.0%
1990		45,629		81,555	46,842	31,559
	18,408		25,897			
	7.4%	18.2%	10.4%	32.6%	18.7%	12.6%
1980		47,237	30,350	63,494	44,156	25,704
	16,458					
	7.2%	20.8%	13.3%	27.9%	19.6%	11.3%
Percent change in age group: 1980–1990	11.8	–3.4	–13.9	28.4	5.2	22.8
1990–2000	–8.2	7.0	–2.6	–0.6	31.0	10.5

surge—then had to cope with excess capacity and loss of revenue when the student-age population dwindled. On the other hand, the fitness industry and food producers who offer low-calorie foods are reaping the benefit of a middle-aged "bulge" in the population.

Medical advances help people live longer and are also adding to the proportion of the population who are **senior citizens**—people age 65 or older. Note from Exhibit 4–6 that the over-65 age group grew by 23 percent in the last decade—and will grow another 10 percent before the turn of the century. Our senior citizens are also more prosperous than ever before. In 1960, about a third of all senior citizens had incomes below the poverty level. Now only about 11 percent are considered poor—lower than the 12.8 percent figure for all adults. These dramatic changes create new opportunities for such industries as tourism, health care, and financial services.[20]

U.S. population is shifting

Exhibit 4–7 shows the population and percentage change in population—growth or decline—in different regions of the United States. The states with the green shading are growing the fastest, and the orange ones are actually losing population. Notice that some of the most populated areas in Exhibit 4–7 are not growing the fastest. For example, people are moving out of the Northeast and the north central states to the Sun Belt of the South and West. California, Texas, and Florida are expected to account for over half of the total U.S. population growth from now until the turn of the century!

Exhibit 4–7   1990 Population (in thousands) and Percent Change in Population (1990–2000) by State

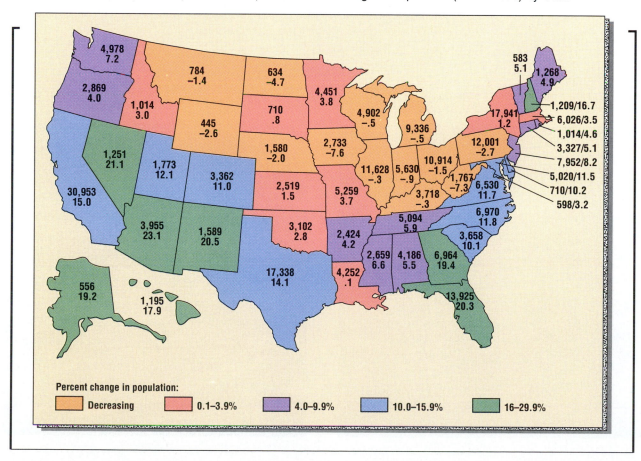

These different rates of growth are especially important to marketers. Sudden growth in an area may create new demand for many goods and services—while retailers in declining areas face tougher competition for a smaller number of customers.[21]

The mobile ones are an attractive market

Of course, none of these population shifts is necessarily permanent. People move, stay awhile, and then move again. In fact, about 18 percent of Americans move each year—about half of them to a new city. Both the long-distance and local mobiles are important market segments. They often must quickly make many purchases—and decisions about where they will shop.[22]

The shift to urban and suburban areas

The extent to which a country's population is clustered around urban areas varies a lot. In the United States, Venezuela, Australia, Israel, and Singapore, for example, a high percentage of people live in urban areas. See Exhibit 4–5. By contrast, in China and Afghanistan less than 20 percent of the people live in major urban areas.

A worldwide trend toward urbanization has prompted increased interest in international markets. Affluent, big-city consumers often have similar lifestyles and needs. Thus, many of the products successful in Toronto, New York, or Paris are likely to be successful in Caracas and Tokyo. More generally, the concentration of people in major cities simplifies Place and Promotion strategy decisions.

In the United States, migration from rural to urban areas has been continuous since 1800. In 1920, about half the population lived in rural areas. By 1950, the number living on farms dropped to 15 percent—and now it is less than 2 percent. During the last 25 years, the middle-income population drifted toward the suburbs rather than the central cities. But clearly we have become an urban and suburban society.[23]

Major cities like Singapore attract many marketers because of their concentration of people and income; by contrast, much of the world's population still lives in poverty in rural villages like this one in China.

Local political boundaries don't define market areas

The growth of sprawling urban and suburban areas in the United States means that the usual practice of reporting population by city and county boundaries can result in misleading descriptions of markets. Marketers are more interested in the size of homogeneous *marketing* areas than in the number of people within political boundaries. To meet this need, the U.S. Census Bureau developed a separate population classification based on metropolitan statistical areas. Much data is reported on the characteristics of people in these areas. The technical definition of these areas has changed over time. But basically a **Metropolitan Statistical Area (MSA)** is an integrated economic and social unit with a large population nucleus. Generally, an MSA centers on one city or urbanized area of 50,000 or more inhabitants and includes bordering urban areas.

The largest MSAs—basically those with a population of more than a million—are called Consolidated Metropolitan Statistical areas. More than a third of all Americans live in the 20 largest consolidated MSAs. You can see why competition for consumer dollars is usually stiff in an MSA.

Metro areas are also attractive markets because they offer greater sales potential than their large population alone suggests. Consumers in these areas have more money to spend because wages tend to be higher. In addition, professionals—with higher salaries—are concentrated there.[24]

There's no market when there's no income

Profitable markets require income—as well as people. The amount of money people can spend affects the products they are likely to buy—and what a society is like.

In many countries, the best available measure of total income is **gross national product (GNP)**—the total market value of goods and services produced in an economy in a year. Exhibit 4–5 gives a GNP estimate for each country listed. You can see that the more developed industrial nations—including the United States, Japan, and Germany—have the biggest share of the world's GNP. This is why so much trade takes place between these countries—and why many firms see them as the more important markets.[25]

Income growth expands markets

However, the fastest *growth* in GNP is not, in general, occurring in the nations with the largest GNPs. For example, total U.S. GNP in 1990 was close to $5 trillion; it has increased approximately 3 percent a year since 1880. This means that GNP doubled—on the average—every 20 years. Recently, this growth slowed—and even declined for a while.

GNP tells us about the income of a whole nation, but in a country with a large population that income must be spread over more people. GNP per person is a useful figure because it gives some idea of the income level of people in a country. Exhibit 4–5 shows, for example, that GNP per capita in the United States is quite high—about $20,000. Japan, Canada, Switzerland, and Germany are among those with the highest GNP per capita. In general, markets like these offer the best potential for products targeted at consumers with higher incomes.

Redistribution of income broadened U.S. market

Family incomes in the United States generally increased with GNP. But even more important to marketers, the *distribution* of income changed drastically over time. Fifty years ago, most U.S. families were bunched together at the low end of the income scale—just over a subsistence level. There were many fewer families in the middle range, and a relative handful formed an elite market at the top. This pattern still exists in many nations. By the 1970s, however, real income (buying power) in the United States rose so much that most families—even those near the bottom of the income distribution—could afford a comfortable standard of living. And the proportion of people with middle incomes was much larger. Such middle-income people enjoyed real choices in the marketplace.

This revolution broadened markets and drastically changed the U.S. marketing system. Products viewed as luxuries in most parts of the world sell to "mass" markets in the

United States. And these large markets lead to economies of scale, which boost our standard of living even more. Similar situations exist in Canada, many Western European countries, Australia, New Zealand, and Japan.

HOW TO EVALUATE OPPORTUNITIES

Developing and applying screening criteria

After you analyze the firm's resources (for strengths and weaknesses), the environmental trends the firm faces, and the objectives of top management, you merge them all into a set of product-market screening criteria. The screening should use both quantitative and qualitative criteria. Quantitative criteria summarize the firm's objectives: sales, profit, and return on investment (ROI) targets. (Note: ROI analysis is discussed briefly in Appendix B, which follows Chapter 16.) The qualitative components summarize what kinds of businesses the firm wants to be in, what businesses it wants to exclude, what weaknesses it should avoid, and what resources (strengths) and trends it should build on.[26]

Developing screening criteria is difficult—but worth the effort. They summarize in one place what the firm wants to accomplish—in quantitative terms—as well as roughly how and where it wants to accomplish it. The criteria should be realistic—that is, they should be achievable. Opportunities that pass the screen should be able to be turned into strategies that the firm can implement with the resources it has.

Exhibit 4–8 illustrates the product-market screening criteria for a small retail and wholesale distributor. These criteria help the firm's managers eliminate unsuitable opportunities—and find attractive ones to turn into strategies and plans.

Exhibit 4–8   An Example of Product-Market Screening Criteria for a Small Retail and Wholesale Distributor ($5 million annual sales)

1. **Quantitative criteria:**
   a. Increase sales by $750,000 per year for the next five years.
   b. Earn ROI of at least 25 percent before taxes on new ventures.
   c. Break even within one year on new ventures.
   d. Opportunity must be large enough to justify interest (to help meet objectives) but small enough so company can handle with the resources available.
   e. Several opportunities should be pursued to reach the objectives—to spread the risks.

2. **Qualitative criteria:**
   a. Nature of business preferred:
      (1) Goods and services sold to present customers.
      (2) Quality products that can be sold at high prices with full margins.
      (3) Competition should be weak and opportunity should be hard to copy for several years.
      (4) Should build on our strong sales skills.
      (5) There should be strongly felt (even unsatisfied) needs—to reduce promotion costs and permit high prices.
   b. Constraints:
      (1) Nature of businesses to exclude:
         (a) Manufacturing.
         (b) Any requiring large fixed capital investments.
         (c) Any requiring many people who must be good all the time and would require much supervision.
      (2) Geographic: limited to United States, Mexico, and Canada only.
      (3) General:
         (a) Make use of current strengths.
         (b) Attractiveness of market should be reinforced by more than one of the following basic trends: technological, demographic, social, economic, or political.
         (c) Market should not be bucking any basic trends.

Whole plans should be evaluated

You need to forecast the probable results of implementing a marketing strategy to apply the quantitative part of the screening criteria because only implemented plans generate sales, profits, and return on investment (ROI). For a rough screening, you only need to estimate the likely results of implementing each opportunity over a logical planning period. If a product's life is likely to be three years, for example, a good strategy may not produce profitable results for 6 to 12 months. But evaluated over the projected three-year life, the product may look like a winner. When evaluating the potential of possible opportunities (product-market strategies) it is important to evaluate similar things—that is, *whole* plans.

Note that managers can evaluate different marketing plans at the same time. Exhibit 4–9 compares a much improved product and product concept (Product A) with a "me-too" product (Product B) for the same target market. In the short run, the me-too product will make a profit sooner and might look like the better choice—if managers consider only one year's results. The improved product, on the other hand, will take a good deal of pioneering—but over its five-year life will be much more profitable.

PLANNING GRIDS HELP EVALUATE A PORTFOLIO OF OPPORTUNITIES

When a firm has many possibilities to evaluate, it usually has to compare quite different ones. This problem is easier to handle with graphical approaches—such as the nine-box strategic planning grid developed by General Electric and used by many other companies. Such grids can help evaluate a firm's whole portfolio of strategic plans or businesses.

General Electric looks for green positions

General Electric's strategic planning grid—see Exhibit 4–10—forces company managers to make three-part judgments (high, medium, and low) about the business strengths and industry attractiveness of all proposed or existing product-market plans. As you can see from Exhibit 4–10, this approach helps a manager organize information about the company's marketing environments (discussed earlier in this chapter) along with information about its strategy.

GE feels opportunities that fall into the green boxes in the upper left-hand corner of the grid are its best growth opportunities. Managers give these opportunities high marks on both industry attractiveness and business strengths. The red boxes in the lower right-hand corner of the grid, on the other hand, suggest a no-growth policy. Existing red businesses may continue to generate earnings, but they no longer deserve much investment. Yellow businesses are borderline cases—they can go either way. GE may continue to support an existing yellow business but will probably reject a proposal for a new one.

Exhibit 4–9   Expected Sales and Cost Curves of Two Strategies over Five-Year Planning Periods

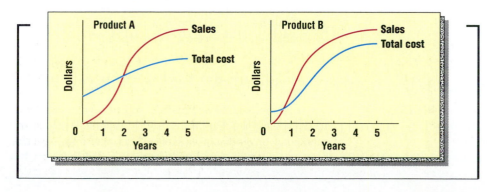

Exhibit 4–10   General Electric's Strategic Planning Grid

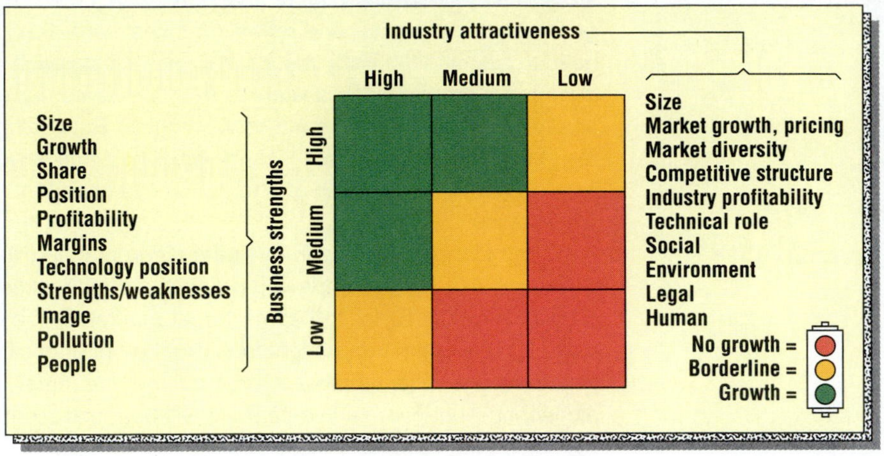

GE's "stop light" evaluation method is a very subjective, multiple-factor approach. It avoids the traps and possible errors of trying to use oversimplified, single-number criteria—like ROI or market share. Instead, top managers review detailed written summaries of many factors that help them make summary judgments. Then they can make a collective judgment. This approach generally leads to agreement. It also helps everyone understand why the company supports some new opportunities and not others.[27]

General Electric considers factors that reflect its objectives. Another firm might modify the evaluation to emphasize other factors—depending on its objectives and the type of product-market plans it is considering. While different firms focus on different factors, using many factors helps ensure that managers consider all the company's concerns when evaluating alternative opportunities.

MULTIPRODUCT FIRMS HAVE A DIFFICULT STRATEGY-PLANNING JOB

Multiproduct firms—like General Electric—obviously have a more difficult strategic planning job than firms with only a few products or product lines aimed at the same or similar target markets. Multiproduct firms have to develop strategic plans for very different businesses. And they have to balance plans and resources so the whole company reaches its objectives. This means they may approve only those plans that make sense for the whole company—even if it means getting needed resources by "milking" some businesses and eliminating others.

Details on how to manage a complicated multiproduct firm are beyond our scope. But you should be aware (1) that there are such firms and (2) that the principles in this text are applicable—they just have to be extended.[28]

EVALUATING OPPORTUNITIES IN INTERNATIONAL MARKETS

Evaluate the risks

The approaches we've discussed so far apply to international markets just as they do to domestic ones. But in international markets it is often harder to fully understand the marketing environment variables. This may make it harder to see the risks involved in

Large multiproduct firms, like Philip Morris, evaluate and pursue a portfolio of strategic opportunities all around the world.

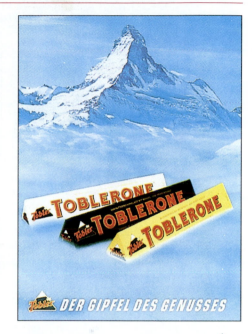

particular opportunities. Some countries are politically unstable; their governments and constitutions come and go. An investment safe under one government might become a takeover target under another. Further, the possibility of foreign exchange controls—and tax rate changes—can reduce the chance of getting profits and capital back to the home country.

To reduce the risk of missing some basic variable that may help screen out a risky opportunity, marketing managers sometimes need a detailed analysis of the market environment they are considering entering. Such an analysis can reveal facts about an unfamiliar market that a manager in a distant country might otherwise overlook. Further, a local citizen who knows the marketing environment may be able to identify an obvious problem ignored even in a careful analysis. Thus, it is very useful for the analysis to include inputs from locals—perhaps cooperative middlemen.[29]

Risks vary with environmental sensitivity

The farther you go from familiar territory, the greater the risk of making big mistakes. But not all products—or marketing mixes—involve the same risk. Think of the risks as running along a "continuum of environmental sensitivity." See Exhibit 4–11.

Exhibit 4–11   Continuum of Environmental Sensitivity

Insensitive		Sensitive
Industrial products	Basic commodity-type consumer products	Consumer products that are linked to cultural variables

Some products, like Ricoh fax machines, are used the same way all over the world. Other products, like chopsticks and noodle soup, are more sensitive to different cultures.

Some products are relatively insensitive to the economic and cultural environment they're placed in. These products may be accepted as is—or may require just a little adaptation to make them suitable for local use. Most industrial products are near the insensitive end of this continuum.

At the other end of the continuum, we find highly sensitive products that may be difficult or impossible to adapt to all international situations. Consumer products closely linked to other social or cultural variables are at this end. For example, some cultures view dieting as unhealthy, so a diet product popular in the United States might be a big failure there.

This continuum helps explain why many of the early successes in international marketing were basic commodities such as gasoline, soap, transportation vehicles, mining equipment, and agricultural machinery. It also helps explain why some consumer products firms have been successful with basically the same promotion and products in different parts of the globe.

Yet some managers don't understand the reason for these successes. They think they can develop a global marketing mix for just about *any* product. They fail to see that firms producing and/or selling products near the sensitive end of the continuum should carefully analyze how their products will be seen and used in new environments—and plan their strategies accordingly.[30]

What if risks are still hard to judge?

If the risks of an international opportunity are hard to judge, it may be wise to look first for opportunities that involve exporting. This gives managers a chance to build experience, know-how, and confidence over time. Then the firm will be in a better position to judge the prospects and risks of taking further steps.

CONCLUSION

Businesses need innovative strategy planning to survive in our increasingly competitive markets. In this chapter, we discussed the variables that shape the environment of marketing strategy planning—and how they may affect opportunities. First we looked at how the firm's own resources and objectives may help guide or limit the search for opportunities. Then we went on to look at the external environments. They are important because changes in these environments present new opportunities—as well as problems—that a marketing manager must deal with in marketing strategy planning.

A manager must study the competitive environment. How well established are competitors? Are there competitive barriers, and what effect will they have? How will competitors respond to a plan?

The economic environment—including chances of recessions or inflation—also affects the choice of strategies. And the marketer must try to anticipate, understand, and deal with these changes—as well as changes in the technological base underlying the economic environment.

The marketing manager must also be aware of legal restrictions—and be sensitive to changing political cli-
mates. The acceptance of consumerism has already forced many changes.

The social and cultural environment affects how people behave and what marketing strategies will be successful.

Developing good marketing strategies within all these environments isn't easy. You can see that marketing management is a challenging job that requires integration of information from many disciplines.

Eventually, managers need procedures for screening and evaluating opportunities. We explained an approach for developing screening criteria—from an analysis of the strengths and weaknesses of the company's resources, the environmental trends it faces, and top management's objectives. We also considered some quantitative techniques for evaluating opportunities. And we discussed ways for evaluating and managing quite different opportunities—using the GE strategic planning grid.

Now we can go on—in the rest of the book—to discuss how to turn opportunities into profitable marketing plans and programs.

QUESTIONS AND PROBLEMS

1. Explain how a firm's objectives may affect its search for opportunities.

2. Specifically, how would various company objectives affect the development of a marketing mix for a new type of baby shoe? If this company were just being formed by a former shoemaker with limited financial resources, list the objectives she might have. Then discuss how they would affect the development of her marketing strategy.

3. Explain how a firm's resources may limit its search for opportunities. Cite a specific example for a specific resource.

4. In your own words, explain how a marketing manager might use a competitor analysis to avoid situations that involve head-on competition.

5. The owner of a small grocery store—the only one in a medium-sized town in the mountains—just learned
that a large chain plans to open a new store nearby. How difficult will it be for the owner to plan for this new competitive threat? Explain your answer.

6. Discuss the probable impact on your hometown if a major breakthrough in air transportation allowed foreign producers to ship into any U.S. market for about the same transportation cost that domestic producers incur.

7. Will the elimination of trade barriers between countries in Europe eliminate the need to consider submarkets of European consumers? Why or why not?

8. What and who is the U.S. government attempting to protect in its effort to preserve and regulate competition?

9. For each of the *major* laws discussed in the text, indicate whether in the long run the law will promote

or restrict competition (see Exhibit 4–4). As a consumer without any financial interest in business, what is your reaction to each of these laws?

10. Drawing on data in Exhibit 4–5, do you think that Egypt would be an attractive market for a firm that produces home appliances? What about Germany? Discuss your reasons.

11. Discuss how the worldwide trend toward urbanization is affecting opportunities for international marketing.

12. Discuss how slower population growth—especially the smaller number of young people—will affect businesses in your local community.

13. Discuss the impact of the aging culture on marketing strategy planning in the United States.

14. Explain the components of product-market screening criteria that can be used to evaluate opportunities.

15. Explain General Electric's strategic planning grid approach to evaluating opportunities.

SUGGESTED CASES

2. Nutra, Inc.
6. Bethlehem Steel Company

30. Metro Medical, Inc.

COMPUTER-AIDED PROBLEM

4. Competitor Analysis

Mediquip, Inc., produces medical equipment and uses its own sales force to sell the equipment to hospitals. Recently, several hospitals have asked Mediquip to develop a laser-beam "scalpel" for eye surgery. Mediquip has the needed resources, and 600 hospitals will probably buy the equipment. But Mediquip managers have heard that Laser Technologies—another quality producer—is thinking of competing for the same business. Mediquip has other good opportunities it could pursue—so it wants to see if it would have a competitive advantage over Laser Tech.

Mediquip and Laser Tech are similar in many ways, but there are important differences. Laser Technologies already produces key parts needed for the new laser product—so its production costs would be lower. It would cost Mediquip more to design the product—and getting parts from outside suppliers would result in higher production costs.

On the other hand, Mediquip has marketing strengths. It already has a good reputation with hospitals—and its sales force calls only on hospitals. Mediquip thinks that each of its current sales reps could spend some time selling the new product—and that it could adjust sales territories so only four more sales reps would be needed for good coverage in the market. In contrast, Laser Tech's sales reps call only on industrial customers, so it would have to add 18 reps to cover the hospitals.

Hospitals have budget pressures—so the supplier with the lowest price is likely to get a larger share of the business. But Mediquip knows that either supplier's price will be set high enough to cover the added costs of designing, producing, and selling the new product—and leave something for profit.

Mediquip gathers information about its own likely costs and can estimate Laser Tech's costs from industry studies and Laser Tech's annual report. Mediquip sets up a spreadsheet to evaluate the proposed new product.

a. The initial spreadsheet results are based on the assumption that Mediquip and Laser Tech will split the business 50/50. If Mediquip can win at least 50 percent of the market, does Mediquip have a competitive advantage over Laser Tech? Explain.

b. Because of economies of scale, both suppliers' average cost per machine will vary depending on the quantity sold. If Mediquip gets only 45 percent of the market and Laser Tech 55 percent, how will their costs (average total cost per machine) compare? What if Mediquip gets 55 percent of the market and Laser Tech only 45 percent? What conclusion do you draw from these analyses?

c. Laser Tech may not enter the market. If Mediquip gets 100 percent of the market, and quantity purchases from its suppliers reduce the cost of producing one unit to $7,000, what price will cover all its costs and contribute $1,250 to profit for every machine sold?

What does this suggest about the desirability of finding your own unsatisfied target markets? Explain.

For additional questions related to this problem, see Exercise 4−4 in the *Learning Aid for use with Essentials of Marketing*, 6th edition.

Getting Information for Marketing Decisions

Chapter 5

When You Finish This Chapter, You Should

❶

Know about marketing information systems.

❷

Understand a scientific approach to marketing research.

❸

Know how to define and solve marketing problems.

❹

Know about getting secondary and primary data.

❺

Understand the role of observing, questioning, and using experimental methods in marketing research.

❻

Understand the important new terms (shown in red).

Marketing managers at Frito-Lay had a problem. They wanted to develop a new snack chip that would appeal to adults. The trick would be to generate new sales, not just take sales away from their other brands, like Cheetos and Fritos, that were already very popular with teens. To develop a strategy, the marketing managers needed good information. And to get that information they turned to marketing research.

A number of focus group interviews provided good ideas. The focus groups liked the concept of a multigrain snack. They also seemed to favor a thin, rectangular chip with ridges and a salty, nutty flavor. The managers then turned to survey research—to see if the opinions of the focus group participants held with larger, more representative samples of target customers. The surveys also provided more details on what consumers liked and didn't like about different versions of the chip and about competitors' products.

Next the Frito-Lay managers tested different variations of the planned marketing mix in specially selected test markets. The test markets provided detailed information from grocery store checkout scanners. The scanner data not only showed how many people tried the new product, but how many came back to buy again. Knowing these repeat purchase rates helped managers estimate the product's real sales potential. Test results also helped managers to choose the Sun Chips brand name and fine-tune other marketing mix decisions. Moreover, the tests confirmed that Sun Chips were attracting the target buyers, especially women in the 25–35 age group.

Now that Sun Chips are distributed nationally, managers need other information to see how well the strategy is working. Much of that information comes from the firm's marketing information system, which is updated daily. In fact, all of Frito-Lay's salespeople are equipped with hand-held computers. Throughout the day they input sales information at the stores they visit. In the evening they send all the data over telephone lines to a central computer, where it is analyzed. Within 24 hours marketing managers at headquarters and in regional offices get reports and graphs that summarize how sales went the day before— broken down by brands and locations. The information system even allows a manager on a computer terminal to zoom in and take a closer look at a problem in Peoria or a sales success in Sacramento.[1]

MARKETING MANAGERS NEED INFORMATION

This example shows that successful planning of marketing strategies requires information—information about potential target markets and their likely responses to marketing mixes as well as about competition and other marketing environment variables. Information is also needed for implementation and control. Without good marketing information, managers have to use intuition or guesses—and in today's fast-changing and competitive markets, this invites failure.

Yet managers seldom have all the information they need. Both customers and competitors can be unpredictable. Getting more information may cost too much or take too long. For example, data on international markets is often incomplete, outdated, or difficult to obtain. So managers often must decide if they need more information and—if so—how to get it. In this chapter, we'll talk about how marketing managers can get the information they need to plan successful strategies.

MARKETING INFORMATION SYSTEMS CAN HELP

Marketing managers for some companies make decisions based almost totally on their own judgment—with very little hard data. When it's time to make a decision, they may wish they had more information. But by then it's too late, so they do without.

MIS makes data available

Some firms like Frito-Lay realize that it doesn't pay to wait until they have important questions they can't answer. They work to develop a *continual flow of information*—and to make it more accessible to managers whenever they need it.

A **marketing information system (MIS)** is an organized way of continually gathering and analyzing data to provide marketing managers with information they need to make decisions. In some companies, an MIS is set up by marketing specialists; in others, by a group that provides *all* departments in the firm with information.

Specialized computer software and hardware help make it easier for companies to gather and analyze marketing information.

The technical details of setting up and running an MIS are beyond the scope of this course. But you should understand what an MIS is so you know some of the possibilities. Exhibit 5–1 shows the elements of a complete MIS.

Decision support systems put managers "online"

An MIS system organizes incoming data in a database so that it's available when needed. Most firms with an MIS have information processing specialists who help managers get standard reports and output from the database.

To get better decisions, some MIS systems provide marketing managers with a decision support system. A **decision support system (DSS)** is a computer program that makes it easy for a marketing manager to get and use information *as he or she is making decisions.* Typically the DSS helps change raw data—like product sales for the previous day—into more *useful information.* For example, it may draw graphs to show relationships in data—perhaps comparing yesterday's sales to the sales on the same day in the last four weeks. The Frito-Lay example illustrates the possibilities.

Some decision support systems go even further. They allow the manager to see how answers to questions might change in various situations. For example, a manager may want to estimate how much sales will increase if the firm expands into a new market area. Drawing on data in the database, the system will make an estimate using a marketing model. A **marketing model** is a statement of relationships among marketing variables.

In short, the decision support system puts managers "online" so they can study available data and make better marketing decisions—faster.[2]

Information makes managers greedy for more

Once marketing managers see how a functioning MIS—and perhaps a DSS—can help their decision making, they are eager for more information. They realize that they can improve all aspects of their planning. Further, they can monitor the implementation of current plans, comparing results against plans and making necessary changes more quickly. Marketing information systems will become more widespread as managers become more sensitive to the possibilities and computer costs continue to drop.[3]

Many firms are not there yet

Of course, not every firm has a complete MIS system. And in some firms that do, managers don't know how to use the system properly. A major problem is that many

Exhibit 5–1   Elements of a Complete Marketing Information System

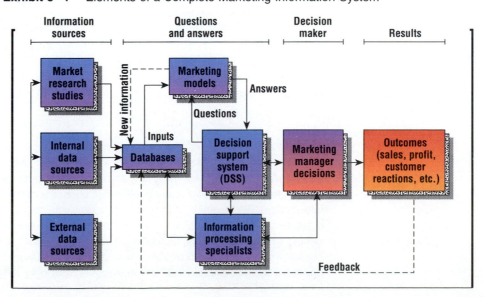

managers are used to working the old way—and they don't think through what information they need.

One sales manager thought he was progressive when he asked his assistant for an MIS report listing each sales rep's sales for the previous month and the current month. The assistant provided the report—but later was surprised to see the sales manager working on the list with a calculator. He was figuring the percentage change in sales for the month and ranking the reps from largest increase in sales to smallest. The computer could have done that—instantly—but the sales manager got what he *asked for* not what he really needed. An MIS can provide information—but only the marketing manager knows what problem needs solving. It's the job of the manager—not the computer or the MIS specialist—to ask for the right information in the right form.

New questions require new answers

MIS systems tend to focus on recurring information needs. Routinely analyzing such information can be valuable to marketing managers. But it shouldn't be their only source of information for decision making. They must try to satisfy ever-changing needs in dynamic markets. So marketing research must be used—to supplement data already available in the MIS.

WHAT IS MARKETING RESEARCH?

Research provides a bridge to customers

The marketing concept says that marketing managers should meet the needs of customers. Yet today, many marketing managers are isolated in company offices—far from potential customers.

This means marketing managers have to rely on help from **marketing research**—procedures to develop and analyze new information to help marketing managers make decisions. One of the important jobs of a marketing researcher is to get the facts not currently available in the MIS.

Who does the work?

Most large companies have a separate marketing research department to plan and carry out research projects. These departments often use outside specialists—including interviewing and tabulating services—to handle technical assignments. Further, they may call in specialized marketing consultants and marketing research organizations to take charge of a research project.

Small companies (those with less than $4 to $5 million in sales) usually don't have separate marketing research departments. They often depend on their salespeople or managers to conduct what research they do.

Some nonprofit organizations are using marketing research—usually with the help of outside specialists. For example, many politicians rely on research firms to conduct surveys of voter attitudes.[4]

? Ethical issues in marketing research

The basic reason for doing marketing research is to get information that people can trust when making decisions. But research often involves many hidden details. A person who wants to misuse marketing research to pursue a personal agenda can often do so.

Perhaps the most common ethical issues concern decisions to withhold certain information. For example, a manager might selectively share only those results that support his or her viewpoint. Others involved in a decision might never know that they are getting only partial truths. Or, during a set of interviews, a researcher may discover that consumers are interpreting a poorly worded question many different ways. If the researcher doesn't admit the problem, an unknowing manager may rely on meaningless results.

Another problem involves more blatant abuses. It is unethical for a firm to contact consumers under the pretense of doing research when the real purpose is to sell something. For example, some political organizations have been criticized for surveying consumers to find out their attitudes about various political candidates and issues. Then, armed with that information, someone else calls back to solicit donations. Legitimate marketing researchers don't do this!

The relationship between the researcher and the manager sometimes creates an ethical conflict. Managers must be careful not to send a signal that the only acceptable results from a research project are ones that confirm their existing viewpoints. Researchers are supposed to be objective, but that objectivity may be swayed if future jobs depend on getting the "right" results.

Effective research usually requires cooperation

Good marketing research requires cooperation between researchers and marketing managers. Researchers must be sure their research focuses on real problems.

Marketing managers must be able to explain what their problems are—and what kinds of information they need. They should be able to communicate with specialists in the specialists' language. They should also know about the basic decisions made during the research process so they know the limitations of the findings.

For this reason, our discussion of marketing research won't emphasize mechanics—but rather how to plan and evaluate the work of marketing researchers.[5]

THE SCIENTIFIC METHOD AND MARKETING RESEARCH

The scientific method can help marketing managers make better decisions. The **scientific method** is a decision-making approach that focuses on being objective and orderly in *testing* ideas before accepting them. With the scientific method, managers don't just *assume* that their intuition is correct. Instead, they use their intuition and observations to develop **hypotheses**—educated guesses about the relationships between things or about what will happen in the future. Then they test their hypotheses before making final decisions.

A manager who relies only on intuition might introduce a new product without testing consumer response. But a manager who uses the scientific method might say, "I think [hypothesize] that consumers currently using the most popular brand will prefer our new product. Let's run some consumer tests. If at least 60 percent of the consumers prefer our product, we can introduce it in a regional test market. If it doesn't pass the consumer test there, we can make some changes and try again."

The scientific method forces an orderly research process. Some managers don't carefully specify what information they need. They blindly move ahead—hoping that research will provide "the answer." Other managers may have a clearly defined problem or question but lose their way after that. These hit-or-miss approaches waste both time and money.

FIVE-STEP APPROACH TO MARKETING RESEARCH

The **marketing research process** is a five-step application of the scientific method that includes:

1. Defining the problem.
2. Analyzing the situation.
3. Getting problem-specific data.
4. Interpreting the data.
5. Solving the problem.

Exhibit 5–2 Five-Step Scientific Approach to Marketing Research Process

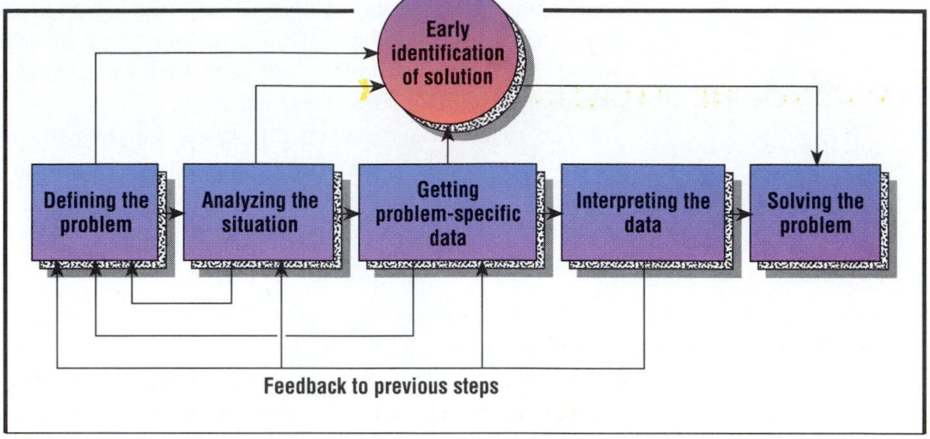

Exhibit 5–2 shows the five steps in the process. Note that the process may lead to a solution before all of the steps are completed. Or, as the feedback arrows show, researchers may return to an earlier step if needed. For example, the interpreting step may point to a new question—or reveal the need for additional information—before a final decision can be made.

DEFINING THE PROBLEM—STEP 1 *The Data Collected Most Answer the Problem*

Defining the problem is often the most difficult step in the marketing research process. But it's important for the objectives of the research to be clearly defined. The best research job on the wrong problem is wasted effort.

Exploratory Research

Finding the right problem level almost solves the problem

Our strategy planning framework is useful for guiding the problem definition step—as well as the whole marketing research process. First, a marketing manager should understand the target market—and what needs the firm can satisfy. Then the manager can focus on lower-level problems—namely, how sensitive the target market is to a change in one or more of the marketing mix ingredients. Without such a framework, marketing researchers can waste time—and money—working on the wrong problem.

Don't confuse problems with symptoms

The problem definition step sounds simple—and that's the danger. It's easy to confuse symptoms with the problem. Suppose a firm's MIS shows that the company's sales are decreasing in certain territories while expenses are remaining the same—resulting in a decline in profits. Will it help to define the problem just by asking: How can we stop the sales decline? Probably not. This is like fitting a hearing-impaired patient with a hearing aid without first trying to find out *why* the patient is having trouble hearing.

It's easy to fall into the trap of mistaking symptoms for the problem, thus confusing the research objectives. Researchers may ignore relevant questions—while analyzing unimportant questions in expensive detail.

Setting research objectives may require more understanding

Sometimes the research objectives are very clear. A manager wants to know if the targeted households have tried a new product and what percentage of them bought it a second time. But research objectives aren't always so simple. The manager might also want to know *why* some didn't buy—or whether they even heard of the product. Companies rarely have enough time and money to study everything so managers must narrow their research objectives. One good way is to develop a research question list that includes all the possible problem areas. Then managers can consider the items on the list more completely—in the situation analysis step—before they set final research objectives.

ANALYZING THE SITUATION—STEP 2

What information do we already have?

When the marketing manager thinks the real problem is beginning to surface, a situation analysis is useful. A **situation analysis** is an informal study of what information is already available in the problem area. It can help define the problem and specify what additional information—if any—is needed.

Pick the brains around you

The situation analysis usually involves informal talks with informed people. Informed people can be others in the firm, a few good middlemen who have close contact with customers, or others knowledgeable about the industry. In business markets—where relationships with customers are close—researchers may even call the customers themselves.

Situation analysis helps educate a researcher

The situation analysis is especially important if the researcher is a research specialist who doesn't know much about the management decisions to be made—or if the marketing manager is dealing with unfamiliar areas. They both must be sure they understand the problem area—including the nature of the target market, the marketing mix, competition, and other external factors. Otherwise, the researcher may rush ahead and make costly mistakes—or simply discover facts that management already knows. The following case illustrates this danger.

A marketing manager at the home office of a large retail chain hired a research firm to do in-store interviews to learn what customers liked most—and least—about some of its stores in other cities. Interviewers diligently filled out their questionnaires. When the results came in, it was apparent that neither the marketing manager nor the researcher did their homework. No one talked with the local store managers! Several of the stores were in the middle of messy remodeling—so all the customers' responses concerned the noise and dust from the construction. The research was a waste of money.

Secondary data may provide the answers— or some background

The situation analysis should also find relevant **secondary data**—information that has been collected or published already. Later, in Step 3, we will cover **primary data**—information specifically collected to solve a current problem. Too often researchers rush to gather primary data when much relevant secondary information is already available—at little or no cost! See Exhibit 5–3.

Much secondary data is available

Ideally, much secondary data is already available from the firm's MIS. Data that has not been organized in an MIS may be available from the company's files and reports. Secondary data also is available from libraries, trade associations, and government agencies.

One of the first places a researcher should look for secondary data—after looking within the firm—is a good library. The *Index of Business Periodicals* helps identify published references to a topic.

Many computerized database and index services are available through libraries and private firms. Lockheed's DIALOGUE system, for example, allows a distant researcher to access a computer and get summaries of articles written on a specific subject. Similarly, ABI Inform is an online service that indexes approximately 800 Canadian and U.S. business periodicals. A computerized search can be a big time saver and help the researcher cover all the bases.

Exhibit 5–3 Sources of Secondary and Primary Data

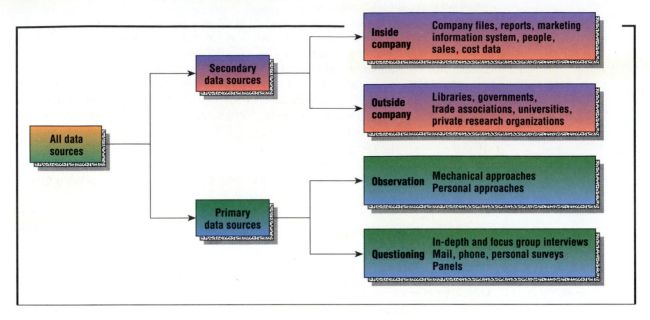

Government data is inexpensive

Federal and state governments publish data on many subjects. Government data is often useful in estimating the size of markets. Almost all government data is available in inexpensive publications. Much is also available in computer form ready for further analysis.

Sometimes it's more practical to use summary publications for leads to more detailed documents. For the U.S. market, one of the most useful summaries is the *Statistical Abstract of the United States*. Like an almanac, it is issued each year and gives 1,500 summary tables from more than 200 published sources. Detailed footnotes guide readers to more specific information on a topic. Similarly, the *United Nations Statistical Yearbook* is one of the finest summaries of worldwide data.

Secondary data is very limited on some international markets. However, most countries with advanced economies have government agencies that help researchers get the data they need. For example, Statistics Canada compiles a great deal of information on the Canadian market. Eurostat, the statistical office for the European Community countries, and the Organization for Economic Cooperation (in Paris) offer many publications packed with data on Europe. In the United States, the Department of Commerce distributes statistics compiled by all other federal departments. Some city and state governments have similar agencies for local data.

Private sources are useful too

Many private research organizations—as well as advertising agencies, newspapers, and magazines—regularly compile and publish data. A good business library is valuable for sources such as *Sales & Marketing Management, Advertising Age,* and the publications of the National Industrial Conference Board.

The *Encyclopedia of Associations* lists 75,000 U.S. and international trade and professional associations that can be a good source of information. For example, the American Marketing Association has an information center with many marketing publications.[6]

Situation analysis yields a lot—for very little

The virtue of a good situation analysis is that it can be very informative but takes little time. And it's inexpensive compared with more formal research efforts—like a large-scale survey. Situation analysis can help focus further research—or even eliminate the need for it entirely. The situation analyst is really trying to determine the exact nature of the situation—and the problem.

Determine what else is needed

At the end of the situation analysis, you can see which research questions—from the list developed during the problem definition step—remain unanswered. Then you have to decide exactly what information you need to answer those questions—and how to get it.

This often requires discussion between technical experts and the marketing manager. Usually companies use a written **research proposal**—a plan that specifies what information will be obtained and how—to be sure no misunderstandings occur later. The research plan may include information about costs, what data will be collected, how it will be collected, who will analyze it and how, and how long the process will take. Then the marketing manager must decide if it makes sense to go ahead—if the time and costs involved seem worthwhile. It's foolish to pay $100,000 for information to solve a $50,000 problem!

GETTING PROBLEM-SPECIFIC DATA—STEP 3

Gathering primary data

The next step is to plan a formal research project to gather primary data. There are different methods for collecting primary data. The best approach depends on the nature of the problem and how much time and money are available.

In most primary data collection, the researcher tries to learn what customers think about some topic—or how they behave under some conditions. There are two basic methods for obtaining information about customers: *questioning* and *observing*. Questioning can range from qualitative to quantitative research. And many kinds of observing are possible.

Qualitative questioning— open-ended with a hidden purpose

Qualitative research seeks in-depth, open-ended responses, not yes or no answers. The researcher tries to get people to share their thoughts on a topic—without giving them many directions or guidelines about what to say.

A researcher might ask different consumers, "What do you think about when you decide where to shop for food?" One person may talk about convenient location, another about service, and others about the quality of the fresh produce. The real advantage of this approach is *depth.* Each person can be asked follow-up questions so the researcher really understands what *that* respondent is thinking. The depth of the qualitative approach gets at the details—even if the researcher needs a lot of judgment to summarize it all.

Exploratory
Descriptive
Causal

Focus groups stimulate discussion

The most widely used form of qualitative questioning in marketing research is the **focus group interview**, which involves interviewing 6 to 10 people in an informal group setting. The focus group also uses open-ended questions, but here the interviewer wants to get group interaction—to stimulate thinking and get immediate reactions.

A skilled focus group leader can learn a lot from this approach. A typical session may last an hour so participants can cover a lot of ground.[7] However, conclusions reached from watching a focus group session vary depending on who watches it! A typical problem—and serious limitation—with qualitative research is that it's hard to measure the results objectively.

To avoid this trap, some researchers use qualitative research to prepare for quantitative research. For example, the Jacksonville Symphony Orchestra wanted to broaden its base of support and increase ticket sales. It hired a marketing research firm to conduct focus group interviews. These interviews helped the marketing managers refine their ideas about what these target "customers" liked and did not like about the orchestra—and what

A skilled leader can learn a lot from a focus group, like this one in which the group is reacting to different brands of toothpaste.

kinds of music future audiences might want. The ideas were then tested with a representative sample. Interviewers telephoned 500 people and asked them how interested they would be in various orchestra programs and guest artists. When the orchestra planned its yearly program based on the research, ticket sales nearly doubled.[8]

As this example suggests, qualitative research can provide good ideas—hypotheses. But we need other approaches—perhaps based on more representative samples and objective measures—to *test* the hypotheses.

Structured questioning gives more objective results

When researchers use identical questions and response alternatives, they can summarize the information quantitatively. Samples can be larger and more representative, and they can use various statistics to draw conclusions. For these reasons, most survey research is **quantitative research**—which seeks structured responses that can be summarized in numbers, like percentages, averages, or other statistics. For example, a marketing researcher might calculate what percentage of respondents have tried a new product—and then figure an average "score" for how satisfied they were.

Fixed responses speed answering and analysis

Survey questionnaires usually provide fixed responses to questions to simplify analysis of the replies. This multiple-choice approach also makes it easier and faster for respondents to reply. Simple fill-in-a-number questions are also widely used in quantitative research. Fixed responses are also more convenient for computer analysis, which is how most surveys are analyzed.

Surveys by mail, phone, or in person

Decisions about what specific questions to ask—and how to ask them—are usually related to how respondents will be contacted—by mail, phone, or in person.

Mail surveys are the most common and convenient

The mail questionnaire is useful when extensive questioning is necessary. With a mail questionnaire, respondents can complete the questions at their convenience. They may be more willing to fill in personal or family characteristics—since a mail questionnaire can be

Cluster Sample —

Simple Random Sample ○ *Stratified Sample — like a weighted average.*

After extensive research with French consumers, including mall intercept interviews like the one shown here, Colgate-France successfully launched its new Axion 2 detergent.

The better your sampling technique, the better sample you will get.

Presidential election 13000 sampled very carefully.

In-Depth
Mail
Telephone
Mall
   Intercept

Observation

Confidence level
95% interval

95% of the sample will have the same characteristics, mean, variance, etc.

returned anonymously. But the questions must be simple and easy to follow since no interviewer is there to help.

A big problem with mail questionnaires is that many people don't complete or return them. The **response rate**—the percentage of people contacted who complete the questionnaire—is often low and people who respond may not be representative.[9]

Mail surveys are economical *if* a large number of people respond. But they may be quite expensive if the response rate is low. Further, it can take a month or more to get the data—too slow for some decisions. Moreover, it is difficult to get respondents to expand on particular points. In markets where illiteracy is a problem, it may be impossible to get any response. In spite of these limitations, the convenience and economy of mail surveys makes them popular for collecting primary data.

Telephone surveys—fast and effective

Telephone interviews are growing in popularity. They are effective for getting quick answers to simple questions. Telephone interviews allow the interviewer to probe and really learn what the respondent is thinking. In addition, with computer-aided telephone interviewing, answers are immediately recorded on a computer, resulting in fast data analysis. On the other hand, some consumers find calls intrusive—and refuse to answer any questions. Moreover, the telephone is usually not a very good contact method if the interviewer is trying to get confidential personal information—such as details of family income. Respondents are not certain who is calling or how such personal information might be used.[10]

Personal interview surveys—can be in-depth

A personal interview survey is usually much more expensive per interview than a mail or telephone survey. But it's easier to get and keep the respondent's attention when the interviewer is right there. The interviewer can also help explain complicated directions—and perhaps get better responses. For these reasons, personal interviews are commonly used for research on business customers. To reduce the cost of locating consumer respondents, interviews are sometimes done at a store or shopping mall. This is called a

LENSCRAFTERS GETS A BETTER VIEW OF ITS MARKET

LensCrafters quickly became one of the largest chains of eyewear stores in the United States and Canada, and now it's testing new stores overseas. A key to its success is that managers use marketing research to better understand target market needs.

When LensCrafters was getting started, focus group interviews and consumer surveys revealed that consumers viewed shopping for glasses as very inconvenient. Frame selections were too small, opticians' shops were closed when customers were off work and had time to shop, and the whole process usually required long waits and repeat trips. So LensCrafters put the labs that make the glasses right in its stores, and kept the stores open nights and weekends. Ads tout LensCrafters' high quality, one-hour service. To be sure that service quality is high, LensCrafters sends a customer satisfaction survey to every customer. Surveys are analyzed by store and used to find out what's going on where. LensCrafters even ties satisfaction results to employee bonuses.

The size and growth rate of various age groups in a market drives demand for vision products. So LensCrafters analyzes demographic data to locate new stores where profit potential is greatest. And each store carries a very large selection of frame styles tailored to the age, gender, and ethnic makeup of the local market.

Research also guides promotion decisions. For example, ad media that work well in Toronto are not used in Atlanta, where other media are better. Similarly, guided by research results, LensCrafters uses direct-mail advertising targeted to customers in segments where interest in its convenient eyeglass service is highest.[11]

mall intercept interview because the interviewer stops a shopper and asks for responses to the survey.

Researchers have to be careful that having an interviewer involved doesn't affect the respondent's answers. Sometimes people won't give an answer they consider embarrassing. Or they may try to impress or please the interviewer. Further, in some cultures people don't want to give any information. For example, many people in Africa, Latin America, and Eastern Europe are reluctant to be interviewed. This is also a problem in many low-income, inner-city areas in the United States; even Census Bureau interviewers have trouble getting cooperation.

Sometimes questioning has limitations. Then observing may be more accurate or economical.

Observing—what you see is what you get

Observing—as a method of collecting data—focuses on a well-defined problem. Here we are not talking about the casual observations that may stimulate ideas in the early steps of a research project. With the observation method, researchers try to see or record what the subject does naturally. They don't want the observing to *influence* the subject's behavior.

A museum director wanted to know which of the many exhibits was most popular. A survey didn't help. Visitors seemed to want to please the interviewer—and usually said that all of the exhibits were interesting. Putting observers near exhibits—to record how long visitors spent at each one—didn't help either. The curious visitors stood around to see what the observer was recording, and that messed up the measures. Finally, the museum floors were waxed to a glossy shine. Several weeks later, the floors around the exhibits were inspected. It was easy to tell which exhibits were most popular—based on how much wax had worn off the floor!

In some situations, consumers are recorded on videotape. Later, researchers can study the tape by running the film at very slow speed or actually analyzing each frame.

Data from electronic scanning at the supermarket helps retailers decide what brand they'll sell.

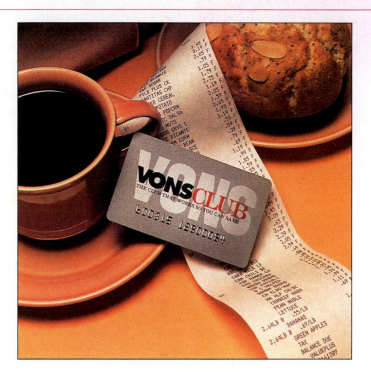

Researchers use this technique to study the routes consumers follow through a grocery store—or how they select products in a department store.

Observation data can be plotted on graphs or maps. A shopping center developer wondered if one of its shopping centers was attracting customers from all the surrounding areas. The developer hired a firm to record the license plate numbers of cars in the parking lot. Using registration information, the firm obtained the addresses of all license holders and plotted them on a map. Very few customers were coming from one large area. The developer aimed direct-mail advertising at that area and generated a lot of new business.

Observation methods are common in advertising research. For example, A. C. Nielsen Company developed a device called the "people meter" that adapts the observation method to television audience research. This machine is attached to the TV set in the homes of selected families. It records when the set is on and what station is tuned in.

Checkout scanners see a lot

Computerized scanners at retail checkout counters, a major breakthrough in observing, help researchers collect very specific—and useful—information. Often this type of data feeds directly into a firm's MIS. Managers of a big department store can see exactly what products have sold each day—and how much money each department earned. But the scanner also has wider applications for marketing research.

Information Resources, Inc., uses **consumer panels**—a group of consumers who provide information on a continuing basis. Whenever a panel member shops for groceries, he or she gives an ID number to the clerk, who keys in the number. Then the scanner records every purchase—including brands, sizes, prices, and any coupons used. For a fee, clients can evaluate actual customer purchase patterns—and answer questions about the effectiveness of their discount coupons. Did the coupons draw new customers, or did current customers simply use them to stock up? If consumers switched from another brand, did they go back to their old brand the next time? The answers to such questions are important in planning marketing strategies—and scanners can help marketing managers get the answers.

Some members of the consumer panel are also tied into a special TV cable system. With this system, a company can direct ads to some houses and not others. Then researchers can evaluate the effect of the ads by comparing the purchases of consumers who saw the ads with those who didn't.

The use of scanners to "observe" what customers actually do is changing consumer research methods. Companies can turn to firms like Information Resources as a *single source* of complete information about customers' attitudes, shopping behavior, and media habits. The information available is so detailed that the possibilities are limited more by imagination—and money—than by technology.[12]

Experimental method controls conditions

A marketing manager can get a different kind of information—with either questioning or observing—using the experimental method. With the **experimental method**, researchers compare the responses of two or more groups that are similar except on the characteristic being tested. Researchers want to learn if the specific characteristic—which varies among groups—*causes* differences in some response among the groups. For example, a researcher might be interested in comparing responses of consumers who saw an ad for a new product with consumers who didn't. The response might be an observed behavior—like the purchase of a product—or the answer to a specific question—like "How interested are you in this new product?"

Marketing managers for Mars—the company that makes Snickers candy bars—used the experimental method to help solve a problem. Other candy and snack foods were taking customers. But why? Surveys showed that many consumers thought candy bars were becoming too small. But they also didn't want to pay more for a larger bar. Mars' managers wanted to know if making their candy bar bigger would increase sales enough to offset the higher cost. To decide, they conducted a marketing experiment.

The company carefully varied the size of candy bars sold in *different* markets. Otherwise, the marketing mix stayed the same. Then researchers tracked sales in each market area to see the effect of the different sizes. They immediately saw a big difference. The added sales more than offset the cost of a bigger candy bar.

Test marketing of new products is another type of marketing experiment. In a typical approach, a company tries variations on its planned marketing mix in a few geographic market areas. The results of the tests help to identify problems or refine the marketing mix—before deciding to go to broader distribution. However, alert competitors may disrupt such tests—perhaps by increasing promotion or offering retailers extra discounts. To avoid these problems, some firms conduct some of their tests in foreign markets.

The producers of Dentax toothbrushes and Pudgies baby wipes did test market experiments in overseas markets—where competitors were less likely to disrupt the results.

Researchers don't use the experimental method as often as surveys and focus groups. Many managers don't understand the valuable information they can get from this method. Further, they don't like the idea of some researcher "experimenting" with their business.[13]

INTERPRETING THE DATA—STEP 4

What does it really mean?

After someone collects the data, it has to be analyzed to decide what it all means. In quantitative research, this step usually involves statistics. Statistical packages—easy-to-use computer programs that analyze data—have made this step easier. As we noted earlier, some firms provide *decision support systems* so managers can use a statistical package to interpret data themselves. More often, however, technical specialists are involved at the interpretation step.

Cross-tabulation is one of the most frequently used approaches for analyzing and interpreting marketing research data. It shows the relationship of answers to two different questions. Exhibit 5–4 is an example. This "cross-tab" analysis shows that customers who moved in the last year were much more likely to have touch-tone phone service.

There are many other approaches for statistical analysis—the best one depends on the situation. The details of statistical analysis are beyond the scope of this book. But a good manager should know enough to understand what a research project can—and can't—do.[14]

Is your sample really representative?

It's usually impossible for marketing managers to collect all the information they want about everyone in a population—the total group they are interested in. Marketing researchers typically study only a sample, a part of the relevant population. How well a sample *represents* the total population affects the results. Results from a sample that isn't representative may give a misleading picture.

The manager of a retail store might want a phone survey to learn what consumers think about the store's hours. If interviewers make all of the calls during the day, the sample will not be representative. Consumers who work outside the home during the day won't have an equal chance of being included. Those interviewed might say the limited store hours are "satisfactory." Yet it would be a mistake to assume that *all* consumers are satisfied.

Research results are not exact

An estimate from a sample—even a representative one—usually varies somewhat from the true value for a total population. Managers sometimes forget this. They assume that survey results are exact. Instead, when interpreting sample estimates, managers should think of them as *suggesting* the approximate value.

Validity problems can destroy research

Even if the sampling is carefully planned, it's also important to evaluate the quality of the research data itself.

Exhibit 5–4   Cross-Tabulation Breakdown of Responses to a Phone Company Consumer Survey

	Have You Moved in the Last Year?		
Answers:	*No*	*Yes*	*Total*
Do You Have Touch-Tone Dialing at Your Home? Yes	10.2%	23.4%	15.5%
No	89.8%	76.6%	84.5%
Total	100.0%	100.0%	100.0%

Interpretation: 15.5% of people in the survey said that they had touch-tone dialing in their homes. However, the percentage was much higher (23.4%) among people who had moved in the last year, and lower (10.2%) among people who had not moved.

SAS *and* STATGRAPHICS *are statistical packages that make it easy to summarize and graph marketing research data.*

Managers and researchers should be sure that research data really measures what it's supposed to measure. Many of the variables marketing managers are interested in are difficult to measure accurately. Questionnaires may let us assign numbers to consumer responses, but that still doesn't mean that the result is precise. An interviewer might ask, "How much did you spend on soft drinks last week?" A respondent may be perfectly willing to cooperate—and be part of the representative sample—but just not be able to remember.

Validity concerns the extent to which data measures what it is intended to measure. Validity problems are important in marketing research because most people want to help and will try to answer—even when they don't know what they're talking about. Further, a poorly worded question can mean different things to different people—and invalidate the results.

Poor interpretation can destroy research

Besides sampling and validity problems, a marketing manager must consider whether the analysis of the data supports the *conclusions* drawn in the interpretation step. Sometimes technical specialists pick the right statistical procedure—their calculations are exact—but they misinterpret the data because they don't understand the management problem. In one survey, car buyers were asked to rank five cars in order from "most preferred" to "least preferred." One car was ranked first by slightly more respondents than any other car so the researcher reported it as the "most liked car." That interpretation, however, ignored the fact that 70 percent of the respondents ranked the car *last*!

Interpretation problems like this can be subtle but crucial. Some people draw misleading conclusions—on purpose—to get the results they want. Marketing managers must decide whether *all* of the results support the interpretation—and are relevant to their problem.

SOLVING THE PROBLEM—STEP 5

The last step is solving the problem

In the problem solution step, managers use the research results to make marketing decisions.

The Hardest Part.

Some researchers—and some managers—are fascinated by the interesting tidbits of information that come from the research process. They are excited if the research reveals

Survey Sampling, Inc., helps marketing researchers develop samples that are really representative of the target market; Donnelley Marketing Information Services provides shared cost data on special markets, including the Hispanic market.

something they didn't know before. But if research doesn't have action implications, it has little value—and suggests poor planning by the researcher and the manager.

When the research process is finished, the marketing manager should be able to apply the findings in marketing strategy planning—the choice of a target market or the mix of the four Ps. If the research doesn't provide information to help guide these decisions, the company wasted research time and money.

We emphasize this step because it is the reason for and logical conclusion to the whole research process. This final step must be anticipated at each of the earlier steps.

HOW MUCH INFORMATION DO YOU NEED?

Information is costly—but reduces risk

We talk about the benefits of good marketing information, but dependable information can be expensive. A big company may spend millions developing an information system. A large-scale survey can cost from $20,000 to $100,000—or even more. The continuing research available from companies such as Information Resources can cost a company well over $100,000 a year. And a market test for 6 to 12 months may cost $200,000 to $500,000 per test market!

Companies willing and able to pay the cost often find that marketing information pays for itself. They are more likely to select the right target market and marketing mix—or see a potential problem before it becomes a costly crisis.

What is the value of information?

The high cost of good information must be balanced against its probable value to management. Managers never get all the information they would like. Very detailed surveys or experiments may be "too good" or "too expensive" or "too late" if all the company needs is a rough sampling of retailer attitudes toward a new pricing plan—by tomorrow. Money is wasted if research shows that a manager's guesses are wrong—and the manager ignores the facts. For example, GM faced an expensive disaster with its 1986 Riviera, which was released even after extensive research predicted a flop.[15]

Marketing managers must take risks because of incomplete information. That's part of their job and always will be. But they must weigh the cost of getting more data against its likely value. If the risk is not too great, the cost of getting more information may be greater than the potential loss from a poor decision. A decision to expand into a new territory with the present marketing mix, for example, might be made with more confidence after a $25,000 survey. But just sending a sales rep into the territory for a few weeks to try to sell potential customers would be a lot cheaper. And, if successful, the answer is in and so are some sales.[16]

CONCLUSION

Marketing managers face difficult decisions in selecting target markets and managing marketing mixes. And managers rarely have all the information they would like to have. But they don't have to rely only on intuition. They can usually obtain good information to improve the quality of their decisions.

Computers are helping marketing managers become full-fledged members of the information age. Both large and small firms are setting up marketing information systems (MIS)—to be certain that routinely needed data is available and accessible quickly.

Marketing managers deal with rapidly changing environments. Available data is not always adequate to answer the detailed questions that arise. Then a marketing research project may be required to gather new information.

Marketing research should be guided by the scientific method. The scientific approach to solving marketing problems involves five steps: defining the problem, analyzing the situation, obtaining data, interpreting data, and solving the problem. This objective and organized approach helps to keep research on target—reducing the risk of doing costly research that isn't necessary or doesn't solve the problem.

Our strategy-planning framework can be helpful in finding the real problem. By finding and focusing on the real problem, the researcher and marketing manager may be able to move quickly to a useful solution—without the cost and risks of gathering primary data in a formal research project. With imagination, they may even be able to find the answers in their MIS or in other readily available secondary data.

QUESTIONS AND PROBLEMS

1. Discuss the concept of a marketing information system and why it is important for marketing managers to be involved in planning the system.

2. In your own words, explain why a decision support system (DSS) can add to the value of a marketing information system. Give an example of how a decision support system might help.

3. Discuss how output from an MIS might differ from the output of a typical marketing research department.

4. Discuss some of the likely problems facing the marketer in a small firm that has just purchased an inexpensive personal computer to help develop a marketing information system.

5. Explain the key characteristics of the scientific method and show why these are important to managers concerned with research.

6. How is the situation analysis different from the data collection step? Can both these steps be done at the same time to obtain answers sooner? Is this wise?

7. Distinguish between primary data and secondary data and illustrate your answer.

8. If a firm were interested in estimating the distribution of income in the state of California, how could it proceed? Be specific.

9. If a firm were interested in estimating sand and clay production in Georgia, how could it proceed? Be specific.

10. Go to the library and find (in some government publication) three marketing-oriented facts on international markets that you did not know existed or were available. Record on one page and show sources.

11. Explain why a company might want to do focus group interviews rather than individual interviews with the same people.

12. Distinguish between qualitative and quantitative approaches to research—and give some of the key advantages and limitations of each approach.

13. Define response rate and discuss why a marketing manager might be concerned about the response rate achieved in a particular survey. Give an example.

14. Prepare a table that summarizes some of the key advantages and limitations of mail, telephone, and personal interview approaches for administering questionnaires.

15. Explain how you might use different types of research (focus groups, observation, survey, and experiment) to forecast market reaction to a new kind of disposable baby diaper, which is to receive no promotion other than what the retailer will give it. Further, assume that the new diaper's name will not be associated with other known products. The product will be offered at competitive prices.

16. Marketing research involves expense—sometimes considerable expense. Why does the text recommend the use of marketing research even though a highly experienced marketing executive is available?

17. Discuss the concept that some information may be too expensive to obtain in relation to its value. Illustrate.

SUGGESTED CASES

8. Emil's Place

9. Sleepy-Inn Motel

COMPUTER-AIDED PROBLEM

5. Marketing Research

Texmac, Inc., has an idea for a new type of weaving machine that could replace the machines now used by many textile manufacturers. Texmac did a telephone survey to estimate how many of the old-style machines are now in use. Respondents using the present machines were also asked if they would buy the improved machine at a price of $25,000.

Texmac researchers identified a population of about 5,000 textile factories as potential customers. A sample of these were surveyed, and Texmac received 500 responses. Researchers think the total potential market is about 10 times larger than the sample of respondents. One hundred and twenty of the respondents indicated that their firms used old machines like the one the new machine was intended to replace. Twenty percent of those firms said that they would be interested in buying the new Texmac machine.

Texmac thinks the sample respondents are representative of the total population, but the marketing manager realizes that estimates based on a sample may not be exact when applied to the whole population. He wants to see how sampling "error" would affect profit estimates. Data for this problem appears in the spreadsheet. Quantity estimates for the whole market are computed from the sample estimates. These quantity estimates are used in computing likely sales, costs, and profit contribution.

a. An article in a trade magazine reports that there are about 4,500 textile factories that use the old-style machine. If the total market is really only 4,500 customers—not 5,000 as Texmac originally thought—how does that affect the total quantity estimate, expected revenue, and profit contribution?

b. Some of the people who responded to the survey didn't know much about different types of machines. If the actual number of old machines in the market is really 140 per 500 firms—not 120 as estimated from survey responses—how much would this affect the expected profit contribution (for 4,500 factories)?

c. The marketing manager knows that the percentage of textile factories that would actually buy the new machine might be different from the 20 percent who said they would in the survey. He estimates that the proportion that will replace the old machine might be as low as 16 and as high as 24 percent—depending on business conditions. Use the What If analysis to prepare a table that shows how expected quantity and profit contribution change when the sample percent varies between a minimum of 16 and a maximum of 24 percent. What does this analysis suggest about the use of estimates from marketing research samples? (Note: Use 4,500 for the number of potential customers and use 140 as the estimate of the number of old machines in the sample.)

For additional questions related to this problem, see Exercise 5–4 in the *Learning Aid for use with Essentials of Marketing*, 6th edition.

Final Consumers and Their Buying Behavior

Chapter

❶

Know how income affects consumer behavior and expenditure patterns.

❷

Understand the economic-buyer model of buyer behavior.

❸

Understand how psychological variables affect an individual's buying behavior.

❹

Understand how social influences affect an individual's and household's buying behavior.

❺

See why the purchase situation has an effect on consumer behavior.

❻

Know how consumers use problem-solving processes.

❼

Have some feel for how a consumer handles all the behavioral variables
and incoming stimuli.

❽

Understand the important new terms (shown in red).

In the summer of 1992, marketing managers at BMW were preparing to roll out their new touring vehicle—a luxury station wagon with the curvy styling and performance of BMW's 525 sedans. The new car was part of BMW's new strategy—prompted by changes in consumer buying behavior.

In the 1980s, BMW targeted the fast-growing group of high-income, urban baby-boomers. Ads focused on the affluent lifestyle of BMW owners—and people who aspired to it. BMW sales grew rapidly, and by their peak in 1986 most consumers thought of BMW as the ultimate yuppie status symbol.

By 1990 consumers had changed—and BMW sales shifted into reverse. Materialism and status symbols were no longer in with the target market. Faced with tough economic times, aging baby-boomers cut back their spending and focused more on family financial security. They based their car buying decisions on finding good value for their money. Safety also became important to more buyers. When BMW's target customers studied their choices, many picked similar Japanese luxury sedans—like the Acura and Lexus—that sold for less.

Marketing managers at BMW knew that they needed to change their strategy. They lowered prices on existing models, introduced two new entry-level models, and launched a $30 million ad campaign to try to convince baby-boomers that BMWs were a good value. The new ads focused on facts about BMW's quality engineering, safety, and new design features; images of lavish lifestyles disappeared altogether. In spite of these changes,

BMW sales continued to slide. Consumer attitudes about BMW developed over a long time—and they weren't changing quickly.

The new touring vehicle was part of BMW's effort to broaden its appeal with luxury buyers—and to show them BMW was responsive to their changing needs. BMW marketers called the new car a touring vehicle because they worried that consumers would think of a station wagon as big and sluggish—and not consistent with BMW's suggested $38,000 price. Moreover, BMW wasn't just aiming at baby-boomer parents who needed to cart around children. The company also targeted luxury buyers who wanted a more versatile, roomy vehicle to haul everything from golf clubs to fly rods. As one BMW marketer put it: "The consumer is evolving, and we're offering a vehicle that's appropriate. It's going to add to the brand an image that we don't have—practicality."

A similar—and popular—BMW touring vehicle has been available in Europe since 1971. But the American target market has different experiences, attitudes, and needs—and different buying behavior. Will BMW's new strategy meet buyers' needs? Only time will tell. Clearly BMW faces a challenge shaking the tarnished image of the ultimate yuppie dream machine.[1]

CONSUMER BEHAVIOR—WHY DO THEY BUY WHAT THEY BUY?

Although many variables influence consumer buying behavior, they differ for different products and target markets. And in today's global markets, the variations are countless. So it's impractical to consider all the possibilities for every market situation. But there are *general* behavioral principles—frameworks—that marketing managers can apply to learn more about their specific target markets. In this chapter, we'll explore some of the thinking from the behavioral disciplines—such as economics, psychology, and sociology—to help develop your skill in working with these frameworks.

Economic needs affect many buying decisions, but for some purchases behavioral influences are more important.

CONSUMER SPENDING PATTERNS ARE RELATED TO INCOME

Markets are made up of people with money to spend. So consumer spending patterns are related to income. Consumer budget studies show that most consumers spend their incomes as part of family or household units. So it makes sense for us to talk about households or family income and how it's spent.

Discretionary income is elusive

Most families spend a good portion of their income on such "necessities" as food, rent or house payments, car and home furnishings payments, and insurance. A family's purchase of "luxuries" comes from **discretionary income**—what is left of income after paying taxes and paying for necessities.

Discretionary income is an elusive concept because the definition of necessities varies from family to family and over time. It depends on what they think is necessary for their lifestyle. A color TV might be purchased out of discretionary income by a lower-income family but be seen as a necessity by a higher-income family. Because of differences like this, marketers often turn to family income and expenditure data to learn more about how their target markets spend their income.

The higher-income groups receive a big share

Exhibit 6–1 divides all U.S. families into five equal-size groups—from lowest income to highest. Higher-income groups receive a very large share of total income. Although the median income of U.S. families in 1990 was about $35,350, the top 20 percent of the families—those with incomes over $61,490—received over 44 percent of the total income. This gave them extra discretionary income and buying power, especially for luxury items like cellular phones, memberships in country clubs, and yachts. Well-to-do families with incomes over $102,358—the top 5 percent nationally—got more than 17 percent of the total income.

At the lower end of the scale, over 13 million families had less than $16,846 income. They account for 20 percent of all families but receive less than 5 percent of total income; half of them live below the poverty level of $13,359 for a family of four. However, these consumers may receive food stamps, medicare, and public housing, which increases their buying power.[2]

Exhibit 6–1   Percent of Total Income Going to Different Income Groups in 1990

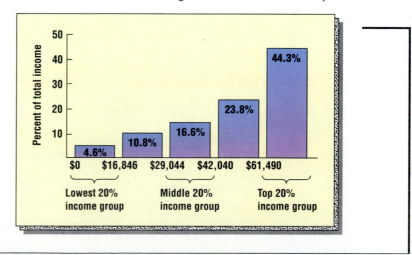

Exhibit 6–2   Family Spending for Several Family Income Levels (in 1989 dollars)

Spending Category	$15,000–$19,999		$20,000–$29,999		$30,000–$39,999	
	$	%	$	%	$	%
Food	3,372	17.0	3,945	15.8	4,803	14.8
Housing	6,247	31.5	7,527	30.1	9,178	28.4
Clothing	972	4.9	1,443	5.8	1,986	6.1
Transportation	3,834	19.3	4,790	19.1	6,915	21.4
Health care	1,384	7.0	1,373	5.5	1,364	4.2
Personal care	318	1.6	339	1.3	424	1.3
Education	150	.8	211	.8	290	.9
Reading	128	.6	142	.6	172	.5
Entertainment	785	3.9	1,180	4.7	1,605	5.0
Alcohol	224	1.1	318	1.3	356	1.1
Tobacco	258	1.3	311	1.2	311	1.0
Insurance and pensions	1,243	6.3	2,047	8.2	3,265	10.1
Contributions	502	2.5	739	2.9	914	2.8
Miscellaneous	440	2.2	669	2.7	783	2.4
Total spending	19,857	100.0	25,024	100.0	32,366	100.0

Expenditure data tells how target markets spend

Exhibit 6–2 shows annual spending by urban families for several family income levels and for major categories of expenditures. The amount spent on major categories—such as food, housing, clothing, transportation, and so on—does vary by income level. And the relationships are logical when you realize that many of the purchases in these categories are necessities.[3]

Such data can help you understand how potential target customers spend their money. Let's make this more concrete. Suppose you are a marketing manager for a swimming pool producer. You're considering a mail advertisement directed to consumers in an urban neighborhood of families with an average annual income of $25,000 a year. Looking at the center column of Exhibit 6–2, you can see how families at this income level spend their money. After paying for housing, transportation, food, clothing, and health care, they have about $6,000 a year left for entertainment, education, personal care, and other expenditures. If a swimming pool costs at least $2,000 a year—including maintenance and depreciation—the average family in this income category would have to make a big change in lifestyle to buy a pool.

Basic data on consumer income and spending patterns can help forecast general *trends* in consumer buying. But when many firms sell similar products, it isn't much help in predicting which *specific* products and brands consumers will purchase. That requires a better understanding of the buying process.

THE BEHAVIORAL SCIENCES HELP UNDERSTAND BUYING PROCESS

Economic needs affect most buying decisions

Most economists assume that consumers are **economic buyers**—people who know all the facts and logically compare choices in terms of cost and value received to get the greatest satisfaction from spending their time and money.

This view assumes that economic needs guide most consumer behavior. **Economic needs** are the factors considered in making the best use of a consumer's time and money—as the consumer sees it. Some consumers look for the lowest price. Others pay extra for convenience. And others may weigh price and quality for the best value. Some economic needs are: economy of purchase or use, convenience, efficiency in operation or use, dependability in use, and improvement of earnings.

Exhibit 6–3   A Model of Buyer Behavior

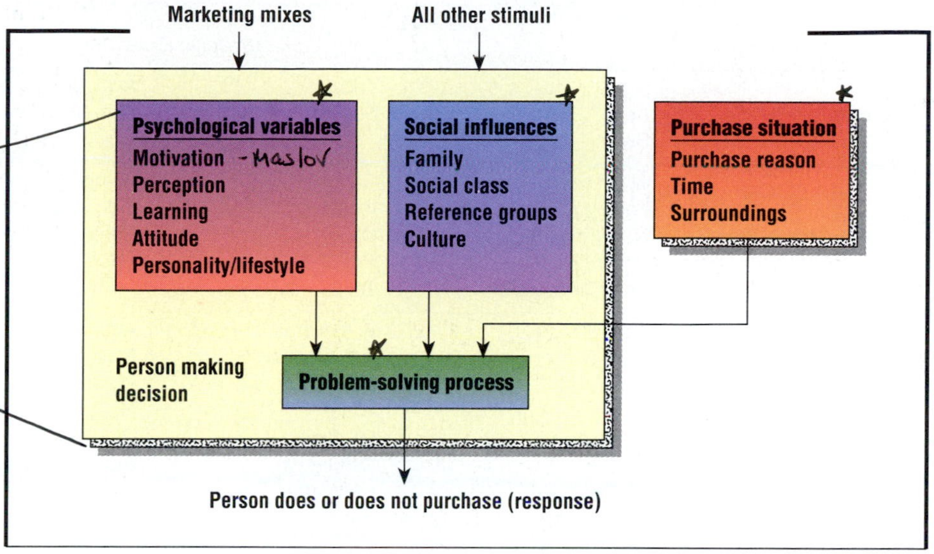

Handwritten annotations (left margin and within figure):

STIMULUS

BLACK BOX

RESPONSE

✱ Decision Making Process

Affects Perceptions
① Stimuli Characteristics
② Our Frame of Mind
③ Surrounding Field of the Stimuli

Marketing mixes   All other stimuli

Psychological variables
Motivation – Maslow
Perception
Learning
Attitude
Personality/lifestyle

Social influences
Family
Social class
Reference groups
Culture

Purchase situation
Purchase reason
Time
Surroundings

Person making decision

Problem-solving process

Person does or does not purchase (response)

Clearly, marketing managers must be alert to new ways to appeal to economic needs. Most consumers appreciate firms that offer them improved value for the money they spend. But improved value does not just mean offering lower and lower prices. Many consumers face a "poverty of time." Carefully planned place decisions can make it easier and faster for customers to make a purchase. Products can be designed to work better, require less service, or last longer. Promotion can explain product benefits in terms of factors like operating costs.

The economic value a purchase offers is an important factor in many purchase decisions. But most marketing managers think that buyer behavior is not as simple as the economic-buyer model suggests. A product that one person sees as a good value—and is eager to buy—is of no interest to someone else. So we can't expect to understand buying behavior without taking a broader view.

How we will view consumer behavior

Many behavioral dimensions influence consumers. Let's try to combine these dimensions into a model of how consumers make decisions. Exhibit 6–3 shows that psychological variables, social influences, and the purchase situation all affect a person's buying behavior. We'll discuss these topics in the next few pages. Then we'll expand the model to include the consumer problem-solving process.

PSYCHOLOGICAL INFLUENCES WITHIN AN INDIVIDUAL

Needs motivate consumers

Everybody is motivated by needs and wants. **Needs** are the basic forces that motivate a person to do something. Some needs involve a person's physical well-being, others the individual's self-view and relationship with others. Needs are more basic than wants. **Wants** are "needs" that are learned during a person's life. For example, everyone needs water or some kind of liquid, but some people also learn to want Perrier with a twist.

When a need is not satisfied, it may lead to a drive. The need for liquid, for example, leads to a thirst drive. A **drive** is a strong stimulus that encourages action to reduce a need. Drives are internal—they are the reasons behind certain behavior patterns. In marketing, a product purchase results from a drive to satisfy some need.

Exhibit 6−4   Possible Needs Motivating a Person to Some Action

Types of Needs	Specific Examples			
Physiological needs	Hunger Sex Rest	Thirst Body elimination	Activity Self-preservation	Sleep Warmth/coolness
Psychological needs	Aggression Family preservation Nurturing Playing-relaxing Self-identification	Curiosity Imitation Order Power Tenderness	Being responsible Independence Personal fulfillment Pride	Dominance Love Playing-competition Self-expression
Desire for . . .	Acceptance Affiliation Comfort Esteem Knowledge Respect Status	Achievement Appreciation Fun Fame Prestige Retaliation Sympathy	Acquisition Beauty Distance—"space" Happiness Pleasure Self-satisfaction Variety	Affection Companionship Distinctiveness Identification Recognition Sociability
Freedom from . . .	Fear Pain Harm	Depression Imitation Ridicule	Discomfort Loss Sadness	Anxiety Illness Pressure

Some critics imply that marketers can somehow manipulate consumers to buy products against their will. But marketing managers can't create internal drives. Most marketing managers realize that trying to get consumers to act against their will is a waste of time. Instead, a good marketing manager studies what consumer drives, needs, and wants already exist and how they can be satisfied better.

Consumers seek benefits to meet needs

We're all a bundle of needs and wants. Exhibit 6−4 lists some important needs that might motivate a person to some action. This list, of course, is not complete. But thinking about such needs can help you see what *benefits* consumers might seek from a marketing mix.

When a marketing manager defines a product-market, the needs may be quite specific. For example, the food need might be as specific as wanting a thick-crust pepperoni pizza—delivered to your door hot and ready to eat.

Several needs at the same time

Some psychologists argue that a person may have several reasons for buying—at the same time. Maslow is well known for his five-level hierarchy of needs. We will discuss a similar four-level hierarchy that is easier to apply to consumer behavior. Exhibit 6−5 illustrates the four levels along with advertising slogans attempting to appeal to each need. The lowest-level needs are physiological. Then come safety, social, and personal needs. As a study aid, think of the PSSP needs.[4]

Physiological needs are concerned with biological needs—food, drink, rest, and sex. **Safety needs** are concerned with protection and physical well-being (perhaps involving health food, medicine, and exercise). **Social needs** are concerned with love, friendship, status, and esteem—things that involve a person's interaction with others. **Personal needs**, on the other hand, are concerned with an individual's need for personal satisfaction—unrelated to what others think or do. Examples include self-esteem, accomplishment, fun, freedom, and relaxation.

Exhibit 6–5   The PSSP Hierarchy of Needs

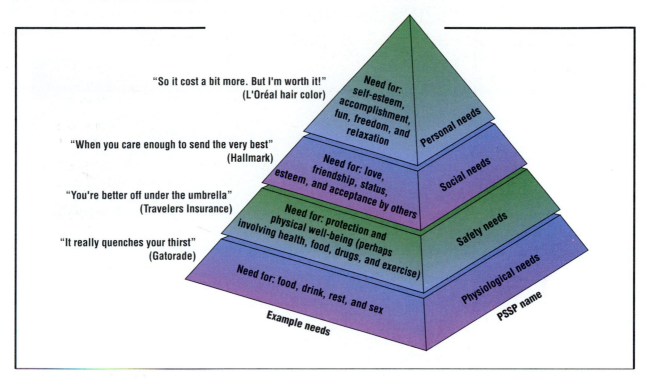

"So it cost a bit more. But I'm worth it!"
(L'Oréal hair color)

Need for: self-esteem, accomplishment, fun, freedom, and relaxation

Personal needs

"When you care enough to send the very best"
(Hallmark)

Need for: love, friendship, status, esteem, and acceptance by others

Social needs

"You're better off under the umbrella"
(Travelers Insurance)

Need for: protection and physical well-being (perhaps involving health, food, drugs, and exercise)

Safety needs

"It really quenches your thirst"
(Gatorade)

Need for: food, drink, rest, and sex

Physiological needs

Example needs

PSSP name

Motivation theory suggests that we never reach a state of complete satisfaction. As soon as we get our lower-level needs reasonably satisfied, those at higher levels become more dominant. This explains why marketing efforts targeted at affluent consumers in advanced economies often focus on higher-level needs. It also explains why these approaches may be useless in parts of the world where consumers' basic needs aren't being met.

It is important to see, however, that a particular product may satisfy more than one need at the same time. In fact, most consumers try to fill a *set* of needs rather than just one need or another in sequence.

Obviously marketers should try to satisfy different needs. Yet discovering these specific consumer needs may require careful analysis. Consider, for example, the lowly vegetable peeler. Marketing managers for OXO International realized that many people, especially young children and senior citizens, have trouble gripping the handle of a typical peeler. OXO redesigned the peeler with a bigger handle that addressed this physical need. OXO also coated the handle with dishwasher-safe rubber. This makes cleanup more convenient—and the sharp peeler is safer to use when the grip is wet. The attractively designed grip also appeals to consumers who get personal satisfaction from cooking—and who want to impress their guests. Even though OXO priced the peeler much higher than most kitchen utensils, it sells very well because it appeals to people with a variety of needs.[5]

Perception determines what consumers see and feel

Consumers sometimes select varying ways to meet their needs because of differences in **perception**—how we gather and interpret information from the world around us.

In promoting its security locks to French consumers, Point Fort appeals to consumers' safety needs. The headline for the ad says: "70% of all burglars do it just like you do; they come in through the door. Come see us first."

We are constantly bombarded by stimuli—ads, products, stores—yet we may not hear or see anything. This is because we apply the following selective processes:

1. **Selective exposure**—our eyes and minds seek out and notice only information that interests us.
2. **Selective perception**—we screen out or modify ideas, messages, and information that conflict with previously learned attitudes and beliefs.
3. **Selective retention**—we remember only what we want to remember.

These selective processes help explain why some people are not affected by some advertising—even offensive advertising. They just don't see or remember it!

Our needs affect these selective processes. And current needs receive more attention. For example, Michelin tire retailers advertise some sale in the newspaper almost weekly. Most of the time we don't even notice these ads—until we need new tires. Only then do we tune in to Michelin's ads.

Marketers are interested in these selective processes because they affect how target consumers get and retain information. This is also why marketers are interested in how consumers *learn*.

Learning determines what response is likely

Learning is a change in a person's thought processes caused by prior experience. Learning is often based on experience: a little girl tastes her first Häagen-Dazs ice cream cone, and learning occurs! Learning may also be based on associations. If you watch an ad that shows other people enjoying a new product, you might conclude that you'd like it too. Consumer learning may result from things that marketers do or from stimuli that have nothing to do with marketing. Either way, almost all consumer behavior is learned.[6]

Experts describe a number of steps in the learning process. We've already discussed the idea of a drive as a strong stimulus that encourages action. Depending on the **cues**—products, signs, ads, and other stimuli in the environment—an individual chooses some specific response. A **response** is an effort to satisfy a drive. The specific response chosen depends on the cues and the person's past experience.

Consumer perceptions of an ad for Scotchgard Fabric Protector might depend on whether they see fabric stains as a big problem.

THERE'S NO SUCH THING AS A LITTLE STAIN.

It may be just a little stain but it sure stands out on your sofa. It could spell ruin.

But professionally-applied, locked-on Scotchgard™ Fabric Protector keeps most seri-

ous spills from becoming stains. Most spills wipe right up. Protects against soiling too.

Scotchgard™ Protectors keep all kinds of things new looking longer. Things like carpeting,

children's clothing, bedspreads, drapes, wooden tabletops, outerwear, car interiors. There's even a Scotchgard™ Protector for leather.

So whenever you shop, always look for

the Scotchgard™ label. Because even a little stain is too much.

Scotchgard

Innovation working for you **3M**

Exhibit 6–6
The Learning Process

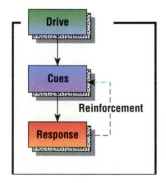

Positive cues help a marketing mix

Many needs are culturally learned

Reinforcement of the learning process occurs when the response is followed by satisfaction—that is, reduction in the drive. Reinforcement strengthens the relationship between the cue and the response. And it may lead to a similar response the next time the drive occurs. Repeated reinforcement leads to development of a habit—making the individual's decision process routine. Exhibit 6–6 shows the relationships of the important variables in the learning process.

The learning process can be illustrated by a thirsty person. The thirst *drive* could be satisfied in a variety of ways. But if the person happened to walk past a vending machine and saw a 7UP sign—a *cue*—then he or she might satisfy the drive with a *response*—buying a 7UP. If the experience is satisfactory, positive *reinforcement* will occur, and our friend may be quicker to satisfy this drive in the same way in the future. This emphasizes the importance of developing good products that live up to the promises of the firm's advertising. People can learn to like or dislike 7UP—reinforcement and learning work both ways.

Sometimes marketers try to identify cues or images that have positive associations from some other situation and relate them to their marketing mix. Many people associate the smell of lemons with a fresh, natural cleanliness. So companies often add lemon scent to household cleaning products—Joy dishwashing detergent and Pledge furniture polish, for example—because it has these associations.

Many needs are culturally (or socially) learned. The need for food, for instance, may lead to many specific food wants. Many Japanese enjoy raw fish, and their children learn to like it. Few Americans, however, have learned to like raw fish.

Some critics argue that marketing efforts encourage people to spend money on learned wants totally unrelated to any basic need. For example, Europeans are less concerned about body odor, and few buy or use a deodorant. Yet Americans spend millions of dollars on such products. Advertising says that using Ban deodorant "takes the worry out of being close." But is marketing activity the cause of the difference in the two cultures? Most research says that advertising can't convince buyers of something contrary to their basic attitudes.

This ad's copy states, "51% of Swedes are prejudiced against fish-balls. You too?" In Sweden, fish-balls are a traditional dish, but most consumers think the canned variety are tasteless and boring. This ad attempts to change these attitudes by showing an attractive way to serve the product. But overcoming negative attitudes is a difficult job.

Attitudes relate to buying

An **attitude** is a person's point of view toward something. The "something" may be a product, an ad, a salesperson, a firm, or an idea. Attitudes are an important topic for marketers because attitudes affect the selective processes, learning, and eventually the buying decisions people make.

Because attitudes are usually thought of as involving liking or disliking, they have some action implications. Beliefs are not so action-oriented. A **belief** is a person's opinion about something. Beliefs may help shape a consumer's attitudes but don't necessarily involve any liking or disliking. It is possible to have a belief—say, that Listerine has a medicinal taste—without really caring what it tastes like.

In an attempt to relate attitude more closely to purchase behavior, some marketers stretched the attitude concept to include consumer "preferences" or "intention to buy." Managers who must forecast how much of their brand customers will buy are particularly interested in the intention to buy. Forecasts would be easier if attitudes were good predictors of intentions to buy. Unfortunately, the relationships usually aren't that simple. A person may have positive attitudes toward a Jacuzzi hot tub but no intention of buying one.

Most marketers work with existing attitudes

Marketers generally try to understand the attitudes of their potential customers and work with them. For now, we want to emphasize that it's more economical to work with consumer attitudes than to try to change them. Attitudes tend to be enduring. Changing present attitudes—especially negative ones—is sometimes necessary. But it's probably the most difficult job marketers face.[7]

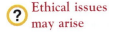 **Ethical issues may arise**

Part of the marketing job is to inform and persuade consumers about a firm's offering. An ethical issue sometimes arises, however, if consumers have *inaccurate* beliefs. For example, many consumers are confused about what foods are really healthy. Marketers for a number of food companies have been criticized for packaging and promotion that take advantage of inaccurate consumer perceptions about the meaning of the words "lite" or

ARE CONSUMERS TRUE-BLUE TO "GREEN" PRODUCTS?

In survey responses, 83 percent of U.S. consumers say they prefer buying environmentally safe products. Many (61 percent) claim they passed up products within the past year due to environmental concerns. They also say they're willing to pay more for products that don't pollute—7.3 percent more, for example, for detergents with a third less pollutants. Moreover, in a recent survey 91 percent felt that business is not concerned enough about the environment, and only 15 percent found current environmental packaging claims believable.

Responses like these have many marketers struggling about how best to respond. Consumer behavior here is less clearcut than it first appears. Part of the problem is that consumers often hold incorrect beliefs about environmental issues. For example, in a 1991 survey, 85 percent of consumers thought aerosol spray cans still use ozone-damaging CFCs. They don't. Moreover, consumers don't always buy what they say they want. For example, most people in a group concerned about plastic packaging said that they preferred ketchup, milk, and soft drinks in plastic bottles.

Of course, some consumers are more "green" than others. And many firms modify their marketing mixes to appeal to these consumers—and to be kinder to the environment. Fast-food restaurants and many other consumer products firms reduce packaging or add labeling to make recycling easier. Manufacturers look for ways to make products that won't spoil the air and water. Oil companies encourage car owners to recycle when it's oil change time. Efforts such as these must continue. But it may take time before the majority of consumers will sacrifice their personal convenience—or the prices they pay. Old habits die hard.

In other countries, habits are different. European and Japanese consumers generate significantly less trash than Americans. For example, they like concentrated detergents that need less packaging. By contrast, many less-developed countries pay very little attention to the environment. They focus on more immediate problems. The environment is a global problem and ultimately will require global efforts—by both marketers and consumers.[8]

"low-fat." A firm's lite donuts may have less fat or fewer calories than its other donuts—but that doesn't mean that the donut is *low* in fat or calories. Similarly, promotion of a "children's cold formula" may play off of parents' fears that adult medicines are too strong—even though the basic ingredients in the children's formula are the same and only the dosage is different.

Marketers must also be careful about promotion that might encourage false beliefs, even if the advertising is not explicitly misleading. For example, Nike doesn't claim that a kid who buys its fancy shoes will be able to fly through the air like Michael Jordan, but some critics argue that the advertising gives that impression.[9]

Personality affects how people see things

Many researchers study how personality affects people's behavior, but the results are generally disappointing to marketers. A trait like neatness can be associated with users of certain types of products—like cleaning materials. But marketing managers haven't found a way to use personality in marketing strategy planning.[10] As a result, they've stopped focusing on personality measures borrowed from psychologists and instead developed life-style analysis.

Psychographics focus on activities, interests, and opinions

Psychographics, or **life-style analysis**, is the analysis of a person's day-to-day pattern of living as expressed in that person's Activities, Interests, and Opinions—sometimes referred to as AIOs. Exhibit 6–7 shows a number of variables for each of the AIO dimensions—along with some demographics used to add detail to the life-style profile of a target market.

Life-style analysis assumes that marketers can plan more effective strategies if they know more about their target markets. Understanding the lifestyle of target customers has

Exhibit 6–7   Life-Style Dimensions (and some related demographic dimensions)

Dimension	Examples		
Activities	Work Hobbies Social events	Vacation Entertainment Club membership	Community Shopping Sports
Interests	Family Home Job	Community Recreation Fashion	Food Media Achievements
Opinions	Themselves Social issues Politics	Business Economics Education	Products Future Culture
Demographics	Income Age Family life cycle	Geographic area City size Dwelling	Occupation Family size Education

been especially helpful in providing ideas for advertising themes. Let's see how it adds to a typical demographic description. It may not help Mercury marketing managers much to know that an average member of the target market for a Sable station wagon is 34.8 years old, married, lives in a three-bedroom home, and has 2.3 children. Lifestyles help marketers paint a more human portrait of the target market. For example, life-style analysis might show that the 34.8-year-old is also a community-oriented consumer with traditional values who especially enjoys spectator sports and spends much time in other family activities. An ad might show the Sable being used by a happy family at a ball game so the target market could really identify with the ad. And the ad might be placed in a magazine like *Sports Illustrated* whose readers match the target life-style profile.[11]

Marketing managers who are interested in learning more about the lifestyle of a target market sometimes turn to specialists for help. For example, SRI International, a research firm, offers a service called VALS 2 (an abbreviation for values, attitudes, and lifestyles). SRI describes a firm's target market in terms of a set of typical VALS life-style groups (segments). An advantage of this approach is that SRI has developed very detailed information about the various VALS groups. For example, the VALS approach has been used to profile consumers in Europe, Japan, and Canada, as well as the United States.[12]

SOCIAL INFLUENCES AFFECT CONSUMER BEHAVIOR

We've been discussing some of the ways needs, attitudes, and other psychological variables influence the buying process. Now we'll look at how the individual interacts with family, social class, and other groups who may have influence.

Family life cycle influences needs

Relationships with other family members influence many aspects of consumer behavior. Family members may share many attitudes and values, consider each other's opinions, and divide various buying tasks. Marital status, age, and the age of any children shape the nature of these family influences. Put together, these dimensions tell us about the life-cycle stage of a family. Exhibit 6–8 shows a summary of stages in the family life cycle.

Young people and families accept new ideas

Although many young people are waiting longer to marry, most do tie the knot eventually. Younger couples seem to be more willing to try new products and brands—and they are careful, price-conscious shoppers. And these younger families—especially those

Exhibit 6–8   Stages in the Modern Family Life Cycles

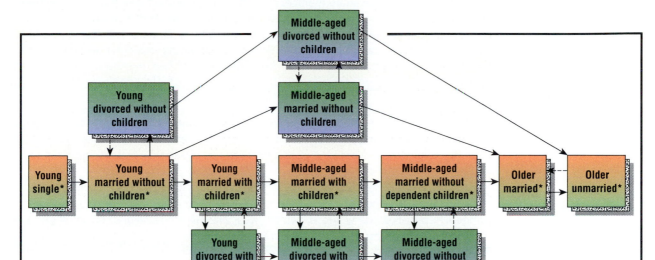

with no children—are still accumulating durable goods, such as automobiles and home furnishings.

As children arrive and grow, family spending shifts to soft goods and services, such as education, medical, and personal care. This usually happens when the family head reaches the 35–44 age group. To meet expenses, people in this age group often make more purchases on credit, and they save less of their income. As children enter the teen years, family influence and spending may shift even more. Teens often earn their own spending money, and many play an important role in family purchase decisions.[13]

Divorce—increasingly a fact of American life—disrupts the family life-cycle pattern. The mother usually has custody of the children, and the father may pay child support. The mother and children typically have much less income than two-parent families. Such families spend a larger percent of their income on necessities—often with little left for discretionary purchases. If a single parent remarries, the family life cycle may start over again.[14]

Selling to the empty nesters

An important category is the **empty nesters**—people whose children are grown and who are now able to spend their money in other ways. Usually these people are in the 50–64 age group. But this is an elusive group because some people marry later and are still raising a family at this age.

Empty nesters are an attractive market for many items. They have paid for their homes, and the big expenses of raising a family are behind them. They are more interested in travel and other things they couldn't afford before. This is a high-income period for many workers—especially white-collar workers.[15]

Who is the real decision maker in family purchases?

Historically, most marketers in the United States targeted the wife as the family purchasing agent. Now, with more women in the work force and with night and weekend shopping becoming more popular, men and older children do more shopping and decision making. In other countries, family roles vary. For example, in Norway women do most of the family shopping.

Buying responsibility and influence vary greatly depending on the product and the family. Although only one family member may go to the store and make a specific purchase, other family members may have influenced the decision or really decided what to buy. Still others may use the product. A marketer trying to plan a strategy will find it helpful to research the specific target market. Remember, many buying decisions are made jointly, and thinking only about who actually buys the product can misdirect the marketing strategy.[16]

Social class affects attitudes, values, and buying

Up to now, we've been concerned with individuals and their family relationships. Now let's consider how society looks at an individual and perhaps the family—in terms of social class. A **social class** is a group of people who have approximately equal social position as viewed by others in the society.

Almost every society has some social class structure. In most countries social class is closely related to a person's occupation, but it may also be influenced by education, community participation, where a person lives, income, possessions, social skills, and other factors—including what family a person is born into.

In most countries—including the United States—there is *some* general relationship between income level and social class. But the income level of people within the same social class can vary greatly, and people with the same income level may be in different social classes. So income by itself is usually not a good measure of social class. And people in different social classes may spend, save, and borrow money in very different ways. For example, spending for clothing, housing, home furnishings, and leisure activities, as well as choices of where and how to shop, often vary with social class.

The U.S. class system is far less rigid than those in most countries. Children start out in the same social class as their parents—but they can move to a different social class depending on their educational levels or the jobs they hold. By contrast, India's social structure is much more rigid, and individuals can't easily move up in the class system.

Marketers want to know what buyers in various social classes are like. In the United States, simple approaches for measuring social class groupings are based on a person's *occupation*, *education*, and *type and location of housing*. By using marketing research surveys or available census data, marketers can get a feel for the social class of a target market. Exhibit 6–9 illustrates a multilevel social class structure for the United States. Note the relative sizes of the groupings and how they differ.

Many people think of America as a middle-class society, but in many marketing situations the social class groups are distinct. Various classes shop at different stores. They prefer different treatment from salespeople. They buy different brands of products—even though prices are about the same. And they have different spending-saving attitudes.

Reference groups are relevant too

A **reference group** is the people to whom an individual looks when forming attitudes about a particular topic. People normally have several reference groups for different topics. Some they meet face-to-face. Others they just wish to imitate. In either case, they may take values from these reference groups and make buying decisions based on what the group might accept.

Reference groups are more important when others will be able to see which product or brand we're using. Influence is stronger for products that relate to status in the group. For one group, owning an expensive fur coat may be a sign of "having arrived." A group of animal lovers might view it as a sign of bad judgment. In either case, a consumer's decision to buy or not buy a fur coat might depend on the opinions of others in that consumer's reference group.[17]

Exhibit 6–9 Characteristics and Relative Size of Different Social Class Groups in the United States

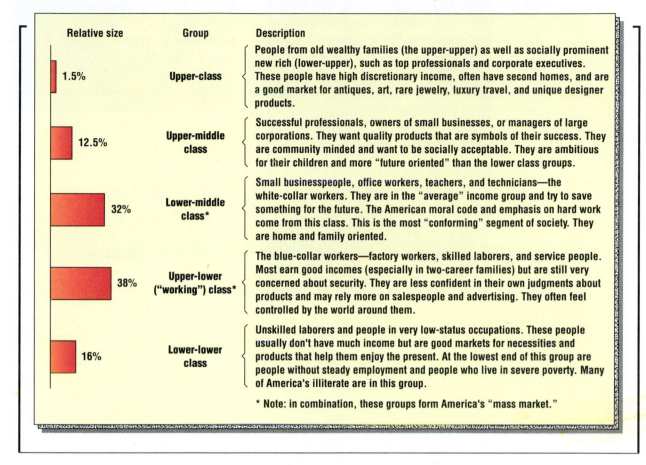

Relative size	Group	Description
1.5%	Upper-class	People from old wealthy families (the upper-upper) as well as socially prominent new rich (lower-upper), such as top professionals and corporate executives. These people have high discretionary income, often have second homes, and are a good market for antiques, art, rare jewelry, luxury travel, and unique designer products.
12.5%	Upper-middle class	Successful professionals, owners of small businesses, or managers of large corporations. They want quality products that are symbols of their success. They are community minded and want to be socially acceptable. They are ambitious for their children and more "future oriented" than the lower class groups.
32%	Lower-middle class*	Small businesspeople, office workers, teachers, and technicians—the white-collar workers. They are in the "average" income group and try to save something for the future. The American moral code and emphasis on hard work come from this class. This is the most "conforming" segment of society. They are home and family oriented.
38%	Upper-lower ("working") class*	The blue-collar workers—factory workers, skilled laborers, and service people. Most earn good incomes (especially in two-career families) but are still very concerned about security. They are less confident in their own judgments about products and may rely more on salespeople and advertising. They often feel controlled by the world around them.
16%	Lower-lower class	Unskilled laborers and people in very low-status occupations. These people usually don't have much income but are good markets for necessities and products that help them enjoy the present. At the lowest end of this group are people without steady employment and people who live in severe poverty. Many of America's illiterate are in this group.

* Note: in combination, these groups form America's "mass market."

Reaching the opinion leaders who are buyers

An **opinion leader** is a person who influences others. Opinion leaders aren't necessarily wealthier or better educated; each social class tends to have its own opinion leaders. And opinion leaders on one subject aren't necessarily opinion leaders on another. Some marketing mixes aim especially at these people since their opinions affect others and research shows that they are involved in many product-related discussions with followers. Favorable word-of-mouth publicity from opinion leaders can really help a marketing mix. But the opposite is also true. If opinion leaders aren't satisfied, they're likely to talk about it.[18]

Culture surrounds the other influences

Culture is the whole set of beliefs, attitudes, and ways of doing things of a reasonably homogeneous set of people. In Chapter 4, we looked at the broad impact of culture.

We can think of the American culture, the French culture, or the Latin American culture. People within these cultural groupings tend to be more similar in outlook and behavior. But sometimes it is useful to think of subcultures within such groupings. For example, within the American culture, there are various religious and ethnic subcultures. And different cultural forces tend to prevail in different regions of the country.

Multicultural diversity is replacing the melting pot

People from different ethnic groups may be influenced by very different cultural variables and have their own ways of thinking. Moreover, rather than disappearing in a melting pot, some important cultural and ethnic dimensions are being preserved and highlighted. This multicultural diversity creates both opportunities and challenges for marketers.

Cultural influences usually differ from one country to another, and each country may also have a number of subcultures.

Some important ethnic differences are obvious. For example, more than 1 out of 10 families in the United States speaks a language other than English at home. Some areas have a much higher rate. In Miami and San Antonio, for example, about one out of three families speaks Spanish. This obviously affects promotion planning.

Stereotypes are common *and* misleading

However, many ethnic influences are not so obvious. This is also an area where stereotyped thinking is common—and misleading. Many firms make the mistake of treating all consumers in a particular ethnic group as homogeneous. For example, some marketing managers treat all 31 million African-American consumers as "the black market," ignoring the great variability among the households on other segmenting dimensions. Just because people share an ethnic or racial origin doesn't mean they fit together into a homogeneous target market.

Ethnic markets are growing fast

The number of ethnic consumers is growing at a much faster rate than the overall society. This growth is due to both immigration and higher birthrates. In combination, these factors have a significant effect. For example, the Asian-American population, now about 7.5 million, more than doubled from 1980 to 1990 and should grow an additional 40 percent by 2000. Similarly, the number of Hispanic consumers more than doubled from about 9 million in 1970 to about 22 million now. To put this in perspective, there are as many Hispanics in the United States as there are Canadians in Canada. By 2010, more than one third of American children will be black, Hispanic, or Asian.

The buying power of ethnic submarkets is also increasing rapidly. Today nearly 1 in 10 black families has an income of $50,000 or more. Hispanic consumers now spend more than $160 billion a year. Moreover, much of this buying power is concentrated in certain cities and states. For example, 70 percent of the Hispanics in the United States live in California, Texas, New York, and Florida. Over 20 percent of San Francisco's residents are Asian-Americans.[19]

Culture varies in international markets

Cultural influences vary even more in international markets. Each foreign market may need to be treated as a separate market with its own submarkets. Ignoring cultural differences—or assuming that they are not important—almost guarantees failure, in international markets. For example, when marketing managers for Procter & Gamble first tried to sell the U.S. version of Cheer to Japanese consumers they promoted it as an effective all-temperature laundry detergent. But many Japanese wash clothes in cold tap water or leftover bath water—so they don't care about all-temperature washing. In addition, Cheer didn't make suds when it was used with popular Japanese fabric softeners. When P&G's marketing managers discovered these problems, they changed Cheer so the fabric softeners didn't affect it. They also changed Cheer ads to promise superior cleaning *in cold water*. Now Cheer is one of P&G's best-selling products in Japan.[20]

From a target marketing point of view, a marketing manager probably wants to aim at people within one culture or subculture. A firm developing strategies for two cultures often needs two different marketing plans.[21]

The attitudes and beliefs that we usually associate with culture tend to change slowly. So once marketers develop a good understanding of the culture they are planning for, they should concentrate on the more dynamic variables discussed above.

INDIVIDUALS ARE AFFECTED BY THE PURCHASE SITUATION

Purchase reason can vary

Why a consumer makes a purchase can affect buying behavior. For example, a student buying a pen to take notes might pick up an inexpensive Bic. But the same student might choose a Cross pen as a gift for a friend.

Time affects what happens

Time influences a purchase situation. *When* consumers make a purchase—and the time they have available for shopping—will influence their behavior. A leisurely dinner induces different behavior than grabbing a quick cup of 7-Eleven coffee on the way to work.

Surroundings affect buying too

Surroundings can affect buying behavior. The excitement of an auction may stimulate impulse buying. Surroundings may discourage buying too. For example, some people don't like to stand in a checkout line where others can see what they're buying—even if the other shoppers are complete strangers.

Needs, benefits sought, attitudes, motivation, and even how a consumer selects certain products all vary depending on the purchase situation. So different purchase situations may require different marketing mixes—even when the same target market is involved.[22]

CONSUMERS USE PROBLEM-SOLVING PROCESSES

The variables discussed affect *what* products a consumer finally decides to purchase. Marketing managers also need to understand *how* buyers use a problem-solving process to select particular products.

Most consumers seem to use the following five-step problem-solving process:

1. Becoming aware of—or interested in—the problem.
2. Recalling and gathering information about possible solutions.
3. Evaluating alternative solutions—perhaps trying some out.
4. Deciding on the appropriate solution.
5. Evaluating the decision.[23]

Exhibit 6–10 presents an expanded version of the buyer behavior model shown in Exhibit 6–3. Note that this exhibit integrates the problem-solving process with the whole set of variables we've been reviewing.

When consumers evaluate information about purchase alternatives, they may weigh not only a product type in relation to other types of products, but also differences in brands

Exhibit 6–10 An Expanded Model of the Consumer Problem-Solving Process

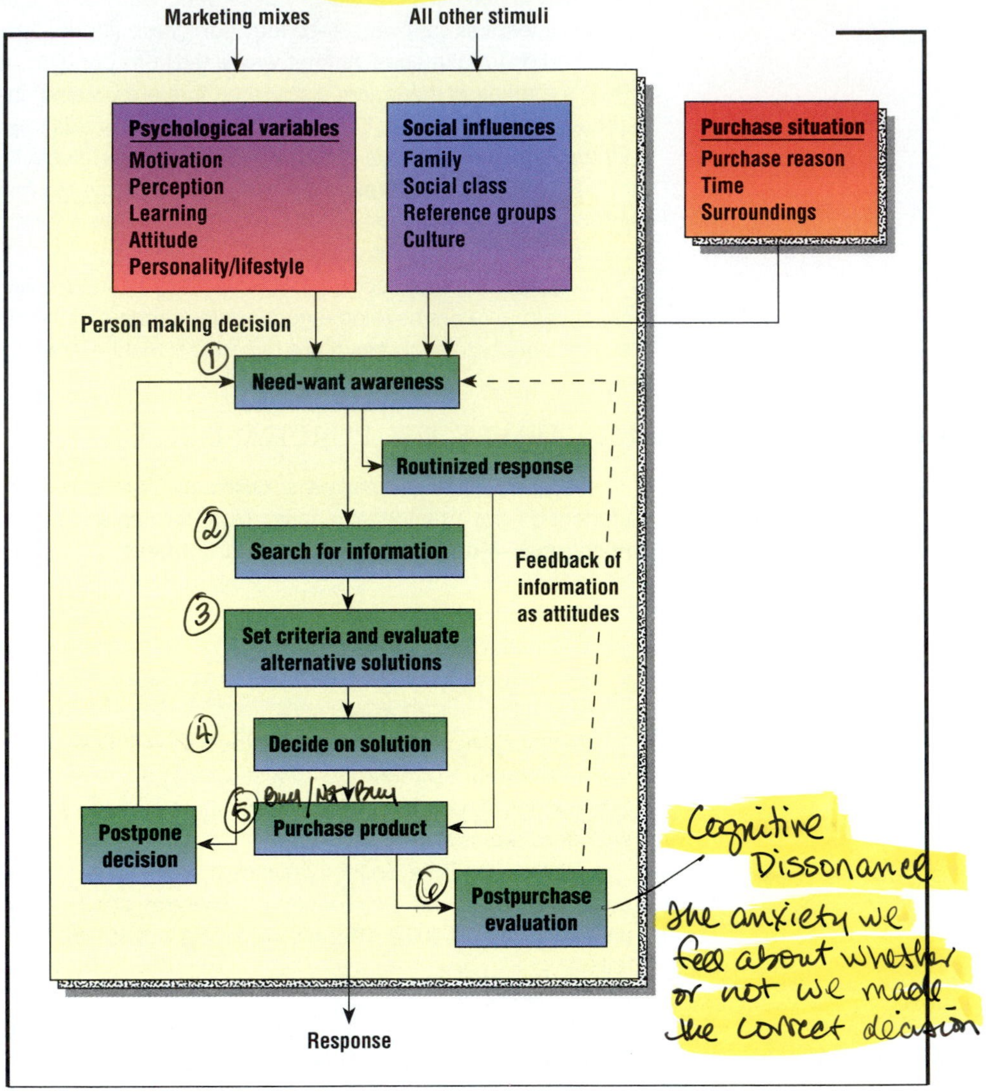

Marketing mixes   All other stimuli

Psychological variables	Social influences	Purchase situation
Motivation	Family	Purchase reason
Perception	Social class	Time
Learning	Reference groups	Surroundings
Attitude	Culture	
Personality/lifestyle		

Person making decision

① Need-want awareness

Routinized response

② Search for information

Feedback of information as attitudes

③ Set criteria and evaluate alternative solutions

④ Decide on solution

⑤ Buy/Not Buy — Purchase product

Postpone decision

⑥ Postpurchase evaluation

Cognitive Dissonance — the anxiety we feel about whether or not we made the correct decision

Response

within a product type *and* the stores where the products may be available. This can be a very complicated evaluation procedure, and, depending on their choice of criteria, consumers may make seemingly irrational decisions. If convenient service is crucial, for example, a buyer might pay list price for an unexciting car from a very convenient dealer. Marketers need a way to analyze these decisions.

Grid of evaluative criteria helps

Based on studies of how consumers seek out and evaluate product information, researchers suggest that marketing managers use an evaluative grid showing features common to different products (or marketing mixes). For example, Exhibit 6–11 shows some of the features common to three different cars a consumer might consider.

The grid encourages marketing managers to view each product as a bundle of features or attributes. The pluses and minuses in Exhibit 6–11 indicate one consumer's attitude toward each feature of each car. If members of the target market don't rate a feature of the marketing manager's brand with pluses, it may indicate a problem. The manager might

Exhibit 6–11   Grid of Evaluative Criteria for Three Car Brands

Brands	Common features			
	Gas mileage	Ease of service	Comfortable interior	Styling
Nissan	–	+	+	–
Saab	+	–	+	+
Toyota	+	+	+	–

Note: Pluses and minuses indicate a consumer's evaluation of a feature for a brand.

want to change the product to improve that feature—or perhaps use more promotion to emphasize an already acceptable feature. The consumer in Exhibit 6–11 has a minus under gas mileage for the Nissan. If the Nissan really gets better gas mileage than the other cars, promotion might focus on mileage to improve consumer attitudes toward this feature and toward the whole product.

Some consumers reject a product if they see *one* feature as substandard—regardless of how favorably they regard the product's other features. The consumer in Exhibit 6–11 might avoid the Saab, which he saw as less than satisfactory on ease of service, even if it were superior in all other aspects. In other instances, a consumer's overall attitude toward the product might be such that a few good features could make up for some shortcomings. The comfortable interior of the Toyota (Exhibit 6–11) might make up for less exciting styling—especially if the consumer viewed comfort as really important.

Of course, consumers don't use a grid like this. However, constructing such a grid helps managers think about what evaluative criteria target consumers consider really important, what consumers' attitudes are toward their product (or marketing mix) on each criteria, and how consumers combine the criteria to reach a final decision.[24]

Three levels of problem solving are useful

The basic problem-solving process shows the steps consumers may go through trying to find a way to satisfy their needs—but it doesn't show how long this process will take or how much thought a consumer will give to each step. Individuals who have had a lot of experience solving certain problems can move quickly through some of the steps or almost directly to a decision.

It is helpful, therefore, to recognize three levels of problem solving: extensive problem solving, limited problem solving, and routinized response behavior. See Exhibit 6–12. These problem-solving approaches are used for any kind of product. Consumers use **extensive problem solving** for a completely new or important need—when they put much effort into deciding how to satisfy it. For example, a music lover who wants higher-quality sound might decide to buy a CD player—but not have any idea what to buy. After talking with friends to find out about good places to buy a player, she might visit several stores to find out about different brands and their features. After thinking about her needs some more, she might buy a portable Sony unit—so she could use it in her apartment and in her car.

Consumers use **limited problem solving** when they're willing to put *some* effort into deciding the best way to satisfy a need. Limited problem solving is typical when a consumer has some previous experience in solving a problem but isn't certain which choice is best at the current time. If our music lover wanted some new disks for her player, she would

Exhibit 6–12 Problem-Solving Continuum

Low involvement		Routinized response behavior	Limited problem solving	Extensive problem solving		High involvement
Frequently purchased						Infrequently purchased
Inexpensive						Expensive
Little risk						High risk
Little information needed						Much information desired

already know what type of music she enjoys. She might go to a familiar store and evaluate what disks they had in stock for her favorite types of music.

Consumers use **routinized response behavior** when they regularly select a particular way of satisfying a need when it occurs. Routinized response behavior is typical when a consumer has considerable experience in how to meet a need and has no need for additional information. For example, our music lover might routinely buy the latest recording by her favorite band as soon as it's available. Most marketing managers would like their target consumers to buy their products in this routinized way.

Routinized response behavior is also typical for **low involvement purchases**—purchases that have little importance or relevance for the customer. Let's face it, buying a box of salt is probably not one of the burning issues in your life.[25]

Problem solving is a learning process

The reason problem solving becomes simpler with time is that people learn from experience—both positive and negative things. As consumers approach the problem-solving process, they bring attitudes formed by previous experiences and social training. Each new problem-solving process may then contribute to or modify this attitude set.

New concepts require an adoption process

When consumers face a really new concept, their previous experience may not be relevant. These situations involve the **adoption process**—the steps individuals go through on the way to accepting or rejecting a new idea. Although the adoption process is similar to the problem-solving process, learning plays a clearer role and promotion's contribution to a marketing mix is more visible.

In the adoption process, an individual moves through some fairly definite steps:

1. Awareness—the potential customer comes to know about the product but lacks details. The consumer may not even know how it works or what it will do.

2. Interest—*if* the consumer becomes interested, he or she will gather general information and facts about the product.

3. Evaluation—a consumer begins to give the product a mental trial, applying it to his or her personal situation.

4. Trial—the consumer may buy the product to experiment with it in use. A product that is either too expensive to try or isn't available for trial may never be adopted.

5. Decision—the consumer decides on either adoption or rejection. A satisfactory evaluation and trial may lead to adoption of the product and regular use. According to psychological learning theory, reinforcement leads to adoption.

6. Confirmation—the adopter continues to rethink the decision and searches for support for the decision—that is, further reinforcement.[26]

Marketing managers for 3M, the company that makes Scotch tape, worked with the adoption process when they introduced Post-It note pads. Test market ads increased awareness—they explained how Post-It notes could be applied to a surface and then easily removed. But test market sales were slow because most consumers were not interested.

Marketers often want to make it easier for consumers to adopt a product. Pittsburgh Paints' Accuvision video system helps customers see how their paint choices will look. Nabisco offers free samples to encourage consumers to try the product.

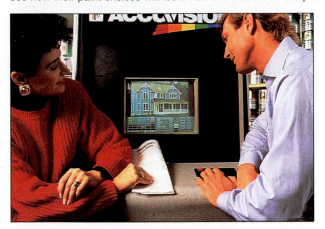

They didn't see the benefit. To encourage trial, 3M distributed free samples. By using the samples, consumers confirmed the benefit—and when they used the samples up they started buying Post-Its. As Post-It distribution expanded to other market areas, 3M used samples to speed consumers through the trial stage and the rest of the adoption process.[27]

Dissonance may set in after the decision

A buyer may have second thoughts after making a purchase decision. The buyer may have chosen from among several attractive alternatives—weighing the pros and cons and finally making a decision. Later doubts, however, may lead to **dissonance**—tension caused by uncertainty about the rightness of a decision. Dissonance may lead a buyer to search for additional information to confirm the wisdom of the decision and so reduce tension. Without this confirmation, the adopter might buy something else next time—or not comment positively about the product to others.[28]

CONCLUSION

In this chapter, we analyzed the individual consumer as a problem solver who is influenced by psychological variables, social influences, and the purchase situation. All of these variables are related, and our model of buyer behavior helps integrate them into one process. Marketing strategy planning requires a good grasp of this material.

Assuming that everyone behaves the way you do— or even like your family or friends do—can lead to expensive marketing errors.

Consumer buying behavior results from the consumer's efforts to satisfy needs and wants. We discussed some reasons why consumers buy and saw that consumer behavior can't be fully explained by only a list of needs.

We also saw that most societies are divided into social classes, a fact that helps explain some consumer

behavior. And we discussed the impact of reference groups and opinion leaders.

We presented a buyer behavior model to help you interpret and integrate the present findings—as well as any new data you might get from marketing research. As of now, the behavioral sciences can only offer insights and theories, which the marketing manager must blend with intuition and judgment to develop marketing strategies.

Companies may have to use marketing research to answer specific questions. But if a firm has neither the money nor the time for research, then marketing managers have to rely on available descriptions of present behavior and guesstimates about future behavior. Popular magazines and leading newspapers often reflect the public's shifting attitudes. And many studies of the changing consumer are published regularly in the business and trade press. This material—coupled with the information in this chapter—will help your marketing strategy planning.

Remember that consumers—with all their needs and attitudes—may be elusive, but they aren't invisible. Re-search has provided more data and understanding of consumer behavior than business managers generally use. Applying this information may help you find your breakthrough opportunity.

QUESTIONS AND PROBLEMS

1. In your own words, explain economic needs and how they relate to the economic-buyer model of consumer behavior. Give an example of a purchase you recently made that is consistent with the economic-buyer model. Give another that is not explained by the economic-buyer model. Explain your thinking.

2. Explain what is meant by a hierarchy of needs and provide examples of one or more products that enable you to satisfy each of the four levels of need.

3. Cut out (or copy) two recent ads: one full-page color ad from a magazine and one large display from a newspaper. In each case, indicate which needs the ads are appealing to.

4. Explain how an understanding of consumers' learning processes might affect marketing strategy planning. Give an example.

5. Briefly describe your own *beliefs* about the potential value of a driver-side air bag, your *attitude* toward air bags, and your *intention* about buying a car with an air bag.

6. Explain psychographics and life-style analysis. Explain how they might be useful for planning marketing strategies to reach college students as opposed to average consumers.

7. A supermarket chain is planning to open a number of new stores to appeal to Hispanics in southern California. Give some examples that indicate how the four Ps might be adjusted to appeal to the Hispanic subculture.

8. How should the social class structure affect the planning of a new restaurant in a large city? How might the four Ps be adjusted?

9. What social class would you associate with each of the following phrases or items?

    a. A gun rack in a pickup truck.
    b. The *National Enquirer.*
    c. New Yorker magazine.
    d. Working Woman magazine.
    e. People watching soap operas.

    f. TV golf tournaments.
    g. Men who drink beer after dinner.
    h. Families who vacation at a Disney theme park.
    i. Families who distrust banks (keep money in socks or mattresses).
    j. Owners of pit bulls.

    In each case, choose one class if you can. If you can't choose one class but think several classes are equally likely, then so indicate. In those cases where you feel that all classes are equally interested or characterized by a particular item, choose all five classes.

10. Illustrate how the reference group concept may apply in practice by explaining how you personally are influenced by some reference group for some product. What are the implications of such behavior for marketing managers?

11. Give two examples of recent purchases where the specific purchase situation influenced your purchase decision. Briefly explain how your decision was affected.

12. Give an example of a recent purchase in which you used extensive problem solving. What sources of information did you use in making the decision?

13. What kind of buying behavior would you expect to find for the following products: (*a*) a haircut, (*b*) a dishwasher detergent, (*c*) a printer for a personal computer, (*d*) a tennis racket, (*e*) a dress belt, (*f*) a telephone answering machine, (*g*) life insurance, (*h*) an ice cream cone (*i*) a new checking account? Set up a chart for your answer with products along the left-hand margin as the row headings and the following factors as headings for the columns: (*a*) how consumers would shop for these products, (*b*) how far they would go, (*c*) whether they would buy by brand, (*d*) whether they would compare with other products, and (*e*) any other factors they should consider. Insert short answers—words or phrases are satisfactory—in the various boxes. Be prepared to discuss how the answers you put in the chart would affect each product's marketing mix.

SUGGESTED CASES

1. McDonald's "Seniors" Restaurant
8. Emil's Place
9. Sleepy-Inn Motel

10. Grand Arena
11. Nike and Fashionable Shoes
28. Grand Foods, Ltd.

COMPUTER-AIDED PROBLEM

6. Selective Processes

Submag, Inc., uses direct-mail promotion to sell magazine subscriptions. Magazine publishers pay Submag $3.40 for each new subscription. Submag's costs include the expenses of printing, addressing, and mailing each direct-mail advertisement plus the cost of using a mailing list. There are many suppliers of mailing lists, and the cost and quality of different lists vary.

Submag's marketing manager, Shandra Debose, is trying to choose between two possible mailing lists. One list has been generated from phone directories. It is less expensive than the other list, but the supplier acknowledges that about 15 percent of the names are out-of-date (addresses of people who moved). A competing supplier offers a list of active members of professional associations. This list costs 10 cents per name more than the phone list, but only 2 percent of the addresses are out-of-date.

In addition to concerns about out-of-date names, not every consumer who receives a mailing buys a subscription. For example, *selective exposure* is a problem. Some target customers never see the offer—they just toss out junk mail without even opening the envelope. Industry studies show that this wastes 9 percent of each mailing.

Selective perception influences some consumers who do open the mailing. Some are simply not interested. Others don't want to deal with a subscription service. Although the price is good, these consumers worry that they'll never get the magazines. Submag's previous experience is that selective perception causes about 70 percent of those who read the offer to reject it.

Of those who perceive the message as intended, many are interested. But *selective retention* can be a problem. Some people set the information aside and then forget to send in the subscription order.

Submag can mail about 25,000 pieces per week. Shandra Debose sets up a spreadsheet to help her study effects of the various relationships discussed above—and to choose between the two mailing lists.

a. If you were Debose, which of the two lists would you buy based on the initial spreadsheet? Why?
b. For the most profitable list, what is the minimum number of items that Submag will have to mail to earn a profit of at least $1,000?
c. For an additional cost of $.02 per mailing, Submag can include a reply card that will reduce the percent of consumers who forget to send in an order (Percent Lost—Selective Retention) to 45 percent. If Submag mails 25,000 items, is it worth the additional cost to include the reply card? Explain your logic.

For additional questions related to this problem, see Exercise 6–5 in the *Learning Aid for use with Essentials of Marketing,* 6th edition.

Business and Organizational Customers and Their Buying Behavior

---

When You Finish This Chapter, You Should

❶

Know who the business and organizational customers are.

❷

Understand the problem-solving behavior of organizational buyers.

❸

See why multiple influence is common in business and organizational
purchase decisions.

❹

Know the basic methods used in organizational buying.

❺

Know about the number and distribution of manufacturers and why they are an important
customer group.

❻

Know how buying by service firms, retailers, wholesalers, and governments is similar
to—and different from—buying by manufacturers.

❼

Understand the important new terms (shown in red).

In 1978, Shahid Kahn used $13,000 in savings and a $50,000 loan to start Bumper Works, a small company that produces lightweight bumpers for pickup trucks. Bumper Works's customers now include major Japanese automakers like Isuzu and Toyota. But success didn't come overnight.

Kahn started to make sales calls on Toyota's purchasing department in 1980, but it was 1985 before he got his first order. And the first order wasn't a big contract. Parts buyers didn't want to risk tarnishing Toyota's reputation for quality by relying too heavily on a new, unproven supplier.

In 1987, Toyota decided to improve the bumpers on its trucks so they would be more durable than those on competing pickups. Toyota engineers developed the specifications for the new bumper, and Toyota buyers selected three suppliers—including Bumper Works—to compete for the business. Kahn developed an economical design that met the specs and won the contract. The contract involved supplying all of the rear bumpers Toyota needed at some of its U.S. facilities.

Although Kahn won the contract, he still faced challenges. Toyota's quality control people were not satisfied with the number of minor defects in Kahn's bumpers. Further, Bumper Works's deliveries were not as dependable as Toyota's production people required. Kahn knew that he would lose the Toyota account if he couldn't meet the demands of these people—and also keep the price low enough to satisfy the purchasing department.

Toyota's purchasing people concluded that Bumper Works wouldn't be able to resolve these problems unless Kahn could make big improvements in his production process. Kahn was stuck because he didn't know what else he could do. However, rather than shift the business to another supplier, Toyota sent a team of experts to show Bumper Works how to build better bumpers faster and cheaper.

Following the advice of Toyota experts, Kahn reorganized all the equipment in his factory to make it more efficient. He also had to retrain all his employees to do their jobs in new ways. But the trouble was worth the effort. Productivity at Bumper Works went up 60 percent, and the number of defects dropped by 80 percent. In 1992, the improvements helped Bumper Works get a big new contract with Isuzu.

Of course, Toyota didn't go to all of its effort just to be friendly. It wanted a committed supplier that could meet its standards. In exchange for its help, Toyota got a big price reduction from Bumper Works.[1]

BUSINESS AND ORGANIZATIONAL CUSTOMERS—A BIG OPPORTUNITY

Most of us think about individual final consumers when we hear the term *customer*. But many marketing managers aim at customers who are not final consumers. In fact, more purchases are made by businesses and other organizations than by final consumers. As the Bumper Works/Toyota case illustrates, the buying behavior of these customers can be very different from the buying behavior of final consumers. Developing marketing strategies

Exhibit 7–1   Examples of Different Types of Business and Organizational Customers

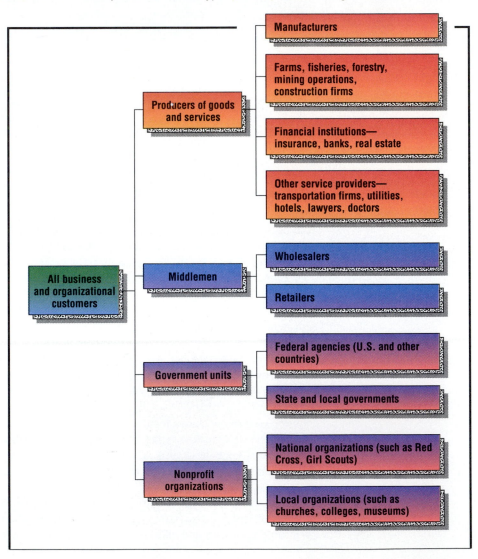

for these markets requires a solid understanding of who these customers are and how they buy. That is the focus of this chapter.

Business and organizational customers are any buyers who buy for resale or to produce other goods and services. Exhibit 7–1 shows the different types of customers in these markets.

Many characteristics of buying behavior are common across different types of organizations. That's why the different kinds of organizational buyers are often loosely referred to as "industrial buyers" or "intermediate buyers." As we discuss organizational buying, we will intermix examples of buying by many different types of organizations. Later in the chapter, however, we will highlight some of the specific characteristics of the different customer groups.

Even small differences are important

Understanding how the buying behavior of a particular organization differs from others can be very important. Even "trivial" differences in buying behavior may be important because success often hinges on fine tuning the marketing mix.

Sellers often approach each organizational customer directly, usually through a sales representative. This gives the seller more chance to adjust the marketing mix for each individual customer. A seller may even develop a unique strategy for each individual customer. This approach carries target marketing to its extreme. But sellers often need unique strategies to compete for large-volume purchases.

In such situations, the individual sales rep takes much responsibility for strategy planning. These jobs are very challenging—and they pay well too.

Serving customers in international markets

Many marketers discover that there are good opportunities to serve business customers in other countries. Specific business customs do vary from one country to another—and the differences can be important. For example, a salesperson working in Japan must know to handle a customer's business card with respect. Japanese consider it rude to write notes on the back of a card or put it in a wallet while the person who presented it is still in the

Hercules, an international supplier of ingredients to food producers, offers its customers expert help in dealing with the differences in tastes in different parts of the world.

room. But the basic approaches marketers use to deal with business customers are much less varied than those required to reach individual consumers.

This is probably why many firms shifted to global markets so rapidly. Their business customers in different countries buy in similar ways and can be reached with similar marketing mixes. Moreover, business customers are often willing to work with a distant supplier.

To keep the discussion specific, we will focus on organizational customers in the United States. But most of the ideas apply to international markets in general.

ORGANIZATIONAL BUYERS ARE PROBLEM SOLVERS

Some people think of organizational buying as entirely different from consumer buying—but there are many similarities. In fact, the problem-solving framework introduced in Chapter 6 can be applied here.

Three kinds of buying processes are useful

In Chapter 6, we discussed problem solving by consumers and how it might vary from extensive problem solving to routine buying. In organizational markets, we can adapt these concepts slightly and work with three similar buying processes: a new-task buying process, a modified rebuy process, or a straight rebuy.[2] See Exhibit 7–2.

New-task buying occurs when an organization has a new need and the buyer wants a great deal of information. New-task buying can involve setting product specifications, evaluating sources of supply, and establishing an order routine that can be followed in the future if results are satisfactory.

A **straight rebuy** is a routine repurchase that may have been made many times before. Buyers probably don't bother looking for new information or new sources of supply. Most of a company's small or recurring purchases are of this type—but they take only a small part of an organized buyer's time.

The **modified rebuy** is the in-between process where some review of the buying situation is done—though not as much as in new-task buying. Sometimes a competitor will get lazy enjoying a straight rebuy situation. An alert marketer can turn these situations into opportunities by providing more information or a better marketing mix.

Customers in a new-task buying situation are likely to seek information from a variety of sources. See Exhibit 7–3. How much information a customer collects also depends on the importance of the purchase and the level of uncertainty about what choice might be

Exhibit 7–2 Organizational Buying Processes

Characteristics	Type of process		
	New-task buying	Modified rebuy	Straight rebuy
Time required	Much	Medium	Little
Multiple influence	Much	Some	Little
Review of suppliers	Much	Some	None
Information needed	Much	Some	Little

best. The time and expense of searching for and analyzing a lot of information may not be justified for a minor purchase. But a major purchase often involves real detective work. After all, the consequences of a mistake can be very important.

Note that a particular product may be bought in any of the three ways. The marketing job may be quite different depending on the buying process. A new-task buy takes much longer than a straight rebuy—and the seller's promotion has much more chance to have an impact.[3]

Purchasing agents are buying specialists

Many organizations, especially large ones, need buying specialists. **Purchasing agents** are buying specialists for their employers. Most purchasing agents and purchasing managers are serious and well educated. In large organizations, they usually specialize by product area and are real experts. Salespeople usually have to see the purchasing agent first—before they contact any other employee.

Rather than being sold, these buyers want salespeople to provide accurate information that will help them buy wisely. They like information on new goods and services, and tips on potential price changes, supply shortages, and other changes in market conditions.

Purchasing may be centralized

If a large organization has facilities at many locations, much of the purchasing work may be done at a central location. With centralized buying, a sales rep may be able to sell to facilities all across a country—or even several countries—without leaving a base city. For example, U.S. Gypsum, one of the largest building materials manufacturers, does most of the buying for over 50 plants from its Chicago offices. Similarly, Wal-Mart handles most of the purchase decisions for stores in its retail chain from its headquarters in Arkansas. Many purchasing decisions for agencies of the U.S. government are handled in Washington, D.C.

Basic purchasing needs are economic

Organizational buyers typically focus on economic factors when they make purchase decisions. They are usually less emotional in their buying than final consumers.

Buyers try to consider the total cost of selecting a supplier and a particular product, not just the initial price of the product. For example, a hospital that needs a new type of X-ray equipment might look at both the original cost and ongoing costs, how it would affect doctor productivity, and of course the quality of the images it produces. The hospital might also consider the seller's reliability, ability to provide speedy repair, and past relationship (including previous favors).

The matter of dependability deserves further emphasis. An organization may not be able to function if purchases don't arrive when they're expected. Dependable product quality is important too. For example, a faulty wire might cause a large piece of equipment to break down. The costs of finding and correcting the problem could be 1,000 times the cost of the wire.

Exhibit 7–3   Major Sources of Information Used by Organizational Buyers

	Marketing sources	Nonmarketing sources
Personal sources	• Salespeople • Others from supplier firms • Trade shows	• Buying center members • Outside business associates • Consultants and outside experts
Impersonal sources	• Advertising in trade publications • Sales literature • Sales catalogs	• Rating services • Trade associations • News publications • Product directories

Business customers usually focus on economic needs when they make purchase decisions.

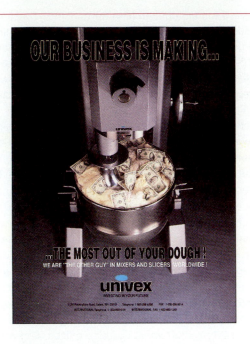

Considering all of the economic factors relevant to a purchase decision is sometimes complex. A supplier or product that is best in one way may not be best in others. To try to deal with these situations, many buyers use **vendor analysis**—a formal rating of suppliers on all relevant areas of performance. By evaluating suppliers and how they are working out, buyers can make better decisions.[4]

Behavioral needs are relevant too

Vendor analysis focuses on economic factors, but purchasing in organizations may also involve many behavioral dimensions. Modern buyers are human—and they want friendly relationships with suppliers. Buyers are also human with respect to protecting their own interests—and their own position in the company. That's why many buyers want to avoid taking risks that might reflect badly on their decisions. They have to buy a wide variety of products from many sources and make decisions involving many factors beyond their control. If a new source delivers late or product quality is poor, you can guess who will be blamed. Marketers who can help the buyer avoid taking risks have a definite appeal. In fact, this may make the difference between a successful and unsuccessful marketing mix.

? Ethical conflicts may arise

Although organizational buyers are influenced by their own needs, most are real professionals who are careful to avoid a conflict between their own self-interest and company outcomes. Marketers must be careful here. A salesperson who offers one of his company pens to a buyer may view the giveaway as a promotional item—but the customer's firm may have a policy against a buyer accepting *any* gift.

Most organizational buyers do their work ethically—and expect marketers to work the same way. Yet there have been highly publicized abuses. For example, NYNEX (the telephone company that serves New York and New England) found out that some of its buyers were giving contracts to suppliers who offered them vacation trips and other personal favors. Abuses of this sort have prompted many organizations, including NYNEX, to set up policies that prohibit a buyer from accepting anything from a potential supplier.[5]

Marketers need to take conflict of interest very seriously. Part of the promotion job in marketing is to identify and persuade different individuals who may influence an organization's purchase decision. Yet the whole marketing effort may be tainted if it even *appears* that a marketer has encouraged a buyer to put personal gain ahead of company interest.

Multiple buying influences in a buying center

Much of the work of the typical purchasing agent consists of straight rebuys. When a purchase requisition comes in, the purchasing agent places an order without consulting anyone else. But in many cases—especially new-task buying—multiple buying influence is important. **Multiple buying influence** means that several people—perhaps even top management—share in making a purchase decision.

An example shows how the different buying influences work. Suppose Electrolux, the Swedish firm that produces vacuum cleaners, wants to buy a machine to stamp out the various metal parts it needs. Different vendors are eager for the business. Several people (influencers) help to evaluate the choices. A finance manager worries about the high cost and suggests leasing the machine. The quality control people want a machine that will do a more accurate job—although it's more expensive. The production manager is interested in speed of operation. The production line workers and their supervisors want the machine that is easiest to use so workers can continue to rotate jobs.

The company president (the decider) asks the purchasing department to assemble all the information but retains the power to select and approve the supplier. The purchasing manager's administrative assistant (a gatekeeper) has been deciding what information to pass on to higher-ups as well as scheduling visits for salespeople. After all these buying influences are considered, one of the purchasing agents for the firm (the buyer) will be responsible for making recommendations and arranging the terms of the sale.

It is helpful to think of a **buying center** as all the people who participate in or influence a purchase. Different people may make up a buying center from one decision to the next. This makes the marketing job difficult.

The salesperson must study each case carefully. Just learning who to talk with may be hard, but thinking about the various roles in the buying center can help. See Exhibit 7–4.

The salesperson may have to talk to every member of the buying center—stressing different topics for each. This not only complicates the promotion job but also lengthens it. On important purchases—a new computer system, a new building, or major equipment—the selling period may stretch out to a year or more.[6]

Exhibit 7–4 Multiple Influence and Roles in the Buying Center

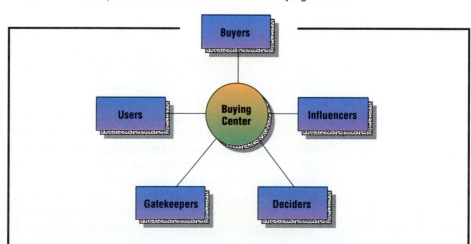

Texaco Chemical Company supplies Owens-Corning with chemicals needed to make insulation—so Texaco's sales reps are in close contact with the different people at Owens-Corning who influence purchase decisions.

BASIC METHODS AND PRACTICES IN ORGANIZATIONAL BUYING

Should you inspect, sample, describe, or negotiate?

Organizational buyers (really, buyers of all types, including final consumers) use four basic approaches to evaluating and buying products: (1) inspection, (2) sampling, (3) description, and (4) negotiated contracts. Understanding the differences in these buying methods is important in strategy planning, so let's look at each approach.

Inspection looks at everything

Inspection buying means looking at every item. It's used for products that are not standardized and require examination. Here each product is different—as in the case of livestock or used equipment. Such products are often sold in open markets—or at auction if there are several potential buyers. Buyers inspect the goods and either haggle with the seller or bid against competing buyers.

Sampling looks at some

Sampling buying means looking at only part of a potential purchase. As products become more standardized—perhaps because of careful grading or quality control—buying by sample becomes possible. For example, a power company might buy miles of heavy electric cable. A sample section might be heated to the melting point to be certain the cable is safe.

People in less-developed economies do a lot of buying by inspection or sampling—regardless of the product. The reason is skepticism about quality—or lack of faith in the seller.

Specifications describe the need

Description (specification) buying means buying from a written (or verbal) description of the product. Most manufactured items are bought this way—often without inspection. When quality can almost be guaranteed, buying by description—grade, brand, or specification—may be satisfactory, especially when there is mutual trust between buyers and sellers. Because this method reduces the cost of buying, buyers use it whenever practical.

Services are usually purchased by description. Since a service is usually not performed until after it's purchased, buyers have nothing to inspect ahead of time.

Buyers may inspect only a portion of a potential fruit purchase, but the quality of the sample may affect the price or acceptability of the whole order. Most manufactured items, including rolls of aluminum, are bought based on written specifications.

Once the purchase needs are specified, it's the buyer's job to get the best deal possible. If several suppliers want the business, the buyer will often request competitive bids. **Competitive bids** are the terms of sale offered by different suppliers in response to the buyer's purchase specifications. If different suppliers' quality, dependability, and delivery schedules all meet the specs, the buyer will select the low-price bid. But a creative marketer needs to look carefully at the purchaser's specs—and the need—to see if other elements of the marketing mix could provide a competitive advantage.

Negotiated contracts handle relationships

Negotiated contract buying means agreeing to a contract that allows for changes in the purchase arrangements.

Sometimes the buyer knows roughly what the company needs but can't fix all the details in advance. Specifications or total requirements may change over time. This situation is common in research and development work and in the building of special-purpose machinery or buildings. In such cases, the general project is described, and a basic price may be agreed on—perhaps even based on competitive bids—but with provision for changes and price adjustments up or down.

Buyers and suppliers form partnerships

To be sure of dependable quality, a buyer may develop loyalty to certain suppliers. This is especially important when buying nonstandardized products. When a supplier and buyer develop a working partnership over the years, the supplier practically becomes a part of the buyer's organization.

A recent purchase by Boeing, the giant airplane manufacturer, illustrates the trend toward closer working partnerships between business customers and their suppliers. Boeing is a big customer for machine tools—the equipment it uses to make airplane parts. Like other manufacturers, Boeing usually designed parts for its planes first and then got competitive bids from machine suppliers. The low-price supplier got the order. Japanese machine tool suppliers were winning in this price-oriented competition.

In today's global economy, organizational buyers prefer dependable suppliers whose products are available when and where they are needed.

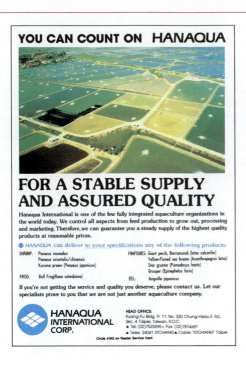

Recently Boeing needed to buy machines to produce landing-gear parts, and it tried a different approach. Boeing invited potential suppliers to study its operations and recommend how the parts should be designed. Ingersol, an American machine-tool company, seized the opportunity. It helped Boeing design the landing-gear parts so that the total cost of both the machines and the parts they produced would be lower. The design also helped speed up Boeing's production process. By helping Boeing develop a better way to make its airplane, Ingersol won the contract.[7]

Buyers may use several sources to spread their risk

Even if a firm develops the best marketing mix possible, it may not get all of a business customer's business. Buyers often look for several dependable sources of supply to protect themselves from unpredictable events, such as a strike or fire at one supplier's plant. Still a good marketing mix is likely to win a larger share of the total business—which can prove to be very important. Moving from a 20 percent share to a 30 percent share may not seem like much from a buyer's point of view, but for the seller it's a 50 percent increase in sales![8]

Most buyers try to routinize buying

To save effort and expense, most firms try to routinize the purchase process whenever they can. When some person or unit wants to buy something, a **requisition**—a request to buy something—is filled out. After approval by some supervisor, the requisition is forwarded to the buyer for placement with the best seller.

Approved requisitions are converted to purchase orders as quickly as possible. Buyers usually make straight rebuys the day they receive the requisition; new-task and modified rebuys take longer. If time is important, the buyer may place the order by telephone, fax, or computer.

Computer buying is becoming common

Many buyers now delegate a large portion of their routine order placing to computers. They program decision rules that tell the computer how to order and leave the details of

CLOROX COMPANY'S SPOTLESS SERVICE BUILDS PARTNERSHIPS

Marketing managers at Clorox Company face a daunting task making good on their objective of "maintaining the highest standards for customer service" in all the product markets they serve. But they must do so to develop and keep strong partnerships with Clorox middlemen (supermarket chains, convenience stores, mass-merchandisers, warehouse clubs, wholesalers) and other business customers (ranging from white tablecloth restaurants to fast-service chains). Clorox deals with more than 100,000 business customers worldwide.

Information shared between Clorox and the firms that buy its products helps make the partnership work. For example, when the bleach buyer for a major retail chain went on vacation, the fill-in person was not familiar with the reorder procedures. As a result, the chain's central distribution center almost ran out of Clorox liquid bleach. But Clorox's distribution people

identified the problem themselves—because of a computer system that allowed Clorox to access the chain's inventory records and sales data for Clorox products. Clorox got a shipment out fast enough to prevent the chain—and Clorox—from losing sales at individual stores. In the future when some other bleach supplier tries to tell buyers for the chain that "bleach is bleach," they'll remember the service Clorox provides.

Business-to-business marketing efforts, whether targeted at middlemen or other types of firms, can be even more demanding than working with final consumers. Building and keeping business partnerships takes constant attention to service quality, not just quality goods. But organizational buyers know that the success of their own firms' marketing strategies depends on such service—so they reward reliable suppliers with their orders.[9]

---

following through to the machine. When economic conditions change, buyers modify the computer instructions. When nothing unusual happens, however, the computer system continues to routinely rebuy as needs develop—printing out new purchase orders to the regular suppliers.

Obviously, it's a big sale to be selected as a major supplier and routinely called up in the buyer's computer program. It's also obvious that such a buyer will be more impressed by an attractive marketing mix for a whole *line* of products than just a lower price for a particular order.[10]

Customers may demand just-in-time delivery

Business customers generally try to maintain an adequate inventory—certainly enough to prevent stockouts or keep production lines moving. There's no greater disaster in a factory than to have a production line close down. And a retailer or wholesaler can lose sales quickly if popular products are not on the shelf.

On the other hand, keeping too much inventory is expensive. Firms now pay more attention to inventory costs—and look to their suppliers for help in controlling them. This often means that a supplier must be able to provide **just-in-time delivery**—reliably getting products there *just* before the customer needs them.

Just-in-time relationships between buyers and sellers require a lot of coordination. For example, an automobile producer may ask a supplier of automobile seats to load the delivery truck so seats are arranged in the color and style of the cars on the assembly line. This reduces the buyer's costs because the seats need to be handled only once. However, it may increase the supplier's costs. Most buyers realize they can't just push costs back onto their suppliers without giving them something in return. Often what they give is a longer-term contract that shares both the costs and benefits of the working partnership.

Ryder, a supplier of transportation services, has a close partnership with Saturn. Ryder helped design Saturn's state-of-the-art system for just-in-time delivery of components to the assembly line—and it also transports finished cars to dealers.

Reciprocity may influence buying

Reciprocity means trading sales for sales—that is, "If you buy from me, I'll buy from you." If a company's customers also can supply products that the firm buys, then the sales departments of both buyer and seller may try to trade sales for sales. Purchasing agents generally resist reciprocity but often face pressure from their sales departments. Reciprocity is often a bigger factor in other countries than it is in the United States. In Japan, for example, reciprocity is very common.[11]

Variations in buying by customer type

We've been discussing dimensions and frameworks that marketing managers often use to analyze buying behavior in many different types of customer organizations—in both the United States and internationally. However, it's also useful to have more detail about specific types of customers.

MANUFACTURERS ARE IMPORTANT CUSTOMERS

There are not many big ones

One of the most striking facts about manufacturers is how few there are compared to final consumers. This is true in every country. In the United States, for example, there are about 363,000 factories. Exhibit 7–5 shows that the majority of these are quite small—almost half have fewer than 10 workers. But these small firms account for only about 3 percent of manufacturing activity. In small plants, the owners often do the buying. And they buy less formally than buyers in the relatively few large manufacturing plants—which employ most of the workers and produce a large share of the value added by manufacturing. For example, plants with 250 or more employees make up only 4 percent of the total—yet they produce over 61 percent of the value added by manufacturers.

The size distribution of manufacturers varies in other countries. But the same conclusion holds: it is often desirable to segment industrial customers on the basis of size because large plants do so much of the buying.

Customers cluster in geographic areas

In addition to concentration by company size, industrial markets are concentrated in certain geographic areas. Internationally, industrial customers are concentrated in coun-

Exhibit 7−5 Size Distribution of Manufacturing Establishments

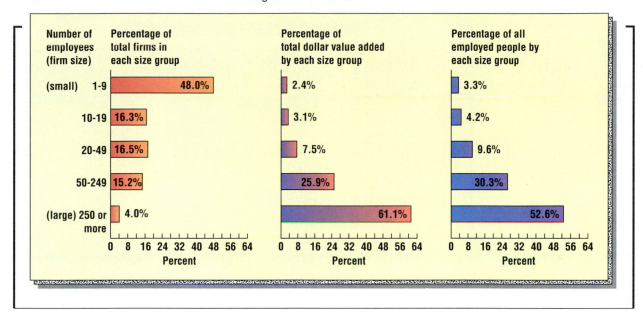

tries that are at the more advanced stages of economic development. Within a country, there is often further concentration in specific areas. In the United States, for example, many factories are concentrated in big metropolitan areas—especially in New York, Pennsylvania, Ohio, Illinois, Texas, and California.[12]

There is also concentration by industry. In Germany, the steel industry is concentrated in the Ruhr Valley. In the United States, it's heavily concentrated in the Pittsburgh, Birmingham (Alabama), and Chicago areas. Similarly, U.S. manufacturers of advanced electronics systems are concentrated in California's famous Silicon Valley near San Francisco and along Boston's Route 128.

Much data is available on industrial markets by SIC codes

What a manufacturer needs to buy depends on the business it is in. Because of this, sales of a product are often concentrated among customers in similar businesses. Marketing managers who can relate their own sales to their customers' type of business can focus their efforts.

Detailed information is often available to help a marketing manager learn more about customers in different lines of business. The U.S. government regularly collects and publishes data by **Standard Industrial Classification (SIC) codes**—groups of firms in similar lines of business. The number of establishments, sales volumes, and number of employees—broken down by geographic areas—are given for each SIC code. A number of other countries collect similar data, and some of them try to coordinate their efforts with an international variation of the SIC system.

In the United States, SIC code breakdowns start with broad industry categories such as food and related products (code 20), tobacco products (code 21), textile mill products (code 22), apparel (code 23), and so on. Within each two-digit industry breakdown, much more detailed data may be available for three-digit and four-digit industries (that is, subindustries of the two- or three-digit industries). Exhibit 7−6 gives an example of more detailed breakdowns within the apparel industry. Four-digit detail isn't available for all industries in every geographic area because the government does not provide data when only one or two plants are located in an area.[13]

Exhibit 7–6 Illustrative SIC Breakdown for Apparel Industries

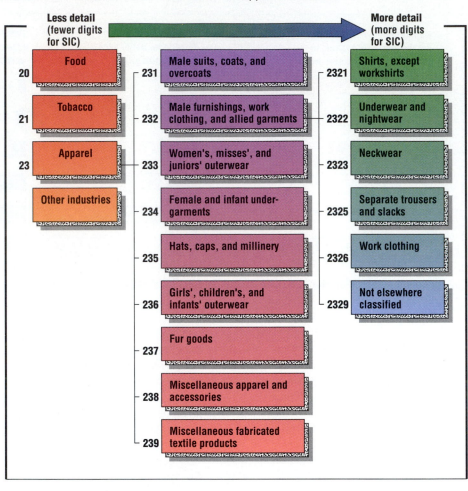

PRODUCERS OF SERVICES—SMALLER AND MORE SPREAD OUT

The service side of the U.S. economy is large and has been growing fast. Service operations are also growing in some other countries. There may be good opportunities providing these companies with the products they need to support their operations. But there are also challenges.

The United States has about 2 million service firms—about six times as many as it has manufacturers. Some of these are big companies with international operations. Examples include AT&T, Hilton Hotels, Prudential Insurance, Citibank, and EDS (Electronic Data Systems). These firms have purchasing departments that are like those in large manufacturing organizations. But, as you might guess given the large number of service firms, most of them are small. They're also more spread out around the country than manufacturing concerns. Factories often locate where transportation facilities are good, where raw materials are available, and where it is less costly to produce goods in quantity. Service operations, in contrast, usually have to be close to their customers.

Buying may not be as formal   Purchases by small service firms are often handled by whoever is in charge. This may be a doctor, lawyer, owner of a local insurance agency, or manager of a hotel. Suppliers who usually deal with purchasing specialists in large organizations may have trouble adjusting to this market. Personal selling is still an important part of promotion, but reaching these customers in the first place often requires more advertising. And small service firms may need much more help in buying than a large corporation.

Canon, the familiar name in office copiers, was successful serving the needs of smaller service firms like law offices. Canon developed promotion materials to help first-time buyers understand differences in copiers. It emphasized that its machines were easy to use and maintain. And Canon also used retail channels to make the copiers available in smaller areas where there wasn't enough business to justify using a sales rep.[14]

RETAILERS AND WHOLESALERS BUY FOR THEIR CUSTOMERS

Most retail and wholesale buyers see themselves as purchasing agents for their target customers—remembering the old saying that "goods well bought are half sold." Typically, retailers do *not* see themselves as sales agents for particular manufacturers. They buy what they think they can sell. And wholesalers buy what they think their retailers can sell.

Reorders are straight rebuys

Most retailers and wholesalers carry a large number of products. A drug wholesaler, for example, may carry up to 125,000 products. Because they deal with so many products, most middlemen buy on a routine reorder basis—as straight rebuys—once they make the initial decision to stock specific items. Sellers to these markets must understand the size of the buyer's job and have something useful to say and do when they call.

Buyers watch computer output closely

Most larger firms now use sophisticated computerized inventory control systems. Scanners at retail checkout counters track what goes out the door—and computers use this data to update the records. Even small retailers and wholesalers use automated control systems that print daily reports showing sales of every product. Buyers with this kind of information know, in detail, the profitability of the different competing products. If a product isn't moving, the retailer isn't likely to be impressed by a salesperson's request for more in-store attention or added shelf space.

The founder of Soft Sheen Products, the most successful marketer of hair care products for African-Americans, calls on a buyer for the Walgreen retail chain. The buyer is a real expert who has helped many suppliers establish new products targeted at ethnic consumers.

Automatic computer ordering is a natural outgrowth of computerized checkout systems. McKesson Corporation—a large wholesaler of drug products—gave computers to drugstores so the stores could keep track of inventory and place orders directly into McKesson's computer. Once a retailer started using the service, McKesson's share of that store's business usually doubled or tripled.[15]

Some are not "open to buy"

Retail buyers are sometimes controlled by a miniature profit and loss statement for each department or merchandise line. In an effort to make a profit, the buyer tries to forecast sales, merchandise costs, and expenses. The figure for "cost of merchandise" is the amount buyers plan to spend over the budget period. If the money is not yet spent, buyers are **open to buy**—that is, the buyers have budgeted funds that can be spent during the current period. However, if the budget is spent, they are no longer in the market and no amount of special promotion or price cutting is likely to induce them to buy.[16]

Buying and selling are closely related

In wholesale and retail firms, there is usually a very close relationship between buying and selling. Buyers are often in close contact with their firm's salespeople and with customers. The housewares buyer for a department store, for example, may supervise the salespeople who sell housewares. Salespeople are quick to tell a buyer if customers want a product that isn't available. A buyer may even buy some items to satisfy the preferences of salespeople. Therefore, salespeople should not be neglected in the promotion effort.

Committee buying is impersonal

Some buyers—especially those who work for big retail chains—are annoyed by the number of wholesalers' and manufacturers' representatives who call on them. Space in their stores is limited, and they simply are not interested in carrying every product that some salesperson wants them to sell. Consider the problem facing grocery chains. In an average week, 150 to 250 new items are offered to the buying offices of a large chain like Safeway. If the chain accepted all of them, it would add 10,000 new items during a single year! Obviously, these firms need a way to deal with this overload.[17]

Decisions to add or drop lines may be handled by a *buying committee*. The seller still calls on and gives a pitch to a buyer—but the buyer does not have final responsibility. Instead, the buyer prepares new-product proposals and passes them on to the committee for evaluation. A seller may not get to make a presentation to the buying committee in person. This rational, almost cold-blooded approach reduces the impact of a persuasive salesperson.

Resident buyers may help a firm's buyers

Resident buyers are independent buying agents who work in central markets (New York, Paris, Rome, Hong Kong, Chicago, Los Angeles, etc.) for several retailer or wholesaler customers based in outlying areas or other countries. They buy new styles and fashions and fill-in items as their customers run out of stock during the year. Resident buying organizations help small channel members (producers and middlemen) reach each other inexpensively. They are usually paid an annual fee based on their purchases.

THE GOVERNMENT MARKET

Size and diversity

Some marketers ignore the government market because they think that government red tape is more trouble than it's worth. They probably don't realize how big the government market really is. Government is the largest customer group in many countries—including the United States. Almost 20 percent of the U.S. gross national product is spent by various government units; the figure is much higher in some economies. Different government units in the United States spend about $1,026,000,000,000 (think about it!) a year to buy almost every kind of product. They run not only schools, police departments, and military

Government agencies are important customers for a wide variety of products.

organizations, but also supermarkets, public utilities, research laboratories, offices, hospitals, and even liquor stores. These huge government expenditures cannot be ignored by an aggressive marketing manager.

Competitive bids may be required

Government buyers in the United States are expected to spend money wisely—in the public interest. To avoid charges of favoritism, most government customers buy by specification using a mandatory bidding procedure. Often the government buyer must accept the lowest bid that meets the specifications. You can see how important it is for the buyer to write precise and complete specifications. Otherwise, sellers may submit a bid that fits the specs but doesn't really match what is needed. By law, a government unit might have to accept the lowest bid—even for an unwanted product. Writing specifications is not easy—and buyers usually appreciate the help of well-informed salespeople.

Rigged specs are an ethical concern

A government customer who wants a specific brand or supplier may try to write the description so that no other supplier can meet all the specs. The buyer may have good reasons for such preferences—a more reliable product, prompt delivery, or better service after the sale. This kind of loyalty sounds great, but marketers must be sensitive to the ethical issues involved. Laws that require government customers to get bids are intended to increase competition among suppliers, not reduce it. Specs that are written primarily to defeat the purpose of these laws may be viewed as illegal bid rigging.

The approved supplier list

Some items that are bought frequently—or for which there are widely accepted standards—are purchased routinely without bids. The government unit simply places an order at a previously approved price. To share in this business, a supplier must be on the list of approved suppliers. The list is updated occasionally, sometimes by a bid procedure. Government units buy school supplies, construction materials, and gasoline this way.

Negotiated contracts are common too

Negotiation is often necessary when there are many intangible factors. Unfortunately, this is exactly where favoritism and influence can slip in. And such influence is not unknown—especially in city and state government. Nevertheless, negotiation is an important buying method in government sales—so a marketing mix should emphasize more than just low price.[18]

Learning what government wants

In the United States, there are more than 83,000 local government units (school districts, cities, counties, and states) as well as many federal agencies that make purchases. Keeping on top of all of them is nearly impossible. Potential suppliers should target the government units they want to cater to and learn the bidding methods of those units. Then it's easier to stay informed since most government contracts are advertised.

A marketer can learn a lot about potential government target markets from various government publications. In the United States, the federal government's *Commerce Business Daily* lists most current purchase bid requests. The Small Business Administration's *U.S. Purchasing, Specifications, and Sales Directory* explains government procedures to encourage competition for such business. Various state and local governments also offer guidance—as do government units in many other countries.

Dealing with foreign governments

Selling to government units in foreign countries can be a real challenge. In many cases, a firm must get permission from its own government to sell to a foreign government. Moreover, most government contracts favor domestic suppliers if they are available. Public sentiment may make it very difficult for a foreign competitor to get a contract. Or the government bureaucracy may simply bury a foreign supplier in so much red tape that there's no way to win.

? Is it unethical to "buy help?"

In some countries, government officials expect small payments ("grease money") just to speed up processing of routine paperwork, inspections, or decisions from the local bureaucracy. Outright influence peddling—where government officials or their friends request bribe money to sway a purchase decision—is also common in some markets. In the past, marketers from some countries looked at such bribes as a cost of doing business. However, the 1977 **Foreign Corrupt Practices Act** prohibits U.S. firms from paying bribes to foreign officials. A person who pays bribes—or authorizes an agent to pay them—can face stiff penalties. However, the law was amended in 1988 to allow small grease money payments if they are customary in a local culture. Further, a manager isn't held responsible if an agent in the foreign country secretly pays bribes.[19]

CONCLUSION

In this chapter, we considered the number, size, location, and buying habits of various types of organizational customers—to try to identify logical dimensions for segmenting markets. We saw that the nature of the buyer and the buying situation are relevant. We also saw that the problem-solving models of buyer behavior introduced in Chapter 6 apply here—with modifications.

The chapter focuses on aspects of buying behavior that are common to different types of organizational customers. However, we also discussed some key differences in the manufacturer, middleman, and government markets.

A clear understanding of organizational buying habits, needs, and attitudes can aid marketing strategy planning. And since there are fewer organizational customers than final consumers, it may even be possible for some marketing managers (and their salespeople) to develop a unique strategy for each potential customer.

This chapter offers some general principles that are useful in strategy planning—but the nature of the products being offered may require adjustments in the plans. Different product classes are discussed in Chapter 8. Variations by product may provide additional segmenting dimensions to help a marketing manager fine-tune a marketing strategy.

QUESTIONS AND PROBLEMS

1. Compare and contrast the problem-solving approaches used by final consumers and organizational buyers.

2. Describe the situations that would lead to the use of the three different buying processes for a particular product—lightweight bumpers for a pickup truck.

3. Compare and contrast the buying processes of final consumers and organizational buyers.

4. Briefly discuss why a marketing manager should think about who is likely to be involved in the buying center for a particular purchase. Is the buying center idea useful in consumer buying? Explain your answer.

5. If a nonprofit hospital were planning to buy expensive MRI scanning equipment (to detect tumors), who might be involved in the buying center? Explain your answer and describe the types of influence different people might have.

6. Why would an organizational buyer want to get competitive bids? What are some of the situations when competitive bidding can't be used?

7. How likely would each of the following be to use competitive bids: (*a*) a small town that needed a road resurfaced, (*b*) a scouting organization that needed a printer to print its scouting handbook, (*c*) a hardware retailer that wants to add a new lawnmower line, (*d*) a grocery store that wants to install a new checkout scanner, (*e*) a sorority that wants to buy a computer to keep track of member dues? Explain your answers.

8. Discuss the advantages and disadvantages of just-in-time supply relationships from an organizational buyer's point of view. Are the advantages and disadvantages merely reversed from the seller's point of view?

9. IBM has a long-term negotiated contract with Microsoft, a supplier that provides the software operating system for IBM computers. Discuss several of the issues that IBM might want the contract to cover.

10. Would a toy manufacturer need a different marketing strategy for a big retail chain, like Toys "R" Us, than for a single toy store run by its owner? Discuss your answer.

11. How do you think a furniture manufacturer's buying habits and practices would be affected by the specific type of product to be purchased? Consider fabric for upholstered furniture, a lathe for the production line, cardboard for shipping cartons, and lubricants for production machinery.

12. Discuss the importance of target marketing when analyzing organizational markets. How easy is it to isolate homogeneous market segments in these markets?

13. Explain how SIC codes might be helpful in evaluating and understanding business markets. Give an example.

14. Considering the nature of retail buying, outline the basic ingredients of promotion to retail buyers. Does it make any difference what kinds of products are involved? Are any other factors relevant?

15. The government market is obviously an extremely large one, yet it is often slighted or even ignored by many firms. Red tape is certainly one reason, but there are others. Discuss the situation and be sure to include the possibility of segmenting in your analysis.

16. Some critics argue that the Foreign Corrupt Practices Act puts U.S. businesses at a disadvantage when competing in foreign markets with suppliers from other countries that do not have similar laws. Do you think that this is a reasonable criticism? Explain your answer.

SUGGESTED CASES

5. General Chemical Company

6. Bethlehem Steel Company

COMPUTER-AIDED PROBLEM

7. Vendor Analysis

CompuTech, Inc., makes circuit boards for microcomputers. It is evaluating two possible suppliers of electronic memory chips.

The chips do the same job. Although manufacturing quality has been improving, some chips are always defective. Both suppliers will replace defective chips. But the only practical way to test for a defective chip is to assemble a circuit board and "burn it in"—run it and see if it works. When one chip on a board is defective at that point, it is impractical to search for the defect, and the whole circuit board must be scrapped. Supplier 1 guarantees a chip failure rate of 1 per 1,000 (that is a defect rate of 0.1 percent). Supplier 2's 0.3 percent defect rate is higher, but its price is lower.

Supplier 1 has been able to improve its quality because it uses a heavier plastic case to hold the chip. The only disadvantage of the heavier case is that it requires CompuTech to use a connector that is somewhat more expensive.

Transportation costs are added to the price quoted by either supplier, but Supplier 2 is further away so transportation costs are higher. And because of the distance, supplies sometimes arrive late. To ensure that a sufficient supply is on hand to keep production going, CompuTech must maintain a backup inventory—and this increases inventory costs. CompuTech figures inventory costs—the expenses of finance and storage—as a percentage of the total order cost.

To make its vendor analysis easier, CompuTech's purchasing agent enters data about the two suppliers on a spreadsheet. He bases his estimates on the quantity he thinks he will need over a full year.

a. Based on the results shown in the initial spreadsheet, which supplier do you think CompuTech should select? Why?

b. CompuTech estimates it will need 100,000 chips a year if sales go as expected. But if sales are slow, fewer chips will be needed. This isn't an issue with Supplier 2; its price is the same at any quantity. However, Supplier 1's price per chip will be $3.09 if CompuTech buys less than 90,000 during the year. If CompuTech only needs 80,000 chips, which supplier would be more economical? Why?

c. If the actual purchase quantity will be 80,000 and Supplier 1's price is $3.09, at what price for Supplier 2 is the total cost to CompuTech from either supplier roughly equal? (Hint: You can enter various prices for Supplier 2 in the spreadsheet—or use the What If analysis to vary Supplier 2's price and display the total costs for both vendors.)

For additional questions related to this problem, see Exercise 7–3 in the *Learning Aid for use with Essentials of Marketing,* 6th edition.

8

Elements of Product Planning for Goods and Services

When You Finish This Chapter, You Should

Understand what "Product" really means.

Know the key differences between goods and services.

Know the key differences among the various consumer and business product classes.

Understand how the product classes can help a marketing manager plan marketing strategies.

Understand what branding is and how to use it in strategy planning.

Understand the importance of packaging and warranties in strategy planning.

Understand the important new terms (shown in red).

Most consumers are fickle when it comes to the shampoo they use. When it's time to buy, they just pick up a brand that's conveniently available where they shop. And they usually have lots of choices. Like it or not, this is the situation that marketing managers for Pert Shampoo faced when they were struggling to increase their 2 percent market share.

Trying to get more space on retail shelves didn't work. Retailers saw little reason to give more space to a brand with a small share. In fact, some retailers pushed Pert off their shelves to make more room for shampoos sold under their own brand names.

In spite of all the competition, Pert's marketing managers saw an opportunity. They realized that many consumers wanted to shampoo *and* condition their hair but disliked the hassle of dealing with two bottles. So the firm's research and development people found a way to combine shampoo and conditioner in a single product. But many marketing questions remained to be answered.

A key decision involved the choice of a brand name. The product could be given a new name. However, over the years, the firm had spent a great deal of money promoting the Pert name in the U.S. market. Another approach was to build on the current name and call the product Pert Plus. That too had problems. Top management wanted to be able to use the same brand name in different countries. However, in some countries the Pert Plus name sounded too similar to other products' names, or it violated trademarks.

To get to market quickly, Pert's marketing managers decided to introduce the product in the United States, Canada, and Latin America as Pert Plus. But they used different names when they expanded distribution to other countries: Rejoy in Japan; Rejoice in Singapore, Hong Kong, and mainland Asia; Vidal Sassoon Wash & Go in the United Kingdom and continental Europe; and Pert 2-in-1 in Australia.

Packaging decisions were also important. Most consumers wanted the convenience and safety of plastic packages with flip-top dispensers. But Pert's marketing managers knew it was also important to use recyclable plastic. Further, they wanted the package design to tie into advertising so consumers would quickly recognize the product when they saw it in stores. And they added the number of toll-free telephone service so consumers could call with questions.

Competitors from several countries quickly imitated Pert's 2-in-1 concept—and many consumers are still fickle about shampoo. But more consumers are insisting on Pert Plus when they shop. In fact, it's now the top-selling brand of shampoo in the world. With the growing popularity of Pert and other brands that include conditioner, sales of "shampoo-only" products are declining.[1]

The Pert case highlights some important topics we'll discuss in this chapter and the next. Here we'll start by looking at how customers see a firm's product. Then we'll talk about product classes to help you better understand marketing strategy planning. We'll also talk about branding and packaging. Most goods need some packaging, and both goods and services should be branded. A successful marketer wants to be sure that satisfied customers know what to ask for the next time.

In summary, we'll cover the strategy planning of producers—and middlemen—who make these Product decisions. Keep in mind that there are many decisions related to the Product area as shown in Exhibit 8–1.

WHAT IS A PRODUCT?

Customers buy satisfaction, not parts

When Honda sells an Acura, is it just selling a certain number of nuts and bolts, some sheet metal, an engine, and four wheels? When Sherwin Williams sells a can of exterior paint, is it just selling a can of chemicals? When Air Jamaica sells a ticket for a flight to the Caribbean, is it just selling so much wear and tear on an airplane and so much pilot fatigue?

Exhibit 8–1   Strategy Planning for Product

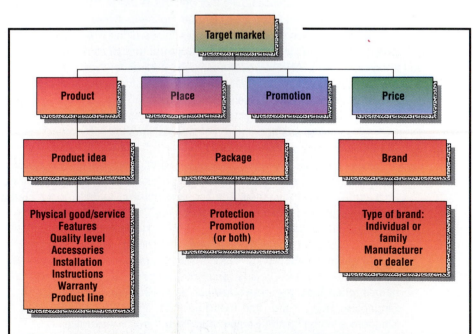

The answer to all these questions is *no*. These companies are really selling the satisfaction, use, or benefit the customer wants.

All customers care about is that their cars look good and keep running. They want to protect their homes with paint—not analyze it. And when they take a trip on Air Jamaica, they don't care how hard it is on the plane or crew. They just want a safe, comfortable trip.

In the same way, when producers and middlemen buy a product, they're interested in the profit they can make from its purchase—through use or resale—not how the product was made.

==Product== means the need-satisfying offering of a firm. ==The idea of Product as potential customer satisfaction or benefits is very important.== Many business managers get wrapped up in the technical details. They think of Product in terms of physical components, like transistors and screws. These are important to *them,* but components have little effect on the way most customers view the product. ==Most customers just want a product that satisfies their needs.== *Can be physical, a service, a person, place, thing, warranty. etc.*

Product quality and customer needs

Product quality should also be determined by how customers view the product. From a marketing perspective, ==quality means a product's ability to satisfy a customer's needs or requirements.== This definition focuses on the customer—and how the customer thinks a product will fit some purpose. For example, the best credit card may not be the one with the highest credit limit but the one that's accepted where a consumer wants to use it. Similarly, the best quality clothing for casual wear on campus may be a pair of jeans—not a pair of dress slacks made of a higher grade fabric.

Among different types of jeans, the one with the strongest stitching and the most comfortable or durable fabric might be thought of as having the highest grade or *relative quality* for its product type. Marketing managers often focus on relative quality when comparing their products to competitors' offerings. However, a product with more features—or even better features—is not a high-quality product if the features aren't what the target market wants or needs.

Quality and satisfaction depend on the total product offering. If potato chips get stale on the shelf because of poor packaging, the consumer will be dissatisfied. A broken button

Because customers buy satisfaction, not just parts, marketing managers must be constantly concerned with the product quality of their goods and services.

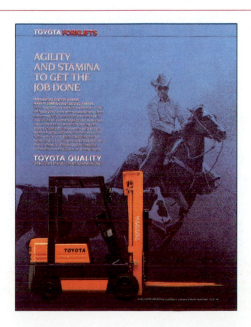

Exhibit 8–2   Examples of Possible Blends of Physical Goods and Services in a Product

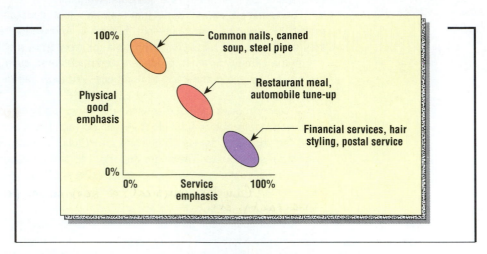

on a shirt will disappoint the customer—even if the laundry did a nice job cleaning and pressing the collar.[2]

Goods and/or services are the product

You already know that a product may be a physical *good* or a *service* or a *blend* of both. You need to understand this view thoroughly. It's too easy to slip into a limited, physical-product point of view. We want to think of a product in terms of the needs it satisfies. If a firm's objective is to satisfy customer needs, service can be part of its product—or service alone may *be* the product—and must be provided as part of a total marketing mix.

Exhibit 8–2 shows this bigger view of Product. It shows that a product can range from a 100 percent emphasis on physical goods—for commodities like common nails—to a 100 percent emphasis on service, like advice from a lawyer. Regardless of the emphasis involved, the marketing manager must consider most of the same elements in planning products and marketing mixes. Given this, we usually won't make a distinction between goods and services but will call all of them *Products*. Sometimes, however, understanding the differences in goods and services can help fine-tune marketing strategy planning. So let's look at some of these differences next.

DIFFERENCES IN GOODS AND SERVICES

How tangible is the Product?

Because a good is a physical thing, it can be seen and touched. You can try on a Benetton shirt, thumb through the latest *People* magazine, smell Colombian coffee as it brews. A good is a *tangible* item. When you buy it, you own it. And it's usually pretty easy to see exactly what you'll get.

On the other hand, a service is a deed performed by one party for another. When you provide a customer with a service, the customer can't keep it. Rather, a service is experienced, used, or consumed. You go see a Touchstone Studios movie, but afterwards all you have is a memory. You ride on a ski lift in the Alps, but you don't own the equipment. Services are not physical—they are *intangible*. You can't hold a service. And it may be hard to know exactly what you'll get when you buy it.

Most products are a combination of tangible and intangible elements. BP gas and the credit card to buy it are tangible—the credit the card grants is not. A McDonald's hamburger is tangible—but the fast service is not.

A good is a physical thing; a service is a deed performed by one party for another.

Is the product produced before it's sold?

Goods are usually produced in a factory and then sold. A Sony TV may be stored in a warehouse or store waiting for a buyer. By contrast, services are often sold first, then produced. And they're produced and consumed in the same time frame. Thus, goods producers may be far away from the customer, but service providers often work in the customer's presence.

Services can't be stored or transported

Services are perishable—they can't be stored. This makes it harder to balance supply and demand. An example explains the problem.

MCI is a major supplier of long-distance telephone services. Even when demand is high—during peak business hours or on Mother's Day—customers expect the service to be available. They don't want to hear "Sorry, all lines are busy." So MCI must have enough equipment and employees to deal with peak demand times. But when customers aren't making many calls, MCI's facilities are idle. MCI might be able to save money with less capacity (equipment and people), but then it will sometimes have to face dissatisfied customers.

It's often difficult to have economies of scale when the product emphasis is on service. Services can't be produced in large, economical quantities and then transported to customers. In addition, *services often have to be produced in the presence of the customer.* So service suppliers often need duplicate equipment and staff at places where the service is actually provided. Merrill Lynch sells investment advice along with financial products worldwide. That advice could, perhaps, be produced more economically in a single building in New York. But Merrill Lynch uses small facilities all over the United States and other countries—to be conveniently available. Customers want a personal touch from the stockbroker telling them how to invest their money.[3]

PRODUCT CLASSES HELP PLAN MARKETING STRATEGIES

You don't have to treat *every* product as unique when planning strategies. Some product classes require similar marketing mixes. These product classes are a useful starting point for developing marketing mixes for new products—and evaluating present mixes. Exhibit 8–3 summarizes the product classes.

Product classes start with type of customer

All products fit into one of two broad groups—based on the type of customer that will use them. **Consumer products** are products meant for the final consumer. **Business**

Exhibit 8–3   Product Classes

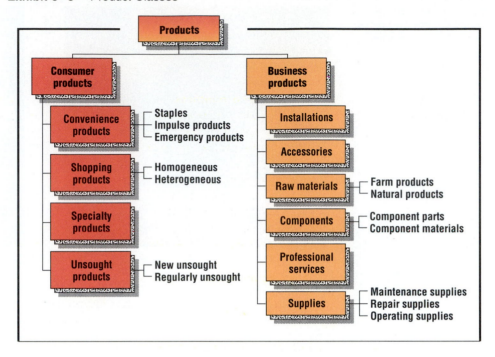

products are products meant for use in producing other products. The same product—like Gatorade—*might* be in both groups. But selling the same product to both final consumers and business customers requires (at least) two different strategies.

There are product classes within each group. Consumer product classes are based on *how consumers think about and shop for products.* Business product classes are based on *how buyers think about products and how they'll be used.*

Gatorade is sold as a consumer product and also as a business product.

CONSUMER PRODUCT CLASSES

Consumer product classes divide into four groups: (1) convenience, (2) shopping, (3) specialty, and (4) unsought. Each class is based on the way people think about and shop for products. See Exhibit 8–4 for a summary of how these product classes relate to typical marketing mixes.[4]

Convenience products—purchased quickly with little effort

Convenience products are products a consumer needs but isn't willing to spend much time or effort shopping for. These products are bought often, require little service or selling, don't cost much, and may even be bought by habit. A convenience product may be a staple, impulse product, or emergency product. *Chewing Gum, Magazines, location more than personal selling.*

Staples—purchased regularly by habit

Bought through Habit

Staples are products that are bought often, routinely, and without much thought—like breakfast cereal, canned soup, and most other packaged foods used almost every day in almost every household. Staples are usually sold in convenient places like food stores, discount stores, or vending machines. Branding is important with staples. It helps customers cut shopping effort and encourages repeat buying of satisfying brands.

Impulse products—bought immediately on sight

location location location

Impulse products are products that are bought quickly—as *unplanned* purchases—because of a strongly felt need. True impulse products are items that the customer hadn't planned to buy, decides to buy on sight, may have bought the same way many times

Exhibit 8–4 Consumer Product Classes and Marketing Mix Planning

Consumer Product Class	Marketing Mix Considerations	Consumer Behavior
Convenience Products		
Staples	Maximum exposure with widespread, low-cost distribution; mass selling by producer; usually low price; branding is important.	Routinized (habitual), low-effort, frequent purchases; low involvement.
Impulse	Widespread distribution with display at point of purchase.	Unplanned purchases bought quickly.
Emergency	Need widespread distribution near probable point of need; price sensitivity low.	Purchase made with time pressure when a need is great.
Shopping Products		
Homogeneous	Need enough exposure to facilitate price comparison; price sensitivity high.	Customers see little difference among alternatives, seek lowest price.
Heterogeneous	Need distribution near similar products; promotion (including personal selling) to highlight product advantages; less price sensitivity.	Extensive problem solving; consumer may need help in making a decision.
Specialty Products	Price sensitivity is likely to be low; limited distribution may be acceptable, but should be treated as a convenience or shopping product (in whichever category product would typically be included) to reach persons not yet sold on its specialty product status.	Willing to expend effort to get specific product, even if not necessary; strong preferences make it an important purchase.
Unsought Products		
New unsought	Must be available in places where similar (or related) products are sought; needs attention getting promotion.	Need for product not strongly felt; unaware of benefits or not yet gone through adoption process.
Regularly unsought	Requires very aggressive promotion, usually personal selling.	Aware of product but not interested; attitude toward product may even be negative.

before, and wants right now. If the buyer doesn't see an impulse product at the right time, the sale may be lost. That's why retailers put candy bars near checkout counters and why life insurance is sold in airports at convenient vending machines.[5]

Emergency products—purchased only when urgently needed

Emergency products are products that are purchased immediately when the need is great. The customer doesn't have time to shop around when a traffic accident occurs, a thunderstorm begins, or an impromptu party starts. The price of the ambulance service, raincoat, or ice cubes won't be important. *Umbrella when its raining. Pricing is not as relevant.*

Shopping products are compared

Usually bought after comparing

Shopping products are products that a customer feels are worth the time and effort to compare with competing products. Shopping products can be divided into two types—depending on what customers are comparing: (1) homogeneous or (2) heterogeneous shopping products.

Homogeneous shopping products—the price must be right

Homogeneous shopping products are shopping products the customer sees as basically the same—and wants at the lowest price. Some consumers feel that certain types of refrigerators, television sets, washing machines, and even cars are very similar. So they just shop for the best price.

Firms may try to emphasize and promote their product differences to avoid head-to-head price competition. For example, Wachovia bank in the Southeast promises customers a "personal banker" who provides information and advice. But if consumers don't think the differences are real or important, they'll just look at price.

Heterogeneous shopping products—the product must be right

Heterogeneous shopping products are shopping products the customer sees as different—and wants to inspect for quality and suitability. Furniture, clothing, dishes, and some cameras are good examples. Often the buyer not only wants—but expects—some kind of help in buying. Quality and style matter more than price.

It's harder—but less important—to compare prices of nonstandardized items. Once the customer has found the right product, price may not matter—as long as it's reasonable. This is also true when service is a major part of the product, as in a visit to a doctor or car repair service.

I don't agree

Branding may be less important for heterogeneous shopping products. The more consumers compare price and quality, the less they rely on brand names or labels. Some retailers carry several brands so consumers won't go to a competitor to compare items.

Specialty products—no substitutes please!

If you are looking for something in part. based on price being lower, that could be a specialty item.

Specialty products are consumer products that the customer really wants—and makes a special effort to find. Shopping for a specialty product doesn't mean comparing—the buyer wants that special product and is willing to search for it. It's the customer's *willingness to search*—not the extent of searching—that makes it a specialty product. Specialty products don't have to be expensive, once-in-a-lifetime purchases. *Any* branded product that consumers insist on by name is a specialty product.

Unsought products—need promotion

Unsought products are products that potential customers don't yet want or know they can buy. So they don't search for them at all. In fact, consumers probably won't buy these products if they see them—unless Promotion can show their value.

There are two types of unsought products. **New unsought products** are products offering really new ideas that potential customers don't know about yet. Informative promotion can help convince customers to accept the product—ending their unsought status. Dannon's Yogurt, Litton's microwave ovens, and Sony's videotape recorders are all popular now, but initially they were new unsought products.

How consumers shop for a product often varies in different countries. In Japan motorists buy oil at an auto supply retailer and then take the four-liter can to be installed. In the United States, the oil and service are usually purchased at the same place.

Regularly unsought products are products—like gravestones, life insurance, and encyclopedias—that stay unsought but not unbought forever. There may be a need, but potential customers aren't motivated to satisfy it. For this kind of product, personal selling is *very* important.

Many nonprofit organizations try to "sell" their unsought products. For example, the Red Cross regularly holds blood drives to remind prospective donors of how important it is to give blood.

One product may be seen several ways

We've been looking at product classes one at a time. But the same product might be seen in different ways by different target markets—at the same time. For example, a product viewed as a staple by most consumers in the United States, Canada, or some similar affluent country might be seen as a heterogeneous shopping product by consumers in another country. The price might be much higher when considered as a proportion of the consumer's budget, and the available choices might be very different. Similarly, a convenient place to shop often means very different things in different countries. In Japan, for example, retail stores tend to be much smaller and carry smaller selections of products.

BUSINESS PRODUCTS ARE DIFFERENT

Business product classes are useful for developing marketing mixes too—since business firms use a system of buying related to these product classes.

Before looking at business product differences, however, we'll note some important similarities that affect marketing strategy planning.

One demand derived from another

The big difference in the business products market is **derived demand**—the demand for business products derive from the demand for final consumer products. For example, car manufacturers buy about one fifth of all steel products. Even a steel company with a good marketing mix will lose sales if demand for cars drops.[6]

Price increases might not reduce quantity purchased

Total *industry* demand for business products is fairly inelastic. To satisfy their customers' needs, business firms buy what they need to produce their own products— almost regardless of price. Even if the cost of buttons doubles, for example, the shirt producer needs them. And the increased cost of the buttons won't have much effect on the price of the shirt—or on the number of shirts consumers demand. But sharp business buyers try to buy as economically as possible. So the demand facing *individual sellers* may be extremely elastic—if similar products are available at a lower price.

Tax treatment affects buying too

How a firm's accountants—and the tax laws—treat a purchase is also important to business customers. An **expense item** is a product whose total cost is treated as a business expense in the year it's purchased. A **capital item** is a long-lasting product that can be used and depreciated for many years. Often it's very expensive. Customers pay for the capital item when they buy it, but for tax purposes the cost is spread over a number of years. This may reduce the cash available for other purchases.

BUSINESS PRODUCT CLASSES—HOW THEY ARE DEFINED

Business product classes are based on how buyers see products—and how the products will be used. The classes of business products are (1) installations, (2) accessories, (3) raw materials, (4) components, (5) supplies, and (6) professional services. Exhibit 8–5 relates these product classes to marketing mix planning.

Installations—a boom-or-bust business

Depreciated over long of life time

Installations—such as buildings, land rights, and major equipment—are important capital items. One-of-a-kind installations—like office buildings and custom-made equipment—generally require special negotiations for each sale. Negotiations often involve top management—and can stretch over months or even years. Standardized equipment may be treated more routinely. But the relative size of a particular purchase can make a difference. A band-saw might be a major purchase for a small cabinet shop—but not for a large furniture manufacturer like Drexel.

Installations are a boom-or-bust business. When sales are high, businesses want to expand capacity rapidly. And if the potential return on an investment in a new installation is very attractive, firms may accept any reasonable price. But during a downswing, buyers have little or no need for new installations, and sales fall off sharply.

Special services may be part of the total product

Suppliers sometimes include special services with an installation at no extra cost. Firms selling (or leasing) equipment to dentists, for example, may install it and help the dentist learn to use it. The service is part of the total product the customer buys.

Accessories—important but short-lived capital items

Depreciated over a shorter amt of time

Accessories are short-lived capital items—tools and equipment used in production or office activities—like Sharp's fax machines, Clark's electric lift trucks, Olivetti's electronic typewriters, and Steelcase's filing cabinets.

Since these products cost less than installations and last a shorter time, multiple buying influence is less important. Operating people and purchasing agents—rather than top managers—may make the purchase decision. As with installations, some customers may wish to lease or rent—to expense the cost.

Accessories are more standardized than installations. And they're usually needed by more customers. For example, IBM sells its robotics systems, which can cost over $1 million, as custom installations to large manufacturers. But IBM's PS/2 desktop computers are accessory equipment for just about every type of modern business all around the world.

Exhibit 8–5   Business Product Classes and Marketing Mix Planning

Business Product Classes	Marketing Mix Considerations	Buying Behavior
Installations	Usually requires skillful personal selling by producer, including technical contacts, and/or understanding of applications; leasing and specialized support services may be required.	Multiple buying influence (including top management) and new-task buying are common; infrequent purchase, long decision period, and boom-or-bust demand are typical.
Accessory Equipment	Need fairly widespread distribution and numerous contacts by experienced and sometimes technically trained personnel; price competition is often intense, but quality is important.	Purchasing and operating personnel typically make decisions; shorter decision period than for installations.
Raw Materials	Grading is important, and transportation and storing can be crucial because of seasonal production and/or perishable products; markets tend to be very competitive.	Long-term contracts may be required to ensure supply.
Component Parts and Materials	Product quality and delivery reliability are usually extremely important; negotiation and technical selling typical on less-standardized items; replacement after market may require different strategies.	Multiple buying influence is common; competitive bids used to encourage competitive pricing.
Maintenance, Repair, and Operating (MRO) Supplies	Typically require widespread distribution or fast delivery (repair items); arrangements with appropriate middlemen may be crucial.	Often handled as straight rebuys, except important operating supplies may be treated much more seriously and involve multiple buying influence.
Professional Services	Services customized to buyer's need; personal selling very important; inelastic demand often supports high prices.	Customer may compare outside service with what internal people could provide; needs may be very specialized.

Raw materials become part of a physical good

Raw materials are unprocessed expense items—such as logs, iron ore, wheat, and cotton—that are moved to the next production process with little handling. Unlike installations and accessories, *raw materials become part of a physical good—and are expense items.*

There are two types of raw materials. **Farm products** are grown by farmers—examples are oranges, wheat, sugar cane, cattle, poultry, eggs, and milk. **Natural products** are products that occur in nature—such as fish and game, timber and maple syrup, and copper, zinc, iron ore, oil, and coal.

The need for grading is one of the important differences between raw materials and other business products. Nature produces what it will—and someone must sort and grade raw materials to satisfy various market segments. Top-graded fruits and vegetables may find their way into the consumer products market. Lower grades—which are treated as business products—are used in juices, sauces, and soups.

Raw materials are usually produced in specific geographic areas. And many raw materials—like oranges and shrimp—are produced seasonally. Yet the demand for raw materials is geographically spread out and fairly constant all year. As a result, storing and transporting are important.

Most buyers of raw materials want ample supplies in the right grades for specific uses—fresh vegetables for Birds Eye's production lines or logs for International Paper's

Procter & Gamble's Flint River plant processes 5,000 tons of wood a day. It is an important raw material for disposable diapers.

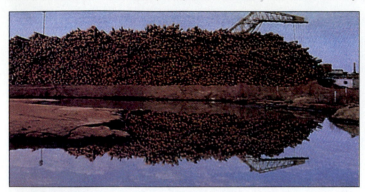

paper mills. To ensure steady quantities, raw materials customers often sign long-term contracts—sometimes at guaranteed prices.

Component parts and materials must meet specifications

Components are processed parts or materials that become part of a finished product. Component *parts* are finished (or nearly finished) items that are ready for assembly into the final product. Disk drives included in personal computers, batteries in cars, and motors for appliances are examples. Component *materials* are items such as wire, paper, textiles, or cement. They have already been processed—but must be processed further before becoming part of the final product. Since components become part of the firm's own product, quality is extremely important.

Some components are custom-made. Much negotiation may be necessary between the engineering staffs of both buyer and seller to arrive at the right specifications. If the price of the item is high—or the item is extremely important to the final product—top managers may be involved. Other standard components are produced in quantity to accepted specifications. Then the buyer may want several dependable sources of supply.

Since component parts go into finished products, a replacement market often develops. This *after market* can be both large and very profitable. Car tires and batteries are two examples of components originally sold in the *OEM* (*original equipment market*) that become consumer products in the after market. The target markets are different—and different marketing mixes are usually necessary.[7]

Supplies—support maintenance, repair, and operations

Supplies are expense items that do not become part of a finished product. Buyers may treat these items less seriously. When a firm cuts its budget, orders for supplies may be the first to go. Supplies can be divided into three types: (1) maintenance, (2) repair, and (3) operating supplies—giving them their common name: MRO supplies.

Operating supplies include lubricating oils and greases, grinding compounds, typing paper, paper clips, coal or electricity, and insurance. If operating supplies are needed regularly—and in large amounts—they receive special treatment. Many companies buy coal and fuel oil in railroad-car quantities; usually there are several sources for such homogeneous products—and large volumes may be purchased in highly competitive international markets.

Maintenance supplies include products such as paint, light bulbs, and sweeping compounds. Maintenance and small operating supplies are like convenience products. An item will be ordered because it is needed—but a buyer won't spend much time worrying about it. Branding can be important for these "nuisance" purchases because it makes

Business customers often compare the cost of purchasing professional services with the cost of doing the work themselves.

buying easier. Breadth of assortment and the seller's dependability are also important. Middlemen usually handle the many supply items.

Repair supplies are parts—like filters, bearings, and gears—needed to fix worn or broken equipment. The original supplier of installations or accessory equipment may be the only source for repair needs. But compared to the cost of a production breakdown, the cost of repairs may be so small that buyers are willing to pay whatever the supplier charges.[8]

Professional services—pay to get it done

Professional services are specialized services that support a firm's operations. They are usually expense items. Engineering or management consulting services can improve the plant layout—or the company's efficiency. Computer services can process data. Design services can supply designs for a physical plant, products, and promotion materials. Advertising agencies can help promote the firm's products—and food services can improve morale.

Here the *service* part of the product is emphasized. Goods may be supplied—as coffee and donuts are with food service—but the customer is primarily interested in the service.

Managers compare the cost of buying professional services outside the firm to the cost of having company people do them. For special skills needed only occasionally, an outsider can be the best source. And the number of service specialists is growing in our complex economy.

BRANDING NEEDS A STRATEGY DECISION TOO

There are so many brands—and we're so used to seeing them—that we take them for granted. Yet branding is an important decision area, so we will treat it in some detail.

What is branding, brand name, and trademark?

Branding means the use of a name, term, symbol, or design—or a combination of these—to identify a product. It includes the use of brand names, trademarks, and practically all other means of product identification.

word
symbol
mark
legally
registered by one comp.
for use

Exhibit 8–6   Recognized Trademarks and Symbols Help in Promotion

 Brand name has a narrower meaning. A **brand name** is a word, letter, or a group of words or letters. Examples include Blockbuster Video, WD-40, 3M Post-its, and IBM PS/2 computers.

Trademark is a legal term. A **trademark** includes only those words, symbols, or marks that are legally registered for use by a single company. A **service mark** is the same as a trademark except that it refers to a service offering.

The word *Buick* can be used to explain these differences. The Buick car is branded under the brand name Buick (whether it's spoken or printed in any manner). When *Buick* is printed in a certain kind of script, however, it becomes a trademark. A trademark need not be attached to the product. It need not even be a word—it can be a symbol. Exhibit 8–6 shows some common trademarks.

These differences may seem technical. But they are very important to business firms that spend a lot of money to protect and promote their brands.

Branding meets needs

Well-recognized brands make shopping easier. Think of trying to buy groceries, for example, if you had to evaluate the advantages and disadvantages of each of 20,000 items every time you went to a supermarket. Many customers are willing to buy new things—but having gambled and won, they like to buy a sure thing the next time.

Brand promotion has advantages for branders as well as for customers. A good brand reduces the marketer's selling time and effort. And sometimes a firm's brand name is the only element in its marketing mix that a competitor can't copy.

CONDITIONS FAVORABLE TO BRANDING

The following conditions are favorable to successful branding:

1. The product is easy to identify by brand or trademark.
2. The product quality is the best value for the price. And the quality is easy to maintain.
3. Dependable and widespread availability is possible.
4. The demand for the general product class is large.
5. The market price can be high enough to make the branding effort profitable.

Encourages Repeat Buying More $ Economies of Scale

6. There are economies of scale. If the branding is really successful, costs should drop and profits should increase.

7. Favorable shelf locations or display space in stores is available.

In general, these conditions are not as common in less-developed economies, and that may explain why efforts to build brands in less-developed nations often fail.

ACHIEVING BRAND FAMILIARITY IS NOT EASY

The earliest and most aggressive brand promoters in America were the patent medicine companies. They were joined by the food manufacturers, who grew in size after the Civil War. Some of the brands started in the 1860s and 1870s (and still going strong) are Borden's Condensed Milk, Quaker Oats, Pillsbury's Best Flour, and Ivory Soap. Today, familiar brands exist for most product categories, ranging from crayons (Crayola) to real estate services (Century 21). However, familiar brands often vary from one country to another.

Brand acceptance must be earned with a good product and regular promotion. **Brand familiarity** means how well customers recognize and accept a company's brand. The degree of brand familiarity affects the planning for the rest of the marketing mix—especially where the product should be offered and what promotion is needed.

Five levels of brand familiarity

Five levels of brand familiarity are useful for strategy planning: (1) rejection, (2) nonrecognition, (3) recognition, (4) preference, and (5) insistence.

⑤ Some brands have been tried and found wanting. **Brand rejection** means that potential customers won't buy a brand unless its image is changed. Rejection may require a change in the product—or perhaps a shift to target customers who have a better image of the brand. Overcoming a negative image is difficult—and can be very expensive.

Brand rejection is a big concern for service-oriented businesses because it's hard to keep consistent quality. A business traveler who gets a dirty room in a Hilton Hotel in Caracas, Venezuela, might not return to any Hilton anywhere. Yet it's difficult for Hilton to ensure that every maid does a good job every time.

④ Some products are seen as basically the same. **Brand nonrecognition** means final consumers don't recognize a brand at all—even though middlemen may use the brand name for identification and inventory control. Examples include school supplies, bed frames, and inexpensive dinnerware.

③ **Brand recognition** means that customers remember the brand. This can be a big advantage if there are many "nothing" brands on the market. Even if consumers can't recall the brand without help, they may be reminded when they see it in a store among other less familiar brands.

② Most branders would like to win **brand preference**—which means that target customers usually choose the brand over other brands, perhaps because of habit or favorable past experience.

① **Brand insistence** means customers insist on a firm's branded product and are willing to search for it. This is an objective of many target marketers. Here the firm may enjoy a very inelastic demand curve.

STRENGTH OF LOYALTY

The right brand name can help

A good brand name can help build brand familiarity. It can help tell something important about the company or its product. Exhibit 8–7 lists some characteristics of a good brand name. Some successful brand names seem to break all these rules, but many of them got started when there was less competition.

Exhibit 8−7   Characteristics of a Good Brand Name

- Short and simple
- Easy to spell and read
- Easy to recognize and remember
- Easy to pronounce
- Can be pronounced in only one way
- Can be pronounced in all languages (for international markets)

- Suggestive of product benefits
- Adaptable to packaging/labeling needs
- Not offensive, obscene, or negative
- Always timely (does not get out of date)
- Adaptable to any advertising medium
- Legally available for use (not in use by another firm)

Companies that compete in international markets face a special problem in selecting brand names. A name that conveys a positive image in one language may be meaningless in another. Or, worse, it may have unintended meanings. This can happen even when different countries use a common language. For example, the brand name for Snickers candy bars was changed to Marathon when they were first introduced in England. Marketing managers were concerned that Snickers sounded too much like knickers, a British term for women's underwear.[9]

A respected name builds brand equity

Because it's difficult and expensive to build brand familiarity, some firms prefer to buy established brands rather than try to build their own. The value of a brand to its current owner or to a firm that wants to buy it is sometimes called **brand equity**—the value of a brand's overall strength in the market. For example, brand equity is likely to be higher if many satisfied customers insist on buying the brand and if middlemen are eager to stock it. That almost guarantees ongoing profits from the brand.

Hellmann's would like Chilean consumers to insist on the Hellmann's brand when they want mayonnaise to go with avocado and other vegetables. This headline asks "Avocado Mayo?"—and then describes Hellmann's as the "real one."

PROTECTING BRAND NAMES AND TRADEMARKS

U.S. common law and civil law protect the rights of trademark and brand name owners. The Lanham Act of 1946 spells out what kinds of marks (including brand names) can be protected and the exact method of protecting them. The law applies to goods shipped in interstate or foreign commerce.

The Lanham Act does not force registration. But registering under the Lanham Act is often a first step toward protecting a trademark to be used in international markets. That's because some nations require that a trademark be registered in its home country before they will register or protect it.

You must protect your own

A brand can be a real asset to a company. Each firm should try to see that its brand doesn't become a common descriptive term for its kind of product. When this happens, the brand name or trademark becomes public property—and the owner loses all rights to it. This happened with the names cellophane, aspirin, shredded wheat, and kerosene.[10]

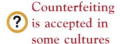 **Counterfeiting is accepted in some cultures**

Even when products are properly registered, counterfeiters may make unauthorized copies. Many well-known brands—ranging from Levi jeans to Rolex watches to Zantax ulcer medicine—face this problem. Unfortunately, counterfeiting is big business in some countries, especially developing nations, so efforts to stop it may meet with limited success.[11]

WHAT KIND OF BRAND TO USE?

Keep it in the family

Branders of more than one product must decide whether they are going to use a **family brand**—the same brand name for several products—or individual brands for each product. Examples of family brands are Keebler snack food products and Sears' Craftsman tools and Kenmore appliances. *Kraft*

The use of the same brand for many products makes sense if all are similar in type and quality. The main benefit is that the goodwill attached to one or two products may help the others. Money spent to promote the brand name benefits more than one product—which cuts promotion costs for each product.

Family brands can also speed acceptance of new products. For example, many consumers quickly tried Snickers Ice Cream Bars when they were introduced because they already liked Snickers candy bars. From a financial perspective, the money spent over the years to promote the candy bar paid off again when consumers tried the ice cream bar. The majority of new products introduced in recent years followed the approach of extending a successful brand name.[12]

A special kind of family brand is a **licensed brand**—a well-known brand that sellers pay a fee to use. For example, the familiar Sunkist brand name is owned by Sunkist Growers, a farmers' cooperative. But the Sunkist brand name has been licensed to many companies for use on more than 400 products in 30 countries.[13]

Individual brands for outside and inside competition

A company uses **individual brands**—separate brand names for each product—when it's important for each product to have a separate identity, as when products vary in quality or type.

If the products are really different, such as Elmer's glue and Borden's ice cream, individual brands can avoid confusion. Some firms use individual brands with similar products to make segmentation and positioning efforts easier. Unilever, for example, markets Aim, Close-Up, and Pepsodent toothpastes, but each involves different positioning efforts.

Procter & Gamble often uses individual brand names; the brand name and product may be changed for international markets.

Sometimes firms use individual brands to encourage competition within the company. Each brand is managed by a different group within the firm. The theory is that if anyone is going to take business away from their firm, it ought to be their own brand. However, many firms that once used this approach have reorganized. Faced with slower market growth, they found they had plenty of competitive pressure from other firms. The internal competition just made it more difficult to coordinate different marketing strategies.[14]

Generic "brands"

Products that some consumers see as commodities may be difficult or expensive to brand. Some manufacturers and middlemen responded to this problem with **generic products**—products that have no brand at all other than identification of their contents and the manufacturer or middleman. Generic products are usually offered in plain packages at lower prices.

A decade ago, some target markets in the United States were interested in buying generic products. But price cuts by branded competitors narrowed the price gap—and won back many customers. Now generics account for only about 1.5 percent of grocery store sales. However, generics still capture significant market share in a few product categories. And they are quite common in less-developed nations.[15]

WHO SHOULD DO THE BRANDING?

Manufacturer brands versus dealer brands

Manufacturer brands are brands created by manufacturers. These are sometimes called "national brands" because the brand is promoted all across the country or in large regions. Note, however, that many manufacturer brands are now distributed globally. Such brands include Kellogg's, Stokely, Whirlpool, Ford, and IBM. Many creators of service-oriented firms—like McDonald's, Orkin Pest Control, and Midas Muffler—promote their brands this way too.

Dealer brands, also called **private brands**, are brands created by middlemen. Examples of dealer brands include the brands of Kroger, Ace Hardware, and Sears. Some of these are advertised and distributed more widely than many national brands.

Who's winning the battle of the brands?

[handwritten: Retailers make more money off dealer brands.]

The **battle of the brands**, the competition between dealer brands and manufacturer brands, is just a question of whose brands will be more popular—and who will be in control.

At one time, manufacturer brands were much more popular than dealer brands. Now sales of both kinds of brands are about equal. But middlemen have some advantages in this battle, and sales of dealer brands are expected to continue growing. With the number of large wholesalers and retail chains increasing, middlemen are better able to arrange reliable sources of supply at low cost. They can also control the point of sale and give their dealer brands special shelf position or promotion.

Consumers benefit from the battle. Competition has already narrowed price differences between manufacturer brands and well-known dealer brands.[16]

THE STRATEGIC IMPORTANCE OF PACKAGING

[handwritten: Generic Brands]

Packaging involves promoting and protecting the product. Packaging can be important to both sellers and customers. Packaging can make a product more convenient to use or store. It can prevent spoiling, tampering, or damage. Good packaging makes products easier to identify and promotes the brand at the point of purchase and even in use.

Packaging can make the difference

A new package can make *the* important difference in a new marketing strategy—by meeting customers' needs better. A better box, wrapper, can, or bottle may help create a "new" product—or a new market. For example, Quaker State oil changed to a twist-off top and pouring spout to make it more convenient for customers of self-service gas stations.

A firm's commitment to recycling is an important packaging issue.

[handwritten notes: Sugar 100 lb bag .01 cost for the bag; 5 lb bag .25 cost for the bag; mini packs .50 cost for envelopes; 1983 $50 billion spent on packaging]

Is your favorite brand packaged for generations to come?

We're looking towards the future.
The environment is part of the future our children will inherit for years to come. And as the makers of Wisk,* Surf,* all,* Snuggle,* Final Touch,* and Sunlight,* we at Lever are taking steps so the plastic in our bottles can be used over and over again.

Now you can enjoy the benefits and convenience of our plastic bottles knowing they can find new life far from landfills.

We're using recycled plastic.
New recycling technology now allows us to include 25% to 35% recycled plastic in many of our bottles of Wisk and "all"

laundry detergents, as well as Snuggle and Final Touch fabric softeners. Through this effort, we will save the equivalent of 50 million plastic bottles a year from going into landfills.

We need your help.
Turning used plastic into new plastic bottles makes a whole lot of sense and a lot less waste. So that all our bottles can help, we've coded them for easy identification and sorting.

But we need more recycled plastic. That's why we've printed an important message on our bottles asking you to support recycling in your community. Because the more plastic collected, the higher levels of recycled plastic we'll be able to use. And that's plastic that won't go to waste.

Together, we can help reshape the future.

LEVER
Shared World,
Shared Responsibility.

© 1990 Lever Brothers Company

Packaging sends a message—even for services

Packaging can tie the product to the rest of the marketing strategy. A good package sometimes gives a firm more promotion effect than it could possibly afford with advertising. Customers see the package in stores—when they're actually buying. Packaging for Eveready batteries features the pink bunny seen in attention-getting TV ads—and reminds consumers that the batteries are durable. Expensive perfume may come in a crystal bottle, adding to the prestige image.[17]

Some firms try to "package" their services so that there is a tangible reminder of the product. For example, the American Express Gold Card sends a signal that is understood worldwide. Disney sends the message that its parks are a good place for family vacations by keeping them spotless.

Packaging may lower distribution costs

Better protective packaging is very important to manufacturers and wholesalers. They often have to pay the cost of goods damaged in shipment, and goods damaged in shipment may also delay production—or cause lost sales.

Retailers need good packaging too. Protective packaging can reduce storing costs by cutting breakage, spoilage, and theft. Packages that are easier to handle can cut costs by speeding price marking, improving handling and display, and saving space.

Universal product codes speed handling

To speed handling of fast-selling products, government and industry representatives developed a **universal product code (UPC)** that identifies each package with marks readable by electronic scanners. A computer then matches each code to the product and its price. Supermarkets and other high-volume retailers are eager to use these codes. They speed the checkout process and reduce the need to mark the price on every item. They also reduce errors by cashiers—and make it easy to control inventory and track sales of specific products. Exhibit 8–8 shows a universal product code mark.[18]

Exhibit 8–8
An Illustration of a Universal Product Code

WHAT IS SOCIALLY RESPONSIBLE PACKAGING?

Laws reduce confusion—and clutter

In the United States, consumer criticism finally led to the passage of the **Federal Fair Packaging and Labeling Act** (of 1966)—which requires that consumer goods be clearly labeled in easy-to-understand terms—to give consumers more information. The law also calls on industry to try to reduce the number of package sizes and make labels more useful. And food products must now show nutrition information as well as weight and volume.

Current laws also offer more guidance on environmental issues. Some states require a consumer to pay a deposit on bottles and cans until they're returned. These laws mean well, but they can cause problems. Channels of distribution are usually set up to distribute products, not return empty packages.[19]

? Ethical decisions remain

Although various laws provide guidance on many packaging issues, many areas still require marketing managers to make ethical choices. For example, some firms design packages that conceal a downsized product, giving consumers less for their money. Similarly, some retailers design packages and labels for their private-label products that look just like—and are easily confused with—manufacturer brands. Are efforts such as these unethical, or are they simply an attempt to make packaging a more effective part of a marketing mix? Different people have different views.

Some marketing managers promote environmentally friendly packaging on some products, but use problematic packages on others. Empty packages now litter our streets, and some plastic packages will lie in a city dump for decades. Yet some consumers like the convenience of such packaging. Is it unethical for a marketing manager to give consumers with different preferences a choice? Some critics argue that it is; others praise firms that give consumers a choice.

Many critics feel that labeling information is too often incomplete or misleading. Do consumers really understand the nutritional information required by new laws? Further, some consumers want information that is difficult—perhaps even impossible—to provide. For example, how can a label accurately describe a product's taste or texture? But the ethical issues usually focus on how far a marketing manager should go in putting potentially negative information on a package. For example, should Häagen-Dazs affix a label that says "this product will clog your arteries"? That sounds extreme, but what type of information *is* appropriate?[20]

Unit-pricing is a possible help

Some retailers—especially large supermarket chains—make it easier for consumers to compare packages with different weights or volumes. They use **unit-pricing**—which involves placing the price per ounce (or some other standard measure) on or near the product. This makes price comparison easier.[21]

WARRANTIES ARE IMPORTANT TOO

Warranty should mean something

U.S. common law says that producers must stand behind their products. The federal **Magnuson-Moss Act** (of 1975) says that producers must provide a clearly written warranty if they choose to offer any warranty. A **warranty** explains what the seller promises about its product. The warranty does not have to be strong. In fact, a written warranty can *reduce* the responsibility a producer would have under common law.

In a competitive market, a product warranty is often a very important part of the marketing mix.

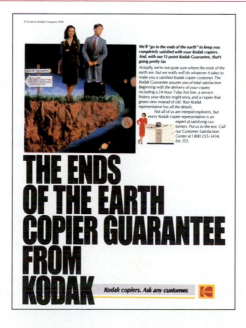

FIRMS GUARANTEE MORE THAN SERVICE WITH A SMILE

It wasn't long ago that companies talked about offering "service with a smile." Often, however, the service wasn't very good, and you didn't get the smile either. Now a number of service companies are putting teeth in their promises by offering customer service guarantees. Pizza Hut guarantees a luncheon pizza in five minutes or it's free. The Hampton Inn motel chain guarantees "100% satisfaction," and if someone fails to provide it the customer gets a discount or refund on the spot. General Motors set up a fast-oil-change guarantee to compete with fast-lube specialists who were taking customers away from dealers. If the dealer doesn't get the job done in 29 minutes or less, the next oil change is free. Delta Dental, an insurance company, has a guarantee that includes one month's free premium if it doesn't provide a new customer with a smooth transition from a previous insurer.

There may be more risk in offering a service guarantee than a guarantee on a physical product. A careless employee or a service breakdown can create a big expense. However, without the guarantee, dissatisfied customers may just go away mad without ever complaining. When customers collect on a guarantee, the company can address the problem so it doesn't happen again to other customers.

A service guarantee is most likely to draw customers when a firm's service quality surpasses the competition. To achieve that objective, more service firms are training employees and giving them the authority to do whatever it takes to make a customer happy. Then employees take greater responsibility to make certain that each customer's "service encounter" goes smoothly in the first place.[22]

Federal Trade Commission (FTC) guidelines try to ensure that warranties are clear and definite—and not deceptive or unfair. Some firms used to say their products were fully warranted or absolutely guaranteed. However, they didn't state the time period or spell out the meaning of the warranty. Now a company has to make clear whether it's offering a full or limited warranty—and the law defines what *full* means. Also, the warranty must be available for inspection before the purchase. Most firms offer a limited warranty—if they offer one at all.

Some firms use warranties to help create different strategies. They design more quality into their goods or services and offer refunds or replacement—not just repair—if there is a problem. In other cases, the basic price for a product may include a warranty that covers a short time period or that covers parts but not labor. Consumers who want more or better protection pay extra for an extended warranty or a service contract.

Deciding on warranty policies is part of strategy planning. Specific decisions should be made about what the warranty will cover—and then the warranty should be communicated clearly to target customers. A warranty can make the difference between success and failure for a whole marketing strategy.[23]

CONCLUSION

In this chapter, we looked at Product very broadly. A product may not be a physical good at all. It may be a service, or it may be some combination of goods and services—like a meal at a restaurant. Most important, we saw that a firm's Product is *what satisfies the needs of its target market.*

We introduced consumer product and business product classes and showed their effect on planning marketing mixes. Consumer product classes are based on consumers' buying behavior. Business product classes are based on how buyers see the products and how they are used. Knowing these product classes—and learning how marketers handle specific products within these classes—will help you develop your marketing sense.

The fact that different people may see the same product in different product classes helps explain why seeming competitors may succeed with very different marketing mixes.

Branding and packaging can create new and more satisfying products. Packaging offers special opportunities to promote the product and inform customers. Variations in packaging can make a product attractive to different target markets. A specific package may have to be developed for each strategy.

Customers see brands as a guarantee of quality, and this leads to repeat purchasing. For marketers, such routine buying means lower promotion costs and higher sales.

Should companies stress branding? The decision depends on whether the costs of brand promotion and honoring the brand guarantee can be more than covered by a higher price or more rapid turnover—or both. The cost of branding may reduce pressure on the other three Ps.

Branding gives marketing managers a choice. They can add brands and use individual or family brands. In the end, however, customers express their approval or disapproval of the whole Product (including the brand). The degree of brand familiarity is a measure of the marketing manager's ability to carve out a separate market. And brand familiarity affects Place, Price, and Promotion decisions.

Warranties are also important in strategy planning. A warranty need not be strong—it just has to be clearly stated. But some customers find strong warranties attractive.

Product is concerned with much more than physical goods and service. To succeed in our increasingly competitive markets, the marketing manager must also be concerned about packaging, branding, and warranties.

QUESTIONS AND PROBLEMS

1. Define, in your own words, what a Product is.

2. Discuss several ways in which physical goods are different from pure services. Give an example of a good and a service that illustrates each of the differences.

3. What products are being offered by a shop that specializes in bicycles? By a travel agent? By a supermarket? By a new car dealer?

4. What kinds of consumer products are the following: (*a*) watches, (*b*) automobiles, (*c*) toothpastes? Explain your reasoning.

5. Consumer services tend to be intangible, and goods tend to be tangible. Use an example to explain how the lack of a physical good in a pure service might affect efforts to promote the service.

6. How would the marketing mix for a staple convenience product differ from the one for a homogeneous shopping product? How would the mix for a specialty product differ from the mix for a heterogeneous shopping product? Use examples.

7. Give an example of a product that is a *new* unsought product for most people. Briefly explain why it is an unsought product.

8. In what types of stores would you expect to find: (*a*) convenience products, (*b*) shopping products, (*c*) specialty products, and (*d*) unsought products?

9. Cite two examples of business products that require a substantial amount of service in order to be useful.

10. Explain why a new law office might want to lease furniture rather than buy it.

11. Would you expect to find any wholesalers selling the various types of business products? Are retail stores required (or something like retail stores)?

12. What kinds of business products are the following: (*a*) lubricating oil, (*b*) electric motors, (*c*) a firm that provides landscaping and grass mowing for an apartment complex? Explain your reasoning.

13. How do raw materials differ from other business products? Do the differences have any impact on their marketing mixes? If so, what specifically?

14. For the kinds of business products described in this chapter, complete the following table (use one or a few well-chosen words).

Products	1	2	3
Installations			
Buildings and land rights			
Major equipment			
Standard			
Custom-made			
Accessories			
Raw materials			
Farm products			
Natural products			
Components			
Supplies			
Maintenance and small operating supplies			
Operating supplies			
Professional services			

1. *Kind of distribution facility(ies) needed and functions provided.*
2. *Caliber of salespeople required.*
3. *Kind of advertising required.*

15. Is there any difference between a brand name and a trademark? If so, why is this difference important?

16. Is a well-known brand valuable only to the owner of the brand?

17. Suggest an example of a product and a competitive situation where it would *not* be profitable for a firm to spend large sums of money to establish a brand.

18. List five brand names and indicate what product is associated with the brand name. Evaluate the strengths and weaknesses of the brand name.

19. Explain family brands. Should Toys "R" Us develop its own dealer brands to compete with some of the popular manufacturer brands it carries? Explain your reasons.

20. In the past Sears emphasized its own dealer brands. Now it carries more well-known manufacturer brands. What are the benefits to Sears of carrying more manufacturer brands?

21. What does the degree of brand familiarity imply about previous and future promotion efforts? How does the degree of brand familiarity affect the Place and Price variables?

22. You operate a small hardware store with emphasis on manufacturer brands and are barely breaking even. Evaluate the proposal of a large wholesaler who offers a full line of dealer-branded hardware items at substantially lower prices. Specify any assumptions necessary to obtain a definite answer.

23. Give an example where packaging costs probably (*a*) lower total distribution costs and (*b*) raise total distribution costs.

24. Is it more difficult to support a warranty for a service than for a physical good? Explain your reasons.

SUGGESTED CASES

1. McDonald's "Seniors" Restaurant
13. Fileco, Inc.

30. Metro Medical, Inc.

COMPUTER-AIDED PROBLEM

8. Branding Decision

Wholesteen Dairy, Inc., produces and sells Wholesteen brand condensed milk to grocery retailers. The overall market for condensed milk is fairly flat, and there's sharp competition among dairies for retailers' business. Wholesteen's regular price to retailers is $9.62 a case (24 cans). FoodWorld—a fast-growing supermarket chain and Wholesteen's largest customer—buys 20,000 cases of Wholesteen's condensed milk a year. That's 20 percent of Wholesteen's total sales volume of 100,000 cases per year.

FoodWorld is proposing that Wholesteen produce private-label condensed milk to be sold with the FoodWorld brand name. FoodWorld proposes to buy the same total quantity as it does now, but it wants half (10,000 cases) with the Wholesteen brand and half with the FoodWorld brand. FoodWorld wants its brand in cans that cost $.01 less than Wholesteen pays for a can now. But FoodWorld will provide preprinted labels with its brand name—which will save Wholesteen an additional $0.02 a can.

Wholesteen spends $90,000 a year on promotion to increase familiarity with the Wholesteen brand. In addition, Wholesteen gives retailers an allowance of $.30 per case for their local advertising, which features the Wholesteen brand. FoodWorld agrees to give up the advertising allowance for its own brand but is only willing to pay $7.94 a case for the milk that will be sold with the FoodWorld brand name. It will continue under the old terms for the rest of its purchases.

Sue Glick, Wholesteen's marketing manager, is considering the FoodWorld proposal. She enters cost and revenue data on a spreadsheet—so she can see more clearly how the proposal might affect revenue and profits.

a. Based on the data in the initial spreadsheet, how will Wholesteen profits be affected if Glick accepts the FoodWorld proposal?

b. Glick is worried that FoodWorld will find another producer for the FoodWorld private label milk if Wholesteen rejects the proposal. This would immediately reduce Wholesteen's annual sales by 10,000 cases.

FoodWorld might even stop buying from Wholesteen altogether. What would happen to profits in these two situations?

c. FoodWorld is growing rapidly—opening one new store each week—and the FoodWorld buyer says that next year's purchases could be 40 percent higher. That might mean a contract for 28,000 cases of Wholesteen's condensed milk. But the Wholesteen manager knows that FoodWorld may stop buying the Wholesteen brand and want all 28,000 cases to carry the FoodWorld private label brand. How will this affect profit? (Hint: Enter the new quantities in the "proposal" column of the spreadsheet.)

d. What should Wholesteen do? Why?

For additional questions related to this problem, see Exercise 8–5 in the *Learning Aid for use with Essentials of Marketing,* 6th edition.

Handwritten notes:

Product Line

		Product Line	
Tide	Gleem	Head + Shoulders ← Product	
Cheer	Crest	Prell	
Duz		Pert	
GAIN			

\# of items in a line = depth

\# of product lines = width

Taxonomy for Goods
   Consumer Goods - based on buying behavior of the consumer to establish strategies.

Chapter

Product Management and New-Product Development

When You Finish This Chapter, You Should

❶
Understand how product life cycles affect strategy planning.

❷
Know what is involved in designing new products and what new products really are.

❸
Understand the new-product development process.

❹
See why safety and product liability must be considered in screening new products.

❺
Understand the need for product or brand managers.

❻
Understand the important new terms (shown in red).

For decades, most companies placed cardboard inserts in shipping cartons to reduce damage. But cardboard didn't protect delicate items very well. Sealed-Air Corporation took business away from cardboard producers when it introduced plastic sheets with built-in air bubbles for cushioning. Although many firms still package their products with air-bubble protection, cheaper polystyrene packing "peanuts" took business away from Sealed-Air. The pellets flow easily around irregularly shaped items—which means they're easier to use. Now, however, the growing use of styrene pellets is prompting many firms to look for more ecologically acceptable products. To meet this need, Storopack, a German firm, developed Renature, the first "flowable" cushioning product that is 100 percent biodegradable. In fact, Renature is made from natural starches found in potatoes—a renewable resource. Sales of Renature (and similar products that competitors are likely to develop) should grow rapidly and replace styrene in thousands of packaging applications.

This life and death cycle is being repeated over and over again in product-markets worldwide. Sales of home movie cameras, lighting systems, projectors, screens, and 8-mm film have all but disappeared as consumers switch to convenient hand-held camcorders. Cassette tapes replaced vinyl records, and now they are, in turn, being replaced by CDs and digital audio tape. Switchboard operators in many firms were replaced with answering machines, and now answering machines are losing ground as phone companies offer new voice mail services.[1]

These innovations show that products, markets, and competition change over time. This makes marketing management an exciting challenge. Developing new products and managing existing products to meet changing conditions is important to the success of every firm. In this chapter, we will look at some important ideas in these areas.

MANAGING PRODUCTS OVER THEIR LIFE CYCLES

Product life cycle has four major stages

Products—like consumers—go through life cycles. The **product life cycle** describes the stages a new product idea goes through from beginning to end. The product life cycle is divided into four major stages: (1) market introduction, (2) market growth, (3) market maturity, and (4) sales decline.

A particular firm's marketing mix usually must change during the product life cycle. There are several reasons why. Customers' attitudes and needs may change over the product life cycle. The product may be aimed at entirely different target markets at different stages. And the nature of competition moves toward pure competition or oligopoly.

Further, total sales of the product—by all competitors in the industry—vary in each of its four stages. They move from very low in the market introduction stage to high at market maturity and then back to low in the sales decline stage. More important, the profit picture changes too. These general relationships can be seen in Exhibit 9–1. Note that sales and profits do not move together over time. *Industry profits decline while industry sales are still rising.*[2]

Market introduction— investing in the future

In the **market introduction** stage, sales are low as a new idea is first introduced to a market. Customers aren't looking for the product. They don't even know about it. Informative promotion is needed to tell potential customers about the advantages and uses of the new product concept.

Even though a firm promotes its new product, it takes time for customers to learn that the product is available. Most companies experience losses during the introduction stage because they spend so much money for Promotion, Product, and Place development. They invest the money in the hope of future profits.

Market growth—profits go up and down

In the **market growth** stage, industry sales grow fast—but industry profits rise and then start falling. The innovator begins to make big profits as more and more customers buy. But competitors see the opportunity and enter the market. Some just copy the most successful product or try to improve it to compete better. Others try to refine their offerings to do a better job of appealing to some target markets. The new entries result in much product variety.

This is the time of biggest profits *for the industry. But it is also when industry profits begin to decline* as competition increases. See Exhibit 9–1.

Exhibit 9–1   Life Cycle of a Typical Product

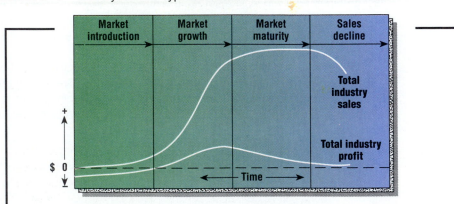

Sony's portable CD-ROM and Grid's pen computer need informative promotion during the market introduction stage of the product life cycle—so customers know about their benefits and uses.

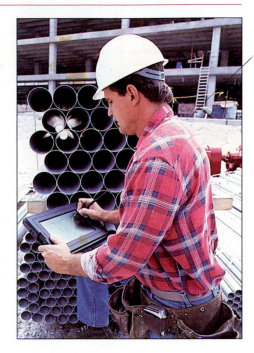

Some firms make big strategy-planning mistakes at this stage by not understanding the product life cycle. They see the big sales and profit opportunities of the early market growth stage but ignore the competition that will soon follow. When they realize their mistake, it may be too late.

Market maturity— sales level off, profits continue down

The **market maturity** stage occurs when industry sales level off—and competition gets tougher. Many aggressive competitors have entered the race for profits—except in oligopoly situations. Industry profits go down throughout the market maturity stage because promotion costs rise and some competitors cut prices to attract business. Less efficient firms that can't compete with this pressure drop out of the market.

New firms may still enter the market at this stage—increasing competition even more. Note that late entries skip the early life-cycle stages, including the profitable market growth stage. And they must try to take a share of the saturated market from established firms, which is difficult and expensive.

Persuasive promotion becomes more important during the market maturity stage. Products may differ only slightly if at all. Most competitors have discovered the most effective appeals—or copied the leaders. The various brands become almost the same in the minds of potential consumers.

In the United States, the markets for most cars, boats, television sets, and many household appliances are in market maturity.[3] This stage may continue for many years—until a basically new product idea comes along—even though individual brands or models come and go.

Sales decline—a time of replacement

During the **sales decline** stage, new products replace the old. Price competition from dying products becomes more vigorous—but firms that successfully differentiated their products may make profits until the end. They may keep some sales by appealing to loyal customers or those who are slow to try new ideas. These buyers might switch later—smoothing the sales decline.

PRODUCT LIFE CYCLES SHOULD BE RELATED TO SPECIFIC MARKETS

Remember that product life cycles describe industry sales and profits for a *product idea* within a particular product-market. The sales and profits of an individual product or brand may not—and often do not—follow the life-cycle pattern. They may vary up and down throughout the life cycle—sometimes moving in the opposite direction of industry sales and profits. Further, a product idea may be in a different life-cycle stage in different markets.

Individual brands may not follow the pattern

A given firm may introduce or withdraw a specific product during any stage of the product life cycle. A me-too brand introduced during the market growth stage, for example, may never get any sales at all and suffer a quick death. Or it may reach its peak and start to decline even before the market maturity stage begins. Market leaders may enjoy high profits during the market maturity stage—even though industry profits are declining. Sometimes the innovator brand loses so much in the introduction stage that it has to drop out just as others are reaping big profits in the growth stage.

Strategy planners who naively expect sales of an individual product to follow the general product life-cycle pattern are likely to be rudely surprised. In fact, it might be more sensible to think in terms of "product-market life cycles" rather than product life cycles—but we will use the term *product life cycle* because it is commonly accepted and widely used.

Each market should be carefully defined

How we see product life cycles depends on how broadly we define a product-market. For example, more than 61 percent of all U.S. households own microwave ovens. Although microwave ovens appear to be at the market maturity stage here, in many other countries they're still early in the growth stage. Even in European countries like Belgium, Denmark,

This ad doesn't focus on primary demand and why consumers should want a pager; rather, it emphasizes selective demand and why a customer might want Motorola's model.

Italy, and Spain, fewer than 10 percent of all households own microwave ovens.[4] Clearly, a firm with a mature product can sometimes find new growth in new markets.

How broadly we define the needs of customers in a product-market also affects how we view product life cycles—and who the competitors are. Consider the needs related to storing and preparing foods. Wax paper sales in the United States started to decline when Dow introduced Saran Wrap. Then in the early 1970s sales of Saran Wrap (and similar products) fell sharply when small plastic storage bags became popular. However, sales picked up again by the end of the decade. The product didn't change, but customers' needs did. Saran Wrap filled a new need because it worked well in microwave cooking.

If a market is defined broadly, there may be many competitors—and the market may appear to be in market maturity. On the other hand, if we focus on a narrow submarket—and a particular way of satisfying specific needs—then we may see much shorter product life cycles as improved product ideas come along to replace the old.

PRODUCT LIFE CYCLES VARY IN LENGTH

How long a whole product life cycle takes—and the length of each stage—vary a lot across products. The cycle may vary from 90 days—in the case of toys like the Ghostbusters line—to possibly 100 years for gas-powered cars.

Some products move fast

A new product idea will move through the early stages of the life cycle more quickly when it has certain characteristics. The fast adoption of NutraSweet low-calorie sweetener in the U.S. market is a good example. NutraSweet offered a real comparative advantage—fewer calories than sugar without the bitter aftertaste of other sweeteners. Free samples of NutraSweet chewing gum made it easy for consumers to try the product without any risk. It was also easy to communicate NutraSweet's benefits, and it worked well in many products—like soft drinks—that were already compatible with consumers' lifestyles. However, in less-developed nations where malnutrition, not dieting, is the problem, NutraSweet does not have the same advantages, and it has not done as well.[5]

Product life cycles are getting shorter

Although the life of different products varies, in general product life cycles are getting shorter. This is partly due to rapidly changing technology. One new invention may make possible many new products that replace old ones. Tiny electronic microchips led to hundreds of new products—from Texas Instruments' calculators and Pulsar digital watches in the early days to microchip-controlled heart valves and fax machines now.

Patents for a new product may not be much protection in slowing down competitors. Competitors can often find ways to copy the product idea without violating a specific patent. Worse, some firms find out that an unethical competitor simply disregarded the patent protection. Patent violations by foreign competitors are very common. A product's life may be over before a case can get through patent-court bottlenecks. By then, the copycat competitor may even be out of business. The patent system, in the United States and internationally, needs significant improvement if it is to really protect firms that develop innovative ideas.[6]

Although life cycles keep moving in the advanced economies, many advances bypass most consumers in less-developed economies. They may struggle at the subsistence level, without an effective macro-marketing system to stimulate innovation.

The early bird usually makes the profits

The increasing speed of the product life cycle means that firms must be developing new products all the time. Further, they must try to have marketing mixes that will make the most of the market growth stage—when profits are highest.

A certain color or style may be in fashion one season and outdated the next.

During the growth stage, competitors are likely to introduce product improvements. Fast changes in marketing strategy may be required here because profits don't necessarily go to the innovator. Sometimes fast copiers of the basic idea jump ahead in the market growth stage. Sony was a pioneer in developing videocassette recorders and one of the first on the market. Other firms quickly followed—and the competition drove down prices and increased demand. But Sony stuck to its Beta format VCRs while most consumers were buying VHS-format machines. When Sony finally offered a VHS-format machine, VCR sales growth had ebbed, and competitors controlled the market.[7]

The short happy life of fashions and fads

The sales of some products are influenced by **fashion**—the currently accepted or popular style. Fashion-related products tend to have short life cycles. What is currently popular can shift rapidly. Marketing managers who work with fashions often have to make really fast product changes.

How fast is fast enough? The Limited, a retail chain that specializes in women's fashions, tracks consumer preferences every day through point-of-sale computers. Based on what's selling, new product designs are sent by satellite to suppliers around the United States and in Hong Kong, South Korea, and Singapore. Within days clothing from those distant points begins to collect in Hong Kong. About four times a week a chartered jet brings it to the Limited's distribution center in Ohio, where items are priced and then shipped to stores within 48 hours. In spite of the speed of this system, a top manager at the Limited has commented that it's "not fast enough" for the 1990s.[8]

PLANNING FOR DIFFERENT STAGES OF THE PRODUCT LIFE CYCLE

Length of cycle affects strategy planning

Where a product is in its life cycle—and how fast it's moving to the next stage—should affect marketing strategy planning. Marketing managers must make realistic plans for the later stages. Exhibit 9–2 shows the relationship of the product life cycle to the marketing mix variables. The technical terms in this figure are discussed later in the book.

Exhibit 9−2 Typical Changes in Marketing Variables over the Product Life Cycle

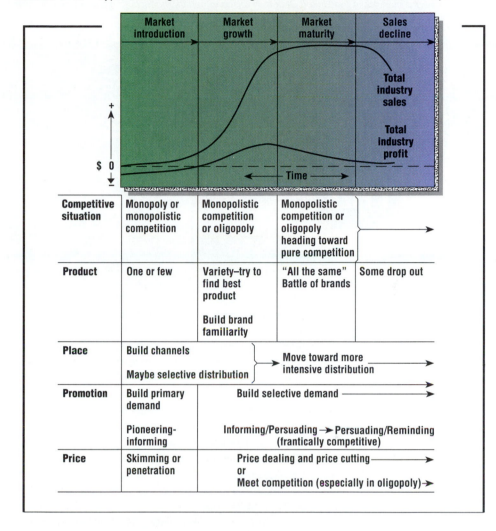

	Market introduction	Market growth	Market maturity	Sales decline
Competitive situation	Monopoly or monopolistic competition	Monopolistic competition or oligopoly	Monopolistic competition or oligopoly heading toward pure competition	
Product	One or few	Variety–try to find best product Build brand familiarity	"All the same" Battle of brands	Some drop out
Place	Build channels Maybe selective distribution	Move toward more intensive distribution		
Promotion	Build primary demand Pioneering-informing	Build selective demand Informing/Persuading → Persuading/Reminding (frantically competitive)		
Price	Skimming or penetration	Price dealing and price cutting or Meet competition (especially in oligopoly) →		

(Graph labels: Total industry sales, Total industry profit, Time, $ 0)

Introducing new products

Exhibit 9−2 shows that a marketing manager has to do a lot of work to introduce a really new product. Money must be spent developing the new product. Even if the product is unique, this doesn't mean that everyone will immediately come running to the producer's door. The firm will have to build channels of distribution—perhaps offering special incentives to win cooperation. Promotion is needed to build demand *for the whole idea*—not just to sell a specific brand. Because all this is expensive, it may lead the marketing manager to try to "skim" the market—charging a relatively high price to help pay for the introductory costs.

The correct strategy, however, depends on how quickly customers will accept the new idea and how quickly competitors will follow with their own products. When the early stages will be fast, a low initial (penetration) price may help develop loyal customers early and keep competitors out.

Also relevant is how quickly the firm can change its strategy as the life cycle moves on. Some firms are very flexible. They can compete effectively with larger, less adaptable competitors by adjusting their strategies more frequently.

Faced with mature markets in the United States, Nabisco varied its products to make them more appealing to some customers—and also looked for new growth opportunities in the Russian market.

Managing maturing products

It's important for a firm to have some competitive advantage as it moves into market maturity. Even a small advantage can make a big difference—and some firms do very well by carefully managing their maturing products. They are able to capitalize on a slightly better product—or perhaps lower production and/or marketing costs. Or they are simply more successful at promotion—allowing them to differentiate their product from competitors. For example, graham crackers were competing in a mature market and sales were flat. Nabisco used the same ingredients to create bite-sized Teddy Grahams and then promoted them heavily. These changes captured new sales and profits.[9]

Industry profits are declining in market maturity. Top management must see this, or they will continue to expect the attractive profits of the market growth stage—profits that are no longer possible. They may set impossible goals for the marketing department—causing marketing managers to think about deceptive advertising or some other desperate attempt to reach impossible objectives.

Product life cycles keep moving. But that doesn't mean a firm should just sit by as its sales decline. There are other choices. A firm can improve its product or develop an innovative new product for the same market. Or it can develop a strategy for its product (perhaps with modifications) targeted at a new market. For example, it might find a market in a country where the life cycle is not so far along, or it might try to serve a new need. Or the firm can withdraw the product before it completes the cycle—and refocus on better opportunities. See Exhibit 9–3.

Develop new strategies for different markets

In a mature market, a firm may be fighting to keep or increase its market share. But if the firm finds a new use for the product, it may be able to stimulate overall demand. Du Pont's Teflon fluorocarbon resin is a good example. Developed more than 50 years ago, it enjoyed sales growth as a nonstick coating for cookware, an insulation for aircraft wiring, and a lining for chemically resistant equipment. But marketing managers for Teflon aren't waiting to be stuck with declining profits in those mature markets. They constantly develop strategies for new markets where Teflon will meet needs. For example, Teflon is now selling well as a special coating for the wires used in high speed communications between computers.[10]

Exhibit 9–3 Examples of Three Marketing Strategy Choices for a Firm in a Mature Product-Market

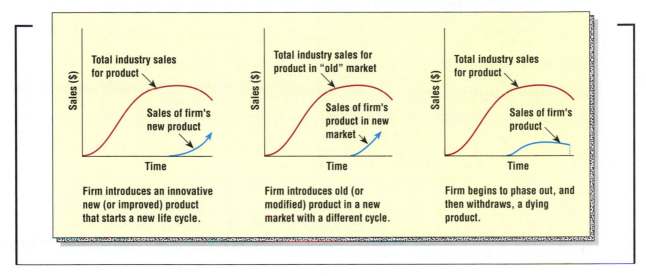

Firm introduces an innovative new (or improved) product that starts a new life cycle.

Firm introduces old (or modified) product in a new market with a different cycle.

Firm begins to phase out, and then withdraws, a dying product.

Phasing out dying products

Not all strategies have to be exciting growth strategies. If prospects are poor in some product-market, a phase-out strategy may be needed. The need for phasing out becomes more obvious as the sales decline stage arrives. But even in market maturity, it may be clear that a particular product is not going to be profitable enough to reach the company's objectives using the current strategy. Then the wisest move may be to develop a strategy that helps the firm phase out of the product-market—perhaps over several years.

Phasing out a product may involve some difficult implementation problems. But phase-out is also a *strategy*—and it must be market-oriented to cut losses. In fact, it's possible to milk a dying product for some time if competitors move out more quickly. This

Du Pont has developed new opportunities by finding new markets for Teflon.

situation occurs when there is still ongoing (though declining) demand—and some customers are willing to pay attractive prices to get their old favorite.

NEW-PRODUCT PLANNING

Competition is strong and dynamic in most markets. So it is essential for a firm to keep developing new products—and improving its current products—to meet changing customer needs and competitors' actions. Not having an active new-product development process means that consciously—or subconsciously—the firm has decided to milk its current products and go out of business. New-product planning is not an optional matter. It has to be done just to survive in today's dynamic markets.

What is a new product?

A **new product** is one that is new *in any way* for the company concerned. A product can become "new" in many ways. A fresh idea can be turned into a new product—and start a new product life cycle. For example, Alza Corporation's time-release skin patches are replacing pills and injections for some medications.

Variations on an existing product idea can also make a product new. Oral B changed its conventional toothbrush to include a strip of colored bristles that fade as you brush; that way you know when it's time for a new brush. Even small changes in an existing product can make it new.[11]

FTC says product is new only six months

A firm can call its product new for only a limited time. Six months is the limit according to the **Federal Trade Commission (FTC)**—the federal government agency that polices antimonopoly laws. To be called new—says the FTC—a product must be entirely new or changed in a "functionally significant or substantial respect." While six months may seem a very short time for production-oriented managers, it may be reasonable, given the fast pace of change for many products.

? Ethical issues in new-product planning

New product decisions—and decisions to abandon old products—often involve ethical considerations. For example, some firms (including the firm that develops drugs used in treating AIDS) have been criticized for holding back important new product innovations until patents run out—or sales slow down—on their existing products. At the same time, others have been criticized for "planned obsolescence"—releasing new products that the company plans to soon replace with improved new versions. Similarly, wholesalers and middlemen complain that producers too often keep their new-product introduction plans a secret and leave middlemen with dated inventory that they can only sell at a loss.

Criticisms are also leveled at firms that constantly release minor variations of products that already saturate markets. Consider what's happening with disposable diapers. Marketing managers may feel that they're serving some customers' needs better when they offer diapers in boys' and girls' versions and in a variety of sizes, shapes, and colors. But many retailers feel that the new products are simply a ploy to get more shelf space. Further, some consumers complain that the bewildering array of choices makes it impossible to make an informed choice.

Different marketing managers might have very different reactions to such criticisms. However, product management decisions often have a significant effect on customers and middlemen. A too casual decision may lead to a negative backlash that affects the firm's strategy or reputation.[12]

AN ORGANIZED NEW-PRODUCT DEVELOPMENT PROCESS IS CRITICAL

Identifying and developing new-product ideas—and effective strategies to go with them—is often the key to a firm's success and survival. But this isn't easy. New-product development demands effort, time, and talent—and still the risks and costs of failure are high. Experts estimate that consumer packaged-goods companies spend at least $20 million to introduce a new brand—and 70 to 80 percent of these new brands flop. In the service sector, the front-end cost of a failed effort may not be as high, but it can have a devastating long-term effect if dissatisfied consumers turn elsewhere for help.[13]

Why new products fail

A new product may fail for many reasons. Most often, companies fail to offer a unique benefit or underestimate the competition. Sometimes the idea is good, but the company has design problems—or the product costs much more to produce than was expected. Some companies rush to get a product on the market without developing a complete marketing plan.[14]

But moving too slowly can be a problem too. With the fast pace of change for many products, speedy entry into the market can be a key to competitive advantage. A few years ago, marketers at Xerox were alarmed that Japanese competitors were taking market share with innovative new copiers. It turned out that competitors were developing new models twice as fast as Xerox and at half the cost. For Xerox to compete, it had to slash its five-year product development cycle.[15]

Five steps to new-product success

To move quickly and also avoid expensive new-product failures, many companies follow an organized new-product development process. The following pages describe such a process, which moves logically through five steps: (1) idea generation, (2) screening, (3) idea evaluation, (4) development (of product and marketing mix), and (5) commercialization.[16] See Exhibit 9–4.

Process tries to kill new ideas—economically

An important element in this new-product development process is continued evaluation of a new idea's likely profitability and return on investment. The process tries to

Speed in the new-product development process can be an important competitive advantage, especially with high-tech products like this cellular Visorphone.

Exhibit 9–4   New-Product Development Process

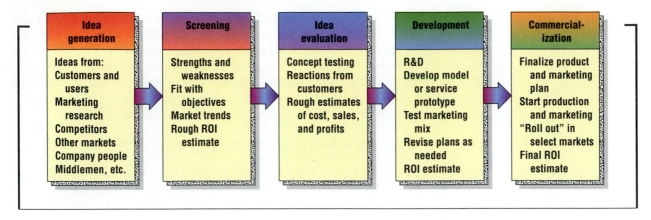

Idea generation	Screening	Idea evaluation	Development	Commercial-ization
Ideas from: Customers and users Marketing research Competitors Other markets Company people Middlemen, etc.	Strengths and weaknesses Fit with objectives Market trends Rough ROI estimate	Concept testing Reactions from customers Rough estimates of cost, sales, and profits	R&D Develop model or service prototype Test marketing mix Revise plans as needed ROI estimate	Finalize product and marketing plan Start production and marketing "Roll out" in select markets Final ROI estimate

uncover why the new idea might *not* be profitable. This puts the burden on the new idea—to prove itself or be rejected. Such a process may seem harsh, but most new ideas have some basic flaw. Marketers try to discover those flaws early, and either find a remedy or reject the idea completely. Applying this process requires much analysis of the idea *before* the company spends money to develop and market a product. This is a major departure from the usual production-oriented approach—in which a company develops a product first and then asks sales to "get rid of it."

Step 1: Idea generation

Finding new product ideas can't be left to chance. Companies need a formal procedure for seeking new ideas. Although later steps eliminate many ideas, a company must have some that succeed.

New ideas can come from a company's own sales or production staff, middlemen, competitors, consumer surveys, or other sources such as trade associations, advertising agencies, or government agencies. By analyzing new and different views of the company's markets and studying present consumer behavior, a marketing manager can spot opportunities that have not yet occurred to competitors—or even to potential customers. For example, ideas for new service concepts may come directly from analysis of consumer complaints.

No one firm can always be first with the best new ideas. So in their search for ideas, companies should pay attention to what competitors are doing. New-product specialists at Ford Motor Company buy other firms' cars as soon as they're available. Then they take the cars apart to get ideas for improvements.[17]

Many firms now shop in international markets for new ideas. Jamaica Broilers, a poultry producer in the Caribbean, moved into fish farming; it learned that many of the techniques it was using to breed chickens were also successful on fish farms in Israel.[18]

Step 2: Screening

Screening involves evaluating the new ideas with the product-market screening criteria described in Chapter 4. Recall that these criteria include the combined output of a resource (strengths and weaknesses) analysis, a long-run trends analysis, and a thorough understanding of the company's objectives. See Exhibit 3–1. Further, a good new idea should eventually lead to a product (and marketing mix) that will give the firm a competitive advantage—hopefully a lasting one.

Screening should also consider how a new product will affect consumers over time. Ideally, the product should increase consumer welfare—not just satisfy a whim. Exhibit 9–5 shows different kinds of new-product opportunities. Obviously, a socially responsible firm tries to find desirable opportunities rather than deficient ones. This may not be as easy as

Exhibit 9–5 Types of New-Product Opportunities

| | | Immediate satisfaction | |
		High	**Low**
Long-run consumer welfare	**High**	Desirable products	Salutary products
	Low	Pleasing products	Deficient products

it sounds, however. Some consumers want pleasing products and give little thought to their own long-term welfare. And some competitors willingly offer what consumers want in the short run. Generating socially responsible new-product ideas is a challenge for new-product planners.

Safety must be considered

Real acceptance of the marketing concept should lead to safe products. The U.S. **Consumer Product Safety Act** (of 1972) set up the Consumer Product Safety Commission to encourage safety in product design and better quality control. The commission has a great deal of power. It can set safety standards for products. It can order costly repairs or return of unsafe products. And it can back up its orders with fines and jail sentences. The Food and Drug Administration has similar powers for food and drugs.

Product safety complicates strategy planning because not all customers—even those who want better safety features—are willing to pay more for safer products. Some features cost a lot to add and increase prices considerably.

A firm can be held liable for unsafe products. **Product liability** means the legal obligation of sellers to pay damages to individuals who are injured by defective or unsafe products. Product liability is a serious matter. Liability settlements may exceed not only a company's insurance coverage but its total assets!

Adopting the marketing concept should lead to the development of safe products.

Relative to most other countries, U.S. courts enforce a very strict product liability standard. Producers may be held responsible for injuries related to their products no matter how the items are used or how well they're designed. Riddell—whose football helmets protect the pros—recently was hit with a $12 million judgment for a high school football player who broke his neck. The jury concluded that Riddell should have put a sticker on the helmet to warn players of the danger of butting into opponents!

Cases and settlements like this are common. Some critics argue that the U.S. rules are so tough that they discourage innovation and economic growth. In contrast, Japan's system discourages consumers from filing complaints because they are required to pay a percentage of any damages they seek as court costs—regardless of whether they win or lose.

Product liability is a serious ethical and legal matter. Many countries are attempting to change their laws so that they will be fair to both firms and consumers. But until product liability questions are resolved, marketing managers must be even more sensitive when screening new-product ideas.[19]

Step 3: Idea evaluation

When an idea moves past the screening step, it is evaluated more carefully. Note that an actual product has not yet been developed—and this can handicap the firm in getting feedback from customers. For help in idea evaluation, firms use **concept testing**—getting reactions from customers about how well a new product idea fits their needs. Concept testing uses market research—ranging from informal focus groups to formal surveys of potential customers.

Product planners must think about wholesaler and retailer reactions as well as final consumers. At the idea evaluation stage, companies often find that other members of the distribution channel won't cooperate. A Utah ice cream maker had to drop his idea for a novelty ice cream product when he learned that grocery store chains wanted payments of $20,000 each just to stock his unproven product in their freezers.[20]

Whatever research methods are used, the idea evaluation step should gather enough information to help decide whether there is an opportunity, whether it fits with the firm's resources, *and* whether there is a basis for a competitive advantage. Then the firm can estimate likely profit from the various market segments and decide whether to continue to the development stage.[21]

Step 4: Development

Product ideas that survive the screening and idea evaluation steps must now be analyzed further. Usually, this involves some research and development (R&D) and engineering to design and develop the physical part of the product. In the case of a new service offering, the firm must work out the details of what training, equipment, staff, and so on will be needed to deliver on the idea. Input from the earlier efforts helps guide this technical work.

New computer-aided design (CAD) systems are sparking a revolution in design work. Designers can develop lifelike 3-D color drawings of packages and products. Then the computer allows the manager to look at different views, just as with a real product. Changes can be made almost instantly. And the final designs feed directly into computer-controlled manufacturing systems. Motorola and Timex found that these systems cut their design development time in half—giving them a leg up on competitors.

Even so, it is still good to test early versions of the product in the market. This process may have several cycles. A manufacturer may build a model of a physical product or produce limited quantities; a service firm may try to train a small group of service providers. Tests with customers may lead to revisions—*before* the firm commits to full-scale efforts.

With actual goods or services, potential customers can react to how well the product meets their needs. Focus groups, panels, and larger surveys can provide reactions to

Computer-aided design is helping to speed up the new-product development process, as in this system that Ford uses in Germany, England, and the United States.

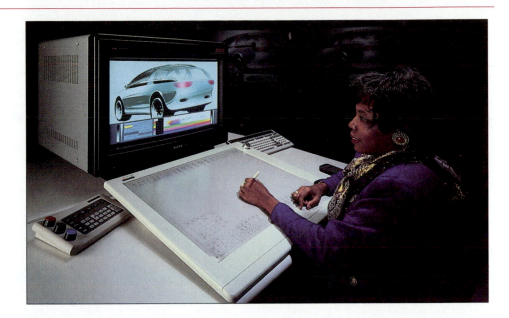

specific features and to the whole product idea. Sometimes that reaction kills the idea. For example, Coca-Cola Foods believed it had a great idea with Minute Maid Squeeze-Fresh, frozen orange juice concentrate in a squeeze bottle. In tests, however, Squeeze-Fresh bombed. Consumers loved the idea but hated the product. It was messy to use, and no one knew how much concentrate to squeeze in the glass.[22]

In other cases, testing can lead to revision of product specifications for different markets. Sometimes a complex series of revisions may be required. Months or even years of research may be necessary to focus on precisely what different market segments will find acceptable. For example, Gillette's Sensor razor took 13 years and over $300 million dollars to develop.[23]

Firms often use full-scale market testing to get reactions in real market conditions or to test variations in the marketing mix. For example, a firm may test alternative brands, prices, or advertising copy in different test cities. Note that the firm is testing the whole marketing mix, not just the product.

Market tests can be very expensive. But *not* testing is risky too. In 1986, Frito-Lay was so sure it understood consumers' preferences that it introduced a cracker snack without market testing. Even with TV ad support, MaxSnax met with overwhelming consumer indifference. By the time Frito-Lay pulled the product from store shelves, it had lost $52 million.[24]

After the market test, the firm can estimate likely ROI for various strategies to determine whether the idea moves on to commercialization.[25]

Step 5: Commercialization

A product idea that survives this far can finally be placed on the market. Putting a product on the market is expensive. Manufacturing or service facilities have to be set up. Goods have to be produced to fill the channels of distribution, or people must be hired and trained to provide services. Further, introductory promotion is costly—especially if the company is entering a very competitive market.

Because of the size of the job, some firms introduce their products city by city or region by region—in a gradual "roll out"—until they have complete market coverage. Roll outs also permit more market testing—although that is not their purpose. But marketing managers also need to pay close attention to control—to ensure that the implementation effort is working and that the strategy is on target.

3M'S SMOOTH-RUNNING INTERNATIONAL INNOVATION MACHINE

Minnesota Mining & Manufacturing (3M) spins out new products faster and better than just about any other company. The company knows that finding new-product opportunities is critical to success. In fact, more than 30 percent of 3M's sales comes from products that did not exist five years ago. That is no accident—it's a company guideline that applies to every division. Another guideline—the "15 percent rule"—allows virtually every employee to spend up to 15 percent of the workweek on anything related to new-product opportunities. Post-it Notes, Scotch Tape, and hundreds of other profitable new products were developed with this "free time."

3M also motivates innovation by rewarding new-product champions, sharing ideas among divisions, and recognizing that many new ideas may need to be considered to come up with one good opportunity. Perhaps most important, 3M works at getting close to customers and their needs. This simple idea has been part of 3M's market orientation for decades—and now it explains why nearly half of 3M's sales come from foreign markets. 3M enters a foreign market with a modest investment and pushes one basic product, such as a new reflective sheeting for traffic signs in the Soviet Union or telecommunications connectors in Hungary. Then it adds new products one at a time, hiring only local managers and workers as sales grow. The native employees help 3M figure out what customers want—and where the best opportunities are for 3M's new and established products. Breakthrough opportunities don't just happen at 3M—the company continually works to find them wherever they are.[26]

NEW-PRODUCT DEVELOPMENT: A TOTAL COMPANY EFFORT

Top-level support is vital

Companies that are particularly successful at developing new goods and services seem to have one trait in common: enthusiastic top-management support for new-product development.[27]

Put someone in charge

In addition, rather than leaving new-product development to anyone who happens to be interested (perhaps in engineering, R&D, or sales), successful companies put someone in charge—a person, department, or committee.

A new-product development department or committee may help ensure that new ideas are carefully evaluated—and profitable ones quickly brought to market. It's important to choose the right people for the job. Overly conservative managers may kill too many—or even all—new ideas. Or committees may create bureaucratic delays that make the difference between a product's success or failure.

Market needs guide R&D effort

From the idea generation stage to the commercialization stage, the R&D specialists, the operations people, and the marketing people must work together to evaluate the feasibility of new ideas. It isn't sensible for a marketing manager to develop elaborate marketing plans for goods or services that the firm simply can't produce—or produce profitably. It also doesn't make sense for R&D people to develop a technology or product that doesn't have potential for the firm and its markets. Clearly, a balancing act is involved here.

NEED FOR PRODUCT MANAGERS

Product variety leads to product managers

When a firm has only one or a few related products, everyone is interested in them. But when many new products are being developed, someone should be put in charge of new-product planning to be sure it is not neglected. Similarly, when a firm has several different kinds of products, management may decide to put someone in charge of each kind—or even each brand—to be sure they aren't lost in the rush of everyday business. **Product managers** or **brand managers** manage specific products—often taking over the jobs formerly handled by an advertising manager. That gives a clue to what is often their major responsibility—Promotion—since the products have already been developed by the new-product people.

Product managers are especially common in large companies that produce many kinds of products. Several product managers may serve under a marketing manager. Sometimes these product managers are responsible for the profitable operation of a particular product's whole marketing effort. Then they have to coordinate their efforts with others—including the sales manager, advertising agencies, production and research people, and even channel members. This is likely to lead to difficulties if product managers have no control over the marketing strategy for other related brands—or authority over other functional areas whose efforts they are expected to direct and coordinate!

To avoid these problems, in some companies the product manager serves mainly as a "product champion"—concerned with planning and getting the promotion effort implemented. A higher-level marketing manager with more authority coordinates the efforts and integrates the marketing strategies for different products into an overall plan.

The activities of product managers vary a lot depending on their experience and aggressiveness—and the company's organizational philosophy. Today companies emphasize marketing *experience*—because this important job takes more than academic training and enthusiasm.[28]

CONCLUSION

New-product planning is an increasingly important activity in a modern economy because it is no longer very profitable to just sell me-too products in highly competitive markets. Markets, competition, and product life cycles are changing at a fast pace.

The product life cycle concept is especially important to marketing strategy planning. It shows that a firm needs different marketing mixes—and even strategies—as a product moves through its cycle. This is an important point because profits change during the life cycle—with most of the profits going to the innovators or fast copiers.

We pointed out that a product is new to a firm if it is new in any way—or to any target market. But the FTC takes a narrower view of what you can call new.

New products are so important to business survival that firms need some organized process for developing them. We discuss such a process—and emphasize that it requires a total-company effort to be successful.

The failure rate of new products is high—but it is lower for better-managed firms that recognize product development and management as vital processes. Some firms appoint product managers to manage individual products and new-product committees to ensure that the process is carried out successfully.

QUESTIONS AND PROBLEMS

1. Explain how industry sales and industry profits behave over the product life cycle.

2. Cite two examples of products that you feel are currently in each of the product life-cycle stages. Consider services as well as physical goods.

3. Explain how you might reach different conclusions about the correct product life-cycle stage(s) in the worldwide automobile market.

4. Explain why individual brands may not follow the product life-cycle pattern. Give an example of a new

brand that is not entering the life cycle at the market introduction stage.

5. Discuss the life cycle of a product in terms of its probable impact on a manufacturer's marketing mix. Illustrate using personal computers.

6. What characteristics of a new product will help it move through the early stages of the product life cycle more quickly? Briefly discuss each characteristic—illustrating with a product of your choice. Indicate how each characteristic might be viewed in some other country.

7. What is a new product? Illustrate your answer.

8. Explain the importance of an organized new-product development process and illustrate how it might be used for (*a*) a new hair care product, (*b*) a new children's toy, (*c*) a new subscribers-only cable television channel.

9. Discuss how you might use the new-product development process if you were thinking about offering some kind of summer service to residents in a beach resort town.

10. Explain the role of product or brand managers. When would it make sense for one of a company's current brand managers to be in charge of the new-product development process? Explain your thinking.

11. If a firm offers one of its brands in a number of different countries, would it make sense for one brand manager to be in charge, or would each country require its own brand manager? Explain your thinking.

12. Discuss the social value of new-product development activities that seem to encourage people to discard products that are not all worn out. Is this an economic waste? How worn out is all worn out? Must a shirt have holes in it? How big?

SUGGESTED CASES

7. Pillsbury's Häagen-Dazs

12. Du Pont

18. Sacramento Sports, Inc.

COMPUTER-AIDED PROBLEM

9. Growth Stage Competition

AgriChem, Inc., has introduced an innovative new product—a combination fertilizer, weed killer, and insecticide that makes it much easier for soybean farmers to produce a profitable crop. The product introduction was quite successful with 900,000 units sold in the year of introduction. And AgriChem's profits are increasing. Total market demand is expected to grow at a rate of 270,000 units a year for the next five years. Even so, AgriChem's marketing managers are concerned about what will happen to sales and profits during this period.

Based on past experience with similar situations, they expect one new competitor to enter the market during each of the next five years. They think this competitive pressure will drive prices down about 6 percent a year. Further, although the total market is growing, they know that new competitors will chip away at AgriChem's market share—even with the 10 percent a year increase planned for the promotion budget. In spite of the competitive pressure, the marketing managers are sure that familiarity with AgriChem's brand will help it hold a large share of

the total market—and give AgriChem greater economies of scale than competitors. In fact, they expect that the ratio of profit to dollar sales for AgriChem should be about 10 percent higher than for competitors.

AgriChem's marketing managers have decided the best way to get a handle on the situation is to organize the data in a spreadsheet. They have set up the spreadsheet so they can change the "years in the future" value and see what is likely to happen to AgriChem and the rest of the industry. The starting spreadsheet shows the current situation with data from the first full year of production.

a. Compare AgriChem's market share and profit for this year with what is expected next year—given the marketing managers' current assumptions. What are they expecting? (Hint: Set number of years in the future to 1.)

b. Prepare a table showing AgriChem's expected profit, and the expected industry revenue and profit, for the current year and the next five years. Briefly explain what happens to industry sales and profits and why. (Hint: Use the What If analysis to vary the number of years in the future value in the spreadsheet from a minimum of 0—the current year—to a maximum of 5. Display the three values requested.)

c. If market demand grows faster than expected—say, at 360,000 units a year—what will happen to AgriChem's profits and the expected industry revenues and profits over the next five years? What are the implications of this analysis?

For additional questions related to this problem, see Exercise 9–4 in the *Learning Aid for use with Essentials of Marketing,* 6th edition.

Place: Channel Systems and Distribution Customer Service

In the spring of 1992, Richard Stewert was frustrated as he looked out at the Sears auto center across the street. Along with 2,500 other independent Goodyear tire distributors in North America, Stewert had just learned that Goodyear planned to sell tires to Sears's 850 auto centers. For the first time, Stewert would have to compete with a big chain in selling Goodyear-brand tires.

Although Stewert focused on the changes in his local market, they were a part of a chain reaction that started with big changes in international competition among tire producers. Goodyear's sales and profits plummeted after France's Michelin and Japan's Bridgestone aggressively expanded distribution in the North American market. Michelin moved quickly by buying Uniroyal; similarly, Bridgestone took over Firestone and its outlets. Goodyear's direct sales to Detroit automakers held up, but the company was having trouble competing in the market for replacement tires.

One reason was that Goodyear sold its brands almost exclusively through its own stores and independent dealers loyal to Goodyear. These stores attracted customers who came in for quality service and specific high-performance tires, like Goodyear Eagles. But many consumers didn't see a difference in tires—they just wanted the best price. They were buying tires from discount retailers that carried several brands.

Goodyear's marketing managers realized they needed to add new distribution channels and change their strategies to reach different target markets. To reach the price-oriented discount shoppers, Goodyear produced private-label tires sold at Wal-Mart and other big chains. Goodyear also converted some of its company-owned stores to no-frills, quick-serve stores operated under the Just Tires name.

Goodyear's marketing managers knew that selling Goodyear tires through retail discounters was risky. It would put even more pressure on Goodyear dealers' profit margins and encourage dealers to push other brands. However, Goodyear felt that many consumers went to Sears for tires without even considering a Goodyear dealer—and Sears sold 10 percent of all replacement tires in the U.S. market. Further, Sears agreed to devote about

20 percent of the tire inventory at each auto center to Goodyear tires. Working with Sears would increase sales by more than 2 million tires a year. For that boost, Goodyear's managers were willing to risk conflict with Richard Stewert and other dealers.

However, to give these dealers a top-quality product that only they could sell, Goodyear introduced a new Aquatred tire designed to be safer on wet roads. Goodyear also increased promotion support by 30 percent. This increased store traffic, but many Goodyear dealers still felt betrayed. They lost sales because they couldn't get timely delivery of popular sizes.[1]

PLACE DECISIONS—AN IMPORTANT PART OF MARKETING STRATEGY

As this example shows, offering customers a good product at a reasonable price is important to a successful marketing strategy. But it's not the whole story. Managers must also think about **Place**—making goods and services available in the right quantities and locations—when customers want them.

In the next three chapters, we'll deal with the many important strategy decisions that a marketing manager must make concerning Place. Exhibit 10–1 gives an overview. We'll start with a discussion of the type of channel that's needed to meet customers' needs. We'll show why specialists are often involved and how they come together to form a **channel of distribution**—any series of firms or individuals who participate in the flow of products from producer to final user or consumer. We'll also consider what level of distribution service to offer—and why firms must coordinate storing and transporting activities to provide the desired service at a reasonable cost. Then in Chapters 11 and 12 we'll take a closer look at the roles of retailers and wholesalers in channels as well as the strategy decisions they make to satisfy their own customers.

Exhibit 10–1   Strategy Decision Areas in Place

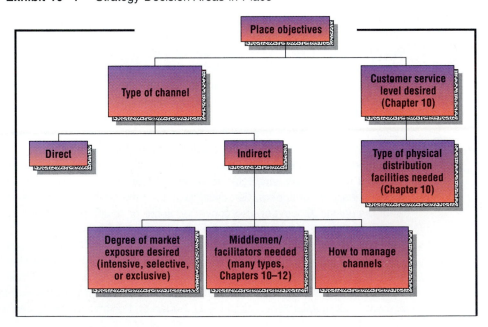

PLACE DECISIONS ARE GUIDED BY "IDEAL" PLACE OBJECTIVES

Product classes suggest place objectives

In Chapter 8 we introduced the product classes—which summarize consumers' urgency to have needs satisfied and willingness to seek information, shop, and compare. Now you should be able to use the product classes to handle Place decisions.

Exhibit 8–4 shows the relationship between consumer product classes and ideal Place objectives. Similarly, Exhibit 8–5 shows the business product classes and how they relate to customer needs. Study these exhibits carefully. They set the framework for making Place decisions. In particular, the product classes help us decide how much market exposure we'll need in each geographic area.

Place system is not automatic

As the Goodyear case shows, several different product classes may be involved if different market segments view a product in different ways. Thus, just as there is no automatic classification for a specific product, we can't automatically decide the one best Place arrangement.

Place decisions have long-run effects

The marketing manager must also consider Place objectives in relation to the product life cycle; see Exhibit 9–3. Place decisions have long-run effects. They're usually harder to change than Product, Price, and Promotion decisions. It can take years and a great deal of money to develop effective channel arrangements. Legal contracts with channel partners may also limit changes. And it's hard to move retail and wholesale facilities once they're set up. Yet as products mature, they typically need broader distribution to reach different target customers.

The producer of Vege Burgers is trying to establish widespread, low-cost distribution throughout Great Britain—because British consumers think of Vege Burgers as a staple product.

CHANNEL SYSTEM MAY BE DIRECT OR INDIRECT

One of the most basic Place decisions producers must make is whether to handle distribution themselves—or use wholesalers, retailers, and other specialists. Middlemen, in turn, must select the producers they'll work with.

Why a firm might want to use direct distribution

Many firms prefer to distribute direct to the final customer or consumer because they want to control the whole marketing job. They may think that they can serve target customers at a lower cost or do the work more effectively than middlemen. Middlemen often carry products of several competing producers. So they may not give any one item the special emphasis its producer wants.

Direct contact with customers

If a firm is in direct contact with its customers, it is more aware of changes in customer attitudes. It is in a better position to adjust its marketing mix quickly because there is no need to convince other channel members to help. If a product needs an aggressive selling effort or special technical service, the marketing manager can ensure that the sales force receives the necessary training and motivation.

Suitable middlemen are not available

A firm may have to go direct if suitable middlemen are not available—or will not cooperate. Middlemen who have the best contacts with the target market may be hesitant to add unproven products, especially really new products that don't fit well with their current business.

Common with business customers and services

Many business products are sold direct-to-customer. Rolm, for example, sells its computerized voice mail systems direct. Direct distribution is often easier in business markets since there are fewer transactions, orders are larger, and customers may be concentrated in a small geographic area.

Many service firms also use direct channels. An accounting firm like Arthur Andersen, for example, must deal directly with its customers.[2]

Don't be confused by the term *direct marketing*

An increasing number of firms now rely on **direct marketing**—direct communication between a seller and an individual customer using a promotion method other than face-to-face personal selling. Sometimes direct marketing promotion is coupled with direct distribution from a producer to consumers. Park Seed Company, for example, sells the seeds it grows direct to consumers with a mail catalog. However, many firms that use direct marketing promotion distribute their products through middlemen. So the term *direct marketing* is primarily concerned with the Promotion area, not Place decisions. We'll talk about direct marketing promotion in more detail in Chapter 13.[3]

When indirect channels are best

Even if a producer wants to handle the whole distribution job, sometimes it's simply not possible. Customers often have established buying patterns. For example, Square D, a producer of electrical supplies, might want to sell directly to big electrical contractors. But if contractors like to make all of their purchases in one convenient stop—at a local electrical wholesaler—the only practical way to reach them is through a wholesaler.

Similarly, consumers are spread throughout many geographic areas and often prefer to shop for certain products at specific places. For example, a consumer may see a local Walgreen drugstore as *the* place to shop for convenience items. This is why most consumer products firms use indirect channels.[4]

Direct distribution usually requires a significant investment in facilities and people. A new company or one that has limited financial resources may want to avoid that investment by working with established middlemen.

The most important reason for indirect channels is that middlemen can often help producers serve customer needs better and at lower cost. Remember that we discussed this briefly in Chapter 1. Now we'll go into more detail so you'll be able to plan different kinds of distribution channels.

DISCREPANCIES AND SEPARATIONS REQUIRE CHANNEL SPECIALISTS

The assortment and quantity of products customers want may be different from the assortment and quantity of products companies produce. Producers are often located far from their customers and may not know how best to reach them. Customers in turn may not know about their choices. Specialists develop to adjust these discrepancies and separations (see Exhibit 1–3).[5]

Middlemen supply needed information

Customers don't always have "perfect information" about all producers—nor do all producers know which customers need what product, where, when, and at what price. Specialists develop to help provide information to bring buyers and sellers together. For example, a local independent insurance agent may help consumers decide which policy—and which insurance company—best fits their needs.

Most producers seek help from specialists when they first enter international markets. Specialists can provide crucial information about customer needs and insights into differences in the marketing environment.

Discrepancies of quantity and assortment

Discrepancy of quantity means the difference between the quantity of products it is economical for a producer to make and the quantity final users or consumers normally want. For example, most manufacturers of golf balls produce large quantities—perhaps 500,000 in a given time period. The average golfer, however, wants only a few balls at a time. Adjusting for this discrepancy usually requires middlemen—wholesalers and retailers.

Producers typically specialize by product—and therefore another discrepancy develops. **Discrepancy of assortment** means the difference between the lines a typical producer makes and the assortment final consumers or users want. Most golfers, for example, need more than golf balls. They want golf shoes, gloves, clubs, a bag, and—of course—a golf course to play on. And they usually don't want to shop for each item separately. So, again, there is a need for wholesalers and retailers to adjust these discrepancies.

Specialists help adjust discrepancies between the quantity that is economical to produce and the quantity a consumer wants to buy.

Channel specialists adjust discrepancies with regrouping activities

Regrouping activities adjust the quantities and/or assortments of products handled at each level in a channel of distribution.

There are four regrouping activities: accumulating, bulk-breaking, sorting, and assorting. When one or more of these activities is needed, a marketing specialist may develop to fill this need.

Adjusting quantity discrepancies by accumulating and bulk-breaking

Accumulating involves collecting products from many small producers. Much of the coffee that comes from Colombia is grown on small farms in the mountains. Accumulating the small crops into larger quantities is a way of getting the lowest transporting rate—and making it more convenient for distant food processing companies to buy and handle it. Accumulating is especially important in less-developed countries and in other situations, like agricultural markets, where there are many small producers.

Accumulating is also important with professional services because they often involve the combined work of a number of individuals, each of whom is a specialized producer. A hospital makes it easier for patients by accumulating the services of a number of health care specialists, many of whom may not actually work for the hospital.

Bulk-breaking involves dividing larger quantities into smaller quantities as products get closer to the final market. A golf ball producer may need 25 wholesalers to help sell its output. And the bulk-breaking may involve several levels of middlemen. Wholesalers may sell smaller quantities to other wholesalers—or directly to retailers. Retailers continue breaking bulk as they sell individual items to their customers.

Adjusting assortment discrepancies by sorting and assorting

Different types of specialists adjust assortment discrepancies. They perform two types of regrouping activities: sorting and assorting.

Sorting means separating products into grades and qualities desired by different target markets. For example, a wholesaler that specializes in serving convenience stores may focus on smaller packages of frequently used products, whereas a wholesaler working with restaurants and hotels might handle only very large institutional sizes.

Assorting means putting together a variety of products to give a target market what it wants. This usually is done by those closest to the final consumer or user—retailers or wholesalers who try to supply a wide assortment of products for the convenience of their customers. A wholesaler selling Yazoo tractors and mowers to golf courses might also carry Pennington grass seed, Scott fertilizer, and even golf ball washers or irrigation systems—for its customers' convenience.

Wholesalers often accumulate products from many producers and then break bulk to provide the smaller quantities needed by retailers.

Watch for changes

Specialists should develop to adjust discrepancies *if they must be adjusted.* But there is no point in having middlemen just because that's the way it's always been done. Sometimes a breakthrough opportunity can come from finding a better way to reduce discrepancies—perhaps eliminating some steps in the channel. For example, Dell Computer found that it could sell computers direct to customers—at very low prices—by advertising in computer magazines and taking orders by mail or phone.[6]

CHANNELS MUST BE MANAGED

The whole channel should have a product-market commitment

Ideally, all of the members of a channel system should have a shared *product-market commitment*—with all members focusing on the same target market at the end of the channel and sharing the various marketing functions in appropriate ways. Unfortunately, many marketing managers overlook this basic idea because it's not the way their firms traditionally handle channel relationships.

Traditional channel systems are common

In **traditional channel systems**—the various channel members make little or no effort to cooperate with each other. They buy and sell from each other—and that's all. Each channel member does only what it considers to be in its own best interest; it doesn't worry about other members of the channel. This is shortsighted, but it's easy to see how it can happen. The objectives of the various channel members may be different. General Electric wants a wholesaler of electrical building supplies to sell GE products. But a wholesaler who works with different producers may not care whose products get sold. The wholesaler just wants happy customers and a good profit margin.

Traditional channel systems are still typical in many industries. The members of these channels have their independence, but they may pay for it too. As we will see, such channels are declining in importance—with good reason.

Glen Raven Mills, the company that produces Sunbrella brand fabrics, gets cooperation from many independent wholesale distributors because it develops marketing strategies that help the whole channel compete more effectively.

Conflict gets in the way of cooperation

Because members of traditional channel systems often have different objectives—and different ideas about how things should be done—conflict is common.

There are two basic types of conflict in channels of distribution. Vertical conflicts occur between firms at different levels of the channel of distribution. For example, a producer and a retailer may disagree about how much shelf space or promotion effort the retailer should give the producer's product.

Horizontal conflicts occur between firms at the same level in the channel of distribution. For example, a furniture store that keeps a complete line of furniture on display isn't happy to find out that a store down the street is offering customers lower prices on special orders of the same items. The discounter is getting a free ride from the competing store's investment in inventory.

Usually the best way to avoid conflict is to get everyone focused on the same basic objective—satisfying the customer at the end of the channel. This leads us away from traditional channels and to the channel captain concept.

Channel captain can guide channel planning

Each channel system should act as a unit, perhaps directed by a **channel captain**—a manager who helps direct the activities of a whole channel and tries to avoid—or solve—channel conflicts.

The concept of a single channel captain is logical. But most traditional channels don't have a recognized captain. The various firms don't act as a coordinated system.

But, like it or not, firms in a channel are interrelated—even if poorly—by their policies. So it makes sense to try to avoid channel conflicts by planning for channel relations. The channel captain arranges for the necessary functions to be performed in the most effective way.

Some producers dominate their channels

In the United States, producers frequently take the lead in channel relations. Middlemen often wait to see what the producer intends to do—and wants them to do. After marketing managers for L'eggs set Price, Promotion, and Place policies, wholesalers and retailers decide whether their roles will be profitable—and whether they want to join in the channel effort.

Some middlemen are channel captains

Some large or well-located wholesalers or retailers do take the lead. These middlemen analyze the types of products their customers want and then seek out producers who can provide these products at reasonable prices. This is becoming more common in the United States—and it is already typical in many foreign markets. In Japan, for example, very large wholesalers (trading companies) are often the channel captains.

Middlemen are closer to the final user or consumer and are in an ideal position to assume the channel captain role. Middlemen—especially large retail chains—may even dominate the marketing systems of the future.[7]

VERTICAL MARKETING SYSTEMS FOCUS ON FINAL CUSTOMERS

Many marketing managers accept the view that a coordinated channel system can help everyone in the channel. These managers are moving their firms away from traditional channel systems and instead developing or joining vertical market systems.

Vertical marketing systems are channel systems in which the whole channel focuses on the same target market at the end of the channel. Such systems make sense—and are growing—because if the final customer doesn't buy the product, the whole channel suffers. There are three types of vertical marketing systems—corporate, administered, and contractual. Exhibit 10–2 summarizes some characteristics of these systems and compares them with traditional systems.

SCIENCE DIET PET FOODS FACE A COMPETITIVE DOGFIGHT

Just as consumers are watching their diets and moving to healthier fare, they're also paying more attention to what they feed their pets. And they're paying more for it too. As a result, Hill's Pet Products, the company that makes Science Diet pet foods for cats and dogs, has enjoyed profitable growth.

Purina, Kal Kan, and most other pet food producers concentrated on collaring pet owners while they shop in supermarkets, where they spend about $6 billion a year. But marketing managers for Science Diet saw an opportunity in a different channel. They concentrated on reaching consumers at nongrocery outlets, primarily pet shops and veterinary offices. They realized that these pet professionals have a lot of influence on what pet owners buy. The choice may also have been part necessity. Prior to 1987, most supermarkets weren't willing to put much emphasis on specialized pet foods.

But now that's changed. By 1991 pet owners were spending over $1 billion a year for premium-priced food from pet stores and vets, where Hill's is the leading brand. What's more, the profit margins on the specialty foods are much higher than on traditional fare.

To reach pet owners who want special pet diet foods, Purina, Kal Kan, and other producers are developing new products and working with supermarkets to set up special "nutrition centers" on the pet food aisle. An executive at Hill's concedes that the new competition from the grocery channel is inevitable. But Hill's plans to stick with its current channels—which have been competing very well. In fact, Hill's is using the same approach for expanding distribution into 28 other countries. In pet stores across Japan, for example, Science Diet is attracting new customers with special displays featuring samples and free literature.[8]

Corporate ownership along the channel

Some corporations develop their own vertical marketing systems by internal expansion and/or by buying other firms. With **corporate channel systems**—corporate ownership all along the channel—we might say the firm is going "direct." But actually the firm may be handling manufacturing, wholesaling, *and* retailing—so it's more accurate to think of the firm as a vertical marketing system.

Corporate channel systems often develop by **vertical integration**—acquiring firms at different levels of channel activity. Bridgestone, for example, has rubber plantations in Liberia, tire plants in Ohio, and wholesale and retail outlets all over the world.

Vertical integration has many possible advantages—stable sources of supply, better control of distribution, better quality control, larger research facilities, greater buying power, and lower executive overhead.

Provided that the discrepancies of quantity and assortment are not too great at each level in a channel—that is, that the firms fit together well—vertical integration can be extremely efficient and profitable. It can also benefit consumers through lower prices and better products.

Firms cooperate in administered and contractual systems

Firms can often gain the advantages of vertical integration without building an expensive corporate channel. A firm can develop administered or contractual channel systems instead. In **administered channel systems**, the channel members informally agree to cooperate with each other. They can agree to routinize ordering, standardize accounting, and coordinate promotion efforts. In **contractual channel systems**, the channel members agree by contract to cooperate with each other. With both of these systems, the members achieve some of the advantages of corporate integration while retaining some of the flexibility of a traditional channel system.

Exhibit 10−2   Characteristics of Traditional and Vertical Marketing Systems

Characteristics	Type of channel			
	Traditional	Vertical marketing systems		
		Administered	Contractual	Corporate
Amount of cooperation	Little or none	Some to good	Fairly good to good	Complete
Control maintained by	None	Economic power and leadership	Contracts	Ownership by one company
Examples	Typical channel of "independents"	General Electric, Miller's Beer, O.M. Scott & Sons (lawn products)	McDonald's, Holiday Inn, IGA, Ace Hardware, Super Valu, Coca-Cola, Chevrolet	Florsheim Shoes, Sherwin Williams

Middlemen in the grocery, hardware, and drug industries develop and coordinate such systems. Computerized checkout systems track sales. The information is sent to the wholesaler's computer, which enters orders automatically when needed. This reduces buying and selling costs, inventory investment, and customer frustration with out-of-stock items throughout the channel.

Vertical marketing systems—compete well

Smoothly operating channel systems are more efficient and successful. In the consumer products field, vertical systems have a healthy majority of retail sales and should continue to increase their share in the future. Vertical marketing systems are becoming the major competitive units in the U.S. distribution system—and they are growing rapidly in other parts of the world as well.[9]

THE BEST CHANNEL SYSTEM SHOULD ACHIEVE IDEAL MARKET EXPOSURE

You may think that all marketing managers want their products to have maximum exposure to potential customers. This isn't true. Some product classes require much less market exposure than others. **Ideal market exposure** makes a product available widely enough to satisfy target customers' needs but not exceed them. Too much exposure only increases the total cost of marketing.

Ideal exposure may be intensive, selective, or exclusive

Intensive distribution means selling a product through all responsible and suitable wholesalers or retailers who will stock and/or sell the product. **Selective distribution** is selling through only those middlemen who will give the product special attention. **Exclusive distribution** is selling through only one middleman in a particular geographic area. As we move from intensive to exclusive distribution, we give up exposure in return for some other advantage—including, but not limited to, lower cost.

Intensive distribution—sell it where they buy it

Intensive distribution is commonly needed for convenience products and business supplies. Customers want such products nearby.

Heath uses intensive distribution, while Godiva uses selective distribution for its high-quality chocolates.

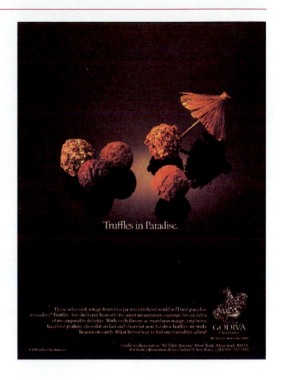

The seller's intent is important here. Intensive distribution refers to the *desire* to sell through *all* responsible and suitable outlets. What this means depends on customer habits and preferences. If target customers normally buy a certain product at a certain type of outlet, ideally you would specify this type of outlet in your Place policies. If customers prefer to buy Sharp portable TVs only at TV stores, you would try to sell all TV stores to achieve intensive distribution. Today, however, many customers buy small portable TVs at a variety of convenient outlets—including Eckerd drugstores, a local Kmart, or over the phone from the Sharper Image catalog. This means that an intensive distribution policy requires use of all these outlets—and more than one channel—to reach one target market.

Selective distribution— sell it where it sells best

Selective distribution covers the broad area of market exposure between intensive and exclusive distribution. It may be suitable for all categories of products. Only the better middlemen are used here. Companies usually use selective distribution to gain some of the advantages of exclusive distribution—while still achieving fairly widespread market coverage.

A selective policy might be used to avoid selling to wholesalers or retailers who (1) have a poor credit rating, (2) have a reputation for making too many returns, (3) place orders that are too small to justify making calls or providing service, or (4) are not in a position to do a satisfactory job.

Selective distribution is becoming more popular than intensive distribution as firms see that they don't need 100 percent coverage of a market to justify or support national advertising. Often the majority of sales come from relatively few customers—and the others buy too little compared to the cost of working with them. That is, they are unprofitable to serve. This is called the 80/20 rule—80 percent of a company's sales often come from only 20 percent of its customers *until it becomes more selective in choosing customers*.

Esprit—a producer of colorful, trendy clothing—was selling through about 4,000 department stores and specialty shops nationwide. But Esprit found that about half of the stores generated most of the sales. Sales analysis also showed that sales in Esprit's own stores were about 400 percent better than sales in other sales outlets. As a result, Esprit cut back to about 2,000 outlets and opened more of its own stores—and profits increased.[10]

Selective distribution makes sense for shopping and specialty products and for those business products that need special efforts from channel members. Wholesalers and retailers are more willing to promote products aggressively if they know they're going to obtain the majority of sales through their own efforts. They may carry more stock and wider lines, do more promotion, and provide more service—all of which lead to more sales.

Exclusive distribution sometimes makes sense

Exclusive distribution is just an extreme case of selective distribution—the firm selects only one middleman in each geographic area. Besides the various advantages of selective distribution, producers may want to use exclusive distribution to help control prices and the service offered in a channel. It's also attractive to middlemen because they know they won't face local competitors selling the same products.

Is limiting market exposure legal?

Exclusive distribution is a vague area in the U.S. antimonopoly laws. Courts currently focus on whether an exclusive distribution arrangement hurts competition.

Horizontal arrangements—among *competing* retailers, wholesalers, or producers—to limit sales by customer or territory are consistently ruled illegal by the U.S. Supreme Court. Courts consider such arrangements obvious collusion that reduces competition and harms customers.

The legality of vertical arrangements—between producers and middlemen—is not as clear-cut. A 1977 Supreme Court decision (involving Sylvania and the distribution of TV sets) reversed an earlier ruling that it was always illegal to set up vertical relationships limiting territories or customers. Now courts can weigh the possible good effects against the possible restrictions on competition. They look at competition between *whole channels*—rather than just focusing on competition at one level of distribution.

The Sylvania decision does *not* mean that all vertical arrangements are legal. Rather, it says that a firm has to be able to legally justify any exclusive arrangements.[11] Thus, firms should be cautious about entering into *any* exclusive distribution arrangement. The courts can force a change in expensively developed relationships. And—even worse—the courts can award triple damages if they rule that competition was hurt.

The same cautions apply to selective distribution. Here, however, less formal arrangements are typical—and the possible impact on competition is more remote. It is now more acceptable to carefully select channel members when building a channel system. Refusing to sell to some middlemen, however, should be part of a logical plan with long-term benefits to consumers.

CHANNEL SYSTEMS CAN BE COMPLEX

Trying to achieve the desired degree of market exposure can lead to complex channels of distribution. Firms may need different channels to reach different segments of a broad product-market—or to be sure they reach each segment.

Exhibit 10–3 shows the many channels used by a company that produces roofing shingles. It also shows (roughly) what percent of the sales go to different channel members. Shingles are both consumer products (sold to do-it-yourselfers) and business products (sold to building contractors and roofing contractors). This helps explain why some channels develop. But note that the shingles go through different wholesalers and retailers—ndependent and chain lumberyards, hardware stores, and mass-merchandisers. This can cause problems because different wholesalers and retailers want different

Exhibit 10–3 Roofing Shingles Are Sold through Many Kinds of Wholesalers and Retailers

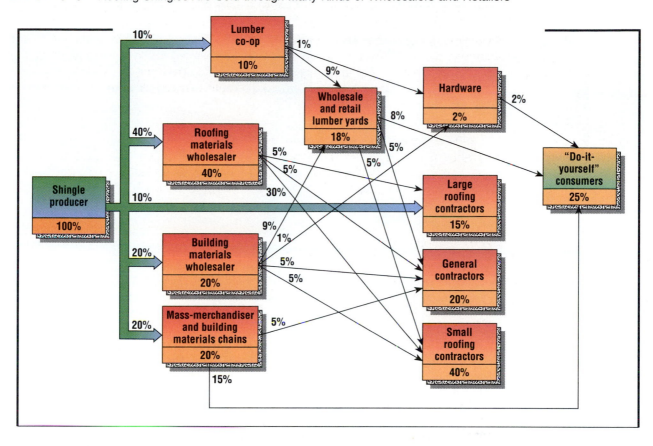

markups. It also increases competition—including price competition. And the competition among different middlemen may result in conflicts between the middlemen and the producer.

Dual distribution systems may be needed

Dual distribution occurs when a producer uses several competing channels to reach the same target market—perhaps using several middlemen in addition to selling directly. Dual distribution is becoming more common. Big retail chains want to deal directly with producers. They want large quantities—and low prices. The producer sells directly to retail chains and relies on wholesalers to sell to smaller accounts. Some established middlemen resent this because they don't appreciate *any* competition—especially price competition set up by their own suppliers.

Other times, producers are forced to use dual distribution because their present channels are doing a poor job or aren't reaching some potential customers. For example, Reebok International had been relying on local sporting goods stores to sell its shoes to high school and college athletic teams. But Reebok wasn't getting much of the business. When it set up its own team-sales department to sell direct to the schools, it got a 30,000 unit increase in sales. Of course, some of the stores weren't happy about their supplier also selling to their potential customers. However, they did get the message that Reebok wanted *someone* to reach that target market.[12]

Ethical decisions may be required

A shared product-market commitment guides cooperation among channel members as long as the whole channel is competitive. However, if customers' place requirements change, the current channel system may not be effective. The changes required to serve

Pepperidge Farm penetrated the Japanese market quickly after Japan's 7-Eleven convenience store chain agreed to carry its cookies; Häagen-Dazs is moving into the Japanese market with its own stores.

customer needs may hurt one or more members of the channel. The most difficult ethical dilemmas in the channels area arise in situations like this—because not everyone can win.

For example, wholesalers and the independent retailers that they serve in a channel of distribution may trust a producer channel-captain to develop marketing strategies that will work for the whole channel. However, the producer may conclude that everyone in the channel will ultimately fail if it continues exclusive distribution. It might decide that consumers—and its own business—are best served by an immediate change (say, dropping current middlemen and selling direct to big retail chains). A move of this sort may not give current middlemen-partners a chance to make adjustments of their own. The more dependent they are on the producer, the more severe the impact is likely to be. It's not easy to determine the best or most ethical solutions in these situations. However, marketing managers must think carefully about the implications of strategy changes in the Place area—because they can have very severe consequences for other channel members. In channels, as in any business dealing, relationships of trust must be treated with care.[13]

Reverse channels should be planned

Most firms focus on getting products to their customers. But some marketing managers must also plan for **reverse channels**—channels used to retrieve products that customers no longer want. The need for reverse channels may arise because of product recalls, errors in completing orders, warranty work, or recycling needs (as with soft-drink bottles). And, of course, at some point or other, most consumers and business customers buy something in error and want to return it.

When marketing managers don't plan for reverse channels, the firm's customers may be left to solve "their" problem. That usually doesn't make sense. So a complete plan for Place may need to consider an efficient way to return products—with policies that different channel members agree on.[14]

PHYSICAL DISTRIBUTION GETS IT TO CUSTOMERS

The right channel of distribution is crucial in getting products to the target market's Place. Whenever the product includes a physical good, Place also requires physical distribution decisions. **Physical distribution (PD)** is the transporting and storing of goods to match target customers' needs with a firm's marketing mix—both within individual firms and along a channel of distribution. **Logistics** is another common name for physical distribution.

Fast and reliable delivery is critical to many business customers.

Logistics costs are very important to both firms and consumers. These costs vary from firm to firm and, from a macro-marketing perspective, from country to country. However, for many goods, firms spend half or more of their total marketing dollars on physical distribution activities. The total amount of money involved is so large that even small improvements in this area can have a big effect on a whole macro-marketing system—and consumers' quality of life.

From the beginning, we've emphasized that marketing strategy planning is based on meeting customers' needs. Planning for physical distribution and Place is no exception. So let's look at PD through a customer's eyes.

Customers want products—not excuses

Customers don't care how a product was moved or stored—or what some channel member had to do to provide it. Rather, customers think in terms of the physical distribution **customer service level**—how rapidly and dependably a firm can deliver what they—the customers—want. Marketing managers need to understand the customer's point of view.

What does this really mean? It means that Toyota wants to have enough windshields delivered to make cars *that* day—not late so production stops *or* early so there are a lot of extras to move around or store. It means that a business executive who rents a car from Hertz wants it to be ready when she gets off the plane. It means you want your Lay's potato chips to be whole when you buy a bag at the snack bar—not crushed into crumbs from rough handling in a warehouse.

In countries where physical distribution systems are inefficient, consumers face shortages and inconvenient waits for the products they need. By contrast, most consumers in the United States and Canada don't think much about physical distribution. This probably means that these market-directed macro-marketing systems work pretty well—that a lot of individual marketing managers made good decisions in this area. But it doesn't mean that the decisions are always clear-cut or simple. In fact, many trade-offs may be required.

Trade-offs of costs, service, and sales

Most customers would prefer very good service at a very low price. But that combination is hard to provide because it usually costs more to provide higher levels of service. So most physical distribution decisions involve trade-offs between costs, the customer service level, and sales.

Exhibit 10–4   Trade-Offs among Physical Distribution Costs, Customer Service Level, and Sales

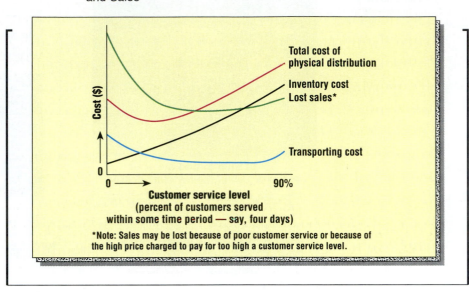

If you want the current top-selling CD and the store where you usually go doesn't have it, you're likely to buy it elsewhere. Perhaps the first store could keep your business by guaranteeing one-day delivery of your CD—using special delivery from the supplier. In this case, the manager is trading the cost of storing a large inventory for the extra cost of speedy delivery.

Exhibit 10–4 illustrates trade-off relationships like those highlighted in the CD example. For example, faster—but more expensive—transportation may reduce the need for costly storing. There is also a trade-off between the service level and sales. If the service level is too low—if products are not available on a timely and dependable basis—customers will buy elsewhere, and sales will be lost. Alternatively, the supplier may hope that a higher service level will attract more customers or motivate them to pay a higher price. But if the service level is higher than customers want or are willing to pay for, sales will be lost.

The important point is that many trade-offs must be made in the PD area. The lowest-cost approach may not be best—if customers aren't satisfied. A higher service level may make a better strategy. Further, if different channel members or target markets want different customer service levels, several different strategies may be needed.[15]

PHYSICAL DISTRIBUTION CONCEPT FOCUSES ON THE WHOLE DISTRIBUTION SYSTEM

The physical
distribution concept

The **physical distribution (PD) concept** says that all transporting and storing activities of a business and a channel system should be coordinated as one system, which should seek to minimize the cost of distribution for a given customer service level. It may be hard to see this as a startling development. But until just a few years ago, even the most progressive companies treated PD functions as separate and unrelated activities.[16]

Decide what service
level to offer

With the physical distribution concept, firms decide what aspects of service are most important to their customers—and what specific service level to provide. Then they focus on finding the least expensive way to achieve the target level of service.

Exhibit 10–5   Examples of Factors that Affect PD Service Level

• Advance information on product availability	• Advance information on delays
• Time to enter and process orders	• Time needed to deliver an order
• Backorder procedures	• Reliability in meeting delivery date
• Where inventory is stored	• Complying with customer's instructions
• Accuracy in filling orders	• Defect-free deliveries
• Damage in shipping, storing, and handling	• How needed adjustments are handled
• Order status information	• Procedures for handling returns

Exhibit 10–5 shows a variety of factors that may influence the customer service level. The most important aspects of customer service depend on target market needs. Xerox might focus on how long it takes to deliver copy machine repair parts once it receives an order. When a copier breaks down, customers want the repair "yesterday." The service level might be stated as "we will deliver emergency repair parts within 24 hours." Such a service level might require that almost all such parts be kept in inventory, that order processing be very fast and accurate, and that the parts be sent by airfreight. Obviously, supplying this service level will affect the total cost of the PD system. But it may also beat competitors who don't provide this service level.[17]

Find the lowest total cost for the right service level

In selecting a PD system, the **total cost approach** involves evaluating each possible PD system—and identifying *all* of the costs of each alternative. This approach uses the tools of cost accounting and economics. Costs that otherwise might be ignored—like inventory carrying costs—are considered. The possible costs of lost sales due to a lower customer service level may also be considered. The following example shows why the total cost approach is useful. *Per Ton Mile + Packaging + Ease of Handling*

A cost comparison of alternative systems

The Good Earth Vegetable Company was shipping produce to distant markets by train. The cost of shipping a ton of vegetables by train averaged less than half the cost of airfreight so the company assumed that rail was the best method. But then Good Earth managers did a more complete analysis. To their surprise, they found the airfreight system was faster and cheaper.

Exhibit 10–6 compares the costs for the two distribution systems—airplane and railroad. Because shipping by train was slow, Good Earth had to keep a large inventory in a warehouse to fill orders on time. And the company was also surprised at the extra cost of carrying the inventory in transit. Good Earth's managers also found that the cost of spoiled vegetables during shipment and storage in the warehouse was much higher when they used rail shipping.

How PD is shared affects the rest of a strategy

How the PD functions are shifted and shared in a channel affects the total cost and also the other three Ps—especially Price. Consider Channel Master, a firm that wanted to take advantage of the growing market for the large dish-like antennas used by motels to receive HBO and other TV signals from satellites. The product looked like it could be a big success, but the small company didn't have the money to invest in a large inventory. So Channel Master decided to work only with wholesalers who were willing to buy (and pay for) several units—to be used for demonstrations and to ensure that buyers got immediate delivery.

In the first few months Channel Master earned $2 million in revenues—just by providing inventory for the channel. And the wholesalers paid the interest cost of carrying inventory—over $300,000 the first year. Here the wholesalers helped share the risk of the

Exhibit 10–6   Comparative Costs of Airplane versus Rail and Warehouse

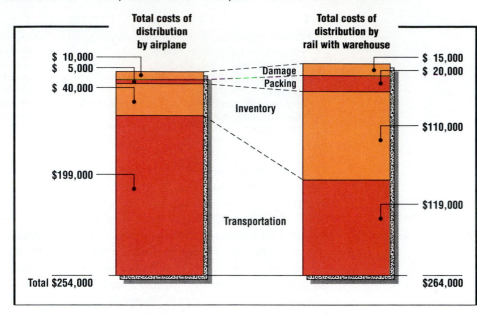

new venture—but they won many sales from a competing channel whose customers had to wait several months for delivery.

Now that you see why the physical distribution concept is important, let's take a closer look at some of the PD decision areas.

THE TRANSPORTING FUNCTION ADDS VALUE TO A MARKETING STRATEGY

Transporting aids economic development and exchange

Transporting is the marketing function of moving goods. Transportation provides time and place utilities—at a cost. But the cost is less than the value added to products by moving them or there is little reason to ship in the first place.

Transporting can help achieve economies of scale in production. If production costs can be reduced by producing larger quantities in one location, these savings may more than offset the added cost of transporting the finished products to customers. Without low-cost transportation, both within countries and internationally, there would be no mass distribution as we know it today.

Transporting can be costly

Transporting costs may limit the target markets a marketing manager can consider. Shipping costs increase delivered cost—and that's what really interests customers. Transport costs add little to the cost of products that are already valuable relative to their size and weight. But transporting costs can be a large part of the total cost for heavy products of low value—like many minerals and raw materials.[18]

WHICH TRANSPORTING ALTERNATIVE IS BEST?

Transporting function must fit the whole strategy

The transporting function should fit into the whole marketing strategy. But picking the best transporting alternative can be difficult. The best alternative depends on the product, other physical distribution decisions, and what service level the company wants to offer. The best alternative should not only be as low-cost as possible but also provide the level of service (for example, speed and dependability) required. Exhibit 10–7 shows that different

Exhibit 10–7 Benefits and Limitations of Different Transport Modes

Mode	Transporting Features					
	Cost	**Delivery speed**	**Number of locations served**	**Ability to handle a variety of goods**	**Frequency of scheduled shipments**	**Dependability in meeting schedules**
Rail	Medium	Average	Extensive	High	Low	Medium
Water	Very low	Very slow	Limited	Very high	Very low	Medium
Truck	High	Fast	Very extensive	High	High	High
Air	Very high	Very fast	Extensive	Limited	High	High
Pipeline	Low	Slow	Very limited	Very limited	Medium	High

modes of transportation have different strengths and weaknesses.[19] Low transporting cost is *not* the only criterion for selecting the best mode.

Railroads—large loads moved at low cost

Railroads are the workhorse of the U.S. transportation system. They carry more freight over more miles than any other mode. In the United States, as in other countries, they carry heavy and bulky goods—such as raw materials, steel, chemicals, cars, canned goods, and machines—over long distances. By handling large quantities, the railroads are able to transport at relatively low cost. Because railroad freight moves more slowly than truck shipments, it is not as well suited for perishable items or those in urgent demand. Railroads are most efficient at handling full carloads of goods. Less-than-carload (LCL) shipments take a lot of handling and rehandling, which means they usually move more slowly and at a higher price per pound than carload shipments.

Competition has forced railroads to innovate

Railroads earned low profits for many years—in part because trucks took a large share of the most profitable business. Now, however, railroads are catering to the needs of new target customers with a variety of specially designed railcars and services—ranging from double-decker railcars to computerized freight-tracking systems.[20]

Another example of a special railroad service is **diversion in transit**, which allows redirection of carloads already in transit. A Florida grower can ship a carload of oranges toward the Northeast as soon as they're ripe. While they head north, the grower can find a buyer or identify the market with the best price. Then—for a small fee—the railroad will reroute the car to this destination.

Trucks are more expensive, but flexible and essential

The flexibility of trucks makes them better at moving small quantities of goods for shorter distances. They can travel on almost any road. They go where the rails can't. That's why at least 75 percent of U.S. consumer products travel at least part of the way from producer to consumer by truck. And in countries with good highway systems, trucks can give extremely fast service.[21]

Ship it overseas— but slowly

Water transportation is the slowest shipping mode—but usually the lowest-cost way of shipping heavy freight. Water transportation is very important for international shipments and often the only practical approach. This explains why port cities like Boston, New York, Rotterdam, Osaka, and Singapore are important centers for international trade.

Inland waterways (such as the Mississippi River and Great Lakes in the United States and the Rhine and Danube in Europe) are also important, especially for bulky, nonperishable products such as iron ore, grain, steel, petroleum products, cement, gravel, sand, and coal. However, when winter ice closes freshwater harbors, alternative transportation must be used.

Pipelines move oil and gas

Pipelines are used primarily to move oil and natural gas. So pipelines are important both in the oil-producing and oil-consuming countries. Only a few major cities in the United States, Canada, Mexico, and Latin America are more than 200 miles from a major pipeline system.

Airfreight is expensive but fast and growing

The most expensive cargo transporting mode is airplane—but it is fast! Airfreight rates normally are at least twice as high as trucking rates—but the greater speed may offset the added cost.

High-value, low-weight goods—like high-fashion clothing and parts for the electronics and metal-working industries—are often shipped by air. Airfreight is also creating new transporting business. Perishable products that previously could not be shipped are now being flown across continents and oceans. Flowers and bulbs from Holland, for example, now are jet-flown to points all over the world.

But airplanes may cut the total cost of distribution

Using planes may help a firm reduce inventory and handling costs, spoilage, theft, and damage. Although the *transporting* cost of air shipments may be higher, the *total* cost of distribution may be lower. As more firms realize this, airfreight firms—like DHL Worldwide Express, Federal Express, Airborne, and Emery Air Freight—are enjoying rapid growth. These firms play an especially important role in the growth of international business.[22]

Put it in a container— and move between modes easily

We've described the modes separately, but products often move by several different modes and carriers during their journey. This is especially common for international shipments. Japanese firms—like Sony—ship stereos to the United States, Canada, and Europe by boat. When they arrive at the dock, they're loaded on trains and sent across the country. Then the units are delivered to a wholesaler by truck or rail.

The growth of airfreight makes it easier and faster for firms to serve customers in foreign markets.

To better coordinate the flow of products between modes, transportation companies like CSX now offer customers a complete choice of different transportation modes. Then CSX, not the customer, figures out the best and lowest-cost way to shift and share transporting functions between the modes.[23]

Loading and unloading goods several times used to be a real problem. Parts of a shipment would become separated, damaged, or even stolen. And handling the goods— perhaps many times—raised costs and slowed delivery. Many of these problems are reduced with **containerization**—grouping individual items into an economical shipping quantity and sealing them in protective containers for transit to the final destination.

THE STORING FUNCTION AND MARKETING STRATEGY

Store it and smooth out sales, increase profits and consumer satisfaction

Storing is the marketing function of holding goods. It provides time utility. **Inventory** is the amount of goods being stored.

Storing is necessary when production of goods doesn't match consumption. This is common with mass production. Nippon Steel, for example, might produce thousands of steel bars of one size before changing the machines to produce another size. Changing the production line can be costly and time-consuming. It's often cheaper to produce large quantities of one size—and store the unsold quantity—than to have shorter production runs. Thus, storing goods allows the producer to achieve economies of scale in production.

Storing varies the channel system

Storing allows producers and middlemen to keep stocks at convenient locations— ready to meet customers' needs. In fact, storing is one of the major activities of some middlemen.

Most channel members provide the storing function for some length of time. Even final consumers store some things for their future needs.

Which channel members store the product—and for how long—affects the behavior of all channel members. For example, the producer of Snapper Lawnmowers tries to get wholesalers to inventory a wide selection of its machines. That way, retailers can carry smaller inventories since they can be sure of dependable local supplies. And they might decide to sell Snapper—rather than Toro or some other brand that they would have to store at their own expense.

Goods are stored at a cost

Storing can increase the value of goods, but *storing always involves costs* too. Car dealers, for example, must store cars on their lots—waiting for the right customer. The interest expense of money tied up in the inventory is a major cost. In addition, if a new car on the lot is dented or scratched, there is a repair cost. If a car isn't sold before the new models come out, its value drops. There is also a risk of fire or theft—so the retailer must carry insurance. And, of course, dealers incur the cost of the display lot where they store the cars.

In today's competitive markets, most firms watch their inventories closely. Taken in total, the direct and indirect costs of unnecessary inventory can make the difference between a profitable strategy and a loser.[24]

Specialized facilities can be very helpful

Specialized storing facilities reduce costs—and serve customers better.

Private warehouses are common

Private warehouses are storing facilities owned or leased by companies for their own use. Most manufacturers, wholesalers, and retailers have some storing facilities either in their main buildings or in a warehouse district.

Firms use private warehouses when a large volume of goods must be stored regularly. Private warehouses can be expensive, however. If the need changes, the extra space may be hard—or impossible—to rent to others.

Public warehouses fill special needs

Public warehouses are independent storing facilities. They can provide all the services that a company's own warehouse can provide. A company might choose a public warehouse if it doesn't have a regular need for space. For example, Tonka Toys uses public warehouses because its business is seasonal. Tonka pays for the space only when it is used. Public warehouses are also useful for manufacturers who must maintain stocks in many locations—including foreign countries.[25]

The right facilities cut handling costs

The cost of physical handling is a major storing cost. To reduce these costs, modern warehouses eliminate the need for elevators—and permit the use of power-operated lift trucks, battery-operated motor scooters, roller-skating order pickers, electric hoists for heavy items, and hydraulic ramps to speed loading and unloading. Most of these new warehouses use lift trucks and pallets (wooden trays that carry many cases) for vertical storage and better use of space. Computers monitor inventory, order needed stock, and track storing and shipping costs. Some warehouses even have computer-controlled order picking systems that speed the process of locating and assembling the assortment required to fill an order.[26]

Discrepancies of assortment or quantity between one channel level and another are often adjusted at the place where goods are stored. It reduces handling costs to regroup and store at the same place—*if both functions are required*. But sometimes regrouping is required when storing isn't.

Don't store it, distribute it

A **distribution center** is a special kind of warehouse designed to speed the flow of goods and avoid unnecessary storing costs. Anchor Hocking moves over a million pounds of its housewares products through its distribution center each day. Faster inventory turnover and easier bulk-breaking reduce the cost of carrying inventory. This is important. These costs may run as high as 35 percent of the value of the average inventory a year. The lower costs and faster turnover lead to bigger profits.

Today, the distribution center concept is widely used by firms at all channel levels.

Mattel's new, computerized distribution center in Germany makes it possible to efficiently consolidate, route, and deliver orders to retailers throughout Europe.

PHYSICAL DISTRIBUTION CHALLENGES AND OPPORTUNITIES

**Coordinating PD
activities among firms**

PD decisions interact with other Place decisions, the rest of the marketing mix, and the whole marketing strategy. As a result, if firms in the channel do not plan and coordinate how they will share PD activities, PD is likely to be a source of conflict rather than a basis for competitive advantage.

**JIT requires
even more cooperation**

We introduced the concept of just-in-time (JIT) delivery in Chapter 7. Now that you know more about PD alternatives, it's useful to consider some of the marketing strategy implications of this approach.

A key advantage of JIT for business customers is that it reduces their PD costs—especially storing and handling costs. However, when a customer doesn't have any backup inventory, there's no security blanket if something goes wrong. Thus, a JIT system requires that a supplier have extremely high quality control in production and in every PD activity, including its PD service.

For example, to control the risk of transportation problems, JIT suppliers often locate their facilities close to important customers. Trucks may make smaller and more frequent deliveries—perhaps even several times a day. As this suggests, a JIT system usually requires a supplier to be able to respond to very short order lead times. In fact, a supplier's production often needs to be based on the customer's production schedule. However, if that isn't possible, the supplier must have adequate inventory to meet the customer's needs.

A JIT system shifts greater responsibility for PD activities backward in the channel—to suppliers. If the supplier can be more efficient than the customer could be in controlling PD costs—and still provide the customer with the service level required—this approach can work well for everyone in the channel. However, it should be clear that JIT is not always the lowest cost—or best—approach. It may be better for a supplier to produce and ship in

CSX uses satellite communications to keep tabs on every container as it moves between different transportation modes.

Another One Of Our
Trains Arrives At The Station.

If you think we're just a railroad, take another look.

We're a lot more. We're Sea-Land, one of the largest container ship lines on earth, serving 76 ports in 64 countries.

We're also trucks. Barges. Pipelines. Energy resources. Fiber optics. Resorts and property development. And, of course, the railroad. And we're developing new technology to make it all work together.

We're CSX, the first true global transporter. If you've never heard of one before, it's because there's never been one before. This is a company on the move.

**CSX
The Company
That Puts Things
In Motion.**
Transportation/Energy/Properties/Technology

larger, more economical quantities—if the savings offset the distribution system's total inventory and handling costs.[27]

Better information helps coordinate PD

Coordinating all of the elements of PD has always been a challenge—even in a single firm. Trying to coordinate PD in the whole channel is even tougher. Keeping track of inventory levels, when to order, and where goods are when they move is difficult. Even so, marketing managers for some firms are finding solutions to these challenges—with help from computers.

Many firms now continuously update their marketing information systems—so they can immediately find out what products have sold, the level of the current inventory, and when goods being transported will arrive. And coordination of physical distribution decisions throughout channels of distribution will continue to improve as more firms are able to have their computers talk to each other directly.

Electronic data interchange sets a standard

Until recently, differences in computer systems from one firm to another hampered the flow of information. Many firms now attack this problem by adopting **electronic data interchange (EDI)**—an approach that puts information in a standardized format easily shared between different computer systems. Purchase orders, shipping or inventory reports, and other paper documents are now being replaced with computerized EDI. With EDI, a customer transmits its order information directly to the supplier's computer. The supplier's computer immediately processes the order—and schedules production, order assembly, and transportation. Inventory information is automatically updated, and status reports are available instantly. The supplier might then use EDI to send the updated information to the transportation provider's computer. This type of system is becoming very common. In fact, almost all international transportation firms rely on EDI links with their customers.[28]

Better coordination of PD activities is a key reason for the success of Pepperidge Farm's line of premium cookies. A few years ago, the company spent a lot of money making the wrong products and delivering them—too slowly—to the wrong market. Poor information was the problem. Delivery truck drivers took orders from retailers, assembled them manually at regional offices, and then mailed them to Pepperidge's bakeries. Now the company has an almost instantaneous EDI link between sales, delivery, inventory, and production. Hundreds of the company's 2,200 drivers use hand-held computers to record the inventory at each stop along their routes. They phone the information into a computer at the bakeries—so that cookies in short supply will be produced. The right assortment of fresh cookies is quickly shipped to local markets, and delivery trucks are loaded with what retailers need that day. Pepperidge Farm now moves cookies from its bakeries to store shelves in about three days; most cookie producers take about 10 days. That means fresher cookies for consumers—and helps to support Pepperidge Farm's high-quality strategy and premium price.[29]

Ethical issues may arise

Most of the ethical issues that arise in the PD area concern communications about product availability. For example, some critics say that marketers too often take orders for products that are not available or which they cannot deliver as quickly as customers expect. Yet a marketing manager can't always know precisely how long it will take before a product will be available. It doesn't make sense for the marketer to lose a customer if it appears that he or she can satisfy the customer's needs. But the customer may be inconvenienced or face added cost if the marketer's best guess isn't accurate.

Some suppliers criticize customers for abusing efforts to coordinate PD activities in the channel. For example, some retailers hedge against uncertain demand by telling suppliers that they plan to place an order, but then they don't *confirm* the order until the last minute. They want to be able to say that it wasn't an order in the first place—if sales in the store are

A marketing manager must be sensitive to the environmental effects of transportation decisions.

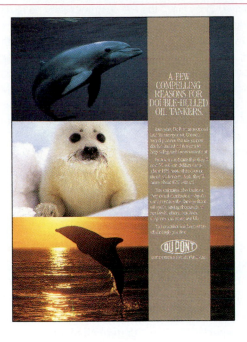

slow. This shifts the uncertainty to the supplier and reduces the retailer's inventory costs. Is this unethical? Some think it is. However, a marketing manager should realize that the firm's order policies can reduce such problems—if the cost of providing the service customers want is higher than what they will pay. In other words, this may simply be another trade-off that the marketer must consider in setting up the PD system.[30]

Transportation choices affect the environment

Marketing managers must be sensitive to the environmental effects of transportation decisions. Some say trucks cause air pollution in already crowded cities. People who live near airports suffer the consequences of noise pollution. A damaged pipeline can spew thousands of gallons of oil before it can be repaired. The Exxon Valdez oil spill in Alaska is a dramatic example of the kind of environmental disaster that can happen when a transportation accident occurs.

Today, the public *expects* companies to manufacture and transport products in an environmentally sound manner. If companies don't meet these expectations, consumers will show their dissatisfaction through their market choices. However, these environmental efforts increase the cost of distribution. Improved technology may help to make trade-offs between cost and environment less difficult. But ultimately, the people in a society must decide whether to bear the consequences of pollution or pay for higher distribution costs.[31]

CONCLUSION

In this chapter, we discussed the role of Place and noted that Place decisions are especially important because they may be difficult and expensive to change.

Marketing specialists—and channel systems—develop to adjust discrepancies of quantity and assort-

ment. Their regrouping activities are basic in any economic system. And adjusting discrepancies provides opportunities for creative marketers.

Channel planning requires firms to decide on the degree of market exposure they want. The ideal level of exposure may be intensive, selective, or exclusive. They also need to consider the legality of limiting market exposure to avoid having to undo an expensively developed channel system or face steep fines.

The importance of planning channel systems was discussed—along with the role of a channel captain. We stressed that channel systems compete with each other—and that vertical marketing systems seem to be winning.

We also considered physical distribution activities—and how they provide *time* and *place* utility. We looked at

the PD customer service level and why it is important. We emphasized the physical distribution concept which focuses on coordinating all the storing and transporting activities into a smoothly working system—to deliver the desired service level at the lowest total cost.

We also discussed how computerized information links—within firms and among firms in the channel—are increasingly important in blending all of the activities into a smooth-running system.[32]

QUESTIONS AND PROBLEMS

1. Review the Goodyear case at the beginning of the chapter and discuss how Goodyear's Place decisions relate to the product class concept. Explain your thinking.

2. Give two examples of service firms that work with other channel specialists to sell their products to final consumers. What marketing functions is the specialist providing in each case?

3. Discuss some reasons why a firm that produces installations might use direct distribution in its domestic market but use middlemen to reach overseas customers.

4. Explain discrepancies of quantity and assortment using the clothing business as an example. How does the application of these concepts change when selling steel to the automobile industry? What impact does this have on the number and kinds of marketing specialists required?

5. Insurance agents are middlemen who help other members of the channel by providing information and handling the selling function. Does it make sense for an insurance agent to specialize and work exclusively with one insurance provider? Why or why not?

6. Discuss the Place objectives and distribution arrangements that are appropriate for the following products (indicate any special assumptions you have to make to obtain an answer):

   a. A postal scale for products weighing up to 2 pounds.
   b. Children's toys: (1) radio-controlled model airplanes costing $80 or more, (2) small rubber balls.
   c. Heavy-duty, rechargeable, battery-powered nut tighteners for factory production lines.
   d. Fiberglass fabric used in making roofing shingles.

7. Give an example of a producer that uses two or more different channels of distribution. Briefly discuss what problems this might cause.

8. Explain how a channel captain can help traditional independent firms compete with a corporate (integrated) channel system.

9. What would happen if retailer-organized channels (either formally integrated or administered) dominated consumer product marketing?

10. How does the nature of the product relate to the degree of market exposure desired?

11. Why would middlemen want to be exclusive distributors for a product? Why would producers want exclusive distribution? Would middlemen be equally anxious to get exclusive distribution for any type of product? Why or why not? Explain with reference to the following products: candy bars, batteries, golf clubs, golf balls, steak knives, televisions, and industrial woodworking machinery.

12. Briefly explain which aspects of customer service you think would be most important for a producer that sells fabric to a firm that manufactures furniture.

13. Discuss the types of trade-offs involved in PD costs, service levels, and sales.

14. Discuss the relative advantages and disadvantages of railroads, trucks, and airlines as transporting methods.

15. Discuss some of the ways that air transportation can change other aspects of a Place system.

16. Indicate the nearest location where you would expect to find large storage facilities. What kinds of products would be stored there? Why are they stored there instead of some other place?

17. Clearly differentiate between a warehouse and a distribution center. Explain how a specific product would be handled differently by each.

18. Discuss some of the ways computers are being used to improve PD decisions.

19. Would a just-in-time delivery system require a supplier to pay attention to quality control? Give an example to illustrate your points.

20. Discuss the problems a supplier might encounter in using a just-in-time delivery system with a customer in a foreign country.

SUGGESTED CASES

13. Fileco, Inc.
15. Samco, Inc.
16. Jenson Company

25. Riverside Packers, Inc.
29. Dalton Olds, Inc.
33. Ladco Mfg. Co.

COMPUTER-AIDED PROBLEM

10. Intensive versus Selective Distribution

Hydropump, Inc., produces and sells high-quality pumps to business customers. Its marketing research shows a growing market for a similar type of pump aimed at final consumers—for use with home hot tubs and jacuzzi tubs. Hydropump will have to develop new channels of distribution to reach this target market because most consumers rely on a retailer for advice about the combination of tub, pump, heater, and related plumbing fixtures they need. Hydropump's marketing manager, Robert Black, is trying to decide between intensive and selective distribution. With intensive distribution, he would try to sell through all the plumbing supply, swimming pool, and hot-tub retailers who will carry the pump. He estimates that about 5,600 suitable retailers would be willing to carry a new pump. With selective distribution, he would focus on about 280 of the best hot-tub dealers (two or three in the hundred largest metropolitan areas).

Intensive distribution would require Hydropump to do more mass selling—primarily advertising in home renovation magazines—to help stimulate consumer familiarity with the brand and convince retailers that Hydropump equipment will sell. The price to the retailer might have to be lower too (to permit a bigger markup) so they will be motivated to sell Hydropump rather than some other brand offering a smaller markup.

With intensive distribution, each Hydropump sales rep could probably handle about 300 retailers effectively. With selective distribution, each sales rep could handle only about 70 retailers because more merchandising help would be necessary. Managing the smaller sales force and fewer retailers—with the selective approach—would require less manager overhead cost.

Going to all suitable and available retailers would make the pump available through about 20 times as many retailers and have the potential of reaching more customers. However, many customers shop at more than one retailer before making a final choice—so selective distribution would reach almost as many potential customers. Further, if Hydropump is using selective distribution, it would get more attention for its pump—and a larger share of pump purchases—at each retailer.

Black decides to use a spreadsheet to analyze the benefits and costs of intensive versus selective distribution.

a. Based on the initial spreadsheet, which approach seems to be the most sensible for Hydropump? Why?
b. A consultant points out that even selective distribution needs national promotion. If Black has to increase advertising and spend a total of $120,000 on mass selling to be able to recruit the retailers he wants for selective distribution, would selective or intensive distribution be more profitable?
c. With intensive distribution, how large a share (percent) of the retailers' total unit sales would Hydropump have to capture to sell enough pumps to earn $220,880 profit?

For additional questions related to this problem, see Exercise 10–4 in the *Learning Aid for use with Essentials of Marketing*, 6th edition.

Retailers and Their Strategy Planning

Chapter 11

When You Finish This Chapter, You Should

❶

Understand how retailers plan their marketing strategies.

❷

Know about the many kinds of retailers that work with producers and wholesalers as members of channel systems.

❸

Understand the differences among the conventional and nonconventional retailers—including those who accept the mass-merchandising concept.

❹

Understand scrambled merchandising and the "wheel of retailing."

❺

See why size or belonging to a chain can be important to a retailer.

❻

Understand why retailing has developed in different ways in different countries.

❼

Understand the important new terms (shown in red).

Toys "R" Us is serious about retailing. Although toy sales in the United States have been flat for a number of years, sales for the Toys "R" Us chain have increased about 25 percent a year. Nearly a quarter of every dollar U.S. consumers spend on toys is now spent at a Toys "R" Us.

Toys "R" Us didn't always enjoy this lofty success. In 1978, it nearly experienced what many other new retailers do: bankruptcy! At that time, most toys were distributed through thousands of small, independent toy stores. Many of them had been working closely with toy producers for years. Moreover, mass-merchandise chains like Kmart were successful offering low prices on the fastest-selling toys. In this highly competitive market, Toys "R" Us pioneered a new retailing format—and it was a real success.

Each store—now more than 500 of them—is conveniently located, and each offers low prices on a mind-boggling selection of 18,000 toys. The company's buying clout helps it to get low prices from toy producers. In addition, it uses computers in each store to spot fast-selling toys before they're hits. This allows the firm to buy early and avoid stockouts that trouble other toy retailers.

Toys "R" Us is also aggressively opening stores in overseas markets—such as the United Kingdom, Hong Kong, and Japan. In many of these countries, small shops and department stores still dominate toy distribution.

To understand how Toys "R" Us is affecting these markets, let's look at what happened when Toys "R" Us opened its first German store in 1987. Small toy retailers criticized Toys "R" Us's self-service approach. They said there would be no expert to warn parents about dangerous toys. Many German toymakers refused to sell to the chain. They feared that its hard-nosed buying would eat into their profits. Consumers, on the other hand, liked Toys "R" Us, and sales grew fast. In fact, as other German retailers began to copy the Toys "R"

Us approach, overall toy sales increased by 50 percent. Toys "R" Us got one fourth of that increase, but competitors got more business too—and consumers got better selections and prices.[1]

THE NATURE OF RETAILING

Retailing covers all of the activities involved in the sale of products to final consumers. Retailers range from large, sophisticated chains of specialized stores—like Toys "R" Us—to individual merchants like the woman who sells baskets from an open stall in the central market in Ibadan, Nigeria.

Retailing is crucial to consumers in every macro-marketing system. For example, consumers spend $1.8 *trillion* (that's $1,800,000,000,000!) a year buying goods and services from U.S. retailers. If the retailing effort isn't effective, everyone in the channel suffers—and some products aren't sold at all.

In this chapter, we'll talk about the major decision areas shown in Exhibit 11–1. We'll emphasize the different types of retailers and how they are evolving. It's important to understand this evolution because the pace of change in retailing is accelerating. Understanding how and why retailing changes will help you know what to expect in the future.

The nature of retailing—and its rate of change—are generally related to the stage and speed of a country's economic development. In the United States, retailing tends to be more varied—and more mature—than in most other countries. By studying the U.S. system—and how it is changing—you will better understand how retailing is evolving in other parts of the world.

PLANNING A RETAILER'S STRATEGY

Retailers interact directly with final consumers—so strategy planning is critical to their survival. If a retailer loses a customer to a competitor, the retailer is the one who suffers. Producers and wholesalers still make *their* sale regardless of which retailer sells the product. Retailers must be guided by the old maxim "Goods well bought are half sold."

Most retailers in developed nations sell more than one kind of product. Think of the retailer's *whole offering*—assortment of goods and services, advice from salesclerks, convenience, and the like—as its "Product." In the case of service retailing—dry cleaning, fast food, or one-hour photo processing, for example—the retailer is also the producer. Now let's look at why customers choose particular retailers.

Exhibit 11–1   Strategy Decision Areas for a Retailer

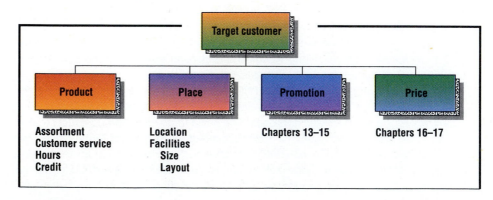

Consumers have reasons for buying from particular retailers

Different consumers prefer different kinds of retailers. But many retailers either don't know or don't care why. All too often, beginning retailers just rent a store and assume customers will show up. As a result, in the United States more than three fourths of new retailing ventures fail during the first year. To avoid this fate, a new retailer—or one trying to adjust to changing conditions—should carefully identify possible target markets and try to understand why these people buy where they do.[2]

Economic needs—which store has the best value?

Consumers consider many factors when choosing a particular retailer. Some of the most important ones relate to their economic needs. Obviously price is relevant, and so are:

1. Convenience.
2. Variety of selection.
3. Quality of products.
4. Help from salespeople.
5. Reputation for integrity and fairness in dealings.
6. Special services offered—delivery, credit, returned-goods privileges.
7. Value offered.

Emotional needs also affect the choice

Consumers may also have important emotional reasons for preferring particular retailers. Some people get an ego boost from shopping in a prestige store. Others just want to shop in a store where they won't feel out of place.

Different stores seem to attract customers from different social classes. People like to shop where salespeople and other customers are similar to themselves. So a store fills the emotional needs of its target market(s). Dollar General—a chain of 1,300 general merchandise stores—succeeds with a "budget" image that appeals to lower-class customers. Tiffany's, on the other hand, works at its upper-class image.

There is no one right answer as to whom a store should appeal. But ignorance about emotional dimensions—including social class appeal—could lead to serious errors in marketing strategy planning.[3]

Product classes help explain store types

We can simplify retail strategy planning by extending our earlier discussion of consumer product classes—convenience, shopping, and specialty products—to define three types of stores.

[handwritten margin note: 3-5 mins travel time (trade area)]

[handwritten margin note: 7-11 owned by Southland didn't move fast enough by putting in gas.]

A **convenience store** is a convenient place to shop—either because it is centrally located near other shopping or because it's "in the neighborhood." Easy parking, fast checkout, and easy-to-find merchandise add to the convenience. **Shopping stores** attract *[handwritten: Macys]* customers from greater distances because of the width and depth of their assortments— *[handwritten: Ricks]* and because of their displays, demonstrations, information, and knowledgeable salesclerks. **Specialty stores** are those for which customers have developed a strong attraction. For whatever reasons—service, selection, or reputation—some customers insist on shopping there. *[handwritten: A particular product, high margins, customers insist on that store.]*

Store types based on how customers see the store

[handwritten margin note: Joint stores. Walmart + McDonalds. Ventures. Cumulative Attraction]

Store types refer to *the way customers think about the store*—not just the kind of products the store carries. Different market segments might see or use a particular store differently. Remember that this was true with the product classes too. So a retailer's strategy planning must consider potential customers' attitudes toward *both* the product and the store. Exhibit 11–2 classifies market segments by how they see both the store type and the product class.

By identifying which competitors are satisfying which market segments, the retailer may see that some boxes in Exhibit 11–2 are already filled or that some are being ignored.

[handwritten note at bottom: Trade Area - Distance, Size of Center, County Barriers, Travel Routes. GA Power will give demographic information for free, because they want biz.]

Exhibit 11–2   How Customers View Store-Product Combinations

Product class	Store type		
	Convenience	**Shopping**	**Specialty**
Convenience	Will buy any brand at most accessible store	Shop around to find better service and/or lower prices	Prefer store. Brand may be important
Shopping	Want some selection but will settle for assortment at most accessible store	Want to compare both products and store mixes	Prefer store but insist on adequate assortment
Specialty	Prefer particular product but like place convenience too	Prefer particular product but still seeking best total product and mix	Prefer both store and product

For example, houseplants used to be sold only by florists or greenhouses. This was fine for customers who wanted a shopping-store variety. But for others, going to such outlets was too much trouble. Then some retailers targeted the convenience-store segment with small houseplant departments or stores in neighborhood shopping centers. They found a big market willing to buy plants—at convenience stores.

Different types of retailers emphasize different strategies

Retailers have an almost unlimited number of ways in which to alter their offerings—their marketing mixes—to appeal to a target market. Because of all the variations, it's oversimplified to classify retailers and their strategies based on a single characteristic—such as merchandise, services, or store size. But it is useful to consider basic types of retailers—and some differences in their strategies.

Let's look first at conventional retailers—and then see how others successfully modify conventional offerings to better meet the needs of *some* consumers. Think about *why* the changes take place. That will help you identify opportunities and plan better marketing strategies.

CONVENTIONAL RETAILERS—TRY TO AVOID PRICE COMPETITION

Single-line, limited-line retailers specialize by product

A hundred and fifty years ago, **general stores**—which carried anything they could sell in reasonable volume—were the main retailers in the United States. But with the growing number of consumer products after the Civil War, general stores couldn't offer enough variety in all their traditional lines. So some stores began specializing in dry goods, apparel, furniture, or groceries.

Now most conventional retailers are **single-line** or **limited-line stores**—stores that specialize in certain lines of related products rather than a wide assortment. Many stores specialize not only in a single line—such as clothing—but also in a *limited-line* within the broader line. For example, within the clothing line, a store might carry *only* shoes, formal wear, men's casual wear, or even neckties—but offer depth in that limited line.

Single-line, limited-line stores are being squeezed

The main advantage of such stores is that they can satisfy some target markets better. Some even achieve specialty-store status by adjusting to suit certain customers. But single-line and limited-line stores face the costly problem of having to stock some

In Japan and Europe, small limited-line stores are still much more common.

slow-moving items in order to satisfy the store's target market. Many of these stores are small—with high expenses relative to sales. They try to avoid competition on identical products so they can keep prices up.

Conventional retailers like this have been around for a long time and are still found in every community. They are a durable lot and clearly satisfy some people's needs. In fact, in most countries conventional retailers still handle the vast majority of all retailing sales.

However, this situation is changing. Nowhere is the change clearer than in the United States. Conventional retailers are being squeezed by retailers who modify their mixes in the various ways suggested in Exhibit 11–3. Let's look closer at some of these other types of retailers.

Exhibit 11–3   Types of Retailers and the Nature of Their Offerings

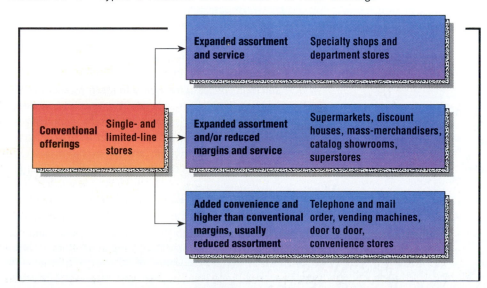

EXPAND ASSORTMENT AND SERVICE—TO COMPETE AT A HIGH PRICE

Specialty shops usually sell shopping products

A **specialty shop**—a type of conventional limited-line store—is usually small and has a distinct "personality." Specialty shops often sell special types of shopping products—such as high-quality sporting goods, exclusive clothing, cameras, or even microwave ovens. They aim at a carefully defined target market by offering a unique product assortment, knowledgeable salesclerks, and better service. For example, specialty shops developed to satisfy people who want help selecting computer software. Expert clerks know the many different software packages available and can explain and demonstrate the advantages of each. These stores also carry computer books and magazines as well as diskettes and other computer accessories.

The specialty shop's major advantage is that it caters to certain types of customers who the management and salespeople come to know well. This simplifies buying, speeds turnover, and cuts costs due to obsolescence and style changes. Specialty shops probably will continue to be a part of the retailing scene as long as customers have varied tastes—and the money to satisfy them.[4]

Don't confuse specialty *shops* with specialty *stores.* A specialty store is a store that for some reason (service, quality, etc.) has become *the* store for some customers. For example, some customers see Sears as a specialty store and regularly buy major appliances there—without shopping anywhere else.

Department stores combine many limited-line stores and specialty shops

Department stores are larger stores that are organized into many separate departments and offer many product lines. Each department is like a separate limited-line store and handles a wide variety of shopping products—such as men's wear or housewares.

Even though department stores account for less than 1 percent of the total number of retail stores, they make almost 10 percent of total retail sales.[5] They also lead in customer services—including credit, merchandise return, and delivery. But their share of retail business has been declining since the 1970s. Well-run limited-line stores compete with good service—and they often carry the same brands. In the United States and many other countries, mass-merchandising retailers pose an even bigger threat.[6] We'll discuss them next.

EVOLUTION OF MASS-MERCHANDISING RETAILERS

Mass-merchandising is different than conventional retailing

So far we've been describing retailers primarily in terms of their product *assortment.* This reflects traditional thinking about retailing. We could talk about supermarkets and discount houses in these terms too. But then we would miss some important differences—just as some conventional retailers did when mass-merchandising retailers first appeared.

Conventional retailers think that demand in their area is fixed—and they have a "buy low and sell high" philosophy. Some modern retailers reject these ideas. They accept the **mass-merchandising concept**—which says that retailers should offer low prices to get faster turnover and greater sales volumes—by appealing to larger markets. To understand mass-merchandising better, let's look at its evolution from the development of supermarkets and discounters to modern mass-merchandisers, like Kmart and Wal-Mart in the United States and Tesco in the United Kingdom.

Supermarkets started the move to mass-merchandising

From a world view, most food stores are relatively small single- or limited-line operations, a situation that makes shopping for food inconvenient and expensive. Many Italians, for example, still go to one shop for pasta, another for meat, and yet another for milk. Although this seems outdated, keep in mind that many of the world's consumers don't

have access to **supermarkets**—large stores specializing in groceries with self-service and wide assortments.

The basic idea for supermarkets developed in the United States during the early Depression years. Some innovators felt they could increase sales by charging lower prices. They also introduced self-service and provided a broad product assortment in large stores. Success and profits came from large-volume sales—not from high traditional markups.[7]

Supermarkets sell convenience products—but in quantity. Newer supermarkets carry 30,000 product items and stores average around 40,000 square feet. According to the Food Marketing Institute, a store must have annual sales of at least $2.5 million to be called a supermarket. However, annual sales for each of the 23,000 supermarkets average about $11 million. Today, supermarkets have reached the saturation level in the United States, but in many countries they are just becoming a force.[8]

Modern supermarkets are planned for maximum efficiency. Scanners at checkout counters make it possible to carefully analyze the sales and profit of each item—and allocate more shelf space to faster-moving and higher-profit items. This helps sell more products—faster. It also reduces the investment in inventory, makes stocking easier, and minimizes the cost of handling products. *Survival* depends on such efficiency. Grocery competition is keen, and net profits after taxes in grocery supermarkets usually run a thin 1 percent of sales—*or less!*

To increase sales volume, some supermarket operators open "super warehouse" stores. These 50,000- to 100,000-square-foot stores carry more items than supermarkets, but they often don't stock perishable items like produce or meat.[9]

Catalog showroom retailers preceded discount houses

Catalog showroom retailers sell several lines out of a catalog and display showroom—with backup inventories. Before 1940, catalog sellers were usually wholesalers who also sold at discounted prices to friends and members of groups—such as labor unions or church groups. In the 1970s, however, these operations expanded rapidly by aiming at final consumers and offering attractive catalogs and improved facilities. Catalog showroom retailers—like Service Merchandise, Consumers Distributing, and Best—offer big price savings and deliver almost all the items in their catalogs from backroom warehouses. They emphasize well-known manufacturer brands of jewelry, gifts, luggage, and small appliances but offer few services.[10]

Early catalog retailers didn't bother conventional retailers because they weren't well publicized and accounted for only a small portion of total retail sales. If the early catalog retailers had moved ahead aggressively—as the current catalog retailers are—the retailing scene might be different. But instead, discount houses developed.

Discount houses upset some conventional retailers

Right after World War II, some retailers moved beyond offering discounts to selected customers. These **discount houses** offered "hard goods" (cameras, TVs, appliances)—at substantial price cuts—to customers who would go to the discounter's low-rent store, pay cash, and take care of any service or repair problems themselves. These retailers sold at 20 to 30 percent off the list price being charged by conventional retailers.

In the early 1950s—with war shortages finally over—manufacturer brands became more available. The discount houses were able to get any brands they wanted—and to offer wider assortments. At this stage, many discounters turned respectable—moving to better locations and offering more services and guarantees. They began to act more like regular retailers. But they kept their prices lower than conventional retailers to keep turnover high.

Mass-merchandisers are more than discounters

Mass-merchandisers are large, self-service stores with many departments that emphasize "soft goods" (housewares, clothing, and fabrics) but still follow the discount house's emphasis on lower margins to get faster turnover. Mass-merchandisers—like Kmart and Wal-Mart—have checkout counters in the front of the store and little sales help on the floor. The average mass-merchandiser has nearly 60,000 square feet of floor space, but many new stores are 100,000 square feet.

Mass-merchandisers grew rapidly. In fact, they expanded so rapidly in some areas that they were no longer taking customers from conventional retailers—but from each other. Some mass-merchandisers—especially Wal-Mart—concentrated on opening stores in smaller towns. This upset some small-town merchants—who thought they were safe from the competitive rat-race.[11]

Superstores meet all routine needs

Some supermarkets and mass-merchandisers have moved toward becoming **superstores (hypermarkets)**—very large stores that try to carry not only foods, but all goods and services that the consumer purchases *routinely*. Such a store may look like a mass-merchandiser, but it's different in concept. A superstore is trying to meet *all* the customer's routine needs—at a low price.

Superstores carry about 50,000 items. In addition to foods, a superstore carries personal care products, medicine, some apparel, toys, some lawn and garden products, gasoline—and services such as dry cleaning, travel reservations, bill paying, and banking. Some superstores are very large—over 200,000 square feet.[12]

New mass-merchandising formats keep coming

The warehouse club is another retailing format gaining in popularity. Price Club, Sam's Warehouse, and Costco are three of the largest. Consumers usually pay an annual membership fee to shop in these large, bare-bones facilities. Among the 3,500 items per store, they carry food, appliances, yard tools, tires, and other items that many consumers see as homogeneous shopping items—and want at the lowest possible price.[13]

Single-line mass-merchandisers are coming on strong

Since 1980 some retailers—focusing on single product lines—have adopted the mass-merchandisers' approach with great success. Toys "R" Us pioneered this trend. Similarly, Hechingers (hardware), Payless Drugstores, B. Dalton Books, Ikea (furniture), Circuit City (electronics), and Sports Unlimited attract large numbers of customers with their large assortment and low prices in a specific product category. These stores are called category killers because it's so hard for less specialized retailers to compete.[14]

SOME RETAILERS FOCUS ON ADDED CONVENIENCE

Supermarkets, discounters, and mass-merchandisers provide many different products at low prices under one roof. But sometimes consumers want more convenience even if the price is a little higher. Let's look at some retailers who meet this need.

Convenience (food) stores must have the right assortment

Convenience (food) stores are a convenience-oriented variation of the conventional limited-line food stores. Instead of expanding their assortment, however, convenience stores limit their stock to pickup or fill-in items like bread, milk, snacks, and beer. Many also sell gas. Stores such as 7-Eleven, Majik Market, and Stop-N-Go fill consumers' needs between major shopping trips to a supermarket. They offer convenience—not assortment—and often charge prices 10 to 20 percent higher than nearby supermarkets.[15]

Single-line mass-merchandisers, like Circuit City, offer selections and prices that make it difficult for traditional retailers to compete.

Vending machines are convenient

Automatic vending is selling and delivering products through vending machines. Although the growth in vending machine sales is impressive, such sales account for only about 1.5 percent of total U.S. retail sales. But for some target markets, this retailing method can't be ignored.

The major disadvantage to automatic vending is high cost. The machines are expensive to buy, stock, and repair relative to the volume they sell. Marketers of similar nonvended products can operate profitably on a margin of about 20 percent. The vending industry requires about 41 percent to cover costs—so they must charge higher prices.[16]

Shop at home—with telephone, TV, and direct-mail retailing

Telephone and direct-mail retailing allow consumers to shop at home—usually placing orders by mail or a toll-free long-distance telephone call—and charging the purchase to a credit card. Typically, catalogs and ads on TV let customers see the offerings, and purchases are delivered by United Parcel Service (UPS). Some consumers really like the convenience of this type of retailing—especially for products not available in local stores.

The early mail-order houses—Sears, Roebuck and Montgomery Ward—pioneered catalog selling. During the 1980s, as many new firms adopted this approach, sales grew at the rapid rate of about 15 percent a year. In 1990, over 13.5 billion catalogs were distributed—an average of 54 for every man, woman, and child! With computer mailing lists to help target customers, companies like Sharper Image, Renovator's Supply, and Horchow Collection are extremely successful with catalogs for narrow lines—electronic gadgets, antique hardware, and expensive gift items.[17]

This approach reduces costs by using warehouse-type buildings and limited sales help. And shoplifting—a big expense for most retailers—isn't a problem. After-tax profits for mail-order retailers average 7 percent of sales—more than twice the profit margins for most other types of retailers. However, increasing competition and slower sales growth are beginning to reduce these margins.

Put the catalog on cable TV or computer

Home Shopping Network and others succeed by devoting cable TV channels to home shopping. Some experts think that as shopping channels become more popular sales will mushroom to $20 billion a year by the end of the decade.[18]

A number of marketers are trying to offer electronic shopping, which allows consumers to connect their personal computers or a push-button phone to central computer systems.

Most of the early efforts in this area fizzled because they proved too complicated for most consumers. Now, however, dial-up systems such as Prodigy—a joint venture between Sears and IBM—seem to be making headway.[19]

Door-to-door retailers—give personal attention

Door-to-door selling means going directly to the consumer's home. It accounts for less than 1 percent of retail sales—but meets some consumers' needs for convenience and personal attention. Door-to-door selling can also be useful with unsought products—like encyclopedias. But with more adults working outside the home, it's getting harder to find someone at home during the day.

RETAILING TYPES ARE EXPLAINED BY CONSUMER NEEDS FILLED

We've talked about many different types of retailers and how they evolved. Earlier, we noted that no single characteristic provided a good basis for classifying all retailers. Now it helps to see the three-dimensional view of retailing presented in Exhibit 11–4. It positions different types of retailers in terms of three consumer-oriented dimensions: (1) width of assortment desired, (2) depth of assortment desired, and (3) a price/service combination. Price and service are combined because they are often indirectly related. Services are costly to provide. So a retailer that wants to emphasize low prices usually has to cut some services—and stores with a lot of service must charge prices that cover the added costs.

We can position most existing retailers within this three-dimensional market diagram. Exhibit 11–4, for example, suggests the *why* of vending machines. Some people—in the front upper left-hand corner—have a strong need for a specific item and are not interested in width of assortment, depth of assortment, or price.

Exhibit 11–4   A Three-Dimensional View of the Market for Retail Facilities and the Probable Position of Some Present Offerings

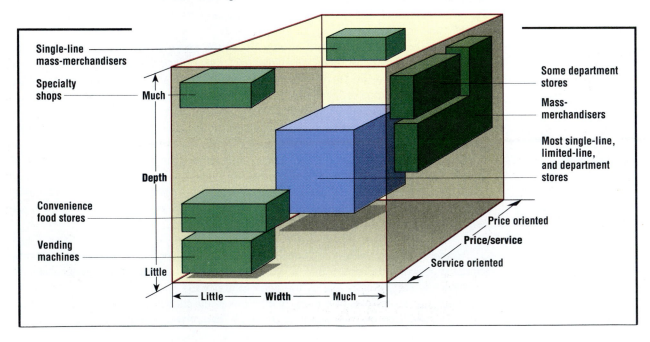

WHY RETAILERS EVOLVE AND CHANGE

Exhibit 11–4 compares different types of *existing* stores. Now we'll look at some ways that retailing is changing.

Scrambled merchandising—mixing product lines for higher profits

Conventional retailers tend to specialize by product line. But most modern retailers are moving toward **scrambled merchandising**—carrying any product lines they think they can sell profitably. Supermarkets and drugstores sell anything they can move in volume—pantyhose, magazines, one-hour photo processing, antifreeze and motor oil, potted plants, and videotapes. Mass-merchandisers don't just sell everyday items but also cameras, jewelry, and even home computers.[20]

The wheel of retailing keeps rolling

The **wheel of retailing theory** says that new types of retailers enter the market as low-status, low-margin, low-price operators and then—if successful—evolve into more conventional retailers offering more services with higher operating costs and higher prices. Then they're threatened by new low-status, low-margin, low-price retailers—and the wheel turns again. Department stores, supermarkets, and mass-merchandisers went through this cycle.

Some innovators start with high margins

The wheel of retailing theory, however, doesn't explain all major retailing developments. Vending machines entered as high-cost, high-margin operations. Convenience food stores are high-priced. Suburban shopping centers don't emphasize low price.

Product life-cycle concept applies to retailer types too

We've seen that people's needs help explain why different kinds of retailers developed. But we have to apply the product life-cycle concept to understand this process better. A retailer with a new idea may have big profits—for a while. But if it's a really good idea, she can count on speedy imitation—and a squeeze on profits. Other retailers will "scramble" their product mix to sell products that offer them higher margins or faster turnover.

The cycle is illustrated by what happened with video movies. As the popularity of VCRs grew, video stores cropped up everywhere. The first ones charged $5 a night for a tape. As

Pantyhose are promoted to grocery chain buyers and microwave popcorn is promoted to video store managers—because many retailers scramble their merchandise lines to earn higher profits.

IKEA'S KNOCK-DOWN COMPETITION WITH TRADITIONAL RETAILERS

During the 1980s, most U.S. department stores stopped carrying furniture because turnover was too slow and costs were too high. That created an opportunity for smaller, limited-line stores specializing in bedding, upholstery, or casual dining. Now the Ikea (pronounced i-KEY-ah) retail chain is, in turn, shaking up these traditional home-furnishings retailers. When Ikea opened its first U.S. store in 1985, it had already developed a low-cost, low-service strategy that was successful in Sweden (where it started) and other parts of Europe. The same mass-merchandising format is proving very popular with price-conscious consumers in the United States.

It's difficult for small retailers to compete with Ikea's low prices or the 12,000-item selection it offers in each of its sprawling, 200,000-square-foot stores. To keep costs low, service is spartan. But Ikea uses a clever store layout that helps consumers get information and make purchase decisions without costly help from salespeople. A couch, for instance, is displayed both in a real-life setting and in a group with other couches so people can compare. A 200-page catalog—mailed to consumers who live within an hour's drive of the store—details prices and specifications. Shoppers wheel the boxes of assemble-it-yourself furniture to the cash register themselves. The store doesn't offer delivery either. But most consumers can carry the "knock-down" furniture designs home in a car. Ikea does offer some services. For example, it staffs a children's playroom—because parents shop better when they don't have their kids in tow. And a restaurant at the store offers consumers low-cost meals and a place to think over big purchase decisions.

Most furniture retailers buy producers' product lines at big wholesale furniture markets. But because Ikea's sales are so large, it designs quality furniture its customers will buy—and then contracts with a producer to make it. This also reduces distribution costs because the furniture is designed so it can be shipped disassembled.[21]

more competitors entered, however, they drove prices (and profits) down. Competition heated up even more as supermarkets and other stores started to rent the most popular tapes—sometimes for as little as 99 cents a night. Many video stores couldn't cover their costs at that price—and they went out of business.

Although the cycle for video stores moved very quickly, it can be much slower. But cycles do exist, and some conventional retailers are far along in their life cycles and may be declining. Recent innovators are still in the market growth stage. See Exhibit 11–5. Some retailing formats that are mature in the United States are only now beginning to grow in other countries.

Some retailers are confused by the scrambling going on around them. They don't see this evolutionary process. And they don't understand that some of their more successful competitors are aiming at different target markets—instead of just selling products.

Some modern retailing successes are firms that moved into a new market and started another life cycle—by aiming at needs along the edges of the market shown in Exhibit 11–4. The convenience food stores, for example, don't just sell food. They deliberately sell a particular assortment-service combination to meet a different need. This is also true of specialty shops and some of the mass-merchandisers and department store chains.[22]

Ethical issues may arise

Most retailers face intense competitive pressure. The desperation that comes with such pressure has pushed some retailers toward questionable marketing practices.

Critics argue, for example, that retailers too often advertise special sale items to bring price-sensitive shoppers into the store but then don't stock enough to meet demand. Other stores are criticized for pushing consumers to trade up to more expensive items. What is ethical and unethical in situations like these, however, is subject to debate. Retailers can't

Exhibit 11–5   Retailer Life Cycles—Timing and Years to Market Maturity

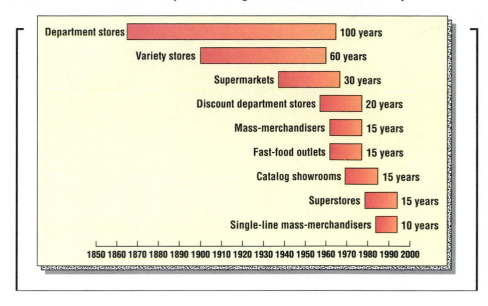

always anticipate demand perfectly, and deliveries may not arrive on time. Similarly, trading up may be a sensible part of a strategy—if it's done honestly.

In retailing, as in other types of business, the marketing concept should guide firms away from unethical treatment of customers. However, a retailer on the edge of going out of business may lose perspective on the need to satisfy customers in both the short and the long term.[23]

RETAILER SIZE AND PROFITS

A few big retailers do most of the business

The large number of retailers might suggest that retailing is a field of small businesses. To some extent this is true. As shown in Exhibit 11–6, about 60 percent of all the retail stores in the United States had annual sales of less than $500,000 during the last census of retailers. But that's only part of the story. Those same retailers accounted for only about 11 cents of every $1 in retail sales!

The larger retail stores—such as supermarkets and other stores selling more than $2.5 million annually—do most of the business. Only about 7 percent of the retail stores are this big, yet they account for about 60 percent of all retail sales.

On the other hand, the many small retailers can't be ignored. They do reach many consumers—and often are valuable channel members. But their large number—and relatively small sales volume—make working with them expensive. They often require separate marketing mixes.[24]

Being in a chain may help

One way for a retailer to achieve economies of scale is with a corporate chain. A **(corporate) chain store** is one of several stores owned and managed by the same firm. Most chains have at least some central buying for different stores. This allows them to take advantage of quantity discounts or opportunities for vertical integration—including developing their own efficient distribution centers. They can use EDI and other computer links to control inventory costs and stockouts. They may also spread promotion and management costs to many stores. Retail chains also have their own dealer brands. Many of these chains are becoming powerful members—or channel captains—in their channel systems.

Exhibit 11–6 Distribution of Stores by Size and Share of Total U.S. Retail Sales

Percent of stores

Small stores — 6.3% (Less than 50,000), 9.8% (50,000–99,999), 23.0% (100,000–249,999), 21.9% (250,000–499,999), 19.0% (500,000–1 million), 12.6% (1–2.5 million), 3.2% (2.5–5 million), 4.2% (Over 5 million) — Large stores

Store size (sales)

Percent of total retail sales

.18% (Less than 50,000), .65% (50,000–99,999), 3.5% (100,000–249,999), 7.1% (250,000–499,999), 12.0% (500,000–1 million), 16.9% (1–2.5 million), 10.1% (2.5–5 million), 49.7% (Over 5 million)

Independents form chains too

The growth of corporate chains encouraged the development of both cooperative chains and voluntary chains.

Cooperative chains are retailer-sponsored groups—formed by independent retailers—that run their own buying organizations and conduct joint promotion efforts. Sales of cooperative chains are rising as they learn how to compete with corporate chains. Examples include Associated Grocers, Certified Grocers, and True Value Hardware.

Voluntary chains are wholesaler-sponsored groups that work with "independent" retailers. Some are linked by contracts stating common operating procedures—and requiring the use of common storefront designs, store names, and joint promotion efforts. Examples include IGA and Super Valu in groceries, and Ace in hardware.

Franchisors form chains too

In a **franchise operation**, the franchisor develops a good marketing strategy, and the retail franchise holders carry out the strategy in their own units. The franchisor acts like a voluntary chain operator—or a producer. Each franchise holder benefits from the experience, buying power, and image of the larger company. In return, the franchise holder usually signs a contract to pay fees and commission—and to strictly follow franchise rules designed to continue the successful strategy. Exhibit 11–7 shows examples of well-known franchise operations.

Voluntary chains tend to work with existing retailers, while some franchisors like to work with—and train—newcomers. For newcomers, a franchise often reduces the risk of starting a new business. Only about 5 percent of new franchise operations fail in the first few years—compared to about 70 percent for other new retailers.

Franchise holders' sales are growing fast and will account for half of all retail sales by the year 2000. One reason is that franchising is especially popular with service firms, one of the fastest-growing sectors of the economy.[25]

Exhibit 11–7   Examples of Some Well-Known Franchise Operations

LOCATION OF RETAIL FACILITIES

Location can spell success or failure for a retail facility. But a good location depends on target markets, competitors, and costs. Let's review some of the ideas a retailer should consider in selecting a location.

Downtown and shopping strips evolve without a plan

Most cities have a central business district with many retail stores. At first, it may seem that such a district developed according to some plan. Actually, the location of individual stores is more an accident of time—and available spaces.

As cities grow, shopping strips of convenience stores develop along major roads. Generally, they emphasize convenience products. But a variety of single-line and limited-line stores may enter too, adding shopping products to the mix. Some retailers dress up the stores in these unplanned strips. The expense of remodeling is small compared to the higher rents at big shopping centers. Even so, strips aren't the planned shopping centers that developed in the last 30 years.

Planned shopping centers—not just a group of stores

A **planned shopping center** is a set of stores planned as a unit to satisfy some market needs. The stores sometimes act together for promotion purposes—and they usually provide free parking. Many centers are in enclosed malls that make shopping more pleasant, especially in harsh weather.

Neighborhood shopping centers consist of several convenience stores. These centers usually include a supermarket, drugstore, hardware store, hairstyling salon, laundry, dry cleaner, gas station, and perhaps others—such as a bakery or video store. They normally serve 7,500 to 40,000 people living within a 6- to 10-minute driving distance.

Community shopping centers are larger and offer some shopping stores as well as the convenience stores found in neighborhood shopping centers. They usually include a small department store that carries shopping products (clothing and home furnishings). But most sales in these centers are convenience products. These centers serve 40,000 to 150,000 people within a radius of five to six miles.

Regional shopping centers are the largest centers and emphasize shopping stores and shopping products. Most of these are enclosed malls, making shopping easier in bad weather. They usually include one or more large department stores and as many as 200 smaller stores. Stores that feature convenience products are often located at the edge of the center—so they won't get in the way of customers primarily interested in shopping.

Some retailers, including Pizza Hut and Home Shopping Network, reach consumers where it's convenient for them to buy—without going to a store.

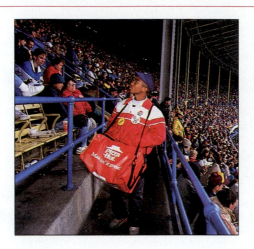 

Regional centers usually serve 150,000 or more people—like the downtown shopping districts of larger cities. However, regional centers usually are found near populated suburban areas. They draw customers from a radius of 7 to 10 miles—or even farther from rural areas where shopping facilities are poor. Regional shopping centers being built now often cover 2 million square feet—as large as 40 football fields![26]

DIFFERENCES IN RETAILING IN DIFFERENT NATIONS

New ideas spread across countries

New retailing approaches that succeed in one part of the world are often quickly adapted to other countries. Self-service approaches that started with supermarkets in the United States are now found in many retail operations around the world. Similarly, mass-merchandising approaches are popular in many countries. In 1969, for example, Kmart entered into a joint venture with Australia's largest department store chain to pioneer mass-merchandising there. The superstore concept, on the other hand, initially developed in Europe.

Mass-merchandising requires mass markets

The low prices, selections, and efficient operations offered by mass-merchandisers and other large chains might be attractive to consumers everywhere. But consumers in less developed nations often don't have the income to support mass distribution. The small shops that survive in these economies sell in very small quantities, often to a small number of consumers.

Some countries block change

The political and legal environment severely limits the evolution of retailing in some nations. Japan is a prime example. For years its Large Store Law—aimed at protecting the country's politically powerful small shopkeepers—has been a real barrier to retail change. The law restricts development of large stores by requiring special permits, which are routinely denied.

Japan says that it is taking steps to change the Large Store Law; in fact, that is why Toys "R" Us was able to enter the Japanese market. Even so, Toys "R" Us must limit its hours and close its stores a month out of every year—like other Japanese retailers. Most experts believe that it will be many years before Japan moves away from its system of small, limited-line shops. The inefficiency of that retail distribution system is an important reason why Japanese consumers pay very high prices for consumer products. Many countries in other parts of Asia, Europe, and South America impose similar restrictions.

The furniture retailing format Ikea developed in Sweden is proving very popular in the United States.

Consumer cooperatives are popular in some countries

Retailing in the United States is more diverse than in most other countries. Even so, some retailing formats, notably consumer cooperatives, are more prominent in other countries. Switzerland's Migros is perhaps the most successful example. Migros runs a variety of different types of stores, ranging from supermarkets to appliance and electronics centers.

Migros accounts for about 22 percent of food sales in Switzerland and nearly 16 percent of all retail sales. Consumer cooperatives probably won't become popular in markets where other types of retailers are already established and meeting customers' needs. However, some experts think consumer cooperatives like Migros will become a dominant form of retailing in central and eastern Europe.[27]

WHAT DOES THE FUTURE LOOK LIKE?

Retailing changed rapidly in the last 30 years—and the changes seem to be continuing. Scrambled merchandising may become even more scrambled. Some people predict even larger stores; others predict smaller ones.

More customer-oriented retailing may be coming

Any effort to forecast trends in such a situation is risky, but our three-dimensional picture of the retailing market (Exhibit 11–4) can help. Those who suggest bigger and bigger stores may be primarily concerned with the center of the diagram. Those who look for more small stores and specialty shops may be anticipating more small—but increasingly wealthy—target markets able to afford higher prices for special goods and services.

To serve small—but wealthy—markets, convenience stores continue to spread. And sales by electronic retailing are expected to grow. For example, Compusave Corporation now has an electronic catalog order system. A videodisc player hooked to a TV-like screen allows the consumer to see pictures and descriptions of thousands of products. The product assortment is similar to that at a catalog store—and the prices are even lower. The consumer makes a selection and inserts a credit card; the computer places the order and routes it to the consumer's home. These machines, being installed in shopping centers around the country, are popular with hurried, cost-conscious consumers.[28]

Many consumers simply don't have as much time to shop as they once did—and a growing number are willing to pay for convenience. Stores will probably continue to make shopping more convenient by staying open later, carrying assortments that make one-stop shopping possible, and being sure stocks don't run out. This interest in convenience and time savings should also lead to the growth of in-home shopping.

A&P's experiment takes self-service retailing a step further—with a scanner-equipped checkout unit consumers operate themselves.

In-home shopping will become more popular

More consumers will "let their fingers do the walking"—and telephone shopping will become more popular too. Mail-order houses and department stores already find phone business attractive. Selling to consumers through a home computer hasn't been very successful so far—but may be popular in the future.

Some retailers are becoming more powerful

We will continue to see growth in retail chains, franchises, and other cooperative arrangements. Such arrangements can help retailers serve their customers better—and also give the retailer more power in the channel.

We may also see more vertical arrangements in channel systems. This will affect present manufacturers—who already see retailers developing their own brands and using manufacturers mainly as production arms.

Changes in technology are also making some retailers more powerful. J. C. Penney, for instance, can spot a great garment in Italy and fly the piece to Dallas, where it is recreated on the computer. While the video image is shown to a focus group, the specs are sent to a manufacturer in the Orient. If the focus group likes the garment, Penney can have it in its stores in weeks rather than months. Similarly, managers for stores like Wal-Mart are showing that computer data can help master distribution costs—while ensuring that a store is never out of stock.

Retailing will continue to be needed, but the role of individual retailers may have to change. Customers will always have needs. But retail *stores* aren't necessarily the only way to satisfy them.

Retailers must face the challenge

One thing is certain—change in retailing is inevitable. For years, conventional retailers' profits declined. Even some of the newer discounters and shopping centers didn't do well. Department stores and food and drug chains saw profits decline. Old-style variety stores faired even worse. Some shifted into mass-merchandising operations, which are also becoming less attractive as limited-line stores try to meet competition with lower margins.

A few firms—such as Wal-Mart, Toys "R" Us, The Gap, and The Limited—are avoiding this general profit squeeze so far. But the future doesn't look too bright for retailers who can't—or won't—change.[29]

CONCLUSION

Modern retailing is scrambled—and we'll probably see more changes in the future. In such a dynamic environment, a producer's marketing manager must choose very carefully among the available kinds of retailers. And retailers must plan their marketing mixes with their target customers' needs in mind—while at the same time becoming part of an effective channel system.

We described many types of retailers—and we saw that each has its advantages and disadvantages. We also saw that modern retailers have discarded conventional practices. The old "buy low and sell high" philosophy is no longer a safe guide. Lower margins with faster turnover is the modern philosophy as more retailers move into mass-merchandising. But even this is no guarantee of success as retailers' product life cycles move on.

Scrambled merchandising will continue as retailing evolves to meet changing consumer demands. But important breakthroughs are still possible because consumers probably will continue to move away from conventional retailers. Convenience products, for example, may be made more easily available by some combination of electronic ordering and home delivery or vending. The big, all-purpose department store may not be able to satisfy anyone's needs exactly. Some combination of mail-order and electronic ordering might make a larger assortment of products available to more people—to better meet their particular needs.

Every society needs a retailing function—but all the present retailers may not be needed. The future retail scene will offer the marketing manager new challenges and opportunities.

QUESTIONS AND PROBLEMS

1. Identify a specialty store selling convenience products in your city. Explain why you think it's that kind of store and why an awareness of this status would be important to a manufacturer. Does it give the retailer any particular advantage? If so, with whom?

2. What sort of a "product" are specialty shops offering? What are the prospects for organizing a chain of specialty shops?

3. Many department stores have a bargain basement. Does the basement represent just another department, like the lingerie department or the luggage department? Or is some whole new concept involved?

4. Distinguish among discount houses, price cutting by conventional retailers, and mass-merchandising. Forecast the future of low-price selling in food, clothing, and appliances.

5. Discuss a few changes in the marketing environment that you think help to explain why telephone and mail-order retailing has been growing so rapidly.

6. Apply the wheel of retailing theory to your local community. What changes seem likely? Will established retailers see the need for change, or will entirely new firms have to develop?

7. What advantages does a retail chain have over a retailer who operates with a single store? Does a small retailer have any advantages in competing against a chain? Explain your answer.

8. Discuss the kinds of markets served by the three types of shopping centers. Are they directly competitive? Do they contain the same kinds of stores? Is the long-run outlook for all of them similar?

9. Many producers are now seeking new opportunities in international markets. Are the opportunities for international expansion equally good for retailers? Explain your answer.

10. Explain the growth and decline of various retailers and shopping centers in your own community. Use the text's three-dimensional drawing (Exhibit 11–4) and the product life-cycle concept. Also, treat each retailer's whole offering as a product.

SUGGESTED CASES

11. Nike and Fashionable Shoes

14. Communication Aids, Inc.

COMPUTER-AIDED PROBLEM

11. Mass-Merchandising

Patrick Burns, the manager of PlayTime Toy Store, is sure a new type of toy will be a big seller in his area. But two brands of the toy are available, so he must decide which to sell—he doesn't have enough shelf space to stock both. In fact, he wants to use as little shelf space as possible for the toy—to save space for other good sellers.

Burns asked his wholesaler how many of these toys he should expect to sell in a year. The wholesaler reported that different stores were adding different dollar markups to the cost—and that lower markups usually sold larger quantities. Based on the experience from other stores, the wholesaler was able to provide Burns with more detailed information:

Markup/Quantity Relationships		
Markup Amount	*Quantity Sold*	
	Brand A	*Brand B*
$1.00	48	36
$1.50	30	30
$2.00	20	16
$2.50	13	12

The wholesaler also advised PlayTime to have a "facing" of at least five of the toys on a shelf—that is, at least five toys should show in the front of the shelf to get enough attention to spark sales. Either toy's package uses the full depth of a standard shelf, but one package is wider than the other.

PlayTime's manager must decide which brand to carry and what markup to use. The spreadsheet gives relevant information, including the wholesaler's quantity estimates based on different markups. (Note: "Contribution" to profit is equal to the markup per toy times the number of toys sold at that markup.)

a. Based on the different markup and "quantity sold" combinations provided by the wholesaler, what markup on Brand A would result in the largest contribution to profit? What markup on Brand B would result in the largest contribution? Based on profit contribution, which brand would you recommend? (Hint: Change the starting markup and quantity values to the combinations reported by the wholesaler.)

b. Given the "best" margin and quantity estimates from (a) above, which brand will earn the highest "contribution" per inch of shelf (assuming a five-package facing as suggested by the wholesaler)?

c. Which brand and markup would you recommend? Why?

For additional questions related to this problem, see Exercise 11–3 in the *Learning Aid for use with Essentials of Marketing,* 6th edition.

Wholesalers and Their Strategy Planning

Chapter **12**

Wholesalers are being squeezed out by mass-marketers who go direct.

wholesalers regroup product

When You Finish This Chapter, You Should

❶

Understand what wholesalers are and the wholesaling functions they *may* provide for others in channel systems.

❷

Know the various kinds of merchant wholesalers and agent middlemen and the strategies that they use.

❸

Understand when and where the various kinds of merchant wholesalers and agent middlemen are most useful to channel planners.

❹

Know what progressive wholesalers are doing to modernize their operations and marketing strategies.

❺

Understand why wholesalers have lasted.

❻

Understand the important new terms (shown in red).

M M M
↓ ↓ M
*   ↓ W*
*   W)*
*   ↓*
*   R*
*   ↓*
*   C*

discrepancy of ~~assor~~ assortment - manufactures make a very narrow asst. of products whereas consumers want a wide asst.

F rieda Caplan and her two daughters, Jackie and Karen, run Produce Specialties, a wholesale firm that each year supplies supermarkets with $20 million worth of exotic fruits and vegetables. It is a sign of the firm's success that kiwifruit, artichokes, alfalfa sprouts, spaghetti squash, pearl onions, and mushrooms no longer seem very exotic. All of these crops were once viewed as unusual. Few farmers grew them, and consumers didn't know about them. Traditional produce wholesalers didn't want to handle them because they had a limited market. Produce Specialties helped to change all that.

Caplan realized that some supermarkets were putting more emphasis on their produce departments and wanted to offer consumers more choice. She looked for products that would help them meet this need. For example, the funny looking, egg-shaped kiwifruit with its fuzzy brown skin was popular in New Zealand but virtually unknown to consumers in other parts of the world. Caplan worked with a number of small farmer-producers to ensure that she could provide her retailer-customers with an adequate supply. She packaged kiwi with interesting recipes and promoted kiwi *and* her brand name to consumers. Because of her efforts, many supermarkets now carry kiwi—which has become a $40 million crop for California farmers.

Because demand for kiwi has grown, other large wholesalers now handle them. But that hasn't slowed Caplan. She still adds new products—like Asian pears and kiwano melons (from New Zealand)—to the 250 products that carry her label. And she continues to have an advantage with many supermarkets because she offers many special services. For example, she was the first to routinely use airfreight for orders, and her firm sends a weekly "hot sheet" to produce managers that tells what's selling. The Caplans even hold seminars to inform produce buyers how to improve their sales.[1]

This example shows that wholesalers are often a vital link in a channel system—and in the whole marketing process—helping both their suppliers and customers. It also shows that wholesalers—like other businesses—must select their target markets and marketing mixes carefully. But you can understand wholesalers better if you look at them as members of channels. Wholesalers are middlemen.

discrepancy of quantity - Qty man. wants to make compared to qty consumer wants to buy.

In this chapter, you will learn more about wholesalers and their strategy planning. You'll see how they have evolved, how they fit into various channels, why they are used, and what functions they perform.

WHAT IS A WHOLESALER?

It's hard to define what a wholesaler is because there are so many different wholesalers doing different jobs. Some of their activities may even seem like manufacturing. As a result, some wholesalers describe themselves as "manufacturer and dealer." Some like to identify themselves with such general terms as merchant, jobber, dealer, or distributor. And others just take the name commonly used in their trade—without really thinking about what it means.

To avoid a long technical discussion on the nature of wholesaling, we'll use the U.S. Bureau of the Census definition:

Wholesaling is concerned with the *activities* of those persons or establishments which sell to retailers and other merchants, and/or to industrial, institutional, and commercial users, but who do not sell in large amounts to final consumers.

So **wholesalers** are firms whose main function is providing *wholesaling activities.* Producers who just take over some wholesaling activities are not considered wholesalers. However, when producers set up branch warehouses at *separate locations,* these establishments basically operate as wholesalers. In fact, they're classified as wholesalers by the U.S. Census Bureau and by government agencies in many other countries.

POSSIBLE WHOLESALING FUNCTIONS

Wholesalers perform certain functions for both their suppliers and the wholesalers' own customers—in short, for those above and below them in the channel. *Wholesaling functions* really are variations of the basic marketing functions. Keep in mind that *not all* wholesalers provide all of the functions.

What a wholesaler might do for customers

Wholesalers perform a variety of activities that benefit their customers. They:

1. Regroup goods—to provide the quantity and assortment customers want at the lowest possible cost.
2. Anticipate needs—forecast customers' demands and buy accordingly.
3. Carry stocks—carry inventory so customers don't have to store a large inventory.
4. Deliver goods—provide prompt delivery at low cost.
5. Grant credit—give credit to customers, perhaps supplying their working capital. This financing function may be very important to small customers.
6. Provide information and advisory service—supply price and technical information as well as suggestions on how to sell and service products.
7. Provide part of the buying function—so customers don't have to hunt for supply sources.
8. Own and transfer title to products—help complete a sale and speed the whole buying and selling process.
9. On Line Service - EDI - for retailers.

A wholesaler often helps its customers by carrying needed products and providing prompt delivery at low cost.

If your store's sales are moving faster than your distributor, make a quick call to us.

For convenience stores, nothing is more inconvenient than running out when customers are running in.

That's why Southland maintains a 99.7% in-stock rate. Why placing an electronic order takes only seconds. Why we deliver on the day we promise, in less than 30 minutes.

Stores with brisk sales need a system that knows how to move.

Call Southland. We're ready to roll.

southland distribution center

To find out more, call the Southland Distribution Center near you:
Northeast—Falmouth, VA (703) 371-5000, Midwest—Champaign, IL (217) 398-1800, West—San Bernardino, CA (714) 887-7921.

What a wholesaler might do for producer-suppliers

Wholesalers also benefit producer-suppliers. They provide producers with access to a target market—the wholesalers' customers. A particular wholesaler may be the only one who reaches certain customers. The producer who wants to reach these customers *may have no choice but to use that wholesaler.*[2] Wholesalers also:

1. Provide part of a producer's selling function—by going to producer-suppliers instead of waiting for their sales reps to call.
2. Store inventory—reduce a producer's need to carry large stocks thus cutting the producer's warehousing expenses.
3. Supply capital—reduce a producer's need for working capital by buying the producer's output and carrying it in inventory until it's sold.
4. Reduce credit risk—by selling to customers the wholesaler knows and taking the loss if these customers don't pay.
5. Provide market information—as an informed buyer and seller closer to the market, the wholesaler reduces the producer's need for market research.[3]

Functions are crucial in many channels

You can see the importance of these wholesaling functions by looking at a specific case. George Mariakakas is a heating contractor. His company sells heating systems—and his crew installs them in new buildings. Mariakakas gets a lot of help from Air Control Company, the wholesaler who supplies this equipment. When Mariakakas isn't certain what type of furnace to install, Air Control's experts give him good technical advice. Air Control also stocks an inventory of products from different producers. This means that Mariakakas can order equipment when he's ready to install it. He doesn't have to tie up capital in a big inventory—or wait for a cross-country delivery from a producer. Air Control even helps finance his business. Mariakakas doesn't have to pay for his purchases till he has been paid by his customers. Mariakakas' whole way of doing business would be different without this wholesaler.

DIFFERENT KINDS OF WHOLESALERS HAVE DIFFERENT COSTS AND BENEFITS

Exhibit 12–1 compares the number, sales volume, and operating expenses of some major types of wholesalers. The differences in operating expenses suggest that each of these types performs—or does not perform—certain wholesaling functions. But which ones and why? And why do manufacturers use merchant wholesalers—costing 14.5 percent of sales—when agent middlemen cost only 4.8 percent?

To answer these questions, we must understand what these wholesalers do—and don't do. Exhibit 12–2 gives a big-picture view of the wholesalers described in more detail below. Note that a major difference is whether they *own* the products they sell.

Learn the pure to understand the real

Although we'll discuss "pure types" of wholesalers, in practice, many wholesalers are mixtures of the pure types. Further, the names commonly used in a particular industry may be misleading. Some so-called brokers actually behave as limited-function merchant wholesalers. And some manufacturers' agents operate as full-service wholesalers. Names also vary by country. This casual use of terms makes it all the more important for you to understand the pure types before trying to understand the blends—and the names they're given in the business world.

Helpful data is sometimes available

In the United States, the Census Bureau publishes detailed data about wholesalers, including breakdowns by kind of business, product line, and geographic territory. Similar information is available for Canada and many other countries, including most of those in the European Community. This kind of data is valuable in strategy planning—especially to learn whether potential channel members are serving a target market. You can also learn what sales volume current middlemen are achieving.

Exhibit 12–1   U.S. Wholesale Trade by Type of Wholesale Operation

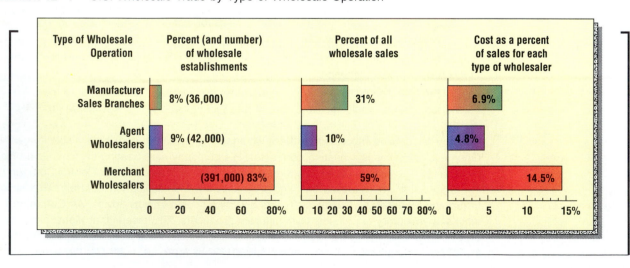

Exhibit 12–2 Type of Wholesalers

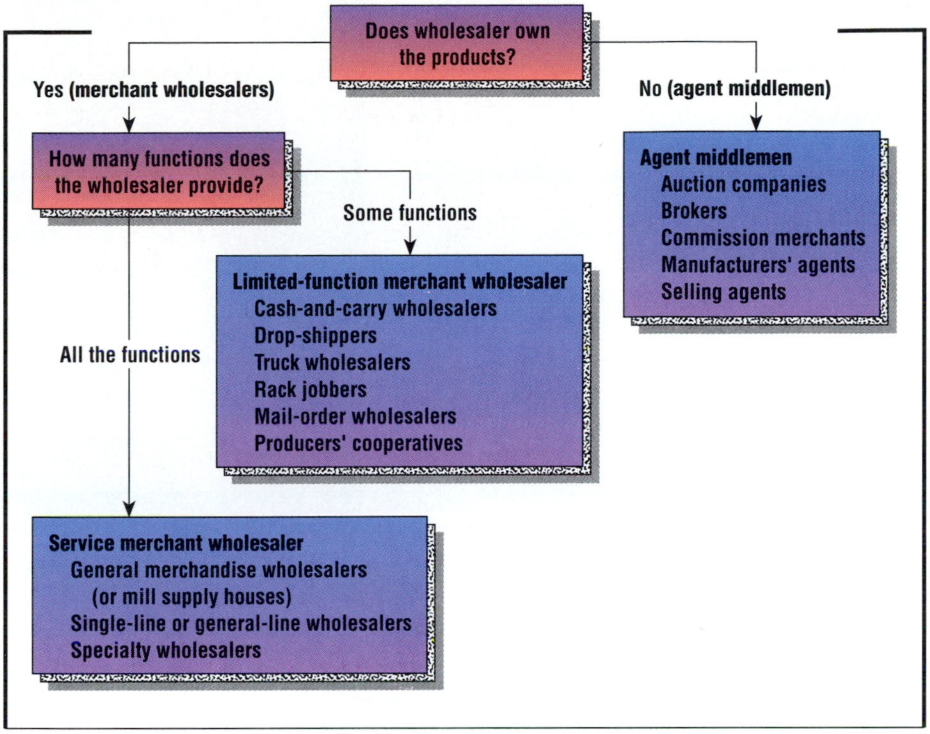

[Flowchart: Type of Wholesalers]

Does wholesaler own the products?

Yes (merchant wholesalers)

How many functions does the wholesaler provide?

Some functions

Limited-function merchant wholesaler
Cash-and-carry wholesalers
Drop-shippers
Truck wholesalers
Rack jobbers
Mail-order wholesalers
Producers' cooperatives

All the functions

Service merchant wholesaler
General merchandise wholesalers
   (or mill supply houses)
Single-line or general-line wholesalers
Specialty wholesalers

No (agent middlemen)

Agent middlemen
Auction companies
Brokers
Commission merchants
Manufacturers' agents
Selling agents

MERCHANT WHOLESALERS ARE THE MOST NUMEROUS

Merchant wholesalers own (take title to) the products they sell. They often specialize by certain types of products or customers. For example, Fastenal is a wholesaler that specializes in distributing threaded fasteners used by a variety of manufacturers. It owns (takes title to) the fasteners for some period before selling to its customers. In Exhibit 12–1, we can see that about four out of five wholesaling establishments in the United States are merchant wholesalers—and they handle about 59 percent of wholesale sales. Merchant wholesalers are even more common in other countries. Japan is an extreme example. In its unusual multitiered distribution system, products are often bought and sold by a series of merchant wholesalers on their way to the business user or retailer.

Many merchant wholesalers service relatively small geographic areas. And several wholesalers may be competing for the same customers. For example, about 3,000 specialized food wholesalers compete for the business of restaurants, hotels, and cafeterias across the United States. Even the largest of these wholesalers—Sysco Corp, Staley Continental, and PYA/Monarch—have only about a 3 percent share each of the total business.[4]

Service wholesalers are merchant wholesalers who provide all the wholesaling functions. Within this basic group are three types: (1) general merchandise, (2) single-line, and (3) specialty.

General merchandise wholesalers are service wholesalers who carry a wide variety of nonperishable items such as hardware, electrical supplies, plumbing supplies, furniture,

Service wholesalers provide all the functions

Merchant wholesalers in Asia are often smaller, carry narrower product lines, and deal with fewer customers than their counterparts in North America.

drugs, cosmetics, and automobile equipment. With their broad line of convenience and shopping products, they serve hardware stores, drugstores, and small department stores. *Mill supply houses* operate in a similar way, but they carry a broad variety of accessories and supplies to serve the needs of manufacturers.

Single-line (or general-line) wholesalers are service wholesalers who carry a narrower line of merchandise than general merchandise wholesalers. For example, they might carry only food, wearing apparel, or certain types of industrial tools or supplies. In

3M produces 1,600 products used by auto body repair shops in the United States, Europe, Japan, and other countries. To reach this target market, 3M works with hundreds of specialty wholesalers.

consumer products, they serve the single- and limited-line stores. In business products, they cover a wider geographic area and offer more specialized service.

Specialty wholesalers are service wholesalers who carry a very narrow range of products—and offer more information and service than other service wholesalers. A consumer products specialty wholesaler might carry only health foods or oriental foods instead of a full line of groceries.

A specialty wholesaler of business products might limit itself to fields requiring special technical knowledge or service. Richardson Electronics is an interesting example. It specializes in distributing replacement parts, such as electron tubes, for old equipment that many manufacturers still use on the factory floor. Richardson describes itself as "on the trailing edge of technology," but its unique products, expertise, and service are valuable to its target customers, many of whom operate in countries where new technologies are not yet common.[5]

Limited-function
wholesalers provide
some functions

Limited-function wholesalers provide only *some* wholesaling functions. Exhibit 12–3 shows the functions typically provided—and not provided. In the following paragraphs, we will discuss the main features of these wholesalers. Less numerous in some countries, nevertheless these wholesalers are very important for some products.

Cash-and-carry
wholesalers want cash

Cash-and-carry wholesalers operate like service wholesalers—except that the customer must pay cash.

Some retailers, such as small auto repair shops, are too small to be served profitably by a service wholesaler. So service wholesalers set a minimum charge—or just refuse to grant credit to a small business that may have trouble paying its bills. The wholesaler can operate at lower cost because the retailers take over many wholesaling functions. These

Exhibit 12–3   Functions Provided by Different Types of Limited-Function Merchant Wholesalers

Functions	Cash-and-Carry	Drop-Shipper	Truck	Mail-Order	Cooperatives	Rack Jobbers
For customers						
Anticipates needs	X		X	X	X	X
"Regroups" products (one or more of four steps)	X		X	X	X	X
Carries stocks	X		X	X	X	X
Delivers products			X		X	X
Grants credit		X	Maybe	Maybe	Maybe	Consignment (in some cases)
Provides information and advisory services		X	Some	Some	X	
Provides buying function		X	X	X	Some	X
Owns and transfers title to products	X	X	X	X	X	X
For producers						
Provides producers' selling function	X	X	X	X	X	X
Stores inventory	X		X	X	X	X
Helps finance by owning stocks	X		X	X	X	X
Reduces credit risk	X	X	X	X	X	X
Provides market information	X	X	Some	X	X	Some

McKESSON'S MARKETING STRATEGY IS A WHOLESALE SUCCESS

(M) cKesson Drug Co. is a full-service merchant wholesaler—and an innovator when it comes to distributing pharmaceutical and health care products to drugstores. A decade ago McKesson's drugstore distribution business was doing so poorly that its owners considered selling it. Since then, sales have tripled, even though McKesson's sales force is now only about half as large.

A top executive at the company says that "everything we've been able to do has been driven by getting the customer on computers." When McKesson put its customers on a direct computer-order hookup, it was easier for them to order and less expensive to maintain the right inventory. McKesson's computers don't just dispatch orders to a warehouse. They also print price stickers and add the precise profit margin that the druggist selects. At the end of the month the druggist even gets a printout that shows the profitability of each department. Other wholesalers now compete with similar systems, but McKesson continues to find new ways to add value in the channel.

In 1991, for example, it modernized its distribution network by installing a state-of-the-art, automated order-picking system in its distribution center. The new system reduces costs, is more accurate, and fills orders faster—at a rate of nearly 1,200 an hour. Changes like this help McKesson reduce the inventory costs of its manufacturer-suppliers while still achieving the product availability that drugstores need. Such efficiency caused a basic shift in the channel of distribution for drugs. In 1973, only 50 percent of sales were handled by distributors, and the rest were direct sales by manufacturers. Now, 75 percent of sales are handled by distributors.

McKesson also strengthened and expanded Valu-Rite, the voluntary chain it set up for independent drugstores. In addition to providing these retailers with computer services and a reliable supply, McKesson provides private-label brands, promotional circulars, and advertising support. Many independent drugstores credit McKesson with giving them the help—and the technology—they need to compete with the big chains. And their loyalty to McKesson explains why sales to members of the Valu-Rite program have grown at 23 percent a year since 1985.

In Canada, direct sales by manufacturers still account for 57 percent of all pharmaceutical sales. That represents a real opportunity for McKesson's Canadian division. McKesson believes that by expanding the use of its approaches in Canada, it will not only increase its own sales and profits, but also reduce the total cost of distributing drugs and thus the prices that consumers pay.[6]

---

cash-and-carry operators are especially common in less-developed nations where very small retailers handle the bulk of retail transactions.

Drop-shipper does not handle the products

Drop-shippers own (take title to) the products they sell—but they do *not* actually handle, stock, or deliver them. These wholesalers are mainly involved in selling. They get orders and pass them on to producers. Then the producer ships the order directly to the customer. Drop-shippers commonly sell bulky products (like lumber) for which additional handling would be expensive and possibly damaging.

Truck wholesalers deliver—at a cost

Truck wholesalers specialize in delivering products that they stock in their own trucks. By handling perishable products in general demand—tobacco, candy, potato chips, and salad dressings—truck wholesalers may provide almost the same functions as full-service wholesalers. Their big advantage is that they promptly deliver perishable products that regular wholesalers prefer not to carry. A 7-Eleven store that runs out of potato chips on a busy Friday night doesn't want to be out of stock all weekend!

Mail-order wholesalers reach outlying areas

Mail-order wholesalers sell out of catalogs that may be distributed widely to smaller industrial customers or retailers who might not be called on by other middlemen. These

Mail-order wholesalers sell out of catalogs—usually to widely dispersed customers.

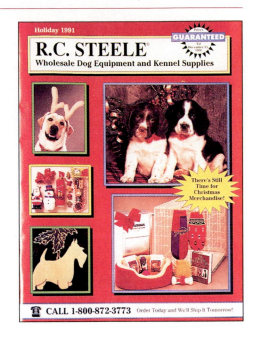

wholesalers operate in the hardware, jewelry, sporting goods, and general merchandise lines.[7] For example, Inmac uses a catalog to sell a complete line of computer accessories. Inmac's catalogs are printed in six languages and distributed to business customers in the United States, Canada, and Europe. Many of these customers don't have a local wholesaler.[8]

Producers' cooperatives do sorting

Producers' cooperatives operate almost as full-service wholesalers—with the profits going to the cooperative's customer-members. Cooperatives develop in agricultural markets where there are many small producers. Cooperatives usually emphasize sorting—to improve the quality of farm products offered to the market. Some also brand these improved products—and then promote the brands. Examples of such organizations are Sunkist (citrus fruits), Sunmaid Raisin Growers Association, and Land O' Lakes Creameries, Inc.[9]

Rack jobbers sell hard-to-handle assortments

Rack jobbers specialize in nonfood products sold through grocery stores and supermarkets—and they often display them on their own wire racks. Most grocers don't want to bother with reordering and maintaining displays of nonfood items (housewares, hardware items, and books and magazines) because they sell small quantities of so many different kinds of products. Rack jobbers are almost service wholesalers—except that they usually are paid cash for what is sold or delivered.

This is a relatively expensive operation—with operating costs of about 18 percent of sales. The large volume of sales from these racks encouraged some large chains to experiment with handling such items themselves. But chains often find that rack jobbers can provide this service as well as—or better than—they can themselves. For example, a rack jobber that wholesales paperback books studies which titles are selling in the local area—and applies that knowledge in many stores. A chain has many stores—but often in different areas where preferences vary.

This video rental store also sells magazines, but the store manager lets a rack jobber decide what magazines to sell.

AGENT MIDDLEMEN ARE STRONG ON SELLING

They don't own the products

Agent middlemen are wholesalers who do not own the products they sell. Their main purpose is to help in buying and selling. They usually provide even fewer functions than the limited-function wholesalers, so they may operate at relatively low cost—sometimes 2 to 6 percent of their selling price.

They are important in international trade

Agent middlemen are common in international trade. Many markets have only a few well-financed merchant wholesalers. The best many producers can do is get local representation through agents—and then arrange financing through banks that specialize in international trade.

Agent middlemen are usually experts on local business customs and rules concerning imported products in their respective countries. Sometimes a marketing manager can't work through a foreign government's red tape without the help of a local agent.

They are usually specialists

Agent middlemen—like merchant wholesalers—normally specialize by customer type and by product or product line. So it's important to determine exactly what each one does. In the following paragraphs, we'll mention only the most important points about each type. Study Exhibit 12–4 for details on the functions provided by each.

Manufacturers' agents—free-wheeling sales reps

Account for over 50% of

A **manufacturers' agent** sells similar products for several noncompeting producers—for a commission on what is actually sold. Such agents work almost as members of each company's sales force—but they're really independent middlemen. More than half of all agent middlemen are manufacturers' agents.

Their big plus is that they already call on some customers and can add another product line at relatively low cost—and at no cost to the producer until something sells! If an area's sales potential is low, a company may use a manufacturers' agent because the agent can

Exhibit 12–4 Functions Provided by Different Types of Agent Middlemen

Functions	Manufacturers' Agents	Brokers	Commission Merchants	Selling Agents	Auction Companies
For customers					
Anticipate needs	Sometimes	Some			
"Regroups" products (one or more of four steps)	Some		X		X
Carries stocks	Sometimes		X		Sometimes
Delivers products	Sometimes		X		
Grants credit			Sometimes	X	Some
Provides information and advisory services	X	X	X	X	
Provides buying function	X	Some	X	X	X
Owns and transfers title to products		Transfers only	Transfers only		
For producer					
Provides selling function	X	Some	X	X	X
Stores inventory	Sometimes		X		X
Helps finance by owning stocks					
Reduces credit risk				X	Some
Provides market information	X	X	X	X	

do the job at low cost. Small producers often use agents everywhere because their sales volume is too small to justify their own sales force.

Agents can be especially useful for introducing new products. For this service, they may earn 10 to 15 percent commission. (In contrast, their commission on large-volume established products may be quite low—perhaps only 2 percent.) A 10 to 15 percent commission rate may seem small for a new product with low sales. Once a product sells well, however, a producer may think the rate is high and begin using its own sales reps. Agents are well aware of this possibility. That's why most try to work for many producers and avoid being dependent on only one line.

Manufacturers' agents are very useful in fields where there are many small manufacturers who need to contact customers. They may cover a very narrow geographic area, such as a city or state. However, they are also important in international marketing, and an agent may take on responsibility for a whole country.

Import and export agents specialize in international trade

While manufacturers' agents operate in every country, **export or import agents** are basically manufacturers' agents who specialize in international trade.

These agent middlemen help international firms adjust to unfamiliar market conditions in foreign markets. A decade ago Brazilian shoe producers had only a small share of footwear sales in the United States. Their low labor costs gave them a big cost advantage, and they could produce a quality product. But the Brazilian producers had trouble anticipating American fashions. So a number of export agents developed. These specialists traveled in the United States, keeping Brazilian producers informed about style changes and finding new retail outlets. With this help, Brazilian firms were able to export $850 million worth of shoes.[10]

Brokers provide information

Brokers bring buyers and sellers together. Brokers usually have a *temporary* relationship with the buyer and seller while a particular deal is negotiated. Their product is

AT&T sometimes relies on wholesalers who specialize in international trade to reach customers in foreign markets.

A Factor buys a clients accts receivables at a discount and then trys to collect on them. Acts receivables do not need to be in arrears

information about what buyers need—and what supplies are available. They may also aid in buyer-seller negotiation. If the transaction is completed, they earn a commission from whichever party hired them. **Export and import brokers** operate like other brokers, but they specialize in bringing together buyers and sellers from different countries.

Usually, some kind of broker develops whenever and wherever market information is inadequate. Brokers are especially useful when buyers and sellers don't come into the market often. A knowledgeable broker is needed to help complete the transaction quickly and inexpensively. In a number of fields, brokers develop computerized databases that make it even cheaper and faster to match sellers with customers.

Selling agents—almost marketing managers

The Firm Needs Caon Wants to reduce cost. Fires present marketers

Do Not Own the product.

Selling agents take over the whole marketing job of producers—not just the selling function. A selling agent may handle the entire output of one or more producers—even competing producers—with almost complete control of pricing, selling, and advertising. In effect, the agent becomes each producer's marketing manager.

Financial trouble is one of the main reasons a producer calls in a selling agent. The selling agent may provide working capital but may also take over the affairs of the business.

A **combination export manager** is a blend of manufacturers' agent and selling agent—handling the entire export function for several producers of similar but noncompeting lines.

Commission merchants handle and sell products in distant markets

Commission merchants and **export or import commission houses** handle products shipped to them by sellers, complete the sale, and send the money—minus their commission—to each seller.

Commission agents are common in agricultural markets where farmers must ship to big-city central markets. They need someone to handle the products there—as well as sell them—since the farmer can't go with each shipment. Although commission merchants don't own the products, they generally are allowed to sell them at the market price—or the best price above some stated minimum.

Commission agents are sometimes used in other trades—such as textiles. Here many small producers want to reach buyers in a central market, perhaps one in a distant country, without having to maintain their own sales force.

Auction companies provide a place where buyers and sellers can come together and complete a transaction. There aren't many auction companies, but they are important in certain lines—such as livestock, fur, tobacco, and used cars. For these products, demand and supply conditions change rapidly—and the product must be seen to be evaluated. The auction company brings buyers and sellers together. Buyers inspect the products—then demand and supply interact to determine the price.

MANUFACTURERS' SALES BRANCHES PROVIDE WHOLESALING FUNCTIONS TOO

Manufacturers' sales branches are separate businesses that producers set up away from their factories. For example, computer producers such as IBM set up local branches in markets around the world to provide service, display equipment, and handle sales.

In the United States, about 8 percent of wholesalers are owned by manufacturers—but they handle 31 percent of total wholesale sales. One reason sales per branch are so high is that the branches are usually placed in the best market areas. This also helps explain why their operating costs are often lower.[11]

WHOLESALERS TEND TO CONCENTRATE TOGETHER

Different wholesalers are found in different places

Most wholesalers are concentrated near transporting, storing, and financing facilities as well as near large populations. In general, that means that they tend to locate in or near large cities. In the United States, about 40 percent of all wholesale sales are made in the 15 largest Metropolitan Statistical Areas. Similar concentrations are found in most countries around the world.

When a number of competing wholesalers are located together, competition can be tough. And channel relations are usually dynamic as producers and middlemen seek lower costs and higher profits.[12]

COMEBACK AND FUTURE OF WHOLESALERS

In earlier days, wholesalers dominated distribution channels in the United States and most other countries. The many small producers and small retailers needed their services. This situation still exists in many countries, especially those with less-developed economies. However, in the developed nations, as producers became larger some bypassed the wholesalers. Similarly, large retail chains often took control of functions that had been handled by wholesalers. In light of these changes, many people predicted a gloomy future for wholesalers.

Producing profits, not chasing orders

Yet partly due to new management and new strategies, wholesalers have held their own, and many are enjoying significant growth. To be sure, many still operate in the old ways—and wholesaling changes less rapidly than retailing. But progressive wholesalers are becoming more concerned with their customers—and with channel systems. Some offer more services. Others develop voluntary chains that bind them more closely to their customers.

Modern wholesalers no longer require all customers to pay for all the services they offer simply because certain customers use them. Now some wholesalers offer basic service at minimum cost—then charge additional fees for any special services required.

Some progressive wholesalers modernize their warehouses and use hand-held computers to reduce costs and improve customer service.

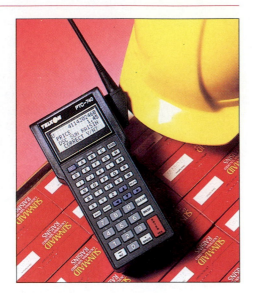

Most modern wholesalers streamlined their operations to cut unnecessary costs and improve profits. To cut costs, they use computers to keep track of inventory—and to order new stock only when it's really needed. Computerized sales analysis helps them identify and drop unprofitable products. Wholesalers are also more selective in picking customers. They use a selective distribution policy—when cost analysis shows that many of their smaller customers are unprofitable. With these less desirable customers gone, wholesalers give more attention to more profitable customers.

Progress—or fail

Many wholesalers are also modernizing their warehouses and physical handling facilities. They mark products with bar codes that can be read with hand-held scanners—so inventory, shipping, and sales records can be easily and instantly updated. Computerized order-picking systems speed the job of assembling orders. New storing facilities are carefully located to minimize the costs of both incoming freight and deliveries. Delivery vehicles travel to customers in a computer-selected sequence that reduces the number of miles traveled. And wholesalers who serve manufacturers are rising to the challenge of just-in-time delivery systems and making renewed efforts to add value in the distribution channel.

Wholesalers are helping retailers reduce costs too. Retailers can wait until they really need a product to order it—and the order can be instantly placed with a fax machine, toll-free telephone line, or computer-to-computer EDI hookups.

Perhaps good-bye to some

Not all wholesalers are progressive, and some of the smaller, less efficient ones may fail. Efficiency and low cost, however, are not all that's needed for success. Some wholesalers will disappear as the functions they provided in the past are shifted and shared in different ways in the channel. Cost-conscious buyers for Wal-Mart, Lowe's, and other chains are refusing to deal with some of the middlemen who represent small producers. They want to negotiate directly with the producer—not just accept the price traditionally available from a wholesaler. Similarly, more producers see advantages in having closer working relationships with fewer suppliers—and they're paring the vendor roles to exclude wholesalers who do a poor job of meeting their needs. Efficient delivery services like UPS

Many modern wholesalers now use bar code labels, which can be quickly read by a computer scanner, to constantly update inventory information.

36-38-AS400

BarCode
Software

No programming experience is necessary when using this versatile, in-house, Barcode Labeling System.

An operator can design new labels using the standard formatting features such as lines, boxes, logos, vertical printing, variable-size characters, and reverse images. Once a label format has been created, it can be recalled at a later time to make changes.

Other systems' features include:
■ Runs on your System 36/38/AS400.
Software resides on your System 36/38/AS400. Uses your existing files.
Label Design or Printing can be done from any terminal, even remote sites.
Several people can use software at the same time.

■ Anyone can design labels.
No programming required.
HELP screens throughout.
Create or change in minutes.

■ Run from your existing procedures and programs. Labels printed with or without operator intervention.

■ Randomly access files for label information.

■ Generate labels for CHEMICAL, MAG, STEEL, PAPER, JEWELRY, LOGMARS, or any other industry.

■ Supports many different printers.

Complete Barcode Printing Solutions Available including software, printer and printer connection, CALL TODAY!

T.L. Ashford & Associates

Fifth Street Center • 525 W. Fifth Street • Covington, KY 41011 • 1-800-541-4893 606-291-7555

Our bar code know-how really stacks up.

When it comes to bar code labeling, we've probably run across a problem that's similar to your own.

And solved it.

That's the reason our bar code know-how stacks up against anybody.

We'll show you how our Legitronic® software/printer combinations make it easy to design and print bar code labels yourself. You can choose from impact, thermal/thermal-transfer and laser systems that print labels anytime you need them.

Or we can print bar code labels for you. Our ECLIPSE® service bureau provides labels to fulfill large-volume and special-ized requirements.

We'll also show you how to collect and use bar code data with our portable scanners and terminals.

We even guarantee you'll meet specifi-cations, because we manufacture labels that are tested and selected to improve bar code readability.

And to support your bar code program, we provide direct service, technical advice and software upgrades whenever you need them.

To arrange a free demonstration of our bar code systems, call **1-800-225-0883.** See for yourself how well we stack up.

Weber®
THE LABELING SPECIALISTS

Weber Marking Systems
711 W. Algonquin Rd. • Arlington Heights, IL 60005-4457
(708) 364-8500 • FAX (708) 364-8575

and Federal Express are also making it easy and inexpensive for many producers to ship directly to their customers—even ones in foreign markets.[13]

? Is it an ethical issue?

There's no doubt that some wholesalers are being squeezed out of business. Some critics—including many of the wholesalers affected by these changes—argue that it's unethical for powerful suppliers or customers to simply cut out wholesalers who spend money and time—perhaps decades—developing markets. Contracts between channel members and laws sometimes define what changes are or are not legal. But in some cases, the ethical issues are more ambiguous.

For example, as part of a broader effort to improve profits, Amana recently notified Cooper Distributing Co. that it intended to cancel their distribution agreement—in 10 days. Cooper had been handling Amana appliances for 30 years, and Amana products repre-sented 85 percent of Cooper's sales. Amana's explanation to Cooper? "It's not because you're doing a bad job: we just think we can do it better."

Situations like this arise often. They may be cold-hearted, but are they unethical? Many argue that it isn't fair for Amana to cut off the relationship with such short notice. But most wholesalers realize that their business is always at risk—if they don't perform channel functions better or cheaper than what their suppliers or customers can do themselves.[14]

Survivors will need effective strategies

The wholesalers who do survive will need to be efficient, but that doesn't mean they'll all have low costs. Some wholesalers' higher operating expenses result from the strategies they select—including the special services they offer to *some* customers.

To survive, each wholesaler must develop a good marketing strategy. Profit margins are not large in wholesaling—typically ranging from less than 1 percent to 2 percent. And they've declined in recent years as the competitive squeeze tightened.

Wholesaling will last—but weaker, less progressive wholesalers may not.

CONCLUSION

Wholesalers can provide functions for those both above and below them in a channel of distribution. These services are closely related to the basic marketing functions. There are many types of wholesalers. Some provide all the wholesaling functions—while others specialize in only a few. Eliminating wholesalers would not eliminate the need for the functions they provide. And we cannot assume that direct channels are more efficient.

Merchant wholesalers are the most numerous and account for the majority of wholesale sales. Their distinguishing characteristic is that they take title to (own) products. Agent middlemen, on the other hand, act more like sales representatives for sellers or buyers—and they do not take title.

Despite various predictions, wholesalers continue to exist. The more progressive ones adapt to a changing environment. Wholesaling hasn't experienced the revolutions we saw in retailing, and none seem likely. But some smaller—and less progressive—wholesalers will probably fail, while larger and more market-oriented wholesalers will continue to provide these necessary functions.

QUESTIONS AND PROBLEMS

1. Discuss the evolution of wholesaling in relation to the evolution of retailing.

2. Does a wholesaler need to worry about new-product planning just as a producer needs to have an organized new-product development process? Explain your answer.

3. What risks do merchant wholesalers assume by taking title to goods? Is the size of this risk about constant for all merchant wholesalers?

4. Why would a manufacturer set up its own sales branches if established wholesalers were already available?

5. What is an agent middleman's marketing mix? Why do you think that many merchant middlemen handle competing products from different producers, while manufacturers' agents usually handle only noncompeting products from different producers?

6. Why would a firm use a manufacturer's representative in a foreign market if it could hire a salesperson for a lower commission rate?

7. Discuss the future growth and nature of wholesaling if low-margin retailing and scrambled merchandising become more important. How will wholesalers have to adjust their mixes if retail establishments become larger and retail managers more professional? Will wholesalers be eliminated? If not, what wholesaling functions will be most important? Are there any particular lines of trade where wholesalers may have increasing difficulty?

8. Which types of wholesalers would be most appropriate for the following products? If more than one type of wholesaler could be used, describe each situation carefully. For example, if size or financial strength of a company has a bearing, then so indicate. If several wholesalers could be used in this same channel, explain this too.

   a. Women's shoes.
   b. Fresh peaches.
   c. Machines to glue packing boxes.
   d. Auto mechanics' tools.
   e. A business accessory machine.
   f. Used construction equipment.
   g. Shoelaces.

9. Would a drop-shipper be desirable for the following products: coal, lumber, iron ore, sand and gravel, steel, furniture, or tractors? Why or why not? What channels might be used for each of these products if drop-shippers were not used?

10. Discuss how computer systems affect wholesalers' operations.

11. Which types of wholesalers are likely to become more important in the next 25 years? Why?

12. What alternatives does a producer have if it is trying to expand distribution in a foreign market and finds that the best existing merchant middlemen won't handle imported products?

SUGGESTED CASES

15. Samco, Inc.

16. Jenson Company

COMPUTER-AIDED PROBLEM

12. Merchant versus Agent Wholesaler

Art Glass Productions, a producer of decorative glass gift items, wants to expand into a new territory. Managers at Art Glass know that unit sales in the new territory will be affected by consumer response to the products. But sales will also be affected by which of two wholesalers Art Glass selects. One wholesaler, Giftware Distributing, is a merchant wholesaler that specializes in gift items. The other, Margaret Degan & Associates, is a manufacturers' agent that calls on many of the gift shops in the territory.

Art Glass makes a variety of glass items, but the cost of making an item is usually about the same—$5.20 a unit. The items would sell to Giftware Distributing at $11.90 each—and in turn the merchant wholesaler's price to retailers would be $14.00—leaving Giftware with a $2.10 markup to cover costs and profit. Giftware Distributing is the only reputable merchant wholesaler in the territory, and it has agreed to carry the line only if Art Glass is willing to advertise in a trade magazine aimed at gift store owners. These ads will cost $6,000 a year.

As a manufacturers' agent, Margaret Degan would cover all of her own expenses and would earn 8 percent of the $14.00 price per unit charged the gift shops. Individual orders would be shipped directly to the retail gift shops by Art Glass—using United Parcel Service. Art Glass would pay the UPS charges at an average cost of $2.00 per item. In contrast, Giftware Distributing would anticipate demand and place larger orders in advance. This would reduce the shipping costs, which Art Glass would pay, to about $.60 a unit.

Art Glass's marketing manager thinks that Degan would only be able to sell about 75 percent as many items as Giftware Distributing—since she doesn't have time to call on all of the smaller shops. On the other hand, the merchant wholesaler's demand for $6,000 worth of supporting advertising requires a significant outlay.

The marketing manager at Art Glass decided to use a spreadsheet to determine how large sales would have to be to make it more profitable to work with Giftware and to see how the different channel arrangements would contribute to profits at different sales levels.

a. Given the estimated unit sales and other values shown on the initial spreadsheet, which type of wholesaler would contribute the most profit to Art Glass Productions?

b. If sales in the new territory are slower than expected, so that the merchant wholesaler is able to sell only 2,500 units—or the agent 1,875 units—which wholesaler will contribute the most to Art Glass's profits? (Note: Assume that the merchant wholesaler only buys what it can sell; i.e., it doesn't carry extra inventory beyond what is needed to meet demand.)

c. Prepare a table showing how the two wholesalers' contributions to profit compare as the quantity sold varies from 2,500 units to 4,500 units for the merchant wholesaler and 75 percent of these numbers for the manufacturers' agent. Discuss these results. (Note: Use the What If analysis to vary the quantity sold by the merchant wholesaler, and the program will compute 75 percent of that quantity as the estimate of what the agent will sell.)

For additional questions related to this problem, see Exercise 12–3 in the *Learning Aid for use with Essentials of Marketing,* 6th edition.

Promotion—Introduction

Chapter

13

*Dual Channels of Distribution.
Setting up retail outlets of
your own, but also selling
to other retailers. Creates
additional competition. Can
cause trouble w/ your other
distributors.*

When You Finish This Chapter, You Should

❶
Know the advantages and disadvantages of the promotion methods a marketing manager can use in strategy planning.

❷
Understand the importance of promotion objectives.

❸
Know how the communication processes should affect promotion planning.

❹
Know how the adoption processes can guide promotion planning.

❺
Know how typical promotion plans are blended.

❻
Know who plans and manages promotion blends.

❼
Understand the importance and nature of sales promotion.

❽
Understand the important new terms (shown in red).

Marketing managers at Ryder Systems faced a challenge. Ryder's move-it-yourself rental trucks were a familiar sight in the United States, Canada, and the United Kingdom. However, demand for rental trucks was down. In the weak economy of 1990, fewer consumers were moving. Further, competing rental firms were cutting prices—hoping for a larger share of the shrinking market. That made things even tougher for Ryder. It had focused on providing quality trucks and service rather than bargain-basement prices. In this market, however, more consumers were just looking for the lowest price.

Ryder's marketers decided that this competitive market called for a new promotion blend. They wanted to communicate to target customers that Ryder's services were better than competitors'. Their objective was to increase rentals and sales of supplies.

To reach consumers considering a move, Ryder first turned to mass selling. Working with an ad agency, it placed attention-getting ads on popular TV shows that appealed to audiences whose demographics matched its target market. The ads offered a free booklet on planning a move. All a consumer had to do was call a toll-free telephone number.

The promotion booklet provided a lot of useful information about moving—including persuasive details on how Ryder's comfortable trucks and helpful services could make the move easier. To promote action, the brochure also included a discount coupon on all Ryder moving supplies—like furniture pads, hand trucks, and boxes—that consumers could redeem at any Ryder dealer.

The list of consumers who called was a very targeted database of prospects for Ryder's telemarketing salespeople. When a salesperson identified a good prospect, the final selling job was turned over to one of Ryder's 4,800 local dealers. Their personal attention helped to resolve consumer questions and get rental contracts.

Ryder's blend of direct-response mass selling, sales promotion, and personal selling succeeded in increasing Ryder's share of rentals even in a very sluggish market. And because the promotion was successful in differentiating Ryder's quality services, Ryder was able to charge a higher price than competitors who relied on discounts alone to pull in customers.[1]

SEVERAL PROMOTION METHODS ARE AVAILABLE

Promotion is communicating information between seller and potential buyer or others in the channel to influence attitudes and behavior. The marketing manager's main promotion job is to tell target customers that the right Product is available at the right Place at the right Price.

What the marketing manager communicates is determined by target customers' needs and attitudes. *How* the messages are delivered depends on what blend of the various promotion methods the marketing manager chooses.

As the Ryder example shows, a marketing manager can choose from several promotion methods—personal selling, mass selling, and sales promotion (see Exhibit 13–1).

Personal selling—
flexibility is its strength

Can alter the message.

Personal selling involves direct spoken communication between sellers and potential customers. Face-to-face selling provides immediate feedback—which helps salespeople to adapt. Although salespeople are included in most marketing mixes, personal selling can be very expensive. So it's often desirable to combine personal selling with mass selling and sales promotion. *The most expensive, but also used in most mixes.*

Mass selling involves
advertising and publicity

Mass selling is communicating with large numbers of potential customers at the same time. It's less flexible than personal selling, but when the target market is large and scattered, mass selling can be less expensive. *The same message to everyone.*

Advertising is the main
form of mass selling

Two forms

① Advertising is any *paid* form of nonpersonal presentation of ideas, goods, or services by an identified sponsor. It includes the use of such media as magazines, newspapers, radio and TV, signs, and direct mail. While advertising must be paid for, another form of mass selling—publicity—is free. *Same to get in good graces w/ the customer. Goodwill*

Publicity avoids
media costs

② Publicity is any *unpaid* form of nonpersonal presentation of ideas, goods, or services. Of course, publicity people are paid. But they try to attract attention to the firm and its offerings *without having to pay media costs*. For example, book publishers try to get authors on TV talk shows because this generates a lot of interest—and book sales—without the publisher paying for TV time. *Firms do pay for PR expertise to get free media.*

Exhibit 13–1   Basic Promotion Methods and Strategy Planning

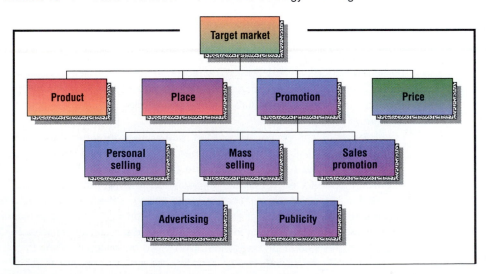

When Coleco introduced its Cabbage Patch dolls, it held press parties for reporters and their children. Many reporters wrote human interest stories about their kids "adopting" the cute dolls. Those stories prompted more media attention—and a very successful product introduction—without Coleco doing any introductory advertising.[2]

If a firm has a really new message, publicity may be more effective than advertising. Trade magazines, for example, may carry articles featuring the newsworthy products of regular advertisers—in part because they *are* regular advertisers. The firm's publicity people write the basic copy and then try to convince magazine editors to print it. Each year, magazines print photos and stories about new cars—and often the source of the information is the auto producers. A consumer might not pay any attention to an ad but carefully read a long magazine story with the same information.

Some companies prepare videotapes designed to get free publicity for their products on TV news shows. For example, one video—distributed to TV stations at Halloween—discussed a government recommendation that parents use makeup rather than masks for young children. The story was effectively tied to a new makeup product for children made by PAAS Products.[3]

Sales promotion tries to spark immediate interest

Sales promotion refers to promotion activities—other than advertising, publicity, and personal selling—that stimulate interest, trial, or purchase by final customers or others in the channel. Sales promotion may be aimed at consumers, at middlemen, or even at a firm's own employees. Examples are listed in Exhibit 13–2.

We'll talk more about sales promotion later in this chapter. First, however, you need to understand the role of the whole promotion blend and how it fits into the rest of the marketing mix.

Less is spent on advertising than on personal selling or sales promotion

Many people think that most promotion money gets spent on advertising because advertising is all around them. The many ads you see in magazines and newspapers and on TV are impressive—and costly. But all the special sales promotions—coupons, sweepstakes, trade shows, sporting events sponsored by firms, and the like—add up to even more money. Similarly, salesclerks complete most retail sales. And behind the scenes, much personal selling goes on in the channels and in other business markets. In total, firms spend less money on advertising than on personal selling or sales promotion.

The emphasis on each promotion method usually varies depending on the target market and other elements of the marketing mix. When planning the marketing strategy, it's important to plan a combination of promotion methods that will work together to achieve specific promotion objectives.

Exhibit 13–2   Example of Sales Promotion Activities

Aimed at final consumers or users	Aimed at middlemen	Aimed at company's own sales force
Contests	Price deals	Contests
Coupons	Promotion allowances	Bonuses
Aisle displays	Sales contests	Meetings
Samples	Calendars	Portfolios
Trade shows	Gifts	Displays
Point-of-purchase materials	Trade shows	Sales aids
Banners and streamers	Meetings	Training materials
Trading stamps	Catalogs	
Sponsored events	Merchandising aids	

Couponing started as a promotion method to get consumers to try a new product. but now a pricing strategy to keep market share.

Rebates

To stimulate an immediate purchase.

Kellogg's marketing managers plan mass selling to communicate with final consumers, but most of their communication with retailers is handled by salespeople.

WHICH METHODS TO USE DEPENDS ON PROMOTION OBJECTIVES

Overall objective is to affect behavior

The different promotion methods are all different forms of communication. Good marketers want promotion to communicate information that will encourage customers to choose *their* product. They know that if they have a better offering, informed customers are more likely to buy. Therefore, they're interested in (1) reinforcing present attitudes that might lead to favorable behavior or (2) actually changing the attitudes and behavior of the firm's target market.

Informing, persuading, and reminding are basic promotion objectives

For a firm's promotion to be effective, its promotion objectives must be clearly defined—because the right promotion blend depends on what the firm wants to accomplish. It's helpful to think of three basic promotion objectives: *informing, persuading,* and *reminding* target customers about the company and its marketing mix. All try to affect buyer behavior by providing more information.

Even more useful is a more specific set of promotion objectives that states *exactly who* you want to inform, persuade, or remind, and *why.* But this is unique to each company's strategy—and too detailed to discuss here. Instead, we'll limit ourselves to the three basic promotion objectives—and how you can reach them.

Informing is educating

Potential customers must know something about a product if they are to buy at all. The informing objective is particularly important during the introduction stage of the product life cycle for a really new product concept. Here, informative promotion must educate consumers and build **primary demand**—demand for the general product idea—not just the company's own brand.

When a product really meets consumer needs better than other products, promotion may not have to do anything but inform consumers. When Mazda introduced its stylish and affordable Miata roadster, the uniqueness of the car simplified the promotion job. Excitement about the product also generated a lot of free publicity in car magazines.

Persuading usually becomes necessary

When competitors offer similar products, the firm must not only inform customers that its product is available but also persuade them to buy it. A *persuading* objective means the firm will try to develop a favorable set of attitudes so customers will buy—and keep buying—its product. The focus here is on building **selective demand**—demand for a company's own brand. Thus, promotion with a persuading objective often focuses on reasons why one brand is better than competing brands. To help convince consumers to

Market Decline — some firms may put lots of money into — to stimulate buying

buy Tylenol rather than some other firm's brand, Johnson & Johnson's ads tout Tylenol as the pain relief medicine most often used in hospitals.

Reminding may be enough, sometimes

If target customers already have positive attitudes about a firm's marketing mix, a *reminding* objective might be suitable. This objective can be extremely important in some cases. Even though customers were attracted and sold once, they are still targets for competitors' appeals. Reminding them of their past satisfaction may keep them from shifting to a competitor. Campbell realizes that most people know about its soup—so much of its advertising is intended to remind.

PROMOTION REQUIRES EFFECTIVE COMMUNICATION

Communication can break down

There are many reasons why a promotion message can be misunderstood—or not heard at all. To understand this, it's useful to think about a whole **communication process**—which means a source trying to reach a receiver with a message. Exhibit 13–3 shows the elements of the communication process. Here we see that a **source**—the sender of a message—is trying to deliver a message to a **receiver**—a potential customer. Research shows that customers evaluate not only the message but also the source of the message in terms of trustworthiness and credibility. For example, American Dental Association (ADA) studies show that Listerine mouthwash helps reduce plaque buildup on teeth. Listerine mentions the ADA endorsement in its promotion to help make the promotion message credible.

A source can use many message channels to deliver a message. A salesperson does it in person. Advertising must do it with magazines, newspapers, radio, TV, and other media.

A major advantage of personal selling is that the source—the seller—can get immediate feedback from the receiver. It's easier to judge how the message is being received—and change it if necessary. Mass sellers must depend on marketing research or total sales figures for feedback—and that can take too long.

The **noise**—shown in Exhibit 13–3—is any distraction that reduces the effectiveness of the communication process. Conversations during TV ads are noise. Advertisers planning messages must recognize that many possible distractions—noise—can interfere with communications.

Encoding and decoding depend on a common frame of reference

The basic difficulty in the communication process occurs during encoding and decoding. **Encoding** means the source deciding what it wants to say and translating it into words or symbols that will have the same meaning to the receiver. **Decoding** is the receiver

Exhibit 13–3 The Communication Process

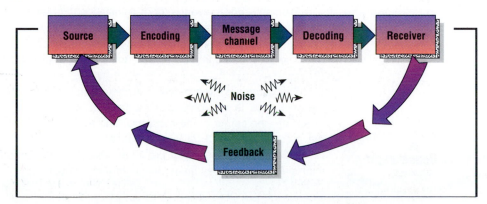

With over 59,000 florists in 140 countries, Interflora promotes the idea that "Flowers speak louder than words—in any language."

translating the message. This process can be very tricky. The meanings of various words and symbols may differ depending on the attitudes and experiences of the two groups.

Maidenform encountered this problem with its promotion aimed at working women. The company ran a series of ads depicting women stockbrokers and doctors wearing Maidenform lingerie. The men in the ads were fully dressed. Maidenform was trying to show women in positions of authority, but some women felt the ad presented them as sex objects. In this case, the promotion people who encoded the message didn't understand the attitudes of the target market—and how they would decode the message.[4]

The same message may be interpreted differently

Different audiences may see the same message in different ways—or interpret the same words differently. Such differences are common in international marketing when translation is a problem. General Motors, for example, had trouble in Puerto Rico with its Nova car. It discovered that, while *nova* means "star" in Spanish, when spoken it sounds like *no va,* meaning "it doesn't go." When the company changed the car's name to Caribe, it sold well. Many other firms make similar mistakes.[5]

Problems occur even without translation problems. For example, a new children's cough syrup was advertised as extra strength. The advertising people thought they were assuring parents that the product worked well. But cautious parents avoided the product because they feared that it might be too strong for their children.

Message channel is important too

The communication process is complicated even more because the receiver knows the message is not only coming from a source but also through some **message channel**—the carrier of the message. The receiver may attach more value to a product if the message comes in a well-respected newspaper or magazine, rather than over the radio. Some consumers buy products advertised in *Good Housekeeping* magazine, for example, because they have faith in its seal of approval.

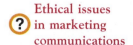

Ethical issues in marketing communications

Promotion is one of the most often criticized areas of marketing, and many of the criticisms focus on whether communications are honest and fair. Marketers must sometimes make ethical judgments in considering these charges and in planning their promotion.

Video publicity releases provide an interesting example. When a TV news program broadcasts a video publicity release, consumers don't know it was prepared to achieve marketing objectives. They think the news staff is the source. That may make the message more credible, but is it fair? Many say yes—as long as the publicity information is truthful. But gray areas still remain.

Critics raise similar concerns about the use of celebrities in advertisements. A person who plays the role of an honest and trustworthy person on a popular TV series may be a credible message source in an ad, but is it misleading to consumers? Some critics believe it is. Others argue that consumers recognize advertising when they see it and know celebrities are paid for their endorsements.

The most common criticisms of promotion relate to promotional messages that make exaggerated claims. Some promotional messages do misrepresent the benefits of a product. However, most marketing managers realize that customers won't come back if the marketing mix doesn't deliver what the promotion promises. Further, consumers are becoming more skeptical about all the claims they hear. As a result, most firms work to make their promotion claims specific and believable.[6]

ADOPTION PROCESSES CAN GUIDE PROMOTION PLANNING

In Chapter 6 we discussed consumer buying as a problem-solving process in which buyers go through six steps on the way to adopting (or rejecting) an idea or product. Now we see that the three basic promotion objectives relate to these six steps. See Exhibit 13–4. *Informing* and *persuading* may be needed to affect the potential customer's knowledge and attitudes about a product—and then bring about its adoption. Later promotion can simply *remind* the customer about that favorable experience—and confirm the adoption decision.

The AIDA model is a practical approach

The basic adoption process fits very neatly with another action-oriented model—called AIDA—which we will use in this and the next two chapters to guide some of our discussion. The **AIDA model** consists of four promotion jobs—(1) to get *Attention*, (2) to hold *Interest*, (3) to arouse *Desire*, and (4) to obtain *Action*. (As a memory aid, note that the first letters of the four key words spell AIDA—the well-known opera.)

Exhibit 13–5 shows the relationship of the adoption process to the AIDA jobs. Getting attention is necessary to make consumers aware of the company's offering. Holding interest gives the communication a chance to build the consumer's interest in the product. Arousing desire affects the evaluation process—perhaps building preference. And obtain-

Exhibit 13–4 Relation of Promotion Objectives, Adoption Process, and AIDA Model

Promotion Objectives	Adoption Process (Chapter 6)	AIDA Model
Informing	Awareness	Attention
	Interest	Interest
Persuading	Evaluation	Desire
	Trial	
Reminding	Decision	Action
	Confirmation	

Exhibit 13–5   The Adoption Curve

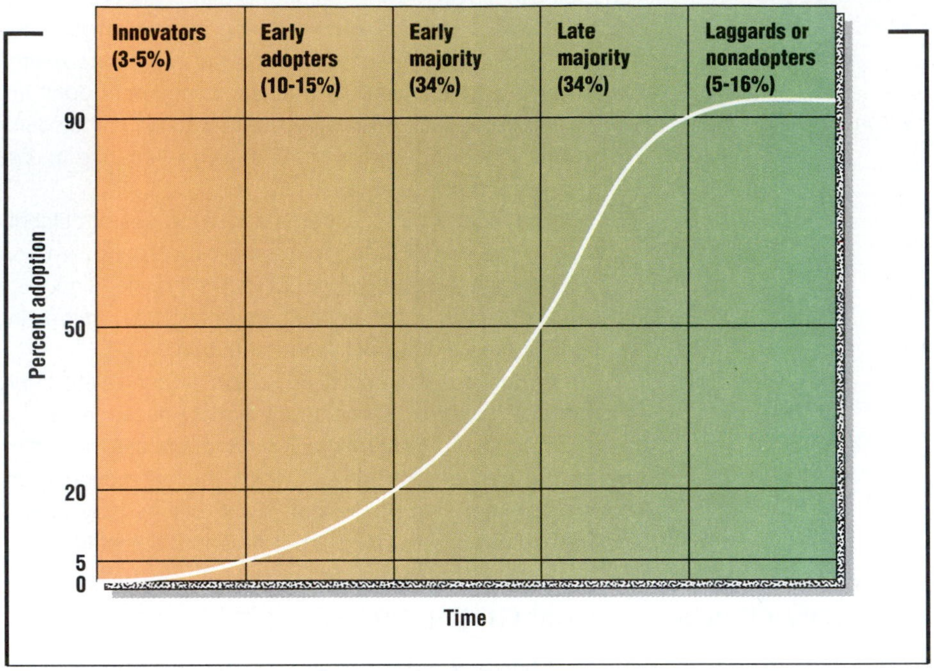

Innovators (3-5%)	Early adopters (10-15%)	Early majority (34%)	Late majority (34%)	Laggards or nonadopters (5-16%)

(Graph: Percent adoption vs. Time, S-shaped adoption curve with y-axis values 0, 5, 20, 50, 90)

ing action includes gaining trial, which may lead to a purchase decision. Continuing promotion is needed to confirm the decision—and encourage additional purchases.

The AIDA and adoption processes look at individuals. This emphasis on individuals helps us understand how people behave. But it's also useful to look at markets as a whole. Different customers within a market may behave differently—with some taking the lead in trying new products and, in turn, influencing others.

Promotion must vary for different adopter groups

Research on how markets accept new ideas has led to the adoption curve model. The adoption curve shows when different groups accept ideas. It shows the need to change the promotion effort as time passes. It also emphasizes the relations among groups—and shows that some groups act as leaders in accepting a new idea.

Exhibit 13–5 shows the adoption curve for a typical successful product. Some of the important characteristics of each of these customer groups are discussed below. Which one are you?

Innovators don't mind taking some risk

The innovators are the first to adopt. They are eager to try a new idea—and willing to take risks. Innovators tend to be young and well educated. They are likely to be mobile and have many contacts outside their local social group and community. Business firms in the innovator group usually are large and rather specialized.

Innovators tend to rely on impersonal and scientific information sources—or other innovators—rather than personal salespeople. They often read articles in technical publications or informative ads in special-interest magazines.

Early adopters are often opinion leaders

Early adopters are well respected by their peers—and often are opinion leaders. They tend to be younger, more mobile, and more creative than later adopters. But unlike innovators, they have fewer contacts outside their own social group or community. Business firms in this category also tend to be specialized.

This UPS ad quickly communicates its message—that UPS is as fast as it is reliable—with an attention-getting photo and simple headline.

Just this once, we'd like to give our vehicles the image they deserve.

Of all the groups, this one tends to have the greatest contact with salespeople. Mass media are important information sources too. Marketers should be very concerned with attracting and selling the early adopter group. Their acceptance is really important in reaching the next group because the early majority look to the early adopters for guidance. The early adopters can help the promotion effort by spreading *word-of-mouth* information and advice among other consumers.[7]

Early majority are deliberate

The **early majority** avoid risk and wait to consider a new idea after many early adopters have tried it—and liked it. Average-sized business firms that are less specialized often fit in this category. If successful companies in their industry adopt the new idea, they will too.

The early majority have a great deal of contact with mass media, salespeople, and early adopter opinion leaders. Members usually aren't opinion leaders themselves.

Late majority are cautious

The **late majority** are cautious about new ideas. Often they are older than the early majority group—and more set in their ways. So they are less likely to follow opinion leaders and early adopters. In fact, strong social pressure from their own peer group may be needed before they adopt a new product. Business firms in this group tend to be conservative, smaller-sized firms with little specialization.

The late majority make little use of marketing sources of information—mass media and salespeople. They tend to be oriented more toward other late adopters rather than outside sources they don't trust.

Laggards or nonadopters hang on to tradition

Laggards or **nonadopters** prefer to do things the way they've been done in the past and are very suspicious of new ideas. They tend to be older and less well educated. They may also be low in social status and income. The smallest businesses with the least specialization often fit this category. They cling to the status quo and think it's the safe way. The main source of information for laggards is other laggards. This certainly is bad news for marketers who are trying to reach a whole market quickly—or who want to use only one promotion method. In fact, it may not pay to bother with this group.[8]

HOW TYPICAL PROMOTION PLANS ARE BLENDED

There is no one right blend

Most business firms develop a *promotion blend* of some kind because the three promotion methods complement each other. And some promotion jobs can be done more economically one way than another. But there is no one *right* promotion blend for all situations. Each one must be developed as part of a marketing mix—and should be designed to achieve the firm's promotion objectives in each marketing strategy.

Get a push in the channel with promotion to middlemen

When a channel of distribution involves middlemen, their cooperation can be crucial to the success of the overall marketing strategy. **Pushing** (a product through a channel) means using normal promotion effort—personal selling, advertising, and sales promotion— to help sell the whole marketing mix to possible channel members. This approach emphasizes the importance of building a channel and securing the wholehearted cooperation of channel members to push the product down the channel to the final user. Producers usually take on much of the responsibility for the pushing effort in the channel. However, most wholesalers also handle at least some of the promotion to retailers or other wholesalers further down the channel.

Promotion to middlemen emphasizes personal selling

Salespeople handle most of the important communication with middlemen. Middlemen don't want empty promises. They want to know what they can expect in return for their cooperation and help. A salesperson can answer questions about what promotion will be directed toward the final consumer, each channel member's part in marketing the product, and important details on pricing, markups, promotion assistance, and allowances.

When a number of suppliers offer similar products and compete for attention and shelf space, the wholesaler or retailer usually pays attention to the one with the best profit potential. In these situations, the sales rep must convince the middleman that demand for the product exists—and that making a profit will be easy.

Promotion planning must consider the whole channel.

Sales promotions targeted at middlemen usually focus on short-term arrangements that will improve the middleman's profits. For example, a soft-drink bottler might offer a convenience store a free case of drinks with each two cases it buys. The free case improves the store's profit margin on the whole purchase. Other types of sales promotions—such as contests that offer vacation trips for high-volume middlemen—are also common.

Firms run ads in trade magazines to recruit new middlemen or to inform channel members about a new offering. Trade ads usually encourage middlemen to contact the supplier for more information, and then a salesperson takes over.

Push within a firm—with promotion to employees

Some firms emphasize promotion to their own employees—especially salespeople or others in contact with customers. This type of *internal marketing* effort is basically a variation on the pushing approach. One objective is to inform employees about important elements of the marketing strategy—so they'll work together as a team to implement it. This is typical in service firms where the quality of the employees' efforts is a big part of the product. Some Delta Airlines' ads, for example, use the theme "We love to fly, and it shows." Although the ads communicate primarily to customers, they remind Delta's employees that the service they provide is crucial to customer satisfaction.

Pulling policy—customer demand pulls the product through the channel

Regardless of what promotion a firm uses to get help from channel members or employees in pushing a product, most producers focus a significant amount of promotion on customers at the end of the channel. This helps to stimulate demand for the firm's offering and can help pull the product through the channel of distribution. **Pulling** means getting customers to ask middlemen for the product.

Pulling and pushing are usually used in combination. However, if middlemen won't handle a product, a producer may try to use a pulling approach by itself. This involves highly aggressive and expensive promotion to final consumers or users—temporarily bypassing middlemen. If the promotion works, the middlemen are forced to carry the product to satisfy customer requests. However, this approach is risky if customers lose interest before reluctant middlemen make the product available. At minimum, middlemen should be told about the planned pulling effort—so they can be ready if the promotion succeeds.[9]

Merrell Dow's consumer advertising informs consumers about Nicorette and helps to pull it through the channel. Merck promotes Mylanta directly to pharmacists to get their help pushing the product through the channel to final consumers.

THE ABC'S OF PROMOTION TO SCHOOL KIDS

Schools are a targeted place for youth-oriented marketers to promote their products to the 45 million elementary and secondary students in the United States. Milky Way provides schools with free book covers—and guess what candy bar appears on the cover. Coke and Pepsi are eager to contribute scoreboards (or is that billboards?) for high school sports fields. In school cafeterias, which serve 30 million meals a day, Kellogg's cereal and Dannon's yogurt sponsor programs to motivate learning (and increase consumption). In-school promotion is not a new idea. The National Dairy Council has distributed information about nutrition—and why students should consume dairy products—since 1915.

To be more effective in reaching students, some consumer products firms turn to promotion specialists, like Sampling Corporation of America (SCA). For example, every Halloween SCA provides schools with safety literature wrapped around product samples or coupons provided by sponsor companies. Many schools are eager to cooperate. In a single year, SCA distributes product coupons and samples to about 70 percent of students aged 6 to 12 and 85 percent of teens in high school.

However, not everyone is happy about marketers targeting promotion at students—even if the schools get something in exchange. For example, when Whittle Communications launched its Channel One television network with special programming for high schools, many parents and teachers criticized its advertising as a crass attempt to exploit captive students. Yet some of these critics are enthusiastic about participating in other promotional programs, such as one in which schools received a contribution of 10 cents for each pound of Jif peanut butter students' families bought.

Some in-school promotion efforts do provide budget-strapped educators with added resources, including useful teaching materials. Yet promotions targeted at students also raise sensitive issues of educational standards, ethics, and taste. Marketers who are not sensitive to these issues can provoke a hostile public backlash.[10]

Promotion to final consumers

The large number of consumers almost forces producers of consumer products and retailers to emphasize advertising and sales promotion. Sales promotion—such as contests or free samples—may build consumer interest and short-term sales of a product. Effective mass selling may build enough brand familiarity so that little personal selling is needed—as in self-service and discount operations.

Personal selling can be effective too. But aggressive personal selling to final consumers usually is found only in relatively expensive channel systems, such as those for fashionable clothing, furniture, consumer electronics, automobiles, and financial services.

Promotion to business customers

Producers and wholesalers who target business customers usually emphasize personal selling. This is practical because these customers are much less numerous than final consumers and their purchases are typically larger. Moreover, a sales rep can be more flexible in adjusting the company's appeal to suit each customer (or member of a buying center)—and personal contact is usually required to close a sale. A salesperson is also able to call back later to follow up with additional information or to resolve any problems.

While personal selling dominates in business markets, mass selling is necessary too. A typical sales call on a business customer costs over $250.[11] That's because salespeople spend less than half their time actually selling. The rest is consumed by such tasks as traveling, paperwork, sales meetings, and strictly service calls. So it's seldom practical for salespeople to carry the whole promotion load.

Ads in trade magazines, for instance, can inform potential customers that a product is available and stimulate inquiries. Domestic and international trade shows also help identify prospects. Even so, in business markets, firms spend only a small percentage of their promotion budget on mass selling and sales promotion.

Each market segment may need a unique blend

Knowing what type of promotion is typically emphasized with different targets is useful in planning the promotion blend. But each unique market segment may need a separate marketing mix—and a different promotion blend. Some mass selling specialists miss this point. They think mainly in mass marketing—rather than target marketing—terms. Aiming at large markets may be desirable in some situations, but promotion aimed at everyone can end up hitting no one.

Promotion blends vary in different situations

The particular promotion blend a firm selects depends on the target of the promotion, but it may be influenced by many other factors including (1) the promotion budget available, (2) the nature of the product and its stage in the product life cycle, and (3) the nature of competition.

SOMEONE MUST PLAN AND MANAGE THE PROMOTION BLEND

Selecting a promotion blend is a strategy decision that should fit with the rest of a company's marketing strategy. Once a firm sets the outlines of its promotion blend, it must develop and implement more detailed plans for the parts of the blend. This is the job of specialists—such as sales managers, advertising managers, and promotion managers.

Sales managers manage salespeople

Sales managers are concerned with managing personal selling. Often the sales manager is responsible for building good distribution channels and implementing Place policies. In smaller companies, the sales manager may also act as the marketing manager—and be responsible for advertising and sales promotion.

Advertising managers work with ads and agencies

Advertising managers manage their company's mass selling effort—in television, newspapers, magazines, and other media. Their job is choosing the right media and developing the ads. Advertising departments within their own firms may help in these efforts—or they may use outside advertising agencies. The advertising manager may handle publicity too. Or it may be handled by an outside agency or by whoever handles **public relations**—communication with noncustomers, including labor, public interest groups, stockholders, and the government.

Sales promotion managers need many talents

Sales promotion managers manage their company's sales promotion effort. They fill the gaps between the sales and advertising managers—increasing their effectiveness. In some companies, sales promotion managers have independent status, reporting to the marketing manager. Sometimes, sales or advertising departments handle a firm's sales promotion effort. But sales promotion activities vary so much that many firms use both inside and outside specialists. If a firm's sales promotion expenses exceed those for advertising, it probably needs a separate sales promotion manager.

Marketing manager talks to all, blends all

Because of differences in outlook and experience, the advertising, sales, and sales promotion managers may have trouble working with each other as partners or equals. So the marketing manager must weigh the pros and cons of the various methods, then devise an effective promotion blend—fitting in the various departments and personalities and coordinating their efforts.

To evaluate a company's promotion blend, you must first know more about the individual areas of promotion decisions. We start in that direction in the next section—with more discussion of sales promotion. Then in the following chapters, we'll take up personal selling and advertising.

SALES PROMOTION: DO SOMETHING DIFFERENT TO STIMULATE CHANGE

Firms generally use sales promotion to complement the other promotion methods. If properly done, it can be very effective. But there are problems in the sales promotion area.

Sales promotion is a weak spot in marketing

Sales promotion is often a weak spot in marketing. Exhibit 13–2 shows that sales promotion includes a wide variety of activities—each of which may be custom-designed and used only once. Thus the typical company develops little skill in sales promotion, and the mistakes caused by lack of experience can be very costly. You can see how in the following example. A promotion jointly sponsored by Polaroid and Trans World Airlines offered a coupon worth 25 percent off the price of any TWA ticket with the purchase of a $20 Polaroid camera. The companies intended to appeal to vacationers who take pictures when they travel. Instead, travel agents bought many of the cameras. For the price of the $20 camera, they made an extra 25 percent on every TWA ticket they sold. And big companies bought thousands of the cameras to save on overseas travel expenses.[12]

Sales promotion problems are likely to be worse when a company has no sales promotion manager. If the personal selling or advertising managers are responsible for sales promotion, they often treat it as a stepchild. They allocate money to sales promotion if there is any left over—or if a crisis develops.

Making sales promotion work is a learned skill—not a sideline for amateurs. In fact, specialists in sales promotion have developed—both inside larger firms and as outside consultants. Some are extremely creative and might be willing to take over the whole promotion job. But it's the marketing manager's responsibility to set sales promotion objectives and policies that will fit with the rest of the company's marketing strategy.[13]

Sales promotion spending is big—and getting bigger

Sales promotion expenditures in the United States now total over $100 billion.[14] You can see why companies need sales promotion experts—and perhaps separate status for sales promotion within their marketing departments.

Spending on sales promotion is growing—sometimes at the expense of other promotion methods—for several reasons. Sales promotion has proved effective in increasingly

---

Employees of the typical company develop little skill in sales promotion because promotion includes a wide variety of activities, each of which may be used only once.

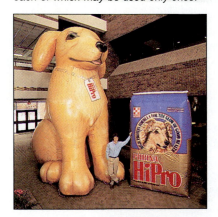  

competitive markets. Sales promotion can usually be implemented quickly and gets results sooner than advertising.[15]

Sales promotion is often designed to get *action*. Act Media—a New York firm specializing in sales promotion—sent representatives to 4,800 stores around the country, where they gave away booklets of coupons for a variety of products. Shoppers quickly redeemed about 12 percent of the coupons—nearly half for products they didn't ordinarily buy![16]

Sales promotion for final consumers or users

Firms use sales promotion aimed at final consumers or users to increase demand or speed up the time of purchase. Sales promotion people may develop displays for retailers' stores—including banners, sample packages, calendars, and various point-of-purchase items—or aisle displays for supermarkets. They might be responsible for sweepstakes contests as well as for coupons designed to get customers to buy a product by a certain date. Total coupon distribution in the United States almost tripled in the last 10 years. Now firms distribute more than 275 billion coupons a year—over 1,100 for every man, woman, and child in America! Coupons and other types of sales promotion targeted at consumers are not yet as common in most other countries, but their use is increasing worldwide.[17]

All these sales promotion efforts aim at specific objectives. For example, if customers already have a favorite brand, it may be hard to get them to try anything new. A free trial-size bottle of mouthwash might be just what it takes to get cautious consumers to try—and like—the new product. Such samples might be distributed house to house, at stores, or attached to other products sold by the firm.

Sales promotion directed at business customers uses the same kinds of ideas. In addition, sales promotion people might set up and staff trade show exhibits. They often use attractive models to encourage buyers to look at a firm's product—especially when it's displayed near other similar products in a circus-like atmosphere.[18]

Sales promotion for middlemen

Sales promotion aimed at middlemen—sometimes called *trade promotion*—stresses price-related matters. The objective may be to encourage middlemen to stock new items, buy in larger quantity, buy early, or put more push behind certain products. The tools used

TV ads and coupons distributed through the mail are popular, but promotion that targets retail customers at the point of purchase may be more likely to prompt action.

include price and/or merchandise allowances, promotion allowances, and perhaps sales contests. Trade promotion is one of the fastest growing elements in the promotion blend for producers of consumer products—especially staples. In fact, one recent study suggests that consumer package goods firms now spend about twice as much on trade promotion as they do on advertising to final consumers.

Sales promotion activities also help a product manager win support from an already overworked sales force. The sales force may be especially receptive to sales promotion in the channels—because competition is growing and middlemen respond to sales promotion. The sales reps can see that their company is willing to help them win more business.[19]

Sales promotion for employees

Sales promotion aimed at the company's own sales force might try to encourage getting new customers, selling a new product, or selling the company's whole line. Depending on the objectives, the tools might be contests, bonuses on sales or number of new accounts, and fancy resorts for sales meetings to raise everyone's spirits.

Ongoing sales promotion work might also be aimed at the sales force—to help sales management. Sales promotion specialists might be responsible for preparing sales portfolios, videotapes on new products, displays, and other sales aids, as well as sales training material.[20]

Sales promotion in mature markets

Some experts think marketing managers—especially those who deal with consumer package goods—emphasize sales promotions too much. They argue that the effect of most sales promotion is temporary and that money spent on advertising and personal selling helps the firm more over the long term. Let's take a closer look at these concerns.

There *is* heavy use of sales promotion in mature markets where competition for customers and attention from middlemen is fierce. Moreover, if the total market is not growing, sales promotions may just encourage deal-prone customers (and middlemen) to switch back and forth among brands. Then the expense of sales promotions and customer swapping simply contributes to lower profits for everyone. However, once a marketing manager is in this situation there may not be any choice. Frequent sales promotions may be needed just to offset the effects of competitors' promotions. To escape from this competitive rat race, the marketing manager must seek new opportunities—with a strategy that doesn't rely solely on short-term sales promotions for competitive advantage.[21]

CONCLUSION

Promotion is an important part of any marketing mix. Most consumers and intermediate customers can choose from many products. To be successful, a producer must not only offer a good product at a reasonable price, but also inform potential customers about the product and where they can buy it. Further, producers must tell wholesalers and retailers in the channel about their product and their marketing mix. These middlemen, in turn, must use promotion to reach their customers.

The promotion blend should fit logically into the strategy being developed to satisfy a particular target market. Strategy planning needs to state *what* should be communicated to them—and *how*.

The overall promotion objective is to affect buying behavior, but the basic promotion objectives are informing, persuading, and reminding.

Three basic promotion methods can be used to reach these objectives. Behavioral science findings can help firms combine various promotion methods for effective communication. In particular, what we know about the communication process and how individuals and groups adopt new products is important in planning promotion blends.

An action-oriented framework called AIDA can help marketing managers plan promotion blends. But the marketing manager has the final responsibility for combining the promotion methods into one promotion blend for each marketing mix.

In this chapter, we considered some promotion basics and went into some detail on sales promotion. Sales promotion spending is big and growing, and it is especially important in prompting action—by customers, middlemen, or salespeople. Many types of sales promotion cause problems for some firms because it's difficult for managers to develop expertise with all of them. However, sales promotion must be managed carefully as part of the overall promotion blend. In the next two chapters, we'll discuss personal selling and advertising in more detail.

QUESTIONS AND PROBLEMS

1. Briefly explain the nature of the three basic promotion methods available to a marketing manager. What are the main strengths and limitations of each?

2. Relate the three basic promotion objectives to the four jobs (AIDA) of promotion using a specific example.

3. Discuss the communication process in relation to a producer's promotion of an accessory product—say, a new electronic security system businesses use to limit access to areas where they store confidential records.

4. If a company wants its promotion to appeal to a new group of target customers in a foreign country, how can it ensure that its communications aren't misinterpreted?

5. Explain how an understanding of the adoption process would help you develop a promotion blend for digital tape recorders, a new consumer electronics product that produces high-quality recordings. Explain why you might change the promotion blend during the course of the adoption process.

6. Promotion has been the target of considerable criticism. What specific types of promotion are probably the object of this criticism? Give a specific example that illustrates your thinking.

7. Would promotion be successful in expanding the general demand for (*a*) raisins, (*b*) air travel, (*c*) tennis rackets, (*d*) cashmere sweaters, (*e*) high-octane unleaded gasoline, (*f*) single-serving, frozen gourmet dinners, (*g*) cement? Explain why or why not in each case.

8. What promotion blend would be most appropriate for producers of the following established products? Assume average- to large-sized firms in each case and support your answer.
   a. Candy bars.
   b. Pantyhose.
   c. Castings for car engines.
   d. Car tires.
   e. A special computer used by manufacturers for computer-aided design of new products.
   f. Inexpensive plastic raincoats.
   g. A camcorder that has achieved specialty-product status.

9. Discuss the potential conflict among the various promotion managers. How could this be reduced?

10. Explain why sales promotion is often a weak spot in marketing and suggest what might be done.

11. If sales promotion spending continues to grow—often at the expense of media advertising—how will this affect the rates charged by mass media for advertising time or space? How will it affect advertising agencies?

SUGGESTED CASES

17. Ledges State Bank

18. Sacramento Sports, Inc.

COMPUTER-AIDED PROBLEM

13. Sales Promotion

As a community service, disk jockeys from radio station WMKT formed a basketball team to help raise money for local nonprofit organizations. The host organization finds or fields a competing team and charges $7.50 admission to the game. Money from ticket sales goes to the nonprofit organization.

Ticket sales were disappointing at recent games—averaging only about 300 people per game. When WMKT's marketing manager, Bruce Miller, heard about the problem, he suggested using sales promotion to improve ticket sales. The PTA for the local high school—the sponsor for the next game—is interested in the idea but is concerned that its budget doesn't include any promotion money. Miller tries to help them by reviewing his idea in more detail.

Specifically, he proposes that the PTA give a free T-shirt (printed with the school name and date of the game) to the first 500 ticket buyers. He thinks the T-shirt giveaway will create a lot of interest. In fact, he says he is almost certain the promotion would help the PTA sell 600 tickets—double the usual number. He speculates that the PTA might even have a sellout of all 900 seats in the school gym. Further, he notes that the T-shirts will more than pay for themselves if the PTA sells 600 tickets.

A local firm that specializes in sales promotion items agrees to supply the shirts and do the printing for $3.50 a shirt—if the PTA places an order for at least 400 shirts. The PTA thinks the idea is interesting but wants to look at it more closely—to see what will happen if the promotion doesn't increase ticket sales. To help the PTA evaluate the alternatives, Miller sets up a spreadsheet with the relevant information.

a. Based on the data from the initial spreadsheet, does the T-shirt promotion look like a good idea? Explain your thinking.

b. The PTA treasurer worries about the up-front cost of printing the T-shirts and wants to know where they would stand if they ordered the T-shirts and still sold only 300 tickets. He suggests it might be safer to order the minimum number of T-shirts (400). Evaluate his suggestion.

c. The president of the PTA thinks the T-shirt promotion will increase sales but wonders if it wouldn't be better just to lower the price. She suggests $4.00 a ticket, which she arrives at by subtracting the $3.50 T-shirt cost from the usual $7.50 ticket price. How many tickets would the PTA have to sell at the lower price to match the money it would make if it used the T-shirt promotion and actually sold 600 tickets? (Hint: Change the selling price in the spreadsheet and then vary the quantity using the What If analysis.)

For additional questions related to this problem, see Exercise 13−3 in the *Learning Aid for use with Essentials of Marketing*, 6th edition.

Personal Selling

Most expensive

Big change in training of salespeople. The focus should be on satisfying the wants & needs of the consumer. Used to be let me sell you what I have instead of let me listen to what you want. Listening skills are important.

Consultative Selling - trained to listen to consumers wants and needs to help them determine what is best.

When You Finish This Chapter, You Should

❶ Understand the importance and nature of personal selling.

❷ Know the three basic sales tasks and what the various kinds of salespeople can be expected to do.

❸ Know what the sales manager must do—including selecting, training, and organizing salespeople—to carry out the personal selling job.

❹ Understand how the right compensation plan can help motivate and control salespeople.

❺ Understand when and where to use the three types of sales presentations.

❻ Understand the important new terms (shown in red).

Advertising helps open doors for personal sales. Helps in intro of new products and opens up channels of distribution. Helps w/ post purchase cognitive dissonance

Mass Selling

① Who's target audience
② What kind of advertising print or TV
③ What kind of media
④ What message
⑤ Who's going to do it. US or advert. agency

A lcoa is a major supplier of sheet aluminum and special metal alloys to manufacturers who make a wide variety of products—ranging from soft-drink cans to airplanes, like Boeing's new 777 jet. The cover of Alcoa's recent annual report reflects the thinking of top management. It states: "Customer satisfaction comes from listening, learning, understanding customer needs, and continuously improving the value we provide. Our best customer relationships become long-term partnerships."

Alcoa's salespeople are at the heart of that listening, learning, and understanding process. They perform many sales tasks to make partnerships a profitable success for both Alcoa and the customer. For example, a salesperson works closely with Boeing engineers, purchasing people, production people, and the other purchase influences to understand their needs. Specialists help resolve the technical challenges. But the salespeople need real skill to get the order and close the deal. That's just the start. An Alcoa salesperson provides technical support after the sale, ensures all orders meet Boeing's quality specifications, and promptly resolves any problems.

To be certain that these challenging jobs are done well, Alcoa recruits good people and then provides sales training to make them even better. Even experienced sales reps get ongoing training. For example, Alcoa gives its salespeople training in the firm's new quality programs and how they relate to customer needs.

Different salespeople have different skills and experience. So Alcoa must carefully match them to particular territories, customers, and product lines. And to be sure that each salesperson is highly motivated, Alcoa's sales managers must make certain that sales compensation arrangements motivate and reward salespeople for producing needed results.[1]

THE IMPORTANCE AND ROLE OF PERSONAL SELLING

Salespeople are communicators

Promotion is communicating with potential customers. As the Alcoa case suggests, personal selling is often the best way to do it. Almost every company can benefit from personal selling. While face-to-face with prospects, salespeople can get more attention than an advertisement or a display. They can adjust what they say or do to take into consideration culture and other behavioral influences on the customer. They can ask questions to find out about a customer's specific interests. They can also stay in tune with the prospect's feedback and adjust the presentation as they move along. If—and when—the prospect is ready to buy, the salesperson is there to ask for the order.

Personal selling requires strategy decisions

In this chapter, we'll discuss the importance and nature of personal selling so you'll understand the strategy decisions sales and marketing managers face. These strategy decisions are shown in Exhibit 14–1.

We'll also discuss frameworks that guide these strategy decisions. Because these approaches apply equally to domestic and international markets—we won't emphasize that distinction in this chapter. This does not mean, however, that personal selling techniques don't vary from one country to another. To the contrary, in dealing with *any* customer, the salesperson must be sensitive to cultural influences and other factors that affect communication. Different customers might respond very differently to subtle aspects of a salesperson's behavior. For example, an Arab customer might expect to be very close to a salesperson, perhaps only 2 feet away, while they talk. A Japanese customer might consider that distance rude. Similarly, what topics of discussion are considered sensitive, how messages are interpreted, and which negotiating styles are used vary among countries. A salesperson must know how to communicate effectively with each customer—wherever and whoever that customer is—but those details are beyond the strategy-planning focus of this text.[2]

Exhibit 14–1 Strategy Planning for Personal Selling

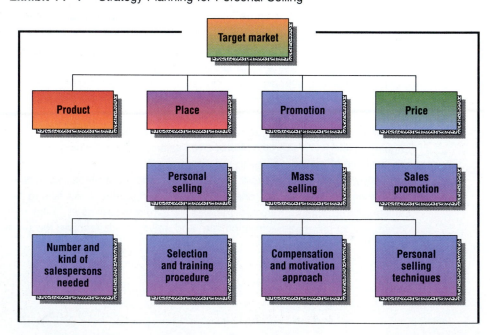

**Personal selling
is important**

We've already seen that personal selling is important in some promotion blends—and absolutely essential in others. You would better appreciate the importance of personal selling if you regularly had to meet payrolls and somehow—almost miraculously—your salespeople kept coming in with orders just in time to keep the business from closing.

Personal selling is often a company's largest single operating expense. This is another reason why it is important to understand the decisions in this area. Bad sales management decisions can be costly not only in lost sales, but also in actual out-of-pocket expenses.

Every economy needs and uses many salespeople. In the United States, 1 person out of every 10 in the total labor force is involved in sales work. By comparison, that's about 20 times more people than are employed in advertising. Any activity that employs so many people—and is so important to the economy—deserves study. Looking at what salespeople do is a good way to start.

**Helping to buy is
good selling**

Good salespeople don't just try to *sell* the customer. Rather, they try to *help the customer buy*—by understanding the customer's needs and presenting the advantages and disadvantages of their products. Such helpfulness results in satisfied customers—and long-term relationships. And strong relationships often form the basis for a competitive advantage, especially for firms that target business markets.

**Salespeople represent
the whole company—
and customers too**

Increasingly, the salesperson is a representative of the whole company—responsible for explaining its total effort to target customers rather than just pushing products. The sales rep is often the only link between the firm and its customers—especially if customers are far away. The salesperson may provide information about products, explain and interpret company policies, and even negotiate prices or diagnose technical problems when a product doesn't work well.

In some cases, salespeople represent their *customers* back inside their own firm too. Recall that feedback is an essential part of both the communication process *and* the basic management process of planning, implementing, and control. For example, the sales rep is the likely one to explain to the production manager why a customer is unhappy with product performance or quality—or to the physical distribution manager why slow shipments are causing problems. As evidence of these changing responsibilities, some companies give their salespeople such titles as field manager, market specialist, account representative, or sales engineer.

While face-to-face with prospects, salespeople can adjust what they say or do to take into consideration culture and other behavioral influences.

Sales force aids in market information function as well

The sales force can aid in the marketing information function too. The sales rep may be the first to hear about a new competitor or a competitor's new product or strategy. And, as the following example shows, sales reps who are well attuned to customers' needs can be a key source of ideas for new products.

Ballard Medical Products is a small producer that competes with international giants in the hospital supply business. A key factor in Ballard's success is that its salespeople all have a lot of say in what products the company produces and how they are designed. Ballard salespeople are trained as information specialists who seek and report on customer feedback. At each hospital, they work closely with the doctor and nurse specialists who use Ballard products. And when one of them says "We need a product to solve this problem," the Ballard sales rep relays the customer's needs back to Ballard's new-product group.[3]

Salespeople can be strategy planners too

Some salespeople are expected to be marketing managers in their own territories. And some become marketing managers by default because top management hasn't provided detailed strategy guidelines. Either way, salespeople may take the initiative to fill the gap. The salesperson may have choices about (1) what target customers to aim at, (2) which particular products to emphasize, (3) which middlemen to call on or to work with the hardest, (4) how to use promotion money, and (5) how to adjust prices.

A salesperson who can put together profitable strategies—and implement them well—can rise very rapidly. The opportunity is there for those prepared and willing to work.[4]

WHAT KINDS OF PERSONAL SELLING ARE NEEDED?

If a firm has too few salespeople—or the wrong kind—some important personal selling tasks may not be completed. And having too many salespeople—or the wrong kind—wastes money. A sales manager needs to find a good balance—the right number and the right kind of salespeople.

One of the difficulties of determining the right number and kind of salespeople is that every sales job is different. While an engineer or accountant can look forward to fairly specific duties, the salesperson's job changes constantly. However, there are three basic types of sales tasks. This gives us a starting point for understanding what selling tasks need to be done—and how many people are needed to do them.

Personal selling is divided into three tasks

The three **basic sales tasks** are order getting, order taking, and supporting. For convenience, we'll describe salespeople by these terms—referring to their primary task—although one person may do all three tasks in some situations.

ORDER GETTERS DEVELOP NEW BUSINESS

Order getters are concerned with getting new business. **Order getting** means seeking possible buyers with a well-organized sales presentation designed to sell a product, service, or idea.

Order getters must know what they're talking about—not just be a personal contact. Order-getting salespeople work for producers, wholesalers, and retailers. They normally are well paid—many earn more than $75,000 a year.

Producers' order getters—find new opportunities

Producers of all kinds of products—especially business products—have a great need for order getters. They use order getters to locate new prospects, open new accounts, see new opportunities, and help establish and build channel relationships.

Top-level customers are more interested in ways to save or make more money than in technical details. Good order getters cater to this interest. They help the customer identify

Consumers interested in shopping products often want help from a well-informed salesperson.

ways to solve problems, and then sell concepts and ideas—not just physical products. The products are merely the means of achieving the customer's end.

For example, Circadian, Inc., sells high-tech medical equipment. Changes in Medicare rules mean that doctors can no longer routinely order expensive tests in hospitals because the costs can't be recovered easily. But the doctors *can* be paid for tests done in their offices—if they have the right equipment. When Circadian order getters call on doctors, they show how the firm's testing equipment can improve patient care—and office profits. Reps can often get a $20,000 order on the spot because they can show that the equipment will pay for itself in the first year. The doctors don't care about technical details as long as the machines are accurate and easy to use.[5]

Order getters for professional services—and other products where service is an important element of the marketing mix—face a special challenge. The customer usually can't inspect a service before deciding to buy. The order getter's communication and relationship with the customer may be the only basis on which to evaluate the quality of the supplier.

Order getters in business markets need the know-how to help solve their customers' problems. Often they need to understand both customers' general business concerns and technical details about the product and its applications. This is especially important for salespeople whose customers are producers. To have technically competent order getters, firms often give special training to business-trained college graduates. Such salespeople can then work intelligently with their specialist customers. In fact, they may be more expert in their narrow specialty than anyone they encounter—so they provide a unique service.

Wholesalers' order getters—almost hand it to the customer

Progressive merchant wholesaler sales reps are developing into counselors and store advisors rather than just order takers. Such order getters may become retailers' partners in the job of moving goods from the wholesale warehouse through the retail store to consumers. These order getters almost become a part of the retailer's staff—helping to check stock, write orders, conduct demonstrations—and plan advertising, special promotions, and other retailing activities.

Agent middlemen often are order getters—particularly the more aggressive manufacturers' agents and brokers. They face the same tasks as producers' order getters. But, unfortunately for them, once the order getting is done and the customers become established and loyal, producers may try to eliminate the agents and save money with their own order takers.

Retail order getters influence consumer behavior

Convincing consumers about the value of products they haven't seriously considered takes a high level of personal selling ability. Order getters for unsought products must help customers see how a new product can satisfy needs now being filled by something else. Without order getters, many of the products we now rely on—such as microwave ovens and air-conditioners—might have died in the market introduction stage. The order getter helps bring products out of the introduction stage into the market growth stage. Without sales and profits in the early stages, the product may fail—and never be offered again.

Order getters are also helpful for selling *heterogeneous* shopping products. Consumers shop for many of these items on the basis of price and quality. They welcome useful information.

ORDER TAKERS—KEEP THE BUSINESS COMING

Order takers sell the regular or typical customers and complete most sales transactions. After a customer becomes interested in a firm's products through an order getter or supporting salesperson or through advertising or sales promotion—an order taker usually answers any final questions and completes the sale. **Order taking** is the routine completion of sales made regularly to the target customers.

Sometimes sales managers or customers use the term *order taker* as a put-down when referring to salespeople who don't take any initiative. While a particular salesperson may perform poorly enough to justify criticism, it's a mistake to downgrade the function of order taking. Order taking is extremely important. Many firms lose sales just because no one ever asks for the order—and closes the sale. Moreover, the order taker's job is not just limited to placing orders. Even in business markets where customers place routine orders with computerized order systems and EDI, order takers do a variety of important jobs.

Producers' order takers—train and explain

After order getters open up industrial, wholesale, or retail accounts, regular follow-up is necessary. Order takers work on improving the whole relationship with the customer, not just on completing a single transaction. Even if computers handle routine reorders, someone has to explain details, make adjustments, handle complaints, explain or negotiate new prices and terms, place sales promotion materials, and keep customers informed of new developments. Someone may have to train customers' employees to use machines or products. In sales to middlemen, someone may have to train wholesalers' or retailers' salespeople. All these activities are part of the order taker's job.

Producers' order takers often have a regular route with many calls. To handle these calls well, they must have energy, persistence, enthusiasm, and a friendly personality that wears well over time. They sometimes have to take the heat when something goes wrong with some other element of the marketing mix.

Firms sometimes use order-taking jobs to train potential order getters and managers. Such jobs give them an opportunity to meet key customers and to better understand their needs. And frequently, they run into some order-getting opportunities.

Order takers who are alert to order-getting opportunities can make the big difference in generating new sales. Averitt Express, a trucking firm, recognized the opportunities. Whenever drivers deliver a shipment to a firm that is not a regular Averitt customer, they call on the shipping manager at the firm. They give the shipping manager sales literature about Averitt services and ask if Averitt can help handle some of that firm's shipping needs. With 700 drivers all helping out as order getters, it's no wonder that Averitt sales have grown rapidly.[6]

A good retail order taker helps to build good relations with customers.

Wholesalers' order takers—not getting orders but keeping them

While producers' order takers usually handle relatively few items—and sometimes even a single item—wholesalers' order takers may sell 125,000 items or more. Most wholesale order takers just sell out of their catalog. They have so many items that they can't possibly give aggressive sales effort to many—except perhaps newer or more profitable items. There are just too many items to single any out for special attention.

The wholesale order taker's main job is to maintain close contact with customers—perhaps once a week—and fill any needs that develop. After writing up the order, the order taker normally checks to be sure the company fills the order promptly and accurately. The order taker also handles any adjustments or complaints and generally acts as a liaison between the company and its customers.

Such salespeople are usually the low-pressure type—friendly and easygoing. Usually these jobs aren't as high paying as the order-getting variety—but they attract many because they aren't as taxing. They require relatively little travel, and there is little or no pressure to get new accounts. There can be a social aspect too. The salesperson sometimes becomes good friends with customers.

Retail order takers— often they are poor salesclerks

Order taking may be almost mechanical at the retail level—for example, at the supermarket checkout counter. Even so, retail order takers play a vital role in a retailer's marketing mix. Customers expect prompt and friendly service. They will find a new place to shop rather than deal with a salesclerk who is rude or acts annoyed by having to complete a sale.

Some retail clerks are poor order takers because they aren't paid much—often only the minimum wage. But they may be paid little because they do little. In any case, order taking at the retail level appears to be declining in quality.

SUPPORTING SALES FORCE—INFORMS AND PROMOTES IN THE CHANNEL

Supporting salespeople help the order-oriented salespeople—but they don't try to get orders themselves. Their activities are aimed at getting sales in the long run. For the short run, however, they are ambassadors of goodwill who may provide specialized services and information. Almost all supporting salespeople work for producers or middlemen who do this supporting work for producers. There are two types of supporting salespeople: missionary salespeople and technical specialists.

Missionary salespeople can increase sales

Missionary salespeople are supporting salespeople who work for producers—calling on their middlemen and their customers. They try to develop goodwill and stimulate demand, help the middlemen train their salespeople, and often take orders for delivery by the middlemen. Missionary salespeople are sometimes called *merchandisers* or *detailers*.

Producers who rely on merchant wholesalers to obtain widespread distribution often use missionary salespeople. The sales rep can give a promotion boost to a product that otherwise wouldn't get much attention from the middlemen because it's just one of many they sell. A missionary salesperson for Vicks cold remedy products, for example, might visit druggists during the cold season and encourage them to use a special end-of-aisle display for Vicks cough syrup—and then help set it up. The wholesaler that supplies the drugstore would benefit from any increased sales, but might not take the time to urge use of the special display.

An imaginative missionary salesperson can double or triple sales. Naturally, this doesn't go unnoticed. Missionary sales jobs are often a route to order-oriented jobs. In fact, this position is often used as a training ground for new salespeople—and recent college grads are often recruited for these positions.

Technical specialists are experts who know product applications

Technical specialists are supporting salespeople who provide technical assistance to order-oriented salespeople. Technical specialists usually are science or engineering graduates with the know-how to understand the customer's applications and explain the advantages of the company's product. They are usually more interested in showing the technical details of their product than in helping to persuade customers to buy it. Before the specialist's visit, an order getter probably has stimulated interest. The technical specialist provides the details.

Three tasks may have to be blended

We described three sales tasks—order getting, order taking, and supporting. However, a particular salesperson might be given two—or all three—of these tasks. Ten percent of a particular job may be order getting, 80 percent order taking, and the additional 10 percent supporting. Another company might have three different people handling the different sales tasks. This can lead to **team selling**—when different sales reps work together on a specific account. Producers of high-ticket items often use team selling. AT&T uses team selling to sell office communications systems for a whole business. Different specialists handle different parts of the job—but the whole team coordinates its efforts to achieve the desired result.[7]

THE RIGHT STRUCTURE HELPS ASSIGN RESPONSIBILITY

A sales manager must organize the sales force so that all the necessary tasks are done well. A large organization might have different salespeople specializing by different selling tasks *and* by the target markets they serve.

Different target markets need different selling tasks

Sales managers often divide sales force responsibilities based on the type of customer involved. For example, Bigelow—a company that makes quality carpet for homes and office buildings—divided its sales force into two groups of specialists. Some Bigelow salespeople call only on architects to help them choose the best type of carpet for new office buildings. Often no selling is involved because the architect only suggests specifications and doesn't actually buy the carpet.

Other Bigelow salespeople call on retail carpet stores. These reps encourage the store manager to keep a variety of Bigelow carpets in stock. They also take orders, help train the store's salespeople, and try to solve any problems that occur.

Big accounts get special treatment

Very large customers often require special selling effort—and are treated differently. Moen, a maker of plumbing fixtures, has a regular sales force to call on building material wholesalers and an elite **major accounts sales force** that sells directly to large accounts—like Lowe's or other major retail chain stores that carry plumbing fixtures.[8]

Some salespeople specialize in telephone selling

Some firms have a group of salespeople who specialize in **telemarketing**—using the telephone to "call" on customers or prospects. A phone call has many of the benefits of a personal visit—including the ability to modify the message as feedback is received. The big advantage of telemarketing is that it saves time and money. Telemarketing is especially useful when customers are small or in hard-to-reach places. It is also important when many prospects have to be contacted to reach one actually interested in buying.

Telemarketing is rapidly growing in popularity. Large and small firms alike find that it allows them to extend their personal selling efforts to new target markets. Telemarketing increases the frequency of contact between the firm and its customers. Convenient toll-free telephone lines make it fast and easy for customers to place orders or get assistance.[9]

Sales tasks are done in sales territories

Often companies organize selling tasks on the basis of a **sales territory**—a geographic area that is the responsibility of one salesperson or several working together. A territory might be a region of a country, a state, or part of a city—depending on the market potential. Companies like Lockheed Aircraft Corporation often consider a whole country as *part* of a sales territory for one salesperson.

Carefully set territories can reduce travel time and the cost of sales calls. Assigning territories can also help reduce confusion about who has responsibility for a set of selling tasks. But sometimes simple geographic division isn't enough. A company may have different products or customers that require very different knowledge or selling skills. For example, Du Pont makes special films for hospital X-ray departments as well as chemicals

Telemarketing helps identify prospects and reach small customers, but technical specialists usually must meet with the customer in person.

used in laboratory blood tests. But it may be unreasonable to expect the same salesperson to talk to a radiologist about X-ray film and also know everything about blood chemistry!

Size of sales force depends on workload

Once the important selling tasks are specified—and the responsibilities divided—the sales manager must decide how many salespeople are needed. The first step is estimating how much work can be done by one person in some time period. Then the sales manager can make an educated guess about how many people are required in total, as the following example shows.

For many years, the Parker Jewelry Company was very successful selling its silver jewelry to department and jewelry stores in the southwestern region of the United States. But management wanted to expand into the big urban markets in the northeastern states. They realized that most of the work for the first few years would require order getters. They felt that a salesperson would need to call on each account at least once a month to get a share of this competitive business. They estimated that a salesperson could make only five calls a day on prospective buyers and still allow time for travel, waiting, and follow-up on orders that came in. This meant that a sales rep who made calls 20 days a month could handle about 100 stores (5 a day × 20 days).

The managers looked at telephone Yellow Pages for their target cities and estimated the total number of jewelry departments and stores. Then they simply divided the total number of stores by 100 to estimate the number of salespeople needed. This also helped them set up territories—by defining areas that included about 100 stores for each salesperson. Obviously, managers might want to fine-tune this estimate for differences in territories—such as travel time. But the basic approach can be applied to many different situations.[10]

When a company is starting a new sales force, managers are concerned about its size. But many established firms ignore this problem. Some managers forget that over time the right number of salespeople may change—as selling tasks change. Then, when a problem becomes obvious, they try to change everything in a hurry—a big mistake. Finding and training effective salespeople takes time—and is an ongoing job.

SOUND SELECTION AND TRAINING TO BUILD A SALES FORCE

Selecting good salespeople takes judgment, plus

It's important to hire good, well-qualified salespeople. But the selection in many companies is a hit-or-miss affair—done without serious thought about exactly what kind of person the firm needs. Managers may hire friends and relations—or whoever is available—because they feel that the only qualifications for sales jobs are a friendly personality and nice appearance. This approach leads to poor sales—and costly sales force turnover.

Progressive companies try to be more careful. They constantly update a list of possible job candidates. They schedule candidates for multiple interviews with various executives, do thorough background checks, and even use psychological tests. Unfortunately, such techniques can't guarantee success. But a systematic approach based on several different inputs results in a better sales force.

One problem in selecting salespeople is that two different sales jobs with identical titles may involve very different selling tasks—and require different skills. A carefully prepared job description helps avoid this problem.

Job descriptions should be in writing and be specific

A **job description** is a written statement of what a salesperson is expected to do. It might list 10 to 20 specific tasks—as well as routine prospecting and sales report writing. Each company must write its own job specifications. And they should provide clear guidelines about what selling tasks the job involves. This is critical to determine the kind of

La-Z-Boy operates a sales training institute to help furniture retailers train their salespeople.

salespeople who should be selected—and later it provides a basis for seeing how they should be trained, how well they are performing, and how they should be paid.

Good salespeople are trained, not born

The idea that good salespeople are born may have some truth—but it isn't the whole story. A salesperson needs to be taught—about the company and its products, and about giving effective sales presentations. But this isn't always done. Many salespeople fail—or do a poor job—because they don't get good training. Firms often hire new salespeople and immediately send them out on the road—or the retail selling floor—with no grounding in the basic selling steps and no information about the product or the customer. They just get a price list and a pat on the back. This isn't enough!

All salespeople need some training

It's up to sales and marketing management to be sure that the salespeople know what they're supposed to do—and how to do it. The kind of initial sales training should be modified based on the experience and skills of the group involved. But the company's sales training program should cover at least the following areas: (1) company policies and practices, (2) product information, and (3) professional selling skills.

Selling skills can be learned

Many companies spend the bulk of their training time on product information and company policy. They neglect training in selling techniques because they think selling is something anyone can do. More progressive companies know that training on selling skills can pay off. For example, training can help salespeople learn how to be more effective cold calling on new prospects, listening carefully to identify a customer's real objections, and closing the sale.

Training on selling techniques often starts in the classroom with lectures, case studies, and videotaped trial presentations and demonstrations. But a complete training program adds on-the-job observation of effective salespeople and coaching from sales supervisors.

SALESPEOPLE WORK SMARTER—WITH THEIR FINGERTIPS

Ⓛaptop computers help more salespeople work smarter, not just harder. Salespeople use computers in many different ways.

Without a laptop, it was impossible for a wholesaler's salespeople to master Cincinnati Milacron's product line. Now a computer asks a series of questions and then helps the salesperson figure out which of 65,000 grinding wheels and hundreds of cutting fluids to sell to each metal shop. Since adding this system, Milacron doubled its market share—without adding new salespeople.

Laptops help keep salespeople for London Fog clothing up-to-date when they're on the road calling on accounts. Early each morning before leaving the hotel, the sales reps call into the company's central computer. It downloads to the laptops all the latest information about product availability, prices, customers' accounts, and the like. Later in the day, when a customer has a question about product delivery, the sales rep can answer it instantly—without scheduling another appointment or even calling the home office.

Salespeople for Metropolitan Life Insurance company use laptops to help customers analyze the financial implications of different investments. For example, when the manager of a pension fund wanted to see what would happen if she switched money from one investment to another, the salesperson used spreadsheet software on the laptop to do the analysis—on the spot. The customer was convinced, and the sales rep closed a $633,000 sale.

When Hewlett Packard equipped a group of salespeople with laptops, the machines helped to improve communications and reduced the amount of time in meetings at the home office. As a result, salespeople were able to spend 27 percent more time with customers—and sales rose by 10 percent.

Results like these explain why the number of companies equipping their salespeople with laptops is expected to triple between 1991 and 1994.[11]

Many companies also use weekly sales meetings, annual sales conventions, and newsletters—as well as ongoing training sessions—to keep salespeople up-to-date.[12]

COMPENSATING AND MOTIVATING SALESPEOPLE

To recruit—and keep—good salespeople, a firm has to develop an attractive compensation plan designed to motivate. Ideally, sales reps should be paid in such a way that what they want to do—for personal interest and gain—is in the company's interest too. Most companies focus on financial motivation—but public recognition, sales contests, and simple personal recognition for a job well done can be highly effective in encouraging greater sales effort.[13] Our main emphasis here, however, will be on financial motivation.[14]

Two basic decisions must be made in developing a compensation plan: (1) the level of compensation and (2) the method of payment.

Compensation varies with job and needed skills

To attract good salespeople, a company must pay at least the going market wage for different kinds of salespeople. To be sure it can afford a specific type of salesperson, the company should estimate—when the job description is written—how valuable such a salesperson will be. A good order getter may be worth $50,000 to $100,000 to one company but only $15,000 to $25,000 to another—just because the second firm doesn't have enough to sell! In such a case, the second company should rethink its promotion plans—because the going rate for order getters is much higher than $15,000 a year.

If a job requires extensive travel, aggressive pioneering, or contacts with difficult customers, the pay may have to be higher. But the salesperson's compensation level should compare—at least roughly—with the pay scale of the rest of the firm. Normally, salespeople earn more than the office or production force but less than top management.

Salespeople use portable computers to save time and improve their communications with both customers and their companies.

Payment methods vary

Once a firm decides on the general level of compensation, it has to set the method of payment. There are three basic methods of payment: (1) *straight salary,* (2) *straight commission,* or (3) a *combination plan.* Straight salary normally supplies the most security for the salesperson—and straight commission the most incentive. These two represent extremes. Most companies want to offer their salespeople some balance between incentive and security, so the most popular method of payment is a combination plan that includes some salary and some commission. Bonuses, profit sharing, pensions, insurance, and other fringe benefits may be included too.

Salary gives control—if there is close supervision

A salesperson on straight salary earns the same amount regardless of how he or she spends time. So the salaried salesperson is expected to do what the sales manager asks—whether it is order taking, supporting sales activities, or completing sales call reports. However, the sales manager maintains control *only* by close supervision. As a result, straight salary or a large salary element in the compensation plan increases the amount of sales supervision needed.

Commission gives incentive—if effort relates to results

If such personal supervision would be difficult, a firm may get better control with a compensation plan that includes some commission—or even a straight commission plan with built-in direction. For example, if a company wants its salespeople to devote more time to developing new accounts, it can pay higher commissions for first orders from a new customer. However, a salesperson on a straight commission tends to be his or her own boss. The sales manager is less likely to get help on sales activities that won't increase the salesperson's earnings.

The incentive effect of compensation works best when there is a direct relationship between a salesperson's effort and results. Otherwise, a salesperson in a growing territory might have rapidly increasing earnings—while the sales rep in a poor area will have little to show for the same work. Such a situation isn't fair—and it can lead to dissatisfaction and high turnover. A sales manager can take such differences into consideration when setting a salesperson's **sales quota**—the specific sales or profit objective a salesperson is expected to achieve.

Exhibit 14−2   Relation between Personal Selling Expenses and Sales Volume
for Three Basic Personal Selling Compensation Alternatives

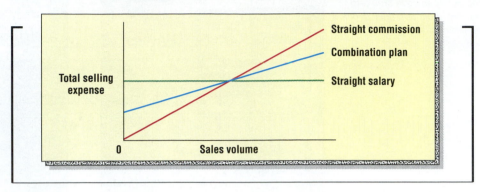

Commissions are paid
only if sales are made

Companies with limited working capital and uncertain markets often prefer straight commission—or combination plans with a large commission element. When sales are low, costs are too. Such flexibility is similar to using manufacturers' agents who get paid only if they deliver sales. This advantage often dominates in selecting a sales compensation method. Exhibit 14−2 shows the general relation between personal selling expense and sales volume for each of the basic compensation alternatives.

Simplicity shows
the link between
effort and income

A final consideration is the need for *simplicity.* Complicated plans are hard for salespeople to understand. Salespeople become dissatisfied if they can't see a direct relationship between their effort and their income. Simplicity is best achieved with straight salary. But in practice, it's usually better to sacrifice some simplicity to gain some incentive, flexibility, and control.[15]

PERSONAL SELLING TECHNIQUES—PROSPECTING AND PRESENTING

When we discussed the need for sales training programs, we stressed the importance of training in selling techniques. Now let's discuss these ideas in more detail so you understand the basic steps each salesperson should follow—including prospecting, planning sales presentations, making sales presentations, and following up after the sale. Exhibit 14−3 shows the steps we'll consider. You can see that the salesperson is just carrying out a planned communication process—as we discussed in Chapter 13.[16]

Prospecting—narrowing
down to the right target

Narrowing the personal selling effort down to the right target requires constant, detailed analysis of markets and much prospecting. Basically, **prospecting** involves following all the leads in the target market to identify potential customers.

Finding live prospects who will help make the buying decision isn't as easy as it sounds. In business markets, for example, the salesperson may need to do some real detective work to find the real purchase decision makers.

Most salespeople use the telephone for much of their detective work. A phone call often saves the wasted expense of personal visits to prospects who aren't interested—or it can provide much useful information for planning a follow-up sales visit. Some hot prospects can even be sold on the phone.

Some companies provide prospect lists to make this part of the selling job easier. For example, one insurance company checks the local newspaper for marriage announcements—then a salesperson calls to see if the new couple is interested in finding out more about life insurance.

Exhibit 14–3 Key Steps in the Personal Selling Process

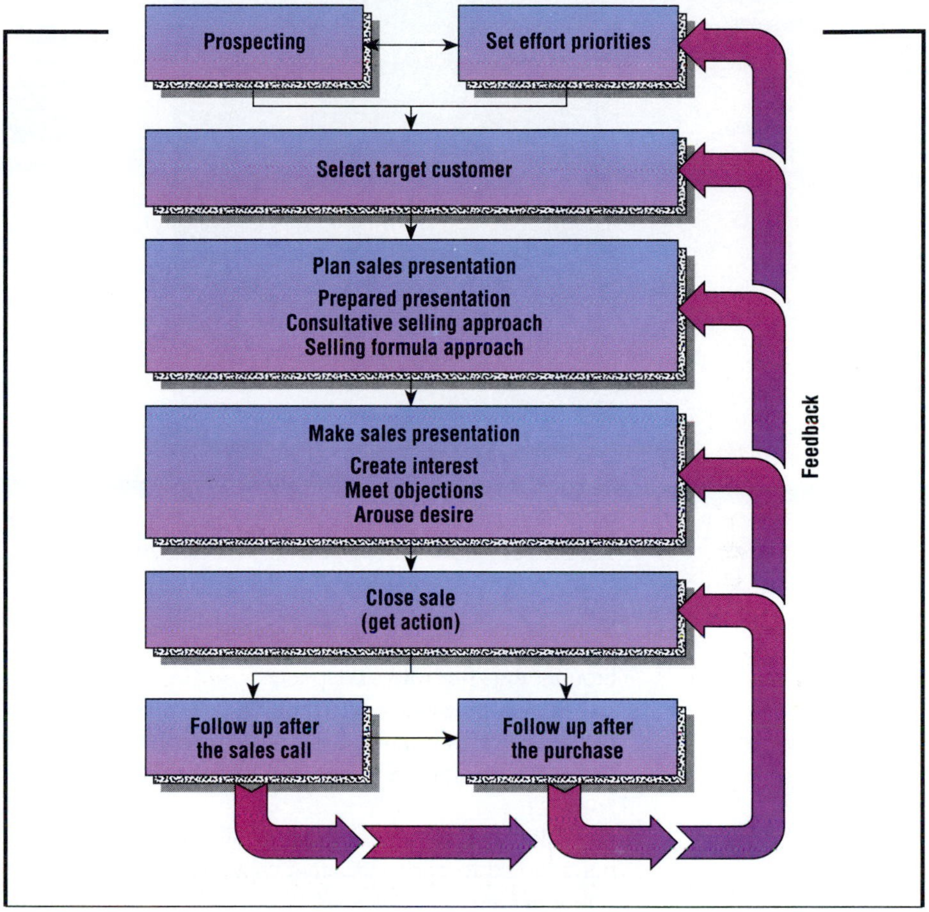

Prospecting

Set effort priorities

Select target customer

Plan sales presentation
Prepared presentation
Consultative selling approach
Selling formula approach

Make sales presentation
Create interest
Meet objections
Arouse desire

Close sale
(get action)

Follow up after
the sales call

Follow up after
the purchase

Feedback

How long to spend with whom?

Once a set of possible prospects is identified, the salesperson must decide how much time to spend on which prospects. A sales rep must qualify prospects—to see if they deserve more effort. The salesperson usually makes these decisions by weighing the potential sales volume—as well as the likelihood of a sale. This requires judgment. But well-organized salespeople usually develop some system because they have too many prospects. They can't wine and dine all of them.[17]

Many firms provide their reps with personal computers—and specially developed computer programs—to help with this process. Most of them use some grading scheme. A sales rep might estimate how much each prospect is likely to purchase—and the probability of getting the business, given the competition. The computer then combines this information and grades each prospect. Attractive accounts may be labeled A—and the salesperson may plan to call on them weekly until the sale is made or they are placed in a lower category. B customers might offer somewhat lower potential—and be called on monthly. C accounts might be called on only once a year—unless they happen to contact the salesperson. And D accounts might be ignored—unless the customer takes the initiative.[18]

Three kinds of sales presentations may be useful

Once a promising prospect is located, it's necessary to make a **sales presentation**—a salesperson's effort to make a sale. But someone has to plan what kind of sales presentation to make. This is a strategy decision. The kind of presentation should be set before the sales rep goes prospecting. And in situations where the customer comes to the

Giltspur offers a training program to help sales people do a better job qualifying prospects; SPC offers software that helps salespeople give more interesting sales presentations.

salesperson—in a retail store, for instance—planners have to make sure that prospects are brought together with salespeople.

A marketing manager can choose two basically different approaches to making sales presentations: the prepared approach or the consultative selling approach. Another approach—the selling formula approach—is a combination of the two. Each of these has its place.

The prepared sales presentation

The **prepared sales presentation** approach uses a memorized presentation that is not adapted to each individual customer. This approach assumes that a customer faced with a particular stimulus will give the desired response—in this case, a yes answer to the salesperson's prepared statement, which includes a **close**, the salesperson's request for an order.

If one trial close doesn't work, the sales rep tries another prepared presentation—and attempts another closing. This can go on for some time—until the salesperson runs out of material or the customer either buys or decides to leave. Exhibit 14–4 shows the relative participation of the salesperson and customer in the prepared approach. Note that the salesperson does most of the talking.

In modern selling, firms commonly use a prepared ("canned") presentation when the prospective sale is low in value and only a short presentation is practical. It's also sensible when salespeople aren't very skilled. The company can control what they say—and in what order. For example, a sales rep for *Time* magazine can call a prospect—perhaps a person whose subscription is about to run out—and basically read the prepared presentation. The caller needs little training or ability.

But a canned approach has a weakness. It treats all potential customers alike. It may work for some and not for others—and the salespeople probably won't know why or learn from experience. A prepared approach may be suitable for simple order taking—but it is no longer considered good selling for complicated situations.

Consultative selling—builds on the marketing concept

The **consultative selling approach** involves developing a good understanding of the individual customer's needs before trying to close the sale. This name is used because the salesperson is almost acting as a consultant to help identify and solve the customer's

Exhibit 14–4
Prepared Approach
to Sales Presentation

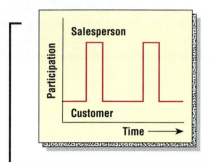

Exhibit 14–5
Consultative Selling Approach
to Sales Presentation

Exhibit 14–6
Selling-Formula Approach
to Sales Presentation

problem. With this approach, the sales rep makes some general benefit statements to get the customer's attention and interest. Then the salesperson asks questions and *listens carefully* to understand the customer's needs. Once they agree on needs, the seller tries to show the customer how the product fills those needs—and to close the sale. This is a problem-solving approach—in which the customer and salesperson work together to satisfy the customer's needs. That's why it's sometimes called the need-satisfaction approach. Exhibit 14–5 shows the participation of the customer and the salesperson during such a sales presentation.

The consultative selling approach is most useful if there are many subtle differences among the customers in one target market. In the extreme, each customer may be thought of as a separate target market—with the salesperson trying to adapt to each one's needs and attitudes. This kind of selling takes more skill—and time. The salesperson must be able to analyze what motivates a particular customer—and show how the company's offering satisfies those needs.

Selling formula approach—some of both

The **selling formula approach** starts with a prepared presentation outline—much like the prepared approach—and leads the customer through some logical steps to a final close. The prepared steps are logical because we assume that we know something about the target customer's needs and attitudes.

Exhibit 14–6 shows the selling formula approach. The salesperson does most of the talking at the beginning of the presentation—to communicate key points early. This part of the presentation may even have been prepared as part of the marketing strategy. As the sales presentation moves along, however, the salesperson brings the customer into the discussion to help clarify just what needs this customer has. The salesperson's job is to discover the needs of a particular customer to know how to proceed. Once it is clear what kind of customer this is, the salesperson comes back to show how the product satisfies this specific customer's needs—and to close the sale.

This approach can be useful for both order-getting and order-taking situations—where potential customers are similar or firms must use relatively untrained salespeople. Some office equipment producers use this approach. They know the kinds of situations their salespeople meet—and roughly what they want them to say. Using this approach speeds training and makes the sales force productive sooner.

AIDA helps plan sales presentations

Most sales presentations follow the AIDA—attention, interest, desire, action—sequence. The how-to-do-it might even be set as part of the marketing strategy. The time a sales rep spends on each of the steps might vary depending on the situation and the selling approach being used. But it is still necessary to begin a presentation by getting the prospect's *attention* and, hopefully, to move the customer to *action* through a close.[19]

Each sales manager—and salesperson—needs to think about this sequence in deciding what sales approach to use and in evaluating a possible presentation. Does the presentation get the prospect's attention quickly? Will the presentation be interesting? Will the benefits be clear so that the prospect is moved to buy the product? Does the presentation consider likely objections—and anticipate problems—so the sales rep can act to close the sale when the time is right? These may seem like simple things. But too frequently they aren't done at all—and a sale is lost.

(?) Ethical issues may arise

As in every other area of marketing communications, ethical issues arise in the personal selling area. The most basic issue, plain and simple, is whether a salesperson's presentation is honest and truthful. But addressing that issue is a no-brainer. No company is served well by a salesperson who lies or manipulates customers to get their business.

On the other hand, most sales reps sooner or later face a sales situation in which they must make more difficult ethical decisions about how to balance company interests, customer interests, and personal interests. Conflicts are less likely to arise if the firm's marketing mix really meets the needs of its target market. Then the salesperson is arranging a happy marriage. Similarly, they are less likely to arise when the firm has a longer-term relationship with the customer. By contrast, they are more likely when the sales rep's personal outcomes (such as commission income) or the selling firm's profits hinge on making sales to customers whose needs are only partially met by the firm's offering. But how close must the fit be between the firm's products and the customer's needs before it is appropriate for the salesperson to push for a sale?

Ideally, companies can avoid the whole problem by supporting their salespeople with a marketing mix that really offers target customers unique benefits. However, marketing managers and salespeople alike should recognize that the ideal may not exist in every sales call. Top executives, marketing managers, and sales managers set the tone for the ethical climate in which a salesperson operates. If they set impossible goals or project a "do-what-you-need-to-do" attitude, a desperate salesperson may yield to the pressure of the moment. When a firm clearly advocates ethical selling behavior, and makes it clear that manipulative selling techniques are not acceptable, the salesperson is not left trying to swim against the flow.[20]

CONCLUSION

In this chapter, we discussed the importance and nature of personal selling. Selling is much more than just getting rid of the product. In fact, a salesperson who is not given strategy guidelines may have to become the strategy planner for the market he or she serves. Ideally, however, the sales manager and marketing manager work together to set some strategy guidelines: the kind and number of salespersons needed, the kind of sales presentation desired, and selection, training, and motivation approaches.

We discussed the three basic sales tasks: (1) order getting, (2) order taking, and (3) supporting. Most sales jobs combine at least two of these three tasks. Once a firm specifies the important tasks, it can decide on the

structure of its sales organization and the number of salespeople it needs. The nature of the job—and the level and method of compensation—also depend on the blend of these tasks. Firms should develop a job description for each sales job. This, in turn, provides guidelines for selecting, training, and compensating salespeople.

Once the marketing manager agrees to the basic plan and sets the budget, the sales manager must implement the plan—including directing and controlling the sales force. This includes assigning sales territories and controlling performance.

We also reviewed some basic selling techniques and identified three kinds of sales presentations. Each has its place—but the consultative selling approach seems best for higher-level sales jobs. In these kinds of jobs, personal selling is achieving a new, professional status because of the skill and personal responsibility required of the salesperson. The day of the old-time glad-hander is passing in favor of the specialist who is creative, industri-ous, persuasive, knowledgeable, highly trained—and therefore able to help the buyer. This type of salesperson always has been—and probably always will be—in short supply. And the demand for high-level salespeople is growing.

QUESTIONS AND PROBLEMS

1. What strategy decisions are needed in the personal selling area? Why should the marketing manager make these strategy decisions?

2. What kind of salesperson (or what blend of the basic sales tasks) is required to sell the following products? If there are several selling jobs in the channel for each product, indicate the kinds of salespeople required. Specify any assumptions necessary to give definite answers.

   a. Laundry detergent.
   b. Costume jewelry.
   c. Office furniture.
   d. Men's underwear.
   e. Mattresses.
   f. Corn.
   g. Life insurance.

3. Distinguish among the jobs of producers', wholesalers', and retailers' order-getting salespeople. If one order getter is needed, must all the salespeople in a channel be order getters? Illustrate.

4. Discuss the potential role of the manufacturers' agent in a marketing manager's promotion plans. What kind of salesperson is a manufacturers' agent? What type of compensation plan is used for a manufacturers' agent?

5. Discuss the future of the specialty shop if producers place greater emphasis on mass selling because of the inadequacy of retail order taking.

6. Compare and contrast missionary salespeople and technical specialists.

7. Explain how a compensation plan could be developed to provide incentives for experienced salespeople and yet make some provision for trainees who have not yet learned the job.

8. Cite an actual local example of each of the three kinds of sales presentations discussed in the chapter. Explain for each situation whether a different type of presentation would have been better.

9. Describe a consultative selling sales presentation that you experienced recently. How could it have been improved by fuller use of the AIDA framework?

10. How would our economy operate if personal salespeople were outlawed? Could the economy work? If so, how? If not, what is the minimum personal selling effort necessary? Could this minimum personal selling effort be controlled by law?

SUGGESTED CASES

19. Mobay Chemical, Inc.
20. Bemis Cable, Inc.

21. Action Furniture Store
26. Cutters, Inc.

COMPUTER-AIDED PROBLEM

14. Sales Compensation

Franco Welles, sales manager for Nanek, Inc., is trying to decide whether to pay a sales rep for a new territory with straight commission or a combination plan. He wants to evaluate possible plans—to compare the compensation costs and profitability of each. Welles knows that sales reps in similar jobs at other firms make about $36,000 a year.

The sales rep will sell two products. Welles is planning a higher commission for Product B—because he wants it to get extra effort. From experience with similar products, he has some rough estimates of expected sales volume under the different plans—and various ideas about commission rates. The details are found in the spreadsheet. The program computes compensation—and how much the sales rep will contribute to profit. Profit contribution is equal to the total revenue generated by the sales rep minus sales compensation costs and the costs of producing the units.

a. For the initial values shown in the spreadsheet, which plan—commission or combination—will give the rep the highest compensation, and which plan will give the greatest profit contribution to Nanek, Inc.?

b. Welles thinks a sales rep might be motivated to work harder and sell 1,100 units of Product B if the commission rate (under the commission plan) is increased to 10 percent. If Welles is right (and everything else stays the same), would the higher commission rate be a good deal for Nanek? Explain your thinking.

c. A sales rep interested in the job is worried about making payments on her new car. She asks if Welles will consider paying her with a combination plan but with more guaranteed income (an $18,000 base salary) in return for taking a 3 percent commission on Products B and A. If this arrangement results in the same unit sales as Welles originally estimated for the combination plan, would Nanek, Inc., be better off or worse off under this arrangement?

d. Do you think the rep's proposal will meet Welles' goals for Product B? Explain your thinking.

For additional questions related to this problem, see Exercise 14–3 in the *Learning Aid for use with Essentials of Marketing*, 6th edition.

Advertising

Handwritten notes:

Product
Trying to sell a
particular product to
final consumer or
distr. channel.
① Pioneering advertising - trys
to develop primary
demand for the product
category. Informs/educates
during market intro. ② Competive
advertising - selective demand
during market growth + maturity.

Institutional -
developing goodwill
for a product or
company. Promotes
the product in
general. Milk.

- Direct Competive Ads - stimulate immediate buying behavior
- Indirect " " - Aimed a future buying behavior
by trying to point out advantages + benefits to
product.

③ Comparative - a
comp. compares their product to another in the ad.

④ Reminder -
keep product
in front of customer

When You Finish This Chapter, You Should

❶ Understand why a marketing manager sets specific objectives to guide the advertising effort.

❷ Understand when the various kinds of advertising are needed.

❸ Understand how to choose the best medium.

❹ Understand how to plan the best message—that is, the copy thrust.

❺ Understand what advertising agencies do—and how they are paid.

❻ Understand how to advertise legally.

❼ Understand the important new terms (shown in red).

Marketing managers for Energizer batteries were concerned that Duracell was taking market share. Duracell's ads showed Duracell-powered toys outrunning ordinary batteries. Although Duracell's race didn't include alkaline batteries like the Energizer, consumers were asking for Duracell. That made it easy for Duracell's salespeople to convince retailers to put special displays at checkout counters. With that extra push, Duracell got even more impulse sales.

By contrast, Energizer sales in Australia were charging ahead. Marketing managers gave much of the credit to a series of ads that featured a popular Australian rugby player. So without much pretesting, the Energizer marketing team ran the same ads in the United States. But consumers hated the ads, and Energizer sales slipped even further.

Energizer's marketing managers and their advertising agency didn't agree about what to do next—so Energizer switched agencies. The new agency knew it would need to cut through the clutter of other TV ads to communicate Energizer's long-life benefit. Their solution was the pink drum-beating Energizer bunny who "keeps going and going and going"—right through phony ads for other products. Almost overnight the bunny ads got more attention than ad campaigns costing ten times as much. But selective perception was still a problem. Research showed that many consumers incorrectly named Duracell as the sponsor of the ads!

To better link the ads with the rest of the marketing mix, Energizer put pictures of the bunny on its packages. Energizer also used the bunny in trade magazine ads—to tell retailers about its special sales promotions, including stuffed-bunny giveaways. Energizer also offered retailers materials for their own local newspaper ads. With help from the rest of the promotion blend, Energizer's salespeople got more display space at checkout counters. And Energizer hopes its sales increases will keep going and going and going.[1]

ADVERTISING PLANNING AND MARKETING STRATEGY DECISIONS

Mass selling makes widespread distribution possible. Although not as flexible as personal selling, advertising can reach large numbers of potential customers at the same time. It can inform and persuade customers—and help position a firm's marketing mix as the one that meets customers' needs.

Advertising contacts vary in cost and results. This means marketing managers—and the advertising managers who work with them—have important strategy decisions to make. As the Energizer case illustrates, they must decide (1) who their target audience is, (2) what kind of advertising to use, (3) how to reach customers (via which types of media), (4) what to say to them (the copy thrust), and (5) who will do the work—the firm's own advertising department or outside agencies. See Exhibit 15–1.

These same basic decision areas apply regardless of where in the world the target market is located. However, the choices available within each of the decision areas may vary dramatically from one country to another. The target audience may be illiterate—making print ads useless. Commercial television may not be available. If it is, governments may place severe limits on the type of advertising permitted or when ads can be shown. Radio broadcasts in a market area may not use the target market's language. Cultural, social, and behavioral influences may limit what type of advertising messages can be communicated. Local advertising agencies may be less than helpful. Throughout this chapter we'll consider a number of these issues, but we'll focus on the array of choices available in the United States and other advanced, market-directed economies.[2]

Exhibit 15–1 Strategy Planning for Advertising

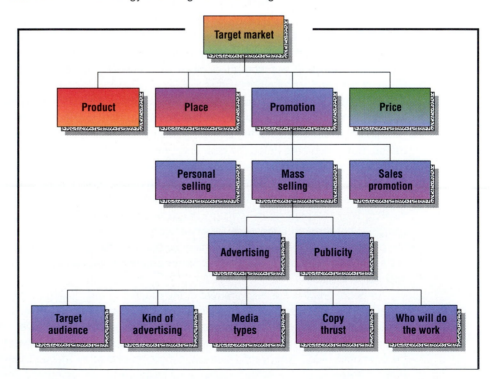

THE IMPORTANCE OF ADVERTISING

Total spending is big—and growing

As an economy grows, advertising becomes more important—because more consumers have income and advertising can get results. But good advertising results cost money. In 1946, U.S. advertising spending was about $3 billion. By 1992 it was about $133 billion, double 1982 spending. Recently, spending in many other parts of the world increased even more rapidly. However, all other nations combined spend only about 25 percent more than the United States alone—and roughly half of that is in Europe.[3]

Most advertisers aren't really spending that much

While total spending on advertising seems high, it represents a small portion of what U.S. consumers pay for the products they buy. U.S. corporations spend an average of only about 2.5 percent of their sales dollar on advertising. Worldwide, the percentage is even smaller.

Exhibit 15–2 shows, however, that advertising spending varies significantly across product categories. Producers of consumer products generally spend a larger percent of sales dollars than producers of business products. For example, U.S. beverage companies spend 8.8 percent, and perfume companies spend 10.1 percent. At the other extreme, companies that sell plastics to manufacturers spend only about 0.7 percent on advertising. Some business products companies—those that depend on personal selling—may spend less than 1/10 of 1 percent.

In general, the percentage is smaller for retailers (and wholesalers) than for producers. Kmart and J. C. Penney spend about 3 percent, but many retailers and wholesalers spend 1 percent or less.

Of course, percentages don't tell the whole story. Nissan spends less than 1 percent of sales on advertising but is among the top 50 advertisers worldwide. The big spenders are

Exhibit 15–2   Advertising Spending as Percent of Sales for Illustrative
Product Categories

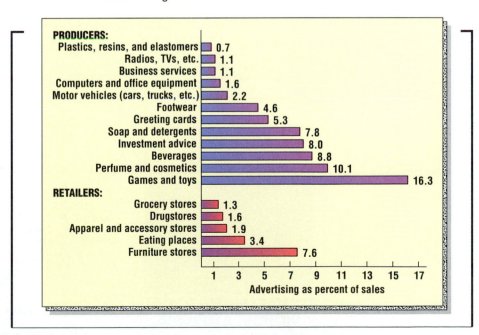

important to the advertising industry because they do a large share of all advertising. For example, Procter & Gamble, Philip Morris, Unilever, General Motors, and Nestle—the five biggest advertisers worldwide—in combination spend about $10 billion. In the United States, the top 100 advertisers (many of which are based in other countries) account for about 25 percent of all advertising spending.[4]

The major advertising expense is for media time and space. In the United States, the largest share of this—26 percent—goes for newspaper space. Television (including cable) takes about 22 percent of the total and direct mail about 18 percent.[5]

Advertising doesn't employ that many people

Many students hope for a glamorous job in advertising, but there are fewer jobs in advertising than you might think. Only about 500,000 people work directly in the U.S. advertising industry. This includes all people who help create or sell advertising or advertising media, those in advertising agencies, and those working for retailers, wholesalers, and producers. Advertising agencies employ only about half of all these people.[6]

ADVERTISING OBJECTIVES ARE A STRATEGY DECISION

Advertising objectives must be specific

Every ad and every advertising campaign should have clearly defined objectives. These should grow out of the firm's overall marketing strategy—and the jobs assigned to advertising. It isn't enough for the marketing manager to say, "Promote the product." The marketing manager must decide exactly what advertising should do.

Advertising objectives should be more specific than personal selling objectives. Salespeople can shift their presentations for each customer. Each ad, however, must be effective for thousands—or millions—of customers.

The marketing manager sets the overall direction

The marketing manager may give the advertising manager one or more of the following specific objectives—along with the budget to accomplish them:

1. Help introduce new products to specific target markets.
2. Help position the firm's brand or marketing mix by informing and persuading target customers or middlemen about its benefits.
3. Help obtain desirable outlets and tell customers where they can buy.

Many nonprofit organizations, including Richmond Public Schools and the U.S. Department of Transportation, rely on advertising to help achieve their objectives.

Exhibit 15–3 Examples of Different Types of Advertising over Adoption Process Stages

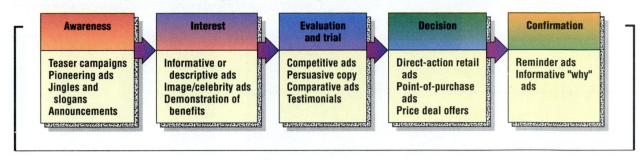

Awareness	Interest	Evaluation and trial	Decision	Confirmation
Teaser campaigns Pioneering ads Jingles and slogans Announcements	Informative or descriptive ads Image/celebrity ads Demonstration of benefits	Competitive ads Persuasive copy Comparative ads Testimonials	Direct-action retail ads Point-of-purchase ads Price deal offers	Reminder ads Informative "why" ads

4. Prepare the way for salespeople.
5. Get immediate buying action.
6. Help buyers confirm their purchase decisions.

If you want half the market, say so!

The objectives listed above are not as specific as they could be. If a marketing manager really wants specific results, they should be clearly stated. A general objective, "To help expand market share," could be rephrased more specifically: "To increase shelf space in our cooperating retail outlets by 25 percent during the next three months."

Objectives guide implementation too

The specific objectives obviously affect implementation. Advertising that might be right for building a good image among opinion leaders might be all wrong for getting typical customers into the retailers' stores. And, as Exhibit 15–3 shows, the type of advertising that achieves objectives for one stage of the adoption process may be off target for another. For example, most advertising for cameras in the United States, Germany, and Japan focuses on foolproof pictures or state-of-the-art design because most consumers in these countries already own *some* camera. In Africa, where less than 20 percent of the population owns a camera, ads must sell the whole concept of picture-taking.

OBJECTIVES DETERMINE THE KINDS OF ADVERTISING NEEDED

The advertising objectives largely determine which of two basic types of advertising to use—product or institutional.

Product advertising tries to sell a product. It may be aimed at final users or channel members.

Institutional advertising tries to promote an organization's image, reputation, or ideas—rather than a specific product. Its basic objective is to develop goodwill or improve an organization's relations with various groups—not only customers but also current and prospective channel members, suppliers, shareholders, employees, and the general public. For example, the British government uses institutional advertising to promote England as a place to do business.

Product advertising—know us, like us, remember us

Product advertising falls into three categories: pioneering, competitive, and reminder advertising.

Pioneering advertising—builds primary demand

Pioneering advertising tries to develop primary demand for a product category rather than demand for a specific brand. Pioneering advertising is usually done early in the product life cycle; it informs potential customers about the new product and helps turn them

Real uses pioneering ads to build primary demand for butter. Plugra uses competitive advertising to develop selective demand for the Plugra brand.

into adopters. When Merrell Dow introduced a prescription drug to help smokers break the habit, it did pioneering advertising to inform both doctors and smokers about its breakthrough. The ad didn't even mention the name of the drug. Instead it informed smokers who wanted to quit that doctors could now help them overcome their nicotine dependence.

Competitive advertising—emphasizes selective demand

Competitive advertising tries to develop selective demand for a specific brand. A firm is forced into competitive advertising as the product life cycle moves along—to hold its own against competitors.

Competitive advertising may be either direct or indirect. The **direct type** aims for immediate buying action. The **indirect type** points out product advantages to affect future buying decisions.

Most of Delta Airlines' advertising is of the direct competitive variety. It tries for immediate sales with prices, timetables, and phone numbers to call for reservations. Some of its ads are the indirect type. They focus on the quality of service and suggest you mention Delta when you talk to a travel agent.

Comparative advertising is even rougher. **Comparative advertising** means making specific brand comparisons—using actual product names. A recent comparative ad for Ford trucks belittles Chevy trucks—by name—as more expensive to buy and worth less later.

Many countries forbid comparative advertising, but that situation is changing. For example, Japan banned comparative advertising until about four years ago. Japan's move followed an earlier change in the United States. The Federal Trade Commission decided to encourage comparative ads—after banning them for years—because it thought they would increase competition and provide consumers with more useful information.

In the United States, superiority claims are supposed to be supported by research evidence—but the guidelines aren't clear. Some firms just keep running tests until they get the results they want. Others talk about minor differences that don't reflect a product's overall benefits.[7]

For years, Michelin used competitive ads to emphasize the safety and durability of its tires. Now that the Michelin brand is more familiar, the company uses more reminder ads.

NO MORE MR. NICE GUY.

Please excuse us, but get out of the way. Because this is the tire that has come to pass. The XGT Series from Michelin. Put a set on your sports car. And teach the world some manners.

MICHELIN
BECAUSE SO MUCH IS
RIDING ON YOUR TIRES®

Reminder advertising—reinforces early promotion

Reminder advertising tries to keep the product's name before the public. It may be useful when the product has achieved brand preference or insistence—perhaps in the market maturity or sales decline stages. Here the advertiser may use soft-sell ads that just mention or show the name—as a reminder.

Institutional advertising—remember our name

Institutional advertising usually focuses on the name and prestige of an organization or industry. It may seek to inform, persuade, or remind.

Large companies sometimes rely on institutional advertising to present the company in a favorable light—perhaps to overcome image problems. Ads for an oil company, for example, might highlight its concern for the environment.

Some organizations use institutional advertising to advocate a specific cause or idea. Insurance companies and organizations like Mothers Against Drunk Driving, for example, use these advocacy ads to encourage people not to drink and drive.[8]

COORDINATING ADVERTISING EFFORTS

Vertical cooperation— advertising allowances, cooperative advertising

Sometimes a producer finds that promotion or advertising can be done more economically by someone further along in the channel. Alternatively, a large retail chain may approach manufacturers with an ad idea and tell them how much it will cost to participate. In either case, the producer may offer **advertising allowances**—price reductions to firms further along in the channel to encourage them to advertise or otherwise promote the firm's products locally.

Cooperative advertising involves middlemen and producers sharing the cost of ads. This helps middlemen compete in their local markets. It also helps the producer get more for the advertising dollar because media usually give local advertisers lower rates than national or international firms. In addition, a retailer or wholesaler who is paying a share of the cost is more likely to follow through.

Coordination in the channel is another reason for cooperative advertising. One big, well-planned advertising effort is often better than many different—perhaps inconsistent—local efforts. KFC, for example, encourages its franchises to use the ads it provides. Before, many used their own local ads—with themes like "Eight clucks for four bucks"—that didn't fit with KFC's overall strategy.[9]

? Ethical concerns may arise

Ethical issues sometimes arise concerning advertising allowance programs. For example, a retailer may run one producer's ad to draw customers to the store but then sell them another brand. Is this unethical? Some producers think it is. A different view is that retailers are obligated to the producer to run the ad—but obligated to consumers to sell them what they want, no matter whose brand it is. A producer can often avoid the problem with a strategy decision—by setting the allowance amount as a percentage of the retailer's *actual purchases*. That way, a retailer who doesn't produce sales doesn't get the allowance.

Some retailers take allowance money but don't run the ads at all. Some producers close their eyes to this problem because they don't know what to do about intense competition from other suppliers for the retailer's attention. But there are also legal and ethical problems with that response. Basically, the allowance may have become a disguised price concession that results in price discrimination, which is illegal in the United States. So smart producers insist on proof that the advertising was really done.

CHOOSING THE BEST MEDIUM—HOW TO DELIVER THE MESSAGE

What is the best advertising medium? There is no simple answer to this question. Effectiveness depends on how well the medium fits with the rest of a marketing strategy—that is, it depends on (1) your promotion objectives, (2) what target markets you want to

Advertising managers always look for cost-effective media that will help them reach the target market.

Competitive parity—
spend what the competition
spends.

reach, (3) the funds available for advertising, and (4) the nature of the media—including who they *reach,* with what *frequency,* with what *impact,* and at what *cost.*

Exhibit 15–4 shows some pros and cons of major kinds of media—and some typical costs. However, some of the advantages noted in this table may not apply in all markets. In less-developed nations, for example, newspapers may *not* be timely. Placing an ad may require a long lead time if only a limited number of pages are available for ads. Similarly, direct mail may not be a flexible choice in a country with a weak postal system or high rate of illiteracy.[10]

Specify promotion objectives

Before you can choose the best medium, you have to decide on your promotion objectives. If the objective is to increase interest and that requires demonstrating product benefits, TV may be the best alternative. If the objective is to inform—telling a long story with precise detail—and if pictures are needed, then print media—including magazines and newspapers—may be better. For example, Jockey switched its advertising to magazines from television when it decided to show the variety of colors, patterns, and styles of its men's briefs. Jockey felt that it was too hard to show this in a 30-second TV spot. Further, Jockey felt that there were problems with modeling men's underwear on television. However, Jockey might have stayed with TV if it had been targeting consumers in France or Brazil—where nudity in TV ads is common.[11]

Match your market with the media

To guarantee good media selection, the advertiser first must *clearly* specify its target market. Then the advertiser can choose media that reach target customers.

The media available in a country may limit the choices. In less-developed nations, for example, radio is often the only way to reach a broad-based market of poor consumers who can't read or afford television.

In most cases, however, the major problem is to select media that effectively reach the target audience. Most media use marketing research to develop profiles of the people who buy their publications—or live in their broadcasting area.

 *Need to Know*

==**Exhibit 15–4**== Relative Size and Costs, and Advantages and Disadvantages of Major Kinds of Media

Kinds of Media	Sales Volume—1991 ($ billions)	Typical Costs—1991	Advantages	Disadvantages
Newspaper	$30.4	$26,055 for one-page weekday, *Atlanta Constitution*	Flexible, timely, local market *believable/creditable in writing*	*ugly* May be expensive, short life, no "pass-along" *to other people*
Television	$27.4	$4,000 for a 30-second spot, prime-time, Atlanta	Demonstrations, good attention, wide reach *stimulates the senses Broad appeal*	Expensive in total, "clutter," *fleeting* less-selective *exposure.* audience *Gone after seconds.*
Direct mail	$24.5	$115/1,000 for listing of 110,200 dentists	Selected audience, *high* flexible, can *Can buy* personalize *mail list.* *little competition*	Relatively expensive per contact, "junk *biggest* mail"—hard to retain *disad* attention *vantage*
Radio	$ 8.5	$300 for one-minute drive time, Atlanta	Wide reach, segmented audiences, inexpensive *demographics available*	Weak attention, many different rates, short exposure *audio only*
Magazine	$ 6.5	$97,090 for one-page, *high* 4-color in *People* *credibility Prestige, long life*	Very targeted, good detail, good *high* "pass-along" *demographic demographics regionl editions*	Inflexible, long lead *fleeting* times *expensive exposure* *no guarantee of position*
Outdoor	$ 1.1	$4,200 (painted) for prime billboard, 30–60-day showings, Atlanta	Flexible, repeat exposure, inexpensive	"Mass market", very short exposure

① Advertising budget - based on percentage of sales. or market average 3-5% norm   ② Affordable
② Objective - gain marketshare how much will you need (difficult to implement)   method - spend what
   + Task   you can.

Another problem is that the audience for media that *do* reach your target market may also include people who are *not* in the target group. But *you pay for the whole audience the media delivers*—including those who aren't potential customers. Levi's, for example, advertised on TV broadcasts of the Olympics because many of the viewers were 18- to 24-year-old jeans buyers. But they were only a portion of the total audience, and the size of the total audience determined the cost of the advertising time.[12]

Because it is so difficult to evaluate alternative media, some media analysts focus on objective measures—such as cost per thousand of audience size or circulation. But advertisers preoccupied with keeping these costs down may ignore the relevant segmenting dimensions—and slip into mass marketing.

Some media help zero in on specific target markets

Today the major media direct more attention to reaching smaller, more defined target markets.

National print media may offer specialized editions. *Time* magazine, for example, offers not only several regional and metropolitan editions but also special editions for college students, educators, doctors, and business managers. Magazines like *Newsweek,* France's *Paris Match International,* and Germany's *Wirtschaftwoche* provide international editions.

Many magazines serve only special-interest groups—such as fishermen, soap opera fans, new parents, professional groups, and personal computer users. In fact, the most profitable magazines seem to be the ones aimed at clearly defined markets.

There are trade magazines in many fields—such as chemical engineering, furniture retailing, electrical wholesaling, farming, and the defense market. *Standard Rate and Data* provides a guide to the thousands of magazines now available in the United States. Similar guides exist in most other countries.

Radio has become a more targeted medium. Some stations cater to particular ethnic and racial groups—such as Hispanics, African-Americans, or French Canadians. Others aim at specific target markets with rock, country, or classical music.

Cable TV channels—like MTV, Cable News Network, Nickelodeon, and ESPN—also target specific audiences. ESPN, for example, has an audience heavily weighted toward affluent, male viewers. British Sky Broadcasting does a good job of reaching housewives with young children.

Specialized media are small—but gaining

The *major* advertising media listed in Exhibit 15–4 attract the vast majority of advertising media budgets. But advertising specialists always look for cost-effective new media that will help advertisers reach their target markets. For example, one company successfully sells space for signs on bike racks that it places in front of 7-Eleven stores. In China, where major media are limited, companies like Kodak pay to put ads on bus shelters.

In recent years, these specialized media gained in popularity. They get the message to the target market close to the point of purchase and away from the usual clutter in the mass media. For example, Actmedia sells advertising space on little message boards that hang on shopping carts and shelves in grocery stores and drugstores.[13]

"Must buys" may use up available funds

Selecting which media to use is still pretty much an art. The media buyer may start with a budgeted amount and try to buy the best blend to reach the target audience.

Some media are obvious "must buys"—such as *the* local newspaper for a retailer in a small or medium-sized town. Most firms serving local markets view a Yellow Pages listing as a must buy. These ads may even use up the available funds.

For many firms—even national advertisers—the high cost of television may eliminate it from the media blend. In the United States, a 30-second commercial on a prime-time show

Most marketing managers serving local markets view Yellow Pages advertising as a must buy—because it usually reaches customers when they're ready to buy.

averages about $125,000—the price goes up rapidly for shows that attract a large audience. A spot on the most popular series costs $200,000 or more, and the Super Bowl costs $800,000.[14]

Integrated direct marketing is very targeted

The challenge of finding media that reach specific target customers has prompted many firms to turn to direct marketing. Early efforts in the direct-marketing area focused on direct-mail advertising. A carefully selected mailing list—from the many available—allowed advertisers to reach a specific target audience. And direct-mail advertising proved to be very effective when the objective was to get a direct response by the customer.

Now it's more than direct-mail advertising

Achieving a measurable, direct response from specific target customers is still the heart of direct marketing. But the advertising medium is evolving to include not just mail but telephone, print, computer, broadcast, or even interactive video. The customer's response may be a purchase (or donation), a question, or a request for more information. More often than not, the customer responds by calling a toll-free telephone number. A knowledgeable salesperson talks with the customer on the phone and follows up. That might involve filling an order and having it shipped to the customer or putting an interested prospect in touch with a salesperson who makes a personal visit. The term *integrated direct marketing* developed because direct-response advertising is closely integrated with the other elements of the marketing mix. However, what distinguishes this general approach is that the marketer targets the advertising at specific individuals who respond directly.

Target customer directly with a database

Direct advertisers rely on a customer (or prospect) database to target specific individuals. The computerized database includes customers' names and addresses (or telephone numbers) as well as past purchases and other segmenting characteristics. Individuals (or segments) who respond to direct advertising are the target for additional ads. For example, BMW and other car companies found that videotapes are a good way to interest consumers in a new model. However, it's too expensive to send tapes to everyone. To target the mailing, BMW first sends likely car buyers (high-income consumers who own a BMW or competing brand) personalized direct-mail ads that offer a free tape. Interested consumers return a card. Then BMW sends the advertising tape and updates its database so a dealer will know to call the consumer.

Direct advertising has become an important part of many marketing mixes, and many customers find it very convenient. But not everyone is enthusiastic. Some critics argue that thousands of acres of trees are consumed each week—just to make the paper for junk mail that consumers don't want. Other critics worry about privacy issues related to how direct-response databases might be used.[15]

PLANNING THE BEST MESSAGE—WHAT TO COMMUNICATE

Specifying the copy thrust

Once you decide *how* the messages will reach the target audience, you have to decide on the **copy thrust**—what the words and illustrations should communicate.

Carrying out the copy thrust is the job of advertising specialists. But the advertising manager and the marketing manager need to understand the process to be sure that the job is done well.

Let AIDA help guide message planning

Basically, the overall marketing strategy should determine *what* the message should say. Then management judgment—perhaps aided by marketing research—can help decide how to encode this content so it will be decoded as intended.

As a guide to message planning, we can use the AIDA concept: getting Attention, holding Interest, arousing Desire, and obtaining Action.

Getting attention

Getting attention is an ad's first job. If an ad doesn't get attention, it doesn't matter how many people see or hear it. Many readers leaf through magazines and newspapers without paying attention to any of the ads. Many listeners or viewers do chores—or get snacks—during radio and TV commercials. When watching a program on videotape, they may zap past the commercial with a flick of the fast-forward button.

Many attention-getting devices are available. A large headline, newsy or shocking statements, attractive models, babies, animals, special effects—anything different or eye-catching—may do the trick. However, the attention-getting device can't detract from—and hopefully should lead to—the next step, holding interest.

Holding interest

Holding interest is more difficult. A humorous ad or an unusual video effect may get your attention—but once you've seen it, then what? If there is no relation between what got your attention and the marketing mix, you'll move on. To hold interest, the tone and language of the ad must fit with the experiences and attitudes of the target customers—and

Billboards are good for getting attention with a simple copy thrust.

their reference groups. As a result, many advertisers develop ads that relate to specific emotions. They hope that the good feeling about the ad will stick—even if its details are forgotten.

To hold interest, informative ads need to speak the target customer's language. Persuasive ads must provide evidence that convinces the customer. Celebrity endorsements may help. TV ads often demonstrate a product's benefits. Layouts for print ads should look right to the customer. Print illustrations and copy should be arranged to encourage the eye to move smoothly through the ad—perhaps from a headline that starts in the upper left-hand corner to the illustration or body copy in the middle and finally to the company or brand name ("signature") at the lower right-hand corner. If all of the elements of the ad work together as a whole, they will help to hold interest and build recall.[16]

Arousing desire

Arousing desire to buy a particular product is one of an ad's most difficult jobs. The ad must convince customers that the product can meet their needs. Testimonials may persuade a consumer that other people—with similar needs—like the product. Product comparisons may highlight the advantages of a particular brand.

Some experts feel that an ad should focus on one *unique selling proposition* that aims at an important unsatisfied need. This can help set the brand apart—and position it as especially effective in meeting the needs of the target market. For example, Wrigley developed a series of ads targeted at smokers—suggesting that Wrigley's gum is a good substitute when smoking is not permitted.

Although products may satisfy emotional needs, many consumers find it necessary to justify their purchases on some logical basis. Snickers candy bar ads help ease the guilt of calorie-conscious snackers by assuring them that "Snickers satisfies you when you need an afternoon energy break."

Obtaining action

Getting action is the final requirement—and not an easy one. From communication research, we now know that prospective customers must be led beyond considering how the product *might* fit into their lives—to actually trying it.

A unique selling proposition can help position a brand as especially effective in meeting the needs of a target market.

GILLETTE'S MEDIUM-CLOSE SHAVE IN IRAN

(G) illette faces sharp competition from other razor producers in most parts of the world. But the situation it faced in Iran was even more prickly. Gillette wanted to introduce its Contour razor with a series of TV ads. Gillette used TV in other countries because it was the best medium for demonstrating the advantages of the Contour razor. And the cost was right; a one-minute ad on Iranian TV cost only $1,000. But TV ads turned out to be impossible as a first step. Since the 1980 Iranian revolution, the Ministry of Guidance, which controls advertising in Iran, prohibited Iran's two TV channels from advertising foreign products. In fact, until 1990 the ministry did not allow any TV advertising, even for local products.

The Ministry of Guidance wasn't Gillette's only obstacle. The Islamic religion discourages its followers from shaving. On the other hand, many Iranians *do* shave—and Gillette figured that people who shave need razors.

Gillette turned to Mormohamad Fathi, head of an Iranian advertising agency, for help. He thought a practical first step would be to try to find a medium that would accept advertising for Gillette's Blue II, a less expensive razor than the Contour. Fathi took a Blue II ad from one Tehran newspaper to another, but they repeatedly turned him down. Fathi thought it was a good omen when he finally found a newspaper advertising manager without a beard—but the man still needed persuading. Fathi explained to him, "Shaving is not just for your face. If you have a car accident and someone has to shave your head, Gillette Blue II is the best." Using this argument, the newspaper's ad manager consulted his clergyman, who gave him permission to take the ad.

Once over that hurdle, other papers followed, and before long Gillette ads appeared regularly in Iranian print media. That helped pave the way for Fathi to plaster Gillette posters on buses all over Tehran. He also handed out hundreds of free samples—to encourage consumers to try the razor and to build repeat sales. Fathi is persistent. With sales momentum building, you can bet it won't be long before Gillette's demonstration ads are showing in Iran's movie theaters.[17]

To communicate more effectively, the ads might emphasize strongly felt customer needs. Careful research on attitudes in the target market may help uncover such strongly felt *unsatisfied* needs.

Appealing to these needs can get more action—and also provide the kind of information buyers need to confirm their decisions. Some customers seem to read more advertising *after* a purchase than before. The ad may reassure them about the correctness of their decision.

Can global messages work?

Many international consumer products firms try to use one global advertising message all around the world. Of course, they translate the message or make other minor adjustments—but they use a global copy thrust. Some do it to cut the cost of developing different ads for each country. Others feel their customers' basic needs are the same, even in different countries. Some just do it because it's fashionable to "go global."

This approach works for some firms. Coca-Cola and Gillette, for example, feel that their products serve similar needs for all consumers. They focus on similarities among consumers in their target market rather than differences. However, many firms have experienced terrible results with this approach. They may have saved money by developing fewer ads, but they lost sales because they did not develop advertising messages—and whole marketing mixes—aimed at specific target markets. They just tried to appeal to a global mass market.

Combining smaller market segments into a single, large target market makes sense if the different segments can be served with a single marketing mix. But when that is not the case, the marketing manager should treat them as different target markets—with specific marketing mixes for each target.[18]

ADVERTISING AGENCIES OFTEN DO THE WORK

An advertising manager manages a company's advertising effort. Many advertising managers—especially those working for large retailers—have their own advertising departments that plan specific advertising campaigns and carry out the details. Others turn over much of the work to specialists—advertising agencies.

Ad agencies are specialists

Advertising agencies are specialists in planning and handling mass-selling details for advertisers. Agencies play a useful role because they are independent of the advertiser and have an outside viewpoint. They bring experience to a client's problems because they work for many other clients. Further, as specialists they can often do a better job than a firm's own department. And an advertiser who is not satisfied can easily switch to a new agency.

Some full-service agencies handle any activities related to advertising. They may even handle overall marketing strategy planning—as well as marketing research, product and package development, and sales promotion.

The biggest agencies handle much of the advertising

The vast majority of advertising agencies are small—with 10 or fewer employees. But the largest agencies account for most of the billings.

Recently, some big agencies merged—creating mega-agencies with worldwide networks. Before the mergers, marketers in one country often had difficulty finding a capable, full-service agency in the country where they wanted to advertise. The mega-agency can offer varied services—wherever in the world a marketing manager needs them. This may be especially important for large corporations—like Toyota, Renault, Unilever, NEC, Phillips, Procter & Gamble, Nestle, and Coca-Cola—which advertise worldwide.[19]

Smaller agencies will continue to play an important role. The really big agencies are less interested in smaller accounts. Smaller agencies will continue to appeal to customers who want more personal attention.

Are they paid too much?

Traditionally, most U.S. advertising agencies are paid a commission of about 15 percent on media and production costs. This arrangement evolved because media usually have two prices: one for national advertisers and a lower rate for local advertisers, such as local retailers. The advertising agency gets a 15 percent commission on national rates—but not on local rates. This makes it worthwhile for producers and national middlemen to use agencies. National advertisers have to pay the full media rate anyway, so it makes sense to let the agency experts do the work—and earn their commission. Local retailers—allowed the lower media rate—seldom use agencies.

There is growing resistance to the idea of paying agencies the same way regardless of the work performed or *the results achieved*. The commission approach also makes it hard for agencies to be completely objective about inexpensive media—or promotion campaigns that use little space or time. Not all agencies are satisfied with the present arrangement either. Some would like to charge additional fees as their costs rise and advertisers demand more services.

Firms that need a lot of service but spend relatively little on media—including most producers of business products—favor a fixed commission system.

Some firms pay the agency based on results

A number of advertisers now "grade" the work done by their agencies—and the agencies' pay depends on the grade. For example, General Foods lowered its basic commission to about 13 percent. However, the company pays the agency a bonus of about 3 percent on campaigns that earn an A rating. If the agency only earns a B, it loses the bonus. If it earns a C, it must improve fast—or GF removes the account. Variations on this approach are becoming common.[20]

? Ethical conflicts may arise

Ad agencies usually work closely with their clients, and they often have access to confidential information. This can create ethical conflicts if an agency is working with two or more competing clients. Most agencies are sensitive to the potential problems and keep people and information from competing accounts separated. But many advertisers don't think that's enough. They refuse to work with an agency that handles any competing accounts, even when they're handled in different offices in different parts of the world. This is a problem for some of the international mega-agencies. Saatchi & Saatchi, for example, gained over $300 million in billings through its mergers but then quickly lost $462 million in billings when old clients departed because Saatchi's new clients included competitors.[21]

MEASURING ADVERTISING EFFECTIVENESS IS NOT EASY

Success depends on the total marketing mix

It would be convenient if we could measure the results of advertising by looking at sales. Certainly some breakthrough ads do have a very direct effect on a company's sales—and the advertising literature is filled with success stories that "prove" advertising increases sales. Unfortunately, we usually can't measure advertising success just by looking at sales. The total marketing mix—not just promotion generally or advertising specifically—is responsible for the sales result. And sales results are also affected by what competitors do and by other changes in the external marketing environment. Only with direct-response advertising can a company make a direct link between advertising and sales results.

Research and testing can improve the odds

Ideally, advertisers should pretest advertising before it runs—rather than relying solely on their own guesses about how good an ad will be. The judgment of creative people or advertising experts may not help much. They often judge only on the basis of originality—or cleverness—of the copy and illustrations.

Some progressive advertisers now demand laboratory or market tests to evaluate an ad's effectiveness. For example, American Express used focus group interviews to get reactions to a series of possible TV ads. The agency prepared picture boards presenting different approaches—as well as specific copy. One idea that seemed to be effective became the basis for an ad that was tested again before being launched on TV.[22]

Split runs on cable TV systems in test markets are now proving to be an important approach for testing ads in a normal viewing environment. Scanner sales data from retailers in those test markets can provide an estimate of how an ad is likely to affect sales. This approach will become even more powerful in the future as more cable systems add new technology that allows viewers to provide immediate feedback as an ad appears on TV.

Hindsight may lead to foresight

After ads run, researchers may try to measure how much consumers recall about specific products or ads. Inquiries from customers may be used to measure the effectiveness of particular ads. The response to radio or television commercials—or magazine readership—can be estimated using various survey methods to check the size and composition of audiences (the Nielsen and Starch reports are examples).[23]

HOW TO AVOID UNFAIR ADVERTISING

Government agencies may say what is fair

In most countries, the government takes an active role in deciding what kinds of advertising are allowed. For example, France and Japan limit the use of cartoon characters in advertising to children, and Sweden and Canada ban *any* advertising targeted directly at children. In Switzerland, an advertiser cannot use an actor to represent a consumer. New Zealand and Switzerland limit political ads on TV. In the United States, print ads must be identified so they aren't confused with editorial matter; in other countries ads and editorial copy can be intermixed. In Italy, a TV ad can be shown only 10 times a year (but this restriction may change as broadcast rules in Europe become more unified).

What is seen as positioning in one country may be viewed as unfair or deceptive in another. For example, in many countries Pepsi advertises its cola as "the choice of the new generation." Japan's Fair Trade Committee doesn't allow it—because right now Pepsi is not "the choice."[24]

Because advertisers face very specific limits in different countries, local experts may be required to ensure that a firm doesn't waste money developing advertising programs that will never be shown—or which consumers will think are deceptive.

FTC controls unfair practices in the United States

In the United States, the Federal Trade Commission has the power to control unfair or deceptive business practices—including deceptive advertising. The FTC has been policing deceptive advertising for many years. And it may be getting results now that advertising agencies as well as advertisers must share equal responsibility for false, misleading, or unfair ads.

This is a serious matter. If the FTC decides that a particular practice is unfair or deceptive, it has the power to require affirmative disclosures—such as the health warnings on cigarettes—or **corrective advertising**—ads to correct deceptive advertising. For

Radio Marketing Services (RMS), a group of private radio stations in Germany, uses a TV spot to show a man being pressured from all sides by state-owned radio. The RMS ad promises potential advertisers: "Your opinions are your own private business."

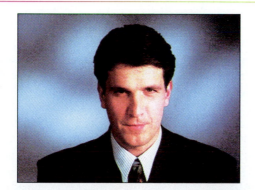
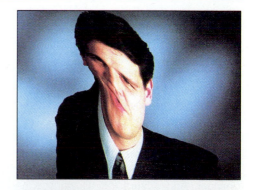

example, the FTC forced Listerine to spend millions of dollars on advertising to "correct" earlier ads that claimed the mouthwash helped prevent colds. The possibility of large financial penalties and/or the need to pay for corrective ads cause more agencies and advertisers to stay well within the law.[25]

When the FTC found fewer outright deceptive ads in national campaigns, the agency moved more aggressively against what it felt to be other "unfair" practices. Some in the FTC felt it was unfair to target advertising at children. And there were questions about whether food and drug advertising should be controlled to protect vulnerable groups, such as the aged, poor, or less educated.

Not everyone agreed with this thrust, however. Congress specifically limits FTC rule making to advertising that is *deceptive* rather than *unfair.* Note, however, that while the FTC is prohibited from using unfairness in a rule affecting a whole industry, unfairness can still be used against an individual company.[26]

Definition of unfair or deceptive is changing

What constitutes unfair and deceptive advertising is a difficult question and one marketing managers will have to wrestle with for years. Sometimes the law provides guidelines, but in most cases the marketing manager must make personal judgments as well. The social and political environment is changing worldwide. Practices considered acceptable some years ago are now questioned—or considered deceptive. Saying or even implying that your product is best may be viewed as deceptive. And a 1988 revision of the Lanham Act protects firms whose brand names are unfairly tarnished in comparative ads.

A little puffing will probably always be acceptable. But advertisers should avoid trying to pass off me-too products as really new or better. Some advertising agencies already refuse such jobs.[27]

CONCLUSION

Theoretically, it may seem simple to develop an advertising campaign. Just pick the media and develop a message. But it's not that easy. Effectiveness depends on using the best available medium and the best message considering (1) promotion objectives, (2) the target markets, and (3) the funds available for advertising.

Specific advertising objectives determine what kind of advertising to use—product or institutional. If product advertising is needed, then the particular type must be decided—pioneering, competitive (direct or indirect), or reminder. And advertising allowances and cooperative advertising may be helpful.

Many technical details are involved in mass selling, and specialists—advertising agencies—handle some of these jobs. But specific objectives must be set for them, or their advertising may have little direction and be almost impossible to evaluate.

Effective advertising should affect sales. But the whole marketing mix affects sales—and the results of advertising can't be measured by sales changes alone. Advertising is only a part of promotion—and promotion is only a part of the total marketing mix a marketing manager must develop to satisfy target customers.

QUESTIONS AND PROBLEMS

1. Identify the strategy decisions a marketing manager must make in the advertising area.

2. Discuss the relation of advertising objectives to marketing strategy planning and the kinds of advertising actually needed. Illustrate.

3. List several media that might be effective for reaching consumers in a developing nation with low per capita income and a high level of illiteracy. Briefly discuss the limitations and advantages of each medium you suggest.

4. Give three examples where advertising to middlemen might be necessary. What are the objectives of such advertising?

5. What does it mean to say that "money is invested in advertising?" Is all advertising an investment? Illustrate.

6. Find advertisements to final consumers that illustrate the following types of advertising: (*a*) institutional, (*b*) pioneering, (*c*) competitive, (*d*) reminder. What objective(s) does each of these ads have? List the needs each ad appeals to.

7. Describe the type of media that might be most suitable for promoting: (*a*) tomato soup, (*b*) greeting cards, (*c*) a business component material, (*d*) playground equipment. Specify any assumptions necessary to obtain a definite answer.

8. Discuss the use of testimonials in advertising. Which of the four AIDA steps might testimonials accomplish? Are they suitable for all types of products? If not, for which types are they most suitable?

9. Find a magazine ad that you think does a particularly good job of communicating to the target audience.

Would the ad communicate well to an audience in another country? Explain your thinking.

10. Johnson & Johnson sells its baby shampoo in many different countries. Do you think baby shampoo would be a good product for Johnson & Johnson to advertise with a single global message? Explain your thinking.

11. Discuss the future of smaller advertising agencies now that many of the largest are merging to form mega-agencies.

12. Does advertising cost too much? How can this be measured?

13. How would your local newspaper be affected if local supermarkets switched their weekly advertising and instead used a service that delivered weekly, free-standing ads directly to each home?

14. Is it unfair to advertise to children? Is it unfair to advertise to less educated or less experienced people of any age? Is it unfair to advertise for "unnecessary" products? Is it unfair to criticize a competitor's product in an ad?

SUGGESTED CASES

17. Ledges State Bank

18. Sacramento Sports, Inc.

COMPUTER-AIDED PROBLEM

15. Advertising Media

Helen Troy, owner of three Sound Haus stereo equipment stores, is deciding what advertising medium to use to promote her newest store. She found direct-mail ads effective for reaching her current customers, but she wants to attract new customers too. The best prospects are professionals in the 25–44 age range with incomes over $38,000 a year. But only some of the people in this group are audiophiles who want the top-of-the-line brands she carries.

Troy narrows her choice to two media: an FM radio station and a biweekly magazine that focuses on entertainment in her city. Many of the magazine's readers are out-of-town visitors interested in concerts, plays, and restaurants. They usually buy stereo equipment at home. But the magazine's audience research shows that many local professionals subscribe too. Troy feels that ads in

six issues will generate good local awareness with her target market. In addition, the magazine's color format will let her present the prestige image she wants to convey in an ad. She thinks that will help convert aware prospects to buyers. A local advertising agency will prepare a high-impact ad for $2,000, and then Troy will pay for the magazine space.

The FM radio station targets an audience similar to Troy's own target market. She knows repeated ads will be needed to be sure that most of her target audience is exposed to her ads. Troy thinks it will take daily ads for several months to create adequate awareness among her target market. The FM station will provide an announcer and prepare a tape of Troy's ad for a one-time fee of $200. All she has to do is tell the station what the ad should say.

Both the radio station and the magazine give Troy reports summarizing recent audience research. She decides that comparing the two media in a spreadsheet will help her make a better decision.

a. Based on the data displayed on the initial spreadsheet, which medium would you recommend to Troy? Why?

b. The agency that offers to prepare Troy's magazine ad will prepare a fully produced radio ad—including a musical jingle—for $2,500. The agency claims its ad will have much more impact than the ad the radio station will create. The agency says its ad should produce the same results as the station ad with 20 percent fewer insertions (airings). If the agency claim is correct, should Troy pay the agency to produce the ad?

c. Troy thinks that the agency-produced ad may create greater awareness, even with the smaller number of insertions. Use the What If analysis to vary the percent of prospects who become aware from 80 to 90 percent. Prepare a table showing how the cost per buyer and cost per aware prospect change with different awareness levels. What are the implications of your analysis?

For additional questions related to this problem, see Exercise 15–3 in the *Learning Aid for use with Essentials of Marketing,* 6th edition.

Pricing Objectives and Policies

When You Finish This Chapter, You Should

❶
Understand how pricing objectives should guide strategy planning for pricing decisions.

❷
Understand choices the marketing manager must make about price flexibility and price levels over the product life cycle.

❸
Understand the legality of price level and price flexibility policies.

❹
Understand the many possible variations of a price structure, including discounts, allowances, and who pays transportation costs.

❺
Understand the important new terms (shown in red).

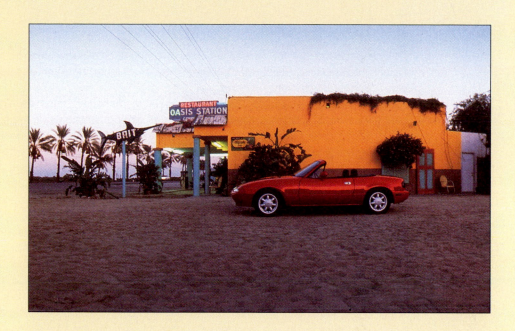

During the 1980s, most American consumers just saw Mazda as a lower-priced Japanese alternative to Toyota and Honda. Mazda's marketing managers knew that they needed to build a more distinct image in the 1990s. Their plan was to offer each of their target markets marketing mixes that clearly established Mazda as a producer of high-performance, affordable cars. The sporty Miata convertible was their first step in that effort. Mazda designers styled the Miata for the preferences of U.S. sports car buffs. Research showed that this target market wanted a back-to-basics two-seater—and it appeared that a low list price of about $14,000 would help Mazda quickly penetrate the market. To ensure profits at that low penetration price, Mazda kept fixed development costs low. It also avoided costly features like digital controls and electronic suspension.

The marketing mix seemed to be on target. Before the Miata was even on the market, magazines praised it as the "best sports car buy in America." Spurred by the publicity, consumers poured into dealer showrooms. However, demand quickly outstripped supply. As a result, Mazda was not as successful in getting dealers to stick to the suggested list price. Most dealers soon had a long waiting list of buyers—and were charging $3,000 or more above the Miata's list price. Other consumers were angry that the dealers expected them to pay a premium even to get on a waiting list. Mazda tried to convince its dealers that selling at list price would be more profitable in the long run. However, most dealers wouldn't listen, and Mazda did not have the legal right to dictate their selling price.

The popularity of the Miata and other new models helped spark sales growth, but 1991 profits still fell short of Mazda's objectives. Mazda needed more profitable sales, not just market share. The company hopes higher margins on its 929 luxury sedan will fill that bill. However, it faces established competitors in a mature market. So how is Mazda pricing it? Below competitors, which is the price for coming late to market.[1]

PRICE HAS MANY STRATEGY DIMENSIONS

Price is one of the four major variables a marketing manager controls. Price level decisions are especially important because they affect both the number of sales a firm makes and how much money it earns.

Guided by the company's objectives, marketing managers must develop a set of pricing objectives and policies. They must spell out what price situations the firm will face and how it will handle them. These policies should explain (1) how flexible prices will be, (2) at what level they will be set over the product life cycle, (3) to whom and when discounts and allowances will be given, and (4) how transportation costs will be handled. See Exhibit 16–1. These Price-related strategy decision areas are the focus of this chapter. In the next chapter, we will discuss how specific prices are set—consistent with the whole marketing strategy.

It's not easy to define price in real-life situations because prices reflect many dimensions. People who don't realize this can make big mistakes.

Suppose you've been saving to buy a new car and you see in an ad that the base price for the new-year model has been dropped to $9,494—5 percent lower than the previous year. At first this might seem like a real bargain. However, your view of this deal might change if you found out you also had to pay an extra $480 for an extended service warranty. The price might look even less attractive if you discovered the options you wanted cost $1,200 more than the previous year. The transportation charge might come as an unpleasant surprise too. Further, how would you feel if you bought the car anyway and then learned that a friend who just bought the same model negotiated a much lower price?[2]

The price equation: price equals something

This example emphasizes that when a seller quotes a price, it is related to *some* assortment of goods and services. So **Price** is what is charged for "something." Of course, price may be called different things in different settings. Colleges charge tuition. Landlords collect rent. Motels post a room rate. Banks ask for interest when they loan money. Transportation companies have fares. Doctors, lawyers, and consultants set fees. Employ-

Exhibit 16–1 Strategy Planning for Price

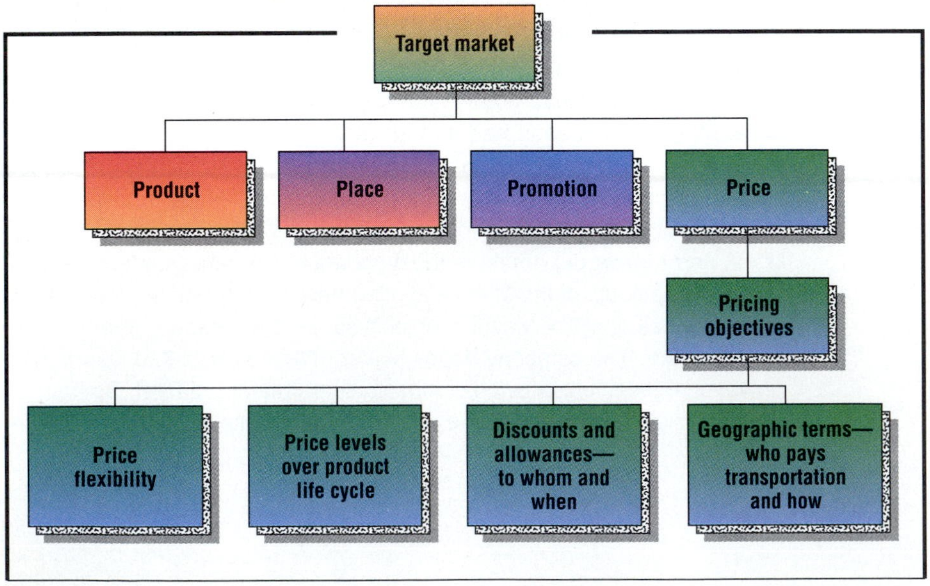

Exhibit 16–2   Price as Seen by Consumers or Users

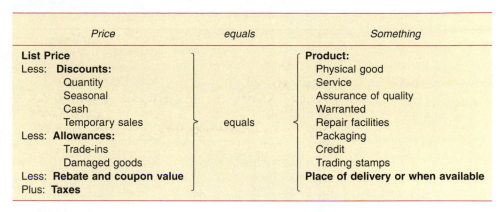

	Price	equals		Something
List Price			**Product:**	
Less:	**Discounts:**			Physical good
	Quantity			Service
	Seasonal			Assurance of quality
	Cash			Warranted
	Temporary sales	*equals*		Repair facilities
Less:	**Allowances:**			Packaging
	Trade-ins			Credit
	Damaged goods			Trading stamps
Less:	**Rebate and coupon value**			**Place of delivery or when available**
Plus:	**Taxes**			

ees want a wage. People may call it different things, but *any business transaction in our modern economy can be thought of as an exchange of money—the money being the Price—for something.*

The something can be a physical product in various stages of completion, with or without supporting services, with or without quality guarantees, and so on. Or it could be a pure service—dry cleaning, a lawyer's advice, or insurance on your car.

The nature and extent of this something determines the amount of money exchanged. Some customers pay list price. Others obtain large discounts or allowances because something is *not* provided. Exhibit 16–2 summarizes some possible variations for consumers or users and Exhibit 16–3 for channel members. These variations are discussed more fully below. But here it should be clear that Price has many dimensions.

OBJECTIVES SHOULD GUIDE STRATEGY PLANNING FOR PRICE

Pricing objectives should flow from—and fit in with—company-level and marketing objectives. Pricing objectives should be *explicitly stated* because they have a direct effect on pricing policies as well as the methods used to set prices.

Exhibit 16–4 shows the various types of pricing objectives we'll discuss.

Exhibit 16–3   Price as Seen by Channel Members

	Price	equals		Something
List price			**Product:**	
Less:	**Discounts:**			Branded—well known
	Quantity			Guaranteed
	Seasonal			Warranted
	Cash			Service—repair facilities
	Trade or functional			Convenient packaging for handling
	Temporary "deals"	*equals*	**Place:**	
Less:	**Allowances:**			Availability—when and where
	Damaged goods		**Price:**	
	Advertising			Price-level guarantee
	Push money			Sufficient margin to allow chance for profit
	Stocking		**Promotion:**	
Plus:	**Taxes and tariffs**			Promotion aimed at customers

Exhibit 16–4 Possible Pricing Objectives

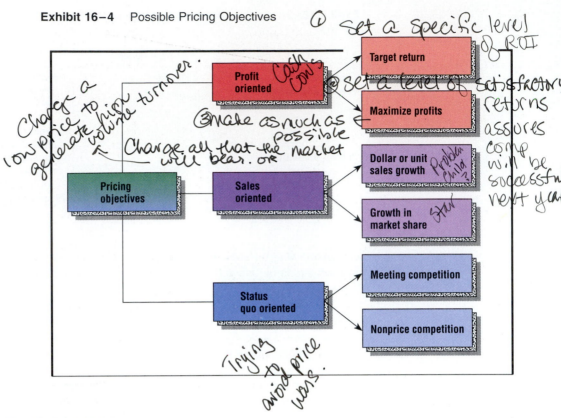

Handwritten annotations:
- ① set a specific level of ROI
- ② set a level of satisfactory returns assures comp will be successful next year
- Charge a low price to generate high volume turnover.
- Cash Cow
- ③ make as much as possible
- Charge all that the market will bear. or
- Problem Child?
- Star
- Trying to avoid price wars.

PROFIT-ORIENTED OBJECTIVES

Target returns provide specific guidelines

A **target return objective** sets a specific level of profit as an objective. Often this amount is stated as a percentage of sales or of capital investment. A large manufacturer like Motorola might aim for a 15 percent return on investment. The target for Safeway and other grocery chains might be a 1 percent return on sales.

A target return objective has administrative advantages in a large company. Performance can be compared against the target. Some companies eliminate divisions—or drop products—that aren't yielding the target rate of return. For example, General Electric sold its small appliance division to Black & Decker because it felt it could earn higher returns in other product-markets.

Some just want satisfactory profits

Some managers aim for only satisfactory returns. They just want returns that ensure the firm's survival and convince stockholders they're doing a good job. Similarly, some small family-run businesses aim for a profit that will provide a comfortable lifestyle.[3]

Many private and public nonprofit organizations set a price level that will just recover costs. In other words, their target return figure is zero. For example, a government agency may charge motorists a toll for using a bridge, but then drop the toll when the cost of the bridge is paid.

Companies that are leaders in their industries—like Alcoa, Du Pont and General Dynamics—sometimes pursue only satisfactory long-run targets. The public—and government officials—expect them to set prices that serve the public interest. Similarly, firms that provide public services—including many utility and insurance companies, transportation firms, and defense contractors—face government agencies that review and approve prices.[4]

But this kind of situation can lead to decisions that don't serve the public interest. For example, before imported cars became popular, many GM managers were afraid of making

Some firms rely primarily on an economical price, rather than other elements of the marketing mix, to attract customers.

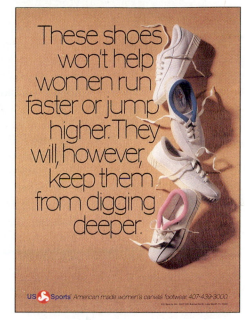

too much profit. They thought if GM lowered its costs—and prices to consumers—the company might gain an even larger market share—and risk antitrust action by the government. When low-cost foreign producers entered the U.S. market, GM was unable to quickly reduce costs—or prices—and ended up losing both profits and market share.

Profit maximization can be socially responsible

A **profit maximization objective** seeks to get as much profit as possible. It might be stated as a desire to earn a rapid return on investment or, more bluntly, to charge all the traffic will bear.

Some people believe that anyone seeking a profit maximization objective will charge high prices—prices that are not in the public interest. However, pricing to achieve profit maximization doesn't always lead to high prices. Low prices may expand the size of the market—and result in greater sales and profits. For example, when prices of VCRs were very high, only innovators and wealthy people bought them. When Sony and its competitors lowered prices, nearly everyone bought one.

If a firm is earning a very large profit, other firms will enter the market. Frequently, this leads to lower prices. IBM sold its original personal computer for about $4,500 in 1981. As Compaq, Dell, and other competitors started to copy IBM, they all added more power and features and cut prices. Ten years later, customers could buy a much better computer for about $600.[5]

SALES-ORIENTED OBJECTIVES

A **sales-oriented objective** seeks some level of unit sales, dollar sales, or share of market—*without referring to profit.*

Sales growth doesn't necessarily mean big profits

Some managers are more concerned about sales growth than profits. They think sales growth always leads to more profits. This kind of thinking causes problems when a firm's costs are growing faster than sales—or when managers don't keep track of their costs. Recently, many major corporations suffered declining profits despite growth in sales. At the extreme, International Harvester kept cutting prices on its tractors—trying to reach its target sales levels in a weak economy—until it had to sell that part of its business. Generally, however, business managers now pay more attention to profits—not just sales.[6]

Some nonprofit organizations set prices to increase market share—precisely because they are *not* trying to earn a profit. For example, many cities set low fares to fill up their buses. Buses cost the same to run empty or full, and there's more benefit when they're full even if the total revenue is no greater.

Market share objectives are popular

Many firms seek to gain a specified share (percent) of a market. A larger market share may give a firm a cost advantage over competitors—because of economies of scale. In addition, it's usually easier to measure a firm's market share than to determine if profits are being maximized.

A company with a longer-run view may aim for increased market share when the market is growing. The hope is that future volume will justify sacrificing some profit in the short run. Companies as diverse as 3M, Coke, and IBM look at opportunities in eastern Europe this way. Of course, market share objectives have the same limitations as straight sales growth objectives. A larger market share—if gained at too low a price—may lead to profitless "success."

STATUS QUO PRICING OBJECTIVES

Don't-rock-the-boat objectives

Managers satisfied with their current market share and profits sometimes adopt **status quo objectives**—don't-rock-the-*pricing*-boat objectives. Managers may want to stabilize prices, or meet competition, or even avoid competition. This don't-rock-the-boat thinking is most common when the total market is not growing.

Or stress nonprice competition instead

A status quo pricing objective may be part of an aggressive overall marketing strategy focusing on **nonprice competition**—aggressive action on one or more of the Ps other than Price. Fast-food chains like McDonald's, Wendy's, and Burger King experienced very profitable growth by sticking to nonprice competition for many years. However, when Taco Bell and others started to take away customers with price-cutting, the other chains also turned to price competition.[7]

MOST FIRMS SET SPECIFIC PRICING POLICIES—TO REACH OBJECTIVES

Administered prices help achieve objectives

Price policies usually lead to **administered prices**—consciously set prices. In other words, instead of letting daily market forces decide their prices, most firms (including *all* of those in monopolistic competition) set their own prices.

If a firm doesn't sell directly to final customers, it usually wants to administer both the price it receives from middlemen and the price final customers pay. After all, the price customers pay ultimately affects its sales. Yet it is often difficult to administer prices throughout the channel. Other channel members may also wish to administer prices to achieve their own objectives.[8]

Some firms don't even try to administer prices. They just meet competition—or worse, mark up their costs with little thought to demand. They act as if they have no choice in selecting a price policy.

Remember that Price has many dimensions. Managers *do* have many choices. They *should* administer their prices. And they should do it carefully because, ultimately, customers must be willing to pay these prices before a whole marketing mix succeeds. In the rest of this chapter, we'll talk about policies a marketing manager must set to do an effective job of administering Price.[9]

PRICE FLEXIBILITY POLICIES

One-price policy—the same price for everyone

One of the first decisions a marketing manager has to make is about price flexibility. A **one-price policy** means offering the same price to all customers who purchase products under essentially the same conditions and in the same quantities. The majority of U.S. firms use a one-price policy—mainly for administrative convenience and to maintain goodwill among customers. *all customers get the same price w/ same level of qty*

A one-price policy makes pricing easier. But a marketing manager must be careful to avoid a rigid one-price policy. This can amount to broadcasting a price that competitors can undercut—especially if the price is somewhat high.

Flexible-price policy— different prices for different customers

Price Problems: Discrimination.

A **flexible-price policy** means offering the same product and quantities to different customers at different prices. Flexible-price policies often specify a *range* in which the actual price charged must fall.

Flexible pricing is most common in the channels, in direct sales of business products, and at retail for expensive shopping products. Retail shopkeepers in less-developed economies typically use flexible pricing. These situations usually involve personal selling—not mass selling. The advantage of flexible pricing is that the salesperson can adjust price—considering competitors' prices, the relationship with the customer, and the customer's bargaining ability.[10]

Flexible pricing does have disadvantages. A customer who finds that others paid lower prices for the same marketing mix will be unhappy. This can cause real conflict in channels. For example, the Winn-Dixie supermarket chain stopped carrying products of some suppliers who refused to give Winn-Dixie the same prices available to chains in other regions of the country.[11]

If buyers learn that negotiating can be in their interest, the time needed for bargaining will increase. This can affect selling costs. In addition, some sales reps let price cutting become a habit. This reduces the role of price as a competitive tool—and leads to a lower price level.

PRICE LEVEL POLICIES—OVER THE PRODUCT LIFE CYCLE

When marketing managers administer prices—as most do—they must consciously set a price level policy. As they enter the market, they have to set introductory prices that may have long-run effects. They must consider where the product life cycle is—and how fast it's moving. And they must decide if their prices should be above, below, or somewhere in between relative to the market.

Skimming pricing— feeling out demand at a high price

downward trend as market expands

A **skimming price policy** tries to sell the top (skim the cream) of a market—the top of the demand curve—at a high price before aiming at more price-sensitive customers. Skimming may maximize profits in the market introduction stage for an innovation, especially if there are few substitutes or if some customers are not price sensitive. Skimming is also useful when you don't know very much about the shape of the demand curve. It's safer to start with a high price that customers can refuse—and then reduce it if necessary.[12]

Used if profit maximization is the goal.

(?) Skimming has critics

Some critics argue that firms should not try to maximize profits by using a skimming policy on new products that have important social consequences—a patent-protected lifesaving drug or a genetic technique that increases crop yields, for example. Many of those who need such a product may not have the money to buy it. This is a serious concern. However, it's also a serious problem if firms don't have incentives to take the risks and develop new products.[13]

Skimming may maximize profits in the market introduction stage, but as more firms enter, market competition typically pushes prices down.

Now UPS delivers for fewer francs, yen or drachmas than our competition.

At UPS, we're changing the face of the international delivery business. Because we've expanded our service to all of Western Europe, the Pacific Rim, New Zealand, Australia and Canada.

And that means delivery door to door to every single address in every country we serve,* with no surcharges for out-of-the-way places.

We'll see that your UPS Letters, Paks and packages move quickly through customs thanks to our Electronic Customs Pre-Alert system that informs of-ficials that your packages are on their way. Our service also includes computerized tracking that enables us to give you a fast reply to your delivery inquiry. Again, we do all this at no added cost.

But what's truly remarkable is that, because of our efficiency, we can do all these things while charging you less than other international delivery companies. Which is important. After all, a drachma saved is a drachma earned.

We run the tightest ship in the shipping business. **UPS**

© 1988 United Parcel Service of America, Inc. *Our apologies: we don't deliver to everyone in the People's Republic of China, just 600 million people. See UPS International Air Service Guide for complete details.

Price moves down the demand curve

A skimming policy usually involves a slow reduction in price over time. See Exhibit 16–5. Note that as price is reduced, new target markets are probably being sought. So as the price level steps down the demand curve, new Place, Product, and Promotion policies may be needed too.

When Hewlett-Packard (HP) introduced its laser printer for personal computers, no close substitute was available. HP initially set a high price—around $4,000 and sold mainly to businesses through authorized HP dealers whose salespeople could explain the printer. As other firms entered the market with similar printers, HP regularly added features and lowered its price. It also did more advertising and added mail-order middlemen to reach new target markets. This is very typical of skimming. It involves changing prices through a series of marketing strategies over the course of the product life cycle.

Penetration pricing—get volume at a low price

A **penetration pricing policy** tries to sell the whole market at one low price. Such an approach might be wise when the elite market—those willing to pay a high price—is small. This is the case when the whole demand curve is fairly elastic. See Exhibit 16–5.

A penetration policy is even more attractive if selling larger quantities results in lower costs because of economies of scale. Penetration pricing may also be wise if the firm expects strong competition very soon after introduction. It discourages competitors from entering the market. For example, when personal computers became popular, Borland International came out with a complete programming language—including a textbook—for under $50. When competitors finally matched Borland's price, its large base of customers weren't interested in switching.

Exhibit 16–5   Alternative Introductory Pricing Policies

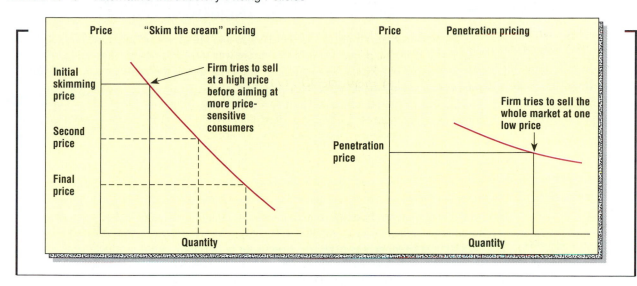

Introductory price dealing—temporary price cuts	Price cuts do attract customers. Therefore, marketers often use **introductory price dealing**—temporary price cuts—to speed new products into a market. However, don't confuse these *temporary* price cuts with low penetration prices. The plan here is to raise prices as soon as the introductory offer is over. Established competitors often choose not to meet introductory price dealing—as long as the introductory period is not too long or too successful.
Meeting competition may be necessary	Regardless of their introductory pricing policy, most firms face competition sooner or later in the product life cycle. When that happens, how high or low a price is may be relative not only to the market demand curve but also to the prices charged by competitors. Meeting competitors' prices may also be the practical choice in mature markets that are moving toward pure competition. Here firms typically face downward pressure on both prices and profits. Profit margins are already thin—and for many firms they would disappear or turn into losses at a lower price. A higher price would simply prompt competitors to promote their price advantage. Similarly, there is little choice in oligopoly situations. Pricing at the market—that is, meeting competition—may be the only sensible policy. Raising prices might lead to a large loss in sales—unless competitors adopt the higher price too. And cutting prices would probably lead to similar reductions by competitors—decreasing revenue for the industry and probably for each firm. The major airlines recently faced these problems. To avoid these problems, each oligopolist may choose a status quo pricing objective—and set its price at the competitive level. Some critics call this pricing behavior conscious parallel action, implying it is unethical and the same as intentional conspiracy among firms. As a practical matter, however, that criticism seems overly harsh. It isn't sensible for firms to ignore their competitors.[14]
There are alternatives in monopolistic competition	In monopolistic competition, there are more pricing options. At one extreme, some firms are clearly above-the-market—they may even brag about it. Tiffany's is well known as one of the most expensive jewelry stores in the world. Other firms emphasize below-the-market prices in their marketing mixes. Prices offered by discounters and mass-merchandisers, such as Kmart and Tesco, illustrate this approach. They may even promote

their pricing policy with catchy slogans like "guaranteed lowest prices" or "we'll beat any advertised price."

Above or below what market?

Do these various strategies promote prices that are above or below the market—or are they really different prices for different target markets or different marketing mixes? In setting price level policies, it is important to clearly define the *relevant target market* and *competitors* when making price comparisons.

Consider Kmart prices again from this view. Kmart may have lower camera prices than conventional camera retailers, but it offers less help in the store and less selection, and it won't take old cameras in trade. Kmart may be appealing to budget-oriented shoppers who compare prices among different mass-merchandisers. A specialty camera store—appealing to different customers—may not be a direct competitor! So it may be better to think of Kmart's price as part of a different marketing mix for a different target market.

Different price level policies through the channel

The price should be set so that channel members can cover costs and make a profit. To achieve its objectives, a manufacturer may set different price level policies for different levels in the channel. For example, a producer of a slightly better product might set a price level that is low relative to competitors when selling to retailers, while suggesting an above-the-market retail price. This encourages retailers to emphasize the product because it yields higher profits.

The price of money may affect the price level

We've been talking about the price level of a firm's product. But a nation's money also has a price level—what it is worth in some other currency. For example, in the summer of 1992 one U.S. dollar was worth 1.48 German marks. In other words, the exchange rate for the German mark against the U.S. dollar was 1.48. Exhibit 16−6 lists exchange rates for money from several countries. Exchange rates change over time—and sometimes the changes are significant. For example, at one point in 1989 a U.S. dollar was worth 1.95 German marks; in 1985 it was as high as 3.3 German marks.

Exchange rate changes can have a significant effect on whether or not a marketing manager's price level has the expected result. As the following example shows, this can be an important factor even for a small firm that sells only in its own local market.

In 1989 the marketing manager for ColorFast—a small firm that mixes and sells special dyes used by textile producers—set a meeting-competition wholesale price at about $100 for a barrel of dye. The wholesalers who distribute her dyes also carried a competing product produced by a German firm. Its wholesale price was also $100, which means that the German firm got about 195 German marks ($100 multiplied times 1.95 marks per dollar) per barrel. However, when the exchange rate for the mark against the

Exhibit 16−6 Exchange Rates for Various Currencies against the U.S. Dollar

Base Currency	Number of Units of Base Currency per U.S. Dollar, July 1992
German (mark)	1.48
Japan (yen)	125.32
France (franc)	4.98
Australia (dollar)	1.34
Canada (dollar)	1.19
United Kingdom (pound sterling)	.52

JAPANESE CONSUMERS YEN FOR CAMPBELL SOUP

I n 1983, marketing managers for Campbell Soup Company mounted a new effort to enter the Japanese market. They developed corn potage and a line of six other soups in Japanese-style packages. In spite of a good product line, Campbell's salespeople struggled to get shelf space in Japan's small, cramped grocery stores. Progress was slow. The firm wasn't achieving its market share objective. In fact, Campbell was shipping less soup to Japan than to Albuquerque, New Mexico! In May of 1985, with a meeting-competition retail price of 220 Japanese yen (about 91 cents) per can, Campbell was barely making a profit.

Over the next two years, there was an 89 percent rise in the exchange rate for the Japanese yen against the U.S. dollar. That meant that Campbell made more dollars for each can of soup sold in Japan—and that its profits would increase simply by holding its price level the same. However, Campbell's marketing managers seized the opportunity to be more aggressive in pursuing their market share objective. They lowered the suggested list price of Campbell soup 16 percent—to a price of 185 yen—and kept retailers' profit margins the same. With those changes, sales volume and market share doubled. Moreover, even at the lower price Campbell made the equivalent of $1.30 a can, up nearly 50 percent from the 1985 level. Campbell used the extra money to increase promotion in the Japanese market to help recruit more retailers.[15]

dollar fell from 1.95 to 1.48, the German producer got 47 fewer marks for each $100 barrel of dye (195 marks – 148 marks = 47 marks).

Because Colorfast's marketing manager was only selling dye to local customers, she didn't pay any attention to the drop in the exchange rate—at first. However, she did pay attention when the German producer decided to raise its wholesale price to $125 a barrel. At the $125 price, the German firm got about 185 marks per barrel ($125 x 1.48 marks per dollar)—less than it was getting before the exchange rate change. Colorfast's sales increased substantially—at the German competitor's expense—because of the lower Colorfast price. Colorfast's marketing manager concluded that it would probably take a while for the German firm to lower its price, even if the exchange rate went up again. So she decided that she could safely raise her price level—and still stay lower than the German firm's price.[16]

Consumers want value pricing

Sooner or later there's competition in most product-markets. And in today's competitive markets, more and more customers are demanding real value. **Value pricing** means setting a fair price level for a marketing mix that really gives customers what they need. Value pricing doesn't necessarily mean bare-bones or low-grade. It doesn't mean high prestige either if the prestige is not accompanied by the right quality. Rather the focus is on the customer's requirements.

Toyota uses value pricing very effectively. It has different marketing mixes for different target markets. But from the $7,000 Tercel to the $42,000 Lexus, the automaker consistently offers better quality and lower prices than its competitors. Among discount retailers, Wal-Mart is a value pricing leader. Its motto says it all: "the low price on the brands you trust."

These companies deliver on their promises. They try to give the consumer pleasant surprises—like an unexpected service or a useful new feature—because it builds customer loyalty. They guarantee to refund the price if the customer isn't completely satisfied. They avoid unrealistic price levels—prices that are high only because consumers already know the brand name.[17]

When you stop to think about it, value pricing is simply the best pricing decision for the type of market-oriented strategy planning we've been discussing throughout this whole text. To build profits and customer satisfaction, the whole marketing mix—including the price level—must meet target customers' needs.

MOST PRICE STRUCTURES ARE BUILT AROUND LIST PRICES

Prices start with a list price

Most price structures are built around a base price schedule or price list. **Basic list prices** are the prices final customers or users are normally asked to pay for products. In this book, unless noted otherwise, list price refers to basic list price.

In the next chapter, we discuss how firms set these list prices. For now, however, we'll consider variations from list price—and why they are made.

DISCOUNT POLICIES—REDUCTIONS FROM LIST PRICES

Discounts are reductions from list price given by a seller to buyers who either give up some marketing function or provide the function themselves. Discounts can be useful in marketing strategy planning. In the following discussion, think about what function the buyers are giving up—or providing—when they get each of these discounts.

Quantity discounts encourage volume buying

Quantity discounts are discounts offered to encourage customers to buy in larger amounts. This lets a seller get more of a buyer's business, or shifts some of the storing function to the buyer, or reduces shipping and selling costs—or all of these. Such discounts are of two kinds: cumulative and noncumulative.

Cumulative quantity discounts apply to purchases over a given period—such as a year—and the discount usually increases as the amount purchased increases. Cumulative discounts are intended to encourage *repeat* buying by a single customer by reducing the customer's cost for additional purchases. For example, a Lowe's lumberyard might give a cumulative quantity discount to a building contractor who is not able to buy all of the needed materials at once. Lowe's wants to reward the contractor's patronage—and discourage shopping around. The discount is small relative to the cost of constantly trying to attract new customers.

Noncumulative quantity discounts apply only to individual orders. Such discounts encourage larger orders—but do not tie a buyer to the seller after that one purchase. Lowe's lumberyard may sell insulation products made by several competing producers. Owens/Corning might try to encourage Lowe's to stock larger quantities of its insulation by offering a noncumulative quantity discount.

While quantity discounts are usually given as price cuts, sometimes they are given as free or bonus products. Airline frequent flier programs use this approach.

Quantity discounts can be a very useful tool for the marketing manager. Some customers are eager to get them. But marketing managers must use quantity discounts carefully. In business markets, they must offer such discounts to all customers on equal terms—to avoid price discrimination.

Noncumulative discounts sometimes produce unexpected results. If the discount is too big, wholesalers or retailers may buy more than they can possibly sell to their own customers—to get the low price. Then they sell the excess at a low price to whoever will buy it—as long as the buyer doesn't compete in the same market area. These "gray market" channels often take customers away from regular channel members, perhaps with a retail price even lower than what most channel members pay.

Cargill uses a seasonal discount to encourage buyers to stock products earlier than present demand requires.

Seasonal discounts— buy sooner and store

Seasonal discounts are discounts offered to encourage buyers to buy earlier than present demand requires. If used by producers, this discount tends to shift the storing function further along in the channel. It also tends to even out sales over the year. For example, Kyota offers wholesalers a lower price on its garden tillers if they buy in the fall—when sales are slow. The wholesalers pass along some of the discount to retailers— who then have a special fall tiller sale.

Payment terms and cash discounts set payment dates

Most sales to businesses are made on credit. The seller sends a bill (invoice), and the buyer's accounting department processes it for payment. Some firms depend on their suppliers for temporary working capital (credit). Therefore, it is very important for both sides to clearly state the terms of payment—including the availability of cash discounts— and to understand the commonly used payment terms.

Net means that payment for the face value of the invoice is due immediately. These terms are sometimes changed to net 10 or net 30—which means payment is due within 10 or 30 days of the date on the invoice.

Cash discounts are reductions in price to encourage buyers to pay their bills quickly. The terms for a cash discount usually modify the net terms.

2/10, net 30 means the buyer can take a 2 percent discount off the face value of the invoice if the invoice is paid within 10 days. Otherwise, the full face value is due within 30 days. And it usually is stated or understood that an interest charge will be added after the 30-day free-credit period.

Why cash discounts are given and should be evaluated

Smart buyers carefully evaluate cash discounts. A discount of 2/10, net 30 may not look like much at first. But the buyer earns a 2 percent discount for paying the invoice just 20 days sooner than it should be paid anyway. By not taking the discount, the company—in effect—is borrowing at an annual rate of 36 percent. That is, assuming a 360-day year and dividing by 20 days, there are 18 periods during which the company could earn 2 percent—and 18 times 2 equals 36 percent a year.

Consumers say "charge it"

Credit sales are also important to retailers. Most retailers use credit card services, such as VISA or MasterCard, and pay a percent of the revenue from each credit sale for the service. For this reason, some retailers offer discounts to consumers who pay cash.

Many consumers like the convenience of credit card buying. But some critics argue that the cards make it too easy for consumers to buy things they really can't afford. Further, because of high interest charges, credit card buying can increase the total costs to consumers.[18]

Trade discounts often are set by tradition

A **trade (functional) discount** is a list price reduction given to channel members for the job they are going to do.

A manufacturer, for example, may allow retailers a 30 percent trade discount from the suggested retail list price to cover the cost of the retailing function and their profit. Similarly, the manufacturer may allow wholesalers a *chain* discount of 30 percent and 10 percent off the suggested retail price. In this case, the wholesalers are expected to pass the 30 percent discount on to retailers.

Special sales reduce list prices—temporarily

A **sale price** is a temporary discount from the list price. Sale price discounts encourage immediate buying. In other words, to get the sale price, customers give up the convenience of buying when they want to buy—and instead buy when the seller wants to sell.

Special sales provide a marketing manager with a quick way to respond to changing market conditions—without changing the basic marketing strategy. For example, a retailer might use a sale to help clear extra inventory. Or a producer might offer a middleman a special deal that makes it more profitable for the middleman to push the product.

In recent years, sale prices and deals have become much more common. At first it may seem that consumers benefit from all this. But prices that change constantly may confuse customers and increase selling costs.

To avoid these problems, some firms that sell consumer convenience products offer **everyday low pricing**—setting a low list price rather than relying on frequent discounts or allowances from a high list price. Many grocery stores use this approach. And some producers, including P&G, use it.

Sale prices should be used carefully, consistent with well thought out pricing objectives and policies. A marketing manager who constantly uses temporary sales to adjust the price level probably didn't do a good job setting the normal price.[19]

ALLOWANCE POLICIES—OFF LIST PRICES

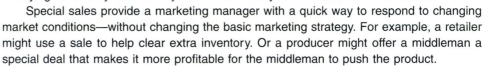

Allowances—like discounts—are given to final consumers, customers, or channel members for doing something or accepting less of something.

Advertising allowances— something for something

Advertising allowances are price reductions given to firms in the channel to encourage them to advertise or otherwise promote the supplier's products locally. For example, General Electric gave an allowance (1.5 percent of sales) to its wholesalers of housewares and radios. They, in turn, were expected to spend the allowance on local advertising.

Stocking allowances—get attention and shelf space

Stocking allowances—sometimes called slotting allowances—are given to a middleman to get shelf space ("slots") for a product. For example, a producer might offer a retailer cash or free merchandise to stock a new item. Stocking allowances are a recent development. So far, they're used mainly to prompt supermarket chains to handle new products. Supermarkets don't have enough slots on their shelves to handle all of the available new products. They're more willing to give space to a new product if the supplier will offset their handling costs and risk.

? Are stocking allowances ethical?

There is much controversy about stocking allowances. Critics say that retailer demands for big stocking allowances slow new product introductions—and make it hard for small producers to compete. Some producers feel that retailers' demands are unethical—just a different form of extortion. Retailers, on the other hand, point out that the fees protect them from producers that simply want to push more me-too products onto their shelves. Perhaps the best way for a producer to cope with the problem is to develop new products that offer consumers a real comparative advantage. Then it will benefit everyone in the channel—including retailers—to get the products to the target market.[20]

PMs—push for cash

Push money (or prize money) allowances—sometimes called PMs or spiffs—are given to retailers by manufacturers or wholesalers to pass on to the retailers' salesclerks for aggressively selling certain items. PM allowances are used for new items, slower-moving items, or higher-margin items. They are often used for pushing furniture, clothing, consumer electronics, and cosmetics. A salesclerk, for example, might earn an additional $5 for each new model Pioneer cassette deck sold.

Bring in the old, ring up the new—with trade-ins

A **trade-in allowance** is a price reduction given for used products when similar new products are bought.

Trade-ins give the marketing manager an easy way to lower the effective price without reducing list price. Proper handling of trade-ins is important when selling durable products.

SOME CUSTOMERS GET EXTRA SOMETHINGS

Clipping coupons— more for less

Many producers and retailers offer discounts (or free items) through coupons distributed in packages, mailings, print ads, or at the store. By presenting a coupon to a retailer, the consumer is given a discount off list price. This is especially common in the consumer packaged goods business—but the use of price-off coupons is growing in other lines of business too.

Retailers are willing to redeem producers' coupons because it increases their sales— and they usually are paid for the trouble of handling the coupon. For example, a retailer who redeems a 50 cents off coupon might be repaid 75 cents.

Cash rebates when you buy

Some producers offer **rebates**—refunds paid to consumers after a purchase. Rebates give the producer a way to be certain that final consumers actually get the price reduction. If the rebate amount were just taken off the price charged middlemen, they might not pass the savings along to consumers. In addition, many consumers buy because of the rebate—but never ask for the refund.[21]

Many trade promotions basically lower the price a business pays.

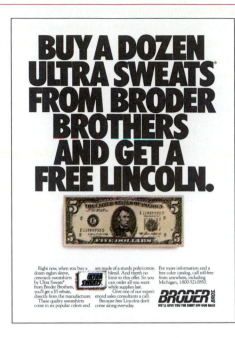

LIST PRICE MAY DEPEND ON GEOGRAPHIC PRICING POLICIES

Retail list prices sometimes include free delivery. Or free delivery may be offered to some customers as an aid to closing the sale. But deciding who pays the freight charge is more important on sales to business customers than to final consumers because more money is involved. Usually purchase orders specify place, time, method of delivery, freight costs, insurance, handling, and other charges. There are many possible variations for an imaginative marketing manager, and some specialized terms have developed.

F.O.B. pricing is easy

A commonly used transportation term is **F.O.B.**—which means free on board some vehicle at some place. Typically, F.O.B. pricing names the place—often the location of the seller's factory or warehouse—as in F.O.B. Taiwan or F.O.B. mill. F.O.B. shipping point means that the seller pays the cost of loading the products onto some vehicle, then title to the products passes to the buyer. The buyer pays the freight and takes responsibility for damage in transit.

If a firm wants to pay the freight for the convenience of customers, it can use F.O.B. delivered or F.O.B. buyer's factory. In this case, title does not pass until the products are delivered. If the seller wants title to pass immediately but is willing to prepay freight (and then include it in the invoice), F.O.B. seller's factory–freight prepaid can be used.

F.O.B. shipping point pricing simplifies the seller's pricing—but it may narrow the market. Since the delivered cost varies depending on the buyer's location, a distant customer must pay more and might buy from closer suppliers.

Zone pricing smooths delivered prices

Zone pricing means making an average freight charge to all buyers within specific geographic areas. The seller pays the actual freight charges and bills each customer for an average charge. For example, a company in Canada might divide the United States into seven zones, then bill all customers in the same zone the same amount for freight even though actual shipping costs vary.

Uniform delivered
pricing—one price to all

Uniform delivered pricing means making an average freight charge to all buyers. It is a kind of zone pricing—an entire country may be considered as one zone—that includes the average cost of delivery in the price. Uniform delivered pricing is most often used when (1) transportation costs are relatively low and (2) the seller wishes to sell in all geographic areas at one price—perhaps a nationally advertised price.

Freight-absorption
pricing—competing
on equal grounds in
another territory

When all firms in an industry use F.O.B. shipping point pricing, a firm usually competes well near its shipping point but not farther away. As sales reps look for business farther away, delivered prices rise and the firm finds itself priced out of the market.

This problem can be reduced with **freight absorption pricing**—which means absorbing freight cost so that a firm's delivered price meets the nearest competitor's. This amounts to cutting list price to appeal to new market segments. Some firms look at international markets this way; they just figure that any profit from export sales is a bonus.

LEGALITY OF PRICING POLICIES

This chapter discusses the many pricing decisions that must be made. However, some pricing decisions are limited by government legislation.

The first step to understanding pricing legislation is to know the thinking of legislators and the courts to get a better idea of the why of legislation. We'll focus on U.S. legislation here, but many other countries have similar pricing laws.[22]

Minimum prices are
sometimes controlled

Unfair trade practice acts put a lower limit on prices, especially at the wholesale and retail levels. They have been passed in more than half the states in the United States. Selling below cost in these states is illegal. Wholesalers and retailers are usually required to take a certain minimum percentage markup over their merchandise-plus-transportation costs. The practical effect of these laws is to protect certain limited-line food retailers—such as dairy stores—from the kind of "ruinous" competition supermarkets might offer if they sold milk as a leader—offering it below cost—for a long time.

The United States and most other countries control the minimum price of imported products with antidumping laws. **Dumping** is pricing a product sold in a foreign market below the cost of producing it or at a price lower than in its domestic market. These laws are designed to protect the country's domestic producers—and jobs. But there is debate about how well they work.

Even very high prices
may be OK

Generally speaking, firms can charge high prices—even outrageously high prices—as long as they don't conspire with their competitors to fix prices, discriminate against some of their customers, or lie.

Of course, there are exceptions. Firms in regulated businesses may need to seek approval for their prices. For example, in the United States, most states regulate automobile insurance rates. Some countries impose more general price controls—to reduce inflation or try to control markets. However, most countries are following the move toward a market-directed economy. That doesn't mean, however, that there aren't important regulations in the pricing area.

You can't lie about prices

Phony list prices are prices customers are shown to suggest that the price has been discounted from list. Some customers seem more interested in the supposed discount than in the actual price. Most businesses, trade associations, and government agencies consider the use of phony list prices unethical. In the United States, the FTC tries to stop such pricing—using the **Wheeler Lea Amendment**, which bans "unfair or deceptive acts in commerce."[23]

Price fixing is illegal—you can go to jail

Difficulties with pricing—and violations of pricing legislation—usually occur when competing marketing mixes are quite similar. When the success of an entire marketing strategy depends on price, there is pressure (and temptation) to make agreements with competitors (conspire). And **price fixing**—competitors getting together to raise, lower, or stabilize prices—is common and relatively easy. *But it is also completely illegal in the United States.* It is considered "conspiracy" under the Sherman Act and the Federal Trade Commission Act. To discourage price fixing, both companies and individual managers are held responsible. Some executives have already gone to jail![24]

Different countries have different rules concerning price fixing, and this creates problems in international trade. Japan, for example, sometimes allows price fixing—especially if it helps Japanese firms in world markets.

U.S. antimonopoly laws ban price discrimination unless. . .

Price level and price flexibility policies can lead to price discrimination. The **Robinson-Patman Act** (of 1936) makes illegal any **price discrimination**—selling the same products to different buyers at different prices—*if it injures competition.* The law does permit some price differences—but they must be based on (1) cost differences or (2) the need to meet competition. Both buyers and sellers are considered guilty if they know they're entering into discriminatory agreements. This is a serious matter—price discrimination suits are common.

What does "like grade and quality" mean?

The Robinson-Patman Act allows a marketing manager to charge different prices for similar products if they are *not* of "like grade and quality." The FTC says that if the physical characteristics of a product are similar, then they are of like grade and quality. A landmark U.S. Supreme Court ruling against the Borden Company upheld the FTC's view that a well-known label *alone* does not make a product different from one with an unknown label. The company agreed that the canned milk it sold at different prices under different labels was the same.

But the FTC's victory in the Borden case was not complete. The U.S. Court of Appeals found no evidence of injury to competition and further noted that there could be no injury unless Borden's price differential exceeded the "recognized consumer appeal of the Borden label." How to measure "consumer appeal" was not spelled out and may lead to additional suits. For now, however, producers who want to sell several brands—or dealer brands at lower prices than their main brand—probably should offer physical differences—and differences that are really useful.[25]

Can cost analysis justify price differences?

The Robinson-Patman Act allows price differences if there are cost differences—say for larger quantity shipments or because middlemen take over some of the physical distribution functions. But justifying cost differences is a difficult job. And the justification must be developed *before* different prices are set. The seller can't wait until a competitor, disgruntled customer, or the FTC brings a charge. At that point, it's too late.[26]

Can you legally meet price cuts?

Under the Robinson-Patman Act, meeting a competitor's price is permitted as a defense in price discrimination cases. A major objective of antimonopoly laws is to protect competition—not competitors. And "meeting competition in good faith" still seems to be legal.

Special promotion allowances might not be allowed

Some firms violate the Robinson-Patman Act by providing push money, advertising allowances, and other promotion aids to some customers and not others. The act prohibits such special allowances—*unless they are made available to all customers on "proportionately equal" terms.*[27]

How to avoid discriminating   Because price discrimination laws are complicated—and penalties for violations heavy—many business managers follow the safest course by offering few or no quantity discounts—and the same cost-based prices to *all* customers. Perhaps this is *too* conservative a reaction. But when firms consider price differences, they may need to include a lawyer in the discussion!

CONCLUSION

The Price variable offers an alert marketing manager many possibilities for varying marketing mixes. What pricing policies should be used depends on the pricing objectives. We looked at profit-oriented, sales-oriented, and status quo-oriented objectives.

A marketing manager must set policies about price flexibility, price levels over the product life cycle, who will pay the freight, and who will get discounts and allowances. While doing this, the manager should be aware of legislation that affects pricing policies.

In most cases, a marketing manager must set prices—that is, administer prices. Starting with a list price, a variety of discounts and allowances may be offered to adjust for the something being offered in the marketing mix.

Throughout this chapter, we talk about what may be included (or excluded) in the something—and what objectives a firm might set to guide its pricing policies. Price setting itself is not discussed. It will be covered in the next chapter—where we show ways to carry out the various pricing objectives and policies.

QUESTIONS AND PROBLEMS

1. Identify the strategy decisions a marketing manager must make in the Price area. Illustrate your answer for a local retailer.

2. How should the acceptance of a profit-oriented, a sales-oriented, or a status quo-oriented pricing objective affect the development of a company's marketing strategy? Illustrate for each.

3. Distinguish between one-price and flexible-price policies. Which is most appropriate for a hardware store? Why?

4. How would differences in exchange rates between different countries affect a firm's decisions concerning the use of flexible-price policies in different foreign markets?

5. Cite two examples of continuously selling above the market price. Describe the situations.

6. Explain the types of competitive situations that might lead to a meeting-competition pricing policy.

7. What pricing objective(s) is a skimming pricing policy most likely implementing? Is the same true for a penetration pricing policy? Which policy is probably most appropriate for each of the following products: (*a*) a new type of home lawn-sprinkling system, (*b*) a

new skin patch drug to help smokers quit, (*c*) a videotape of a best-selling movie, (*d*) a new children's toy?

8. Would consumers be better off if all nations dropped their antidumping laws? Explain your thinking.

9. How would our marketing system change if manufacturers were required to set fixed prices on *all* products sold at retail and *all* retailers were required to use these prices? Would a manufacturer's marketing mix be easier to develop? What kind of an operation would retailing be in this situation? Would consumers receive more or less service?

10. Is price discrimination involved if a large oil company sells gasoline to taxicab associations for resale to individual taxicab operators for 2 1/2 cents a gallon less than the price charged to retail service stations? What happens if the cab associations resell gasoline not only to taxicab operators but to the general public as well?

11. Do stocking allowances increase or reduce conflict in a channel of distribution? Explain your thinking.

12. Are seasonal discounts appropriate in agricultural businesses (which are certainly seasonal)?

13. What are the effective annual interest rates for the following cash discount terms: *(a)* 1/10, net 20; *(b)* 1/5, net 10; *(c)* net 25?

14. Why would a manufacturer offer a rebate instead of lowering the suggested list price?

15. How can a marketing manager change her F.O.B. terms to make her otherwise competitive marketing mix more attractive?

16. What type of geographic pricing policy is most appropriate for the following products (specify any assumptions necessary to obtain a definite answer): *(a)* a chemical by-product, *(b)* nationally advertised candy bars, *(c)* rebuilt auto parts, and *(d)* tricycles?

17. How would a ban on freight absorption (that is, requiring F.O.B factory pricing) affect a producer with substantial economies of scale in production?

SUGGESTED CASES

13. Fileco, Inc.
23. AAA Photo Labs, Inc.

24. Kelman Mfg., Inc.

COMPUTER-AIDED PROBLEM

16. Cash Discounts

Joe Tulkin owns Tulkin Wholesale Co. He sells paper, tape, file folders, and other office supplies to about 120 retailers in nearby cities. His average retailer customer spends about $1,200 a month. When Tulkin started business in 1986, competing wholesalers were giving retailers invoice terms of 3/10, net 30. Tulkin never gave the issue much thought—he just used the same invoice terms when he billed customers. At that time, about half of his customers took the discount. Recently he notices a change in the way his customers pay their bills. Checking his records, he finds that 85 percent of the retailers are taking the cash discount. With so many retailers taking the cash discount, it seems to have become a price reduction. In addition, Tulkin learns that other wholesalers are changing their invoice terms.

Tulkin decides he should rethink his invoice terms. He knows he could change the percent rate on the cash discount, the number of days the discount is offered, or the number of days before the face amount is due. Changing any of these—or any combination—will change the interest rate at which a buyer is, in effect, borrowing money if he does not take the discount. Tulkin decides that it will be easier to evaluate the effect of different

invoice terms if he sets up a spreadsheet to let him change the terms and quickly see the effective interest rate for each change.

a. With 85 percent of Tulkin's customers now taking the discount, what is the total monthly cash discount amount?

b. If Tulkin changes his invoice terms to 1/10, net 30, what interest rate is each buyer paying by not taking the cash discount? With these terms, will fewer buyers take the discount? Why?

c. Tulkin thinks 10 customers will switch to other wholesalers if he changes his invoice terms to 2/10, net 30, while 65 percent of the remaining customers will take the discount. What interest rate does a buyer pay by not taking this cash discount?

For this situation, what will the total gross sales (total invoice) amount be? The total cash discount? The total net sales receipts after the total cash discount? Compare Tulkin's current situation with what will happen if he changes his invoice terms to 2/10, net 30.

For additional questions related to this problem, see Exercise 16–3 in the *Learning Aid for use with Essentials of Marketing,* 6th edition.

Marketing Arithmetic

Appendix **B**

When You Finish This Appendix, You Should

❶

Understand the components of an operating statement (profit and loss statement).

❷

Know how to compute the stockturn rate.

❸

Understand how operating ratios can help analyze a business.

❹

Understand how to calculate markups and markdowns.

❺

Understand how to calculate return on investment (ROI) and return on assets (ROA).

❻

Understand the basic forecasting approaches and why they are used.

❼

Understand the important new terms (shown in red).

Marketing students must become familiar with the essentials of the language of business. Businesspeople commonly use accounting terms when talking about costs, prices, and profit. And using accounting data is a practical tool in analyzing marketing problems.

THE OPERATING STATEMENT

An **operating statement** is a simple summary of the financial results of a company's operations over a specified period of time. Some beginning students may feel that the operating statement is complex, but as we'll soon see, this really isn't true. *The main purpose of the operating statement is determining the net profit figure—and presenting data to support that figure.* This is why the operating statement is often referred to as the *profit and loss statement*.

Exhibit B–1 shows an operating statement for a wholesale or retail business. The statement is complete and detailed so you will see the framework throughout the discussion, but the amount of detail on an operating statement is *not* standardized. Many companies use financial statements with much less detail than this one. They emphasize clarity and readability rather than detail. To really understand an operating statement, however, you must know about its components.

Only three basic components

The basic components of an operating statement are *sales*—which come from the sale of goods and services; *costs*—which come from the making and selling process; and the balance—called *profit or loss*—which is just the difference between sales and costs. So there are only three basic components in the statement: sales, costs, and profit (or loss). Other items on an operating statement are there only to provide supporting details.

Time period covered may vary

There is no one time period an operating statement covers. Rather, statements are prepared to satisfy the needs of a particular business. This may be at the end of each day or at the end of each week. Usually, however, an operating statement summarizes results for one month, three months, six months, or a full year. Since the time period does vary, this information is included in the heading of the statement as follows:

SMITH COMPANY
Operating Statement
For the (Period) Ended (Date)

Also, see Exhibit B–1.

Management uses of operating statements

Before going on to a more detailed discussion of the components of our operating statement, let's think about some of the uses for such a statement. Exhibit B–1 shows that a lot of information is presented in a clear and concise manner. With this information, a manager can easily find the relation of net sales to the cost of sales, the gross margin, expenses, and net profit. Opening and closing inventory figures are available—as is the amount spent during the period for the purchase of goods for resale. Total expenses are listed to make it easier to compare them with previous statements—and to help control these expenses.

All this information is important to a company's managers. Assume that a particular company prepares monthly operating statements. A series of these statements is a valuable tool for directing and controlling the business. By comparing results from one month to the next, managers can uncover unfavorable trends in the sales, costs, or profit areas of the business—and take any needed action.

Exhibit B–1 An Operating Statement (profit and loss statement)

SMITH COMPANY
Operating Statement
For the Year Ended December 31, 199X

Gross sales..			$540,000
Less: Returns and allowances			40,000
Net Sales			$500,000
Cost of Sales:			
Beginning inventory at cost		$ 80,000	
Purchases at billed cost	$310,000		
Less: Purchase discounts	40,000		
Purchase at net cost	270,000		
Plus freight-in	20,000		
Net cost of delivered purchases		290,000	
Cost of products available for sale		370,000	
Less: Ending inventory at cost		70,000	
Cost of sales			300,000
Gross margin (gross profit)			200,000
Expenses:			
Selling expenses:			
Sales salaries..................................	60,000		
Advertising expense	20,000		
Delivery expense	20,000		
Total selling expense		100,000	
Administrative expense			
Office salaries	30,000		
Office supplies	10,000		
Miscellaneous administrative expense	5,000		
Total administrative expense		45,000	
General expense:			
Rent expense..................................	10,000		
Miscellaneous general expenses	5,000		
Total general expense		15,000	
Total expenses			160,000
Net profit from operation			$ 40,000

A skeleton statement gets down to essential details

Let's refer to Exhibit B–1 and begin to analyze this seemingly detailed statement to get first-hand knowledge of the components of the operating statement.

As a first step, suppose we take all the items that have dollar amounts extended to the third, or right-hand, column. Using these items only, the operating statement looks like this:

Gross sales	$540,000
Less: Returns and allowances	40,000
Net sales	500,000
Less: Cost of sales	300,000
Gross margin	200,000
Less: Total expenses	160,000
Net profit (loss)	$ 40,000

Is this a complete operating statement? The answer is **yes.** This skeleton statement differs from Exhibit B–1 only in supporting detail. All the basic components are included. In fact, the only items we must list to have a complete operating statement are:

Net sales	$500,000
Less: Costs	460,000
Net profit (loss)	$ 40,000

These three items are the essentials of an operating statement. All other subdivisions or details are just useful additions.

Meaning of sales

Now let's define the meaning of the terms in the skeleton statement.

The first item is sales. What do we mean by sales? The term **gross sales** is the total amount charged to all customers during some time period. However, there is always some customer dissatisfaction—or just plain errors in placing and filling orders. This results in returns and allowances—which reduce gross sales.

A **return** occurs when a customer sends back purchased products. The company either refunds the purchase price or allows the customer dollar credit on other purchases.

An **allowance** occurs when a customer is not satisfied with a purchase for some reason. The company gives a price reduction on the original invoice (bill), but the customer keeps the goods and services.

These refunds and price reductions must be considered when the firm computes its net sales figure for the period. We're mainly interested in the revenue the company manages to keep. This is **net sales**—the actual sales dollars the company receives. Therefore, all reductions, refunds, cancellations, and so forth—made because of returns and allowances—are deducted from the original total (gross sales) to get net sales. This is shown below:

Gross sales	$540,000
Less: Returns and allowances	40,000
Net sales	$500,000

Meaning of cost of sales

The next item in the operating statement—**cost of sales**—is the total value (at cost) of the sales during the period. We'll discuss this computation later. Meanwhile, note that after we obtain the cost of sales figure, we subtract it from the net sales figure to get the gross margin.

Meaning of gross margin and expenses

Gross margin (gross profit) is the money left to cover the expenses of selling the products and operating the business. Firms hope that a profit will be left after subtracting these expenses.

Selling expense is commonly the major expense below the gross margin. Note that in Exhibit B–1, **expenses** are all the remaining costs subtracted from the gross margin to get the net profit. The expenses in this case are the selling, administrative, and general expenses. (Note that the cost of purchases and cost of sales are not included in this total expense figure—they were subtracted from net sales earlier to get the gross margin. Note, also, that some accountants refer to cost of sales as cost of goods sold.)

Net profit—at the bottom of the statement—is what the company earned from its operations during a particular period. It is the amount left after the cost of sales and the expenses are subtracted from net sales. *Net sales and net profit are not the same.* Many firms have large sales and no profits—they may even have losses! That's why understanding costs—and controlling them—is important.

DETAILED ANALYSIS OF SECTIONS OF THE OPERATING STATEMENT

Cost of sales for a wholesale or retail company

The cost of sales section includes details that are used to find the cost of sales ($300,000 in our example).

In Exhibit B–1, you can see that beginning and ending inventory, purchases, purchase discounts, and freight-in are all necessary to calculate costs of sales. If we pull the cost of sales section from the operating statement, it looks like this:

Cost of sales:		
Beginning inventory at cost		$ 80,000
Purchases at billed cost	$310,000	
Less: Purchase discounts	40,000	
Purchases at net cost	270,000	
Plus: Freight-in	20,000	
Net cost of delivered purchases		290,000
Cost of goods available for sale		370,000
Less: Ending inventory at cost		70,000
Cost of sales		$300,000

Cost of sales is the cost value of what is *sold*—not the cost of goods on hand at any given time.

Inventory figures merely show the cost of goods on hand at the beginning and end of the period the statement covers. These figures may be obtained by physically counting goods on hand on these dates—or estimated from perpetual inventory records that show the inventory balance at any given time. The methods used to determine the inventory should be as accurate as possible because these figures affect the cost of sales during the period—and net profit.

The net cost of delivered purchases must include freight charges and purchase discounts received since these items affect the money actually spent to buy goods and bring them to the place of business. A **purchase discount** is a reduction of the original invoice amount for some business reason. For example, a cash discount may be given for prompt payment of the amount due. We subtract the total of such discounts from the original invoice cost of purchases to get the *net* cost of purchases. To this figure we add the freight charges for bringing the goods to the place of business. This gives the net cost of *delivered* purchases. When we add the net cost of delivered purchases to the beginning inventory at cost, we have the total cost of goods available for sale during the period. If we now subtract the ending inventory at cost from the cost of the goods available for sale, we get the cost of sales.

One important point should be noted about cost of sales. The way the value of inventory is calculated varies from one company to another—and can cause big differences in the cost of sales and the operating statement. (See any basic accounting textbook for how the various inventory valuation methods work.)

Cost of sales for a manufacturing company

Exhibit B–1 shows the way the manager of a wholesale or retail business arrives at his cost of sales. Such a business *purchases* finished products and resells them. In a manufacturing company, the purchases section of this operating statement is replaced by a section called cost of production. This section includes purchases of raw materials and parts, direct and indirect labor costs, and overhead charges (such as heat, light, and power) that are necessary to produce finished products. The cost of production is added to the beginning finished products inventory to arrive at the cost of products available for sale. Often a separate cost of production statement is prepared, and only the total cost of production is shown in the operating statement. See Exhibit B–2 for an illustration of the cost of sales section of an operating statement for a manufacturing company.

Expenses

Expenses go below the gross margin. They usually include the costs of selling and the costs of administering the business. They do not include the cost of sales—either purchased or produced.

There is no right method for classifying the expense accounts or arranging them on the operating statement. They can just as easily be arranged alphabetically or according to amount, with the largest placed at the top and so on down the line. In a business of any size, though, it is clearer to group the expenses in some way and use subtotals by groups for analysis and control purposes. This was done in Exhibit B–1.

Summary on operating statements

The statement presented in Exhibit B–1 contains all the major categories in an operating statement—together with a normal amount of supporting detail. Further detail

Exhibit B–2   Cost of Sales Section of an Operating Statement for a Manufacturing Firm

Cost of sales:		
Finished products inventory (beginning)	$ 20,000	
Cost of production (Schedule 1)	100,000	
Total cost of finished products available for sale	120,000	
Less: Finished products inventory (ending)	30,000	
Cost of sales		$ 90,000
Schedule 1, Schedule of cost of production		
Beginning work in process inventory		15,000
Raw materials		
Beginning raw materials inventory	10,000	
Net cost of delivered purchases	80,000	
Total cost of materials available for use	90,000	
Less: Ending raw materials inventory	15,000	
Cost of materials placed in production	75,000	
Direct labor	20,000	
Manufacturing expenses		
Indirect labor	$4,000	
Maintenance and repairs	3,000	
Factory supplies	1,000	
Heat, light, and power	2,000	
Total manufacturing expenses	10,000	
Total manufacturing costs		105,000
Total work in process during period		120,000
Less: Ending work in process inventory		20,000
Cost of production		$100,000

can be added to the statement under any of the major categories without changing the nature of the statement. The amount of detail normally is determined by how the statement will be used. A stockholder may be given a sketchy operating statement—while the one prepared for internal company use may have a lot of detail.

COMPUTING THE STOCKTURN RATE

A detailed operating statement can provide the data needed to compute the **stockturn rate**—a measure of the number of times the average inventory is sold during a year. Note that the stockturn rate is related to the *turnover during a year*—not the length of time covered by a particular operating statement.

The stockturn rate is a very important measure because it shows how rapidly the firm's inventory is moving. Some businesses typically have slower turnover than others. But a drop in turnover in a particular business can be very alarming. It may mean that the firm's assortment of products is no longer as attractive as it was. Also, it may mean that the firm will need more working capital to handle the same volume of sales. Most businesses pay a lot of attention to the stockturn rate—trying to get faster turnover (and lower inventory costs).

Three methods—all basically similar—can be used to compute the stockturn rate. Which method is used depends on the data available. These three methods—which usually give approximately the same results—are shown below.*

$$(1) \quad \frac{\text{Cost of sales}}{\text{Average inventory at cost}}$$

$$(2) \quad \frac{\text{Net sales}}{\text{Average inventory at selling price}}$$

$$(3) \quad \frac{\text{Sales in units}}{\text{Average inventory in units}}$$

Computing the stockturn rate will be illustrated only for Formula 1 since all are similar. The only difference is that the cost figures used in Formula 1 are changed to a selling price or numerical count basis in Formulas 2 and 3. Note: regardless of the method used, you must have both the numerator and denominator of the formula in the same terms.

If the inventory level varies a lot during the year, you may need detailed information about the inventory level at different times to compute the average inventory. If it stays at about the same level during the year, however, it's easy to get an estimate. For example, using Formula 1, the average inventory at cost is computed by adding the beginning and ending inventories at cost and dividing by 2. This average inventory figure is then divided into the cost of sales (in cost terms) to get the stockturn rate.

For example, suppose that the cost of sales for one year was $1,000,000. Beginning inventory was $250,000 and ending inventory $150,000. Adding the two inventory figures and dividing by 2, we get an average inventory of $200,000. We next divide the cost of sales by the average inventory ($1,000,000 ÷ $200,000) and get a stockturn rate of 5. The stockturn rate is covered further in Chapter 17.

---

*Differences occur because of varied markups and nonhomogeneous product assortments. In an assortment of tires, for example, those with low markups might have sold much better than those with high markups. But with Formula 3, all tires would be treated equally.

OPERATING RATIOS ANALYZE THE BUSINESS

Many businesspeople use the operating statement to calculate **operating ratios**—the ratio of items on the operating statement to net sales—and compare these ratios from one time period to another. They can also compare their own operating ratios with those of competitors. Such competitive data is often available through trade associations. Each firm may report its results to a trade association, which then distributes summary results to its members. These ratios help managers control their operations. If some expense ratios are rising, for example, those particular costs are singled out for special attention.

Operating ratios are computed by dividing net sales into the various operating statement items that appear below the net sales level in the operating statement. The net sales is used as the denominator in the operating ratio because it shows the sales the firm actually won.

We can see the relation of operating ratios to the operating statement if we think of there being another column to the right of the dollar figures in an operating statement. This column contains percentage figures—using net sales as 100 percent. This approach can be seen below:

Gross sales	$540,000	
Less: Returns and allowances	40,000	
Net sales	500,000	100%
Cost of sales	300,000	60
Gross margin	200,000	40
Expenses	160,000	32
Net profit	$ 40,000	8%

The 40 percent ratio of gross margin to net sales in the above example shows that 40 percent of the net sales dollar is available to cover sales expenses and administering the business—and provide a profit. Note that the ratio of expenses to sales added to the ratio of profit to sales equals the 40 percent gross margin ratio. The net profit ratio of 8 percent shows that 8 percent of the net sales dollar is left for profit.

The value of percentage ratios should be obvious. The percentages are easily figured—and much easier to compare than large dollar figures.

Note that because these operating statement categories are interrelated, only a few pieces of information are needed to figure the others. In this case, for example, knowing the gross margin percent and net profit percent makes it possible to figure the expenses and cost of sales percentages. Further, knowing just one dollar amount and the percentages lets you figure all the other dollar amounts.

MARKUPS

A **markup** is the dollar amount added to the cost of sales to get the selling price. The markup usually is similar to the firm's gross margin because the markup amount added onto the unit cost of a product by a retailer or wholesaler is expected to cover the selling and administrative expenses—and to provide a profit.

The markup approach to pricing is discussed in Chapter 17, so it will not be discussed at length here. But a simple example illustrates the idea. If a retailer buys an article that costs $1 when delivered to his store, he must sell it for more than this cost if he hopes to make a profit. So he might add 50 cents onto the cost of the article to cover his selling and other costs and, hopefully, to provide a profit. The 50 cents is the markup.

The 50 cents is also the gross margin or gross profit from that item *if* it is sold. But note that it is *not* the net profit. Selling expenses may amount to 35 cents, 45 cents, or even 55 cents. In other words, there is no guarantee the markup will cover costs. Further, there is no guarantee customers will buy at the marked-up price. This may require markdowns, which are discussed later in this appendix.

Markup conversions

Often it is convenient to use markups as percentages rather than focusing on the actual dollar amounts. But markups can be figured as a percentage of cost or selling price. To have some agreement, *markup (percent)* will mean percentage of selling price unless stated otherwise. So the 50-cent markup on the $1.50 selling price is a markup of 33⅓ percent. On the other hand, the 50-cent markup is a 50 percent markup on cost.

Some retailers and wholesalers use markup conversion tables or spreadsheets to easily convert from cost to selling price—depending on the markup on selling price they want. To see the interrelation, look at the two formulas below. They can be used to convert either type of markup to the other.

$$\frac{SP - C}{SP} \times 100 = MU\% \quad (4)$$

$$\text{Percent markup on selling price} = \frac{\text{Percent markup on cost}}{100\% + \text{Percent markup on cost}}$$

$$(5) \quad \text{Percent markup on cost} = \frac{\text{Percent markup on selling price}}{100\% - \text{Percent markup on selling price}}$$

In the previous example, we had a cost of $1, a markup of 50 cents, and a selling price of $1.50. We saw that the markup on selling price was 33⅓ percent—and on cost, it was 50 percent. Let's substitute these percentage figures—in Formulas 4 and 5—to see how to convert from one basis to the other. Assume first of all that we only know the markup on selling price and want to convert to markup on cost. Using Formula 5, we get:

$$\text{Percent markup on cost} = \frac{33\frac{1}{3}\%}{100\% - 33\frac{1}{3}\%} = \frac{33\frac{1}{3}\%}{66\frac{2}{3}\%} = 50\%$$

On the other hand, if we know only the percent markup on cost, we can convert to markup on selling price as follows:

$$\text{Percent markup on selling price} = \frac{50\%}{100\% + 50\%} = \frac{50\%}{150\%} = 33\frac{1}{3}\%$$

These results can be proved and summarized as follows:

Markup $0.50 =	50% of cost, or 33⅓% of selling price
+ Cost $1.00 =	100% of cost, or 66⅔% of selling price
Selling price $1.50 =	150% of cost, or 100% of selling price

It is important to see that only the percentage figures change while the money amounts of cost, markup, and selling price stay the same. Note, too, that when selling price is the base for the calculation (100 percent), then the cost percentage plus the markup percentage equal 100 percent. But when the cost of the product is used as the base figure (100 percent), the selling price percentage must be greater than 100 percent by the markup on cost.

MARKDOWN RATIOS HELP CONTROL RETAIL OPERATIONS

The ratios we discussed above were concerned with figures on the operating statement. Another important ratio, the **markdown ratio**, is a tool many retailers use to measure the efficiency of various departments and their whole business. But note that it is *not directly related to the operating statement*. It requires special calculations.

[Handwritten margin notes:]

Cost orient approach

aver. cost pricing only good if you are a good forecaster of demand. Doesn't acct for econ. of scale or higher cost at lower qtys. history

experience curve pricing the more you do something the better you get + w/ experience you become efficient. Aver. cost pricing using an estimate of future costs. predicting

target return pricing the price setter is looking for a specific ROI. Target return objective

Breakeven analysis Evaluate the level of price + product necessary to cover all costs.

BE = TC = TR

marginal Analysis The change in total cost for producing one more unit. Marginal rev is the change in rev that results from one more unit. The Δ in cost + Rev from

A **markdown** is a retail price reduction required because customers won't buy some item at the originally marked-up price. This refusal to buy may be due to a variety of reasons—soiling, style changes, fading, damage caused by handling, or an original price that was too high. To get rid of these products, the retailer offers them at a lower price.

Markdowns are generally considered to be due to business errors—perhaps because of poor buying, original markups that are too high, and other reasons. (Note, however, some retailers use markdowns as a way of doing business rather than a way to correct errors. For example, a store that buys out overstocked fashions from other retailers may start by marking each item with a high price and then reduce the price each week until it sells.) Regardless of the reason, however, markdowns are reductions in the original price—and they are important to managers who want to measure the effectiveness of their operations.

Markdowns are similar to allowances because price reductions are made. Thus, in computing a markdown ratio, markdowns and allowances are usually added together and then divided by net sales. The markdown ratio is computed as follows:

$$\text{Markdown \%} = \frac{\$ \text{ Markdowns} + \$ \text{ Allowances}}{\$ \text{ Net sales}} \times 100$$

The 100 is multiplied by the fraction to get rid of decimal points.

Returns are *not* included when figuring the markdown ratio. Returns are treated as consumer errors—not business errors.

Retailers who use markdown ratios usually keep a record of the amount of markdowns and allowances in each department and then divide the total by the net sales in each department. Over a period of time, these ratios give management one measure of the efficiency of buyers and salespeople in various departments.

It should be stressed again that the markdown ratio is not calculated directly from data on the operating statement since the markdowns take place before the products are sold. In fact, some products may be marked down and still not sold. Even if the marked-down items are not sold, the markdowns—that is, the reevaluations of their value—are included in the calculations in the time period when they are taken.

The markdown ratio is calculated for a whole department (or profit center)—*not* individual items. What we are seeking is a measure of the effectiveness of a whole department—not how well the department did on individual items.

RETURN ON INVESTMENT (ROI) REFLECTS ASSET USE

Another off-the-operating-statement ratio is **return on investment (ROI)**—the ratio of net profit (after taxes) to the investment used to make the net profit, multiplied by 100 to get rid of decimals. Investment is not shown on the operating statement. But it is on the **balance sheet** (statement of financial condition)—another accounting statement—that shows a company's assets, liabilities, and net worth. It may take some digging or special analysis, however, to find the right investment number.

Investment means the dollar resources the firm has invested in a project or business. For example, a new product may require $4 million in new money—for inventory, accounts receivable, promotion, and so on—and its attractiveness may be judged by its likely ROI. If the net profit (after taxes) for this new product is expected to be $1 million in the first year, then the ROI is 25 percent—that is, ($1 million ÷ $4 million) × 100.

There are two ways to figure ROI. The *direct* way is:

$$\text{ROI (in \%)} = \frac{\text{Net profit (after taxes)}}{\text{Investment}} \times 100$$

The *indirect* way is:

$$\text{ROI (in \%)} = \frac{\text{Net profit (after taxes)}}{\text{Sales}} \times \frac{\text{Sales}}{\text{Investment}} \times 100$$

This way is concerned with net profit margin and turnover—that is:

$$\text{ROI (in \%)} = \text{Net profit margin} \times \text{Turnover} \times 100$$

This indirect way makes it clearer how to *increase* ROI. There are three ways:

1. Increase profit margin (with lower costs or a higher price).
2. Increase sales.
3. Decrease investment.

Effective marketing strategy planning and implementation can increase profit margins and/or sales. And careful asset management can decrease investment.

ROI is a revealing measure of how well managers are doing. Most companies have alternative uses for their funds. If the returns in a business aren't at least as high as outside uses, then the money probably should be shifted to the more profitable uses.

Some firms borrow more than others to make investments. In other words, they invest less of their own money to acquire assets—what we called investments. If ROI calculations use only the firm's own investment, this gives higher ROI figures to those who borrow a lot—which is called leveraging. To adjust for different borrowing proportions—to make comparisons among projects, departments, divisions, and companies easier—another ratio has come into use. **Return on assets (ROA)** is the ratio of net profit (after taxes) to the assets used to make the net profit—times 100. Both ROI and ROA measures are trying to get at the same thing—how effectively the company is using resources. These measures became increasingly popular as profit rates dropped and it became more obvious that increasing sales volume doesn't necessarily lead to higher profits—or ROI or ROA. Inflation and higher costs for borrowed funds also force more concern for ROI and ROA. Marketers must include these measures in their thinking or top managers are likely to ignore their plans—and requests for financial resources.

FORECASTING TARGET MARKET POTENTIAL AND SALES

Estimates of target **market potential**—what a whole market segment might buy—and a **sales forecast**—an estimate of how much an industry or firm hopes to sell to a market segment—are necessary for effective strategy planning. Without such information, it's hard to know if a strategy is potentially profitable.

We must first try to judge market potential before we can estimate what share a particular firm may be able to win with its particular marketing mix.

Three levels of forecast are useful

We're interested in forecasting the potential in specific market segments. To do this, it helps to make three levels of forecasts.

Some economic conditions affect the entire global economy. Others may influence only one country or a particular industry. And some may affect only one company or one product's sales potential. For this reason, a common approach to forecasting is to:

1. Develop a *national income forecast* (for each country in which the firm operates) and use this to:
2. Develop an *industry sales forecast,* which then is used to:
3. Develop *specific company* and *product forecasts.*

[handwritten margin note:] Leader Pricing. Set low prices to lure customers in to buy other goods. Grocery stores.

Generally, a marketing manager doesn't have to make forecasts for a national economy or the broad industry. This kind of forecasting—basically trend projecting—is a specialty in itself. Such forecasts are available in business and government publications, and large companies often have their own technical specialists. Managers can use just one source's forecast or combine several. Unfortunately, however, the more targeted the marketing manager's earlier segmenting efforts have been, the less likely that industry forecasts will match the firm's product-markets. So managers have to move directly to estimating potential for their own companies—and for their specific products.

Two approaches to forecasting

Many methods are used to forecast market potential and sales, but they can all be grouped into two basic approaches: (1) extending past behavior and (2) predicting future behavior. The large number of methods may seem confusing at first, but this variety has an advantage. Forecasts are so important that managers often develop forecasts in two or three different ways and then compare the differences before preparing a final forecast.

Extending past behavior can miss important turning points

[handwritten margin note:] Value + Use Pricing. Firm will set prices that will capture savings that customer will achieve by using the firm's product instead of the one they currently using. Word processors eliminate 3 salaries. Refrigerators.

When we forecast for existing products, we usually have some past data to go on. The basic approach—called **trend extension**—extends past experience into the future. With existing products, for example, the past trend of actual sales may be extended into the future. See Exhibit B–3.

Ideally, when extending past sales behavior, we should decide why sales vary. This is the difficult and time-consuming part of sales forecasting. Usually we can gather a lot of data about the product or market—or about changes in the marketing environment. But unless we know the *reason* for past sales variations, it's hard to predict in what direction—and by how much—sales will move. Graphing the data and statistical techniques—including correlation and regression analysis—can be useful here. (These techniques, which are beyond our scope, are discussed in beginning statistics courses.)

Once we know why sales vary, we can usually develop a specific forecast. Sales may be moving directly up as population grows, for example. So we can just estimate how population is expected to grow and project the impact on sales.

The weakness of the trend extension method is that it assumes past conditions will continue unchanged into the future. In fact, the future isn't always like the past. For example, for years the trend in sales of disposable diapers moved closely with the number of new births. However, as the number of women in the work force increased and as more women returned to jobs after babies were born, use of disposable diapers increased, and the trend changed. As in this example, trend extension estimates will be wrong whenever big changes occur. For this reason—although they may extend past behavior for one

Exhibit B–3   Straight-Line Trend Projection—Extends Past Sales into the Future

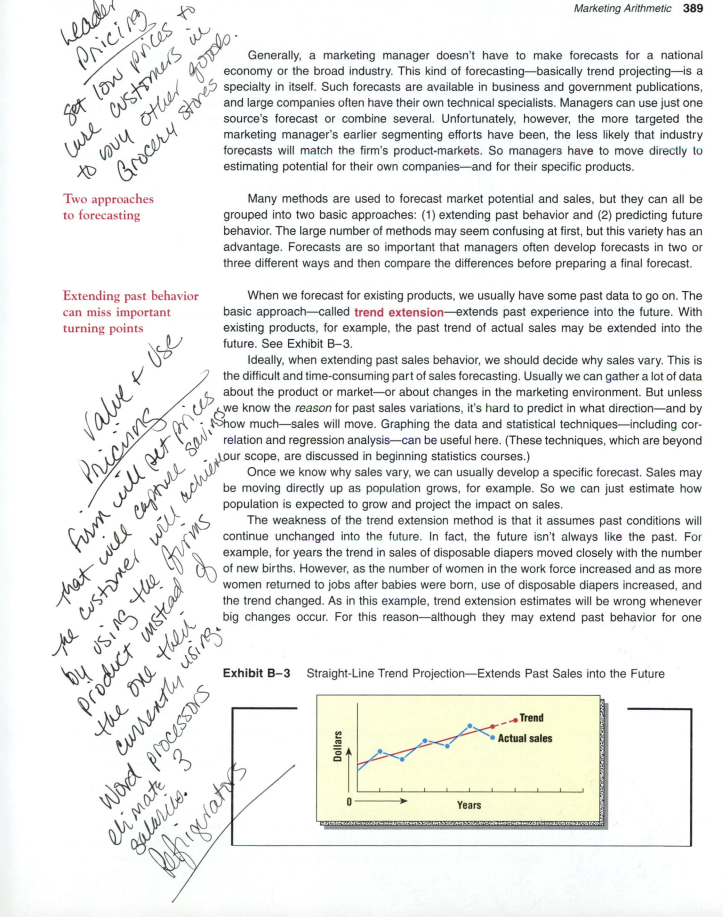

estimate—most managers look for another way to help them forecast sharp economic changes.

Predicting future behavior takes judgment

When we try to predict what will happen in the future—instead of just extending the past—we have to use other methods and add a bit more judgment. Some of these methods (to be discussed later) include juries of executive opinion, salespeople's estimates, surveys, panels, and market tests.

FORECASTING COMPANY AND PRODUCT SALES BY EXTENDING PAST BEHAVIOR

Past sales can be extended

At the very least, a marketing manager ought to know what the firm's present markets look like—and what it has sold to them in the past. A detailed sales analysis—for products and geographic areas—helps to project future results.

Just extending past sales into the future may not seem like much of a forecasting method. But it's better than just assuming that next year's total sales will be the same as this year's.

Factor method includes more than time

A simple extension of past sales gives one forecast. But it's usually desirable to tie future sales to something more than the passage of time.

The **factor method** tries to forecast sales by finding a relation between the company's sales and some other factor (or factors). The basic formula is: something (past sales, industry sales, etc.) *times* some factor *equals* sales forecast. A **factor** is a variable that shows the relation of some other variable to the item being forecast. For instance, in our example above, both the birthrate and the number of working mothers are factors related to sales of disposable diapers.

A bread producer example

The following example—about a bread producer—shows how firms can make forecasts for many geographic market segments—using the factor method and available data. This general approach can be useful for any firm—producer, wholesaler, or retailer.

Analysis of past sales relationships showed that the bread manufacturer regularly sold one tenth of 1 percent (0.001) of the total retail food sales in its various target markets. This is a single factor. By using this single factor, a manager could estimate the producer's sales for the coming period by multiplying a forecast of expected retail food sales by 0.001.

Sales & Marketing Management magazine makes retail food sales estimates each year. Exhibit B–4 shows the kind of geographically detailed data available.

Let's carry this bread example further—using the data in Exhibit B–4 for Las Vegas, Nevada. Las Vegas's food sales were $1,253,589,000 for the last year. By simply accepting last year's food sales as an estimate of next year's sales—and multiplying the food sales estimate for Las Vegas by the 0.001 factor (the firm's usual share of food purchases in such markets), the manager would have an estimate of next year's bread sales in Las Vegas. That is, last year's food sales estimate ($1,253,589,000) times 0.001 equals this year's bread sales estimate of $1,253,589.

Factor method can use several factors

The factor method is not limited to just one factor; several factors can be used together. For example, *Sales & Marketing Management* regularly gives a "buying power index" (BPI) as a measure of the potential in different geographic areas. See Exhibit B–4. This index considers (1) the population in a market, (2) the market's income, and (3) retail sales in that market. The BPI for the Las Vegas, Nevada, metro area, for example, is 0.3068—that is, Las Vegas accounts for 0.3068 percent of the total U.S. buying power. This means that consumers who live in Las Vegas do not have particularly high buying power. We know this because Las Vegas accounts for about 0.3084 percent of the U.S. population, so its buying power is about average relative to other cities that size.

[Handwritten margin notes: "Prestige Pricing / High price for Quality or Status." and "Price Lining / A few price levels to sell all products. Shoe store co's" and "Full line pricing / one price"]

Exhibit B–4   Sample of Pages from *Sales & Marketing Management's* Survey of Buying Power

Nevada

POPULATION

S&MM ESTIMATES: 12/31/90

METRO AREA County City	Total Population (Thousands)	% Of U.S.	Median Age Of Pop.	% of Pop. by Age Group				House-holds Thousands)
				18-24 Years	25-34 Years	35-49 Years	50 & Over	
LAS VEGAS	**773.4**	**.3084**	**33.2**	**10.1**	**18.5**	**22.1**	**24.6**	**299.6**
Clark	773.4	.3084	33.2	10.1	18.5	22.1	24.6	299.6
Henderson	67.7	.0270	31.8	8.8	18.9	23.5	20.4	24.2
• Las Vegas	269.4	.1074	32.6	10.0	19.4	21.6	23.9	104.0
North Las Vegas . . .	49.8	.0199	27.1	11.9	17.7	17.9	18.1	15.2
SUBURBAN TOTAL . . .	504.0	.2010	33.5	10.1	18.2	22.3	25.0	195.6
RENO	**260.0**	**.1036**	**33.7**	**10.4**	**18.8**	**23.8**	**23.7**	**104.5**
Washoe	260.0	.1036	33.7	10.4	18.8	23.8	23.7	104.5
• Reno	136.7	.0545	33.5	12.1	20.0	22.1	24.9	58.5
Sparks	54.5	.0217	32.6	10.2	18.8	23.6	21.9	21.0
SUBURBAN TOTAL . . .	123.3	.0491	33.9	8.5	17.6	25.8	22.3	46.0

RETAIL SALES BY STORE GROUP

Total Retail Sales ($000)	Food ($000)	Eating & Drinking Places ($000)	General Mdse. ($000)	Furniture/ Furnish. Appliance ($000)	Auto-motive ($000)	Drug ($000)
5,806,823	1,253,589	665,294	643,750	281,602	1,148,885	185,522
5,806,823	1,253,589	665,294	643,750	281,602	1,148,885	185,522
191,539	83,997	17,558	16,224	3,228	31,722	9,112
2,500,988	492,197	266,658	265,790	134,966	492,144	93,202
186,843	49,765	23,906	13,066	3,937	45,132	10,890
3,305,835	761,392	398,636	377,960	146,636	656,741	92,320
2,548,478	452,327	195,172	384,341	118,224	562,079	119,111
2,548,478	452,327	195,172	384,341	118,224	562,079	119,111
1,882,030	314,619	135,035	259,005	95,318	490,366	75,150
470,379	100,539	35,870	121,107	15,986	23,391	41,276
666,448	137,708	60,137	125,336	22,906	71,713	43,961

EFFECTIVE BUYING INCOME

S&MM ESTIMATES: 12/31/90

METRO AREA County City	Total EBI ($000)	Median Hsld. EBI	% of Hslds. by EBI Group: (A) $10,000-$19,999 (B) $20,000-$34,999 (C) $35,000-$49,999 (D) $50,000 & Over				Buying Power Index
			A	B	C	D	
LAS VEGAS	**10,408,999**	**28,175**	**21.2**	**27.0**	**18.5**	**20.0**	**.3068**
Clark	10,408,999	28,175	21.2	27.0	18.5	20.0	.3068
Henderson	848,258	32,288	15.4	25.9	23.3	21.7	.0207
• Las Vegas	3,518,216	27,087	21.0	26.1	18.0	19.1	.1133
North Las Vegas . . .	446,333	24,748	24.0	29.1	18.7	13.0	.0135
SUBURBAN TOTAL . . .	6,890,783	28,748	21.3	27.5	18.7	20.5	.1935
RENO	**3,941,398**	**30,460**	**19.6**	**26.6**	**18.6**	**24.1**	**.1193**
Washoe	3,941,398	30,460	19.6	26.6	18.6	24.1	.1193
• Reno	2,060,185	27,309	22.0	27.0	16.9	20.9	.0716
Sparks	785,946	33,102	18.5	26.0	21.5	25.5	.0234
SUBURBAN TOTAL . . .	1,881,203	34,423	16.6	25.9	20.9	28.2	.0477

EFFECTIVE BUYING INCOME

METRO AREA County City	Total EBI ($000)	Median Hsld. EBI	% of Hslds. by EBI Group: (A) $10,000-$19,999 (B) $20,000-$34,999 (C) $35,000-$49,999 (D) $50,000 & Over				Buying Power Index
			A	B	C	D	
Douglas	462,540	33,384	16.3	28.4	21.6	25.1	.0113
Elko	421,170	27,388	19.4	28.0	17.9	19.1	.0116
Esmeralda	27,098	39,800	14.0	15.0	25.6	33.7	.0006
Eureka	19,953	26,000	21.0	24.3	13.2	21.2	.0004
Humboldt	143,743	21,759	29.6	25.1	14.7	14.3	.0046
Lander	87,258	33,156	15.1	25.8	22.1	24.0	.0021
Lincoln	35,394	22,667	24.9	30.6	13.3	12.2	.0009
Lyon	225,105	23,230	24.4	27.8	16.1	12.9	.0061
Mineral	82,488	27,437	19.6	28.8	18.2	17.2	.0023
Nye	199,662	24,820	21.9	27.5	18.6	13.2	.0053
Pershing	60,442	27,094	17.5	27.2	15.5	22.1	.0016

Using several factors rather than only one uses more information. And in the case of the BPI, it gives a single measure of a market's potential. Rather than falling back to using population only, or income only, or trying to develop a special index, the BPI can be used in the same way that we used the 0.001 factor in the bread example.

PREDICTING FUTURE BEHAVIOR CALLS FOR MORE JUDGMENT AND SOME OPINIONS

These past-extending methods use quantitative data—projecting past experience into the future and assuming that the future will be like the past. But this is risky in competitive markets. Usually, it's desirable to add some judgment to other forecasts before making the final forecast yourself.

⑥ Most of the factors that contribute to ROI also contribute to long term value.

Jury of executive opinion adds judgment

One of the oldest and simplest methods of forecasting—the **jury of executive opinion**—combines the opinions of experienced executives—perhaps from marketing, production, finance, purchasing, and top management. Each executive estimates market potential and sales for the *coming years.* Then they try to work out a consensus.

The main advantage of the jury approach is that it can be done quickly and easily. On the other hand, the results may not be very good. There may be too much extending of the past. Some of the executives may have little contact with outside market influences. But their estimates could point to major shifts in customer demand or competition.

Estimates from salespeople can help too

Using salespeople's estimates to forecast is like the jury approach. But salespeople are more likely than home office managers to be familiar with customer reactions—and what competitors are doing. Their estimates are especially useful in some business markets where the few customers may be well known to the salespeople. But this approach may be useful in any type of market. Good retail clerks have a feel for their markets—their opinions shouldn't be ignored.

However, managers who use estimates from salespeople should be aware of the limitations. For example, new salespeople may not know much about their markets. Even experienced salespeople may not be aware of possible changes in the economic climate or the firm's other environments. And if salespeople think the manager is going to use the estimates to set sales quotas, the estimates may be low!

Surveys, panels, and market tests

Special surveys of final buyers, retailers, and/or wholesalers can show what's happening in different market segments. Some firms use panels of stores—or final consumers—to keep track of buying behavior and to decide when just extending past behavior isn't enough.

Surveys are sometimes combined with market tests when the company wants to estimate customers' reactions to possible changes in its marketing mix. A market test might show that a product increased its share of the market by 10 percent when its price was dropped one cent below competition. But this extra business might be quickly lost if the price were increased one cent above competition. Such market experiments help the marketing manager make good estimates of future sales when one or more of the four Ps is changed.

Accuracy depends on the marketing mix

Forecasting can help a marketing manager estimate the size of possible market opportunities. But the accuracy of any sales forecast depends on whether the firm selects and implements a marketing mix that turns these opportunities into sales and profits.[1]

(Conclusion)

QUESTIONS AND PROBLEMS

80% of the variability & profitability could be explained by 37 of the variables. Of the 37, 7 were most valuable/significant.

1. Distinguish between the following pairs of items that appear on operating statements: *(a)* gross sales and net sales, and *(b)* purchases at billed cost and purchases at net cost.

2. How does gross margin differ from gross profit? From net profit?

3. Explain the similarity between markups and gross margin. What connection do markdowns have with the operating statement?

4. Compute the net profit for a company with the following data:

Beginning inventory (cost)	$ 150,000
Purchases at billed cost	330,000
Sales returns and allowances	250,000
Rent	60,000
Salaries	400,000
Heat and light	180,000
Ending inventory (cost)	250,000
Freight cost (inbound)	80,000
Gross sales	1,300,000

② Market share + profitability are strongly related. Big units w/ over 5% share had rate of return 3x greater than a firm w/ less than 10% share. & economies of scale

① In the long run – quality of products + services relative to the competition. ⓑ Increased biz allows economies of scale. In the short run – a price premium.

③ High investment intensive acts as a powerful drag or negative effect on the comp.

④ Many Dog + ? firms generate cash + cash cows are dry. The BCG Matrix is an over simplified model. Growth + share are important but should not be used solely to predict cash flow.

⑤ Vertical Integration is a profitable strategy for some biz but not for others. Regardless of the cost of such. V.I. there are other factors to consider for profitability

5. Construct an operating statement from the following data:

Returns and allowances	$150,000
Expenses	20%
Closing inventory at cost	600,000
Markdowns	2%
Inward transportation	30,000
Purchases	1,000,000
Net profit (5%)	300,000

6. Compute net sales and percent of markdowns for the data given below:

Markdowns	$ 40,000
Gross sales	400,000
Returns	32,000
Allowances	48,000

7. (a) What percentage markups on cost are equivalent to the following percentage markups on selling price: 20, 37½, 50, and 66⅔? (b) What percentage markups on selling price are equivalent to the following percentage markups on cost: 33⅓, 20, 40, and 50?

START

8. What net sales volume is required to obtain a stock-turn rate of 20 times a year on an average inventory at cost of $100,000 with a gross margin of 25 percent?

9. Explain how the general manager of a department store might use the markdown ratios computed for her various departments. Is this a fair measure? Of what?

10. Compare and contrast return on investment (ROI) and return on assets (ROA) measures. Which would be best for a retailer with no bank borrowing or other outside sources of funds; i.e., the retailer has put up all the money that the business needs?

11. Explain the difference between a forecast of market potential and a sales forecast.

12. Suggest a plausible explanation for sales fluctuations for (a) bicycles, (b) ice cream, (c) lawnmowers, (d) tennis rackets, (e) oats, (f) disposable diapers, and (g) latex for rubber-based paint.

13. Explain the factor method of forecasting. Illustrate your answer.

14. Based on data in Exhibit B–4, discuss the relative market potential of Reno and Las Vegas, Nevada, for: (a) prepared cereals, (b) automobiles, and (c) furniture.

PIMS Profit Impact of Market Strategy.
Started by GE in 1960. Now Harvard Marketing Science Institute. Now at Univ of Mass.

Look for commonalities among comps. that made those comps. successful. What do the firms do to be successful. Gathers + aggregates data to determine profitability. 450 firms contributing data represent 3000 SBU's (single biz units). A cross sectional study + longitudinal study (over long time) (many firms)

Appx 200 pcs per comp. Market condit., sales, share, comp, cost, degree of vertical integration, etc.
where a retailer may purchase a manufacturer

Large & small comps, US & international, wide range products candy to heavy equip.

Regression Analysis (drop some out)

Dependent Variable   Factors

Profitability = $X_1 + X_2 + X_3 \dots X_{200}$

Price Setting in the Business World

Chapter

17

When You Finish This Chapter, You Should

❶

Understand how most wholesalers and retailers set their prices—using markups.

❷

Understand why turnover is so important in pricing.

❸

Understand the advantages and disadvantages of average cost pricing.

❹

Know how to find the most profitable price and quantity for a marketing strategy.

❺

Know the many ways that price setters use demand estimates in their pricing.

❻

Understand the important new terms (shown in red).

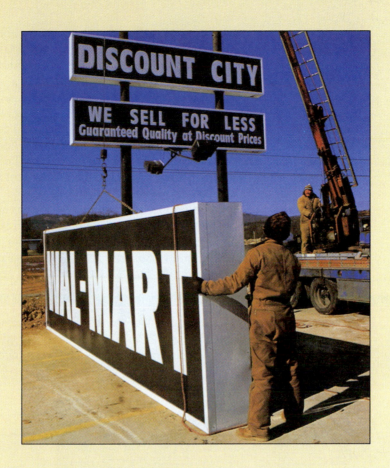

In 1991, Wal-Mart and Kmart, the two giant mass-merchandisers, both had similar sales volume. Although Wal-Mart generally had lower prices, it made about twice as much profit. It was also growing faster—with both sales and profits more than doubling between 1988 and 1992.

How could Wal-Mart have higher profits when it has about the same total sales as Kmart and is at the same time selling at lower prices? Part of the answer is that Wal-Mart has more sales volume *in each store*. Wal-Mart's $250 sales per square foot is almost twice Kmart's. Wal-Mart's lower prices increase demand. That also reduces its fixed operating costs as a percentage of sales. That means it can add a smaller markup, still cover its operating expenses, and make a larger profit. And as lower prices pull in more customers, its percent of overhead costs to sales continues to drop—from about 17.5 percent in 1985 to less than 16 percent now.

But Wal-Mart is not content to just add a standard percentage markup because it's convenient. The company was one of the first retailers to install computerized checkout counters that gave managers in every department in every store detailed sales reports. They dropped items that were collecting dust and put even lower prices on the items with the fastest turnover. That further cut inventory costs. The reports also list special VPIs (volume producing items). For example, Equate Baby Oil is a VPI in the pharmacy area. Each store gives its VPIs special display space—to get a bigger profit boost.

Wal-Mart's buyers are tough in negotiating prices with their suppliers. But Wal-Mart also works closely with producers to reduce costs in the channel. For example, Wal-Mart was one of the first major retailers to insist that all orders be placed by computer.

It also works with producers to create private-label brands, such as Sam's Choice Cola. Wal-Mart store managers wanted this store-brand to have an everyday low price about 15 percent below what consumers pay for Coke and Pepsi. They didn't expect it to make big profits but rather wanted it to draw customers into the stores. When customers come to buy the cola, they also pick up other—more profitable—products.

Many firms just add a standard markup to the average cost of the products they sell. But this is changing. More managers are realizing that they should set prices by evaluating the effect of a price decision not only on the profit margin for a given item but also on demand and therefore on sales volume and costs. In Wal-Mart's very competitive markets, this approach often leads to low prices that increase profits *and* at the same time reduce customers' costs. For firms in different market situations, careful price setting leads to a premium price for a marketing mix that offers customers something unique.[1]

PRICE SETTING IS A KEY STRATEGY DECISION

In the last chapter, we discussed the idea that pricing objectives and policies should guide pricing decisions. Now we'll see how the basic list price is set in the first place—based on information about costs, demand, and profit margins. See Exhibit 17–1.

Exhibit 17–1   Key Factors that Influence Price Setting

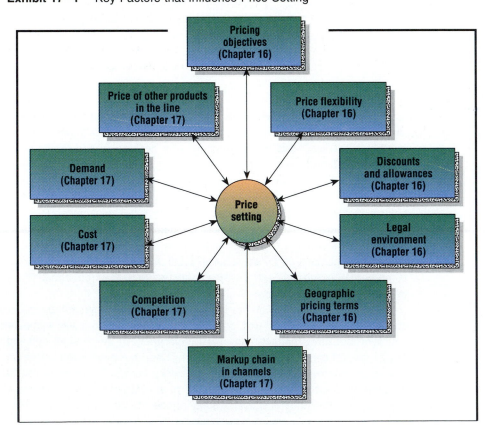

There are many ways to set list prices. But—for simplicity—they can be reduced to two basic approaches: *cost-oriented* and *demand-oriented* price setting. We will discuss cost-oriented approaches first because they are most common. Also, understanding the problems of relying on a cost-oriented approach shows why a marketing manager must also consider demand to make good price decisions. Let's begin by looking at how most retailers and wholesalers set cost-oriented prices.

SOME FIRMS JUST USE MARKUPS

Markups guide pricing by middlemen

Some firms—including most retailers and wholesalers—set prices by using a **markup**—a dollar amount added to the cost of products to get the selling price. For example, suppose that a Revco drugstore buys a bottle of Prell shampoo for $1. To make a profit, the drugstore obviously must sell the shampoo for more than $1. If it adds 50 cents to cover operating expenses and provide a profit, we say that the store is marking up the item 50 cents.

Markups, however, usually are stated as percentages rather than dollar amounts. And this is where confusion sometimes arises. Is a markup of 50 cents on a cost of $1 a markup of 50 percent? Or should the markup be figured as a percentage of the selling price—$1.50—and therefore be 33⅓ percent? A clear definition is necessary.

Markup percent is based on selling price— a convenient rule

Unless otherwise stated, **markup (percent)** means percentage of selling price that is added to the cost to get the selling price. So the 50-cent markup on the $1.50 selling price is a markup of 33⅓ percent. Markups are related to selling price for convenience.

There's nothing wrong with the idea of markup on cost. However, to avoid confusion, it's important to state clearly which markup percent you're using.

Managers often want to change a markup on cost to one based on selling price—or vice versa. The calculations used to do this are simple (see the section on markup conversion in Appendix B on marketing arithmetic—it follows Chapter 16).[2]

Products for which consumers do extensive comparisons put pressure on everyone in the channel to be more price competitive.

Many use a standard markup percent

Many middlemen select a standard markup percent and then apply it to all their products. This makes pricing easier. When you think of the large number of items the average retailer and wholesaler carry—and the small sales volume for many items—this approach may make sense. Spending the time to find the best price to charge on every item might not pay.

Markups are related to gross margins

How do managers decide on a standard markup in the first place? A standard markup is usually set close to the firm's *gross margin.* Managers regularly see gross margins on their operating (profit and loss) statements. (See Appendix B on marketing arithmetic if you are unfamiliar with these ideas.) Our Revco manager knows that there won't be any profit if the gross margin is not large enough. For this reason, Revco might accept a markup percent on Prell shampoo that is close to the store's usual gross margin.

Smart producers pay attention to the gross margins and standard markups of middlemen in their channel. They usually plan trade (functional) discounts similar to the standard markups these middlemen expect.

Markup chain may be used in channel pricing

Different firms in a channel often use different markups. A **markup chain**—the sequence of markups firms use at different levels in a channel—determines the price structure in the whole channel. The markup is figured on the *selling price* at each level of the channel.

For example, Black & Decker's selling price for an electric drill becomes the cost the Ace Hardware wholesaler pays. The wholesaler's selling price becomes the hardware retailer's cost. And this cost plus a retail markup becomes the retail selling price. Each markup should cover the costs of running the business—and leave a profit.

Exhibit 17–2 illustrates the markup chain for an electric drill at each level of the channel system. The production (factory) cost of the drill is $21.60. In this case, the producer takes a 10 percent markup and sells the product for $24. The markup is 10 percent of $24 or $2.40. The producer's selling price now becomes the wholesaler's cost—$24. If the wholesaler is used to taking a 20 percent markup on selling price, the markup is $6—and the wholesaler's selling price becomes $30. $30 now becomes the cost for the hardware retailer. The retailer, who is used to a 40 percent markup, adds $20, so the retail selling price becomes $50.

High markups don't always mean big profits

Some people—including many traditional retailers—think high markups mean big profits. Often this isn't true. A high markup may result in a price that's too high—a price at which few customers will buy. And you can't earn much if you don't sell much—no matter how high your markup on a single item. So high markups may lead to low profits.

Exhibit 17–2 Example of a Markup Chain and Channel Pricing

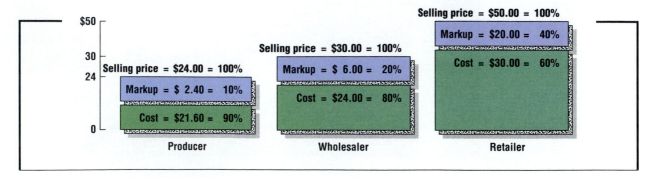

Lower markups can speed turnover—and the stockturn rate

Some retailers and wholesalers, however, try to speed turnover to increase profit—even if this means reducing their markups. They realize that a business runs up costs over time. If they can sell a much greater amount in the same time period, they may be able to take a lower markup—and still earn higher profits at the end of the period.

An important idea here is the **stockturn rate**—the number of times the average inventory is sold in a year. Various methods of figuring stockturn rates can be used (see the section "Computing the Stockturn Rate" in Appendix B). A low stockturn rate may be bad for profits.

At the very least, a low stockturn increases inventory carrying cost and ties up working capital. If a firm with a stockturn of 1 (once per year) sells products that cost it $100,000, it has that much tied up in inventory all the time. But a stockturn of 5 requires only $20,000 worth of inventory ($100,000 cost ÷ 5 turnovers a year).

Whether a stockturn rate is high or low depends on the industry and the product involved. A NAPA auto parts wholesaler may expect an annual rate of 1—while an A&P store might expect 10 to 12 stockturns for soaps and detergents and 50 to 60 stockturns for fresh fruits and vegetables.

Mass-merchandisers run in fast company

Although some middlemen use the same standard markup percent on all their products, this policy ignores the importance of fast turnover. Mass-merchandisers know this. They put low markups on fast-selling items and higher markups on items that sell less frequently. For example, Wal-Mart may put a small markup on fast-selling health and beauty aids (like toothpaste or shampoo) but higher markups on appliances and clothing.

Where does the markup chain start?

Some markups eventually become standard in a trade. Most channel members tend to follow a similar process—adding a certain percentage to the previous price. But who sets price in the first place?

The firm that brands a product is usually the one that sets its basic list price. It may be a large retailer, a large wholesaler, or, most often, the producer.

Some producers just start with a cost per unit figure and add a markup—perhaps a standard markup—to obtain their selling price. Or they may use some rule-of-thumb formula such as:

$$\text{Selling price} = \text{Average production cost per unit} \times 3$$

A producer who uses this approach might develop rules and markups related to its own costs and objectives. Yet even the first step—selecting the appropriate cost per unit to build on—isn't easy. Let's discuss several approaches to see how cost-oriented price setting really works.

Items with a high stockturn rate may have a lower markup.

AVERAGE-COST PRICING IS COMMON AND DANGEROUS

Average-cost pricing means adding a reasonable markup to the average cost of a product. A manager usually finds the average cost per unit by studying past records. Dividing the total cost for the last year by all the units produced and sold in that period gives an estimate of the average cost per unit for the next year. If the cost was $32,000 for all labor and materials and $30,000 for fixed overhead expenses—such as selling expenses, rent, and manager salaries—then the total cost is $62,000. If the company produced 40,000 items in that time period, the average cost is $62,000 divided by 40,000 units, or $1.55 per unit. To get the price, the producer decides what "target" profit per unit to add to the average cost per unit. If the company considers 45 cents a reasonable profit for each unit, it sets the new price at $2.00. Exhibit 17–3A shows that this approach produces the desired profit—if the company sells 40,000 units.

It does not make allowances for cost variations as output changes

Average-cost pricing is simple. But it can also be dangerous. It's easy to lose money with average-cost pricing. To see why, let's follow this example further.

First, remember that the average cost of $2.00 per unit was based on 40,000 units. But if the firm is only able to produce and sell 20,000 units in the next year, it may be in trouble. Twenty thousand units sold at $2.00 each ($1.55 cost plus 45 cents for expected profit) yield a total revenue of only $40,000. The overhead is still fixed at $30,000, and the variable material and labor cost drops by half to $16,000—for a total cost of $46,000. This means a loss of $6,000, or 30 cents a unit. The method that was supposed to allow a profit of 45 cents a unit actually causes a loss of 30 cents a unit! See Exhibit 17–3B.

The basic problem with the average-cost approach is that it doesn't consider cost variations at different levels of output. In a typical situation, costs are high with low output, and then economies of scale set in—the average cost per unit drops as the quantity

Exhibit 17–3   Results of Average-Cost Pricing

A. Calculation of Planned Profit if 40,000 Items Are Sold		B. Calculation of Actual Profit if Only 20,000 Items Are Sold	
Calculation of Costs:		**Calculation of Costs:**	
Fixed overhead expenses	$30,000	Fixed overhead expenses	$30,000
Labor and materials	32,000	Labor and materials	16,000
Total costs	$62,000	Total costs	$46,000
"Planned" target profit	18,000		
Total costs and planned profit	$80,000		
Calculation of profit (or loss):		**Calculation of profit (or loss):**	
Actual unit sales × price ($2.00)*	$80,000	Actual unit sales × price ($2.00)*	$40,000
Minus: total costs	62,000	Minus: total costs	46,000
Profit (loss)	$18,000	Profit (loss)	($6,000)
Result:		**Result:**	
Planned profit of $18,000 is earned if 40,000 items are sold at $2.00 each.		Planned profit of $18,000 is not earned. Instead, $6,000 loss results if 20,000 items are sold at $2.00 each.	

*Calculation of "reasonable" price: $\dfrac{\text{Expected total costs and planned profit}}{\text{Planned number of items to be sold}} = \dfrac{\$80,000}{40,000} = \$2.00$

ARE WOMEN CONSUMERS BEING TAKEN TO THE CLEANERS?

Diane Dunlap was annoyed when a local laundry charged more to wash and iron her white blouses than to clean her husband's white shirts. Actually, she was more than just annoyed. She telephoned 61 cleaners and asked each one's price to launder a no-frills, white oxford cotton blouse the same style and size as a man's shirt. Twenty-one of them quoted higher prices for blouses. Then she did an experiment. She cut the label out of a blouse, sewed in the label for a man's shirt, and took the blouse to the cleaner along with three of her husband's shirts. The cleaner charged her $1.25. Later she did the same thing but with a blouse that had the original label. The cleaner charged her $2.25. Dunlap feels that the cleaners' pricing is unethical—that they are discriminating against women and charging arbitrarily higher prices. She wants her local city government to pass an ordinance that prohibits laundry and dry-cleaning businesses from discriminatory pricing based on gender.

The president of the Association of Launderers and Cleaners in Dunlap's state has a different view. "The automated equipment we use fits a certain range of standardized shirts," he said. "A lot of women's blouses have different kinds of trim, different kinds of buttons, and lots of braid work, and it all has to be hand-finished. If it involves hand-finishing, we charge more." In other words, some cleaners charge more for doing women's blouses because the average cost is higher than the average cost for men's shirts. Of course, the cost of cleaning and ironing any specific shirt may be higher or lower than the average.

A consumer-protection specialist in the attorney general's office in Dunlap's state said that there were no federal or state laws to regulate what the cleaners could charge. She said that customers who don't like a particular cleaner's rates are free to visit a competitor who may charge less.

Many firms face the problem of how to set prices when the costs are different to serve different customers. For example, poor, inner-city consumers often pay higher prices for food. But inner-city retailers also face higher average costs for facilities, shoplifting, and insurance. Some firms don't like to charge different consumers different prices, but they also don't want to charge everyone a higher average price—to cover the expense of serving high-cost customers.[3]

produced increases. This is why mass production and mass distribution often make sense. It's also why it's important to develop a better understanding of the different types of costs a marketing manager should consider when setting a price.

MARKETING MANAGER MUST CONSIDER VARIOUS KINDS OF COSTS

Average-cost pricing may lead to losses because there are a variety of costs—and each changes in a *different* way as output changes. Any pricing method that uses cost must consider these changes. To understand why, we need to define six types of costs.

There are three kinds of total cost

1. **Total fixed cost** is the sum of those costs that are fixed in total—no matter how much is produced. Among these fixed costs are rent, depreciation, managers' salaries, property taxes, and insurance. Such costs stay the same even if production stops temporarily.

2. **Total variable cost**, on the other hand, is the sum of those changing expenses that are closely related to output—expenses for parts, wages, packaging materials, outgoing freight, and sales commissions.

Average fixed costs are lower when a larger quantity is produced.

At zero output, total variable cost is zero. As output increases, so do variable costs. If Wrangler doubles its output of jeans in a year, its total cost for denim cloth also (roughly) doubles.

3. **Total cost** is the sum of total fixed and total variable costs. Changes in total cost depend on variations in total variable cost—since total fixed cost stays the same.

There are three kinds of average cost

The pricing manager usually is more interested in cost per unit than total cost because prices are usually quoted per unit.

1. **Average cost** (per unit) is obtained by dividing total cost by the related quantity (that is, the total quantity that causes the total cost).
2. **Average fixed cost** (per unit) is obtained by dividing total fixed cost by the related quantity.
3. **Average variable cost** (per unit) is obtained by dividing total variable cost by the related quantity.

An example shows cost relations

A good way to get a feel for these different types of costs is to extend our average-cost pricing example (Exhibit 17–3A). Exhibit 17–4 shows the six types of cost and how they vary at different levels of output. The line for 40,000 units is highlighted because that was the expected level of sales in our average-cost pricing example. For simplicity, we assume that average variable cost is the same for each unit. Notice, however, that total variable cost increases when quantity increases.

Exhibit 17–5 shows the three average cost curves from Exhibit 17–4. Notice that average fixed cost goes down steadily as the quantity increases. Although the average variable cost remains the same, average cost decreases continually too. This is because average fixed cost is decreasing. With these relations in mind, let's reconsider the problem with average-cost pricing.

Exhibit 17–4   Cost Structure of a Firm

Quantity (Q)	Total Fixed Costs (TFC)	Average Fixed Costs (AFC)	Average Variable Costs (AVC)	Total Variable Costs (TVC)	Total Cost (TC)	Average Cost (AC)
0	$30,000	—	—	—	$ 30,000	—
10,000	30,000	$3.00	$0.80	$ 8,000	38,000	$3.80
20,000	30,000	1.50	0.80	16,000	46,000	2.30
30,000	30,000	1.00	0.80	24,000	54,000	1.80
40,000	30,000	0.75	0.80	32,000	62,000	1.55
50,000	30,000	0.60	0.80	40,000	70,000	1.40
60,000	30,000	0.50	0.80	48,000	78,000	1.30
70,000	30,000	0.43	0.80	56,000	86,000	1.23
80,000	30,000	0.38	0.80	64,000	94,000	1.18
90,000	30,000	0.33	0.80	72,000	102,000	1.13
100,000	30,000	0.30	0.80	80,000	110,000	1.10

$$\begin{bmatrix} 110,000 \ (TC) \\ -80,000 \ (TVC) \\ \hline 30,000 \ (TFC) \end{bmatrix} \quad (Q)\ 100,000 \overline{\begin{array}{l} 0.30\ (AFC) \\ 30,000\ (TFC) \\ \hline 0.80\ (AVC) \end{array}} \quad \begin{bmatrix} 100,000\ (Q) \\ \times 0.80\ (AVC) \\ \hline 80,000\ (TVC) \end{bmatrix} \quad \begin{bmatrix} 30,000\ (TFC) \\ +80,000\ (TVC) \\ \hline 110,000\ (TC) \end{bmatrix} \quad (Q)\ 100,000 \overline{\begin{array}{l} 1.10\ (AC) \\ 110,000\ (TC) \end{array}}$$

Ignoring demand is the major weakness of average-cost pricing

Average-cost pricing works well if the firm actually sells the quantity it used to set the average cost price. Losses may result, however, if actual sales are much lower than expected. On the other hand, if sales are much higher than expected, then profits may be very good. But this will only happen by luck—because the firm's demand is much larger than expected.

To use average-cost pricing, a marketing manager must make *some* estimate of the quantity to be sold in the coming period. Without a quantity estimate, it isn't possible to compute average cost. But unless this quantity is related to price—that is, unless the firm's

Exhibit 17–5   Typical Shape of Cost (per unit) Curves when AVC Is Assumed Constant per Unit

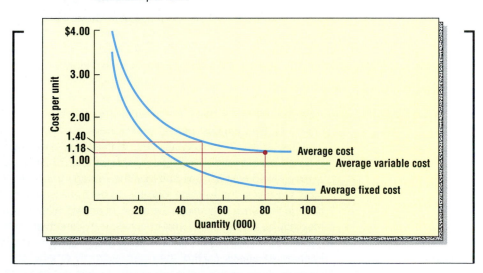

Exhibit 17–6   Evaluation of Various Prices along a Firm's Demand Curve

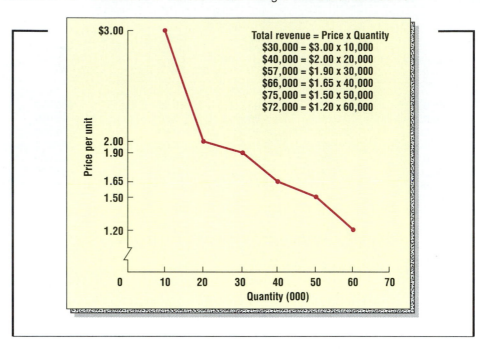

demand curve is considered—the marketing manager may set a price that doesn't even cover a firm's total cost! You saw this happen in Exhibit 17–3B, when the firm's price of $2.00 resulted in demand for only 20,000 units—and a loss of $6,000.

The demand curve is still important even if management doesn't take time to think about it. For example, Exhibit 17–6 shows the demand curve for the firm we're discussing. This demand curve shows *why* the firm lost money when it tried to use average-cost pricing. At the $2.00 price, quantity demanded is only 20,000. With this demand curve and the costs in Exhibit 17–4, the firm will incur a loss whether management sets the price at a high of $3 or a low of $1.20. At $3, the firm will sell only 10,000 units for a total revenue of $30,000. But total cost will be $38,000—for a loss of $8,000. At the $1.20 price, it will sell 60,000 units—at a loss of $6,000. However, the curve suggests that at a price of $1.65 consumers will demand about 40,000 units, producing a profit of about $4,000.

In short, average-cost pricing is simple in theory—but often fails in practice. In stable situations, prices set by this method may yield profits—but not necessarily *maximum* profits. And note that such cost-based prices may be higher than a price that would be more profitable for the firm—as shown in Exhibit 17–6. When demand conditions are changing, average-cost pricing is even more risky.

Exhibit 17–7 summarizes the relationships discussed above. Cost-oriented pricing requires an estimate of the total number of units to be sold. That estimate determines the *average* fixed cost per unit and thus the average total cost. Then the firm adds the desired profit per unit to the average total cost to get the cost-oriented selling price. How customers react to that price determines the actual quantity the firm will be able to sell. But that quantity may not be the quantity used to compute the average cost! Further, the quantity the firm actually sells (times price) determines total revenue (and total profit or loss). A decision made in one area affects each of the others—directly or indirectly. Average-cost pricing does not consider these effects.[4] A manager who forgets this can make serious pricing mistakes.

Exhibit 17–7   Summary of Relationships among Quantity, Cost, and Price Using Cost-oriented Pricing

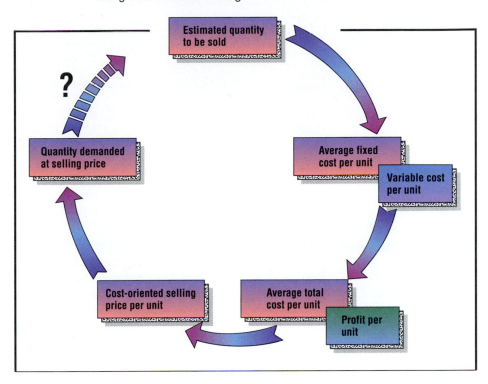

FINDING THE MOST PROFITABLE PRICE AND QUANTITY TO PRODUCE

Marketing managers must choose only one price (for a time period). The problem is which price to choose. The price, of course, sets the quantity customers will buy.

To maximize profit, marketing managers should choose the price that will lead to the greatest difference between total revenue and total cost. To find the best price and quantity, they need to estimate the firm's demand curve. A practical approach here is to list a wide range of possible prices. Then, for each price, they estimate the quantity that might be sold. You can think of this as a summary of the answers to a series of what-if questions—*what* quantity will be sold *if* a particular price is selected? By multiplying each price by its related quantity, marketing managers can find the total revenue for that price. Then they estimate the firm's likely costs at each of the quantities. Finally, they get the profit for each price and quantity by subtracting the related total cost from the total revenue. See Exhibit 17–8 for an example.

In Exhibit 17–9, which graphs the data from Exhibit 17–8, you can see that the best price is the one that has the greatest distance between the total revenue and total cost curves. In this example, the best price is $79. At that price, the related quantity is 6 units, and profit would be $106.

A profit range is reassuring

Estimating the quantity a firm might sell at each price isn't easy. But we need some estimate of the demand to set prices. This is just one of the tough jobs a marketing manager faces. Ignoring demand curves doesn't make them go away! So some estimates must be made.

Exhibit 17–8   Revenue, Cost, and Profit for an Individual Firm

(1) Price P	(2) Quantity Q	(3) Total Revenue TR	(4) Total Cost TC	(5) Profit (TR–TC)
$150	0	$ 0	$200	$–200
140	1	140	296	–156
130	2	260	316	– 56
117	3	351	331	+ 20
105	4	420	344	+ 76
92	5	460	355	+105
79	6	474	368	+106
66	7	462	383	+ 79
53	8	424	423	+ 1
42	9	378	507	–129
31	10	310	710	–400

Note that demand estimates don't have to be exact. Exhibit 17–10 shows that there is a range of profitable prices. The price that would result in the highest profit is $79, but this strategy would be profitable all the way from a price of $53 to $117.

The marketing manager should try to estimate the best price—the one that earns the highest profit. But a slight miss doesn't mean failure. The effort of trying to estimate demand will probably lead to being some place in the range. In contrast, mechanical use of average-cost pricing could lead to a price that is much too high—or much too low. This is why estimating demand isn't just desirable—it's essential.[5]

Exhibit 17–9   Graphic Determination of the Price Giving the Greatest Total Profit for a Firm

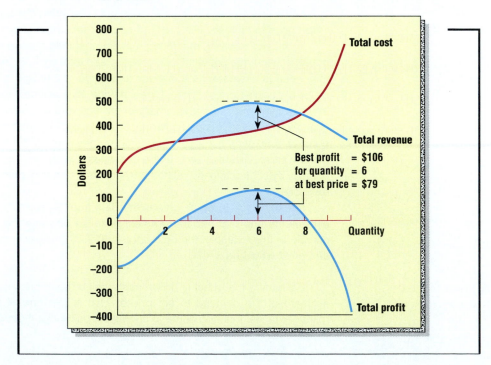

Exhibit 17–10   Range of Profitable Prices for Illustrative Data in Exhibits 17–8 and 17–9

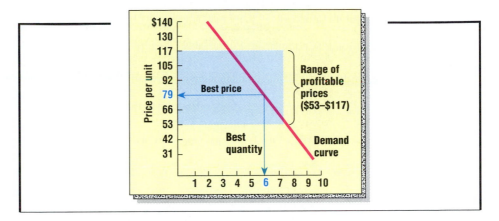

DEMAND-ORIENTED APPROACHES FOR SETTING PRICES

Value in use pricing—how much will the customer save?

Organizational buyers think about how a purchase will affect their total costs. Many marketers who aim at business markets keep this in mind when estimating demand and setting prices. They use **value in use pricing**—which means setting prices that will capture some of what customers will save by substituting the firm's product for the one currently being used.

For example, a producer of computer-controlled machines used to assemble cars knows that the machine doesn't just replace a standard machine. It also reduces labor costs, quality control costs, and—after the car is sold—costs of warranty repairs or dissatisfied customers. The marketer can estimate what each auto producer will save by using the machine—and then set a price that makes it less expensive for the auto producer to buy the computerized machine than to stick with the old methods. The number of

Value in use pricing considers what a customer will save by buying a product.

customers who have different levels of potential savings also provides some idea about the shape of the demand curve.[6]

Customers may have reference prices

Some people don't devote much thought to what they pay for the products they buy—including some frequently purchased goods and services. But most consumers have a **reference price**—the price they expect to pay—for many of the products they purchase. And different customers may have different reference prices for the same basic type of purchase. For example, a person who really enjoys reading might have a higher reference price for a popular paperback book than another person who is only an occasional reader. Marketing research can sometimes identify different segments with different reference prices.[7]

Leader pricing—make it low to attract customers

Leader pricing means setting some very low prices—real bargains—to get customers into retail stores. The idea is not to sell large quantities of the leader items but to get customers into the store to buy other products.[8] Certain products are picked for their promotion value and priced low—but above cost. In food stores, the leader prices are the "specials" that are advertised regularly to give an image of low prices. Leader items are usually well-known, widely used items that customers don't stock heavily—milk, butter, eggs, or coffee—but on which they will recognize a real price cut. In other words, leader pricing is normally used with products for which consumers do have a specific reference price.

Leader pricing may try to appeal to customers who normally shop elsewhere. But it can backfire if customers buy only the low-price leaders. To avoid hurting profits, managers often select leader items that aren't directly competitive with major lines—as when bargain-priced recording tape is the leader for a stereo equipment store.

Bait pricing—offer a steal, but sell under protest

Bait pricing is setting some very low prices to attract customers—but trying to sell more expensive models or brands once the customer is in the store. For example, a furniture store may advertise a color TV for $199. But once bargain hunters come to the store, salesclerks point out the disadvantages of the low-price TV and try to convince them to trade up to a better (and more expensive) set. Bait pricing is something like leader pricing. But here the seller *doesn't* plan to sell many at the low price.

If bait pricing is successful, the demand for higher-quality products expands. This approach may be a sensible part of a strategy to trade-up customers. And customers may be well served if—once in the store—they find a higher-priced product offers features better suited to their needs. But bait pricing is also criticized as unethical.

? Is bait pricing ethical?

Extremely aggressive and sometimes dishonest bait-pricing advertising has given this method a bad reputation. Some stores make it very difficult to buy the bait item. The Federal Trade Commission considers this type of bait pricing a deceptive act and has banned its use in interstate commerce. Even Sears, one of the nation's most trusted retail chains, has been criticized for bait-and-switch pricing. But some unethical retailers who operate only within one state continue to advertise bait prices on products they won't sell.

Psychological pricing—some prices just seem right

Psychological pricing means setting prices that have special appeal to target customers. Some people think there are whole ranges of prices that potential customers see as the same. So price cuts in these ranges do not increase the quantity sold. But just below this range, customers may buy more. Then, at even lower prices, the quantity demanded stays the same again—and so on. Exhibit 17–11 shows the kind of demand curve that leads to psychological pricing. Vertical drops mark the price ranges that customers see as the same. Pricing research shows that there *are* such demand curves.[9]

Exhibit 17–11 Demand Curve when Psychological Pricing Is Appropriate

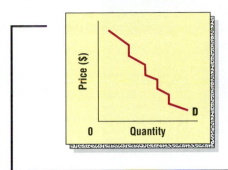

Exhibit 17–12 Demand Curve Showing a Prestige Pricing Situation

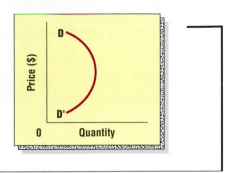

Odd-even pricing is setting prices that end in certain numbers. For example, products selling below $50 often end in the number 5 or the number 9—such as 49 cents or $24.95. Prices for higher-priced products are often $1 or $2 below the next even dollar figure—such as $99 rather than $100. Some marketers use odd-even pricing because they think consumers react better to these prices—perhaps seeing them as "substantially" lower than the next highest even price. Marketers using these prices seem to assume that they have a rather jagged demand curve—that slightly higher prices will substantially reduce the quantity demanded. Long ago, some retailers used odd-even prices to force their clerks to make change. Then the clerks had to record the sale and could not pocket the money. Today, however, it's not always clear why firms use these prices—or whether they really work. Perhaps it's done simply because everyone else does it.[10]

Prestige pricing indicates quality

Prestige pricing is setting a rather high price to suggest high quality or high status. Some target customers want the best, so they will buy at a high price. But if the price seems cheap, they worry about quality and don't buy.[11] Prestige pricing is most common for luxury products—such as jewelry and perfume.

It is also common in service industries—where the customer can't see the product in advance and relies on price to judge its quality. Target customers who respond to prestige pricing give the marketing manager an unusual demand curve. Instead of a normal down-sloping curve, the curve goes down for a while and then bends back to the left again. See Exhibit 17–12.

Price lining—a few prices cover the field

Price lining is setting a few price levels for a product line and then marking all items at these prices. This approach assumes that customers have a certain reference price in mind that they expect to pay for a product. For example, most neckties are priced between $10 and $40. In price lining, there are only a few prices within this range. Ties will not be priced at $10.00, $10.50, $11.00, and so on. They might be priced at four levels—$10, $20, $30, and $40.

Price lining has advantages other than just matching prices to what consumers expect to pay. The main advantage is simplicity—for both clerks and customers. It is less confusing than having many prices. Some customers may consider items in only one price class. Their big decision, then, is which item(s) to choose at that price.

Demand-backward pricing

Demand-backward pricing is setting an acceptable final consumer price and working backward to what a producer can charge. It is commonly used by producers of final consumer products—especially shopping products, such as women's and children's

Prestige pricing is most common for luxury products such as jewelry and perfume.

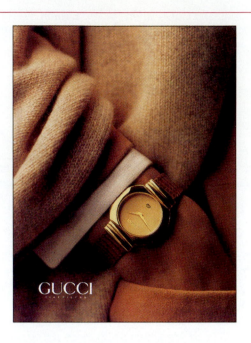

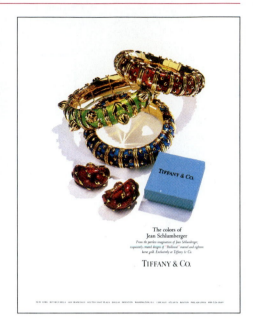

clothing and shoes. It is also used for toys or gifts for which customers will spend a specific amount—because they are seeking a $5 or a $10 gift. Here a reverse cost-plus pricing process is used. This method has been called market-minus pricing.

The producer starts with the retail (reference) price for a particular item and then works backward—subtracting the typical margins that channel members expect. This gives the approximate price the producer can charge. Then the average or planned marketing expenses can be subtracted from this price to find how much can be spent producing the item. Candy companies do this. They alter the size of the candy bar to keep the bar at the expected price.

Demand estimates are needed for demand-backward pricing to be successful. The quantity that will be demanded affects production costs—that is, where the firm will be on its average cost curve.

PRICING A FULL LINE

Our emphasis has been—and will continue to be—on the problem of pricing an individual product mainly because this makes our discussion clearer. But most marketing managers are responsible for more than one product. In fact, their product may be the whole company line! So we'll discuss this matter briefly.

Full-line pricing—market- or firm-oriented?

Full-line pricing is setting prices for a whole line of products. How to do this depends on which of two basic situations a firm is facing.

In one case, all products in the company's line are aimed at the same general target market, which makes it important for all prices to be related. For example, a producer of TV sets can offer several price and quality levels to give its target customers some choice. The different prices should appear reasonable when the target customers are evaluating them.

In the other case, the different products in the line are aimed at entirely different target markets so there doesn't have to be any relation between the various prices. A chemical

Demand-backward pricing starts with the retail price for a particular item and then works backward—subtracting the typical margins that channel members expect.

producer of a wide variety of products with several target markets, for example, probably should price each product separately.

Cost is not much help in full-line pricing

The marketing manager must try to recover all costs on the whole line—perhaps by pricing quite low on competitive items and much higher on less competitive items. Estimating costs for each product is a big problem because there is no single right way to assign a company's fixed costs to each of the products. Further, if any cost-oriented pricing method is carried through without considering demand, it can lead to very unrealistic prices. To avoid mistakes, the marketing manager should judge demand for the whole line as well as demand for each individual product in each target market.

Complementary product pricing

Complementary product pricing is setting prices on several products as a group. This may lead to one product being priced very low so that the profits from another product will increase—and increase the product group's total profits. A new Gillette shaver, for example, may be priced low to sell the blades, which must be replaced regularly.

Complementary product pricing differs from full-line pricing because different production facilities may be involved—so there's no cost allocation problem. Instead, the problem is really understanding the target market and the demand curves for each of the complementary products. Then various combinations of prices can be tried to see what set will be best for reaching the company's pricing objectives.

Product-bundle pricing—one price for several products

A firm that offers its target market several different products may use **product-bundle pricing**—setting one price for a set of products. Firms that use product-bundle pricing usually set the overall price so that it's cheaper for the customer to buy the products at the same time rather than separately. Drugstores sometimes bundle the cost of a roll of film and the cost of the processing. A bank may offer a product-bundle price for a safe deposit box, travelers checks, and a saving account. Bundling encourages customers to spend more and buy products that they might not otherwise buy—because the "added cost" of the extras is not as high as it would normally be.

Most firms that use product-bundle pricing also set individual prices for the unbundled products. This may increase demand by attracting customers who want one item in a product assortment but don't want the extras. Many firms treat services this way. A software company may have a product-bundle price for its software and access to a toll-free telephone assistance service. However, customers who don't need help can pay a lower price and get just the software.[12]

BID PRICING AND NEGOTIATED PRICING DEPEND HEAVILY ON COSTS

A new price for every job

Bid pricing means offering a specific price for each possible job rather than setting a price that applies for all customers. Building contractors, for example, must bid on possible projects. And many companies selling services (like cleaning or data processing) must submit bids for jobs they would like to have.

The big problem in bid pricing is estimating all the costs that will apply to each job. This may sound easy, but a complicated bid may involve thousands of cost components. Further, management must include an overhead charge and a charge for profit.

Sometimes it isn't even possible to figure out costs in advance. This may lead to a contract where the customer agrees to pay the supplier's total cost plus an agreed-on profit figure (say, 10 percent of costs or a dollar amount)—after the job is finished.

? Ethical issues in cost-plus bid pricing

Some unethical sellers give bid prices based on cost-plus contracts a bad reputation by faking their records to make costs seem higher than they really are. In other cases, there may be honest debate about what costs should be allowed.

Demand must be considered too

Competition must be considered when adding in overhead and profit for a bid price. Usually, the customer will get several bids and accept the lowest one. So unthinking addition of typical overhead and profit rates should be avoided. Some bidders use the same overhead and profit rates on all jobs—regardless of competition—and then are surprised when they don't get some jobs.[13]

Negotiated prices— what will a specific customer pay?

Sometimes a customer asks for bids and then singles out the company that submits the *most attractive* bid—not necessarily the lowest—for further bargaining. What the customer will buy—if the customer buys at all—depends on the **negotiated price**, a price set based on bargaining between the buyer and seller. As with simple bid pricing, negotiated pricing is most common in situations where the marketing mix is adjusted for each customer—so bargaining may involve the whole marketing mix, not just the price level.

Sellers must know their costs to negotiate prices effectively. However, negotiated pricing *is* a demand-oriented approach. Here, the seller is very carefully analyzing a particular customer's position on a demand curve—or on different possible demand curves based on different offerings—rather than the overall demand curve for a group of customers.

CONCLUSION

In this chapter, we discussed various approaches to price setting. Generally, retailers and wholesalers use traditional markups. Some use the same markups for all their items. Others find that varying the markups increases turnover and profit. In other words, they consider demand and competition!

Many firms use average-cost pricing to help set their prices. But this approach sometimes ignores demand completely. A more realistic approach to average-cost pricing requires a sales forecast—maybe just assuming that sales in the next period will be roughly the same as in the last period. This approach *does* enable the marketing manager to set a price—but the price may or may not cover all costs and earn the desired profit.

The major difficulty with demand-oriented pricing is estimating the demand curve. But experienced managers—aided perhaps by marketing research—can estimate the nature of demand for their products. Such estimates are useful—even if they aren't exact. They get you thinking in the right ballpark. Sometimes, when all you need is a decision about raising or lowering price, even rough demand estimates can be very revealing. Further, a firm's demand curve does not cease to exist simply because it's ignored. Some information is better than none at all. And it appears that some marketers do consider demand in their pricing. We see this with value in use pricing, leader pricing, bait pricing, odd-even pricing, psychological pricing, full-line pricing, and even bid pricing.

Throughout the book, we stress that firms must consider the customer before they do anything. This certainly applies to pricing. It means that when managers are setting a price, they have to consider what customers will be willing to pay. This isn't always easy. But it's nice to know that there is a profit range around the best price. Therefore, even rough estimates about what potential customers will buy at various prices will probably lead to a better price than mechanical use of traditional markups or cost-oriented formulas.

While our focus in this chapter is on price setting, it's clear that pricing decisions must consider the cost of offering the whole marketing mix. Smart marketers don't just accept costs as a given. Target marketers always look for ways to be more efficient—to reduce costs while improving what they offer customers.[14]

QUESTIONS AND PROBLEMS

1. Why do many department stores seek a markup of about 40 percent when some discount houses operate on a 20 percent markup?

2. A producer distributed its riding lawnmowers through wholesalers and retailers. The retail selling price was $800, and the manufacturing cost to the company was $312. The retail markup was 35 percent and the wholesale markup 20 percent. (*a*) What was the cost to the wholesaler? To the retailer? (*b*) What percentage markup did the producer take?

3. Relate the concept of stock turnover to the growth of mass-merchandising. Use a simple example in your answer.

4. If total fixed costs are $200,000 and total variable costs are $100,000 at the output of 20,000 units, what are the probable total fixed costs and total variable costs at an output of 10,000 units? What are the average fixed costs, average variable costs, and average costs at these two output levels? Explain what additional information you would want to determine what price should be charged.

5. Construct an example showing that mechanical use of a very large or very small markup might still lead to unprofitable operation while some intermediate price would be profitable.

6. Discuss the idea of drawing separate demand curves for different market segments. It seems logical because each target market should have its own marketing mix. But won't this lead to many demand curves and possible prices? And what will this mean with respect to functional discounts and varying prices in the marketplace? Will it be legal? Will it be practical?

7. How does a prestige pricing policy fit into a marketing mix? Would exclusive distribution be necessary?

8. Cite a local example of odd-even pricing and evaluate whether it makes sense.

9. Cite a local example of psychological pricing and evaluate whether it makes sense.

10. Distinguish between leader pricing and bait pricing. What do they have in common? How can their use affect a marketing mix?

11. Is a full-line pricing policy available only to producers? Cite local examples of full-line pricing. Why is full-line pricing important?

SUGGESTED CASES

22. Texco, Inc.

29. Dalton Olds, Inc.

COMPUTER-AIDED PROBLEM

17. Price Setting

Lazar Forino, marketing manager for Tool Technologies, Inc. (TTI), is considering a new opportunity. TTI designs specialized tools for industrial customers. Recently TTI developed a new design for an electric drill. Forino is considering producing the safer-to-use drill for the consumer market. Two retail chains—Tool Depot and D.I.Y. Hardware—have expressed interest in carrying the product and selling it under their own brand names. Forino must decide which chain TTI should work with and what price to charge.

D.I.Y. Hardware is a chain of traditional hardware stores that caters to do-it-yourself homeowners. D.I.Y. uses a 40 percent markup on tools. On the other hand, Tool Depot carries only tools—and sells all of its tools at a "discount" price. Tool Depot usually uses a 33 percent markup. In both cases, markup percents are based on selling price.

Forino estimates that either chain might sell about 3,000 drills the first year. But, he knows that demand for the drill—and the actual number sold by either chain—would depend on the retail selling price. Forino also thinks that sales of the drill will depend on the promotion effort that the retailers will devote to the drill—and that effort will be affected by how much the retailer will earn by handling the drills.

Forino knows that there are limitations to average-cost pricing, but he also thinks that analyzing costs—and the desired profit level from selling the drill—will help him to evaluate pricing possibilities. He estimates that the fixed cost of producing the new drill would be $24,000, and that the average variable production cost per drill would be $16. In the first year, Forino would like to make about $18,000 profit from sales of the drill.

To assist with his analysis, Forino has set up a spreadsheet that computes the price he would need to charge—based on his quantity estimate—to cover his costs and earn his desired profit. The spreadsheet also computes the retail price that would result from the retailer's markup and the total markup dollars the retailer would earn by carrying the product. Finally, the spreadsheet can be used to analyze how costs, revenue and profit might change if the actual demand varies from his initial sales quantity estimate.

a. Given Forino's estimated sales quantity of 3,000 units and his $18,000 profit objective—as shown on the initial spreadsheet—what retail price would D.I.Y. charge? What retail price would Tool Depot charge? Using information from the spreadsheet, calculate the markup percent (on selling price) TTI would earn if it sells 3,000 units. Show your work and label your calculations.

b. If TTI were to set a price based on the 3,000-unit estimate, but Tool Depot could actually sell 3,300 drills, how would TTI's actual profit differ from its planned profit? If D.I.Y. could only sell 2,400 drills—because of its higher retail price—what would happen to TTI's planned profit? Briefly discuss the implications of these results.

c. Forino is thinking about selling the drill through Tool Depot. He is interested in seeing how the estimate of TTI's average fixed cost per unit might change for estimates of quantity sold ranging between 2,800 and 3,800. He is also interested in how the different quantity sold estimates might effect TTI's price and Tool Depot's price. Do a What If analysis to prepare a table that summarizes this information and then discuss the pattern you observe.

d. Forino is thinking about setting a price assuming that Tool Depot will sell 3,300 units. However, he thinks that actual demand (units sold) at that price might be as low as 3,000 units and as high as 3,600 units. How would TTI's actual profit differ from the desired profit over that range? How would Tool Depot's total dollar markup (from TTI drill sales) vary over this same range? Prepare a table summarizing the analysis and discuss the results.

For additional questions related to this problem, see Exercise 17–3 in the *Learning Aid for use with Essentials of Marketing,* 6th edition.

Ethical Marketing in a Consumer-Oriented World: Appraisal and Challenges

Chapter

When You Finish This Chapter, You Should

❶

Understand why marketing must be evaluated differently at the micro and macro levels.

❷

Understand why the text argues that micro-marketing sometimes costs too much.

❸

Understand how quality management approaches can help make implementation of micro-marketing more effective.

❹

Understand why the text argues that macro-marketing does not cost too much.

❺

Know some of the challenges marketers face as they work to develop ethical marketing strategies that serve consumers' needs.

(M) ore than ever, the macro-marketing systems of the world are interconnected. The collapse of communism and the worldwide drive toward market-directed economies is dramatic evidence that consumer-citizens want freedom and choices—not only in politics but in markets. Centrally planned economies simply weren't able to meet needs.

Although there's much talk about the world as a global village, we're not there yet. People in a *real* village on the plains of Niger may be able to crowd around a TV and glimpse the life that we enjoy, but for them it isn't real. What is real is their struggle to meet the basic physical needs of life—to survive starvation, malnutrition, and epidemics. The plight of consumers doesn't seem quite as severe in the fragile and emerging democracies, like those in Latin America and Eastern Europe. But the vast majority of consumer-citizens in those societies can only wonder if they'll ever have varied choices among goods and services—and the income to buy them—that consumers take for granted in the advanced economies.[1]

The challenges faced by consumers—and marketing managers—in the advanced economies seem minor by contrast. When we worry about products being available, we're more likely thinking about instant gratification. We expect the corner convenience store to have a nice selection of frozen gourmet dinners that we can prepare in minutes in a microwave oven. Or perhaps that's too much hassle. After all, Domino's will deliver a pizza in less than 30 minutes. We want supermarkets and drugstores handy. And we expect everything from fresh tropical fruits to batteries for our Walkman to be available when—and where—we want them. Few of the world's consumers can expect so much—and get so much of what they expect. All of this has a price, of course—and we, as consumers, pay the bill.[2]

When you think about these contrasts, it's not hard to decide which set of consumers is better off. But are we making a straw man comparison? Is the first situation one extreme, with the system in the United States and similar societies just as extreme—only in a different way? Would we be better off if we didn't put quite so much emphasis on marketing? Do firms spend too much money advertising trivial differences between their brands? Does marketing encourage us to want too much of the wrong products? Are there too many retailers and wholesalers—all taking "too big" markups? More generally, does marketing cost too much? Some people feel strongly that marketing *does* cost too much—that it's a waste of resources we could better use elsewhere. Do you agree?

Now that you have a better understanding of what marketing is all about—and how it contributes to the *macro*-marketing process—you should be able to decide whether marketing costs too much. That's what this chapter is about.

Your answer is very important. It will affect your own business career and the economy in which you live.

HOW SHOULD MARKETING BE EVALUATED?

We must evaluate at two levels

As we saw in Chapter 1, it's useful to distinguish between two levels of marketing: the *micro* level (how individual firms run) and the *macro* level (how the whole system works). Some complaints against marketing are aimed at only one of these levels at a time. In other cases, the criticism *seems* to be directed to one level—but actually is aimed at the other. Some critics of specific ads, for example, would probably be happier if there wasn't *any* advertising. When evaluating marketing, we must treat each of the macro and micro levels separately.

Nation's objectives affect evaluation

Different nations have different social and economic objectives. Dictatorships, for example, may be mainly concerned with satisfying the needs of society as seen by the political elite. In a socialist state, the objective might be to satisfy society's needs as defined by government planners. In a society that has just broken the chains of communism, the objective may be to make the transition to a market-directed economy as quickly as possible—before there are more revolts.

Consumer satisfaction is the objective in the United States

In the United States, *the basic objective of our market-directed economic system has been to satisfy consumer needs as they—the consumers—see them.* This objective implies that political freedom and economic freedom go hand in hand—and that citizens in a free society have the right to live as they choose. The majority of American consumers would be unwilling to give up the freedom of choice they now enjoy. The same can be said for

The lifestyle of a middle-class, urban family in Russia (on left) is a stark contrast to the lifestyle of a middle-class family in the United States (on right).

Canada, Great Britain, and most other countries in the European community. However, for focus we will concentrate on marketing as it exists in American society.

Therefore, let's try to evaluate the operation of marketing in the American economy—where the present objective is to satisfy consumer needs *as consumers see them*. This is the essence of our system. The business firm that ignores this fact is asking for trouble.

CAN CONSUMER SATISFACTION BE MEASURED?

Since consumer satisfaction is our objective, marketing's effectiveness must be measured by *how well* it satisfies consumers. Unfortunately, consumer satisfaction is hard to define—and even harder to measure.

Satisfaction depends on individual aspirations

There have been various efforts to measure overall consumer satisfaction not only in the United States but also in other countries. However, measuring consumer satisfaction is difficult because satisfaction depends on your level of aspiration or expectation. Less prosperous consumers begin to expect more out of an economy as they see the higher living standards of others. Also, aspiration levels tend to rise with repeated successes—and fall with failures. Products considered satisfactory one day may not be satisfactory the next day, or vice versa. A few years ago, most of us were more than satisfied with a 19-inch color TV that pulled in three or four channels. But once you've watched one of the newer large-screen models and enjoyed all the options possible with a cable hook-up or VCR, that old TV is never the same again. And when high-definition TVs become readily available, today's satisfying units won't seem quite so acceptable. So consumer satisfaction is a highly personal concept—and looking at the satisfaction of a whole society does not provide a reliable standard for evaluating macro-marketing effectiveness.[3]

Measuring macro-marketing must be subjective

If the objective of macro-marketing is maximizing consumer satisfaction, then we must measure total satisfaction—of everyone. But there's no good way to measure aggregate consumer satisfaction. At a minimum, some consumers are more satisfied than others. So our evaluation of macro-marketing effectiveness has to be subjective.

Probably the supreme test is whether the macro-marketing system satisfies enough individual consumer-citizens so that they vote—at the ballot box—to keep it running. So far, we've done so in the United States.

Measuring micro-marketing can be less subjective

Measuring micro-marketing effectiveness is also difficult, but it can be done. Individual business firms can and should try to measure how well their marketing mixes satisfy their customers (or why they fail). In fact, most large firms now have some type of ongoing effort to determine whether they're satisfying their target markets. Many large and small firms measure customer satisfaction with attitude research studies. For example, the J. D. Powers marketing research firm is well known for its studies of consumer satisfaction with different makes of automobiles and computers. Other widely used methods include unsolicited consumer responses (usually complaints), opinions of middlemen and salespeople, market test results, and profits. Of course, customers may be very satisfied about some aspects of what a firm is doing but dissatisfied about other dimensions of performance.[4]

In our market-directed system, it's up to each customer to decide how effectively individual firms satisfy his or her needs. Usually, customers will buy more of the products that satisfy them—and they'll do it repeatedly. Thus, efficient marketing plans can increase profits—and profits can be used as a rough measure of a firm's efficiency in satisfying customers. Nonprofit organizations have a different bottom line, but they too will fail if they don't satisfy supporters and get the resources they need to continue to operate.

Evaluating marketing effectiveness is difficult—but not impossible

Because it's hard to measure consumer satisfaction—and, therefore, the effectiveness of micro- and macro-marketing—it's easy to see why opinions differ. If the objective of the economy is clearly defined, however—and the argument is stripped of emotion—the big questions about marketing effectiveness probably *can* be answered.

In this chapter, we argue that micro-marketing (how individual firms and channels operate) frequently *does* cost too much but that macro-marketing (how the whole marketing system operates) *does not* cost too much, *given the present objective of the American economy—consumer satisfaction.* Don't accept this position as *the* answer—but rather as a point of view. In the end, you'll have to make your own decision.[5]

MICRO-MARKETING OFTEN *DOES* COST TOO MUCH

Throughout the text, we've explored what marketing managers could or should do to help their firms do a better job of satisfying customers—while achieving company objectives. Many firms implement highly successful marketing programs, but others are still too production-oriented and inefficient. For customers of these latter firms, micro-marketing often does cost too much.

Research shows that many consumers are not satisfied. But you know that already. All of us have had experiences when we weren't satisfied—when some firm didn't deliver on its promises. And the problem is much bigger than some marketers want to believe. Research suggests that the majority of consumer complaints are never reported. Worse, many complaints that are reported never get fully resolved.

The failure rate is high

Further evidence that too many firms are too production-oriented—and not nearly as efficient as they could be—is the fact that so many new products fail. New and old businesses fail regularly too.

Generally speaking, marketing inefficiencies are due to one or more of three reasons:

1. Lack of interest in—or understanding of—the sometimes fickle customer.
2. Improper blending of the four Ps—caused in part by overemphasis on production and/or internal problems as contrasted with a customer orientation.
3. Lack of understanding of—or adjustment to—the marketing environment, especially what competitors do.

The high cost of poor marketing mixes

Perhaps lack of concern for the customer is most noticeable in the ways the four Ps are sometimes combined—or forced—into a marketing mix. This can happen in many ways.

Too many firms develop a new product to satisfy some manager's pet idea—not to meet the needs of certain target customers. Or they see another company with a successful product and try to jump into the market with another me-too imitation—without even thinking about the competition they'll encounter. Often they don't worry about quality. In fact, until very recently, most U.S. manufacturers lacked *any* quality control procedures even in the production of goods or services. The idea of using total quality management to implement marketing plans to meet customers' requirements was foreign.

Some marketing managers don't pay attention to getting needed support from middlemen. Too many producers don't even consider the possibility that a big retail chain may see better value for its customers—and greater profit potential—in someone else's product.

Firms often ignore demand and set prices on a cost-plus basis. While margins are fairly definite, firms can only predict volume. So they choose high margins—which may lead to high prices and reduced volume.

Du Pont tries to meet the needs of its target markets—so that retailers will want to carry its products and the success of its strategies don't just rely on promotion.

If a product is poorly designed—or if a firm uses inadequate channels or pricing that isn't competitive—it's easy to see why promotion may be costly. Aggressive spending on promotion doesn't make up for the other types of mistakes.

Top-management decisions on company objectives may increase the cost of marketing unnecessarily. Seeking growth for growth's sake, for example, often leads to too much spending for promotion.

Another sign of failure is the inability of firms to identify new target markets and new opportunities. A new marketing mix that isn't offered doesn't fail—but the lost opportunity can be significant for both a firm and society. Too many seize on whatever strategy seems easiest rather than seeking really new ways to satisfy customers.

Micro-marketing does cost too much—but things are changing

For reasons like these, marketing does cost too much in many firms. Despite much publicity, the marketing concept is not really applied in many places.

But not all firms and marketers deserve criticism. More of them *are* becoming customer-oriented. And many are paying more attention to market-oriented planning to carry out the marketing concept more effectively. Throughout the text, we've highlighted firms and strategies that are making a difference. The successes of innovative firms—like Baldor, Wal-Mart, Toys "R" Us, ITW, McKesson Drug Co., Dell, 3M, and Science Diet—do not go unnoticed. Yes they make some mistakes. That's human—and marketing is a human enterprise. But they have also showed the results that market-oriented strategy planning can produce.

Another encouraging sign is the end of the idea that anybody can run a business successfully. This never was true. Today, the growing complexity of business draws more and more professionals—not only business managers but computer and communications specialists, psychologists, statisticians, and economists.

Managers who adopt the marketing concept as a way of business life do a better job. They look for target market opportunities and carefully blend the elements of the marketing mix to meet their customers' needs. As more of these managers rise in business, we can look forward to much lower micro-marketing costs—and strategies that do a better job of satisfying customer needs.

IMPROVING MARKETING BY BUILDING QUALITY INTO THE IMPLEMENTATION EFFORT

From the start, our focus has been on developing effective marketing strategies. As we evaluate the costs of micro-marketing, it's important to recognize that problems—and much costly waste—also arise because of poor implementation. Without effective implementation, even the best planned strategy may end up missing the mark—neither satisfying customers nor covering the firm's costs. Yet, just as there's reason to be encouraged that many firms are getting better at market-oriented strategy planning, many are getting better at implementation. The details of implementation are covered in advanced courses—and are beyond the scope here. However, it's useful to briefly review what some firms are doing in this area—to open your eyes to the possibilities.

Total quality management meets customer requirements

There are many different ways to improve implementation in each of the four Ps decision areas, but here we will focus on total quality management, which you can use to improve *any* marketing implementation effort. With **total quality management (TQM)**, everyone in the organization is concerned about quality, throughout all of the firm's activities, to better serve customer needs.

In Chapter 8 we explained that product quality means the ability of a product to satisfy a customer's needs or requirements. Now we'll expand that idea and think about the quality of the whole marketing mix and how it is implemented—to meet customer requirements.

Total quality management is not just for factories

Most of the early attention in quality management focused on reducing defects in goods produced in factories. Reliable goods are important, but clearly there's a lot more to marketing implementation than that. Yet if we start by considering product defects, you'll see how the total quality management idea has evolved and how it applies to implementing a marketing program. At one time most firms assumed defects were an inevitable part of mass production. They assumed the cost of replacing defective parts or goods was just a cost of doing business—an insignificant one compared to the advantages of mass production. However, many firms were forced to rethink this assumption when Japanese producers of cars, electronics, and cameras showed that defects weren't inevitable. Much to the surprise of some production-oriented managers, the Japanese experience showed that it is less expensive to do something right the first time rather than pay to do it poorly and *then* pay again to fix problems. And their success in taking customers away from established competitors made it clear that the cost of poor quality wasn't just the cost of fixing the defects.

Having dissatisfied customers is costly

From the customer's point of view, getting a defective product and having to complain about it is a big headache. The customer can't use the defective product and suffers the inconvenience of waiting for someone to fix the problem—if *someone* gets around to it. That erodes goodwill and leaves customers dissatisfied. The big cost of poor quality is the cost of lost customers.

Firms that adopted TQM methods to reduce manufacturing defects soon used the same approaches to overcome many other implementation problems. Their success brought attention to what is possible with TQM—whether the implementation problem concerns unreliable delivery schedules, poor customer service, advertising that appears on the wrong TV show, or salespeople who can't answer customers' questions. Of course, all of these problems increase the cost of micro-marketing.

Getting a handle on doing things right— the first time

The idea of doing things right the first time seems obvious, but it's easier said than done. Problems always come up, and it's not always clear what isn't being done as well as it could be. Most people tend to ignore problems that don't pose an immediate crisis. But firms that adopt TQM always look for ways to improve implementation with **continuous improvement**—a commitment to constantly make things better one step at a time. Once you accept the idea that there *may* be a better way to do something and you look for it, you may just find it! The place to start is to clearly define "defects" in the implementation process—from the customers' point of view.

Things gone right and things gone wrong

Managers who use the TQM approach think of quality improvement as a sorting process—a sorting out of things gone right and things gone wrong. The sorting process calls for detailed measurements related to a problem. Then managers use a set of statistical tools to analyze the measurements and identify the problem areas that are the best candidates for fixing. The statistical details are beyond our focus here, but it's useful to get a feel for how managers use the tools.

Starting with customer needs

Let's consider the case of a restaurant that does well during the evening hours but wants to improve its lunch business. The restaurant develops a strategy that targets local businesspeople with an attractive luncheon buffet. The restaurant decides on a buffet because research shows that target customers want a choice of good healthy food and are willing to pay reasonable prices for it—as long as they can eat quickly and get back to work on time.

As the restaurant implements its new strategy, the manager wants a measure of how things are going. So she encourages customers to fill out comment cards that ask, "How did we do today?" After several months, business is not as brisk as it was at first. The manager reads the comment cards and divides the ones with complaints into categories—to count up different reasons why customers weren't satisfied.

Slay the dragons first

Then the manager creates a graph showing a frequency distribution for the different types of complaints. Quality people call this a **Pareto chart**—a graph that shows the number of times a problem cause occurs, with problem causes ordered from most frequent to least frequent. The manager's Pareto chart, shown in Exhibit 18–1, reveals that

Exhibit 18–1 Pareto Chart Showing Frequency of Different Complaints

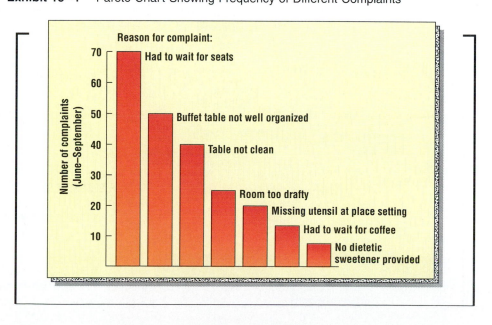

customers complain most frequently that they have to wait for a seat. There were other common complaints—the buffet was not well organized, the table was not clean, and so on. However, the first complaint is much more common.

This pattern is typical. The worst problems often occur over and over again. This focuses the manager's attention on which implementation problem to fix first. A rule of quality management is to slay the dragons first—which simply means start with the biggest problem. After removing that problem, the battle moves on to the next most frequent problem. If you do this *continuously*, you solve a lot of problems—and you don't just satisfy customers, you delight them.

Figure out why things go wrong

So far, our manager has only identified the problem. To solve it, she creates a **fishbone diagram**—a visual aid that helps organize cause-and-effect relationships for "things gone wrong."

Our restaurant manager, for example, discovers that customers wait to be seated because tables aren't cleared soon enough. In fact, the Pareto chart (Exhibit 18–1) shows that customers also complain frequently about tables not being clean. So the two implementation problems may be related.

The manager's fishbone diagram (Exhibit 18–2) summarizes the various causes for tables not being cleaned quickly. There are different basic categories of causes—restaurant policy, procedures, people problems, and the physical environment. With this overview of different ways the service operation is going wrong, the manager can decide what to fix. She establishes different formal measures. For example, she counts how frequently different causes delay customers from being seated. She finds that the cashier's faulty credit card machine holds up check processing. The fishbone diagram shows that restaurant policy is to clear the table after the entire party leaves. But customers have to

Exhibit 18–2   Fishbone Diagram Showing Cause and Effect for "Why Tables Are Not Cleared Quickly"

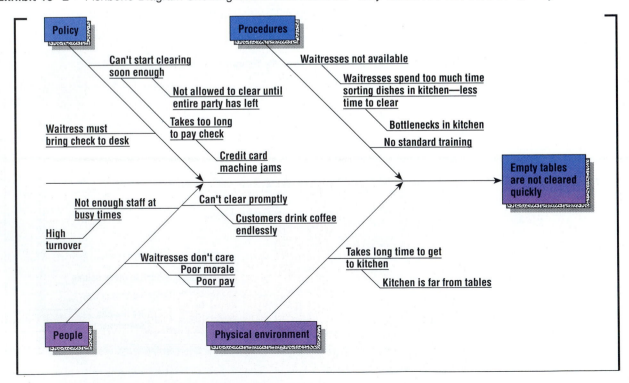

wait at their tables while the staff deals with the jammed credit card machine, and cleaning is delayed. With the credit card machine replaced, the staff can clear the tables sooner— and because they're not so hurried they do a better cleaning job. Two dragons are on the way to being slayed!

Our case shows that people in different areas of the restaurant affect customer satisfaction. The waitperson couldn't do what was needed to satisfy customers because the cashier had trouble with the credit card machine. The TQM approach helps everyone see—and understand—how their job affects what others do—and the customer's satisfaction.[6]

Building quality into services

The restaurant case illustrates how a firm can improve implementation with TQM approaches. We used a service example because providing customer service is often a difficult area of implementation. Recently, marketers in service businesses have been paying a lot of attention to improving service quality.

But some managers seem to forget that almost every firm must implement service quality as part of its plan—whether its product is primarily a service, primarily a physical good, or a blend of both. For example, a manufacturer of ball bearings isn't just providing wholesalers or producers with round pieces of steel. Customers need information about deliveries, they need orders filled properly, and they may have questions to ask the firm's accountant, receptionist, or engineers. Because almost every firm must manage the service it provides customers, let's focus on some of the special concerns of implementing quality service.

Train people and empower them to serve

Customer service is hard to implement because the server is inseparable from the service. A person doing a specific service job may perform one specific task correctly but still annoy the customer in a host of other ways. Customers will not be satisfied if employees are rude or inattentive—even if they "solve the customer's problem." There are two keys to improving how people implement quality service: (1) training and (2) empowerment.

This ad uses humor to make it clear Gert Boyle, the top executive for Columbia Sportswear, is serious about implementing the marketing plan to give her customers the quality they want.

Firms that commit to customer satisfaction realize that all employees who have any contact with customers need training—many firms see 40 hours a year of training as a minimum. Simply showing customer-contact employees around the rest of the business—so that they learn how their contribution fits in the total effort—can be very effective. Good training usually includes role playing on handling different types of customer requests and problems. This is not just sales training! A rental car attendant who is rude when a customer is trying to turn in a car may leave the customer dissatisfied—even if the rental car was perfect.

Companies can't afford an army of managers to inspect how each employee implements a strategy—and such a system usually doesn't work anyway. Quality cannot be "inspected in." It must come from the people who do the service jobs. So firms that commit to service quality empower employees to satisfy customers' needs. **Empowerment** means giving employees the authority to correct a problem without first checking with management. At a Guest Quarters hotel, an empowered room-service employee knows it's OK to run across the street to buy the specific mineral water a guest requests. In the new Saturn car manufacturing plant, employees can stop the assembly line to correct a problem rather than passing it down the line. At Upton's clothing stores, a salesclerk can make an immediate price adjustment if there's a flaw in an item the customer wants.

Manage expectations— with good communication

Some customers end up dissatisfied because they expect much more than it is possible for any firm to deliver. Some firms react to this by faulting customers for being unreasonable. However, these problems often go away if marketers clearly communicate what they are offering. Customers are satisfied when the service matches their expectations, and careful communication leads to reasonable expectations. For example, most airline passengers are mad if a plane is late taking off—but they're happy to wait patiently if they know the delay is caused by a thunderstorm high over the airport.

Separate the routine and plan for the special

Implementation usually involves some routine services and some that require special attention. Customer satisfaction increases when the two types of service encounters are separated. For example, banks set up special windows for commercial deposits, and supermarkets have cash only lines. In developing the marketing plan, it's important to analyze the types of service customers will need and plan for both types of situations. In some cases, completely different strategies may be required.

Increasingly, firms try to use computers and other equipment to handle routine services. ATMs are quick and convenient for dispensing cash. American Airlines's Dial a Flight system allows customers to use a touchtone phone to check fares, schedules, and arrival times—without the need for an operator.

Firms that study special service requests can use training so that even unusual customer requests become routine to the staff. Every day, hotel guests lose their keys, bank customers run out of checks, and supermarket shoppers leave their wallets at home. A well-run service operation anticipates these special events so service providers can respond in a way that satisfies customers' needs.

Managers lead the quality effort

Quality implementation doesn't just happen by itself. Managers must show that they are committed to doing things right to satisfy customers—and that quality is everyone's job. Without top level support, some people won't get beyond their business as usual attitude—and TQM won't work.

TQM is not the only method for improving marketing implementation, but it is an important approach. Some firms don't yet use TQM; they may be missing an opportunity.

Other firms apply some quality methods—but act like they are the private property of a handful of "quality specialists" who want to control things. That's not good either. Everyone must own a TQM effort. As more marketing managers see the benefits of TQM, it will become a more important part of marketing thinking, especially marketing implementation. And, in combination with better strategy planning, that may reduce some of the unnecessary costs of micro-marketing.[7]

MACRO-MARKETING DOES NOT COST TOO MUCH

We've been talking about the problem of planning and implementing micro-marketing, but many critics of marketing take aim at the whole macro-marketing system. They typically argue that the macro-marketing system causes poor use of resources and leads to an unfair distribution of income. Most of these complaints imply that some micro-marketing activities should not be permitted—and because they are, our macro-marketing system does a poor job. Let's look at some of these positions to help you form your own opinion.

Micro-efforts help the economy grow

Some critics feel that marketing helps create monopoly or at least monopolistic competition. Further, they think this leads to higher prices, restricted output, and reduction in national income and employment.

It's true that firms in a market-directed economy try to carve out separate monopolistic markets for themselves with new products. However, this is simply a response to consumer preferences. Consumers do have a choice. They don't *have* to buy the new product unless they think it's a better value. The old products are still available. In fact, to meet the new competition, prices of the old products usually drop. And that makes them even more available.

Marketing stimulates innovation and the development of new ways to meet customers' needs.

The innovator's profits may rise—but rising profits also encourage further innovation by competitors. This leads to new investments—which contribute to economic growth and higher levels of national income and employment. Around the world, many countries failed to achieve economic growth under centrally planned systems because this type of profit incentive didn't exist.

Increased profits also attract competition. Profits then begin to drop as new competitors enter the market and begin producing somewhat similar products. (Recall the rise and fall of industry profit during the product life cycle.)

Is advertising a waste of resources?

Advertising is the most criticized of all micro-marketing activities. Indeed, many ads *are* annoying, insulting, misleading, and downright ineffective. This is one reason why micro-marketing often does cost too much. However, advertising can also make both the micro- and macro-marketing processes work better.

Advertising is an economical way to inform large numbers of potential customers about a firm's products. Provided that a product satisfies customer needs, advertising can increase demand for the product—resulting in economies of scale in production, distribution, and sales. Because these economies may more than offset advertising costs, advertising can actually *lower* prices to the consumer.[8]

Does marketing make people buy things they don't need?

Some critics feel that advertising manipulates consumers into buying products that they don't need.[9] This, of course, raises a question. How should a society determine which products are unnecessary—and shouldn't be produced or sold? One critic suggested that Americans could and should do without such items as pets, newspaper comic strips, second family cars, motorcycles, snowmobiles, campers, recreational boats and planes, pop and beer cans, and hats.[10] You may agree with some of these. But who should determine the basic requirements of life—consumers or critics?

Should consumers be left to decide what needs are important and what products should be available—or should those decisions be made by social critics?

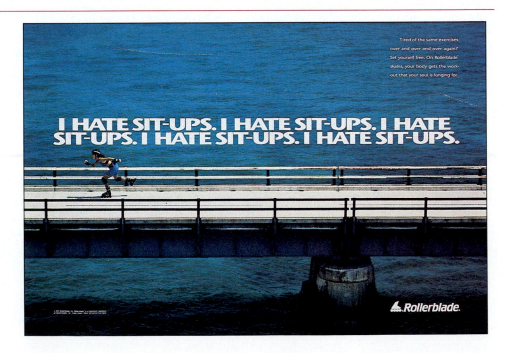

The idea that firms can manipulate consumers to buy anything the company chooses to produce simply isn't true. A consumer who buys a soft drink that tastes terrible won't buy another can of that brand—regardless of how much it's advertised. In fact, many new products fail the test of the market. And if powerful corporations know some way to get people to buy products against their will, would General Motors have recently tallied the biggest loss in history?

It is true that marketing stimulates interest in new products—including products consumers might never have considered. But consumer needs and wants change constantly. Few of us would care to live the way our grandparents lived when they were our age. Marketing's job is not just to satisfy consumer wants as they exist at any particular point in time. Rather, marketing must keep looking for new—and better—ways to serve consumers.[11]

Does marketing make people materialistic?

There is no doubt that marketing caters to materialistic values. However, people disagree as to whether marketing creates these values—or simply appeals to values already there.

Even in the most primitive societies, people want to accumulate possessions. In fact, in some tribal villages, social status is measured by how many goats or sheep a person owns. Further, the tendency for ancient pharaohs and kings to surround themselves with wealth and treasures can hardly be attributed to the persuasive powers of advertising agencies!

Experts who study materialism seem to agree that marketing reflects social values in the short run, while—in the long run—it enhances and reinforces them. One expert pointed out that consumers vote for what they want in the marketplace and in the polling place. To

The idea that firms can manipulate consumers to buy anything the company chooses to produce simply isn't true.

In the 1920s, few consumers saw the need for an electric icebox. Now we all feel a refrigerator is a necessity—but some consumers don't see the need for special features. Who should decide what you need?

say that what they choose is wrong, he said, is to criticize the basic idea of free choice and democracy.[12]

Clearly, the quality of life can't be measured just in terms of quantities of material goods. But when we view products as the means to an end—rather than the end itself—they *do* make it possible to satisfy higher-level needs. Microwave ovens, for example, greatly reduced the amount of time and effort people must spend preparing meals—leaving them free to pursue other interests. And more dependable cars expanded people's geographic horizons—affecting where they can live and work and play.

Not all needs are met

Some critics argue that our macro-marketing system is flawed because it does not provide solutions to important problems, such as how to help the homeless, the uneducated, dependent children, minorities who have suffered discrimination, the elderly poor, and the sick. Many of these people do live in dire circumstances, and these are important societal issues. However, consumer-citizens in a market-directed system assign some responsibilities to business and some to government. Ultimately, consumer-citizens vote in the ballot box for how they want government to deal with these concerns. As more managers in the public sector understand and apply marketing concepts, we should be able to do a better job meeting the needs of all people.

Is it the responsibility of business to meet the needs of all people, including the homeless and others who have no money to spend?

CHALLENGES FACING MARKETERS

We've said that our macro-marketing system does *not* cost too much—given the present objective of our economy. But we admit that the performance of many business firms leaves a lot to be desired. This presents a challenge to serious-minded students and marketers. What needs to be done—if anything?

We need better performance at the micro level

We need better market-oriented planning

Many firms are still production-oriented. Some hardly plan at all, and others simply extend one year's plans into the next. Progressive firms are beginning to realize that this doesn't work in our fast-changing markets. Market-oriented strategy planning is becoming more important in many companies. Firms are paying more attention to changes in the market—including trends in the marketing environment—and how marketing strategies need to be adapted to consider these changes. Exhibit 18−3 lists some of the trends and changes we've discussed throughout this text.

Most of the changes and trends summarized in Exhibit 18−3 are having a positive effect on how marketers serve society. Whether it's because marketers are applying new approaches to solve old marketing problems or applying classic marketing concepts to new kinds of opportunities, consumers are better off. And this ongoing improvement is self-directing. As consumers shift their support to firms that do meet their needs, laggard businesses are forced to either improve or get out of the way.

We need continuous improvement

Good marketing strategy planning needs to focus on a specific target market and a marketing mix to meet its needs. The basic frameworks and ideas about how to do that haven't changed as much as the long list in Exhibit 18−3 seems to suggest. At the same time, thinking about all these changes highlights the fact that marketing is dynamic. Marketing managers must constantly evaluate their strategies to be sure they're not being left in the dust by competitors who see new and better ways of doing things.

Exhibit 18–3 Some Important Changes and Trends Affecting Marketing Strategy Planning

Communication Technologies
Computer-to-computer data exchange
Satellite communications
FAX machine transmissions
Cable television
Telemarketing
Cellular

Role of Computerization
Personal computers and laptops
Spreadsheet analysis
Computer networks
Checkout scanners
Bar codes for tracking inventory
Computer-to-computer ordering (EDI)

Marketing Research
Growth of marketing information systems
Decision support systems
Single source data
People meters
Use of scanner data
Easy-to-use statistical packages

Demographic Patterns
Aging of the baby boomers
Slowdown in U.S. population growth
Growth of ethnic submarkets
Geographic shifts in population
Slower real income growth in U.S.

Business and Organizational Customers
Closer buyer/seller relationships
Just-in-time inventory systems
More single-vendor sourcing

Product Area
More attention to innovation/new-product development
Faster new-product development
Computer-aided package/product design
Market-driven focus on research and development
More attention to quality and quality control
More attention to services
Advances in packaging
Extending established family brand names
   to new products

Channels and Logistics
More vertical market systems
Larger, more powerful retail chains
More conflict between producers/chains
More attention to physical distribution service
Better inventory control
Automated warehouses
Integrated distribution centers
More competition among transportation companies
Coordination of logistics in the channnel

Channels and Logistics (continued)
Growing role of air freight
Growth of mass-merchandising
Catalog, TV retailing

Sales Promotion
Increased promotion to middlemen
Event sponsorships
Greater use of coupons
Stocking allowances

Personal Selling
Automated order taking
Use of portable computers
More specialization:
   Major accounts
   Telemarketing
   Team selling

Mass Selling
More targeted mass media:
   Specialty publications
   Cable, satellite TV
   Specialty media, especially in-store
Shorter TV commercials
Larger advertising agencies
Changing agency compensation
Growth of direct-response advertising
Shrinking percentage of total promotion budgets

Pricing
Value pricing
Less reliance on traditional markups by middlemen
Overuse of sales and deals on consumer products
Bigger differences in functional discounts
More attention to exchange rate effects
Focus on higher stockturn at lower margins

International Marketing
Collapse of communism worldwide
More international market development
New and different competitors—at home and abroad
Need to adjust to unfamiliar markets, cultures
Widely spread markets
Changing trading restrictions (unification of Europe, tariffs,
   quotas, etc.)
More attention to exporting by small firms
Growth of multinational corporations

General
Less regulation of business
More attention to marketing ethics
Shift of emphasis away from diversification
More attention to profitability, not just sales
Greater attention to competitive advantage
Implementation of total quality management
Greater attention to environmental issues

It's crazy for a marketing manager to constantly change a strategy that's working well. But too many fail to see or plan for needed changes. They're afraid to do anything different and adhere to the idea that "if it ain't broke, don't fix it." But a firm can't always wait until a problem becomes completely obvious to do something about it. When customers move on and profits disappear, it may be too late to fix the problem. Marketing managers who take the lead in finding innovative new markets and approaches get a competitive advantage.

We need to welcome international competition

Increasingly, marketing managers face global competition. Some managers hate that thought. Worldwide competition creates even more pressure on marketing managers to figure out what it takes to gain a competitive advantage—both at home and in foreign markets. But with the challenge comes opportunities. The forces of competition in and among market-directed economies will help speed the diffusion of marketing advances to consumers everywhere. As macro-marketing systems improve worldwide, more consumers will have income to buy products—wherever in the world the products come from.

Marketers can't afford to bury their heads in the sand and hope that international competition will go away. Rather, they must realize that it is part of today's marketing environment—and they must do marketing strategy planning that rises to the challenges it poses.

May need more social responsibility

Good business managers put themselves in the consumer's position. A useful rule to follow might be: Do unto others as you would have others do unto you. In practice, this means developing satisfying marketing mixes for specific target markets. It may mean building in more quality or more safety. The consumer's long-run satisfaction should be considered too. How will the product hold up in use? What about service guarantees? While trying to serve the needs of some target market, does the marketing strategy disregard the rights and needs of other consumers—or create problems that will be left for future generations?

The environment is everyone's need

Marketers need to work harder and smarter at finding ways to satisfy consumer needs without sacrificing the current or future environment. All consumers need the environment—whether they realize it yet or not. We are only beginning to understand the environmental damage that's already been done. Acid rain, the ozone layer, and toxic waste in water supplies—to mention but a few current environmental problems—have catastrophic effects. Many top executives now say that protecting the environment will be *the* major challenge of business firms in the next decade.

In the past, most firms didn't pass the cost of environmental damage on to consumers in the prices that they paid. Pollution was a hidden and unmeasured cost for most companies. That is changing rapidly. Firms are already paying billions of dollars to correct problems—including problems created years ago. The government isn't accepting the excuse that "nobody knew it was a big problem." Consider yourself warned: businesspeople who fail to anticipate the coming public backlash on this issue put their careers and businesses at risk!

May need attention to consumer privacy

Marketers also must be sensitive to consumers' rights to privacy. Today, sophisticated marketing research and new technologies make it easier to abuse these rights. For example, credit card records—which reveal much about consumers' purchases and private lives—are routinely computerized and sold to anybody who pays for the list. Marketing managers should use technology responsibly to improve the quality of life—not disrupt it.

Need to rethink some present laws

One of the advantages of a market-directed economic system is that it operates automatically. But in our version of this system, consumer-citizens provide certain con-

SMITH & HAWKEN TRASHES JUNK MAIL

The U.S. Postal Service says that consumers throw out over 10 billion pieces of *unopened* third-class junk mail each year. That's another million cubic yards of paper dumped in overtaxed landfills—and over 5 million trees consumed to make the paper. But that's just the start of the waste. In total, consumers get over 60 billion pieces of unsolicited third-class mail each year—and they quickly trash 95 percent or more of it. Ironically, nonprofit environmental groups—like Greenpeace—are heavy users of direct-mail advertising for fund-raising. They say that there's less waste with direct-mail than with most print media.

Even so, Paul Hawken has declared war on junk mail waste. "It doesn't matter how 'beautiful' the catalog or how 'important' the cause," he says, "if you don't want it, it's junk." Oh, we forgot to tell you. Hawken is head of Smith & Hawken Ltd.—a firm that uses direct-mail catalogs to market garden supplies. Perhaps you're wondering if Hawken is planning a move to a different business. He's not.

Instead, Smith & Hawken (S&H) is taking steps to reduce waste and increase environmentally sound practices in direct-mail marketing. The firm uses selective mailings, giving customers a choice of which S&H catalogs they will receive. Customers are encouraged to keep catalogs longer; in turn, S&H carries products longer and has stopped "remailing"—the common practice of repackaging old catalogs to make them seem new. S&H even offers a $5 gift certificate to consumers who alert the firm that they've received a duplicate catalog. To further reduce waste, S&H catalogs carry postcards that make it easier for customers to remove their names from the company's mailing list and other firms' lists.

S&H doesn't pretend it has all the answers to the rising mountain of junk mail, but it hopes that other firms will follow its lead. In the meantime, S&H is doing a better job of zeroing in on the target market that actually wants its mailings.[13]

---

straints (laws), which can be modified at any time. Managers who ignore consumer attitudes must realize that their actions may cause new restraints.

Before piling on too many new rules, however, some of the ones we have need to be revised and others may need to be enforced more carefully. Antitrust laws, for example, are often applied to protect competitors from each other—when they were really intended to encourage competition.

On the other hand, U.S. antitrust laws were originally developed so that all firms in a market would compete on a level playing field. That is no longer always true. In many markets individual U.S. firms compete with foreign firms whose governments urge them to cooperate with each other.

Laws should affect top managers

Strict enforcement of present laws could have far-reaching results if more price fixers, fraudulent or deceptive advertisers, and others who violate existing laws—thus affecting the performance of the macro-marketing system—were sent to jail or given heavy fines. A quick change in attitudes might occur if unethical top managers—those who plan strategy—were prosecuted, instead of the salespeople or advertisers expected to deliver on weak or undifferentiated strategies.

Laws merely define minimal ethical standards

As we discussed ethical issues in marketing throughout the text, we emphasized that a marketing manager doesn't face an ethical dilemma about complying with laws and regulations. Whether a marketer is operating in his or her own country or in a foreign nation, the legal environment sets the *minimal* standards of ethical behavior as defined by a society. In addition, the American Marketing Association's code of ethics (Exhibit 2–3) provides a checklist of basic guidelines that a marketing manager should observe. But

As more private and nonprofit organizations adopt the marketing concept, they should be able to do a better job of meeting the needs of those they serve.

marketing managers constantly face ethical issues where there are no clearly defined answers. Every marketing manager should make a personal commitment to carefully evaluate the ethical consequences of marketing strategy decisions.

On the other hand, innovative new marketing strategies *do* sometimes cause problems for those who have a vested interest in the old ways. Some of these people portray anything that disrupts their own personal interest as unethical. But that is not an appropriate ethical standard; the most basic ethical charge to marketers is to find new and better ways to serve society's needs.

Need socially responsible consumers

We've stressed that marketers should act responsibly—but consumers have responsibilities too.[14] Some consumers abuse policies about returning goods, change price tags in self-service stores, and are downright rude to salespeople. Others think nothing of ripping off businesses because "they're rich." Shoplifting is a major problem for most retailers—and honest consumers pay for the cost of shoplifting in higher prices.

Americans tend to perform their dual role of consumer-citizens with a split personality. We often behave one way as consumers—then take the opposite position at the ballot box. For example, we cover our beaches and parks with garbage and litter, while urging our legislators to take stiff action to curb pollution. We protest sex and violence in the media—and then flock to see the latest R- or X-rated movies. Parents complain about advertising aimed at children—then use TV as a Saturday morning babysitter.

Consumers share the responsibility for preserving an effective macro-marketing system. And they should take this responsibility seriously.

Should marketing managers limit consumers' freedom of choice?

Achieving a better macro-marketing system is certainly a desirable objective. But what part should a marketer play in deciding what products to offer?

This is extremely important because some marketing managers—especially those in large corporations—can have an impact far larger than they do in their role as a consumer-citizen. For example, should they refuse to produce hazardous products—like skis or motorcycles—even though such products are in strong demand? Should they install safety devices that increase costs—but that customers don't want?

These are difficult questions to answer. Clearly, some things marketing managers do benefit both the firm and consumers because they lower costs and/or improve consumers' options. But other choices may actually reduce consumer choice and conflict with a desire to improve the effectiveness of our macro-marketing system.

Consumer-citizens should vote on the changes

It seems fair to suggest, therefore, that marketing managers should be expected to improve and expand the range of goods and services they make available to consumers—always trying to better satisfy their needs and preferences. This is the job we've assigned to business.

If pursuing this objective makes excessive demands on scarce resources—or has an unacceptable ecological effect—then consumer-citizens have the responsibility to vote for laws restricting individual firms that are trying to satisfy consumers' needs. This is the role that we, as consumers, have assigned to the government—to ensure that the macro-marketing system works effectively.

It is important to recognize that some *seemingly minor* modifications in our present system *might* result in very big, unintended problems. Allowing some government agency to prohibit the sale of products for seemingly good reasons could lead to major changes we never expected—and could seriously reduce consumers' present rights to freedom of choice—including the right to make "bad" choices.[15]

CONCLUSION

Macro-marketing does *not* cost too much. Consumers have assigned business the role of satisfying their needs. Customers find it satisfactory—and even desirable—to permit businesses to cater to them and even to stimulate wants. As long as consumers are satisfied, macro-marketing will not cost too much—and business firms will be permitted to continue as profit-making entities.

But business exists at the consumer's discretion. It's mainly by satisfying the consumer that a particular firm—and our economic system—can justify its existence and hope to keep operating.

In carrying out this role—granted by consumers—business firms are not always as effective as they could be. Many business managers don't understand the marketing concept—or the role that marketing plays in our way of life. They seem to feel that business has a God-given right to operate as it chooses. And they proceed in their typical production-oriented ways. Further, many managers have had little or no training in business management—and are not as competent as they should be. Others fail to adjust to the changes taking place around them. And a few dishonest or unethical managers can do a great deal of damage before consumer-citizens take steps to stop them. As a result, micro-marketing

often *does* cost too much. But the situation is improving. More business training is now available, and more competent people are being attracted to marketing and business generally. Clearly, *you* have a role to play in improving marketing activities in the future.

Total quality management can help the firm get the type of implementation it needs—implementation that continuously improves and does a better job of meeting customers' needs and at a lower cost.

Marketing has new challenges to face in the future. *Our* consumers may have to settle for a lower standard of living. Resource shortages, slower population growth, and a larger number of elderly—with a smaller proportion of the population in the workforce—may all combine to reduce our income growth. This may force consumers to shift their consumption patterns—and politicians to change some of the rules governing business. Even our present market-directed system may be threatened.

To keep our system working effectively, individual firms should implement the marketing concept in a more efficient, ethical, and socially responsible way. At the same time, we—as consumers—should consume goods and services in an intelligent and socially responsible way. Further, we have the responsibility to vote and ensure that we get the kind of macro-marketing system we want. What kind do you want? What should you do to ensure that fellow consumer-citizens will vote for your system? Is your system likely to satisfy you as well as another macro-marketing system? You don't have to answer these questions right now—but your answers will affect the future you'll live in and how satisfied you'll be.

QUESTIONS AND PROBLEMS

1. Explain why marketing must be evaluated at two levels. What criteria should be used to evaluate each level of marketing? Defend your answer. Explain why your criteria are better than alternative criteria.

2. Discuss the merits of various economic system objectives. Is the objective of the American economic system sensible? Could it achieve more consumer satisfaction if sociologists—or public officials—determined how to satisfy the needs of lower-income or less-educated consumers? If so, what education or income level should be required before an individual is granted free choice?

3. Should the objective of our economy be maximum efficiency? If your answer is yes, efficiency in what? If not, what should the objective be?

4. Discuss the conflict of interests among production, finance, accounting, and marketing executives. How does this conflict affect the operation of an individual firm? The economic system? Why does this conflict exist?

5. Why does adoption of the marketing concept encourage a firm to operate more efficiently? Be specific about the impact of the marketing concept on the various departments of a firm.

6. In the short run, competition sometimes leads to inefficiency in the operation of our economic system. Many people argue for monopoly in order to eliminate this inefficiency. Discuss this solution.

7. How would officially granted monopolies affect the operation of our economic system? Consider the effect on allocation of resources, the level of income and employment, and the distribution of income. Is the effect any different if a firm obtains monopoly by winning out in a competitive market?

8. What are the major advantages of total quality management as an approach for improving implementation of marketing plans? What limitations can you think of?

9. Comment on the following statement: "Ultimately, the high cost of marketing is due only to consumers."

10. How far should the marketing concept go? How should we decide this issue?

11. Should marketing managers, or business managers in general, refrain from producing profitable products that some target customers want but that may not be in their long-run interest? Should firms be expected to produce "good" but less profitable products? What if they are unprofitable but the company makes other profitable products—so on balance it still makes some profit? What criteria are you using for each of your answers?

12. Should a marketing manager or a business refuse to produce an energy-gobbling appliance that some consumers are demanding? Should a firm install an expensive safety device that will increase costs but that customers don't want? Are the same principles involved in both these questions? Explain.

13. Discuss how one or more of the trends or changes shown in Exhibit 18–3 is affecting marketing strategy planning for a specific firm that serves the market where you live.

14. Discuss how slower economic growth or no economic growth would affect your college community—in particular, its marketing institutions.

SUGGESTED CASES

15. Riverside Packers, Inc.
26. Cutters, Inc.
27. KASTORS, Inc.
28. Grand Foods, Ltd.

30. Metro Medical, Inc.
31. Lever, Ltd.
32. Chase & Arnold, P.C.

Career Planning in Marketing

Appendix **C**

When You Finish This Appendix, You Should

❶

Know that there is a job—or a career—for you in marketing.

❷

Know that marketing jobs can be rewarding, pay well, and offer opportunities for growth.

❸

Understand the difference between "people-oriented" and "thing-oriented" jobs.

❹

Know about the many marketing jobs you can choose from.

One of the hardest jobs most college students face is the choice of a career. Of course, we can't make this decision for you. You must be the judge of your own objectives, interests, and abilities. Only you can decide what career *you* should pursue. However, you owe it to yourself to at least consider the possibility of a career in marketing.

THERE'S A PLACE IN MARKETING FOR YOU

We're happy to tell you that many opportunities are available in marketing. There's a place in marketing for everyone—from a service provider in a fast-food restaurant to a vice president of marketing in a large consumer products company such as Procter & Gamble or General Foods. The opportunities range widely—so it will help to be more specific. In the following pages, we'll discuss (1) the typical pay for different marketing jobs, (2) setting your own objectives and evaluating your interests and abilities, and (3) the kinds of jobs available in marketing.

MARKETING JOBS CAN PAY WELL

There are many interesting and challenging jobs for those with marketing training. Fortunately, marketing jobs open to college-level students do pay well! At the time this went to press, marketing undergraduates were being offered starting salaries ranging from $15,000 to $36,000 a year. Of course, these figures are extremes. Starting salaries can vary considerably—depending on your background, experience and location. But many jobs are in the $22,000–$26,000 range.

Starting salaries in marketing compare favorably with many other fields. They are lower than those in such fields as computer science and engineering where college graduates are currently in very high demand. But there is even better opportunity for personal growth, variety, and income in many marketing positions. *The American Almanac of Jobs and Salaries* ranks the median income of marketers number 10 in a list of 125 professions. Marketing also supplies about 50 percent of the people who achieve senior management ranks.

However, many factors affect how far and fast your career and income rise above the starting level—including your willingness to work, how well you get along with people, and your individual abilities. But most of all, success depends on *getting results*—individually and through other people. And this is where many marketing jobs offer the newcomer great opportunities. It's possible to show initiative, ability, and judgment in marketing jobs. And some young people move up very rapidly in marketing. Some even end up at the top in large companies—or as owners of their own businesses.

Marketing is often the route to the top

Marketing is where the action is! In the final analysis, a firm's success or failure depends on the effectiveness of its marketing program. This doesn't mean the other functional areas aren't important. It merely reflects the fact that a firm won't have much need for accountants, finance people, production managers, and so on, if it can't successfully sell its products.

Because marketing is so vital to a firm's survival, many companies look for people with training and experience in marketing when filling key executive positions. A survey of the nation's largest corporations shows that the greatest proportion of chief executive officers have backgrounds in marketing and distribution (see Exhibit C–1).

Exhibit C–1   Main Career Emphasis of Corporate Chief Executive Officers*

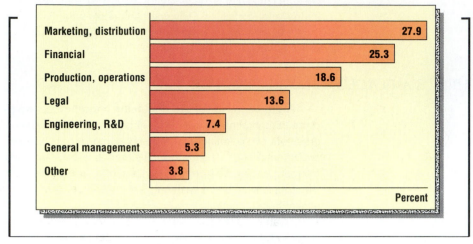

	Percent
Marketing, distribution	27.9
Financial	25.3
Production, operations	18.6
Legal	13.6
Engineering, R&D	7.4
General management	5.3
Other	3.8

*Based on a survey of the chief executive officers of the nation's 500 largest industrial corporations and 300 nonindustrial corporations (including commercial banks, life insurance firms, retailers, transportation companies, utilities, and diversified financial enterprises).

DEVELOP YOUR OWN PERSONAL MARKETING STRATEGY

Now that you know there are many opportunities in marketing, your problem is matching the opportunities to your own personal objectives and strengths. Basically the problem is a marketing problem: developing a marketing strategy to sell a product—yourself—to potential employers. Just as in planning strategies for products, developing your own strategy takes careful thought. Exhibit C–2 shows how you can organize your

Exhibit C–2   Organizing Your Own Personal Marketing Strategy Planning

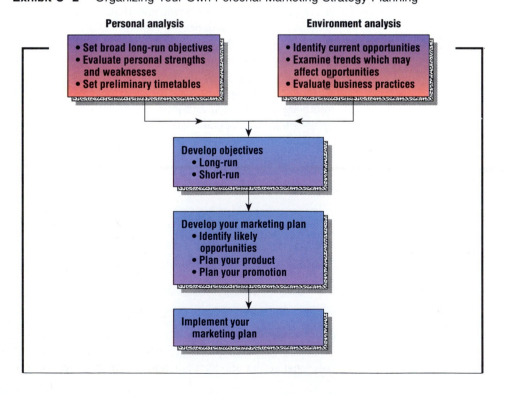

own strategy planning. This exhibit shows that you should evaluate yourself first—a personal analysis—and then analyze the environment for opportunities. This will help you sharpen your own long- and short-run objectives—which will lead to developing a strategy. And, finally, you should start implementing your own personal marketing strategy. These ideas are explained more fully below.

CONDUCT YOUR OWN PERSONAL ANALYSIS

First you have to decide what your long-run objectives are—what you want to do, how hard you want to work, and how quickly you want to reach your objectives. Be honest with yourself—or you will eventually face frustration. Evaluate your own personal strengths and weaknesses—and decide what factors may become the key to your success. Finally, as part of your personal analysis, set some preliminary timetables to guide your strategy planning and implementation efforts. Let's spell this out in detail.

Set broad long-run objectives

Strategy planning requires much trial-and-error decision making. But at the very beginning, you should make some tentative decisions about your own objectives—what you want out of a job—and out of life. At the very least, you should decide whether you are just looking for a job—or whether you want to build a career. Beyond this, do you want the position to be personally satisfying—or is the financial return enough? And just how much financial return do you need? Some people work only to support themselves and their leisure-time activities. Others work to support themselves and their families. These people seek only financial rewards from a job. They try to find job opportunities that provide adequate financial returns but aren't too demanding of their time or effort.

Other people look first for satisfaction in their job—and they seek opportunities for career advancement. Financial rewards may be important too, but these are used only as measures of success. In the extreme, the career-oriented individual may be willing to sacrifice a lot—including leisure and social activities—to achieve success in a career.

Once you've tentatively decided these matters, you can get more serious about whether you should seek a job—or a career—in marketing. If you decide to pursue a career, you should set your broad long-run objectives to achieve it. For example, one long-run objective might be to pursue a career in marketing management (or marketing research). This might require more academic training than you planned—as well as a different kind of training. If your objective is to get a job that pays well, on the other hand, this calls for a different kind of training and different kinds of job experiences before completing your academic work.

What kind of a job is right for you?

Because of the great variety of marketing jobs, it's hard to generalize about what aptitudes you should have to pursue a career in marketing. Different jobs attract people with various interests and abilities. We'll give you some guidelines about what kinds of interests and abilities marketers should have. However, if you're completely lost about your own interests and abilities, see your campus career counselor and take some vocational aptitude and interest tests. These tests will help you to compare yourself with people who are now working in various career positions. They will *not* tell you what you should do, but they can help—especially in eliminating possibilities you're less interested in and/or less able to do well in.

Are you "people-oriented" or "thing-oriented"?

One of the first things you need to decide is whether you are basically "people-oriented" or "thing-oriented." This is a very important decision. A thing-oriented person might be very happy in an inventory management job, for example, but miserable in a personal selling or retail management job that involves a lot of customer contact.

Marketing has both people-oriented and thing-oriented jobs. People-oriented jobs are primarily in the promotion area—where company representatives must make contact with potential customers. This may be direct personal selling or customer service activities—for example, in technical service or installation and repair. Thing-oriented jobs focus more on creative activities and analyzing data—as in advertising and marketing research—or on organizing and scheduling work—as in operating distribution centers, transportation agencies, or the back-end of retailers.

People-oriented jobs tend to pay more, in part because such jobs are more likely to affect sales—the life blood of any business. Thing-oriented jobs, on the other hand, are often seen as cost-generators rather than sales-generators. Taking a big view of the whole company's operations, the thing-oriented jobs are certainly necessary—but without sales no one is needed to do them.

Thing-oriented jobs are usually done at a company's facilities. Further, especially in lower-level jobs, the amount of work to be done—and even the nature of the work—may be spelled out quite clearly. The time it takes to design questionnaires and tabulate results, for example, can be estimated with reasonable accuracy. Similarly, running a warehouse, totaling inventories, scheduling outgoing shipments, and so on, are more like production operations. It's fairly easy to measure an employee's effectiveness and productivity in a thing-oriented job. At least, time spent can be used to measure an employee's contribution.

A sales rep, on the other hand, might spend all weekend thinking and planning how to make a half-hour sales presentation on Monday. For what should the sales rep be compensated—the half-hour presentation, all of the planning and thinking that went into it, or the results? Typically, sales reps are rewarded for their sales results—and this helps account for the sometimes extremely high salaries paid to effective order getters. At the same time, some people-oriented jobs can be routinized and are lower paid. For example, salesclerks in some retail stores are paid at or near the minimum wage.

Managers needed for both kinds of jobs

Here we have oversimplified deliberately to emphasize the differences among types of jobs. Actually, of course, there are many variations between the two extremes. Some sales reps must do a great deal of analytical work before they make a presentation. Similarly, some marketing researchers must be extremely people-sensitive to get potential customers to reveal their true feelings. But the division is still useful because it focuses on the primary emphasis in different kinds of jobs.

Managers are needed for the people in both kinds of jobs. Managing others requires a blend of both people and analytical skills—but people skills may be the more important of the two. Therefore, people-oriented persons are often promoted into managerial positions.

What will differentiate your Product?

After deciding whether you're generally people-oriented or thing-oriented, you're ready for the next step—trying to identify your specific strengths (to be built on) and weaknesses (to be avoided or remedied). It is important to be as specific as possible so you can develop a better marketing plan. For example, if you decide you are more people-oriented, are you more skilled in oral *or* written communication? Or if you are more thing-oriented, what specific analytical or technical skills do you have? Are you good at working with numbers, solving complex problems, or coming to the root of a problem? Other possible strengths include past experience (career-related or otherwise), academic performance, an outgoing personality, enthusiasm, drive, motivation, and so on.

Your plan should build on your strengths. An employer will be hiring you to do something—so promote yourself as someone who is able to do something *well*. In other words, find your competitive advantage in your unique strengths—and then communicate these unique things about *you* and what you can do.

Large companies like Kraft and Colgate-Palmolive regularly recruit college graduates in marketing and other fields.

While trying to identify strengths, you also must realize that you may have some important weaknesses—depending on your objectives. If you are seeking a career that requires technical skills, for example, then you need to get these skills. Or if you are seeking a career that requires independence and self-confidence, then you should try to develop these characteristics in yourself—or change your objectives.

Set some timetables

At this point in your strategy planning process, set some timetables to organize your thinking and the rest of your planning. You need to make some decisions at this point to be sure you see where you're going. You might simply focus on getting your first job, or you might decide to work on two marketing plans: (1) a short-run plan to get your first job and (2) a longer-run plan—perhaps a five-year plan—to show how you're going to accomplish your long-run objectives. People who are basically job-oriented may get away with only a short-run plan—just drifting from one opportunity to another as their own objectives and opportunities change. But those interested in careers need a longer-run plan. Otherwise, they may find themselves pursuing attractive first job opportunities that satisfy short-run objectives—but quickly leave them frustrated when they realize that they can't achieve their long-run objectives without additional training or other experiences.

ENVIRONMENT ANALYSIS

Strategy planning is a matching process. For your own strategy planning, this means matching yourself to career opportunities. So let's look at opportunities available in the marketing environment. (The same approach applies, of course, in the whole business area.) Exhibit C–3 shows some of the possibilities and salary ranges.

Identifying current opportunities in marketing

Because of the wide range of opportunities in marketing, it's helpful to narrow your possibilities. After deciding on your own objectives, strengths, and weaknesses, think about where in the marketing system you might like to work. Would you like to work for manufacturers, or wholesalers, or retailers? Or does it really matter? Do you want to be

Exhibit C–3   Some Career Paths and Salary Ranges

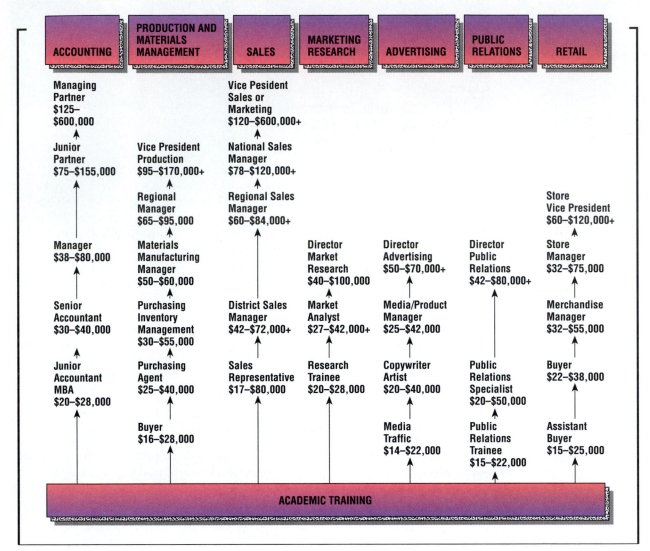

involved with consumer products or business products? By analyzing your feelings about these possibilities, you can begin to zero in on the kind of job and the functional area that might interest you most.

One simple way to get a better idea of the kinds of jobs available in marketing is to review the chapters of this text—this time with an eye for job opportunities rather than new concepts. The following paragraphs briefly describe job areas that marketing graduates are often interested in and give references to specific chapters in the text. Some, as noted below, offer good starting opportunities, while others do not. While reading these paragraphs, keep your own objectives, interests, and strengths in mind.

Marketing manager (Chapter 2)

This is usually not an entry-level job, although aggressive students may move quickly into this role in smaller companies.

Marketing research opportunities (Chapter 5)

There are entry-level opportunities at all levels in the channel (but especially in large firms where more formal marketing research is done) and in advertising agencies and marketing research firms. Quantitative and behavioral science skills are extremely important in marketing research, so many firms prefer to hire statistics or psychology graduates rather than business graduates. But there still are many opportunities in marketing research for marketing graduates. A recent graduate might begin in a training program—conducting interviews or summarizing open-ended answers from questionnaires—before being promoted to assistant project manager and subsequent management positions.

Customer or market analyst (Chapters 3 and 5)

Opportunities as consumer analysts and market analysts are commonly found in large companies, marketing research organizations, and advertising agencies. Beginners start in thing-oriented jobs until their judgment and people-oriented skills are tested. The job may involve collecting or analyzing secondary data or preparation of reports and plans. Because knowledge of statistics, computer software, and/or the behavioral sciences is very important, marketing graduates often find themselves competing with majors in fields such as psychology, sociology, statistics, and computer science. Graduates who have courses in marketing *and* one or more of these areas may have the best opportunities.

Purchasing agent/buyer (Chapter 7)

Entry-level opportunities are commonly found in large companies. Beginners start as trainees or assistant buyers under the supervision of experienced buyers. That's good preparation for a promotion to more responsibility.

Product planner (Chapter 9)

This is usually not an entry-level position. Instead, people with experience on the technical side of the business and/or in sales might be moved into new-product development as they demonstrate judgment and analytical skills.

Product/brand manager (Chapters 8 and 9)

Many multiproduct firms have brand or product managers handling individual products—in effect, managing each product as a separate business. Some firms hire marketing graduates as assistant brand or product managers, although typically only MBAs are considered. Most firms prefer that recent college graduates spend some time in the field doing sales work before moving into brand or product management positions.

Packaging specialists (Chapter 8)

Packaging manufacturers tend to hire and train interested people from various backgrounds—there is little formal academic training in packaging. There are many sales opportunities in this field—and with training, interested people can become specialists fairly quickly in this growing area.

Distribution channel management (Chapter 10)

This work is typically handled or directed by sales managers—and therefore is not an entry-level position.

Physical distribution opportunities (Chapter 10)

There are many sales opportunities with physical distribution specialists—but there are also many thing-oriented jobs involving traffic management, warehousing, and materials handling. Here training in computers, accounting, finance, and quantitative methods could be very useful. These kinds of jobs are available at all levels in the channels of distribution.

Retailing opportunities (Chapter 11)

Most entry-level marketing positions in retailing involve some kind of sales work. Retailing positions tend to offer lower-than-average starting salaries—but they often provide opportunities for very rapid advancement. Most retailers require new employees to have some selling experience before managing others—or buying. A typical marketing graduate can expect to do some sales work and manage one or several departments before advancing to a store management position—or to a staff position that might involve buying, advertising, marketing research, and so on.

Wholesaling opportunities (Chapter 12)

Entry-level jobs with merchant wholesalers typically fall into one of two categories. The first is in the logistics area—working with transportation management, inventory control, distribution customer service, and related activities. The other category usually involves personal selling and customer support. Agent wholesalers typically focus on selling, and entry-level jobs often start out with order-taking responsibilities that grow into order-getting responsibilities.

Sales promotion opportunities (Chapter 13)

There are not many entry-level positions in this area. Creativity and judgment are required, and it is difficult for an inexperienced person to demonstrate these skills. A beginner would probably move from sales or advertising jobs into sales promotion.

Personal sales opportunities (Chapter 14)

Most of the job opportunities—especially entry-level jobs—are in personal selling. This might be order getting, order taking, or missionary selling. Many students are reluctant to get into personal selling—but this field offers benefits that are hard to match in any other field. These include the opportunity to earn extremely high salaries and commissions quickly, a chance to develop your self-confidence and resourcefulness, an opportunity to work with minimal supervision—almost to the point of being your own boss—and a chance to acquire product and customer knowledge that many firms consider necessary for a successful career in product/brand management, sales management, and marketing management. Many salespeople spend their entire careers in selling—preferring the freedom and earning potential that go with a sales job over the headaches and sometimes lower salaries of sales management positions.

Advertising opportunities (Chapter 15)

Job opportunities are varied in this area—and highly competitive. And because the ability to communicate and knowledge of the behavioral sciences are important, marketing graduates often find themselves competing with majors from fields such as English, journalism, psychology, and sociology. There are thing-oriented jobs such as copywriting, media buying, art, and so on. Competition for these jobs is very competitive—and they go to people with a track record. So the entry-level positions are as assistant to a copywriter, media buyer, or art director. There are also people-oriented positions involving work with clients—which are probably of more interest to marketing graduates. This is a glamorous but small and extremely competitive industry where young people can rise very rapidly—but they can also be as easily displaced by new bright young people. Entry-level salaries in advertising are typically low. There are sometimes good opportunities to get started in advertising with a retail chain that prepares its advertising internally. Another way to get more experience with advertising is to take a sales job with one of the media. Selling advertising space in a newspaper or for a magazine may not seem as glamorous as developing TV ads, but media salespeople help their customers solve promotion problems—and get experience dealing with both the business and creative sides of advertising.

Pricing opportunities (Chapters 16 and 17)

Pricing is generally handled by experienced executives, so there are no entry-level opportunities here. However, in a few large companies there are opportunities for marketing graduates who have accounting and quantitative skills as pricing analysts. These people work as assistants to higher-level executives and collect and analyze information about competitors' prices and costs as well as the firm's own costs. The route to these jobs is usually through experience in marketing research or product management.

Credit management opportunities

Specialists in credit have a continuing need for employees who are interested in evaluating customers' credit ratings and ensuring that money gets collected. Both people skills and thing skills can be useful here. Entry positions normally involve a training program—and then working under the supervision of others until your judgment and abilities are tested.

International marketing opportunities

Many marketing students are intrigued with the adventure and foreign travel promised by careers in international marketing. Some firms hire recent college graduates for positions in international marketing, but more often these positions go to MBA graduates. However, that is changing as more and more firms are pursuing international markets. It's an advantage in seeking an international marketing job to know a second language and to know about the culture of the countries where you would like to work. Your college may have courses that would help in these areas. Graduates aiming for a career in international marketing usually must spend time mastering the firm's domestic marketing operations before being sent abroad. So a good way to start is to focus on firms that are already involved in international marketing or planning to move in that direction soon.

Customer relations/consumer affairs opportunities (Chapters 14 and 18)

Most firms are becoming more concerned about their relations with customers and the general public. Employees in this kind of work, however, usually have held various positions with the firm before doing customer relations.

Study trends that may affect your opportunities

A strategy planner should always be evaluating the future because it's easier to go along with trends than to buck them. This means you should watch for political, technical, or economic changes that might open—or close—career opportunities.

If you can spot a trend early, you may be able to prepare yourself to take advantage of it as part of your long-run strategy planning. Other trends might mean you should avoid certain career options. For example, rapid technological changes in computers and communications are likely to lead to major changes in retailing and advertising—as well as in personal selling. Cable television, telephone selling, and direct-mail selling may reduce the need for routine order takers—while increasing the need for higher-level order getters. More targeted and imaginative sales presentations for delivery by mail, phone, or TV screen may be needed. The retailers who survive may need a better understanding of their target markets. And they may need to be supported by wholesalers and manufacturers who can plan targeted promotions that make economic sense. This will require a better understanding of the production and physical distribution side of business—as well as the financial side. And this means better training in accounting, finance, inventory control, and so on. So plan your personal strategy with such trends in mind.

Evaluate business practices

Finally, you need to know how businesses really operate—and the kind of training required for various jobs. We've already seen that there are many opportunities in marketing—but not all jobs are open to everyone, and not all jobs are entry-level jobs. Positions such as marketing manager, brand manager, and sales manager are higher rungs on the marketing career ladder. They become available only when you have a few years of experience and have shown leadership and judgment. Some positions require more education than others. So take a hard look at your long-run objectives—and then see what degree you may need for the kinds of opportunities you might like.

DEVELOP OBJECTIVES

Once you've done a personal analysis and environment analysis—identifying your personal interests, your strengths and weaknesses, and the opportunities in the environment—define your short-run and long-run objectives more specifically.

Develop long-run objectives

Your long-run objectives should clearly state what you want to do—and what you will do for potential employers. You might be as specific as indicating the exact career area you want to pursue over the next 5 to 10 years. For example, your long-run objective might be to apply a set of marketing research and marketing management tools to the food manufacturing industry—with the objective of becoming director of marketing research in a small food manufacturing company.

Your long-run objectives should be realistic and attainable. They should be objectives you have thought about and for which you think you have the necessary skills (or the capabilities to develop those skills) as well as the motivation to reach the objectives.

Develop short-run objectives

To achieve your long-run objective(s), you should develop one or more short-run objectives. These should spell out what you need to reach your long-run objective(s). For example, you might need to develop a variety of marketing research skills *and* marketing management skills—because both are needed to reach the longer-run objective. Or you might need an entry-level position in marketing research for a large food manufacturer—to gain experience and background. An even shorter-run objective might be to take the academic courses necessary to get that desired entry-level job. In this example, you would probably need a minimum of an undergraduate degree in marketing—with an emphasis on marketing research. (Note that, given the longer-run objective of managerial responsibility, a business degree would probably be better than a degree in statistics or psychology.)

DEVELOPING YOUR MARKETING PLAN

Now that you've developed your objectives, move on to developing your own personal marketing plan. This means zeroing in on likely opportunities and developing a specific marketing strategy for these opportunities. Let's talk about that now.

Identify likely opportunities

An important step in strategy planning is identifying potentially attractive opportunities. Depending on where you are in your academic training, this can vary all the way from preliminary exploration to making detailed lists of companies offering the kinds of jobs that interest you. If you're just getting started, talk to your school's career counselors and placement officers about the kinds of jobs being offered to your school's graduates. Your marketing instructors can also help you be realistic about ways you can match your training, abilities, and interests to job opportunities. Also, it helps to read business publications such as *Business Week, Fortune, The Wall Street Journal,* and *Advertising Age.* If you're interested in opportunities in a particular industry, check at your library to see if there are trade publications that can bring you up to speed on the marketing issues in that area. Don't overlook the business sections of your local newspapers to keep in touch with marketing developments in your area. And take advantage of any opportunity to talk with marketers directly. Ask them what they're doing—and what satisfactions they find in their jobs. Also, if your college has a marketing club, join it and participate actively in the club's programs. It will help you meet marketers and students with serious interest in the field. Some may have had interesting job experiences and can provide you with leads on part-time jobs or exciting career opportunities.

If you're far along in your present academic training, list companies that you know something about or are willing to investigate—trying to match your skills and interests with possible opportunities. Narrow your list to a few companies you might like to work for.

If you have trouble narrowing down to specific companies, make a list of your personal interest areas—sports, travel, reading, music, or whatever. Think about the companies that compete in markets related to these interests. Often your own knowledge about these areas—and interest in them—can give you a competitive advantage in getting a job. This helps you focus on companies that serve needs you think are important or interesting.

Then do some research on these companies. Find out how they're organized, their product lines, and their overall strategies. Try to get clear job descriptions for the kinds of positions you're seeking. Match these job descriptions against your understanding of these jobs and your objectives. Jobs with similar titles may offer very different opportunities. By researching job positions and companies in depth, you should begin to have a feel for where you would be comfortable as an employee. This will help you narrow your target market of possible employers to perhaps five firms. For example, you may decide that your target market for an entry position is large corporations with (1) in-depth training programs, (2) a wide product line, and (3) a wide variety of marketing jobs that will enable you to get a range of experiences and responsibilities within the same company.

Planning your Product   Just like any strategy planner, you must decide what Product features are necessary to appeal to your target market. Identify which credentials are mandatory—and which are optional. For example, is your present academic program enough, or will you need more training? Also identify what technical skills are needed—such as computer programming or accounting. Further, are there any business experiences or extracurricular activities that might help make your Product more attractive to employers? This might involve active participation in college organizations or work experience—either on the job or in internships.

Planning your promotion   Once you identify target companies and develop a Product you hope will be attractive to them, you have to tell these potential customers about your Product. You can write directly to prospective employers—sending a carefully developed resume that reflects your strategy planning. Or you can visit them in person (with your résumé). Many colleges run well-organized interviewing services. Seek their advice early in your strategy-planning effort.

IMPLEMENTING YOUR MARKETING PLAN

When you complete your personal marketing plan, you have to implement it—starting with working to accomplish your short-run objectives. If, as part of your plan, you decide that you need specific outside experience, arrange to get it. This may mean taking a low-paying job—or even volunteering to work in political organizations or volunteer organizations where you can get that kind of experience. If you decide that you need skills you can learn in academic courses, plan to take these courses. Similarly, if you don't have a good understanding of your opportunities, then learn as much as you can about possible jobs by talking to professors, taking advanced courses, and talking to businesspeople. And, of course, trends and opportunities can change—so continue to read business publications, talk with professionals in your areas of interest, and be sure that the planning you've done still makes sense.

Strategy planning must adapt to the environment. If the environment changes or your personal objectives change, you have to develop a new plan. This is an ongoing process—and you may never be completely satisfied with your strategy planning. But even trying will make you look much more impressive when you begin your job interviews. Remember, while all employers would like to hire a Superman or a Wonder Woman, they are also impressed with candidates who know what they want to do and are looking for a place where they can fit in—and make a contribution. So planning a personal strategy and implementing it almost guarantee you'll do a better job of career planning, and this will help ensure that you reach your own objectives—whatever they are.

Whether or not you decide to pursue a marketing career, the authors wish you the best of luck in your search for a challenging and rewarding career—wherever your interests and abilities may take you.

Cases

Guide to the Use of These Cases

Cases can be used in many ways. And the same case can be analyzed several times for different purposes.

"Suggested cases" are listed at the end of most chapters, but these cases can also be used later in the text. The main criterion for the order of these cases is the amount of technical vocabulary—or text principles—which are needed to read the case meaningfully. The first cases are easiest in this regard. This is why an early case can easily be used two or three times—with different emphasis. Some early cases might require some consideration of Product and Price, for example, and might be used twice, perhaps regarding product planning and, later, pricing. In contrast, later cases, which focus more on Price, might be treated more effectively *after* the Price chapters are covered.

1 McDonald's "Seniors" Restaurant

Patty Maloney is manager of a McDonald's restaurant in a city with many "seniors." She has noticed that some senior citizens have become not just regular patrons—but patrons who come for breakfast and stay on until about 3 P.M. Many of these older customers were attracted initially by a monthly breakfast special for people aged 55 and older. The meal costs $.99, and refills of coffee are free. Every fourth Monday, between 100 and 150 seniors jam Patty's McDonald's for the special offer. But now almost as many of them are coming every day—turning the fast-food restaurant into a meeting place. They sit for hours with a cup of coffee, chatting with friends. On most days, as many as 100 will stay from one to four hours.

Patty's employees have been very friendly to the seniors, calling them by their first names and visiting with them each day. In fact, Patty's McDonald's is a happy place—with her employees developing close relationships with the seniors. Some employees have even visited customers who have been hospitalized. "You know," Patty says, "I really get attached to the customers. They're like my family. I really care about these people." They are all "friends" and being friendly with the customers is a part of McDonald's corporate philosophy.

These older customers are an orderly group—and very friendly to anyone who comes in. Further, they are neater than most customers, and carefully clean up their tables before they leave. Nevertheless, Patty is beginning to wonder if anything should be done about her growing "non-fast-food" clientele. There's no crowding problem yet, during the time when the seniors like to come. But if the size of the senior citizen group continues to grow, crowding could become a problem. Further, Patty is concerned that her restaurant might come to be known as an "old people's" restaurant—which might discourage some younger customers. And if customers felt the restaurant was crowded, some might feel that they wouldn't get fast service. On the other hand, a place that seems busy might be seen as "a good place to go" and a "friendly place."

Patty also worries about the image she is projecting. McDonald's is a fast-food restaurant, and normally customers are expected to eat and run. Will allowing people to stay and visit change the whole concept? In the extreme, Patty's McDonald's might become more like a European-style restaurant where the customers are never rushed—and feel very comfortable about lingering over coffee for an hour or two! Patty knows that the amount her senior customers spend is similar to the average customer's purchase—but the seniors do use the facilities for a much longer time. However, most of the older customers leave McDonald's by 11:30—before the noon crowd comes in.

Patty is also concerned about another possibility. If catering to seniors is OK, then should she do even more with this age group? In particular, she is considering offering bingo games during the slow morning hours—9 A.M. to 11 A.M. Bingo is popular with some seniors, and this could be a new revenue source—beyond the extra food and drink purchases which probably would result. She figures she could charge $3 per person for the two-hour period and run it with two underutilized employees. The prizes would be coupons for purchases at her store (to keep it legal) and would amount to about two thirds of the bingo receipts (at retail prices). The party room area of her McDonald's would be perfect for this use and could hold up to 150 persons.

Evaluate Patty Maloney's current strategy regarding senior citizens. Does this strategy improve this McDonald's image? What should she do about the senior citizen market—should she encourage, ignore, or discourage her seniors? What should she do about the bingo idea? Explain.

2 Nutra, Inc.

It is 1991, and Dan Martin, newly elected president of Nutra, Inc., faces a severe decline in profits. Nutra, Inc., is a 123-year-old California-based food processor. Its multiproduct lines are widely accepted under the Nutra brand. The company and its subsidiaries prepare, package, and sell canned and frozen foods—including fruits, vegetables, pickles, and condiments. Nutra, which operates more than 27 processing plants in the United States, is one of the largest U.S. food processors—with annual sales (in 1990) of about $650 million.

Until 1989, Nutra was a subsidiary of a major midwestern food processor (Swift, Inc.), and many of the present managers came from the parent company. Nutra's last president recently said: "Swift's influence is still with us. As long as new products look like they will increase the company's sales volume, they are produced. Traditionally, there has been little, if any, attention paid to margins. We are well aware that profits will come through good products produced in large volume."

Fred Lynch, a 25-year employee and now production manager, agrees with the multiproduct-line policy. Mr. Lynch says: "Volume comes from satisfying needs. We will can or freeze any vegetable or fruit we think consumers might want." He also admits that much of the expansion in product lines was encouraged by economics. The typical plants in the industry are not fully used. By adding new products to use this excess capacity, costs are spread over greater volume. So the production department is always looking for new ways to make more effective use of its present facilities.

The wide expansion of product lines, coupled with Nutra's line-forcing policy, has resulted in 88 percent of the firm's sales coming from supermarket chain stores—such as Safeway, Kroger, and A&P. Smaller stores are generally not willing to accept the Nutra policy—which requires that any store wanting to carry its brand name must be willing to carry all 65 items in the line. Mr. Lynch explains: "We know that only large stores can afford to stock all our products. But the large stores are the volume! We give consumers the choice of any Nutra product they want, and the result is maximum sales." Many small retailers have complained about Nutra's policy, but they have been ignored because they are considered too small in potential sales volume per store to be of any significance.

In 1991, a stockholders' revolt over low profits (in 1990, they were only $500,000) resulted in Nutra's president and two of its five directors being removed. Dan Martin, an accountant from the company's outside auditing firm, was brought in as president. One of the first things he focused on was the variable and low levels of profits in the past several years. A comparison of Nutra's results with comparable operations of some large competitors supported Mr. Martin's concern. In the past 13 years, Nutra's closest competitors had an average profit return on shareholder's investment of 6 to 12 percent, while Nutra averaged only 2.5 percent. Further, Nutra's sales volume, $650 million in 1990, has not increased much from the 1956 level (after adjusting for inflation)—while operating costs have soared upward. Profits for the firm were about $8 million in 1956. The closest Nutra has come since then is about $6 million—in 1964.

The outgoing president blamed his failure on an inefficient sales department. He said: "Our sales department has deteriorated. I can't exactly put my finger on it, but the overall quality of salespeople has dropped, and morale is bad. The team just didn't perform." When Mr. Martin confronted Jose Lopez—the vice president of sales—with this charge, his reply was: "It's not our fault. I think the company made a key mistake after World War II. It expanded horizontally—by increasing its number of product offerings—while major competitors were expanding vertically, growing their own raw materials and making all of their packing materials. They can control quality and make profits in manufacturing that can be used in promotion. I lost some of my best people from frustration. We just aren't competitive enough to reach the market the way we should with a comparable product and price."

In further conversation with Jose Lopez, Mr. Martin learned more about the nature of Nutra's market. Although all the firms in the food-processing industry advertise heavily, the size of the market for most processed foods hasn't grown much for many years. Further, most consumers aren't very selective. If they can't find the brand of food they are looking for, they'll pick up another brand rather than go without a basic part of their diet. No company in the industry has much effect on the price at which its products are sold. Chain store buyers are very knowledgeable about prices and special promotions available from all the competing suppliers, and they are quick to play one supplier against another to keep the price low. Basically, they have a price they are willing to pay—and they won't exceed it. However, the chains will charge any price they wish on a given brand sold at retail. (That is, a 48-can case of beans might be purchased from any supplier for $18.10, no matter whose product it is. Generally, the shelf price for each is no more than a few pennies different, but chain stores occasionally attract customers by placing a well-known brand on sale.)

Besides insisting that processors meet price points, like for the canned beans, some chains require price allowances if special locations or displays are desired. They also carry nonadvertised brands and/or their own brands at lower price—to offer better value to their customers. And most will willingly accept producers' cents-off coupons—which are offered by Nutra as well as most of the other major producers of full lines.

At this point, Mr. Martin is trying to decide why Nutra, Inc., isn't as profitable as it once was. And he is puzzled about why some competitors are putting products on the market with low potential sales volume. (For example, one major competitor recently introduced a line of gourmet vegetables with sauces.) And others have been offering frozen dinners or entrees with vegetables for several years. Apparently, Nutra's managers considered trying such products several years ago but decided against it because of the small potential sales volumes and the likely high costs of new-product development and promotion.

Evaluate Nutra's present situation. What would you advise Mr. Martin to do to improve Nutra's profits? Explain why.

3 Gerber Products Company

Andrea Kelly, president of Kelly Research, Inc., wants to develop a research proposal for Gerber Products Company's CEO, David Johnson, who is seriously looking for new product-market opportunities which might make sense for Gerber. As the new CEO, David Johnson has just cleaned out some weak diversification efforts—including trucking, furniture, and toy ventures—which tended to take the company away from its core baby food business. Now he is looking for new opportunities close to the food business. But Mr. Johnson has also made it clear that Gerber may want to move beyond baby foods because only about 4 percent of U.S. households have babies—and the baby food market is *very* competitive.

Mr. Johnson (according to trade press articles) would like new ideas for "premium-quality, value-added products in niche markets." It might be possible, for example, to extend the sales of its baby food products to adults (in general) and/or senior citizens. Some of its current chunky food items are intended for older tots and might be attractive to some adults. They are no-salt, easy-to-chew items. But care may be needed in expanding into these markets. Gerber had troubles in the 1970s with some products that were intended for adult tastes—one was beef stroganoff in a baby-food jar. Yet Mr. Johnson now wonders, "How come we can't develop food products that target everyone over the toddler age?"

Recent new Gerber product offerings include a line of applesauce-based fruit cups, bottled water, and shelf-stable homogenized milk. All three of these seem to fit with Gerber's growth plans—offering more premium-quality, value-added products to niche markets. Further growth efforts might include products that will enable the company to get enough experience to understand a market area and be able to pursue joint ventures or acquisitions. This might include activities other than food, or at least baby food—which has become almost a commodity business. The feeling of some Gerber executives is that "opportunities must be better elsewhere—in niches that haven't been worked as hard as baby food." Some market possibilities that have been mentioned in the food-oriented trade press for a company like Gerber are canned or frozen food items for restaurants, military commissaries, gourmet food stores, or specialty departments in chain food stores.

Mr. Johnson's background includes not only domestic but international marketing with major companies that sell cleaning products, health and beauty aids, drug products, and baked goods. So it is likely that he will be willing to consider going quite far from baby foods. And given that Gerber is a major U.S. food processor—with sales over $1 billion—it is clear the company has the production, distribution, and financial resources to consider a good-sized product-market opportunity. But are there any attractive new opportunities—or must Gerber simply copy someone else's earlier developments?

Andrea Kelly wants to develop a research proposal to find and evaluate some new opportunities for Gerber. But she wants to narrow the scope of the search somewhat so she doesn't seem to be "fishing in the whole ocean." She also wants to suggest some attractive-sounding possibilities to catch Mr. Johnson's attention. So she is asking her staff for ideas—to make her proposal more attractive.

Explain how Andrea Kelly should go about selecting possible "attractive opportunities." Suggest five product-market opportunities that might make sense for Mr. Johnson and Gerber Products Company, and explain why.

4 Jim's Service, Inc.

Jim Dickson is getting desperate about his new business. He's not sure he can make a go of it—and he really wants to stay in his hometown of Petoskey, Michigan, a beautiful summer resort area along the eastern shore of Lake Michigan. The area's permanent population of 10,000 more than triples in the summer months and doubles at times during the winter skiing and snowmobiling season.

Jim spent seven years in the Marines after high school graduation, returning home in June 1991. He decided to go into business for himself because he couldn't find a good job in the Petoskey area. He set up Jim's Service, Inc. He thought that his savings would allow him to start the business without borrowing any money. His estimates of required expenditures were $7,000 for a used panel truck, $625 for a steam-cleaning machine adaptable to carpets and furniture, $400 for a heavy-duty commercial vacuum cleaner, $50 for special brushes and attachments, $100 for the initial supply of cleaning fluids and compounds, and $200 for insurance and other incidental expenses. This total of $8,375 still left Jim with about $3,000 in savings to cover living expenses while getting started.

One of the reasons Jim chose the cleaning business was his previous work experience. From the time he was 16, Jim had worked part-time for Joel Bullard. Mr. Bullard operates the only successful complete (carpet, furniture, walls, etc.) cleaning company in Petoskey. (There is one other cleaning company in Petoskey, but it is rumored to be near bankruptcy.)

Mr. Bullard prides himself on quality work and has a loyal clientele. Specializing in residential carpet cleaning and furniture care, Bullard has built a strong customer franchise. For 40 years, Bullard's major source of new business—besides retailer recommendations—has been satisfied customers who tell friends about his quality service. He is so highly thought of that the leading carpet and furniture stores in Petoskey always recommend Bullard for preventive maintenance in quality carpet and furniture care. Often Bullard is given the keys to the area's finest homes for months at a time—when owners are out of town and want his services. Bullard's customers are so loyal, in fact, that Vita-Clean—a national household carpet-cleaning franchise—found it impossible to compete with him. Even price cutting was not an effective weapon against Mr. Bullard.

Jim Dickson thought that he knew the business as well as Mr. Bullard—having worked for him many years. Jim was anxious to reach his $60,000-per-year sales objective because he thought this would provide him with a comfortable living in Petoskey. While aware of cleaning opportunities in businesses such as office buildings and motels, Jim felt that the sales volume available there was small because most businesses had their own cleaning staffs. As Jim saw it, his only opportunity was direct competition with Mr. Bullard.

To get started, Jim spent $1,000 to advertise his business in the local newspaper. With this money he bought two large announcement ads and 52 weeks of daily ads in the classified section—listed under Miscellaneous Residential Services. He painted a sign on his truck and waited for business to take off.

Jim had a few customers and was able to gross about $130 a week. Of course, he had expected much more. These customers were usually Bullard regulars who, for one reason or another (usually stains, spills, or house guests), weren't able to wait the two weeks until Bullard could work them in. While these people agreed that Jim's work was of the same quality as Mr. Bullard's, they preferred Bullard's "quality-care" image. Sometimes Jim did get more work than he could handle. This happened during April and May—when seasonal businesses were preparing for summer openings and owners of summer homes and condos were ready to "open the cottage." The same rush occurred in September and October—as many of these places were being closed for the winter. During these months, Jim was able to gross about $130 to $150 a day—working 10 hours.

Toward the end of his discouraging first year in business, Jim Dickson is thinking about quitting. While he hates to think about leaving Petoskey, he can't see any way of making a living there in the carpet and furniture-cleaning business. Mr. Bullard seems to have dominated the market—except in the rush seasons and for people who need emergency cleaning. And the resort housing market is not growing very fast, so there is little hope of a big increase in potential customers.

Evaluate Jim Dickson's strategy planning for his new business. Why wasn't he able to reach his objective of $60,000? What should Jim do now? Explain.

5 General Chemical Company

Kim Lu, a chemist in General Chemical's polymer resins laboratory, is trying to decide how hard to fight for the new product he has developed. Lu's job is to find new, more profitable applications for the company's present resin products—and his current efforts are running into unexpected problems.

During the last four years, Lu has been under heavy pressure from his managers to come up with an idea that will open up new markets for the company's foamed polystyrene.

Two years ago, Lu developed the "foamed-dome concept"—a method of using foamed polystyrene to make dome-shaped roofs and other structures. He described the procedure for making domes as follows: The construction of a foamed dome involves the use of a specially designed machine that bends, places, and bonds pieces of plastic foam together into a predetermined dome shape. In forming a dome, the machine head is mounted on a boom, which swings around a pivot like the hands of a clock, laying and bonding layer upon layer of foam board in a rising spherical form.

According to Lu, polystyrene foamed boards have several advantages:

1. Foam board is stiff—but can be formed or bonded to itself by heat alone.
2. Foam board is extremely lightweight and easy to handle. It has good structural rigidity.
3. Foam board has excellent and permanent insulating characteristics. (In fact, the major use for foam board is as an insulator.)
4. Foam board provides an excellent base on which to apply a variety of surface finishes.

Using his good selling abilities, Lu easily convinced his managers that his idea had potential.

According to a preliminary study by the marketing research department, the following were areas of construction that could be served by the domes:

1. Bulk storage.
2. Cold storage.
3. Educational construction.
4. Covers for industrial tanks.
5. Light commercial construction.
6. Planetariums.
7. Recreational construction (such as a golf-course starter house).

The marketing research study focused on uses for existing dome structures. Most of the existing domes are made of cement-based materials. The study showed that large savings would result from using foam boards—due to the reduction of construction time.

Because of the new technology involved, the company decided to do its own contracting (at least for the first four to five years). Lu thought this was necessary to make sure that no mistakes were made by inexperienced contractor crews. (For example, if not applied properly, the plastic may burn.)

After building a few domes in the United States to demonstrate the concept, Lu contacted some leading U.S. architects. Reactions were as follows:

"It's very interesting, but we're not sure the fire marshall of Chicago would ever give his OK."

"Your tests show that foamed domes can be protected against fires, but there are no good tests for unconventional building materials as far as I am concerned."

"I like the idea, but foam board does not have the impact resistance of cement."

"We design a lot of recreational facilities, and kids will find a way of poking holes in the foam."

"Building codes in our area are written for wood and cement structures. Maybe we'd be interested if the codes change."

After this unexpected reaction, management didn't know what to do. Lu still thinks they should go ahead with the project. He wants to build several more demonstration projects in the United States and at least three each in Europe and Japan to expose the concept in the global market. He thinks architects outside the United States may be more receptive to really new ideas. Further, he says, it takes time for potential users to "see" and accept new ideas. He is sure that more exposure to more people will speed acceptance. And he is convinced that a few reports of well-constructed domes in leading trade papers and magazines will go a long way toward selling the idea. He is working on getting such reports right now. But his managers aren't sure they want to OK spending more money on "his" project. His immediate boss is supportive, but the rest of the review board is less sure about more demonstration projects or going ahead at all—just in the United States or in global markets.

Evaluate how they got into the present situation. What should Kim Lu do? What should Lu's managers do? Explain.

6 Bethlehem Steel Company

Bethlehem Steel Company is one of the two major producers of wide-flange beams in the United States. The other major producer is the U.S. Steel Corporation (now USX). A few small and lower-cost firms compete, and have tended to push prices lower in a flat construction market. Typically, all interested competitors charge the same delivered price, which varies some depending on how far the customer is from either of the two major producers. In other words, local prices are higher in more remote geographic markets.

Wide-flange beams are one of the principal steel products used in construction. They are the modern version of what are commonly known as I-beams. U.S. Steel rolls a full range of wide flanges from 6 to 36 inches. Bethlehem entered the field about 30 years ago—when it converted an existing mill to produce this product. Bethlehem's mill is limited to flanges up to 24 inches, however. At the time of the conversion, Bethlehem felt that customer usage of sizes over 24 inches was likely to be small. In the past few years, however, there has been a definite trend toward the larger and heavier sections.

The beams produced by the various competitors are almost identical—since customers buy according to standard dimensional and physical-property specifications. In the smaller size range, there are a number of competitors. But above 14 inches, only U.S. Steel and Bethlehem compete. Above 24 inches, U.S. Steel has no competition.

All the steel companies sell these beams through their own sales forces. The customer for these beams is called a structural fabricator. This fabricator typically buys unshaped beams and other steel products from the mills and shapes them according to the specifications of each customer. The fabricator sells to the contractor or owner of the structure being built.

The structural fabricator usually must sell on a competitive-bid basis. The bidding is done on the plans and specifications prepared by an architectural or structural engineering firm—and forwarded to the fabricator by the contractor who wants the bid. Although thousands of structural fabricators compete in the U.S., relatively few account for the majority of wide-flange tonnage in the various geographical regions. Since the price is the same from all producers, they typically buy beams on the basis of availability (i.e., availability to meet production schedules) and performance (i.e., reliability in meeting the promised delivery schedule).

Several years ago, Bethlehem's production schedulers saw that they were going to have an excess of hot-rolled plate capacity in the near future. At the same time, a new production technique allowed a steel company to weld three plates together into a section with the same dimensional and physical properties and almost the same cross-section as a rolled wide-flange beam. This development appeared to offer two advantages to Bethlehem. (1) It would enable Bethlehem to use some of the excess plate capacity. (2) Larger sizes of wide-flange beams could be offered. Cost analysts showed that by using a fully depreciated plate mill and the new welding process it would be possible to produce and sell larger wide-flange beams at competitive prices—at the same price charged by U.S. Steel.

Bethlehem's managers were excited about the possibilities because customers usually appreciate having a second source of supply. Also, the new approach would allow the production of up to a 60-inch flange. With a little imagination, these larger sizes might offer a significant breakthrough for the construction industry.

Bethlehem decided to go ahead with the new project. As the production capacity was converted, the salespeople were kept well informed of the progress. They, in turn, promoted this new capability to their customers—emphasizing that soon they would be able to offer a full range of beam products. Bethlehem sent several general information letters to a broad mailing list but did not advertise. The market development section of the sales department was very busy explaining the new possibilities of the process to fabricators—at engineering trade associations and shows.

When the new production line was finally ready to go, the market reaction was disappointing. No orders came in and none were expected. In general, customers were wary of the new product. The structural fabricators felt they couldn't use it without the approval of their customers—because it would involve deviating from the specified rolled sections. And as long as they could still get the rolled section, why make the extra effort for something unfamiliar—especially with no price advantage. The salespeople were also bothered with a very common question: How can you take plate that you sell for about $460 per ton and make a product that you can sell for $470? This question came up frequently and tended to divert the whole discussion to the cost of production—rather than to the way the new product might be used.

Evaluate Bethlehem's situation. What should Bethlehem do?

7 Pillsbury's Häagen-Dazs

Carol Hodgman is the newly hired ice-cream product-market manager for the United States for Häagen-Dazs—the market leader in the U.S. super premium ice cream market. The company has seen its sales continue to grow during the 1980s and early 1990s, but the markets may be on the edge of significant change and very aggressive competition. Ms. Hodgman is now responsible for Häagen-Dazs's ice cream strategy planning for the United States.

Other product-market managers are responsible for Europe, Japan, and other global markets—where very rapid growth is expected, following on what happened (and happens) in the United States. Therefore, Ms. Hodgman will be expected to focus only on the United States while knowing that "everyone" will be watching her (and the United States) for clues about what may happen elsewhere.

Sales growth in super premium ice cream is slowing down in the United States, in part because of competition from other products, such as lower-calorie yogurts and ice milk. Some producers' sales, including Häagen-Dazs, are continuing to grow at attractive rates—10 to 50 percent a year. But other U.S. super premium producers are reporting flat sales—and some are going out of business.

There is also some evidence that Americans are becoming more concerned with diet and health and reducing or even eliminating super desserts. And "dessert junkies" who want to indulge without too much guilt are turning to soft frozen yogurt and low-calorie ice milk. This has encouraged some super premium ice cream competitors to offer these products too. Pillsbury's Häagen-Dazs, International Dairy Queen, Inc., and Baskin and Robbins are selling frozen yogurt. And Kraft, Inc., which makes Frusen Glädjé, and Dreyer's Grand Ice Cream, Inc., are among many other ice cream makers who are promoting gourmet versions of ice milk. Some producers are even seeking government approval to call such ice milk "light ice cream."

Most ice cream products are considered economy and regular brands—priced at $2 to $3 a half gallon. But the higher priced—and higher profit—super premium products provided most of the growth in the ice cream market in the 1980s. The super premium ice cream category accounted for about 12 percent of total ice cream sales ($7 billion) in 1990 compared to almost 5 percent in 1980.

Super premium ice cream, with more than 14 percent butter fat (economy ice cream has a minimum of 10 percent) is the ultimate ice cream product—rich, indulgent, and fashionable. It retails for $2 to $2.50 a *pint, or* $8 to $10 a half gallon.

The rapid growth of the U.S. super premium market may be over, as more and more consumers become concerned about cholesterol (and ice cream is high in cholesterol). Some of the super premium producers remain optimistic, however. Häagen-Dazs, for example, feels that because "people like to make every calorie count—they want wonderful food." But other competitors are more concerned because they see many close competitors going out of business. The easy availability of super premium ice cream in supermarkets has hurt some competitors who sell through ice cream stores, which specialize in take-out cones, sundaes, and small containers of ice cream.

Many U.S. ice cream producers are turning to frozen yogurt for growth. A fad in the 1970s, frozen yogurt went into a long slump because many people didn't like the tart taste. But now the product has been reformulated and is winning customers. The difference is that today's frozen yogurt tastes more like ice cream.

The yogurt market leader, TCBY Enterprises, Inc., which had sales of only about $2 million in 1983, has risen to over $100 million in sales. U.S. yogurt makers are using aggressive promotion against ice cream. TCBY ads preach: "Say goodbye to high calories—say goodbye to ice cream" and "All the pleasure, none of the guilt." And the ads for its nonfat frozen yogurt emphasize: "Say goodbye to fat and high calories with the great taste of TCBY Nonfat Frozen Yogurt."

Baskin Robbins has introduced yogurt in many of its U.S. stores and has even changed its name to Baskin Robbins Ice Cream and Yogurt. Häagen-Dazs also offers yogurt in most of its stores.

A new threat to super premium ice cream comes from ice milk. Traditionally, ice milk was an economical product for families on a budget. The butter fat content was at the low end of the 2 to 7 percent range. And, in part because of this, it was dense, gummy, stringy, and had a coarse texture. But the new "gourmet" ice milk products taste better due to 6 to 7 percent butter fat, less air content, and improved processing. And they still have only about half the calories of ice cream. Some U.S. producers of these products find their sales increasing nicely. Dreyer's, for example, is experiencing rapid growth of its Dreyer's Light, which retails for about $4.30 a half gallon.

Other ice cream producers, including Häagen-Dazs, have been saying they are not planning to offer ice milk—under any name. These firms feel their brands stand for high quality and the best ingredients and they do not want to offer a cheap product. As one marketing manager put it, "Ice milk is a failure, and that is why some producers are trying to reposition it as light ice cream."

Evaluate what is happening in the ice cream market, especially regarding the apparent leveling off of the super premium ice cream market and the possible growth of the ice milk market. Should Carol Hodgman plan to have Häagen-Dazs offer an ice milk product in the near future—either under the Häagen-Dazs brand or another brand? Why?

8 Emil's Place

Emil Fortino, the owner of Emil's Place, is reviewing the slow growth of his restaurant. He's also thinking about the future and wondering if he should change his strategy. In particular, he is wondering if he should join a fast food or family restaurant franchise chain. Several are located near him, but there are many franchisors without local restaurants. He has heard that with help from the franchisors, some of these places gross $500,000 to $1 million a year. Of course, he would have to follow someone else's strategy—and thereby lose his independence, which he doesn't like to think about. But those sales figures do sound good, and he has also heard that the return to the owner-manager (including salary) can be over $100,000 per year.

Emil's Place is a fairly large restaurant—about 2,000 square feet—located in the center of a small shopping center completed early in 1990. In addition to Emil's restaurant, other businesses in the shopping center include a supermarket, a beauty shop, a liquor store, a hardware-variety store, and a video rental store. Ample parking space is available.

The shopping center is located in a residential section of a growing suburb in the East—along a heavily traveled major traffic route. The nearby population is mostly middle-income Italian-American families.

Emil's sells mainly full-course "home-cooked" Italian-style dinners (no bar) at moderate prices. Emil's is owned and managed by Emil Fortino. He graduated from a local high school and a nearby university and has lived in this town with his wife and two children for many years. He has been self-employed in the restaurant business since his graduation from college in 1962. His most recent venture—before opening Emil's—was a large restaurant that he operated successfully with his brother from 1980 to 1986. In 1986, Emil sold out his share because of illness. Following his recovery, Emil was anxious for something to do and opened the present restaurant in April 1990.

Emil feels his plans for the business and his opening were well thought out. When he was ready to start his new restaurant, he looked at several possible locations before finally deciding on the present one. Emil explained: "I looked everywhere, but here I particularly noticed the heavy traffic when I first looked at it. This is the crossroads for practically every main road statewide. So obviously the potential is here."

Having decided on the location, Emil signed a 10-year lease with option to renew for 10 more years, and then eagerly attacked the problem of outfitting the almost empty store space in the newly constructed building. He tiled the floor, put in walls of surfwood, installed plumbing and electrical fixtures and an extra washroom, and purchased the necessary restaurant equipment. All this cost $70,000—which came from his own cash savings. He then spent an additional $1,500 for glassware, $2,000 for an initial food stock, and $1,625 to advertise Emil's Place's opening in the local newspaper. The paper serves the whole metro area, so the $1,625 bought only three quarter-page ads. These expenditures also came from his own personal savings. Next he hired five waitresses at $150 a week and one chef at $300 a week. Then, with $20,000 cash reserve for the business, he was ready to open. (His wife—a high school teacher—was willing to support the family until the restaurant caught on.) Reflecting his sound business sense, Emil knew he would need a substantial cash reserve to fall back on until the business got on its feet. He expected this to take about one year. He had no expectations of getting rich overnight.

The restaurant opened in April and by August had a weekly gross revenue of only $1,800. Emil was a little discouraged with this, but he was still able to meet all his operating expenses without investing any new money in the business. By September business was still slow, and

Emil had to invest an additional $2,000 in the business just to survive.

Business had not improved in November, and Emil stepped up his advertising—hoping this would help. In December, he spent $600 of his cash reserve for radio advertising—10 late evening spots on a news program at a station that aims at middle-income America. Emil also spent $1,100 more during the next several weeks for some metro newspaper ads.

By April 1991, the situation had begun to improve, and by June his weekly gross was up to between $2,100 and $2,300. By March of 1992, the weekly gross had risen to about $2,800. Emil increased the working hours of his staff six to seven hours a week—and added another cook to handle the increasing number of customers. Emil was more optimistic for the future because he was finally doing a little better than breaking even. His full-time involvement seemed to be paying off. He had not put any new money into the business since the summer of 1991 and expected business to continue to rise. He had not yet taken any salary for himself, even though he had built up a small surplus of about $5,000. Instead, he planned to put in a bigger air-conditioning system at a cost of $4,000—and was also planning to use what salary he might have taken for himself to hire two new waitresses to handle the growing volume of business. And he saw that if business increased much more he would have to add another cook.

Evaluate Emil's past and present marketing strategy. What should he do now? Should he seriously consider joining some franchise chain?

⑨ Sleepy-Inn Motel

Jack Roth is trying to decide whether he should make some minor changes in the way he operates his Sleepy-Inn Motel or if he should join either the Days Inn or Holiday Inn motel chains. Some decision must be made soon because his present operation is losing money. But joining either of the chains will require fairly substantial changes, including new capital investment if he goes with Holiday Inn.

Jack bought the recently completed 60-room motel two years ago after leaving a successful career as a production manager for a large producer of industrial machinery. He was looking for an interesting opportunity that would be less demanding than the production manager job. The Sleepy-Inn is located at the edge of a very small town near a rapidly expanding resort area and about one-half mile off an interstate highway. It is 10 miles from the tourist area, with several nationally franchised full-service resort motels suitable for "destination" vacations. There is a Best Western, a Ramada Inn, and a Hilton Inn, as well as many "mom and pop" and limited service–lower price motels in the tourist area. The interstate highway near the Sleepy-Inn carries a great deal of traffic since the resort area is between several major metropolitan areas. No development has taken place around the turnoff from the interstate highway. The only promotion for the tourist area along the interstate highway is two large signs near the turnoffs. They show the popular name for the area and that the area is only 10 miles to the west. These signs are maintained by the tourist area's Tourist Bureau. In addition, the state transportation department maintains several small signs showing (by symbols) that near this turnoff one can find gas, food, and lodging. Jack does not have any signs advertising Sleepy-Inn except the two on his property. He has been relying on people finding his motel as they go towards the resort area.

Initially, Jack was very pleased with his purchase. He had traveled a lot himself and stayed in many different hotels and motels—so he had some definite ideas about what travelers wanted. He felt that a relatively plain but modern room with a comfortable bed, standard bath facilities, and free cable TV would appeal to most customers. Further, Jack thought a swimming pool or any other non-revenue-producing additions were not necessary. And he felt a restaurant would be a greater management problem than the benefits it would offer. However, after many customers commented about the lack of convenient breakfast facilities, Jack served a free continental breakfast of coffee, juice, and rolls in a room next to the registration desk.

Day-to-day operations went fairly smoothly in the first two years, in part because Jack and his wife handled registration and office duties—as well as general management. During the first year of operation, occupancy began to stabilize around 55 percent of capacity. But according to industry figures, this was far below the average of 68 percent for his classification—motels without restaurants.

After two years of operation, Jack was concerned because his occupancy rates continued to be below average. He decided to look for ways to increase both occupancy rate and profitability—and still maintain his independence.

Jack wanted to avoid direct competition with the full-service resort motels. He stressed a price appeal in his signs and brochures—and was quite proud of the fact that he had been able to avoid all the "unnecessary expenses" of the full-service resort motels. As a result, Jack was able to offer lodging at a very modest price— about 40 percent below the full-service hotels and comparable to the lowest-priced resort area motels. The customers who stayed at Sleepy-Inn said they found it quite acceptable. But he was troubled by what seemed to be a large number of people driving into his parking lot, looking around, and not coming in to register.

Jack was particularly interested in the results of a recent study by the regional tourist bureau. This study revealed the following information about area vacationers:

1. 68 percent of the visitors to the area are young couples and older couples without children.
2. 40 percent of the visitors plan their vacations and reserve rooms more than 60 days in advance.
3. 66 percent of the visitors stay more than three days in the area and at the same location.
4. 78 percent of the visitors indicated that recreational facilities were important in their choice of accommodations.
5. 13 percent of the visitors had family incomes of less than $20,000 per year.
6. 38 percent of the visitors indicated that it was their first visit to the area.

After much thought, Jack began to seriously consider affiliating with a national motel chain in hopes of attracting more customers and maybe protecting his motel from the increasing competition. There were constant rumors that more motels were being planned for the area. After some investigating, he focused on two national chain possibilities: Days Inn and Holiday Inn. Neither had affiliates in the area.

Days Inn of America, Inc., is an Atlanta-based chain of economy lodgings. It has been growing rapidly—and is willing to take on new franchisees. A major advantage of Days Inn is that it would not require a major capital investment by Jack. The firm is targeting people interested in lower-priced motels—in particular senior citizens, the military, school sports teams, educators, and business travelers. In contrast, Holiday Inn would probably require Jack to upgrade some of his facilities, including adding a swimming pool. The total new capital investment would be between $300,000 and $500,000 depending on how fancy he got. But then Jack would be able to charge higher prices—perhaps $70 per day on the average, rather than the $40 per day per room he's charging now.

The major advantages of going with either of these national chains would be their central reservation system—and their national names. Both companies offer toll-free reservation lines—nationwide—which produce about 40 percent of all bookings in affiliated motels.

A major difference between the two national chains is their method of promotion. Days Inn uses little TV advertising and less print advertising than Holiday Inn. Instead, Days Inn emphasizes sales promotions. In a recent campaign, for example, Blue Bonnet margarine users could exchange proof-of-purchase seals for a free night at a Days Inn. This tie-in led to the Days Inn system *selling* an additional 10,000 rooms. Further, Days Inn operates a September Days Club for over 300,000 senior citizens who receive such benefits as discount rates and a quarterly travel magazine. This club accounts for about 10 percent of the chain's room revenues.

Both firms charge 8 percent of gross room revenues for belonging to their chain—to cover the costs of the reservation service and national promotion. This amount is payable monthly. In addition, franchise members must agree to maintain their facilities—and make repairs and improvements as required. Failure to maintain facilities can result in losing the franchise. Periodic inspections are conducted as part of supervising the whole chain and helping the members operate more effectively.

Evaluate Jack Roth's present strategy. What should he do? Explain.

10 Grand Arena

Matt O'Keefe, the manager of Grand Arena, is trying to decide what strategies to use to increase profits.

Grand Arena is an ice-skating rink with a conventional hockey rink surface (85 feet × 200 feet). It is the only indoor ice rink in a northern U.S. city of about 450,000. The city operates some outdoor rinks in the winter, but they don't offer regular ice skating programs because of weather variability.

Matt runs a successful hockey program that is more than breaking even—but this is about all he can expect if he only offers hockey. To try to increase his profits, Matt is trying to expand and improve his public skating program. With such a program, he could have as many as 700 people in a public session at one time, instead of limiting the use of the ice to 12 to 24 hockey players per hour. While the receipts from hockey can be as high as $140 an hour (plus concession sales), the receipts from a two-hour public skating session—charging $3 per person—

could yield up to $2,100 for a two-hour period (plus much higher concession sales). The potential revenue from such large public skating sessions could make Grand Arena a really profitable operation. But, unfortunately, just scheduling public sessions doesn't mean that a large number will come. In fact, only a few prime times seem likely: Friday and Saturday evenings and Saturday and Sunday afternoons.

Matt has included 14 public skating sessions in his ice schedule, but so far they haven't attracted as many people as he hoped. In total, they only generate a little more revenue than if the times were sold for hockey use. Offsetting this extra revenue are extra costs. More staff people are needed to handle a public skating session—guards, a ticket seller, skate rental, and more concession help. So the net revenue from either use is about the same. He could cancel some of the less attractive public sessions—like the noon-time daily sessions which have very low attendance—and make the average attendance figures look a lot better. But he feels that if he is going to offer public skating he must have a reasonable selection of times. He does recognize, however, that the different public skating sessions do seem to attract different people and, really, different kinds of people.

The Saturday and Sunday afternoon public skating sessions have been the most successful—with an average of 200 people attending during the winter season. Typically, this is a "kid-sitting" session. More than half of the patrons are young children who have been dropped off by their parents for several hours, but there are also some family groups.

In general, the kids and the families have a good time—and a fairly loyal group comes every Saturday and/or Sunday during the winter season. In the spring and fall, however, attendance drops about in half, depending on how nice the weather is. (Matt schedules no public sessions in the summer—focusing instead on hockey clinics and figure skating.)

The Friday and Saturday evening public sessions are a big disappointment. The sessions run from 8 until 10—a time when he had hoped to attract teenagers and young adult couples. At $3 per person, plus 75 cents for skate rental, this would be an economical date. In fact, Matt has seen quite a few young couples—and some keep coming back. But he also sees a surprising number of 8- to 12-year-olds who have been dropped off by their parents. The younger kids tend to race around the rink playing tag. This affects the whole atmosphere—making it less appealing for dating couples and older patrons.

Matt has been hoping to develop a teenage and young-adult market for a "social activity"—adapting the format used by roller-skating rinks. Their public skating sessions feature a variety of couples-only and group games as well as individual skating to dance music. Turning ice skating sessions into such social activities is not common, however, although industry rumors suggest that a few ice-rink operators have had success with the roller-skating format. Seemingly, the ice skating sessions are viewed as active recreation, offering exercise and/or a sports experience.

Matt installed some soft lights to try to change the evening atmosphere. The music was selected to encourage people to skate to the beat and couples to skate together. Some people complained about the "old" music; but it was "danceable," and some skaters really liked it. For a few sessions, Matt even tried to have some couples-only skates. The couples liked it, but this format was strongly resisted by the young boys who felt that they had paid their money and there was no reason why they should be kicked off the ice. Matt also tried to attract more young people and especially couples by bringing in a local rock radio station disk jockey to broadcast from Grand Arena—playing music and advertising the Friday and Saturday evening public sessions. But this had no effect on attendance—which varies from 50 to 100 per two-hour session during the winter.

Matt seriously considered the possibility of limiting the Friday and Saturday evening sessions to people age 13 and over—to try to change the environment. He knew it would take time to change people's attitudes. But when he counted the customers, he realized this would be risky. More than a quarter of his customers on an average weekend night appear to be 12 or under. This means that he would have to make a serious commitment to building the teenage and young-adult market. And, so far, his efforts haven't been successful. He has already invested over $3,000 in lighting changes and over $8,000 promoting the sessions over the rock music radio station—with very disappointing results. Although the station's sales rep said they reached teenagers all over town, an on-air offer for a free skating session did not get a single response!

Some days, Matt feels it's hopeless. Maybe he should accept that most public ice skating sessions are a mixed bag. Or maybe he should just sell the time to hockey groups. Still he keeps hoping that something can be done to improve weekend evening public skating attendance, because the upside potential is so good. And

the Saturday and Sunday afternoon sessions are pretty good money-makers.

Evaluate Grand Arena's situation. What should Matt O'Keefe do? Why?

11 Nike and Fashionable Shoes

Tamara Lang, owner of the Runners World, is trying to decide what she should do with her retail store and how committed she should be to function over fashion.

Tamara is a runner herself—and Runners World grew with the jogging boom. But that has now flattened out and may actually be declining as many people find that jogging is hard work—and hard on the body, especially the knees. The jogging boom helped make Runners World a profitable business. Throughout this period, Tamara emphasized Nike shoes, which were well accepted and seen as top quality. This positive image made it possible to get $5 to $7 above the market for Nike shoes—and some of this was left with the retailers, which led to attractive profits for Tamara Lang.

Committing so heavily to Nike seemed like a good idea when its quality was up and the name was good. But around 1985, Nike quality began to slip. It hurt not only Nike but retailers, such as Tamara, who were heavily committed to them. Now Nike has gotten its house in order again. But it is working on developing other kinds of athletic shoes, including walking shoes, and emphasizing engineering function rather than fashion. This is forcing Tamara to reconsider the emphasis in her store and to question whether she should continue committing so completely to Nike.

Nike's move into the walking market is supported by U.S. Census Bureau estimates that between 50 and 80 million Americans walk for exercise—with between 15 and 20 million of these considering themselves serious "health" walkers. After several years of internal research, Nike is introducing shoes designed specifically for walkers. Nike found that walkers' feet are on the ground more often than a runner's feet—but receive about half the impact. So Nike reduced the size of its mid-sole and grooved it for flexibility. Nike also eliminated inside seams at the toe to avoid irritation and lowered the back tab of the shoe to avoid pressure on the Achilles tendon. The manager of the Nike walking shoe effort is optimistic about the potential for walking shoes. In fact, she's convinced it's a lot larger than the jogging market—especially since no experience or practice is necessary to be good right away.

Many competitors are entering the walking shoe market, but the exact nature and size of the market isn't too clear. For one thing, it's likely that some ex-runners may just stop exercising—especially if they've damaged their knees. Further, the medical and biomechanical evidence about the need for specific walking shoes is not at all clear. One problem is that a shoe made for running can be used for walking, but not vice versa. Only very serious walkers may be interested in "only a walking shoe." Further, fashion has invaded the athletic shoe markets, so it may be necessary to have many different colors and quality levels. But Nike has tended to emphasize function rather than fashion. This may be a problem because about 75 percent of current walkers are women, many of them older, and many women seem to be more interested in fashion.

An important question that Tamara is debating is whether there really is a market for walking shoes. Further, is there a market for the Nike version of walking shoes—that will emphasize function more than fashion? What she must decide is whether she should give a lot of emphasis to walking shoes—while continuing to carry jogging shoes for her regular customers—and perhaps carry running shoe brands other than Nike. And should she put much greater emphasis on fashion rather than function? This would require, at the least, retraining current salespeople and perhaps hiring more fashion-oriented salespeople.

Just a small shift in emphasis probably won't make much of a difference. But a real shift to a heavy emphasis on walking shoes and fashion might require Tamara to change the name of her store—and perhaps even hire salespeople who will be more sympathetic with nonjoggers and their needs. One of the reasons she might want to broaden her line beyond Nike is that many other companies have entered the running shoe market—with many different designs and styles. And many customers purchase running shoes with no intention of ever running in them. In fact, one study suggested that 80 percent of consumers buy sneakers just for looks. Running shoes are the new casual shoe. Prices have dropped. And many producers are emphasizing fashion over function.

Still another problem that worries Tamara is whether she really wants to help pioneer a specialty walking shoe market. Those people who accept the need for quality walking shoes seem to be satisfied with running shoes—or hiking boots. Selling a whole new walking shoe concept will require a lot of expensive introductory promotion. And if it is successful, lower-priced versions will probably enter the market and be sold in most sporting goods stores—as well as large shoe stores. So the larger margins currently available will erode as the size of the specialty walking shoe market becomes clearer. The basic questions bothering Tamara are: Is there really a specialty walking shoe market? If so, how big is it? To get a better idea of how people feel about specialty walking shoes, she started asking some of her present customers how they felt about special shoes for walking. The following are representative responses:

> *"What? I can walk in my running shoes!"*
> *"I might be interested if I could really notice the difference, but I think my running shoes will work fine."*
> *"No, my running shoes walk good!"*

To get a better feel for how noncustomers felt, she talked to some friends and neighbors and a few people in a nearby shopping mall. Typical responses were:

> *"My regular shoes are fine for walking."*
> *"I really don't do much walking and don't see any need for such things!"*
> *"I might be interested if you could explain to me why they were better than my present running shoes, which I got at Wal-Mart."*
> *"My hiking boots work pretty well, but I'd be willing to hear how yours are better."*
> *"I do a lot of walking and might be really interested if they were a lot better than the running shoes I'm using now."*
> *"I'm always interested in looking at new products!"*

Evaluate Tamara Lang's present strategy. Evaluate the alternative strategies she is considering. What should she do? Why?

12 Du Pont

Tiffany Chin, a new product manager for Du Pont, must decide what to do with a new engine cooling system product that is not doing well compared to the company's other cooling system products. Du Pont is one of the large chemical companies in the United States—making a wide line of organic and inorganic chemicals and plastics. Technical research has played a vital role in the company's growth.

Recently, one of Du Pont's researchers developed a new engine cooling system product—EC-301. Much time and money was spent on the technical phase, involving various experiments concerned with the quality of the new product. Then Tiffany Chin took over and has been trying to develop a strategy for the product.

The engine coolant commonly used now is ethylene glycol. If it leaks into the crankcase oil, it forms a thick, pasty sludge that can cause bearing damage, cylinder scoring, or a dozen other costly and time-consuming troubles for both the operator and the owner of heavy-duty engines.

Du Pont researchers believed that the new product—EC-301—would be very valuable to the owners of heavy-duty diesel and gasoline trucks—as well as other heavy-equipment owners. Chemically, EC-301 uses a propanol base—instead of the conventional glycol and alcohol bases. It cannot prevent leakage, but if it does get into the crankcase, it won't cause any problems.

The suggested list price of EC-301 is $22 per gallon—more than twice the price of regular coolants. The higher price was set because of higher production costs and to obtain a "premium" for making a better engine coolant.

At first, Chin thought she had two attractive markets for EC-301: (1) the manufacturers of heavy-duty trucks and (2) the users of heavy-duty trucks. Du Pont sales reps have made numerous calls. So far neither type of customer has shown much interest, and the sales reps' sales manager is discouraging any more calls for EC-301. He feels there are more profitable uses for their time. The truck manufacturer prospects are reluctant to show interest in the product until it has been proven in actual use. The buyers for construction companies and other users of heavy-duty trucks have also been hesitant. Some say the suggested price is far too high for the advantages offered. Others don't understand what is wrong with the present coolants—and refuse to talk any more about paying extra for just another me-too product.

Explain what has happened so far. What should Tiffany Chin do? Why?

13 Fileco, Inc.*

Mary Miller, marketing manager for Fileco, Inc., must decide whether she should permit her largest customer to buy some of Fileco's commonly used file folders under the customer's brand rather than Fileco's own FILEX

brand. She is afraid that if she refuses, this customer—Natcom, Inc.—will go to another file folder producer and Fileco will lose this business.

Natcom, Inc., is a major distributor of office supplies and has already managed to put its own brand on more than 45 large-selling office supply products. It distributes these products—as well as the branded products of many manufacturers—through its nationwide distribution network, which includes 50 retail stores. Now Tom Lupe, vice president of marketing for Natcom, is seeking a line of file folders similar in quality to Fileco's FILEX brand, which now has over 60 percent of the market.

This is not the first time that Natcom has asked Fileco to produce a file folder line for Natcom. On both previous occasions, Mary Miller turned down the requests and Natcom continued to buy. In fact, Natcom not only continued to buy the file folders but the rest of Fileco's lines. And total sales continued to grow. Natcom accounts for about 30 percent of Mary Miller's business. And FILEX brand file folders account for about 35 percent of this volume.

Fileco has consistently refused such dealer-branding requests—as a matter of corporate policy. This policy was set some years ago because of a desire (1) to avoid excessive dependence on any one customer and (2) to sell its own brands so that its success is dependent on the quality of its products rather than just a low price. The policy developed from a concern that if it started making products under other customers' brands, those customers could shop around for a low price and the business would be very fickle. At the time the policy was set, Mary Miller realized that it might cost Fileco some business. But it was felt wise nevertheless—to be better able to control the firm's future.

Fileco, Inc., has been in business 25 years and now has a sales volume of $35 million. Its primary products are file folders, file markers and labels, and a variety of indexing systems. Fileco offers such a wide range of size, color, and type that no competition can match it in its part of the market. About 40 percent of Fileco's file folder business is in specialized lines such as: files for oversized blueprint and engineer drawings; see-through files for medical markets; and greaseproof and waterproof files for marine, oil field, and other hazardous environmental markets. Fileco's competitors are mostly small paper converters. But excess capacity in the industry is substantial, and these converters are always hungry for orders and willing to cut price. Further, the raw materials for the FILEX line of file folders are readily available.

Fileco's distribution system consists of 10 regional stationery suppliers (40 percent of total sales), Natcom,

*Adapted from a case written by Professor Hardy, University of Western Ontario, Canada.

Inc. (30 percent), and more than 40 local stationers who have wholesale and retail operations (30 percent). The 10 regional stationers each have about six branches, while the local stationers each have one wholesale and three or four retail locations. The regional suppliers sell directly to large corporations and to some retailers. In contrast, Natcom's main volume comes from retail sales to small businesses and walk-in customers in its 50 retail stores.

Mary Miller has a real concern about the future of the local stationers' business. Some are seriously discussing the formation of buying groups to obtain volume discounts from vendors and thus compete more effectively with Natcom's 50 retail stores, the large regionals, and the superstore chains, which are spreading rapidly. These chains—such as Staples, Office World, Office Max, and Office Square—operate stores of 16,000 to 20,000 square feet (i.e., large stores compared to the usual office supply stores) and let customers wheel through high-stacked shelves to supermarket-like checkout counters. These chains generate $5 million to $15 million in annual business—stressing convenience, wide selection, and much lower prices than the typical office supply retailers. They buy directly from manufacturers, such as Fileco, bypassing wholesalers like Natcom. It is likely that growing pressure from these chains is causing Natcom to renew its proposal to buy a file line with its own name.

None of Mary's other accounts is nearly as effective in retailing as Natcom—which has developed a good reputation in every major city in the country. Natcom's profits have been the highest in the industry. Further, its brands are almost as well known as those of some key producers—and its expansion plans are aggressive. And now, these plans are being pressured by the fast-growing superstores—which some expect will knock out many local stationers.

Mary is sure that Fileco's brands are well entrenched in the market, despite the fact that most available money has been devoted to new-product development rather than promotion of existing brands. But Mary is concerned that if Natcom brands its own file folders, it will sell them at a discount and may even bring the whole market price level down. Across all the lines of file folders, Mary is averaging a 35 percent gross margin, but the commonly used file folders sought by Natcom are averaging only a 20 percent gross margin. And cutting this margin further does not look very attractive to Mary.

Mary is not sure whether Natcom will continue to sell Fileco's FILEX brand of folders along with Natcom's own file folders if Natcom is able to find a source of supply. Natcom's history has been to sell its own brand and a major brand side by side, especially if the major brand offers high quality and has strong brand recognition.

Mary is having a really hard time deciding what to do about the existing branding policy. Fileco has excess capacity and could easily handle the Natcom business. And she fears that if she turns down this business, Natcom will just go elsewhere and its own brand will cut into Fileco's existing sales at Natcom stores. Further, what makes Natcom's offer especially attractive is that Fileco's variable manufacturing costs would be quite low in relation in any price charged to Natcom—i.e., there are substantial economies of scale, so the "extra" business could be very profitable—if Mary doesn't consider the possible impact on the FILEX line. This Natcom business will be easy to get, but it will require a major change in policy, which Mary will have to sell to Bob Butcher, Fileco's president. This may not be easy. Bob is primarily interested in developing new and better products so the company can avoid the "commodity end of the business."

Evaluate Fileco's current strategy. What should Mary Miller do about Natcom's offer? Explain.

14 Communication Aids, Inc.

Rich Monash, manager of Communication Aids, Inc. (CA), is looking for ways to increase profits. But he's turning cautious after the poor results of his last effort—during the previous Christmas season. CA is located along a busy cross-town street about two miles from the downtown of a metropolitan area of 1 million and near a large university. It sells high-quality still, movie, and video cameras, accessories, and projection equipment—including 8-mm and 16-mm movie projectors, 35-mm slide projectors, opaque and overhead projectors, and a large assortment of projection screens. Most of the sales of this specialized equipment are made to area school boards for classroom use, to industry for use in research and sales, and to the university for use in research and instruction.

CA also offers a wide selection of film, developing and printing equipment and supplies, and a specialized film-processing service. Instead of processing film on a mass production basis, CA gives each order individual attention—to bring out the particular features requested by a customer. This service is really appreciated by local firms that need high-quality pictures of lab or manufacturing processes for analytical and sales work.

To encourage the school and industrial trade, CA offers a graphics consultation service. If a customer wants to build a display—whether large or small—

professional advice is readily available. In support of this free service, CA carries a full line of graphic arts supplies.

CA has four full-time store clerks and two outside sales reps. The sales reps call on business firms, attend trade shows, make presentations for schools, and help both present and potential customers in their use and choice of visual aids. Most purchases are delivered by the sales reps or the store's delivery truck. Many orders come in by phone or mail.

The people who make most of the over-the-counter purchases are (1) serious amateur photographers and (2) some professional photographers who buy in small quantities. CA gives price discounts of up to 25 percent of the suggested retail price to customers who buy more than $1,500 worth of goods per year. Most regular customers qualify for the discount.

In recent years, many amateurs have been buying relatively light-weight and inexpensive video cameras to capture family events and "memories." Frequently, the buyer is a first-time father who wants to record the birth and early development of his new baby. CA has not offered the lower-priced quality models such buyers commonly want. But Rich Monash knew that lots of such video cameras are bought and felt that there ought to be a good opportunity to expand sales during the coming Christmas gift-giving season. Therefore, he planned a special pre-Christmas sale of two of the most popular brands of video cameras and discounted the prices to competitive discount store levels—about $500 for one and $800 for the other. To promote the sale, he posted large signs in the store windows and ran ads in a Christmas gift-suggestion edition of the local newspaper. This edition appeared each Wednesday during the four weeks before Christmas. At these prices and with this promotion, Rich hoped to sell at least 100 cameras. However, when the Christmas returns were in, total sales were five cameras. Rich was extremely disappointed with these results—especially because trade experts suggested that sales of video cameras in these price and quality ranges were up 200 percent over last year—during the Christmas selling season.

Evaluate what Communication Aids is doing and what happened with the special promotion. What should Rich Monash do to increase sales and profits?

15 Samco, Inc.

Sam Melko, owner of Samco, Inc., is deciding whether to take on a new line. He is very concerned, however, because although he wants more lines he feels that something is wrong with his latest possibility.

Sam Melko graduated from a large midwestern university in 1988 with a B.S. in business. He worked as a car salesman for a year. Then Sam decided to go into business for himself and formed Samco, Inc. Looking for opportunities, Sam placed several ads in his local newspaper in Columbus, Ohio, announcing that he was interested in becoming a sales representative in the area. He was quite pleased to receive a number of responses. Eventually, he became the sales representative in the Columbus area for three local computer software producers: Accto Company, which produces accounting-related software; Saleco, Inc., a producer of sales management software; and Invo, Inc., a producer of inventory control software. All of these companies were relatively small—and were represented in other areas by other sales representatives like Sam Melko.

Sam's main job was to call on possible customers. Once he made a sale, he would send the order to the respective producer, who would ship the programs directly to the customer. The producer would bill the customer, and Melko would receive a commission varying from 5 percent to 10 percent of the dollar value of the sale. Melko was expected to pay his own expenses. And the producers would handle any user questions—using 800 numbers for out-of-town calls.

Melko called on anyone in the Columbus area who might use the products he sold. At first, his job was relatively easy, and sales came quickly because he had little competition. Many national companies offer similar products, but at that time, they were not well represented in the Columbus area.

In 1990, Melko sold $250,000 worth of Accto software, earning a 10 percent commission; $100,000 worth of Saleco software, also earning a 10 percent commission; and $200,000 worth of Invo software, earning a 5 percent commission. He was encouraged with his progress and looked forward to expanding sales in the future. He was especially optimistic because he had achieved these sales volumes without overtaxing himself. In fact, he felt he was operating at about 60 percent of his capacity and could easily take on new lines. So he began looking for other products he could sell in the Columbus area. A manufacturer of small lift trucks had recently approached him, but Sam wasn't too enthusiastic about this offer because the commission was only 2 percent on potential annual sales of $150,000.

Now Sam Melko is faced with another decision. The Metclean Company, also in Columbus, has made what looks like an attractive offer. They heard what a fine job Sam was doing and felt that he could help them solve their present problem. Metclean is having trouble with its whole marketing effort and would like Sam Melko to take over.

Metclean, Inc., produces solvents used to make coatings for metal products. It sells mainly to industrial customers in the mid-Ohio area and faces many competitors selling essentially the same products and charging the same low prices. Metclean is a small manufacturer. Last year's sales were $400,000. It could handle at least four times this sales volume with ease—and is willing to expand to increase sales—its main objective in the short run. Metclean is offering Sam a 12 percent commission on all sales if he will take charge of their pricing, advertising, and sales efforts. Sam is flattered by their offer, but he is a little worried because the job might require a great deal more traveling than he is doing now. For one thing, he would have to call on new potential customers in mid-Ohio, and he might have to travel up to 200 miles around Columbus to expand the solvent business. Further, he realizes that he is being asked to do more than just sell. But he did have marketing courses in college, and thinks the new opportunity might be challenging.

Evaluate Sam Melko's current strategy and how the proposed solvent line fits in with what he is doing now. What should he do? Why?

16 Jenson Company

Frank Jenson, owner of Jenson Company, feels his business is threatened by a tough new competitor. And now Frank must decide quickly about an offer that may save his business.

Frank Jenson has been a sales rep for lumber mills for about 20 years. He started selling in a clothing store but gave it up after two years to work in a lumber yard because the future looked much better in the building materials industry. After drifting from one job to another, Frank finally settled down and worked his way up to manager of a large wholesale building materials distribution warehouse in Buffalo, New York. In 1972, he formed Jenson Company and went into business for himself, selling carload lots of lumber to lumber yards in western New York and Pennsylvania.

Frank works with five large lumber mills on the West Coast. They notify him when a carload of lumber is available to be shipped, specifying the grade, condition, and number of each size board in the shipment. Frank isn't the only person selling for these mills—but he is the only one in his area. He isn't required to take any particular number of carloads per month—but once he

tells a mill he wants a particular shipment, title passes to him and he has to sell it to someone. Frank's main function is to find a buyer, buy the lumber from the mill as it's being shipped, and have the railroad divert the car to the buyer.

Frank has been in this business for 20 years, so he knows all of the lumber yard buyers in his area very well—and is on good working terms with them. He does most of his business over the telephone from his small office, but he tries to see each of the buyers about once a month. He has been marking up the lumber between 4 and 6 percent—the standard markup, depending on the grades and mix in each car—and has been able to make a good living for himself and his family. The going prices are widely publicized in trade publications, so the buyers can easily check to be sure Frank's prices are competitive.

In the last few years, the regional building market slowed down. Frank's profits did too, but he decided to stick it out—figuring that people still needed housing and that business would pick up again.

Six months ago, an aggressive young salesman set up in the same business, covering about the same area but representing different lumber mills. This new salesman charges about the same prices as Frank but undersells him once or twice a week in order to get the sale. Many lumber buyers—feeling that they were dealing with a homogeneous product—seem to be willing to buy from the lowest-cost source. This has hurt Frank financially and personally—because even some of his old friends are willing to buy from the new competitor if the price is lower. The near-term outlook seems dark, since Frank doubts that there is enough business to support two firms like his, especially if the markup gets shaved any closer. Now they seem to be splitting the business about equally—as the newcomer keeps shaving his markup.

A week ago, Frank was called on by Mr. Talbott of Bear Mfg. Co., a large manufacturer of windows and accessories. Talbott knows that Frank is well acquainted with the local lumber yards and wants him to become Bear's exclusive distributor (sales rep) of residential windows and accessories in his area. Talbott gave Frank several brochures on the Bear product lines. He also explained Bear's new support program which will help train and support Frank and interested lumber yards on how to sell the higher-markup accessories. Talbott explained that this program will help Frank and interested lumberyards differentiate themselves in this very competitive market.

Most residential windows of specified grades are basically "commodities" which are sold on the basis of price and availability, although some premium and very low end windows are sold also. Lumber yards usually do not stock windows because there are so many possible sizes. Instead, the lumber yards custom order from the stock sizes each factory offers. Stock sizes are not set by industry standards; they vary from factory to factory, and some offer more sizes. Bear Mfg. Co., for example, offers many variations in ⅛-inch increments to cater to remodelers who must adjust to many situations. Most factories can deliver these custom orders in two to six weeks—which is usually adequate to satisfy contractors who buy and install them according to architectural plans. This part of the residential window business is well established, and most lumber yards buy from several different window manufacturers—to assure sources of supply in case of strikes, plant fires, etc. How the business is split depends on price and the personality and persuasiveness of the sales reps. And, given that prices are usually similar, the sales rep–customer relationship can be quite important. One reason Talbott has approached Frank Jenson is because of Frank's many years in the business. But the other reason is that Bear is aggressively trying to expand—relying on its accessories and newly developed factory support system to help differentiate it from the many other window manufacturers.

To give Frank a quick big picture of the opportunity he is offering, Talbott explained the window market as follows:

1. For commercial construction, the usual building code ventilation requirements are satisfied with mechanical ventilation. So the windows do not have to operate to permit natural ventilation. They are usually made with heavy grade aluminum framing. Typically, a distributor furnishes and installs the windows. As part of its service, the distributor provides considerable technical support including engineered drawings and diagrams to the owners, architects, and/or contractors.

2. For residential construction, on the other hand, windows must be operable to provide ventilation. Residential windows are usually made of wood, frequently with light-gauge aluminum or vinyl on the exterior. Lumber yards are the most common source of supply for contractors in Frank's area, and these lumber yards do not provide any technical support or engineered drawings. A few residential window manufacturers do have their own sales centers in selected geographic areas, which provide a full range of support and engineering services, but none are anywhere near Frank's area.

Bear Mfg. Co. feels a big opportunity exists in the commercial building repair and rehabilitation market—sometimes called the retrofit market—for a crossover of residential windows to commercial applications—and it has designed some accessories and a factory support program to help lumber yards get this commercial business. For applications such as nursing homes and dormitories (which must meet commercial codes), the wood interior of a residential window is desired, but the owners and architects are accustomed to commercial grades and building systems. And in some older facilities, the windows may have to provide supplemental ventilation for a deficient mechanical system. So, what is needed is a combination of the residential *operable* window with a heavy-gauge commercial exterior frame that is easy to specify and install. And this is what Bear Mfg. Co. is offering with a combination of its basic windows and easily adjustable accessory frames. Two other residential window manufacturers offer a similar solution, but neither has pushed its products aggressively and neither offers technical support to lumber yards or trains sales reps like Frank to do the necessary job. Talbott feels this could be a unique opportunity for Frank.

The sales commission on residential windows would be about 5 percent of sales. Bear Mfg. Co. would do the billing and collecting. By getting just 20 to 30 percent of his lumber yards' residential window business, Frank could earn about half of his current income. But the real upside would come from increasing his residential window share. To do this, Frank would have to help the lumber yards get a lot more (and more profitable) business by invading the commercial market with residential windows and the bigger markup accessories needed for this market. Frank would also earn a 20 percent commission on the accessories—adding to his profit potential.

Frank is somewhat excited about the opportunity because the retrofit market is growing. And owners and architects are seeking ways of reducing costs (which Bear's approach does—over usual commercial approaches). But he is also concerned that a lot of sales effort will be needed to introduce this new idea. He is not afraid of work, but he is concerned about his financial survival.

Frank thinks he has three choices:

1. Take Talbott's offer and sell both products.
2. Take the offer and drop lumber sales.
3. Stay strictly with lumber and forget the offer.

Talbott is expecting an answer within one week, so Frank has to decide soon.

Evaluate Frank Jenson's current strategy and how the present offer fits in. What should he do now? Why?

17 Ledges State Bank

Tom Nason isn't having much luck convincing his father that their bank needs the new look and image he is proposing.

Tom Nason was recently appointed director of marketing by his father, Bob Nason, long-time president of the Ledges State Bank. Tom is a recent marketing graduate of the nearby state college. He worked in the bank during summer vacations, but this is his first full-time job.

The Ledges State Bank is a profitable, family-run business located in Ledges—the county seat. The town itself has a population of only 15,000, but it serves suburbanites and farmers as far away as 20 miles. About 10 miles east is a metropolitan area of 350,000—to which many in the Ledges area commute. Banking competition is quite strong there. But Ledges has only one other downtown full-service bank—of about the same size—and two small limited-service branches of two metro banks on the main highway going east. The Ledges State Bank has been quite profitable, last year earning about $400,000—or 1 percent of assets—a profit margin that would look very attractive to big-city bankers.

Ledges State Bank has prospered over the years by emphasizing its friendly, small-town atmosphere. The employees are all local residents and are trained to be friendly with all customers—greeting them on a first-name basis. Even Tom's father tries to know all the customers personally and often comes out of his office to talk with them. The bank has followed a conservative policy—for example, insisting on 25 percent downpayments on homes and relatively short maturities on loans. The interest rates charged are competitive or slightly higher than in the nearby city, but they are similar to those charged by the other full-service bank in town. In fact, the two local banks seem to be following more or less the same approach—friendly, small-town service. Since they both have fairly convenient downtown locations, Tom feels that the two banks will continue to share the business equally unless some change is made.

Tom has an idea that he thinks will attract a greater share of the local business. At a recent luncheon meeting with his father, he presented his plan and was disappointed when it wasn't enthusiastically received. Nevertheless, he has continued to push the idea.

Basically, Tom wants to differentiate the bank by promoting a new look and image. His proposal is to try to get all the people in town to think of the bank as "The Friendly Bank." And Tom wants to paint the inside and outside of the bank in current designers' colors (e.g., pastels) and have all the bank's advertising and printed materials refer to "The Friendly Bank" campaign. The bank would give away pastel shopping bags, offer pastel deposit slips, mail out pastel interest checks, advertise on pastel billboards, and have pastel stationery for the bank's correspondence. And all the employees will be trained to be friendly or even more friendly to everyone. Tom knows that his proposal is different for a conservative bank. But that's exactly why he thinks it will work. He wants people to notice his bank instead of just assuming that both banks are alike. He is sure that after the initial surprise, the local people will think even more positively about Ledges State Bank. Its reputation is very good now, but he would like it to be recognized as different. Tom feels that this will help attract a larger share of new residents and businesses. Further, he hopes that his "The Friendly Bank" campaign will cause people to talk about Ledges State Bank—and given that word-of-mouth comments are likely to be positive, the bank might win a bigger share of the present business.

Bob Nason is less excited about his son's proposal. He thinks the bank has done very well under his direction—and he is concerned about changing a good thing. He worries that some of the older townspeople and farmers who are loyal customers will question the integrity of the bank. His initial request to Tom was to come up with some way of differentiating the bank without offending present customers. Further, Bob Nason thinks that Tom is talking about an important change that will be hard to undo once the decision is made. On the plus side, Bob agrees that the proposal will make the bank appear quite different from its competitor. Further, people are continuing to move into the Ledges area, and he wants an increasing share of this business.

Evaluate Ledges State Bank's situation and Tom's proposal. What should the bank do to increase its market share?

18 Sacramento Sports, Inc.

Ben Huang, owner of Sacramento Sports, Inc., is worried about his business' future. He has tried various strategies for two years now, and he's still barely breaking even.

Two years ago, Ben Huang bought the inventory, supplies, equipment, and business of Sacramento Sports—located on the edge of Sacramento, California. The business is in an older building along a major highway leading out of town—several miles from any body of water. The previous owner had sales of about $400,000 a year—but was just breaking even. For this reason—plus the desire to retire to southern California—the owner sold to Ben for roughly the value of the inventory.

Sacramento Sports had been selling two well-known brands of small pleasure boats, a leading outboard motor, two brands of snowmobiles and jet-skis, and a line of trailer and pickup-truck campers. The total inventory was valued at $140,000—and Ben used all of his own savings and borrowed some from two friends to buy the inventory and the business. At the same time, he took over the lease on the building—so he was able to begin operations immediately.

Ben had never operated a business of his own before, but he was sure that he would be able to do well. He had worked in a variety of jobs—as a used-car salesman, an auto repair man, and a jack-of-all-trades in the maintenance departments of several local businesses.

Soon after starting his business, Ben hired his friend, Larry, who had a similar background. Together, they handle all selling and set-up work on new sales and do maintenance work as needed. Sometimes the two are extremely busy—at the peaks of each sport season. Then both sales and maintenance keep them going up to 16 hours a day. At these times it's difficult to have both new and repaired equipment available as soon as customers want it. At other times, however, Ben and Larry have almost nothing to do.

Ben usually charges the prices suggested by the various manufacturers—except at the end of a weather season when he is willing to make deals to clear the inventory. He is annoyed that some of his competitors sell mainly on a price basis—offering 10 to 30 percent off a manufacturer's suggested list prices—even at the beginning of a season! Ben doesn't want to get into that kind of business, however. He hopes to build a loyal following based on friendship and personal service. Further, he doesn't think he really has to cut price because all of his lines are exclusive for his store. No stores within a 10-mile radius carry any of his brands, although nearby retailers offer many brands of similar products.

To try to build a favorable image for his company, Ben occasionally places ads in local papers and buys some radio spots. The basic theme of this advertising is that Sacramento Sports is a friendly, service-oriented place to buy the equipment needed for the current season. Sometimes he mentions the brand names he carries, but generally Ben tries to build an image for concerned, friendly service—both in new sales and repairs—stressing, "We do it right the first time." He chose this approach because, although he has exclusives on the brands he carries, there generally are 10 to 15 different manufacturers' products being sold in the area in each product category—and most of the products are quite similar. Ben feels that this similarity among competing products almost forces him to try to differentiate himself on the basis of his own store's services.

The first year's operation wasn't profitable. In fact, after paying minimal salaries to Larry and himself, the business just about broke even. Ben made no return on his $140,000 investment.

In hopes of improving profitability, Ben jumped at a chance to add a line of lawn mowers, tractors, and trimmers as he was starting into his second year of business. This line was offered by a well-known equipment manufacturer who wanted to expand into the Sacramento area. The equipment is similar to that offered by other lawn equipment manufacturers. The manufacturer's willingness to do some local advertising and to provide some point-of-purchase displays appealed to Ben. And he also liked the idea that customers probably would want this equipment sometime earlier than boats and other summer items. So he thought he could handle this business without interfering with his other peak selling seasons.

It's two years since Ben bought Sacramento Sports—and he's still only breaking even. Sales have increased a little, but costs have gone up too because he had to hire some part-time help. The lawn equipment helped to expand sales—as he had expected—but unfortunately, it did not increase profits as he had hoped. Ben needed part-time helpers to handle this business—in part because the manufacturer's advertising had generated a lot of sales inquiries. Relatively few inquiries resulted in sales, however, because many people seemed to be shopping for deals. So Ben may have even lost money handling the new line. But he hesitates to give it up because he doesn't want to lose that sales volume, and the manufacturer's sales rep has been most encouraging—assuring Ben that things will get better and that his company will be glad to continue its promotion support during the coming year.

Ben is now considering the offer of a mountain bike producer that has not been represented in the area. The bikes have become very popular with students and serious bikers in the last several years. The manufacturer's sales rep says industry sales are still growing (but not as fast as in the first two to three years) and probably will grow for many more years. The sales rep has praised Ben's service orientation and says this could help him sell lots of bikes because many mountain bikers are serious about buying a quality bike and then keeping it serviced. He says Ben's business approach would be a natural fit with bike customers' needs and attitudes. As a special inducement to get Ben to take on the line, the sales rep says Ben will not have to pay for the initial inventory of bikes, accessories, and repair parts for 90 days. And, of course, the company will supply the usual promotion aids and a special advertising allowance of $10,000 to help introduce the line to Sacramento. Ben kind of likes the idea of carrying mountain bikes because he has one himself and knows that they do require some service year-round. But he also knows that the proposed bikes are very similar in price and quality to the ones now being offered by the bike shops in town. These bike shops are service- rather than price-oriented, and Ben feels that they are doing a good job on service—so, he is concerned with how he could be different.

Evaluate Ben Huang's overall strategy(ies) and the mountain bike proposal. What should he do now?

19 Mobay Chemical, Inc.

Mobay Chemical, Inc., is a multinational producer of various chemicals and plastics with plants in the United States, England, France, and Germany. It is run from its headquarters in New Jersey.

Gerry Mason is marketing manager of Mobay's global plastic business. Gerry is reconsidering his promotion approach. He is evaluating what kind of promotion—and how much—should be directed to car producers and to other major customers worldwide. Currently, Gerry has one salesperson who devotes most of his time to the U.S. car industry. This man is based in the Detroit area and focuses on the Big Three—GM, Ford, Chrysler—and the various molders who supply the car industry. This approach was adequate as long as relatively little plastic was used in each car *and* the auto producers did all of the designing themselves and then sent out specifications for very price-oriented bidding. But now the whole product planning and buying system is changing—and foreign producers in the United States are becoming more important.

The new system can be explained in terms of Ford's "program management" approach—developed in 1980 and used on the Taurus-Sable project. Instead of the normal five-year process of creating a new automobile in sequential steps, the new system is a team approach. Under the old system, product planners would come up with a general concept and then expect the design team to give it artistic form. Next Engineering would develop the specifications and pass them on to Manufacturing and suppliers. There was little communication between the groups—and no overall project responsibility. Under the new program management approach, representatives

from all the various functions—Planning, Design, Engineering, Marketing, and Manufacturing—work together. The whole team takes final responsibility for a car. Because all of the departments are involved from the start, problems are resolved as the project moves on—before they cause a crisis. Manufacturing, for example, can suggest changes in design that will result in higher productivity—or better quality.

In the Taurus-Sable project, Ford engineers followed the Japanese lead and did some reverse engineering of their own. This helped them learn how the parts were assembled—and how they were designed. Ford actually bought several Japanese cars and dismantled them, piece by piece, looking for ideas they could copy or improve. Further, Ford engineers carefully analyzed over 50 similar cars to find the best parts of each. The Audi 5000 had the best accelerator-pedal feel. The Toyota Supra was best for fuel-gauge accuracy. The best tire and jack storage was in the BMW 228e. Eventually, Ford incorporated almost all of the best features into its Taurus-Sable.

In addition to reverse engineering, Ford researchers conducted the largest series of market studies the company had ever done. This led to the inclusion of additional features, such as oil dipsticks painted a bright yellow for faster identification and a net in the trunk to hold grocery bags upright.

At the same time, a five-member ergonomics group studied ways to make cars more comfortable and easier to operate. They took seats from competing cars and tested them in Ford cars to learn what customers liked—and disliked. They tested dashboard instruments and controls. Eventually the best elements in competing models were incorporated into the Taurus-Sable.

Ford also asked assembly-line workers for suggestions before the car was designed—and then incorporated their ideas into the new car. All bolts had the same-size head, for example, so workers didn't have to switch from one wrench to another.

Finally, Ford consulted its suppliers as part of the program management effort. Instead of turning to a supplier after the car's design was completed, the Ford team signed long-term contracts with suppliers—and invited them to participate in product planning. This project was so successful that it appears most auto producers will follow a similar approach in the future.

The suppliers selected for the Taurus project were major suppliers who had already demonstrated a serious commitment to the car industry. They had not only the facilities, but the technical and professional managerial staff who could understand—and become part of—the program management approach. Ford expected that these major suppliers would be able to provide the just-in-time delivery system pioneered by the Japanese—and that the suppliers could apply statistical quality-control procedures in their manufacturing processes. These criteria led Ford to ignore suppliers whose primary sales technique was to entertain buyers and then submit bids on standard specifications.

Assuming that the program management approach will spread through the car industry and to other industries as well, Gerry Mason is trying to determine if Mobay's present effort is still appropriate. Gerry's strategy has focused primarily on responding to inquiries and bringing in Mobay technical people as the situation seems to require. Potential customers with technical questions are sometimes referred to other customers already using the materials or to a Mobay plant—to be sure that all questions are answered. But basically, all producer customers are treated more or less alike. The sales rep makes calls and tries to find good business wherever it is.

Usually each sales rep has a geographic area. If an area like Detroit needs more than one rep, each may specialize in one or several similar industries. But Mobay uses the same basic approach—call on present users of plastic products and try to find opportunities for getting a share (or bigger share) of existing purchases or new applications. The sales reps are supposed to be primarily order getters rather than technical specialists. Technical help can be brought in when the customer wants it.

Gerry now sees that some of his major competitors—including General Electric and Dow Chemical—are becoming more aggressive. They are seeking to affect specifications and product design from the start, rather than after a product design is completed. This takes a lot more effort and resources, but Gerry thinks it may get better results. A major problem he sees, however, is that he may have to drastically change the nature of Mobay's promotion. Instead of focusing primarily on buyers and responding to questions, it may be necessary to try to contact *all* the multiple buying influences and not only answer their questions but help them understand what questions to raise—and help answer them. Such a process may even require more technically trained sales reps.

Contrast Ford Motor Company's previous approach to designing and producing cars to its program management approach, especially as it might affect suppliers' *promotion efforts. Assuming most major producers move in the program management direction, what promotion effort should Gerry Mason develop for Mobay? Should every producer in every geographic area be treated alike—regardless of size? Explain.*

20 Bemis Cable, Inc.

Jack Meister, vice president of marketing for Bemis Cable, Inc., is deciding how to organize and train his sales force—and what to do about Tom Brogs.

At its plant in Pittsburgh, Pennsylvania, Bemis Cable, Inc., produces wire cable—ranging from one-half inch to four inches in diameter. Bemis sells across the United States and Canada. Customers include firms that use cranes and various other overhead lifts in their own operations—ski resorts and amusement parks, for example. The company's main customers, however, are cement plants, railroad and boat yards, heavy-equipment manufacturers, mining operations, construction companies, and steel manufacturers.

Bemis employs its own sales specialists to call on and try to sell the buyers of potential users. All of Bemis's sales reps are engineers who go through an extensive training program covering the different applications, product strengths, and other technical details concerning wire rope and cable. Then they are assigned their own district—the size depending on the number of potential customers. They are paid a good salary plus generous travel expenses—with small bonuses and prizes to reward special efforts.

Tom Brogs went to work for Bemis in 1961, immediately after receiving a civil engineering degree from the University of Wisconsin. After going through the training program, he took over as the only company rep in the Illinois district. His job was to call on and give technical help to present customers of wire cable. He was also expected to call on new customers, especially when inquiries came in. But his main activities were to (1) service present customers and supply the technical assistance needed to use cable in the most efficient and safe manner, (2) handle complaints, and (3) provide evaluation reports to customers' management regarding their use of cabling.

Tom Brogs soon became Bemis's outstanding representative. His exceptional ability to handle customer complaints and provide technical assistance was noted by many of the firm's customers. This helped Tom bring in more sales dollars per customer and more in total from present customers than any other rep. He also brought in many new customers—mostly heavy equipment manufacturers in northern Illinois. Over the years, his sales have been about twice the sales rep average, and always at least 20 percent higher than the next best rep—even though each district is supposed to have about the same sales potential.

Tom's success established Illinois as Bemis's largest-volume district. Although the company's sales in Illinois have not continued to grow as fast in the last few years because Tom seems to have found most of the possible applications and won a good share for Bemis, the replacement market has been steady and profitable. This fact is mainly due to Tom Brogs. As one of the purchasing agents for a large machinery manufacturer mentioned, "When Tom makes a recommendation regarding use of our equipment and cabling, even if it is a competitor's cable we are using, we are sure it's for the best of our company. Last week, for example, a cable of one of his competitors broke, and we were going to give him a contract. He told us it was not a defective cable that caused the break, but rather the way we were using it. He told us how it should be used and what we needed to do to correct our operation. We took his advice and gave him the contract as well!"

Four years ago, Bemis introduced a unique and newly patented wire sling device for holding cable groupings together. The sling makes operations around the cable much safer—and its use could reduce hospital and lost-time costs due to accidents. The slings are expensive—and the profit margin is high. Bemis urged all its representatives to push the sling, but the only sales rep to sell the sling with any success was Tom Brogs. Eighty percent of his customers are currently using the wire sling. In other areas, sling sales are disappointing.

As a result of Tom's success, Jack Meister is now considering forming a separate department for sling sales and putting Tom Brogs in charge. His duties would include traveling to the various sales districts and training other representatives to sell the sling. The Illinois district would be handled by a new rep.

Evaluate Jack Meister's strategy(ies). What should he do about Tom Brogs—and his sales force? Explain.

21 Action Furniture Store

Jean Mead, owner of Action Furniture Store, is discouraged with her salespeople and is even thinking about hiring some new blood. Mrs. Mead has been running Action Furniture Store for 10 years and has slowly built the sales to $3,500,000 a year. Her store is located on the outskirts of a growing city of 275,000 population. This is basically a factory city, and she has deliberately selected blue-collar workers as her target market. She carries some higher-priced furniture lines but emphasizes budget combinations and easy credit terms.

Mrs. Mead is concerned that she may have reached the limit of her sales growth—her sales have not been increasing during the last two years even though total furniture sales have been increasing in the city as new people move in. Her newspaper advertising seems to attract her target customers, but many of these people come in, shop around, and leave. Some of them come back—but most do not. She thinks her product selections are very suitable for her target market and is concerned that her salespeople don't close more sales with potential customers. She has discussed this matter several times with her 10 salespeople. Her staff feels they should treat all customers alike—the way they personally want to be treated. They argue that their role is just to answer questions when asked—not to make suggestions or help customers make decisions. They think this would be too "hard sell."

Mrs. Mead says their behavior is interpreted as indifference by the customers attracted to the store by her advertising. She has tried to convince her salespeople that customers must be treated on an individual basis—and that some customers need more help in looking and deciding than others. Moreover, Mrs. Mead is convinced that some customers actually appreciate more help and suggestions than the salespeople themselves might. To support her views, she showed her staff the data from a study of furniture store customers (Tables 1 and 2, p. 474). She tried to explain the differences in demographic groups and pointed out that her store was definitely trying to aim at specific people. She argued that they (the salespeople) should cater to the needs and attitudes of their customers—and think less about how they would like to be treated themselves. Further, Mrs. Mead announced that she is considering changing the sales compensation plan or hiring new blood if the present employees can't do a better job. Currently, the sales reps are paid $20,000 per year plus a 5 percent commission on sales.

Contrast Mrs. Mead's strategy and thoughts about her salespeople with their apparent view of her strategy and especially their role in it. What should she do now? Explain.

Table 1

In Shopping for Furniture I Found (find) That	Demographic Groups			
	Group A	Group B	Group C	Group D
I looked at furniture in many stores before I made a purchase.	78%	72%	52%	50%
I went (am going) to only one store and bought (buy) what I found (find) there.	2	5	10	11
To make my purchase I went (am going) back to one of the stores I shopped in previously.	63	59	27	20
I looked (am looking) at furniture in no more than three stores and made (will make) my purchase in one of these.	20	25	40	45
I like a lot of help in selecting the right furniture.	27	33	62	69
I like a very friendly salesperson.	23	28	69	67

Table 2   The Sample Design

Demographic Status
Upper class (Group A); 13% of sample
This group consisted of managers, proprietors, or executives of large businesses. Professionals, including doctors, lawyers, engineers, college professors and school administrators, research personnel. Sales personnel, including managers, executives, and upper-income salespeople above level of clerks.
Family income over $40,000.
Middle class (Group B); 37% of sample
Group B consists of white-collar workers including clerical, secretarial, salesclerks, bookkeepers, etc. It also includes school teachers, social workers, semiprofessionals, proprietors or managers of small businesses; industrial foremen and other supervisory personnel.
Family income between $20,000 and $50,000.
Lower middle class (Group C); 36% of sample
Skilled workers and semiskilled technicians were in this category along with custodians, elevator operators, telephone linemen, factory operatives, construction workers, and some domestic and personal service employees.
Family income between $10,000 and $40,000.
No one in this group had above a high school education.
Lower class (Group D); 14% of sample
Nonskilled employees, day laborers. It also includes some factory operatives and domestic and service people.
Family income under $18,000.
None had completed high school; some had only grade school education.

22   Texco, Inc.

Myra Martinez, marketing manager of consumer products for Texco, Inc., is trying to set a price for her most promising new product—a space-saving shoe rack suitable for small homes or apartments.

Texco, Inc.—located in Ft. Worth, Texas—is a custom producer of industrial wire products. The company has a lot of experience bending wire into many shapes—and also can chrome- or gold-plate finished products. The company was started 13 years ago and has slowly built its sales volume to $2.5 million a year. Just one year ago, Myra Martinez was appointed marketing manager of the consumer products division. It is her responsibility to develop this division as a producer and marketer of the company's own branded products—as distinguished from custom orders, which the industrial division produces for others.

Ms. Martinez has been working on a number of different product ideas for almost a year now and has developed several designs for CD holders, cassette holders, plate holders, doll stands, collapsible book ends, and other such products. Her most promising product is a shoe rack for crowded homes and apartments. It is very similar to one the industrial division produced for a number of years for another company. In fact, it was experience with the sales volume of that product that interested Texco in the market—and led to the development of the consumer products division.

Ms. Martinez has sold hundreds of the shoe racks to various local grocery and general merchandise stores and wholesalers on a trial basis, but each time the price has been negotiated, and no firm policy has been set. Now she must determine what price to set on the shoe rack—which she plans to push aggressively wherever she can. Actually, she hasn't decided on exactly which channels of distribution to use. But trials in the local area have been encouraging, and, as noted above, the experience in the industrial division suggests that there is a large market for this type of product. The manufacturing cost on this product—when made in reasonable quantities—is approximately 40 cents if it is painted black and 50 cents if it is chromed. Similar products have been selling at retail in the $1.50 to $3 range. The sales and administrative overhead to be charged to the division will amount to $80,000 a year. This will include Ms. Martinez's salary and some office expenses. She expects that a number of other products will be developed in the near future. But for the coming year, she hopes the shoe rack will account for about half the consumer products division's sales volume.

Evaluate Myra Martinez's strategy planning so far. What should she do now? What price should she set for the shoe rack? Explain.

23 AAA Photo Labs, Inc.

Kevin Masters, marketing manager of AAA Photo Labs, is faced with price-cutting and wants to fight fire with fire. But his boss feels that they should promote harder to retailers and/or final consumers and maybe add mini-mini-labs in some stores to combat the mini-lab competition.

AAA Photo Labs, Inc., is one of the three major Colorado-based photofinishers—each with annual sales of about $8 million. AAA has company-owned plants in five cities in Colorado and western Kansas. They are located in Boulder, Pueblo, Denver, and Colorado Springs, Colorado, and Hays, Kansas.

AAA does all of its own black-and-white processing. While it has color-processing capability, AAA finds it more economical to have most color film processed by the regional Kodak processing plant. The color film processed by AAA is either off-brand film—or special work done for professional photographers. AAA has always given its customers fast, quality service. All pictures—including those processed by Kodak—can be returned within three days of receipt by AAA.

AAA's major customers are drugstores, camera stores, grocery stores, and any other retail outlets that offer photofinishing to consumers. These retailers insert film rolls, cartridges, negatives, and so on, into separate bags—marking on the outside the kind of work to be done. The customer gets a receipt but seldom sees the bag into which the film has been placed. The bag has the retailer's name on it—not AAA's.

Each processing plant has a small retail outlet for drop-in customers who live near the plant. This is a minor part of AAA's business.

Table 1

Type of Business	Percent of Dollar Volume
Sales to retail outlets	80%
Direct-mail sales	17
Retail walk-in sales	3
	100%

The company also does direct-mail photofinishing within the state of Colorado. The Denver plant processes direct-mail orders from consumers. All film received is handled in the same way as the other retail business.

A breakdown of the dollar volume by type of business is shown in Table 1.

All retail prices are set by local competition—and all major competitors charge the same prices. AAA sets a retail list price and offers each retailer a trade discount based on the volume of business generated. Table 2 shows the pricing schedule used by each of the major competitors in the Colorado–Kansas market.

All direct-mail processing for final consumers is priced at 33⅓ percent discount off the usual store price. But this is done under the Mountain Prints name—not the AAA name—to avoid complaints from retailer customers. Retail walk-in accounts are charged the full list price for all services.

Retail stores offering photofinishing are served by AAA's own sales force. Each processing plant has at least three people servicing accounts. Their duties include daily visits to all present accounts to pick up and deliver all photofinishing work. These sales reps also make daily trips to the nearby bus terminals to drop off color film to be processed by Kodak and pick up color slides or prints from Kodak. The reps are not expected to call on possible new accounts.

Since the final consumer does not come in contact with AAA, it has not advertised its retail store servicing business to final consumers. Similarly, possible retailer

Table 2

Monthly Dollar Volume (12-month average)	Discount (2/10, net 30)
$ 0–$ 100	33⅓%
$ 101–$ 500	40
$ 501–$1,000	45
$1,001–above	50

accounts are not called on or advertised to—except that AAA Photo Labs is listed under "Photofinishing: Wholesale"—in the Yellow Pages of all telephone books in cities and towns served by the five plants. Any phone inquiries are followed up by the nearest sales rep.

The direct-mail business—under the Mountain Prints name—is generated by regular ads in the Sunday pictorial sections of newspapers serving Pueblo, Denver, Colorado Springs, and Boulder. These ads usually stress low price, fast service, and fine quality. Mailers are provided for consumers to send to the plant. Some people in the company feel this part of the business might have great potential if pursued more aggressively.

AAA's president, Mr. Zang, is worried about the loss of several retail accounts in the $501 to $1,000 monthly sales volume range (See Table 2). He has been with the company since its beginning—and has always stressed quality and rapid delivery of the finished products. Demanding that all plants produce the finest quality, Mr. Zang personally conducts periodic quality tests of each plant through the direct-mail service. Plant managers are advised of any slips in quality.

To find out what is causing the loss in retail accounts, Mr. Zang is reviewing sales reps' reports and talking to employees. In their weekly reports, AAA's sales reps report a major threat to the company—price cutting. Speedpro, Inc.—a competitor of equal size that offers the same services as AAA—is offering an additional 5 percent trade discount in each sales volume category. This really makes a difference at some stores—because these retailers think that all the major processors do an equally good job. Further, they note, consumers apparently feel that the quality is acceptable because no complaints have been heard so far.

AAA has faced price cutting before—but never by an equally well established company. Mr. Zang can't understand why these retailer customers would leave AAA because AAA is offering higher quality and the price difference is not that large. Mr. Zang thinks the sales reps should sell quality a lot harder. He is also considering a radio or TV campaign to consumers to persuade them to demand AAA's quality service from their favorite retailer. Mr. Zang is convinced that consumers demanding quality will force retailers to stay with—or return to—AAA Photo Labs. He says: "If we can't get the business by convincing the retailer of our fine quality, we'll get it by convincing the consumer."

Mr. Zang also feels that Kevin Masters should seriously consider the pros and cons of offering AAA's customers the opportunity of installing a mini-mini-lab in their stores—to serve customers who want immediate processing of color film into color prints. Many consumers have gone to one-hour mini-lab operators in the last decade. In fact, over 30 percent of photofinishing work is now done by such operators—companies like Fotomart and Moto Photo, which are often located in shopping centers. Over 15,000 such mini-labs are operating now and have taken almost all of the growth in photofinishing in recent years. As a result, AAA and similar operators have seen flat sales and increasingly aggressive sales efforts as they fight for market share. Mr. Zang feels the development of more or less self-service mini-mini-labs, which can process and print a roll of color film in about 30 minutes, may help AAA succeed in this increasingly competitive market. Mr. Zang is thinking of installing one of these $35,000 machines in every logical retail store willing to operate the service along with AAA's present three-day photo service. The machines are the size of a small office copier, and the whole system requires as little as 18 square feet. The machines need no plumbing hookup and little monitoring after a few hours of training (which probably could be done by the sales reps who already call on the stores). Installing these machines in AAA's larger volume stores might win back some of the 30 percent of the market using mini-labs—without cutting much into the three-day customer business.

Kevin Masters, the marketing manager, disagrees with Mr. Zang regarding the price-cutting problem. Kevin thinks AAA ought to at least meet the price cut or cut prices up to another 5 percent wherever Speedpro has taken an AAA account. This would do two things: (1) get the business back and (2) signal that continued price cutting will be met by still deeper price cuts. Further, he says: "If Speedpro doesn't get the message, we ought to go after a few of their big accounts with 10 percent discounts. That ought to shape them up."

With respect to installing mini-mini-labs, Kevin Masters has serious reservations. His sales reps might have to become service reps and lose their effectiveness as sales reps. Also, that might slow up the pick-up and delivery activity and cause the three-day system to slip into a four-day cycle—which could open AAA accounts to three-day supplier competitors—a disaster! Also, he worries that the stores would have little incentive to promote the use of the machines because it is not their $35,000 machine! Finally, most of AAA's stores—being in outlying areas—don't compete with shopping centers so they have not really felt the impact of the mini-labs. But offering an in-store mini-lab might result in a large shift in business and loss of the present system's production economies of scale. Further, more investment will be required, but it probably won't be possible to raise the retail price much (if at all—the one-hour mini-lab operators usually meet the market price).

Evaluate AAA's present and proposed strategies. What should they do now? Explain.

(24) Kelman Mfg., Inc.

Al Kelman, the marketing manager of Kelman Mfg., Inc., wants to increase sales by adding sales reps rather than playing with price. That's how Al describes what Henry Kelman, his father and Kelman's president, is suggesting. Henry is not sure what to do either. But he does want to increase sales, so something new is needed.

Kelman Mfg., Inc.—of Long Beach, California—is a leading producer in the plastic forming machinery industry. It has patents covering over 200 variations, but Kelman's customers seldom buy more than 30 different types in a year. The machines are sold to plastic forming manufacturers to increase production capacity or replace old equipment.

Established in 1952, the company has enjoyed a steady growth to its present position with annual sales of $50 million.

Twelve U.S. firms compete in the U.S. plastic forming machinery market. Several Japanese, German, and Swedish firms compete in the global market, but the Kelmans have not seen them on the West Coast. Apparently the foreign firms rely on manufacturers' agents who have not provided an on-going presence. They don't follow up on inquiries, and their record for service on the few sales they have made on the East Coast is not good. So the Kelmans are not worried about them right now.

Each of the 12 U.S. competitors is about the same size and manufactures basically similar machinery. Each has tended to specialize in its own geographic area. None has exported much because of high labor costs in the United States. Six of the competitors are located in the East, four in the Midwest, and two—including Kelman—on the West Coast. The other West Coast firm is in Tacoma, Washington. All of the competitors offer similar prices and sell F.O.B. their factories. Demand has been fairly strong in recent years. As a result, all of the competitors have been satisfied to sell in their geographic areas and avoid price-cutting. In fact, price-cutting is not a popular idea in this industry. About 20 years ago, one firm tried to win more business and found that others immediately met the price cut—but industry sales (in units) did not increase at all. Within a few years, prices returned to their earlier level, and since then competition has tended to focus on promotion and avoid price.

Kelman's promotion depends mainly on six company sales reps, who cover the West Coast. In total, these reps cost about $660,000 per year including salary, bonuses, supervision, travel, and entertaining. When the sales reps are close to making a sale, they are supported by two sales engineers—at a cost of about $120,000 per year per engineer. Kelman does some advertising in trade journals—less than $50,000—and occasionally uses direct mailings. But the main promotion emphasis is on personal selling. Any personal contact outside the West Coast market is handled by manufacturers' agents who are paid 4 percent on sales—but sales are very infrequent. Henry Kelman is not satisfied with the present situation. Industry sales have leveled off and so have Kelman's sales—although the firm continues to hold its share of the market. Henry would like to find a way to compete more effectively in the other regions because he sees great potential outside of the West Coast.

Competitors and buyers agree that Kelman is the top-quality producer in the industry. Its machines have generally been somewhat superior to others in terms of reliability, durability, and productive capacity. The difference, however, usually has not been great enough to justify a higher price—because the others are able to do the necessary job—unless a Kelman sales rep convinces the customer that the extra quality will improve the customer's product and lead to fewer production line breakdowns. The sales rep also tries to sell Kelman's better sales engineers and technical service people—and sometimes is successful. But if a buyer is only interested in comparing delivered prices for basic machines—the usual case—Kelman's price must be competitive to get the business. In short, if such a buyer has a choice between Kelman's and another machine *at the same price,* Kelman will usually win the business in its part of the West Coast market. But it's clear that Kelman's price has to be at least competitive in such cases.

The average plastic forming machine sells for about $220,000, F.O.B. shipping point. Shipping costs within any of the three major regions average about $4,000—but another $3,000 must be added on shipments between the West Coast and the Midwest (either way) and another $3,000 between the Midwest and the East.

Henry Kelman is thinking about expanding sales by absorbing the extra $3,000 to $6,000 in freight cost that occurs if a midwestern or eastern customer buys from his West Coast location. By doing this, he would not be cutting price in those markets but rather reducing his net return. He thinks that his competitors would not see this as price competition—and therefore would not resort to cutting prices themselves.

Al Kelman, the marketing manager, disagrees. Al thinks that the proposed freight absorption plan would stimulate price competition in the Midwest and East—and perhaps on the West Coast. He proposes instead that Kelman hire some sales reps to work the Midwest and Eastern regions—selling quality—rather than relying on the manufacturers' agents. He argues that two additional sales reps in each of these regions would not increase costs too much—and might greatly increase the sales from these markets over that brought in by the agents. With this plan, there would be no need to absorb the freight and risk disrupting the status quo. Adding more of Kelman's own sales reps is especially important, he argues, because competition in the Midwest and East is somewhat hotter than on the West Coast—due to the number of competitors (including foreign competitors) in those regions. A lot of expensive entertaining, for example, seems to be required just to be considered as a potential supplier. In contrast, the situation has been rather quiet in the West—because only two firms are sharing this market and each is working harder near its home base. The eastern and midwestern competitors don't send any sales reps to the West Coast—and if they have any manufacturers' agents, they haven't gotten any business in recent years.

Henry Kelman agrees that his son has a point, but industry sales are leveling off and Henry wants to increase sales. Further, he thinks the competitive situation may change drastically in the near future anyway, as global competitors get more aggressive and some possible new production methods and machines become more competitive with existing ones. He would rather be a leader in anything that is likely to happen—rather than a follower. But he is impressed with Al's comments about the greater competitiveness in the other markets and therefore is unsure about what to do.

Evaluate Kelman's current strategies. Given Henry Kelman's sales objective, what should Kelman Mfg. do? Explain.

25 Riverside Packers, Inc.

Jon Dow, president of Riverside Packers, Inc., is not sure what he should propose to the board of directors. His recent strategy change isn't working. And Bill Jacobs, Riverside's only sales rep (and a board member), is so frustrated that he refuses to continue his discouraging sales efforts. Jacobs wants Jon Dow to hire a sales force or *something*.

Riverside Packers, Inc., is a long-time processor in the highly seasonal vegetable canning industry. Riverside packs and sells canned beans, peas, carrots, corn, peas and carrots mixed, and kidney beans. It sells mainly through food brokers to merchant wholesalers, supermarket chains (such as Kroger, Safeway, A&P, and Jewel), cooperatives, and other outlets—mostly in the Chicago area. Of less importance, by volume, are sales to local institutions, grocery stores, and supermarkets—and sales of dented canned goods at low prices to walk-in customers.

Riverside is located in Wisconsin's Devil's River Valley. The company has more than $28 million in sales annually (exact sales data is not published by the closely held corporation). Plants are located in strategic places along the valley—with main offices in Riverside. The Riverside brand is used only on canned goods sold in the local market. Most of the goods are sold and shipped under a retailer's label or a broker's/wholesaler's label.

Riverside is well known for the consistent quality of its product offerings. And it's always willing to offer competitive prices. Strong channel relations were built by Riverside's former chairman of the board and chief executive officer, Fritz Allshouse. Mr. Allshouse—who owns controlling interest in the firm—worked the Chicago area as the company's sales rep in its earlier years—before he took over from his father as president in 1950. Allshouse was an ambitious and hard-working top manager—the firm prospered under his direction. He became well known within the canned food processing industry for technical/product innovations.

During the off-canning season, Mr. Allshouse traveled widely. In the course of his travels, he arranged several important business deals. His 1968 and 1982 trips resulted in the following two events: (1) inexpensive pineapple was imported from Formosa and sold by Riverside—primarily to expand the product line, and (2) a technically advanced continuous process cooker (65 feet high) was imported from England and installed at the Riverside plant in February-March 1985. It was the first of its kind in the United States and cut processing time sharply.

Mr. Allshouse retired in 1989 and named his son-in-law, 35-year-old Jon Dow, as his successor. Mr. Dow is intelligent and hardworking. He was concerned primarily with the company's financial matters and only recently with marketing problems. During his seven years as financial director, the firm received its highest credit rating—and was able to borrow working capital ($5 million to meet seasonal can and wage requirements) at the lowest rate ever.

The fact that the firm isn't unionized allows some competitive advantage. However, changes in minimum wage laws have increased costs. And these and other rising costs have squeezed profit margins. This led to the recent closing of two plants—as they became less efficient to operate. Riverside expanded capacity of the remaining two plants (especially warehouse facilities) so they could operate more profitably with maximum use of existing processing equipment.

Shortly after Mr. Allshouse's retirement, Jon Dow reviewed the company's situation with his managers. He pointed to narrowing profit margins, debts contracted for new plant and equipment, and an increasingly competitive environment. Even considering the temporary labor-saving competitive advantage of the new cooker system, there seemed to be no way to improve the status quo unless the firm could sell direct—as they do in the local market—thereby eliminating the food brokers' 5 percent commission on sales. This was the plan decided on, and Bill Jacobs was given the new sales job. An inside sales clerk was retained to handle incoming orders.

Bill Jacobs, the only full-time outside sales rep for the firm, lives in Riverside. Other top managers do some selling—but not much. Being a nephew of Mr. Allshouse, Bill Jacobs is also a member of the board of directors. He is well qualified in technical matters and has a college degree in food chemistry. Although Bill Jacobs formerly did call on some important customers with the brokers' sales reps, he is not well known in the industry or even by Riverside's usual customers.

It is now five months later. Bill Jacobs is not doing very well. He has made several selling trips and hundreds of telephone calls with discouraging results. He is unwilling to continue sales efforts on his own. There seem to be too many potential customers for one person to reach. And much wining and dining seems to be needed—certainly more than he can or wants to do. Jacobs insists that Riverside hire a sales force to continue the present way of operating. Sales are down in comparison both to expectations and to the previous year's results. Some regular supermarket chain customers have stopped buying—though basic consumer demand has not changed. Further, some potential new customers have demanded quantity guarantees much larger than the firm can supply. Expanding supply would be difficult in the short run—because the firm typically must contract with

growers to assure supplies of the type and quality they normally offer.

Mr. Allshouse, still the controlling stockholder, has asked for a special meeting of the board in two weeks to discuss the present situation.

Evaluate Riverside's past and current strategy planning. What should Jon Dow tell Mr. Allshouse? What should Riverside do now?

26 Cutters, Inc.

Tony Kenny, president and marketing manager of Cutters, Inc., is deciding what strategy—or strategies—to pursue.

Cutters, Inc., is a manufacturer of industrial cutting tools. These tools include such items as lathe blades, drill press bits, and various other cutting edges used in the operation of large metal cutting, boring, or stamping machines. Tony Kenny takes great pride in the fact that his company—whose $5,200,000 sales in 1991 is small by industry standards—is recognized as a producer of a top-quality line of cutting tools.

Competition in the cutting-tool industry is intense. Cutters competes, not only with the original machine manufacturers, but also with many other larger domestic and foreign manufacturers offering cutting tools as one of their many different product lines. This has had the effect, over the years, of standardizing the price, specifications, and, in turn, the quality of the competing products of all manufacturers. It has also led to fairly low prices on standard items.

About a year ago, Tony was tiring of the financial pressure of competing with larger companies enjoying economies of scale. At the same time, he noted that more and more potential cutting-tool customers were turning to small tool-and-die shops because of specialized needs that could not be met by the mass production firms. Tony thought perhaps he should consider some basic strategy changes. Although he was unwilling to become strictly a custom producer, he thought that the recent trend toward buying customized cutting edges suggested new markets might be developing—markets too small for the large, multiproduct-line companies to serve profitably but large enough to earn a good profit for a flexible company of Cutters's size.

Tony hired a marketing research company, Holl Associates, to study the feasibility of serving these markets. The initial results were encouraging. It was estimated that Cutters might increase sales by 65 percent and profits by

90 percent by serving the emerging markets. This research showed that many large users of standard cutting tools buy directly from large cutting-tool manufacturers (domestic or foreign) or wholesalers who represent these manufacturers. This is the bulk of the cutting-tool business (in terms of units sold and sales dollars). But there are also many smaller users all over the United States who buy in small but regular quantities. And some of these needs are becoming more specialized. That is, a special cutting tool may make a machine and/or worker much more productive, perhaps eliminating several steps with time-consuming set-ups. This is the area that the research company sees as potentially attractive.

Next, Tony had the sales manager hire two technically oriented market researchers (at a total cost of $60,000 each per year, including travel expenses) to maintain continuous contact with potential cutting-tool customers. The researchers were supposed to identify any present—or future—needs that might exist in enough cases to make it possible to profitably produce a specialized product. The researchers were not to take orders or sell Cutters's products to the potential customers. Tony felt that only through this policy could these researchers talk to the right people.

The initial feedback from the market researchers was most encouraging. Many firms (large and small) had special needs—although it often was necessary to talk to the shop foreman or individual machine operators to find these needs. Most operators were making do with the tools available. Either they didn't know customizing was possible or doubted that their supervisors would do anything about it if they suggested that a more specialized tool would increase productivity. But these operators were encouraging because they said that it would be easier to persuade supervisors to order specialized tools if the tools were already produced and in stock than if they had to be custom-made. So Tony decided to continually add high-quality products to meet the ever-changing, specialized needs of users of cutting tools and edges.

Cutters's potential customers for specialized tools are located all over the United States. The average sale per customer is likely to be less than $500, but the sale will be repeated several times within a year. Because of the widespread market and the small order size, Tony doesn't think that selling direct—as is done by small custom shops—is practical. At the present time, Cutters sells 90 percent of its regular output through a large industrial wholesaler—National Mill Supplies, Inc.—which serves the area east of the Mississippi River and carries a very complete line of industrial supplies (to "meet every industrial need"). Each of National's sales reps sells over 10,000 items from a 910-page catalog. National Mill Supplies, although very large and well known, is having trouble moving cutting tools. National is losing sales of cutting tools in some cities to newer wholesalers specializing in the cutting-tool industry. The new wholesalers are able to give more technical help to potential customers and therefore better service. National's president is convinced that the newer, less-experienced concerns will either realize that a substantial profit margin can't be maintained along with their aggressive strategies, or they will eventually go broke trying to overspecialize.

From Tony's standpoint, the present wholesaler has a good reputation and has served Cutters well in the past. National Mill Supplies has been of great help in holding down Tony's inventory costs—by increasing the inventory in National's 35 branch locations. Although Tony has received several complaints about the lack of technical assistance given by National's sales reps—as well as their lack of knowledge about Cutters's new special products—he feels that the present wholesaler is providing the best service it can. All its sales reps have been told about the new products at a special training session, and a new page has been added to the catalog they carry with them. So regarding the complaints, Tony says: "The usual things you hear when you're in business."

Tony thinks there are more urgent problems than a few complaints. Profits are declining, and sales of the new cutting tools are not nearly as high as forecast—even though all research reports indicate that the company's new products meet the intended markets' needs perfectly. The high costs involved in producing small quantities of special products and in adding the market research team—together with lower-than-expected sales—have significantly reduced Cutters's profits. Tony is wondering whether it is wise to continue to try to cater to the needs of many specific target markets when the results are this discouraging. He also is considering increasing advertising expenditures in the hope that customers will pull the new products through the channel.

Evaluate Cutters's situation and Tony Kenny's present strategy. What should he do now?

27 KASTORS, Inc.

Rick Moore, marketing manager for KASTORS, Inc., is trying to figure out how to explain to his boss why a proposed new product line doesn't make sense for them. Rick is sure it's wrong for KASTORS, Inc.—but isn't able to explain why.

KASTORS, Inc., is a producer of malleable iron castings for automobile and aircraft manufacturers—and a variety of other users of castings. Last year's sales of castings amounted to over $70 million.

KASTORS also produces about 30 percent of all the original-equipment bumper jacks installed in new U.S.-made automobiles each year. This is a very price-competitive business, but KASTORS has been able to obtain its large market share with frequent personal contact between the company's executives and its customers—supported by very close cooperation between the company's engineering department and its customers' buyers. This has been extremely important because the wide variety of models and model changes frequently requires alterations in the specifications of the bumper jacks. All of KASTORS's bumper jacks are sold directly to the automobile manufacturers. No attempt has been made to sell bumper jacks to final consumers through hardware and automotive channels—although they are available through the manufacturers' automobile dealers.

Tim Owen, KASTORS's production manager, now wants to begin producing hydraulic garage jacks for sale through automobile-parts wholesalers to retail auto parts stores. Owen saw a variety of hydraulic garage jacks at a recent automotive show—and knew immediately that his plant could produce these products. This especially interested him because of the possibility of using excess capacity—now that auto sales are down. Further, he says "jacks are jacks," and the company would merely be broadening its product line by introducing hydraulic garage jacks. (Note: Hydraulic garage jacks are larger than bumper jacks and are intended for use in or around a garage. They are too big to carry in a car's trunk.)

As Tim Owen became more enthusiastic about the idea, he found that KASTORS's engineering department already had a design that appeared to be at least comparable to the products now offered on the market. None of these products have any patent protection. Further, Owen says that the company would be able to produce a product that is better made than the competitive products (i.e., smoother castings, etc.)—although he agrees that most customers probably wouldn't notice the difference. The production department estimates that the cost of producing a hydraulic garage jack comparable to those currently offered by competitors would be about $48 per unit.

Rick Moore, the marketing manager, has just received a memo from Bill Borne, the company president, explaining the production department's enthusiasm for broadening KASTORS's present jack line into hydraulic jacks. Bill Borne seems enthusiastic about the idea too, noting that it would be a way to make fuller use of the company's resources and increase its sales. Borne's memo asks for Rick's reaction, but Bill Borne already seems sold on the idea.

Given Borne's enthusiasm, Rick Moore isn't sure how to respond. He's trying to develop a good explanation of why he isn't excited about the proposal. He knows he's already overworked and couldn't possibly promote this new line himself—and he's the only sales rep the company has. So it would be necessary to hire someone to promote the line. And this sales manager would probably have to recruit manufacturers' agents (who probably will want 10 to 15 percent commission on sales) to sell to automotive wholesalers who would stock the jack and sell to the auto parts retailers. The wholesalers will probably expect trade discounts of about 20 percent, trade show exhibits, some national advertising, and sales promotion help (catalog sheets, mailers, and point-of-purchase displays). Further, Rick Moore sees that KASTORS's billing and collection system will have to be expanded because many more customers will be involved. It will also be necessary to keep track of agent commissions and accounts receivable.

Auto parts retailers are currently selling similar hydraulic garage jacks for about $99. Rick Moore has learned that such retailers typically expect a trade discount of about 35 percent off of the suggested list price for their auto parts.

All things considered, Rick Moore feels that the proposed hydraulic jack line is not very closely related to the company's present emphasis. He has already indicated his lack of enthusiasm to Tim Owen, but this made little difference in Tim's thinking. Now it's clear that Rick will have to convince the president or he will soon be responsible for selling hydraulic jacks.

Contrast KASTORS's current strategy and the proposed strategy. What should Rick Moore say to Bill Borne to persuade him to change his mind? Or should he just plan to sell hydraulic jacks? Explain.

28 Grand Foods, Ltd.*

Jessica Walters, marketing manager of Grand Foods, Ltd.—a Canadian company—is being urged to approve the creation of a separate marketing plan for Quebec.

---

*Adapted from case written by Professor Roberta Tamilia, University of Windsor, Canada.

This would be a major policy change because Grand Foods's international parent is trying to move towards a global strategy for the whole firm and Jessica has been supporting Canada-wide planning.

Jessica Walters has been the marketing manager of Grand Foods, Ltd., for the last four years—since she arrived from international headquarters in Minneapolis. Grand Foods, Ltd.—headquartered in Toronto—is a subsidiary of a large U.S.-based consumer packaged-food company with worldwide sales of more than $2 billion in 1991. Its Canadian sales are just over $350 million—with the Quebec and Ontario markets accounting for 69 percent of the company's Canadian sales.

The company's product line includes such items as cake mixes, puddings, pie fillings, pancakes, prepared foods, and frozen dinners. The company has successfully introduced at least six new products every year for the last five years. Products from Grand Foods are known for their high quality and enjoy much brand preference throughout Canada—including the Province of Quebec.

The company's sales have risen every year since Jessica Walters took over as marketing manager. In fact, the company's market share has increased steadily in each of the product categories in which it competes. The Quebec market has closely followed the national trend except that, in the past two years, total sales growth in that market began to lag.

According to Mrs. Walters, a big advantage of Grand Foods over its competitors is the ability to coordinate all phases of the food business from Toronto. For this reason, Mrs. Walters meets at least once a month with her product managers—to discuss developments in local markets that might affect marketing plans. While each manager is free to make suggestions—and even to suggest major changes—Jessica Walters is finally responsible for all plans.

One of the product managers, Marie LeMans, expressed great concern at the last monthly meeting about the poor performance of some of the company's products in the Quebec market. While a broad range of possible reasons—ranging from inflation and the threat of job losses to politics—were reviewed to try to explain the situation, Ms. LeMans insisted that it was due to a basic lack of understanding of that market. She felt not enough managerial time and money had been spent on the Quebec market—in part because of the current emphasis on developing all-Canada plans on the way to having one global strategy.

Marie LeMans felt the current marketing approach to the Quebec market should be reevaluated because an inappropriate marketing plan may be responsible for the sales slowdown. "After all," she said, "80 percent of the market is French-speaking. It's in the best interest of the company to treat that market as being separate and distinct from the rest of Canada."

Marie LeMans supported her position by showing that Quebec's per capita consumption of many product categories (in which the firm competes) is above the national average (Table 1). Research projects conducted by Grand Foods also support the "separate and distinct" argument. Over the years, the firm has found many French-English differences in brand attitudes, lifestyles, usage rates, and so on.

Ms. LeMans argued that the company should develop a unique Quebec marketing plan for some or all of its brands. She specifically suggested that the French-language advertising plan for a particular brand be developed independently of the plan for English Canada. Currently, the Toronto agency assigned to the brand just translates its English-language ads for the French market. Jessica Walters pointed out that the present advertising approach assured Grand Foods of a uniform brand image across Canada. Marie LeMans said she knew what the agency is doing, and that straight translation into Canadian-French may not communicate the same brand image. The discussion that followed suggested that a different brand image might be needed in the French market if the company wanted to stop the brand's decline in sales.

The managers also discussed the food distribution system in Quebec. The major supermarket chains have their lowest market share in that province. Independents are strongest there—the "mom-and-pop" food stores fast disappearing outside Quebec remain alive and well in the province. Traditionally, these stores have stocked a higher proportion (than supermarkets) of their shelf space with national brands—an advantage for Grand Foods.

Finally, various issues related to discount policies, pricing structure, sales promotion, and cooperative advertising were discussed. All of this suggested that things were different in Quebec—and that future marketing

Table 1   Per Capita Consumption Index, Province
of Quebec (Canada = 100)

Cake mixes	107	Soft drinks	126
Pancakes	87	Pie fillings	118
Puddings	114	Frozen dinners	79
Salad dressings	85	Prepared packaged foods	83
Molasses	132	Cookies	123

plans should reflect these differences to a greater extent than they do now.

After the meeting, Jessica Walters stayed in her office to think about the situation. Although she agreed with the basic idea that the Quebec market was in many ways different, she wasn't sure how far the company should go in recognizing this fact. She knew that regional differences in food tastes and brand purchases existed not only in Quebec but in other parts of Canada as well. But people are people, after all, with far more similarities than differences, so a Canadian and eventually a global strategy makes some sense too.

Jessica Walters was afraid that giving special status to one region might conflict with top management's objective of achieving standardization whenever possible—one global strategy for Canada, on the way to one worldwide global strategy. She was also worried about the long-term effect of such a policy change on costs, organizational structure, and brand image. Still, enough product managers had expressed their concern over the years about the Quebec market to make her wonder if she shouldn't modify the current approach. Perhaps they could experiment with a few brands—and just in Quebec. She could cite the language difference as the reason for trying Quebec rather than any of the other provinces. But Mrs. Walters realizes that any change of policy could be seen as the beginning of more change, and what would Minneapolis think? Could she explain it successfully there?

Evaluate Grand Foods, Ltd.'s present strategy. What should Jessica Walters do now? Explain.

29 Dalton Olds, Inc.

Bob Dalton owns Dalton Olds, Inc., an Oldsmobile/Nissan dealership in suburban Dallas, Texas. Bob is seriously considering moving into a proposed auto mall—a large display and selling area for 10 to 15 auto dealers, none handling the same car brands. This mall will be a few miles away from his current location but easily available to his present customers and quite convenient to many more potential customers. He can consider moving now because the lease on his current location will be up in one year. He is sure he can renew the lease for another five years, but he feels the building owner is likely to want to raise the lease terms so his total fixed costs will be about $100,000 more per year than his current fixed costs of $650,000 per year. Moving to the new mall will probably increase his total fixed costs to about $1,100,000 per year. Further, fixed costs—wherever he is—will probably continue to rise with inflation. But he doesn't see this as a

major problem. Car prices tend to rise at about the same rate as inflation, so these rising revenues and costs tend to offset each other.

Bob Dalton is considering moving to an auto mall because he feels this is the future trend. Already, about 125 such malls operate in the United States. And the number should double in the next 5 to 10 years because they do seem to increase sales per dealership. Some dealers in auto malls have reported sales increases of as much as 30 percent over what they were doing in their former locations outside the mall. The auto mall concept seems to be a continuing evolution from isolated car dealerships to car dealer strips along major traffic arteries to more customer-oriented clusters of dealerships that make it easier for customers to shop.

Bob is considering moving to a mall because of the growing number of competing brands and the desire of some consumers to shop more conveniently. Instead of just the Big Three, now over 30 different brands of cars and 15 brands of trucks compete in the U.S. market—not including specialty cars such as Lamborghini and Rolls-Royce. Increasing competition is already taking its toll on some domestic and foreign car dealers as they have to take less profit on each sale. For example, even owners of luxury car franchises such as Porsche, Audi, and Acura are having troubles, and some have moved into malls. Dealer ranks have thinned considerably too. Once there were 50,000 dealerships in the United States. Now, there are less than half that number—and failures are reported all the time. Recently, some dealers tried to become "mega-dealers" operating in several markets, but this did not work too well because they could not achieve economies of scale. Now owners of multiple dealerships seem to be going to malls to reduce their overhead and promotion costs. And if customers begin to go to these malls, then this may be *the* place to be—even for a dealer with only one or two auto franchises. That's the position that Bob Dalton is in—with his Oldsmobile and Nissan franchises. And he wonders if he should become well positioned in a mall before it is too late.

Bob Dalton's dealership is now selling between 550 and 700 new and used cars per year—at an average price of about $11,000. With careful management, he is grossing about $1,000 per car. This $1,000 is not all net profit, however. It must go towards covering his fixed costs of about $650,000 per year. So if he sells more than 650 cars he will more than cover his fixed costs and make a profit. Obviously, the more cars he sells beyond 650, the bigger the profit—assuming he controls his costs. So he is thinking that moving to a mall might increase his sales and therefore lead to a larger profit. A major question is whether he is likely to sell enough extra cars in a mall to help pay for the increase in fixed costs. He is also concerned about how his Oldsmobile products will stand up against all of the other cars when consumers can more easily shop around and compare. Right now, Bob has some loyal customers who regularly buy from him because of his seasoned, helpful sales force *and* his dependable repair shop. But he worries that making it easy for these customers to compare other cars might lead to brand switching or put greater pressure on price to keep some of his loyal customers.

Another of Bob's concerns is whether the Big Three car manufacturers will discourage dealers from going into auto malls. Now these auto manufacturers do not encourage dealers to go into a supermarket setting. Instead, they prefer their dealers to devote their full energies to one brand in a free-standing location. But as real estate prices rise, it becomes more and more difficult to insist on free-standing dealerships in all markets—and still have profitable dealerships. The rising number of bankruptcies or dealerships in financial difficulties has caused the manufacturers to be more relaxed about insisting on a free-standing location. Oldsmobile and Nissan seem to be accepting this change, so this is not Bob's main concern right now.

Adding to the competitiveness in the U.S. auto market—which is Bob's biggest concern—is the increasing aggressiveness of foreign auto importers as well as Japanese-owned U.S. car producers like Honda. As they increase their penetration on the East and West Coasts, they are moving into the center of the United States. While imports represent more than half of car sales in some east and west coast markets, they account for as little as 15 to 25 percent of the market in the middle of the United States. But now they are setting up more dealers in this area and competition is likely to become even more intense. In Texas, imports account for over 25 percent of the market, but this share will probably rise in the future. And Bob wants to be able to survive in this increasingly competitive market. That is why he added the Nissan franchise recently—to give his sales reps more to sell and increase his chances for making a profit.

Evaluate Bob Dalton's present and possible new strategy. What should Bob Dalton do? Why?

30 Metro Medical, Inc.

Jackie Johnson, executive director of Metro Medical, Inc., is trying to clarify her strategies. She's sure some changes are needed, but she's less sure about how *much*

change is needed and/or whether it can be handled by her people.

Metro Medical, Inc. (MM), is a nonprofit organization that has been operating—with varying degrees of success—for 25 years—offering nursing services in clients' homes. Some of its funding comes from the local United Way—to provide emergency nursing services for those who can't afford to pay. The balance of the revenues—about 90 percent of the $1.8 million annual budget—comes from charges made directly to the client or to third-party payers—including insurance companies and the federal government—for Medicare or Medicaid services.

Jackie Johnson has been executive director of MM for two years. She has developed a well-functioning organization able to meet most requests for service that come from some local doctors and from the discharge officers at local hospitals. Some business also comes by self-referral—the client finds the MM name in the Yellow Pages of the local phone directory.

The last two years have been a rebuilding time—because the previous director had personnel problems. This led to a weakening of the agency's image with the local referring agencies. Now the image is more positive. But Jackie is not completely satisfied with the situation. By definition, Metro Medical is a nonprofit organization. But it still must cover all its costs: payroll, rent payments, phone expenses, and so on—including Jackie's own salary. She can see that while MM is growing slightly and is now breaking even, it doesn't have much of a cash cushion to fall back on if (1) the demand for MM nursing services declines, (2) the government changes its rules about paying for MM's kind of nursing services—either cutting back what it will pay for or reducing the amount it will pay for specific services—or (3) new competitors enter the market. In fact, the last possibility concerns Jackie greatly. Some hospitals—squeezed for revenue—are expanding into home health care—especially nursing services as patients are being released earlier from hospitals because of new government payment guidelines. For-profit organizations (e.g., Kelly Home Care Services) are expanding around the country to provide a complete line of home health-care services—including nursing services of the kind offered by MM. These for-profit organizations appear to be efficiently run—offering good service at competitive and sometimes even lower prices than some nonprofit organizations. And they seem to be doing this at a profit—which suggests that it would be possible for these for-profit companies to lower their prices if nonprofit organizations try to compete on price.

Jackie is considering whether she should ask her board of directors to let her offer a complete line of home health care services—to move beyond just nursing services into what she calls "care and comfort" services.

Currently, MM is primarily concerned with providing professional nursing care in the home. But MM nurses are much too expensive for routine home health-care activities—helping fix meals, bathing and dressing patients, and other care and comfort activities. The full cost of a nurse to MM (including benefits and overhead) is about $60 per hour. But, a registered nurse is not needed for care and comfort services. All that is required is someone who can get along with all kinds of people and is willing to do this kind of work. Generally, any mature person can be trained fairly quickly to do the job—following the instructions and under the general supervision of a physician, a nurse, or family members. The full cost of aides is $6 to $10 per hour for short visits—and as low as $50 per 24 hours for a live-in aide who has room and board supplied by the client.

The demand for all kinds of home health-care services seems to be growing as more women join the work force and aren't available to take over home health care when the need arises—due to emergencies or long-term disabilities. And with people living longer, there are more single-survivor family situations where there is no one nearby to take care of the needs of these older people. But often some family members—or third-party payers such as the government or insurers—are willing to pay for some home health-care services. Now Jackie occasionally recommends other agencies, or suggests one or another of three women who have been doing care and comfort work on their own—part-time. But with growing demand, Jackie wonders if MM should get into this business—hiring aides as needed.

Jackie is concerned that a new, full-service home health-care organization may come into her market and provide both nursing services *and* less-skilled home care and comfort services. This has happened already in two nearby but somewhat larger cities. Jackie fears that this might be more appealing than MM to the local hospitals and other referrers. In other words, she can see the possibility of losing nursing service business if MM does not begin to offer a complete home health-care service. This would cause real problems for MM—because overhead costs are more or less fixed. A loss in revenue of as little as 10 percent would require some cutbacks—perhaps laying off some nurses or secretaries, giving up part of the office, and so on.

Another reason for expanding beyond nursing services—using paraprofessionals and relatively unskilled personnel—is to offer a better service to present customers *and* make more effective use of the organization structure that she has developed over the last two years. Jackie estimates that the administrative and office capabilities could handle twice as many clients without straining the system. It would be necessary to add some clerical help—if the expansion were quite large—as well as expanding the hours when the switchboard is open. But these increases in overhead would be minor compared to the present proportion of total revenue that goes to covering overhead. In other words, additional clients or more work for some clients could increase revenue and assure the survival of MM, provide a cushion to cover the normal fluctuations in demand, and assure more job security for the administrative personnel.

Further, Jackie thinks that if MM were successful in expanding its services—and therefore could generate some surplus—it could extend services to those who aren't now able to pay. Jackie says one of the worst parts of her job is refusing service to clients whose third-party benefits have run out or for whatever reason can no longer afford to pay. She is uncomfortable about having to cut off service, but she must schedule her nurses to provide revenue-producing services if she's going to meet the payroll every two weeks. By expanding to provide more services, she might be able to keep serving more of these nonpaying clients. This possibility excites Jackie because her nurse's training has instilled a deep desire to serve people—whether they can pay or not. This continual need to cut off service because people can't pay has been at the root of many disagreements—and even arguments—between the nurses serving the clients and Jackie, as executive director and representative of the board of directors.

Jackie knows that expanding into care and comfort services won't be easy. Some decisions would be needed about relative pay levels for nurses, paraprofessionals, and aides. MM would also have to set prices for these different services and tell the present customers and referral agencies about the expanded services.

These problems aren't bothering Jackie too much, however—she thinks she can handle them. She is sure that care and comfort services are in demand and could be supplied at competitive prices.

Her primary concern is whether this is the right thing for Metro Medical—basically a nursing organization—to do. MM's whole history has been oriented to supplying *nurses' services*. Nurses are dedicated professionals who bring high standards to any job they undertake. The question is whether MM should offer less-professional services. Inevitably, some of the aides will not be as dedicated as the nurses might like them to be. And this could reflect unfavorably on the nurse image. At the same time, however, Jackie worries about the future of MM—and her own future.

Evaluate MM's present strategy. What should Jackie Johnson do? Explain.

31 Lever, Ltd.*

Joe Hall is product manager for Guard Deodorant Soap. He was just transferred to Lever, Ltd., a Canadian subsidiary of Lever Group, Inc., from world headquarters in New York. Joe is anxious to make a good impression because he is hoping to transfer to Lever's London office. He is working on developing and securing management approval of next year's marketing plan for Guard. His first job is submitting a draft marketing plan to Sarah Long—his recently appointed group product manager—who is responsible for several such plans from product managers like Joe.

Joe's marketing plan is the single most important document he will produce on this assignment. This annual marketing plan does three main things:

1. It reviews the brand's performance in the past year, assesses the competitive situation, and highlights problems and opportunities for the brand.

---

*Adapted from a case prepared by Daniel Aronchick, who at the time of its preparation was marketing manager at Thomas J. Lipton, Limited.

2. It spells out marketing strategies and the plan for the coming year.

3. Finally, and most importantly, the marketing plan sets out the brand's sales objectives and advertising/promotion budget requirements.

In preparing this marketing plan, Joe gathered the information in Table 1.

Joe was somewhat surprised at the significant regional differences in the bar soap market:

a. The underdevelopment of the deodorant bar segment in Quebec, with a corresponding overdevelopment of the beauty bar segment. But some past research suggested that this is due to cultural factors—English-speaking people have been more interested than others in cleaning, deodorizing, and disinfecting. A similar pattern is seen in most European countries, where the adoption of deodorant soaps has been slower than in North America. For similar reasons, the perfumed soap share is highest in French-speaking Quebec.

b. The overdevelopment of synthetic bars in the Prairies. These bars, primarily in the deodorant segment, lather better in the hard water of the Prairies. Nonsynthetic bars lather very poorly in hard-water areas—and leave a soap film.

c. The overdevelopment of the "all-other" segment in Quebec. This segment, consisting of smaller brands, fares better in Quebec where 43 percent of the grocery trade is done by independent stores. Conversely, large chain grocery stores dominate in Ontario and the Prairies.

Table 1 Past 12-month Share of Bar Soap Market (percent)

	Maritimes	Quebec	Ontario	Manitoba/Saskatchewan	Alberta	British Columbia
Deodorant segment						
Zest	21.3%	14.2%	24.5%	31.2%	30.4%	25.5%
Dial	10.4	5.1	12.8	16.1	17.2	14.3
Lifebuoy	4.2	3.1	1.2	6.4	5.8	4.2
Guard	2.1	5.6	1.0	4.2	4.2	2.1
Beauty bar segment						
Camay	6.2	12.3	7.0	4.1	4.0	5.1
Lux	6.1	11.2	7.7	5.0	6.9	5.0
Dove	5.5	8.0	6.6	6.3	6.2	4.2
Lower-priced bars						
Ivory	11.2	6.5	12.4	5.3	5.2	9.0
Sunlight	6.1	3.2	8.2	4.2	4.1	8.0
All others						
(including stores' own brands)	26.9	30.8	18.6	17.2	16.0	22.6
Total bar soap market	100.0	100.0	100.0	100.0	100.0	100.0

Table 2 Standard Cases of Three-Ounce Bars Consumed per 1,000 People in 12 Months

	Maritimes	Quebec	Ontario	Manitoba/ Saskatchewan	Alberta	British Columbia
Guard	4.1	10.9	1.9	8.1	4.1	6.2
Sales Index	66	175	31	131	131	100

Joe's brand, Guard, is a highly perfumed deodorant bar. His business is relatively weak in the key Ontario market. To confirm this share data, Joe calculated consumption of Guard per thousand people in each region (see Table 2). These differences are especially interesting since per capita sales of all bar soap products are roughly equal in all provinces.

A consumer attitude and usage research study was conducted approximately a year ago. This study revealed that consumer "top-of-mind" awareness of the Guard brand differed greatly across Canada. This was true despite the even—by population—expenditure of advertising funds in past years. Also, trial of Guard was low in the Maritimes, Ontario, and British Columbia (Table 3).

The attitude portion of the research revealed that consumers who had heard of Guard were aware that its deodorant protection came mainly from a high fragrance level. This was the main selling point in the copy, and it was well communicated by Guard's advertising. The other important finding was that consumers who had tried Guard were satisfied with the product. About 70 percent of those trying Guard had repurchased the product at least twice.

Joe has also discovered that bar soap competition is especially intense in Ontario. It is Canada's largest market, and many competitors seem to want a share of it. The chain stores are also quite aggressive in promotion and pricing—offering specials, in-store coupons, etc. They want to move goods. And because of this, two key Ontario chains have put Guard on their pending delisting sheets. These chains, which control about half the grocery volume in Ontario, are dissatisfied with how slowly Guard is moving off the shelves.

Now Joe feels he is ready to set a key part of the brand's marketing plan for next year: how to allocate the advertising/sales promotion budget by region.

Guard's present advertising/sales promotion budget is 20 percent of sales. With forecast sales of $4 million, this would amount to an $800,000 expenditure. Traditionally such funds have been allocated in proportion to population (Table 4).

Joe feels he should spend more heavily in Ontario, where the grocery chain delisting problem exists. Last year, 36 percent of Guard's budget was allocated to Ontario, which accounted for only 12 percent of Guard's sales. Joe wants to increase Ontario spending to 48 percent of the total budget by taking funds evenly from all other areas. Joe expects this will increase business in the key Ontario market, which has over a third of Canada's population, because it is a big increase and will help Guard "out-shout" the many other competitors who are promoting heavily.

Joe presented this idea to Sarah, his newly appointed group product manager. Sarah strongly disagrees. She has also been reviewing Guard's business and feels that promotion funds have historically been misallocated. It is her strong belief that, to use her words, "a brand should spend where its business is." Sarah believes that the first priority in allocating funds regionally is to support the areas of strength. She suggested to Joe that there may be more business to be had in the brand's strong areas, Quebec and the Prairies, than in chasing sales in Ontario. The needs and attitudes toward Guard, as well as competitive pressures, may vary a lot among the provinces. Therefore, Sarah suggested that spending for Guard in the coming year be proportional to the brand's sales by region rather than to regional population.

Joe is convinced this is wrong, particularly in light of the Ontario situation. He asked Sarah how the Ontario market should be handled. Sarah said that the conservative way to build business in Ontario is to invest incremental promotion funds. However, before these incremental

Table 3 Usage Results (in percent)

	Maritimes	Quebec	Ontario	Manitoba/ Saskatchewan	Alberta	British Columbia
Respondents aware of Guard	20%	58%	28%	30%	32%	16%
Respondents ever trying Guard	3	18	2	8	6	4

Table 4 Allocation of Advertising/Sales Promotion Budget, by Population

	Maritimes	Quebec	Ontario	Manitoba/ Saskatchewan	Alberta	British Columbia	Canada
Percent of population	10%	27%	36%	8%	8%	11%	100%
Possible allocation of budget based on population (in 000s)	$80	$216	$288	$64	$64	$88	$800
Percent of Guard business at present	7%	51%	12%	11%	11%	8%	100%

funds are invested, a test of this Ontario investment proposition should be conducted. Sarah recommended that some of the Ontario money should be used to conduct an investment-spending market test in a small area or town in Ontario for 12 months. This will enable Joe to see if the incremental spending results in higher sales and profits—profits large enough to justify higher spending. In other words, an investment payout should be assured before spending any extra money in Ontario. Similarly, Sarah would do the same kind of test in Quebec—to see if more money should go there.

Joe feels this approach would be a waste of time and unduly cautious, given the importance of the Ontario market and the likely delistings in two key chains.

Evaluate the present strategy for Guard and Joe's and Sarah's proposed strategies. How should the promotion money be allocated? Should investment-spending market tests be run first? Why? Explain.

32 Chase & Arnold P.C.

The partners of Chase & Arnold are having a serious discussion about what the firm should do in the near future.

Chase & Arnold P.C. (C&A) is a large regional certified public accounting firm based in Grand Rapids, Michigan—with branch offices in Lansing and Detroit. Chase & Arnold has 9 partners and a professional staff of approximately 105 accountants. Gross service billings for the fiscal year ending June 30, 1992, were $6,900,000. Financial data for 1990, 1991, and 1992 are presented in Table 1.

C&A's professional services include auditing, tax preparation, and bookkeeping. Its client base includes municipal governments (cities, villages, and townships), manufacturing companies, professional organizations (attorneys, doctors, and dentists), and various other small businesses. A good share of revenue comes from the firm's municipal practice. Table 1 gives C&A's gross revenue by service area and client industry for 1990, 1991, and 1992.

Table 1 Fiscal Year Ending June 30

	1992	1991	1990
Gross billings	$6,900,000	$6,400,000	$5,800,000
Gross billings by service area:			
Auditing	3,100,000	3,200,000	2,750,000
Tax preparation	1,990,000	1,830,000	1,780,000
Bookkeeping	1,090,000	745,000	660,000
Other	720,000	625,000	610,000
Gross billings by client industry:			
Municipal	3,214,000	3,300,000	2,908,000
Manufacturing	2,089,000	1,880,000	1,706,000
Professional	1,355,000	1,140,000	1,108,000
Other	242,000	80,000	78,000

At the monthly partners' meeting held in July 1992, Pat Hogan, the firm's managing partner (CEO), expressed concern about the future of the firm's municipal practice. Hogan's presentation to his partners appears below:

Although our firm is considered to be a leader in municipal auditing in our geographic area, I am concerned that as municipals attempt to cut their operating costs, they will solicit competitive bids from other public accounting firms to perform their annual audits. Due to the fact that the local offices of most of the Big 6 firms* in our area concentrate their practice in the manufacturing industry—which typically has December 31 fiscal year-ends—they have available staff during the summer months.[†]

---

*The Big 6 firms are a group of the six largest public accounting firms in the United States. They maintain offices in almost every major U.S. city. Until recently, these firms were known as the Big 8, but after several mergers they have come to be known as the Big 6.

†Organizations with December fiscal year-ends require audit work to be performed during the fall and in January and February. Those with June 30 fiscal year-ends require auditing during the summer months.

Therefore, they can afford to low-ball competitive bids to keep their staffs busy and benefit from on-the-job training provided by municipal clientele. I am concerned that we may begin to lose clients in our most established and profitable practice area.

Ann Yost, a senior partner in the firm and the partner in charge of the firm's municipal practice, was the first to respond to Pat Hogan's concern.

Pat, we all recognize the potential threat of being underbid for our municipal work by our Big 6 competitors. However, C&A is a recognized leader in municipal auditing in Michigan, and we have much more local experience than our competitors. Furthermore, it is a fact that we offer a superior level of service to our clients—which goes beyond the services normally expected during an audit to include consulting on financial and other operating issues. Many of our less sophisticated clients depend on our nonaudit consulting assistance. Therefore, I believe, we have been successful in differentiating our services from our competitors. In many recent situations, C&A was selected over a field of as many as 10 competitors even though our proposed prices were much higher than those of our competitors.

The partners at the meeting agreed with Ann Yost's comments. However, even though C&A had many success stories regarding their ability to retain their municipal clients—despite being underbid—they had lost three large municipal clients during the past year. Ann Yost was asked to comment on the loss of those clients. She explained that the lost clients are larger municipalities with a lot of in-house financial expertise—and therefore less dependent on C&A's consulting assistance. As a result, C&A's service differentiation went largely unnoticed. Ann explained that the larger, more-sophisticated municipals regard audits as a necessary evil and usually select the low-cost reputable bidder.

Pat Hogan then requested ideas and discussion from the other partners at the meeting. One partner, Joe Reid, suggested that C&A should protect itself by diversifying. Specifically, he felt a substantial practice development effort should be directed toward manufacturing. He reasoned that since manufacturing work would occur during C&A's off-season, C&A could afford to price very low to gain new manufacturing clients. This strategy would also help to counter (and possibly discourage) Big 6 competitors' low-ball pricing for municipals.

Another partner, Bob LaMott, suggested that "if we have consulting skills, we ought to promote them more, instead of hoping that the clients will notice and come to appreciate us. Further, maybe we ought to be more aggressive in calling on smaller potential clients."

Another partner, John Smith, agreed with LaMott, but wanted to go further. He suggested that they recognize that there are at least two types of municipal customers and that two (at least) different strategies be implemented, including lower prices for auditing only for larger municipal customers and/or higher prices for smaller customers who are buying consulting too. This caused a big uproar from some who said this would lead to price-cutting of professional services and C&A didn't want to be price cutters: "One price for all is the professional way."

However, another partner, Megan Cullen, agreed with John Smith and suggested they go even further—pricing consulting services separately. In fact, she suggested that the partners consider setting up a separate department for consulting—like the Big 6 have done. This can be very profitable business. But it is a different kind of business and eventually may require different kinds of people and a different organization. For now, however, it may be desirable to appoint a manager for consulting services—with a budget—to be sure it gets proper attention. This suggestion too caused serious disagreement. Some of the partners knew that having a separate consulting arm had led to major conflicts in some firms. The main problem seemed to be that the consultants brought in more profit than the auditors, but the auditors controlled the partnership and did not properly reward the successful consultants—at least as they saw it!

Pat Hogan thanked everyone for their comments and charged them with thinking hard about the firm's future before coming to a one-day retreat (in two weeks) to continue this discussion and come to some conclusions.

Evaluate Chase & Arnold's situation. What strategy(ies) should the partners select? Why?

33 Ladco Mfg. Co.*

Ed Mackey, newly hired VP of Marketing for Ladco Mfg. Co., is reviewing the firm's international distribution arrangements because they don't seem to be very well thought out. He is not sure if anything is wrong, but he feels that the company should follow a global strategy rather than continuing its current policies.

Ladco, based in Atlanta, Georgia, produces finished aluminum products, such as aluminum ladders, umbrella-type clothes racks, scaffolding, and patio tables and

*Adapted from a case written by Professor Peter Banting, McMaster University, Hamilton, Ontario, Canada.

chairs that fold flat. Sales in 1991 reached $25 million—primarily to U.S. customers.

In 1987, Ladco decided to try foreign markets. The sales manager, Ruth Ways, believed the growing affluence of European workers would help the company's products gain market acceptance quickly. And she wanted to develop relationships before the 1992 target for forming the European Community.

Ruth's first step in investigating foreign markets was to join a trade mission to Europe—a tour organized by the U.S. Department of Commerce. This trade mission visited Italy, Germany, Denmark, Holland, France, and England. During this trip, Ruth was officially introduced to leading buyers for department store chains, import houses, wholesalers, and buying groups. The two-week trip convinced Ruth that there was ample buying power to make exporting a profitable opportunity.

On her return to Atlanta, Ruth's next step was to obtain credit references for the firms she considered potential distributors. To those who were judged creditworthy, she sent letters expressing interest and samples, brochures, prices, and other relevant information.

The first orders were from a French wholesaler. Sales in this market totaled $70,000 in 1988. Similar success was achieved in Germany and England. Italy, on the other hand, did not produce any sales. Ruth felt the semi-luxury nature of the company's products and the lower incomes in Italy encouraged a "making do" attitude rather than purchase of goods and services that would make life easier.

In the United States, Ladco distributes through fairly aggressive and well-organized merchant hardware distributors and buying groups, such as cooperative and voluntary hardware chains, who have taken over much of the strategy planning for cooperating producers and retailers. In its foreign markets, however, there is no recognizable pattern. Channel systems vary from country to country. To avoid mixing channels of distribution, Ladco has only one account in each country. The chosen distributor is the exclusive distributor.

In France, Ladco distributes through a wholesaler based in Paris. This wholesaler has five salespeople covering the country. The firm specializes in small housewares and has contacts with leading buying groups, wholesalers, and department stores. Ruth is impressed with the firm's aggressiveness and knowledge of merchandising techniques.

In Germany, Ladco sells to a Hamburg-based buying group for hardware wholesalers throughout the country. Ruth felt this group would provide excellent coverage of the market because of its extensive distribution network.

In Denmark, Ladco's line is sold to a buying group representing a chain of hardware retailers. This group recently expanded to include retailers in Sweden, Finland, and Norway. Together this group purchases goods for about 500 hardware retailers. The buying power of Scandinavians is quite high, and it is expected that Ladco's products will prove very successful there.

In the United Kingdom, Ladco uses an importer-distributor, who both buys on his own account and acts as a sales agent. This firm sells to department stores and hardware wholesalers. This firm has not done very well overall, but it has done very well with Ladco's line of patio tables and chairs.

Australia is handled by an importer who operates a chain of discount houses. It heard about Ladco from a United Kingdom contact. After much correspondence, this firm discovered it could land aluminum patio furniture in Melbourne at prices competitive with Japanese imports. So it started ordering because it wanted to cut prices in a high-priced garden furniture market.

The Argentina market is handled by an American who came to the United States from Buenos Aires in search of new lines. Ladco attributes success in Argentina to the efforts of this aggressive and capable agent. He has built a sizable trade in aluminum ladders.

In Trinidad and Jamaica, Ladco's products are handled by traders who carry such diversified lines as insurance, apples, plums, and fish. They have been successful in selling aluminum ladders. This business grew out of inquiries sent to the U.S. Department of Commerce, which Ruth Ways followed up by mail.

Ruth Ways's export policies for Ladco are as follows:

1. Product: No product modifications will be made in selling to foreign customers. This may be considered later after a substantial sales volume develops.

2. Price: The company does not publish suggested list prices. Distributors add their own markup to their landed costs. Supply prices will be kept as low as possible. This is accomplished by (a) removing advertising expenses and other strictly domestic overhead charges from price calculations, (b) finding the most economical packages for shipping (smallest volume per unit), and (c) bargaining with carriers to obtain the lowest shipping rates possible.

3. Promotion: The firm does no advertising in foreign markets. Brochures and sales literature already being used in the United States are supplied to foreign distributors. Ladco will continue to promote its products by participating in overseas trade shows. These are handled by

the sales manager. All inquiries are forwarded to the firm's distributor in that country.

4. Distribution: New distributors will be contacted through foreign trade shows. Ruth Ways considers large distributors desirable. She feels, however, that they are not as receptive as smaller distributors to a new, unestablished product line. Therefore, she prefers to appoint small distributors. Larger distributors may be appointed after the company has gained a strong consumer franchise in a country.

5. Financing: Ladco sees no need to provide financial help to distributors. The company views its major contribution as providing good products at the lowest possible prices.

6. Marketing and Planning Assistance: Ruth Ways feels that foreign distributors know their own markets best. Therefore, they are best equipped to plan for themselves.

7. Selection of Foreign Markets: The evaluation of foreign market opportunities for the company's products is based primarily on disposable income and life-style patterns. For example, Ruth fails to see any market in North Africa for Ladco's products, which she thinks are of a semi-luxury nature. She thinks that cheaper products such as wood ladders (often homemade) are preferred to prefabricated aluminum ladders in regions such as North Africa and Southern Europe. Argentina, on the other hand, she thinks is a more highly industrialized market with luxury tastes. Thus, Ruth sees Ladco's products as better suited for more highly industrialized and affluent societies.

Evaluate Ladco's present foreign markets strategies. Should it develop a global strategy? What strategy or strategies should Ed Mackey (the new VP of Marketing) develop? Explain.

Computer-Aided Problems

Guide to the Use of the Computer-Aided Problems

COMPUTER-AIDED PROBLEM SOLVING

Marketing managers are problem solvers who must make many decisions. Solving problems and making good decisions usually involves analysis of marketing information. This information is often in numbers. For example, a marketing manager needs to know how many customers are in the target market—and how many units of a product will be sold at a certain price—to estimate how much profit is likely to be earned with a marketing strategy. Marketing managers also analyze marketing-related costs—to help control their marketing plans.

Many marketing managers now use personal computers to help them analyze information. The speed of computer calculations means that managers can look at a problem from many different angles. They can see how a change in one aspect of the plan may affect the rest of the plan.

The computer can only take a manager so far. It can help keep track of the numbers and speed through tedious calculations. But the manager is the one who puts it all together. It takes skill to decide what the information means.

The computer-aided problems at the end of each chapter in this text—and the accompanying computer program that you will use to solve them—were specially developed by the authors to help you develop this skill. The computer program is named *PLUS*—an abbreviation for *Professional Learning Units Systems*. PLUS is similar to other programs that marketing managers use to analyze decisions—but it is easier to use. A master diskette with the computer program and all of the problems is available to instructors from the publisher.

Most of the problems are short descriptions of decisions faced by marketing managers. Each description includes information to help make the decision. The information for each problem is in the PLUS computer program. There are several questions for you to answer for each problem. The *Learning Aid for use with Essentials of Marketing* includes additional exercises related to each problem. You should use the computer program to do an analysis. But most problems ask you to indicate what decision you would make—and why. Thus, in these problems—as in the marketing manager's job—the computer program is just a tool to help you make better decisions.

Each of the problems focuses on one or more of the marketing decision areas discussed in that chapter. The earlier problems require less marketing knowledge and are simpler in terms of the analysis involved. The later problems build on the principles already covered in the text. The problems can be used in many ways. And the same problem can be analyzed several times for different purposes. While it is not necessary to do all of the problems or to do them in a particular order, you will probably want to start with the first problem. This practice problem is simpler than the others. In fact, you could do the calculations quite easily without a computer. But this problem will help you see how the program works—and how it can help you solve the more complicated problems that come later.

SPREADSHEET ANALYSIS OF MARKETING PROBLEMS

Marketing managers often use *spreadsheet analysis* to evaluate their alternatives—and the PLUS program does computerized spreadsheet analysis. In spreadsheet analysis, costs, revenue, and other data related to a marketing problem are organized into a data table—a spreadsheet. Spreadsheet analysis allows you to change the value of one or more of the variables in the data table—to see how each change affects the value of other variables.

This is possible because the relationships among the variables are programmed in the computer. Let's look at an overly simple example.

You are a marketing manager interested in the total revenue that will result from a particular marketing strategy. You are considering selling your product at $10.00 per unit. You expect to sell 100 units. In our PLUS analysis, this problem might be shown in a (very simple) spreadsheet that looks like this:

Variable	Value
Selling price	$ 10.00
Units sold	100
Total revenue	$1,000.00

There is only one basic relationship in this spreadsheet: total revenue is equal to the selling price multiplied by the number of units sold. If that relationship has been programmed in the computer (as it is in these problems), you can change the selling price, or the number of units you expect to sell, and the program will compute the new value for total revenue.

But now you can ask questions like: "What if I raise the price to $10.40 and still sell 100 units? What will happen to total revenue?" To get the answer, all you have to do is enter the new price in the spreadsheet and the program will compute the total revenue for you.

You may also want to do many "What If" analyses— for example, to see how total revenue changes over a range of prices. Computerized spreadsheet analysis allows you to do this quickly and easily. For example, if you want to see what happens to total revenue as you vary the price between some minimum value (say, $8.00) and a maximum value (say, $12.00), the program will provide a What If analysis showing total revenue for 11 different prices in the range from $8.00 to $12.00.

In a problem like this—with easy numbers and a simple relationship between the variables—the spreadsheet does not do that much work for you. You could do it in your head. But, with more complicated problems, the spreadsheet program can be a big help—making it very convenient to more carefully analyze different alternatives or situations.

USING THE PLUS PROGRAM

Don't worry. *You don't have to know about computers to use the PLUS program!* It was designed to be easy to learn and use. The program will give you "help" information whenever you need it.

A menu box gives directions—and help

When you use the program, information is displayed on the computer's screen. The screen looks different in different parts of the program. But every screen has a title at the top to make it easy to keep track of where you are. And each screen has a "menu box" at the bottom. Pay attention to the menu box because that's where the program displays directions for you. A sample of a screen (the Problem Selection Screen)—and what you will see in the menu box for this screen—is shown in Exhibit 1.

As you can see in Exhibit 1, the directions in the menu box are brief. The first few times you use the program you may want more help than these summaries provide. This is not a problem. In the menu box you will see the word **H**elp—and the letter H will be highlighted. If you press the H key (short for the **H**elp command) on the computer keyboard, a screen with more detailed instructions will quickly appear. This quick help information is specific to where you are in the program.

If you still have a question after reading the Quick Help Screen, look in the menu box and you will see the phrase "General **H**elp." Again, the letter H will be highlighted. If you press the H key again, a General Help Menu Screen will appear. It offers more information. Select the topic you want and the information will appear on the screen. When you are finished with general help you can press the R key (to "**R**eturn to the Program" where you left off). Remember, you can get back to this general help from any point in the program. Just press H to get the Quick Help Screen, and then press H again to get the General Help Menu Screen.

Along with the **H**elp command, the menu box also has other words or phrases that summarize different commands—what you can do at that point in the program. Here, as with **H**elp, just press the key for the highlighted letter to select the command you want. For example, on some screens you will see the phrase **Q**uit—and the letter Q is highlighted. If you are finished with your work, press the Q key and the program will end. Don't worry about accidentally hitting the Q key and losing your work. Before the program actually ends, it will ask you if that's really what you want to do and you will have to press another key to end the program.

IMPORTANT! Try things out. A mistake won't hurt anything! If you press a key that isn't useful at that point in the program, the computer will beep at you or display a message. In that case, just check the message in the menu box—or the help information—and try again! The following pages give some additional instructions—but all of the information you need is available by simply pressing the H key. So, you may want to go ahead and try the

Exhibit 1   The PLUS Computer Program Problem Selection Screen

```
                    P L U S  -  Problem Selection
                1. Revenue, Cost, and Profit Relationships
                2. Target Marketing
                3. Segmenting Customers
                4. Competitor Analysis
                5. Marketing Research
                6. Selective Processes
                7. Vendor Analysis
                8. Branding Decision
                9. Growth Stage Competition
               10. Intensive vs. Selective Distribution
               11. Mass-Merchandising
               12. Merchant versus Agent Wholesaler
               13. Sales Promotion
               14. Sales Compensation
               15. Advertising Media
              ↓16. Cash Discounts

   ┌─────────────────────────────────────────────────────────────┐
   │ Use the arrow keys to highlight the desired problem. Press P to │
   │ "Work the Highlighted Problem." Press the H key if you need Help. │
   │                                                                 │
   │ Highlight Down · Highlight Up    Work Highlighted Problem   Help   Quit │
   │ Use PgDn or PgUp key to see more of problem list                │
   └─────────────────────────────────────────────────────────────┘
```

practice problem now—especially if you've used a computer before.

Start at the problem selection screen

When you use the program, the first screen displayed is the Title Screen. By pressing any key, you will move on to the Problem Selection Screen—the real starting point of the program. The Problem Selection Screen (see Exhibit 1) shows a list of problems. The problem at the top of the list will be highlighted. In the menu box at the bottom of the screen, you will see the phrase "Work Highlighted **P**roblem" and the letter P will be highlighted. If you want to work the problem which is highlighted on the list, simply press the P key, and the program will display a short description of the problem you selected. The questions for each problem appear in this book—so you will want to have this book with you at the computer when you are actually doing the problem.

If you want to work another problem on the list—instead of the highlighted one—look again at the menu box at the bottom of the Problem Selection Screen. You will see the phrase "Highlight **D**own," with the letter D highlighted and "Highlight **U**p," with the letter U highlighted. Press the letter D to move the highlighting down to the next problem on the list. Press the D key again to move even further down the list. Pressing the U key will move the highlighting up the list of problems.

Most personal computers have special keys labelled with left, right, up, and down arrows. You can also use these special arrow keys to move up or down the problem list. If you've never used a computer, you will probably find it useful to look at Exhibit 2 and Exhibit 3. They provide labelled drawings of two typical keyboards—and briefly explain the purpose of the special keys. They also show the normal location of the arrow keys and other keys mentioned in these instructions.

On the Problem Selection Screen, you will also see a small down-pointing arrow near the bottom of the list of problems. You will see an arrow like this on other screen displays as well. The arrow means that additional information is available—but won't all fit on the screen at the same time. For example, on the Problem Selection Screen the down-pointing arrow means that the list of problems continues beyond what you see on the screen. To bring the additional information onto the screen—continue to press the D key (to move "highlighting **D**own"). Similarly, you will sometimes see a small up-pointing arrow on the screen. When this appears, you can use the U key ("Highlight **U**p") to move back to the top of the information. The special keys marked PgDn (which stands for "Page Down") and PgUp (which stands for "Page Up") can also be used when the down arrow or up arrow appears on a screen. The best way to see what they do is to try them out when a small arrow appears on the screen.

Exhibit 2   Diagram of a Typical Keyboard for an IBM PC, IBM XT, or IBM AT Personal Computer

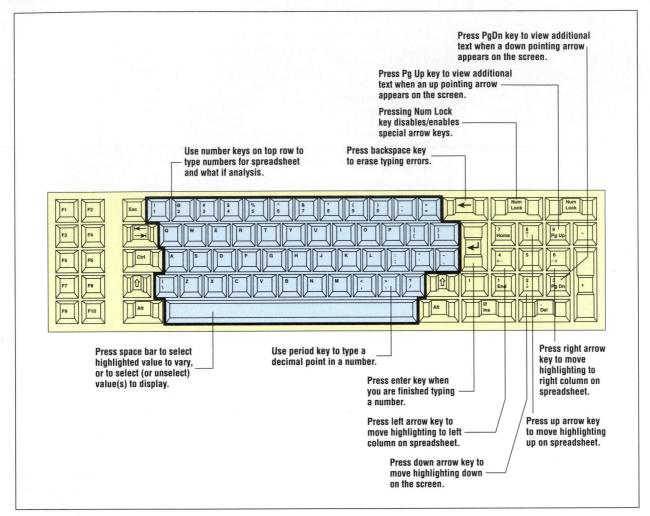

Press PgDn key to view additional text when a down pointing arrow appears on the screen.

Press Pg Up key to view additional text when an up pointing arrow appears on the screen.

Pressing Num Lock key disables/enables special arrow keys.

Use number keys on top row to type numbers for spreadsheet and what if analysis.

Press backspace key to erase typing errors.

Press space bar to select highlighted value to vary, or to select (or unselect) value(s) to display.

Use period key to type a decimal point in a number.

Press enter key when you are finished typing a number.

Press left arrow key to move highlighting to left column on spreadsheet.

Press down arrow key to move highlighting down on the screen.

Press right arrow key to move highlighting to right column on spreadsheet.

Press up arrow key to move highlighting up on spreadsheet.

Moving to the problem description and spreadsheet screens

Once you select a problem from the Problem Selection Screen, a Problem Description Screen will appear. This gives a brief description of that problem. Then you can continue to the Spreadsheet Screen for that problem by following the menu box instructions. The spreadsheet displays the starting values for the problem.

Each spreadsheet consists of one or two columns of numbers. Each column and row is labelled. Look at the row and column labels carefully to see what variable is represented by the value (number) in the spreadsheet. Study the layout of the spreadsheet, and get a feel for how it organizes the information from the printed problem description in this text. You will see that some of the values in the spreadsheet are marked with an asterisk (*).

These are usually values related to the decision variables in the problem you are solving. *You can change any value (number) that is marked with an asterisk.* When you make a change, the rest of the values (numbers) in that column are recalculated to show how a change in the value of one variable affects the others.

Making changes in values is easy. When the Spreadsheet Screen appears, you will see that one of the values in the spreadsheet is highlighted. As on the Problem Selection Screen, think of the highlighting as a pointer that shows where you are in the spreadsheet. Use the D key to move **D**own, the U key to move **U**p, the R key to move **R**ight, and the L key to move **L**eft until you are highlighting the value you want to change. (Note: You can also use the up, down, left and right arrow keys to move around on the screen.)

Exhibit 3   Diagram of a Typical Keyboard for an IBM PS/2 Computer

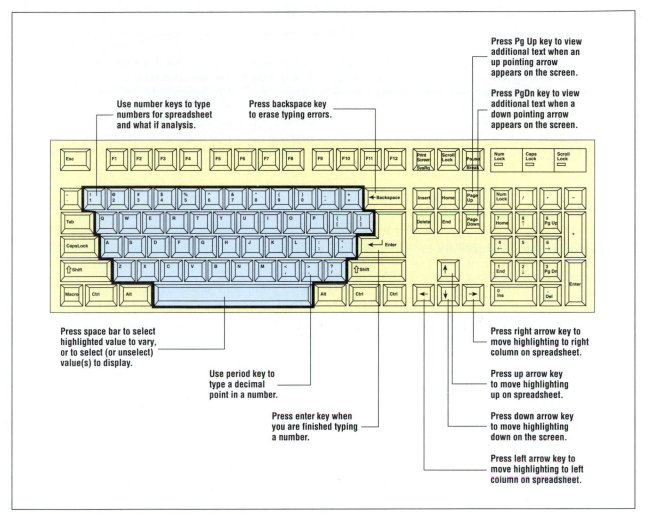

When you have highlighted the value (number) you want to change, just type in your new number. This number will show in the menu box at the bottom of the screen as you type. When you are finished typing the number, press the enter key and the other values in the spreadsheet will be recalculated to show the effect of your new value. (Note: the enter key is much like a "carriage return" key on a typewriter. It is usually larger than other keys and is located on the right side of the keyboard. Usually, a bent arrow is printed on the enter key (Exhibits 2 and 3 show the normal location of the enter key).

When you are typing numbers into the PLUS program, you type the numbers and the decimal point as you would on a typewriter. For example, a price of one thousand dollars and 50 cents would be typed as 1000.50

or just 1000.5—*using the number keys on the top row of the keyboard* and the period key for the decimal point. *Do not type in the dollar sign or the commas to indicate thousands.* Be careful not to type the letters o or l (lower case L) instead of the numbers 0 or 1.

Typing percent values is a possible point of confusion—since there are different ways to think about a percent. For example, "ten and a half" percent might be represented by 10.5 or .105. To avoid confusion, the program always expects you to enter percents using the first approach—which is the way percents are discussed in the problems. Thus, if you want to enter the value for ten and a half percent you would type 10.5.

A set of permitted values is programmed in the computer for each problem to help prevent errors. For

NOTE ON RESETTING VALUES ON THE SPREADSHEET

Once a value on the spreadsheet has been changed, the change stays in effect unless it is changed again. Sometimes, after making one or more changes, it is useful to be able to reset the values for *all* of the variables as they were at the start of a problem. For example, this is useful when answering a series of questions based on a problem description.

To reset all of the values at the same time, press the P key (Select another Problem) at the Spreadsheet Screen. You will be returned to the Problem Selection Screen, and the title of the problem you have been working will be highlighted. Simply press P (or the enter key) and you will be returned to the same problem—but the Spreadsheet Screen will be reset to the initial values.

example, you cannot accidentally type a letter when the computer program expects a number. Or, if you type a number that is outside of the permitted range, the program will display a message in the menu box. Just read the message—to see the range of permitted values—and then use the backspace key to erase what you have typed. (Note: The backspace key is usually toward the right side of the top row of the keyboard—along with the number keys—and usually it is marked with a left-pointing bold arrow. See Exhibits 2 and 3.) After you use the backspace key to erase what you typed earlier, retype a new number that is in the permitted range—and then press the enter key to recompute the spreadsheet.

For example, if you try to type –10.00 as the price of a product, the menu box might display a message that you can only enter a value that is greater than 1 and less than 20 for that variable. (It doesn't make sense to set the price as a negative number!) You could then backspace to erase what you typed, type in a new value, and finally press the enter key.

In addition to changing values (numbers) in the spreadsheet itself, the selections in the menu box have other uses. If you press the O key for " **O**utput to printer," the current spreadsheet will be printed. (Before you press the O key, make sure that your computer has a printer, that it is plugged into both power and the computer, that it is turned on, and that the paper is loaded where you want it to start printing. The first time you use the printer, the program will ask you to type in your name. That way, each printout will have your name at the top.)

The menu box may also show the phrase "Select another **P**roblem," with the letter P highlighted. If you press the P key, you will be returned to the Problem Selection Screen. Similarly, you may see the phrase "Do **W**hat If" with the letter W highlighted. If you press the W

key, you will see a new screen that starts a What If analysis.

What If analysis

The What If part of the program allows you to study in more detail the effect of changing the value of a particular variable. It systematically changes the value of a variable—and displays the effect that variable has on other variables. As before, all you have to do is follow the instructions in the menu box at the bottom of the screen. You could do the same thing "manually" at the Spreadsheet Screen—by entering a value for a variable, checking the effect on other variables, and then repeating the process over and over again. But the manual approach is time-consuming and requires you to keep track of the results after each change. A What If analysis does all this very quickly and presents the results on the screen.

Now, let's go through the What If analysis part of the PLUS program step-by-step. Remember that you don't have to memorize this. The menu box will remind you what to do and you can press the H key (for help) to get additional detail while you are using the program. You start a What If analysis by pressing the W key when "Do **W**hat If" is an option in the menu box. The Select Value to Vary Screen will appear. It shows the values for those variables which you can change (ones which are marked with an asterisk on the original Spreadsheet Screen). One value on the Select Value to Vary Screen will be highlighted. As with other screens, you can use the D, U, R, or L keys (or the up, down, right, or left arrow keys) to "move" the highlighting to some other variable. When the value (number) you want to change is highlighted, simply press the space bar (the long key across the bottom center of the keyboard). The letter V will appear beside that value—to remind you what variable you have selected to vary.

The menu box at the bottom of the screen will then prompt you to type in a new minimum value for that variable. It will also show a suggested minimum value. This suggested minimum value is usually 20% smaller than the value from the initial spreadsheet. If you press the enter key at this point, this suggested value will be used as the minimum value in the analysis. You might want to do this your first time through to get some quick results. Later, you can type in your own minimum value in the same way as you do in the Spreadsheet Screen. Remember that you can use the backspace key to correct any errors. Press the enter key when you are finished typing.

Next you will be prompted to provide the largest value for the analysis. Here again, you can accept the program's suggested maximum value by pressing the enter key. Or if you wish, you can type in your own value.

After you have entered the minimum and maximum values for the variable you want to change, the screen will change to the Select Values to Display Screen. You will be prompted to select the variables for which you want summary results to be displayed. Typically, you will want to display the results (computed values) for variables that will be affected by the variable you select to vary. Remember the example we used earlier. If you had specified that price was going to vary, you might want to display total revenue—to see how it changes at different price levels.

You select a variable to display in the same way that you select the variable you are going to change. Use the arrow keys to move from one value (number) to another. The highlighting moves to show you where you are. If you want the values of the highlighted variable to appear in the results table, press the space bar. The letter D will appear beside that value—as a reminder of the variable you selected to be displayed. If you change your mind, you can press the space bar again to "unselect" the highlighted value. The D will disappear—and that variable will not be displayed in the results table.

You can use this approach to select up to three variables to be displayed as the output of a What If analysis. When you have completed this step, you will see a V beside the variable you chose to vary, and a D beside one, two or three variables that you want to display.

Now you can let the computer take over. In the menu box at the bottom of the screen you will see the phrase "**A**nalyze and Display Data," and the letter A will be highlighted. If you press the A key, the results of the What If analysis will appear on the screen. Each row in the first column of the table will show a different value for the variable you wanted to vary. The minimum value you specified will be in the first row. The maximum value will be in the bottom row. Evenly spaced values between the minimum and maximum will be in the middle rows. The other column(s) show the calculated results for the values you selected to display. Each column of values is labeled at the top to identify the column and row from the spreadsheet. The row portion of the label is a short version of the label from the spreadsheet. The results are based on the values that were on the Spreadsheet Screen when you started the What If analysis—except for the value you selected to vary.

At this point you will want to study the results of your analysis. As with the Spreadsheet Screen, you can output a printed copy of the results. The menu box shows other possibilities. For example, if you press the C key to **C**ontinue with the What If analysis, the Select Value to Vary Screen will reappear. The screen will show the values you selected in the previous analysis. The value you varied before will be highlighted. You can select the same value again by pressing the space bar, or highlight and select another value. If you want to display the values you selected before, press the A key (**A**nalyze and Display Data). Or, you can "**C**lear" those selections by pressing the C key and then you can highlight and select new values to display.

At any point in the What If analysis, you can return to the Spreadsheet Screen. From there you can make additional changes in the values in the spreadsheet, do a new What If analysis, or select another problem to work. Or, if your computer has the right equipment, you can look at (and print) a graph of values on the What If Display Screen.

Viewing a graph of your results

You can create a graph of values on the What If Display Screen by pressing the G key (for **G**raph Data). The horizontal axis for the graph will be the variable in the first column of the display. The vertical axis is based on the column that is highlighted when you press the G key. Before you press the G key, you can use the right arrow key (or the R key for **R**ight) to change which column is highlighted and will be graphed. From the Graph View Screen you can print the graph, or you can go back and select other values to vary or select another column to graph. Or you can go back to the Spreadsheet Screen.

For the Graph Data feature to work properly, your computer must be equipped with the correct type of graphics display (monitor) and printer. If you press G for

Exhibit 4   Glossary of Menu Box Selections

Analyze & display data   Appears on the Select Values to Display Screen. After you have selected the value(s) you want to display in the What If analysis, press the A key and the results will be displayed.

Approaches for Working Problems   Appears on the General Help Menu Screen. This selection reviews some ideas about using the PLUS program to solve problems.

Clear Selections   Appears on the What If Screen where you select values to display after you have selected one or more values. A "D" appears by the values you have selected; if you change your mind and want to select new values to display, you can press the C key and all of the "Ds" will be cleared. You can clear a single selection by highlighting it and pressing the space bar.

Continue to Spreadsheet   Appears on the Problem Description Screen. When you are finished reading the description, press the C key to continue on to the spreadsheet for that problem. (From the spreadsheet, you can return to the Problem Selection Screen—if you want to select another problem).

Continue with last problem   Appears on the Problem Selection Screen. Press the C key and you will return to the problem description for the problem you have been working. From there, you can continue to the spreadsheet for that problem. The values on the spreadsheet will be the same as they were when you left the problem (i.e., any changes you made will be preserved)—if you have not started another problem in between.

Do What If   Appears on the Spreadsheet Screen. Press the W key and the first screen for the What If analysis will appear. The What If analysis will be based on values on the spreadsheet screen from which it is called—except that you will use the program to automatically vary one of the values.

General Help   Appears on most "Quick Help" Screens. If the Quick Help Screen does not have the information you want, pressing the H key again will display a selection of more general help information that is available.

General Information   Appears on the General Help Menu Screen. It reviews a number of introductory ideas about using the PLUS program.

Glossary of Menu Box Selections   Appears on the General Help Menu and displays the information you are now reading.

Graph Data   Appears on the What If Data Display Screen Menu and displays a graph. The horizontal axis plots the values of the first column of data, and vertical axis plots values of the column of data that is highlighted on the screen. Highlighting can be moved to a different column by using the right or left arrow keys.

Help   The Help command appears on almost every screen. Press the H key to get additional information ("Quick Help") and directions about what to do at that point in the program. If you want more general help than is available on the "Quick Help" Screen, press the H key again—see the discussion of "General Help" above. You can return to where you left off from either type of help screen.

Highlight Down   Appears on the Problem Selection Screen. Press the D key (or the Down arrow key) to move highlighting down the problem list to the problem you want to work. When a small down arrow appears on a Help Screen, you can also use the D key to "page down" through the help information. You can use the D key (instead of the down arrow key) to move the highlighting down on the Spreadsheet Screen or on any screen in the What If section of the program.

Highlight Up   Appears on the Problem Selection Screen. Press the U key (or the Up arrow key) to move highlighting up the problem list to the problem you want to work. When a small up arrow appears on a Help Screen, you can also use the U

Graph Data and your computer does not have the correct type of graphics monitor, the Graph View Screen will not appear and instead you will see a message indicating that your computer can't display the type of graphs produced by the PLUS program. For a graph to print properly, your computer must be attached to a standard IBM graphics printer (or another printer that is 100 percent compatible with IBM graphics standards).

What to do next

The next section gives additional tips on the PLUS program. You will probably want to look through it after you have done some work with the practice problem. Exhibit 4 lists all of the menu box commands and provides a summary of what they do. For now, however,

you're probably tired of reading instructions. So work a problem or two. It's easier and faster to use the program than to read about it! Give it a try, and don't be afraid to experiment. If you have problems, remember that the H key will bring you **H**elp in a hurry.

SPECIAL TIPS ON USING THE PLUS PROGRAM

Hardware requirements

The PLUS computer program is designed to work on IBM personal computers (microcomputers) and other true IBM-compatible microcomputers with at least 256k of memory. Almost all IBM computers have this much memory. But you don't have to know how much memory your computer has.

Exhibit 4   (*continued*)

key to "page up" through the help information you have already seen. You can use the U key (instead of the up arrow key) to move the highlighting up on the Spreadsheet Screen or on any What If Analysis Screen.

How the Program is Organized   Appears on the General Help Menu Screen. Press the O key for a description of the different sections of the PLUS program and a quick summary of the different screens that are displayed in each section.

Making Changes on the Spreadsheet   Appears on the General Help Menu Screen. Press the S key to get general information about making changes on the Spreadsheet Screen.

More Description   Appears on the Problem Description Screen. At the end of each problem description is the note "End of description." If the problem description continues beyond what will show on one screen, you can press the D key to bring additional information onto the screen. You can also use the down arrow key and the PgDn key for the same purpose. You can go back to review parts of the description you have already read by pressing the U key (for up), the up arrow key, or the PgUp key.

New Graph   Appears on the Graph View Screen. If you press the G key, you will return to the What If Graph Selection Screen and you can use the left or right arrow keys to highlight a different column of numbers to graph.

Output to printer   Appears on the Spreadsheet Screen, the screen showing the results of the What If analysis, and the Graph View Screen. If you press the O key, you will be prompted to type in your name. Then your name and a summary of the screen information will be printed. Before you press the O key, make certain that the printer is hooked up, turned on, and that paper has been loaded where you want the printing to start. Remember that you can only print graphs on printers that have a graphics capability (and some older

printers, especially daisy wheel printers, can only be used to print text and numbers, not graphics).

Quit   Appears on a number of screens. In fact, it will also work from some screens where it does not actually appear in the menu box. Press the Q key if you want to leave the PLUS program. You will be given a prompt to verify that you are through doing your work. If you do not want to leave the PLUS program at that point, press the letter N (for no) in response to the prompt.

Return to Program   Appears on the General Help Menu Screen. Press the R key when you are ready to return to where you left off in the program (that is, the point at which you pressed the H key to get help).

Return to What If   Appears on the Screen that displays the results of a What If analysis. If you press the R key, you will return to the "Selection of Value to Vary" Screen—and you can redo the What If analysis for a different set of values.

Select another Problem   Appears in the menu box for the Spreadsheet Screen. Pressing the letter P will return you to the Problem Selection Screen. From there, you can select another problem to work—or return to the problem you just left.

Selecting Menu Items   Appears on the General Help Menu Screen. Press the M key to review information about the Menu box—which is where the commands reviewed in this glossary appear on a screen.

Strategy for Working Problems   Appears on the General Help Menu Screen. Press the P key to review ideas and suggestions on how to approach analyzing a problem.

Work Highlighted Problem   Appears on the Problem Selection Screen. Use the arrow keys to highlight the problem you want to work from the list that appears on the screen. Then press the P key and the Problem Description Screen for the highlighted problem will appear.

The program will tell you if your computer doesn't have enough memory to make the program work. Some problems will work with less memory than others; even if your computer has less than 256k of memory, the program will work if the computer has enough memory for the problem on which you are working. The software operates faster if it is run from a hard disk, but a hard disk is not necessary.

Typically, all you need to do to start the PLUS software is put the disk in the disk drive, type PLUS and press return. However, if the software has been set up for your use on a computer with a hard disk or in a computer lab, the person who has set it up will give you instructions on starting it. If your computer does not have a color monitor, the highlighting may not show on your screen. In that case, just press Q to exit the program. Then start the

software over again by entering PLUS NOCOLOR at the DOS prompt. That should correct the problem.

Checking the computer's calculations

Some values appear in the spreadsheet as whole numbers, and others appear with one or more digits to the right of a decimal point. For example, dollar values usually have two digits to the right of the decimal point—indicating how many cents are involved. A value indicating, say, number of customers, however, will appear as a whole number.

When you are doing arithmetic by hand (or with a calculator) you sometimes have to make decisions about how much detail is necessary. For example, if you divide

13 by 3 the answer is 4.33, 4.333, 4.3333, 4.3333 or perhaps 4.33333, depending on how important it is to be precise. Usually we round off the number to keep things manageable. Similarly, computers usually display results after rounding off the numbers. This has the potential to create confusion and seeming inaccuracy when many calculations are involved. If the computer uses a lot of detail in its calculations and then displays intermediate results after rounding off, the numbers may appear to be inconsistent. To illustrate this, let's extend the example above. If you multiply 4.33 times 2640, you get 11431.20. But if you multiply 4.333 by 2640, you get 11439.12. To make it easier for you to check relationships between the values on a spreadsheet, the PLUS program does not use a lot of hidden detail in calculations. If it rounds off a number to display it in the spreadsheet, the rounded number is used in subsequent calculations. It would be easy for the computer to keep track of all of the detail in its calculations—but that would make it harder for you to check the results yourself. If you check the results on a spreadsheet (with outside calculations) and find that your numbers are close but do not match exactly, it is probably because you are making different decisions about rounding than were programmed into PLUS.

Resetting the spreadsheet screen to initial values

The initial spreadsheet for each problem gives the "starting values" for the problem. While working a problem, you will often change one or more of the starting values to a new number. A changed value stays in effect—unless you change it again. This is a handy feature. But, after you have made several changes you may not be able to remember the starting values. There is a simple solution—you can return to the Problem Selection Screen, highlight the problem again, and press the P key. The spreadsheet will appear with the original set of starting values. If you return to the Problem Selection Screen after working on a problem—but then change your mind and decide you want to return to the Spreadsheet Screen that contains the changes you had already made—just press the C key (you will see from the menu

box at the bottom of the screen that this is short for "**C**ontinue with Last problem.")

Remember that a value stays changed until you change it again. Some of the questions that accompany the problems ask you to evaluate results associated with different sets of values. It's good practice to check that you have entered all the correct values on a spreadsheet before interpreting the results.

A warning that you've made an error

The PLUS program was designed and tested to be easy to use and error free. In fact, it is programmed to help prevent the user from making typing errors. But it is impossible to anticipate every possible combination of numbers which you might enter—and some combinations of numbers can cause problems. For example, a certain combination of numbers might result in an instruction for the computer to divide a number by zero—which is a mathematical impossibility! When a problem of this sort occurs, the word ERROR will appear in the spreadsheet (or in the What If results) instead of a number. If this happens, recheck the numbers in the spreadsheet and redo the analysis—to make certain that the numbers you typed in were what you intended. That should straighten out the problem in almost every case. Yet any computer program can have hidden bugs that surface only in unusual situations—or on certain computers. Thus, if you think you have found a bug, we would like to know so that we can track down the source of the difficulty.

Glossary of menu box selections

Exhibit 4 is basically a glossary; it reviews the choices that appear in the menu box at the bottom of different screens. This information is provided here for completeness, *but you do not need to study the exhibit. All of this information is available to you on screen at any time* by pressing the H key twice (to get to the General Help Screen) and then pressing the G key (for **G**lossary of Menu Box selections). All of the terms are organized in alphabetical order. The letter in bold print is the key you push to activate that selection.

Notes

Chapter 1

1. Christopher H. Lovelock and Charles B. Weinberg, *Marketing for Public and Nonprofit Managers* (New York: John Wiley & Sons, 1984); Ruby Roy Dholakia, "A Macromarketing Perspective on Social Marketing: The Case of Family Planning in India," *Journal of Macromarketing* 4, no. 1 (1984), pp. 53–61.

2. Gregory D. Upah and Richard E. Wokutch, "Assessing Social Impacts of New Products: An Attempt to Operationalize the Macromarketing Concept," *Journal of Public Policy and Marketing* 4 (1985), pp. 166–78.

3. An American Marketing Association committee developed a similar—but more complicated—definition of marketing: "Marketing is the process of planning and executing conception, pricing, promotion, and distribution of ideas, goods, and services to create exchanges that satisfy individual and organizational objectives." See *Marketing News*, March 1, 1985, p. 1. See also Ernest F. Cooke, C. L. Abercrombie, and J. Michael Rayburn, "Problems with the AMA's New Definition of Marketing Offer Opportunity to Develop an Even Better Definition," *Marketing Educator*, Spring 1986, p. 1ff.; O. C. Ferrell and George H. Lucas, Jr., "An Evaluation of Progress in the Development of a Definition of Marketing," *Journal of the Academy of Marketing Science*, Fall 1987, pp. 12–23.

4. George Fisk, "Editor's Working Definition of Macromarketing," *Journal of Macromarketing* 2, no. 1 (1982), pp. 3–4; Shelby D. Hunt and John J. Burnett, "The Macromarketing/Micromarketing Dichotomy: A Taxonomical Model," *Journal of Marketing*, Summer 1982, pp. 11–26; J. F. Grashof and A. Kelman, *Introduction to Macro-Marketing* (Columbus, Ohio: Grid, 1973).

5. For a more complete discussion of this topic see Y. H. Furuhashi and E. J. McCarthy, *Social Issues of Marketing in the American Economy* (Columbus, Ohio: Grid, 1971), pp. 4–6.

6. "The Battle against the Bottlenecks," *Newsweek*, January 27, 1992, p. 31; "Businesses Learn How to Skip Old Laws," *USA Today*, November 5, 1991, p. 1Bff.; "As Socialism Wanes, a Soviet Family Waits in Line, and Worries," *The Wall Street Journal*, October 22, 1991, p. A1ff.; "Capitalism Moscow-Style: Down and Dirty," *USA Today*, October 22, 1991, p. 6A; "Two Moscow Grocery Stores Are Aisles Apart," *USA Today*, September 27, 1991, p. 5A; "Soviet Managers Woo American Investment against Heavy Odds," *The Wall Street Journal*, September 26, 1991, p. A1ff.; "Let's Do Business," *Fortune*, September 23, 1991, pp. 62–68; "After the Soviet Union," *Business Week*, September 9, 1991, pp. 26–38; "Soviet Economy Holds Potential for Disaster as the Union Weakens," *The Wall Street Journal*, September 4, 1991, p. A1ff.; "As Independence Nears, the Baltic States Face Raft of New Challenges," *The Wall Street Journal*, September 3, 1991, p. A1ff.; "Yeltsin's Triumph," *Business Week*, September 2, 1991, pp. 20–29; "The Russian Revolution," *Time*, September 2, 1991, pp. 20–31; "Soviet Upheaval Stirs Worry that U.S.S.R. Just Might Unravel," *The Wall Street Journal*, August 26, 1991, p. A1ff.; "Rewriting Communism," *Newsweek*, August 5, 1991, pp. 36–38; "Soviets Pin Hopes on Mom 'n' Pop Stores," *The Wall Street Journal*, April 23, 1991, p. A19; "Reawakening: A Market Economy Takes Root in Eastern Europe," *Business Week*, April 15, 1991, pp. 46–58; "The New Russian Revolution," *Fortune*, November 19, 1990, pp. 127–34; "A Day in the Death of the Soviet Union," *Insight*, November 19, 1990, pp. 8–21;

Patricia E. Goeke, "State Economic Development Programs: The Orientation Is Macro But the Strategy Is Micro," *Journal of Macromarketing*, Spring 1987, pp. 8–21; Jacob Naor, "Towards A Socialist Marketing Concept—The Case of Romania," *Journal of Marketing*, January 1986, pp. 28–39; Coskun Samli, *Marketing and Distribution Systems in Eastern Europe* (New York: Praeger Publishers, 1978).

7. Eric H. Shaw, "A Review of Empirical Studies of Aggregate Marketing Costs and Productivity in the United States," *Journal of the Academy of Marketing Science*, Fall 1990, pp. 285–92; James M. Carman and Robert G. Harris, "Public Regulation of Marketing Activity, Part III: A Typology of Regulatory Failures and Implications for Marketing and Public Policy," *Journal of Macromarketing*, Spring 1986, pp. 51–64; Venkatakrishna V. Bellur et al., "Strategic Adaptations to Price Controls: The Case of Indian Drug Industry," *Journal of the Academy of Marketing Science*, Winter/Spring 1985, pp. 143–59.

8. Van R. Wood and Scott J. Vitell, "Marketing and Economic Development: Review, Synthesis and Evaluation," *Journal of Macromarketing* 6, no. 1 (1986), pp. 28–48; Robert W. Nason and Phillip D. White, "The Visions of Charles C. Slater: Social Consequences of Marketing," *Journal of Macromarketing* 1, no. 2 (1981), pp. 4–18; Franklin S. Houston and Jule B. Gassenheimer, "Marketing and Exchange," *Journal of Marketing*, October 1987, pp. 3–18; Suzanne Hosley and Chow Hou Wee, "Marketing and Economic Development: Focusing on the Less Developed Countries," *Journal of Macromarketing*, Spring 1988, pp. 43–53.

9. John S. McClenahen, "The Third World Challenge," *Industry Week*, May 28, 1984, pp. 90–95.

10. "Exports: Ship 'Em Out," *Fortune*, Special Issue (The New American Century), Spring/Summer 1991, p. 58; Christopher M. Korth, "Managerial Barriers to U.S. Exports," *Business Horizons*, March/April 1991, pp. 18–26; "America's Growing Economic Lead," *The Wall Street Journal*, February 7, 1991, p. A14; Cynthia Fraser and Robert E. Hite, "Impact of International Marketing Strategies on Performance in Diverse Global Markets," *Journal of Business Research*, May, 1990, pp. 249–62; Refik Culpan, "Export Behavior of Firms: Relevance of Firm Size," *Journal of Business Research*, May 1989, pp. 207–18; M. Frank Bradley, "Nature and Significance of International Marketing: A Review," *Journal of Business Research*, June 1987, pp. 205–20.

11. "Invasion of the Booty Snatchers," *Business Week*, June 24, 1991, pp. 66–69; "Viva Free Trade with Mexico!" *Fortune*, June 17, 1991, pp. 97–100; "How Latin America Is Opening Up," *Fortune*, April 8, 1991, pp. 84–90; Paul A. Dion and Peter M. Banting, "What Industrial Marketers Can Expect from U.S.–Canadian Free Trade," *Industrial Marketing Management*, February 1990, pp. 77–80; "Rethinking Japan: The New, Harder Line Toward Tokyo," *Business Week*, August 7, 1989, pp. 44–52; "Where Global Growth Is Going," *Fortune*, July 31, 1989, pp. 71–92; "Perils of Getting Tough on Korea," *Fortune*, June 5, 1989, pp. 263–68; "Export Barriers the U.S. Hates Most," *Fortune*, February 27, 1989, pp. 88–93; "As EC Markets Unite, U.S. Exporters Face New Trade Barriers," *The Wall Street Journal*, January 19, 1989, p. A1ff.; "An $85,000 Lincoln Will Become Reality Soon in South Korea," *The Wall Street Journal*, March 22, 1988, p. 53.

12. Aspy P. Palia and Oded Shenkar, "Countertrade Practices in China," *Industrial Marketing Management* 20, no. 1 (1991), pp. 57–66; Matt

Schaffer, "Countertrade as an Export Strategy," *The Journal of Business Strategy,* May/June 1990, pp. 33–38; "Ship Me a Pepsi, Please!" *Time,* April 23, 1990, p. 64; "PepsiCo Signs a 10-Year Trade Accord with Moscow that Includes Soviet Ships," *The Wall Street Journal,* April 10, 1990, p. A12; Arnold Reisman, Raj Aggarwal, and Duu-Cheng Fuh, "Seeking Out Profitable Countertrade Opportunities," *Industrial Marketing Management,* February 1989, pp. 65–72; Arnold Reisman, Duu-Cheng Fuh, and Gang Li, "Achieving an Advantage with Countertrade," *Industrial Marketing Management,* February 1988, pp. 55–64; David Shipley and Bill Neale, "Industrial Barter and Countertrade," *Industrial Marketing Management,* February 1987, pp. 1–8.

13. William McInnes, "A Conceptual Approach to Marketing," in *Theory in Marketing,* second series, ed. Reavis Cox, Wroe Alderson, and Stanley J. Shapiro (Homewood, Ill.: Richard D. Irwin, 1964), pp. 51–67.

14. *1990 Annual Report,* Tandem; "The New Germany's Glowing Future," *Fortune,* December 3, 1990, pp. 146–54; "Berlin Tries to Raze Its Great Divide," *Insight,* October 15, 1990, pp. 8–17; "West Brands Rain on East's Parade," *Advertising Age,* October 1, 1990, p. 15ff.; "Speeding over the Bumps," *Time,* July 30, 1990, pp. 30–31; "A New Germany," *Newsweek,* July 9, 1990, pp. 28–36; "One Germany," *Business Week,* April 2, 1990, pp. 46–54; "Dealmakers Are Pouring through the Brandenburg Gate," *Business Week,* February 12, 1990, pp. 42–43; "Freedom!" *Time,* November 20, 1989, pp. 24–33; "The Wall Comes Down," *Newsweek,* November 20, 1989, pp. 24–30.

15. Reed Moyer, *Macro Marketing: A Social Perspective* (New York: John Wiley & Sons, 1972), pp. 3–5; see also Roger A. Layton, "Measures of Structural Change in Macromarketing Systems," *Journal of Macromarketing,* Spring 1989, pp. 5–15.

Chapter 2

1. "New Selling Tool: The Acura Concept," *Fortune,* February 24, 1992, pp. 88–89; *1990 Annual Report,* Black & Decker.

2. J. David Lichtenthal and David T. Wilson, "Becoming Market Oriented," *Journal of Business Research,* May, 1992, pp. 191–208; Caron H. St. John and Ernest H. Hall, Jr., "The Interdependency between Marketing and Manufacturing," *Industrial Marketing Management* 20, no. 3 (1991), pp. 223–30; Regis McKenna, "Marketing Is Everything," *Harvard Business Review,* January/February 1991, pp. 65–79; Sandra Vandermerwe and Douglas Gilbert, "Making Internal Services Market Driven," *Business Horizons,* November/December 1989, pp. 83–89; "Marketing: The New Priority," *Business Week,* November 21, 1983, pp. 96–106; Neal Gilliatt and Pamela Cuming, "The Chief Marketing Officer: A Maverick Whose Time Has Come," *Business Horizons,* January/February 1986, pp. 41–48. For an early example of how the marketing revolution affected one firm, see Robert J. Keith, "The Marketing Revolution," *Journal of Marketing,* January 1960, pp. 35–38. For an overview of some of Procter & Gamble's recent marketing efforts, see "Procter & Gamble Is Following Its Nose," *Business Week,* April 22, 1991, p. 28; "P&G Is Turning into Quite a Makeup Artist," *Business Week,* April 8, 1991, pp. 66–67ff.; "Health and Beauty Aids: P&G Gives Itself a Makeover," *Sales and Marketing Management,* June 1990, pp. 66–67ff.; "P&G Rewrites the Marketing Rules," *Fortune,* November 6, 1989, pp. 34–36ff.; "Stalking the New Consumer," *Business Week,* August 28, 1989, pp. 54–62; "The Marketing Revolution at Procter & Gamble," *Business Week,* July 25, 1988, pp. 72–73ff. See also Thomas Masiello, "Developing Market Responsiveness throughout Your Company," *Industrial Marketing Management,* May 1988, pp. 85–94; Robert R. Lusch and Gene R. Laczniak, "The Evolving Marketing Concept, Competitive Intensity and Organizational Performance," *Journal of the Academy of Marketing Science,* Fall 1987, pp. 1–11; Franklin S. Houston, "The Marketing Concept: What It Is and What It Is Not," *Journal of Marketing,* April 1986, pp. 81–87.

3. For more on the marketing concept in the banking industry, see "Despite the Mergers of Many Big Banks, Tiny Ones May Thrive," *The Wall Street Journal,* October 9, 1991, p. A1ff.; "Banking Soft-Sells the Rich," *Adweek's Marketing Week,* June 10, 1991, pp. 24–25; "Mellon Bank Shops for Customers at Local Supermarket," *The Wall Street Journal,* October 5, 1990, p. A4; "Taking a Tip from Retailing, Branch Banks Get Gussied Up," *Insight,* July 16, 1990, pp. 38–39; "Banks

Discover the Consumer," *Fortune,* February 12, 1990, pp. 96–104; "Making Change for a Segmented Market, Banks Package Services to Woo Target Groups," *The Wall Street Journal,* November 2, 1989, p. B1ff. For more on the marketing concept and the legal profession, see "Mixed Verdict: Prepaid Legal Services Draw Plenty of Customers and Criticism," *The Wall Street Journal,* August 6, 1991, p. B1ff.; " 'I Love My Lawyer' Ads May Spread to More States," *The Wall Street Journal,* December 7, 1990, p. B1ff.; F. G. Crane, Carolyn Meacher, and T. K. Clarke, "Lawyers' Attitudes towards Legal Services Advertising in Canada," *International Journal of Advertising* 8, no. 1 (1989), pp. 71–78. For more on the marketing concept and the accounting profession, see "Accountants Adopt Pushier Standards," *The Wall Street Journal,* September 17, 1991, p. B1; "Consulting Concerns, Competing Hard, Learn the Business of Selling Themselves," *The Wall Street Journal,* September 27, 1990, p. B1ff.; "Accountants Struggle as Marketers," *The Wall Street Journal,* July 10, 1989, p. B1. For more on the marketing concept and the academic community, see "Business Schools Revamp to Win Students," *The Wall Street Journal,* August 21, 1991, p. B1ff.; "Ailing College Treats Student as Customer, and Soon Is Thriving," *The Wall Street Journal,* July 17, 1991, p. A1ff. For more on the marketing concept and the medical profession, see William A. Schaffer, "Physician Advertising in the United States Since 1980," *International Journal of Advertising* 8, no. 1 (1989), pp. 25–34; "Pediatric Centers Spring Up to Provide Off-Hour Care," *The Wall Street Journal,* February 13, 1989, p. B1. For more on other service industries, see Gary D. Hailey, "The Federal Trade Commission, the Supreme Court, and Restrictions on Professional Advertising," *International Journal of Advertising* 8, no. 1 (1989), pp. 1–16; Valarie A. Zeithaml, A. Parasuraman, and Leonard L. Berry, "Problems and Strategies in Services Marketing," *Journal of Marketing,* Spring 1985, pp. 33–46; Paul N. Bloom, "Effective Marketing for Professional Services," *Harvard Business Review,* September/October 1984, pp. 102–10; Betsy D. Gelb, Samuel V. Smith, and Gabriel M. Gelb, "Service Marketing Lessons from the Professionals," *Business Horizons,* September/October 1988, pp. 29–34.

4. Larry C. Giunipero, William Crittenden, and Vicky Crittenden, "Industrial Marketing in NonProfit Organizations," *Industrial Marketing Management,* August 1990, p. 279; "Profiting from the Nonprofits," *Business Week,* March 26, 1990, pp. 66–74; "Nonprofits Learn How-To's of Marketing," *Marketing News,* August 14, 1989, pp. 1–2; Peter F. Drucker, "What Business Can Learn from Nonprofits," *Harvard Business Review,* July/August 1989, pp. 88–93; Alan R. Andreasen, "Nonprofits: Check Your Attention to Customers," *Harvard Business Review,* May/June 1982, pp. 105–10; Jeffrey A. Barach, "Applying Marketing Principles to Social Causes," *Business Horizons,* July/August 1984, pp. 65–69; C. Scott Greene and Paul Miesing, "Public Policy, Technology, and Ethics: Marketing Decisions for NASA's Space Shuttle," *Journal of Marketing,* Summer 1984, pp. 56–67; Regina E. Herzlinger and William S. Krasker, "Who Profits from Nonprofits?" *Harvard Business Review,* January/February 1987, p. 93ff.

5. *1990 Annual Report,* Du Pont; "Chemical Firms Press Campaigns to Dispel Their 'Bad Guy' Image," *The Wall Street Journal,* September 20, 1988, p. 1ff.; "CFC Curb to Save Ozone Will Be Costly," *The Wall Street Journal,* March 28, 1988, p. 6.

6. "A Matter of Ethics," *Industry Week,* March 16, 1992, pp. 57–62; Michael R. Hyman, Robert Skipper, and Richard Tansey, "Ethical Codes Are Not Enough," *Business Horizons,* March/April 1990, pp. 15–22; Alan J. Dubinsky and Barbara Loken, "Analyzing Ethical Decision Making in Marketing," *Journal of Business Research,* September 1989, pp. 83–108; John Tsalikis and David J. Fritzsche, "Business Ethics: A Literature Review with a Focus on Marketing Ethics," *Journal of Business Ethics,* September 1989, pp. 695–702; Donald Robin et al., "A Different Look at Codes of Ethics," *Business Horizons,* January/February 1989, pp. 66–73; "Ethics Codes Spread Despite Skepticism," *The Wall Street Journal,* July 15, 1988, p. 17; G. R. Laczniak, R. F. Lusch, and P. E. Murphy, "Social Marketing: Its Ethical Dimensions," *Journal of Marketing,* Spring 1979, pp. 29–36.

7. Mary Anne Raymond and Hiram C. Barksdale, "Corporate Strategic Planning and Corporate Marketing: Toward an Interface," *Business Horizons,* September/October 1989, pp. 41–48; David W. Cravens, "Strategic Forces Affecting Marketing Strategy," *Business Horizons,* September/October 1986, pp. 77–86; Joel E. Ross and Ronnie Silverblatt, "Developing the Strategic Plan," *Industrial Marketing Management,* May 1987, pp. 103–8; Barton A. Weitz and Robin

Wensley, eds., *Strategic Marketing: Planning, Implementation and Control* (Boston: Kent, 1984); William A. Cohen, "War in the Marketplace," *Business Horizons,* March/April 1986, pp. 10–20.

8. "King Customer," *Business Week,* March 12, 1990, pp. 88–94; "Here's the Maine Store for the Great Outdoors," *The Blade,* (Toledo, Ohio), August 26, 1990; "L. L. Bean Scales Back Expansion Goals to Ensure Pride in Its Service Is Valid," *The Wall Street Journal,* July 31, 1989, p. B3; "Training at L. L. Bean," *TRAINING, The Magazine of Human Resources Development,* October 1988; "Using the Old (L. L.) Bean," *The Reader's Digest,* June 1986.

9. *1990 Annual Report,* Baldor; "Baldor's Success: Made in the U.S.A.," *Fortune,* July 17, 1989, pp. 101–4.

10. Orville C. Walker, Jr., and Robert W. Ruekert, "Marketing's Role in the Implementation of Business Strategies: A Critical Review and Conceptual Framework," *Journal of Marketing,* July 1987, pp. 15–33; Thomas V. Bonoma, "A Model of Marketing Implementation," *1984 AMA Educators' Proceedings* (Chicago: American Marketing Association, 1984), pp. 185–89.

11. *1990 Annual Report,* Gillette Company.

12. "And if It Matters, They Also Tell Time," *The Wall Street Journal,* September 20, 1991, p. B1; "High Time for Timex," *Adweek's Marketing Week,* July 29, 1991, p. 24; "Timex Hopes 'True Story' Ads Will Keep Watch Sales Ticking," *The Wall Street Journal,* October 30, 1990, p. B7; "Swatch Says It's Time to Reach Older Crowd," *The Wall Street Journal,* July 2, 1990, p. B1; "Watchmakers Put Emphasis on Technology," *Advertising Age,* April 3, 1989, p. 28; "Timex, Swatch Push Fashion," *Advertising Age,* July 18, 1988, p. 4.

Chapter 3

1. "The Ultimate Nuts and Bolts Company," *Fortune,* July 16, 1990, pp. 70–73.

2. Michael E. Raynor, "The Pitfalls of Niche Marketing," *The Journal of Business Strategy,* March/April 1992, pp. 29–32; George S. Day and Robin Wensley, "Assessing Advantage: A Framework for Diagnosing Competitive Superiority," *Journal of Marketing,* April 1988, pp. 1–20; Kevin P. Coyne, "Sustainable Competitive Advantage—What It Is, What It Isn't," *Business Horizons,* January/February 1986, pp. 54–61; Michael E. Porter, *Competitive Advantage—Creating and Sustaining Superior Performance* (New York: Free Press, MacMillan, 1986).

3. "Visa, MasterCard Make Inroads Wooing American Express's Corporate Clients," *The Wall Street Journal,* July 3, 1991, p. B1ff.; "Rivalry Rages among Big Credit Cards," *The Wall Street Journal,* May 3, 1991, p. B1ff.; "Visa Explores New Frontiers," *Adweek's Marketing Week,* January 7, 1991, pp. 18–19; "AT&T Tweaks MCI's 'Friends,' " *Advertising Age,* March 2, 1992, p. 4; "MCI, Sprint Ads Hit AT&T Outage," *Advertising Age,* September 23, 1991, p. 3ff.; "Phone Firms Again Spark a Price War," *USA Today,* March 19, 1991, p. 1Bff.; "US Sprint's Troubles Come Amid Ferment in Long Distance Field," *The Wall Street Journal,* July 31, 1990, p. A1ff.; "Long-Distance Battle Shifts to Homes, Small Businesses," *The Wall Street Journal,* December 20, 1989, p. B1–2; *1990 Annual Report,* McDonald's Corporation; "Soviet McDonald's Tastes Success," *USA Today,* November 22, 1991, p. 8B; "McDonald's Beats Lenin 3 to 1," *Fortune,* December 17, 1990, p. 11; "McRisky," *Business Week,* October 21, 1991, pp. 114–22; "McLifestyle," *Adweek's Marketing Week,* September 16, 1991, pp. 4–5; "Play Centers May Be on Menu for McDonald's," *The Wall Street Journal,* August 30, 1991, p. B1ff.; "Pizza Hut Gains Fast-Food Entree to Institutions," *The Wall Street Journal,* November 29, 1991, p. B1ff.; "High-Flying Retail Takes off at Airports," *USA Today,* June 18, 1991, p. 6B; "Consumers in Airports Eat Up Name-Brand Food," *The Wall Street Journal,* May 13, 1991, p. B1; "McDonald's Takes Nip at Supermarkets," *Advertising Age,* March 11, 1991, p. 1ff.; "Microsoft," *Business Week,* February 24, 1992, pp. 60–65; "How Bill Gates Keeps the Magic Going," *Fortune,* June 18, 1990, pp. 82–89; "Will Sony Make It in Hollywood?" *Fortune,* September 9, 1991, pp. 158–66; "Media Colossus," *Business Week,* March 25, 1991, pp. 64–74; "From Walkman to Showman," *Time,* October 9, 1989, pp. 70–71; "A Changing Sony Aims to Own the 'Software' That Its Products Need," *The Wall Street Journal,* December 30, 1988, p. A1ff.; "Holiday Inn Scrambles for New Profits," *The New York Times,* April 22, 1984.

4. "The Little Guys Are Making It Big Overseas," *Business Week,* February 27, 1989, pp. 94–96.

5. This point of view is discussed at much greater length in a classic article by T. Levitt, "Marketing Myopia," *Harvard Business Review,* September/October 1975, p. 1ff. See also George S. Day, A. D. Shocker, and R. K. Srivastava, "Customer-Oriented Approaches to Identifying Product-Markets," *Journal of Marketing,* Fall 1979, pp. 8–19; Rajendra K. Srivastava, Mark I. Alpert, and Allan D. Shocker, "A Customer-Oriented Approach for Determining Market Structures," *Journal of Marketing,* Spring 1984, pp. 32–45.

6. "The Riches in Market Niches," *Fortune,* April 27, 1987, pp. 227–30.

7. Terry Elrod and Russell S. Winer, "An Empirical Evaluation of Aggregation Approaches for Developing Market Segments," *Journal of Marketing,* Fall 1982, pp. 32–34; Frederick W. Winter, "A Cost-Benefit Approach to Market Segmentation," *Journal of Marketing,* Fall 1979, pp. 103–11.

8. James W. Harvey, "Benefit Segmentation for Fund Raisers," *Journal of the Academy of Marketing Science,* Winter 1990, pp. 77–86; Steven A. Sinclair and Edward C. Stalling, "How to Identify Differences between Market Segments with Attribute Analysis," *Industrial Marketing Management,* February 1990, pp. 31–40; Peter R. Dickson and James L. Ginter, "Market Segmentation, Product Differentiation, and Marketing Strategy," *Journal of Marketing,* April 1987, pp. 1–10; Russell I. Haley, "Benefit Segmentation—20 Years Later," *Journal of Consumer Marketing* 1, no. 2 (1984), pp. 5–14. See also "The Mass Market Is Splitting Apart," *Fortune,* November 28, 1983, pp. 76–82; Lynn R. Kahle, "The Nine Nations of North America and the Value Basis of Geographic Segmentation," *Journal of Marketing,* April 1986, pp. 37–47.

9. "U.S. Aid Plan for Poor Helps Big Food Firms," *The Wall Street Journal,* March 29, 1991, p. B1ff.; "Breakthrough in Birth Control May Elude Poor," *The Wall Street Journal,* March 4, 1991, p. B1ff.; "American Home Infant-Formula Giveaway to End," *The Wall Street Journal,* February 4, 1991, p. B1ff.; "Selling to Kids," *Adweek,* February 10, 1992, pp. 37–44; "The Littlest Shoppers," *American Demographics,* February 1992, pp. 48–53; "Gatorade for Kids," *Adweek's Marketing Week,* July 15, 1991, pp. 4–5; James U. McNeal, "Planning Priorities for Marketing to Children," *The Journal of Business Strategy,* May/June 1991, pp. 12–15; "Fast-Food Vendors Get Serious with Kids," *The Wall Street Journal,* January 19, 1990, p. B1ff.; "Malt Liquor Makers Find Lucrative Market in the Urban Young," *The Wall Street Journal,* March 9, 1992, p. A1ff.; "Malt Advertising That Touts Firepower Comes under Attack by U.S. Officials," *The Wall Street Journal,* July 1, 1991, p. B1ff.; "Sneaker Makers Face Scrutiny from PUSH," *The Wall Street Journal,* July 19, 1990, p. B1; "Don't Blame Sneakers for Inner-City Crime," *Adweek's Marketing Week,* May 7, 1990, p. 65; "Tobacco Critics See a Subtle Sell to Kids," *The Wall Street Journal,* May 3, 1990, p. B1ff.; "Under Fire from All Sides," *Time,* March 5, 1990, p. 41; "After Uptown, Are Some Niches Out?" *The Wall Street Journal,* January 22, 1990, p. B1ff.

10. Girish Punj and David W. Stewart, "Cluster Analysis in Marketing Research: Review and Suggestions for Application," *Journal of Marketing Research,* May 1983, pp. 134–48; Fernando Robles and Ravi Sarathy, "Segmenting the Computer Aircraft Market with Cluster Analysis," *Industrial Marketing Management,* February 1986, pp. 1–12; Rajendra K. Srivastava, Robert P. Leone, and Allen D. Shocker, "Market Structure Analysis: Hierarchical Clustering of Products Based on Substitution-in-Use," *Journal of Marketing,* Summer 1981, pp. 38–48.

11. David A. Aaker and J. Gary Shansby, "Positioning Your Product," *Business Horizons,* May/June 1982, pp. 56–62; Al Ries and Jack Trout, *Positioning: The Battle for Your Mind* (New York: McGraw-Hill, 1981), p. 53.

Chapter 4

1. "Rubbermaid Turns Up Plenty of Profit in the Mundane," *The Wall Street Journal,* March 27, 1992, p. B4; "The Art of Rubbermaid," *Adweek's Marketing Week,* March 16, 1992, pp. 22–25; "Tupperware Takes Fresh Approach," *USA Today,* March 3, 1992, p. 5B; "Move Over Honda, Cozy Coupe's No. 1," *Adweek's Marketing Week,* December 9, 1991, p. 19; "At Rubbermaid, Little Things Mean a Lot," *Business Week,* November 11, 1991, p. 126; "Little Tikes with a Grown-Up Dilemma,"

Adweek's Marketing Week, September 10, 1991, pp. 18–19; "Rubbermaid Packs an Ecological Lunch," *Adweek's Marketing Week,* September 9, 1991, p. 10; "Rubbermaid Tries Its Hand at Bristles and Wood," *Adweek's Marketing Week,* March 5, 1990, pp. 20–21; *1990 Annual Report,* Rubbermaid; "Rubbermaid Moves beyond the Kitchen," *The Wall Street Journal,* February 3, 1989, p. B2.

2. See Peter F. Drucker, *Management: Tasks, Responsibilities, Practices, and Plans* (New York: Harper and Row, 1973).

3. "Reichhold Chemicals: Now the Emphasis Is on Profits rather than Volume," *Business Week,* June 20, 1983, pp. 178–79; Carolyn Y. Woo, "Market-Share Leadership—Not Always So Good," *Harvard Business Review,* January/February 1984, pp. 50–55; Robert Jacobson and David A. Aaker, "Is Market Share All that It's Cracked Up to Be?" *Journal of Marketing,* Fall 1985, pp. 11–22.

4. "Harley-Davidson's U-Turn," *USA Today,* March 2, 1990, p. 1Bff.; "How Harley Beat Back the Japanese," *Fortune,* September 25, 1989, pp. 155–64.

5. "No Air Bags for Passengers; Ford Stores 3,000 Lincolns," *Automotive News,* March 26, 1990, p. 1ff.; "TRW Says Air Bag Supply OK Despite Factory Explosions," *Automotive News,* August 7, 1989, p. 4.

6. "Still Battling the Ozone Stigma," *Adweek's Marketing Week,* March 16, 1992, pp. 18–19. For more on the competitive environment, see Klaus Brockhoff, "Competitor Technology Intelligence in German Companies," *Industrial Marketing Management* 20, no. 2 (1991), pp. 91–98; John L. Haverty and Myroslaw J. Kyj, "What Happens When New Competitors Enter an Industry," *Industrial Marketing Management* 20, no. 1 (1991), pp. 73–80; David W. Cravens and Shannon H. Shipp, "Market-Driven Strategies for Competitive Advantage," *Business Horizons,* January/February 1991, pp. 53–61; Roger J. Calantone and C. Anthony di Benedetto, "Defensive Industrial Marketing Strategies," *Industrial Marketing Management,* August 1990, pp. 267–78; Paul N. Bloom and Torger Reve, "Transmitting Signals to Consumers for Competitive Advantage," *Business Horizons,* July/August 1990, pp. 58–66; Fahri Karakaya and Michael J. Stahl, "Barriers to Entry and Market Entry Decisions in Consumer and Industrial Goods Markets," *Journal of Marketing,* April 1989, pp. 80–91.

7. "P&G Wins Lawsuit, Loses Market," *Advertising Age,* September 18, 1989, p. 72.

8. "Most U.S. Companies Are Innocents Abroad," *Business Week,* November 16, 1987, pp. 168–69.

9. "The Global Economy: Can You Compete?" (Special Report), *Business Week,* December 17, 1990, pp. 60–93; "Markets of the World Unite," *Fortune,* July 30, 1990, pp. 101–20.

10. "In Niches, Necessity Can Be the Mother of Reinvention," *The Wall Street Journal,* April 30, 1991, p. B2.

11. "Cutting Edge: Using Advanced Technology, Gillette Has Managed an Unusual Feat," *The Wall Street Journal,* April 6, 1992, p. R6; "Almost Like Being There: Virtual-Reality Technology Is Finally Moving Out of the Lab," *The Wall Street Journal,* April 6, 1992, p. R10; "Designing Drugs: Computers Promise to Speed up the Development, and Improve the Effectiveness, of New Medicines," *The Wall Street Journal,* April 6, 1992, p. R20; "From Technology to Market—First," *Fortune,* March 23, 1992, p. 108; "The Videophone Era May Finally Be Near, Bring Big Changes," *The Wall Street Journal,* March 10, 1992, p. A1ff.; "Readin', Writin' & Multimedia: Slowly, Teachers Are Turning to a New Tool," *The Wall Street Journal,* October 21, 1991, p. R12ff.; "Get Smart: Everyday Products Will Soon Come with Built-In Intelligence," *The Wall Street Journal,* October 21, 1991, p. R18; "Technology in the Year 2000," *Fortune,* July 18, 1988, pp. 92–98; John D. Ela and Manley R. Irwin, "Technology Changes Market Boundaries," *Industrial Marketing Management,* July 1983, pp. 153–56; Geoffrey Kiel, "Technology and Marketing: The Magic Mix?" *Business Horizons,* May/June 1984, pp. 7–14; Noel Capon and Rashi Glazer, "Marketing and Technology: A Strategic Coalignment," *Journal of Marketing,* July 1987, pp. 1–14. For more on privacy, see "Nowhere To Hide," *Time,* November 11, 1991, pp. 34–40; "Caller I. D. vs. Privacy: Now There's a Middle Road," *Business Week,* April 1, 1991, p. 87; "Caller ID Service Barred by Pennsylvania Appeals Court," *The Wall Street Journal,* May 31, 1990, p. B1ff.; "Drink Box Firms to Pay $75,000 to Settle Ad Suit," *USA*

Today, August 29, 1991, p. 1B; "Lunch-Box Staple Runs Afoul of Activists," *The Wall Street Journal,* March 14, 1991, p. B1ff.

12. "Consumers: Quality Still Comes First," *USA Today,* March 9, 1992, p. 1Bff.; "Patriotism and the Pocketbook," *USA Today,* March 9, 1992, p. 3B; "Do You Drive an American Car? Don't Be So Sure," *USA Today,* March 2, 1992, p. 1Bff.; " 'Buy American' Is Easier Said Than Done," *The Wall Street Journal,* January 28, 1992, p. B1ff.; "Growing Movement to 'Buy American' Debates the Term," *The Wall Street Journal,* January 24, 1992, p. A1ff.; "Honda, Is It an American Car?" *Business Week,* November 18, 1991, pp. 105–12; "Foreign or Domestic? Car Firms Play Games with the Categories," *The Wall Street Journal,* November 11, 1991, p. A1ff.

13. "As EC Leaders Gather, the Program for 1992 Is Facing Big Problems," *The Wall Street Journal,* December 6, 1991, p. A1ff.; "Now the New Europe," *Fortune,* December 2, 1991, pp. 136–72; "The New Europeans," *The Economist,* November 16, 1991, pp. 65–66; "Tearing Down Even More Fences in Europe," *Business Week,* November 4, 1991, pp. 50–52; Andrew I. Millington and Brian T. Bayliss, "Non-Tariff Barriers and U.K. Investment in the European Community," *Journal of International Business Studies,* Fourth Quarter, 1991, pp. 695–710; Alan Wolfe, "The Single European Market: National or Euro-Brands?" *International Journal of Advertising* 10, no. 1 (1991), pp. 49–58; "Europe Hits the Brakes on 1992," *Fortune,* December 17, 1990, pp. 133–40; Jack G. Kaikati, "Opportunities for Smaller U.S. Industrial Firms in Europe," *Industrial Marketing Management,* November, 1990, pp. 339–48; "Europeans Foresee Era of Prosperity, Unity and Growing Power," *The Wall Street Journal,* July 5, 1990, p. A1; "World Business: The Uncommon Market," *The Wall Street Journal,* September 22, 1989, pp. R1–12. See also John R. Darling and Danny R. Arnold, "Foreign Consumers' Perspective of the Products and Marketing Practices of the United States versus Selected European Countries," *Journal of Business Research,* November 1988, pp. 237–48; Sandra Vandermerwe and Marc-Andre L'Huillier, "Euro-Consumers in 1992," *Business Horizons,* January/February 1989, pp. 34–40; James M. Higgins and Timo Santalainen, "Strategies for Europe 1992," *Business Horizons,* July/August 1989, pp. 54–58.

14. Alan Morrison, "The Role of Litigation in Consumer Protection," *The Journal of Consumer Affairs,* Winter 1991, pp. 209–20; "Educating the Customer," *American Demographics,* September 1991, pp. 44–47; "Nader Suits Up to Strike Back Against 'Slapps,' " *The Wall Street Journal,* July 9, 1991, p. B1ff.; "The Resurrection of Ralph Nader," *Fortune,* May 22, 1989, pp. 106–16; "Attorneys General Flex Their Muscles: State Officials Join Forces to Press Consumer and Antitrust Concerns," *The Wall Street Journal,* July 13, 1988, p. 25; "Consumers Union Tests Products in Ways Manufacturers Don't," *The Wall Street Journal,* January 14, 1985, p. 19.

15. "What Led Beech-Nut Down the Road to Disgrace," *Business Week,* February 22, 1988, pp. 124–28. See also Louis W. Stern and Thomas L. Eovaldi, *Legal Aspects of Marketing Strategy: Antitrust and Consumer Protection Issues* (Englewood Cliffs, N.J.: Prentice Hall, 1984).

16. "Getting Tougher with Toxics," *Industry Week,* February 17, 1992, pp. 46–51; "Labels We Can Live By," *Newsweek,* November 18, 1991, p. 90; "Large Food Companies Express Relief at FDA's Truth-in-Labeling Proposals," *The Wall Street Journal,* November 7, 1991, p. B9; "Making Shoppers Conversant in the Language of Nutrition," *USA Today,* November 7, 1991, p. 6D; "FDA Proposes Relabeling Most Packaged Food," *The Wall Street Journal,* June 24, 1991, p. B1ff.; "The Cholesterol Is in the Fire Now," *Business Week,* June 10, 1991, pp. 34–35; "FDA Takes on 'No Cholesterol' Claims," *The Wall Street Journal,* May 15, 1991, p. B1ff., "FDA Finds Bunk in Bottled-Water Claims," *The Wall Street Journal,* April 10, 1991, p. B1ff.; "Generic Drug Scandal at the FDA Linked to Deregulation Drive," *The Wall Street Journal,* September 13, 1989, p. A1ff.; "Generic Drug Scandal Creates Opening," *The Wall Street Journal,* September 6, 1989, p. B1; Joseph C. Miller and Michael D. Hutt, "Assessing Societal Effects of Product Regulations: Toward An Analytic Framework," in *1983 American Marketing Association Educators' Proceedings,* ed. P. E. Murphy et al. (Chicago: American Marketing Association, 1983), pp. 364–68; Rachel Dardis and B. F. Smith, "Cost-Benefit Analysis of Consumer Product Safety Standards," *Journal of Consumer Affairs,* Summer 1977, pp. 34–46; Paul Busch, "A Review and Critical Evaluation of the Consumer Product Safety Commission: Marketing Management Implications," *Journal of Marketing,* October 1976, pp. 41–49.

17. John Tsalikis and Osita Nwachukwu, "A Comparison of Nigerian to American Views of Bribery and Extortion in International Commerce," *Journal of Business Ethics,* February 1991, pp. 85–98; "Marketing Law: A Marketer's Guide to Alphabet Soup," *Business Marketing,* January 1990, pp. 56–58; Ray O. Werner, "Marketing and the Supreme Court in Transition, 1982–1984," *Journal of Marketing,* Summer 1985, pp. 97–105; Ray O. Werner, "Marketing and the United States Supreme Court, 1975–1981," *Journal of Marketing,* Spring 1982, pp. 73–81; Dorothy Cohen, "Trademark Strategy," *Journal of Marketing,* January 1986, pp. 61–74; A. R. Beckenstein, H. L. Gabel, and Karlene Roberts, "An Executive's Guide to Antitrust Compliance," *Harvard Business Review,* September/October 1983, pp. 94–102; Susan L. Holak and Srinivas K. Reddy, "Effects of a Television and Radio Advertising Ban: A Study of the Cigarette Industry," *Journal of Marketing,* October 1986, pp. 219–27.

18. Based on U.S. Census data, United Nations statistical data, and *The World Market Atlas* (New York, N.Y.: Business International Corp., 1990); "Projected World Population," *USA Today,* October 2, 1991, p. 1A.

19. Based on U.S. Census data, United Nations statistical data, and PCGLOBE software (Tempe, Arizona: PC Globe, Inc., 1990); "We Can Hope It's Getting Wiser, Too," *The Wall Street Journal,* February 28, 1992, p. B1; "Superpowers Lose Population Momentum," *The Wall Street Journal,* April 23, 1990, p. B1; James V. Koch, "An Economic Profile of the Pacific Rim," *Business Horizons,* March/April 1989, pp. 18–25; "Economic and Social Indicators on the Pacific Rim," *Business Horizons,* March/April 1989, pp. 14–15.

20. Based on U.S. Census data and William H. Frey, "Boomer Magnets," *American Demographics,* March 1992, pp. 34–37; "Boomers Leave a Challenge," *Advertising Age,* July 8, 1991, p. 1ff.; "Those Aging Boomers," *Business Week,* May 20, 1991, pp. 106–12; Jeff Ostroff, "An Aging Market: How Businesses Can Prosper," *American Demographics,* May 1989, pp. 26–33ff.; "Special Report: Marketers Slow to Catch Age Wave," *Advertising Age,* May 22, 1989, pp. S1–S6; "Firms Seek To Ring in New Customers," *The Wall Street Journal,* March 23, 1989, p. B1; "Marketers Err by Treating Elderly as Uniform Group," *The Wall Street Journal,* October 31, 1988, p. B1.

21. Based on U.S. Census data and "The North Shall Rise," *American Demographics,* March 1992, p. 55; "American Diversity," *American Demographics,* (supplement) July 1991; "South Paces Decade's Growth," *USA Today,* March 6, 1991, p. 6A; "Turnaround States," *American Demographics,* March 1991, p. 55; "Census '90," *The Wall Street Journal Reports,* March 9, 1990, pp. R1–36; "More than It Grows, the Population Flows," *The Wall Street Journal,* March 2, 1990, p. B1; Cheryl Russell, *100 Predictions for the Baby Boom: The Next 50 Years* (Ithaca, NY: American Demographics Press, 1988).

22. "Mobility of U.S. Society Turns Small Cities into Giants," *The Wall Street Journal,* February 8, 1991, p. B1ff.; "Americans on the Move," *American Demographics,* June 1990, pp. 46–49; James R. Lumpkin and James B. Hunt, "Mobility as an Influence on Retail Patronage Behavior of the Elderly: Testing Conventional Wisdom," *Journal of the Academy of Marketing Science,* Winter 1989, pp. 1–12; Michael R. Hyman, "Long-Distance Geographic Mobility and Retailing Attitudes and Behaviors: An Update," *Journal of Retailing,* Summer 1987, pp. 187–208.

23. Based on U.S. Census data and "Beliefs Bound to the Land Hold Firm as Times Change," *Insight,* December 7, 1987, pp. 10–11.

24. Based on U.S. Census data and "Census: City Growth Booming," *USA Today,* December 18, 1991, p. 3A; Joel Garreau, "Edge Cities: Life on the New Frontier," *American Demographics,* September 1991, pp. 24–53; "America's Megamarkets," *American Demographics,* June 1991, p. 59; Joe Schwartz and Thomas Exter, "This World Is Flat," *American Demographics,* April 1991, pp. 34–39; "The MSA Mess," *American Demographics,* January 1989, pp. 53–56.

25. U.S. Bureau of the Census, *Statistical Abstract of the United States 1991* (Washington, D.C.: U.S. Government Printing Office, 1991), p. 841; U.S. Arms Control and Disarmament Agency, *World Military Expenditures and Arms Transfers 1990* (Washington, D.C.: U.S. Government Printing Office, 1991), pp. 35–46; PCGLOBE software (Tempe, Arizona: PC Globe, Inc., 1990); "The Global Economy: Can You Compete?" (Special Report), *Business Week,* December 17, 1990, pp. 60–93; "Markets of the World Unite," *Fortune,* July 30, 1990,

pp. 101–20; "Where Global Growth Is Going," *Fortune,* July 31, 1989, pp. 71–92.

26. Frank R. Bacon, Jr., and Thomas W. Butler, Jr., *Planned Innovation,* rev. ed. (Ann Arbor: Institute of Science and Technology, University of Michigan, 1980).

27. Paul F. Anderson, "Marketing, Strategic Planning, and the Theory of the Firm," *Journal of Marketing,* Spring 1982, pp. 15–26; George S. Day, "Analytical Approaches to Strategic Market Planning," in *Review of Marketing 1981,* ed. Ben M. Enis and Kenneth J. Roering (Chicago: American Marketing Association, 1981), pp. 89–105; Ronnie Silverblatt and Pradeep Korgaonkar, "Strategic Market Planning in a Turbulent Business Environment," *Journal of Business Research,* August 1987, pp. 339–58.

28. *1990 Annual Report,* Sara Lee; *1990 Annual Report,* Philip Morris; Richard N. Cardozo and David K. Smith, Jr., "Applying Financial Portfolio Theory to Product Portfolio Decisions: An Empirical Study," *Journal of Marketing,* Spring 1983, pp. 110–19; Yoram Wind, Vijay Mahajan, and Donald J. Swire, "An Empirical Comparison of Standardized Portfolio Models," *Journal of Marketing,* Spring 1983, pp. 89–99; Philippe Haspeslagh, "Portfolio Planning: Uses and Limits," *Harvard Business Review,* January/February 1982, pp. 58–73; Samuel Rabino and Arnold Wright, "Applying Financial Portfolio and Multiple Criteria Approaches to Product Line Decisions," *Industrial Marketing Management,* October 1984, pp. 233–40.

29. "Soviet Breakup Stymies Foreign Firms," *The Wall Street Journal,* January 23, 1992, p. B1ff.; "Some Americans Take the Steppes in Stride," *The Wall Street Journal,* January 23, 1992, p. B1ff.; "Some U.S. Firms Profit in Booming Far East Despite Mighty Japan," *The Wall Street Journal,* January 8, 1992, p. A1ff.; "U.S. Food Firms Find Europe's Huge Market Hardly a Piece of Cake," *The Wall Street Journal,* May 15, 1990, p. A1ff.; "Rewriting the Export Rules," *Fortune,* April 23, 1990, pp. 89–96; "You Can Make Money in Japan," *Fortune,* February 12, 1990, pp. 85–92; "What's Next for Business in China," *Fortune,* July 17, 1989, pp. 110–12; "U.S. Importers Aren't Jumping Ship—Yet," *Business Week,* June 26, 1989, p. 78; "Myth and Marketing in Japan," *The Wall Street Journal,* April 6, 1989, p. B1; Thomas W. Shreeve, "Be Prepared for Political Changes Abroad," *Harvard Business Review,* July/August 1984, pp. 111–18; Victor H. Frank, Jr., "Living with Price Control Abroad," *Harvard Business Review,* March/April 1984, pp. 137–42; Michael G. Harvey and James T. Rothe, "The Foreign Corrupt Practices Act: The Good, the Bad and the Future," in *1983 American Marketing Association Educators' Proceedings,* ed. P. E. Murphy et al. (Chicago: American Marketing Association, 1983), pp. 374–79.

30. Kamran Kashani, "Beware the Pitfalls of Global Marketing," *Harvard Business Review,* September/October 1989, pp. 91–98; "How to Go Global—and Why," *Fortune,* August 28, 1989, pp. 70–76; "Coke to Use 'Can't Beat the Feeling' as World-Wide Marketing Theme," *The Wall Street Journal,* December 12, 1988, p. 35; "Marketers Turn Sour on Global Sales Pitch Harvard Guru Makes," *The Wall Street Journal,* May 12, 1988, p. 1ff.; John A. Quelch and E. J. Hoff, "Customizing Global Marketing," *Harvard Business Review,* May/June 1986, pp. 59–68; Barbara Mueller, "Reflections of Culture: An Analysis of Japanese and American Advertising Appeals," *Journal of Advertising Research,* June/July 1987, p. 51ff.; Subhash C. Jain, "Standardization of International Marketing Strategy: Some Research Hypotheses," *Journal of Marketing,* January 1989, pp. 70–79.

Chapter 5

1. "In the Chips: At Frito-Lay, the Consumer Is an Obsession," *The Wall Street Journal,* March 22, 1991, pp. B1–2; "Frito-Lay Adds High-Tech Crunch," *American Demographics,* March 1991, pp. 18–20; "Frito-Lay Bets Big with Multigrain Chips," *The Wall Street Journal,* February 28, 1991, p. B1ff.; "What the Scanner Knows about You," *Fortune,* December 3, 1990, pp. 51–52; "Hand-Held Computers Help Field Staff Cut Paper Work and Harvest More Data," *The Wall Street Journal,* January 30, 1990, p. B1ff.; "Frito-Lay Shortens Its Business Cycle," *Fortune,* January 15, 1990, p. 11; *1990 Annual Report,* PepsiCo.

2. John T. Mentzer and Nimish Gandhi, "Expert Systems in Marketing: Guidelines for Development," *Journal of the Academy of Marketing*

Science, Winter 1992, pp. 73–80; J. M. McCann, W. G. Lahti, and J. Hill, "The Brand Manager's Assistant: A Knowledge-based System Approach to Brand Management," *International Journal of Research in Marketing,* April 1991, pp. 51–74; A. A. Mitchell, J. E. Russo, and D. R. Wittink, "Issues in the Development and Use of Expert Systems for Marketing Decisions," *International Journal of Research in Marketing,* April 1991, pp. 41–50; "Marketers Increase Their Use of Decision Support Systems," *Marketing News,* May 22, 1989, p. 29; Thomas H. Davenport, Michael Hammer, and Tauno J. Metsisto, "How Executives Can Shape Their Company's Information Systems," *Harvard Business Review,* March/April 1989, pp. 130–34; Martin D. Goslar and Stephen W. Brown, "Decision Support Systems in Marketing Management Settings," in *1984 American Marketing Association Educators' Proceedings,* ed. R. W. Belk et al. (Chicago: American Marketing Association, 1984), pp. 217–21.

3. Nancy J. Merritt and Cecile Bouchy, "Are Microcomputers Replacing Mainframes in Marketing Research Firms?" *Journal of the Academy of Marketing Science,* Winter 1992, pp. 81–86; Michael R. Czinkota, "International Information Needs for U.S. Competitiveness," *Business Horizons,* November/December 1991, pp. 86–91; Naresh K. Malhotra, Armen Tashchian, and Essam Mahmoud, "The Integration of Microcomputers in Marketing Research and Decision Making," *Journal of the Academy of Marketing Science,* Summer 1987, pp. 69–82; Martin D. J. Buss, "Managing International Information Systems," *Harvard Business Review,* September/October 1982, pp. 153–62; Lindsay Meredith, "Developing and Using a Customer Profile Data Bank," *Industrial Marketing Management,* November 1985, pp. 255–68.

4. Lawrence B. Chonko, John F. Tanner, Jr., and Ellen Reid Smith, "Selling and Sales Management in Action: The Sales Force's Role in International Marketing Research and Marketing Information Systems," *Journal of Personal Selling and Sales Management,* Winter 1991, pp. 69–80; "Focusing on Customers' Needs and Motivations," *Business Marketing,* March 1991, pp. 41–43; James M. Sinkula, "Perceived Characteristics, Organizational Factors, and the Utilization of External Market Research Suppliers," *Journal of Business Research,* August 1990, pp. 1–18; Earl Naumann and Douglas J. Lincoln, "Systems Theory Approach to Conducting Industrial Marketing Research," *Journal of Business Research,* September 1989, p. 151; Bruce Stern and Scott Dawson, "How to Select a Market Research Firm," *American Demographics,* March 1989, p. 44; Bodo B. Schlegelmilch, K. Boyle, and S. Therivel, "Marketing Research in Medium-Sized U.K. and U.S. Firms," *Industrial Marketing Management,* August 1986, pp. 177–86.

5. For a discussion of ethical issues in marketing research, see "Studies Galore Support Products and Positions, but Are They Reliable?" *The Wall Street Journal,* November 14, 1991, p. A1ff.; Ishmael P. Akaah, "Attitudes of Marketing Professionals Toward Ethics in Marketing Research: A Cross-National Comparison," *Journal of Business Ethics,* January 1990, pp. 45–54; Ishmael P. Akaah and Edward A. Riordan, "Judgments of Marketing Professionals About Ethical Issues in Marketing Research: A Replication and Extension," *Journal of Marketing Research,* February 1989, pp. 112–20. For more details on doing marketing research, see Harper W. Boyd, Jr., Ralph Westfall, and Stanley F. Stasch, *Marketing Research: Text and Cases* (Homewood, Ill.: Richard D. Irwin, 1988). See also James R. Krum, Pradeep A. Rau, and Stephen K. Keiser, "The Marketing Research Process: Role Perceptions of Researchers and Users," *Journal of Advertising Research,* December 1987–January 1988, pp. 9–22.

6. For a discussion of European secondary data, see "The New Europeans," *The Economist,* November 16, 1991, pp. 65–66; "Reaching the Real Europe," *American Demographics,* October 1990, pp. 38–43ff.; Alfred C. Holden, "How to Locate and Communicate with Overseas Customers," *Industrial Marketing Management* 20, no. 3 (1991), pp. 161–68. An excellent review of commercially available secondary data may be found in Donald R. Lehmann, *Marketing Research and Analysis,* 3rd ed. (Homewood, Ill.: Richard D. Irwin, 1988), pp. 231–72. See also Ronald L. Vaughn, "Demographic Data Banks: A New Management Resource," *Business Horizons,* November/December 1984, pp. 38–56.

7. Jeffrey Durgee, "Richer Findings from Qualitative Research," *Journal of Advertising Research,* August/September 1986, pp. 36–44; Kathleen M. Wallace, "The Use and Value of Qualitative Research Studies," *Industrial Marketing Management,* August 1984, pp. 181–86. For more on focus groups see "Focus Groups Key to Reaching Kids," *Advertising*

Age, February 10, 1992, p. S1ff.; "Focus Group Spurt Predicted for the '90s," *Marketing News,* January 8, 1990, p. 21; Joe L. Welch, "Researching Marketing Problems and Opportunities with Focus Groups," *Industrial Marketing Management,* November 1985, pp. 245–54.

8. "Symphony Strikes a Note for Research as It Prepares to Launch a New Season," *Marketing News,* August 29, 1988, p. 12.

9. Frederick Wiseman and Maryann Billington, "Comment on a Standard Definition of Response Rates, *Journal of Marketing Research,* August 1984, pp. 336–38; Jolene M. Struebbe, Jerome B. Kernan, and Thomas J. Grogan, "The Refusal Problem in Telephone Surveys," *Journal of Advertising Research,* June/July 1986, pp. 29–38.

10. "The 'Bloodbath' in Market Research," *Business Week,* February 11, 1991, pp. 72–74; Tyzoon T. Tyebjee, "Telephone Survey Methods: The State of the Art," *Journal of Marketing,* Summer 1979, pp. 68–77; Nicolaos E. Synodinos and Jerry M. Brennan, "Computer Interactive Interviewing in Survey Research," *Psychology and Marketing,* Summer 1988, pp. 117–38; A. Dianne Schmidley, "How to Overcome Bias in a Telephone Survey," *American Demographics,* November 1986, pp. 50–51.

11. " 'SuperOpticals' Edge out the Corner Optician," *Adweek's Marketing Week,* October 1, 1990, p. 36; "LensCrafters Takes the High Road," *Adweek's Marketing Week,* April 30, 1990, pp. 26–27; *1990 Annual Report,* U.S. Shoe; "The Big Battle over Eyewear," *The New York Times,* November 26, 1989, Sect. 6, p. 4.

12. For more detail on observational approaches, see "Kmart Testing 'Radar' to Track Shopper Traffic," *The Wall Street Journal,* September 24, 1991, p. B1ff.; "Information Resources Wires the Drugstores; MarketSource and Roper also Announce Expanded Programs," *Adweek's Marketing Week,* May 27, 1991, p. 34; *1990 Annual Report,* Information Resources; "Targeting the Grocery Shopper," *The New York Times,* May 26, 1991, Sect. 3, p. 1ff.; J. Bayer and R. Harter, " 'Miner', 'Manager', and 'Researcher': Three Modes of Analysis of Scanner Data," *International Journal of Research in Marketing,* April, 1991, pp. 17–28; "Using Hidden Eyes to Mind the Store," *Insight,* February 25, 1991, p. 50; "Buy the Numbers," *Inc.,* March 1985; Eugene Webb et al., *Unobtrusive Measures: Nonreactive Research in the Social Sciences* (Chicago: Rand McNally, 1966); "Single-Source Ad Research Heralds Detailed Look at Household Habits," *The Wall Street Journal,* February 16, 1988, p. 39; "Collision Course: Stakes High in People-Meter War," *Advertising Age,* July 27, 1987, p. 1ff.

13. "America's Next Test Market? Singapore," *Adweek's Marketing Week,* February 4, 1991, p. 22; Alan G. Sawyer, Parker M. Worthing, and Paul E. Fendak, "The Role of Laboratory Experiments to Test Marketing Strategies," *Journal of Marketing,* Summer 1979, pp. 60–67; "Bar Wars: Hershey Bites Mars," *Fortune,* July 8, 1985, pp. 52–57.

14. For more detail on data analysis techniques, see Naresh Malhotra, *Marketing Research: An Applied Orientation* (New York: Prentice Hall, 1993) or other current marketing research texts.

15. "GM Seeks Revival of Buick and Olds," *The Wall Street Journal,* April 12, 1988, p. 37.

16. Alan R. Andreasen, "Cost-Conscious Marketing Research," *Harvard Business Review,* July/August, 1983, pp. 74–81; A. Parasuraman, "Research's Place in the Marketing Budget," *Business Horizons,* March/April 1983, pp. 25–29; Danny N. Bellenger, "The Marketing Manager's View of Marketing Research," *Business Horizons,* June 1979, pp. 59–65.

Chapter 6

1. "BMW Rolls Out a Luxury Station Wagon," *The Wall Street Journal,* April 2, 1992, p. B1; "BMW Puts $30M Behind Ads to Drive Away Yuppie Image," *Advertising Age,* June 24, 1991, p. 3ff.; "BMW Will Try to Shed Its Image as the Ultimate 'Yuppie' Machine," *The Wall Street Journal,* June 21, 1991, p. B2; "Turning Conservative, Baby Boomers Reduce Their Frivolous Buying," *The Wall Street Journal,* June 19, 1991, p. A1ff.; "The Simple Life," *Time,* April 8, 1991, pp. 58–65; "Reality of the '90s Hits Yuppie Brands," *The Wall Street Journal,* December 20, 1990, p. B1ff.; "BMW Down-Shifts to Safety Sell," *Adweek's Marketing Week,* July 16, 1990, p. 17.

2. Based on U.S. Census data and "Apartheid, American Style," *Newsweek,* March 23, 1992, p. 61; "The Middle Class Boom of the 1980s," *The Wall Street Journal,* March 12, 1992, p. A10; "The 'Fortunate Fifth' Fallacy," *The Wall Street Journal,* January 28, 1992, p. A14; "A Class Structure that Won't Stay Put," *The Wall Street Journal,* November 20, 1991, p. A16; Jan Larson, "Reaching Downscale Markets," *American Demographics,* November 1991, pp. 38–40ff.; "What Happened to the American Dream?" *Business Week,* August 19, 1991, pp. 80–85; "Why the Middle Class Is Anxious," *Fortune,* May 21, 1990, pp. 106–12; "The Rich Are Different from One Another," *The Wall Street Journal,* November 12, 1990, p. B1; "The New Middle Class: How It Lives," *Fortune,* August 13, 1990, pp. 104–13; "The Rise and Fall of Family Incomes," *The Wall Street Journal,* August 3, 1990, p. B1; "Downscale Consumers, Long Neglected, Start to Get Some Respect from Marketers," *The Wall Street Journal,* May 31, 1990, p. B1ff.

3. U.S. Department of Labor, *Consumer Expenditure Survey 1988–89* (Washington, D.C.: U.S. Government Printing Office, 1991), pp. 15–17; Gail DeWeese and Marjorie J. T. Norton, "Impact of Married Women's Employment on Individual Household Member Expenditures for Clothing," *The Journal of Consumer Affairs,* Winter 1991, pp. 235–57; Margaret Ambry, "The Age of Spending," *American Demographics,* November 1990, pp. 16–23ff.; "What Does It Take to Get Along?" *American Demographics,* May 1990, pp. 36–39.

4. K. H. Chung, *Motivational Theories and Practices* (Columbus, Ohio: Grid, 1977), pp. 40–43; A. H. Maslow, *Motivation and Personality* (New York: Harper & Row, 1970). See also M. Joseph Sirgy, "A Social Cognition Model of Consumer Problem Recognition," *Journal of the Academy of Marketing Science,* Winter 1987, pp. 53–61.

5. "What Works for One Works for All," *Business Week,* April 20, 1992, pp. 112–13.

6. Frances K. McSweeney and Calvin Bierley, "Recent Developments in Classical Conditioning," *Journal of Consumer Research,* September 1984, pp. 619–31; Walter R. Nord and J. Paul Peter, "A Behavior Modification Perspective on Marketing," *Journal of Marketing,* Spring 1980, pp. 36–47; James R. Bettman, "Memory Factors in Consumer Choice: A Review," *Journal of Marketing,* Spring 1979, pp. 37–53; Richard Weijo and Leigh Lawton, "Message Repetition, Experience and Motivation," *Psychology and Marketing,* Fall 1986, pp. 165–80.

7. For just a few references, see Alvin A. Achenbaum, "Advertising Doesn't Manipulate Consumers," *Journal of Advertising Research,* April 1972, pp. 3–14; Sharon E. Beatty and Lynn R. Kahle, "Alternate Hierarchies of the Attitude-Behavior Relationship: The Impact of Brand Commitment and Habit," *Journal of the Academy of Marketing Science,* Summer 1988, pp. 1–10; Calvin P. Duncan and Richard W. Olshavsky, "External Search: The Role of Consumer Beliefs," *Journal of Marketing Research,* February 1982, pp. 32–43; M. Joseph Sirgy, "Self-Concept in Consumer Behavior: A Critical Review," *Journal of Consumer Research,* December 1982, pp. 287–300; Joel E. Urbany, Peter R. Dickson, and William L. Wilkie, "Buyer Uncertainty and Information Search," *Journal of Consumer Research,* September 1989, pp. 208–15.

8. "Americans Flunk Test on Environment," *The Wall Street Journal,* November 8, 1991, p. B3A; "Consciously Green: Consumers Question Marketers' Commitment," *Advertising Age,* September 16, 1991, p. 14; "Americans Passionate about the Environment? Critic Says That's 'Nonsense,' " *Marketing News,* September 16, 1991, p. 8; "Eight of 10 Americans Are Environmentalists, at Least So They Say," *The Wall Street Journal,* August 2, 1991, p. A1ff.; "The Green Marketing Revolution," *Advertising Age,* (Special Issue) January 29, 1991; "How to Deal with Tougher Customers," *Fortune,* December 3, 1990, pp. 38–48; "Consumers Turning Green: JWT Survey," *Advertising Age,* November 12, 1990, p. 74.

9. "Milky Way Light," *Fortune,* February 24, 1992, p. 103; "Labels Lose the Fat," *Advertising Age,* June 10, 1991, p. 3ff.; "Yolkless Dunkin' Donuts," *Fortune,* April 8, 1991, p. 70; "Most Coors Labels Will Drop Claim to Rockies Water," *The Wall Street Journal,* March 15, 1991, p. B3; "FTC Is Cracking Down on Misleading Ads," *The Wall Street Journal,* February 4, 1991, p. B6; "How to Pig Out but Avoid Fat," *Time,* February 5, 1990, p. 65.

10. Harold H. Kassarjian and Mary Jane Sheffet, "Personality and Consumer Behavior: An Update," in H. Kassarjian and T. Robertson, *Perspectives in Consumer Behavior* (Glenview, Ill.: Scott, Foresman,

1981), p. 160; Raymond L. Horton, *Buyer Behavior: A Decision Making Approach* (Columbus, Ohio: Charles E. Merrill, 1984).

11. "Lifestyle Study: Who We Are, How We Live, What We Think," *Advertising Age,* January 20, 1992, pp. 16–18; Robert A. Mittelstaedt, "Economics, Psychology, and the Literature of the Subdiscipline of Consumer Behavior," *Journal of the Academy of Marketing Science,* Fall 1990, pp. 303–12; William D. Danko and Charles M. Schaninger, "An Empirical Evaluation of the Gilly-Enis Updated Household Life Cycle Model," *Journal of Business Research,* August 1990, pp. 39–58; Martha Farnsworth Riche, "Psychographics For the 1990s," *American Demographics,* July 1989, pp. 24–31; W. D. Wells, "Psychographics: A Critical Review," *Journal of Marketing Research,* May 1975, pp. 196–213; Jack A. Lesser and Marie Adele Hughes, "The Generalizability of Psychographic Market Segments Across Geographic Locations," *Journal of Marketing,* January 1986, pp. 18–27.

12. "New VALS 2 Takes Psychological Route," *Advertising Age,* February 13, 1989, p. 24; Lynn R. Kahle, Sharon E. Beatty, and Pamela Homer, "Alternative Measurement Approaches to Consumer Values: The List of Values (LOV) and Values and Life Styles (VALS)," *Journal of Consumer Research,* December 1986, pp. 405–10.

13. "How Spending Changes During Middle Age," *The Wall Street Journal,* January 14, 1992, p. B1; "How the Average American Gets By," *Fortune,* October 21, 1991, pp. 52–64; "Here Come the Brides," *American Demographics,* June 1990, p. 4; "Feathering the Empty Nest," *American Demographics,* June 1990, p. 8; Patrick E. Murphy and William A. Staples, "A Modernized Family Life Cycle," *Journal of Consumer Research,* June 1979, pp. 12–22; William D. Wells and George Gubar, "Life Cycle Concept in Marketing Research," *Journal of Marketing Research,* November 1966, pp. 355–63.

14. "Breaking the Divorce Cycle," *Newsweek,* January 13, 1992, pp. 48–53; "Marrying Age Higher than Ever Before," *USA Today,* June 7, 1991, p. 1D; " 'I Do' Is Repeat Refrain for Half of Newlyweds," *USA Today,* February 15, 1991, p. 1A; "As Baby Boomers Age, Fewer Couples Untie the Knot," *The Wall Street Journal,* November 7, 1990, p. B1ff.; "Delaying Marriage, Time and Again," *The Wall Street Journal,* May 31, 1990, p. B1; "The Life of a Marriage," *American Demographics,* February 1989, p. 12.

15. "What Works for One Works for All," *Business Week,* April 20, 1992, pp. 112–13; "Geritol Extend Goes for the Old," *Adweek's Marketing Week,* February 17, 1992, pp. 30–31; "Ads for Elderly May Give Wrong Message," *The Wall Street Journal,* December 31, 1991, p. B4; "School Days for Seniors," *Newsweek,* November 11, 1991, pp. 60–65; Charles E. Longino, Jr., and William H. Crown, "Older Americans: Rich or Poor?" *American Demographics,* August 1991, pp. 48–53; "Wild at Heart," *Adweek,* July 22, 1991, pp. 21–24; "Designers Try to Get a Grip on Safety Caps," *The Wall Street Journal,* April 9, 1991, p. B1; "Three Strategies for Reaching Older Consumers in the 1990s," *Adweek's Marketing Week,* December 3, 1990, pp. 30–31; "Older Readers Prove Elusive as Magazines Rethink Strategies for the 'Mature Market,' " *The Wall Street Journal,* July 12, 1990, p. B1ff.; "Going for the Gold," *Newsweek,* April 23, 1990, pp. 74–76; John J. Burnett, "Retirement versus Age: Assessing the Efficacy of Retirement as a Segmentation Variable," *Journal of the Academy of Marketing Science,* Fall 1989, pp. 333–44; Ellen Day et al., "Reaching the Senior Citizen Market(s)," *Journal of Advertising Research,* December 1987–January 1988, pp. 23–30.

16. For more on kids' influence in purchase decisions, see William Dunn, "Hanging Out with American Youth," *American Demographics,* February 1992, pp. 24–35; James U. McNeal, "The Littlest Shoppers," *American Demographics,* February 1992, pp. 48–56; "Getting 'Em While They're Young," *Business Week,* September 9, 1991, pp. 94–95. For more on men's influence, see Diane Crispell, "The Brave New World of Men," *American Demographics,* January 1992, pp. 38–43; "Mr. Mom May Be a Force to Reckon With," *The Wall Street Journal,* October 3, 1991, p. B6; Charles Wiles and Anders Tjernlund, "A Comparison of Role Portrayal of Men and Women in Magazine Advertising in the USA and Sweden," *International Journal of Advertising* 10, no. 3 (1991), pp. 259–68; "Special Report: Marketing to Men," *Advertising Age,* April 15, 1991, pp. S1–S12. For more on women's influence, see "Woman's Work Is Never Done," *Newsweek,* July 31, 1989, p. 65; "The Lasting Changes Brought by Women Workers," *Business Week,* March 15, 1982, p. 59–67; Michael D. Reilly, "Working

Wives and Convenience Consumption," *Journal of Consumer Research,* March 1982, pp. 407–18; W. Keith Bryant, "Durables and Wives' Employment Yet Again," *Journal of Consumer Research,* June 1988, pp. 37–47. For more on family decision-making, see Ellen R. Foxman, Patriya S. Tansuhaj, and Karin M. Ekstrom, "Adolescents' Influence in Family Purchase Decisions: A Socialization Perspective," *Journal of Business Research,* March 1989, pp. 159–72; Daniel T. Seymour, "Forced Compliance in Family Decision-Making," *Psychology and Marketing,* Fall 1986, pp. 223–40; Thomas C. O'Guinn, Ronald J. Faber, and Giovann Imperia, "Subcultural Influences on Family Decision Making," *Psychology and Marketing,* Winter 1986, pp. 305–18.

17. George P. Moschis, "Social Comparison and Informal Group Influence," *Journal of Marketing Research,* August 1976, pp. 237–44; James H. Donnelly, Jr., "Social Character and Acceptance of New Products," *Journal of Marketing Research,* February 1970, pp. 111–16; Jeffrey D. Ford and Elwood A. Ellis, "A Reexamination of Group Influence on Member Brand Preference," *Journal of Marketing Research,* February 1980, pp. 125–32; Dennis L. Rosen and Richard W. Olshavsky, "The Dual Role of Informational Social Influence: Implications for Marketing Management," *Journal of Business Research,* April 1987, pp. 123–44.

18. "Survey: If You Must Know, Just Ask One of These Men," *Marketing News,* August 19, 1991, p. 13; James H. Myers and Thomas S. Robertson, "Dimensions of Opinion Leadership," *Journal of Marketing Research,* February 1972, pp. 41–46; Charles W. King and John O. Summers, "Overlap of Opinion Leadership across Consumer Product Categories," *Journal of Marketing Research,* February 1970, pp. 43–50.

19. For an overview of ethnic populations in the United States, see "Immigrant Impact Grows on U.S. Population," *The Wall Street Journal,* March 16, 1992, p. B1; "Cosmetic Firms Wake Up to Minorities," *USA Today,* January 3, 1992, pp. 1B–2B; "Ethnics Gain Market Clout," *Advertising Age,* August 5, 1991, pp. 3ff.; "Classrooms of Babel," *Newsweek,* February 11, 1991, pp. 56–57; "Beyond the Melting Pot," *Time,* April 9, 1990, pp. 28–35. For more on the African-American market, see "Waking Up to a Major Market," *Business Week,* March 23, 1992, pp. 72–73; "Black Middle Class Debates Merits of Cities and Suburbs," *The Wall Street Journal,* August 6, 1991, p. B1ff.; "Special Report: Marketing to African-Americans," *Advertising Age,* July 1, 1991; "Six Myths about Black Consumers," *Adweek's Marketing Week,* May 6, 1991, pp. 16–19; "African-Americans," *Adweek's Marketing Week,* January 21, 1991, pp. 18–21; "A Long Way from 'Aunt Jemima,' " *Newsweek,* August 14, 1989, pp. 34–35; "The Black Middle Class," *Business Week,* March 14, 1988, pp. 62–70. For more on the Hispanic market, see "The United States of Miami," *Adweek's Marketing Week,* July 15, 1991, pp. 19–22; "The New 'Multilingual' Pitch," *Adweek's Marketing Week,* April 22, 1991, p. 35; "Survey Shows Hispanic Diversity," *USA Today,* April 11, 1991, p. 3A; "Hispanic Growth Booms," *USA Today,* February 6, 1991, p. 1Aff.; "Special Report: Marketing to Hispanics," *Advertising Age,* October 15, 1990, pp. 42–47; "In a Society Awash with Coupons, Marketers Try to Reach Hispanics," *The Wall Street Journal,* April 25, 1990, p. B6; "Hispanic Market Strong, but Often Ignored," *Marketing News,* February 19, 1990, p. 1ff.; Humberto Valencia, "Hispanic Values and Subcultural Research," *Journal of the Academy of Marketing Science,* Winter 1989, pp. 23–28. For more on the Asian-American market, see "Taking the Pulse of Asian-Americans," *Adweek's Marketing Week,* August 12, 1991, p. 32; "Suddenly, Asian-Americans Are a Marketer's Dream," *Business Week,* June 17, 1991, pp. 54–55; "Asian-Americans Become More Heterogeneous," *The Wall Street Journal,* March 13, 1991, p. B1.

20. "After Early Stumbles, P&G Is Making Inroads Overseas," *The Wall Street Journal,* February 6, 1989, p. B1.

21. Grant McCracken, "Culture and Consumption: A Theoretical Account of the Structure and Movement of the Cultural Meaning of Consumer Goods," *Journal of Consumer Research,* June 1986, pp. 71–84; Walter A. Henry, "Cultural Values Do Correlate with Consumer Behavior," *Journal of Marketing Research,* May 1976, pp. 121–27. See also Lynn R. Kahle, "The Nine Nations of North America and the Value Basis of Geographic Segmentation," *Journal of Marketing,* April 1986, pp. 37–47.

22. Russell W. Belk, "Situational Variables and Consumer Behavior," *Journal of Consumer Research* 2, 1975, pp. 157–64; John F. Sherry, Jr., "Gift Giving in Anthropological Perspective," *Journal of Consumer Research,* September 1983, pp. 157–68; C. Whan Park, Easwar S. Iyer,

and Daniel C. Smith, "The Effects of Situational Factors on In-Store Grocery Shopping Behavior: The Role of Store Environment and Time Available for Shopping," *Journal of Consumer Research,* March 1989, pp. 422–33.

23. Adapted and updated from James H. Myers and William H. Reynolds, *Consumer Behavior and Marketing Management* (Boston: Houghton Mifflin, 1967), p. 49. See also Judith Lynne Zaichkowsky, "Consumer Behavior: Yesterday, Today, and Tomorrow," *Business Horizons,* May/June 1991, pp. 51–58.

24. Wayne D. Hoyer, "An Examination of Consumer Decision Making for a Common Repeat Purchase Product," *Journal of Consumer Research,* December 1984, pp. 822–29; James R. Bettman, *An Information Processing Theory of Consumer Choice* (Reading, Mass.: Addison-Wesley Publishing, 1979); Richard W. Olshavsky and Donald H. Granbois, "Consumer Decision Making—Fact or Fiction?" *Journal of Consumer Research,* September 1979, pp. 93–100; Lawrence X. Tarpey, Sr., and J. Paul Peter, "A Comparative Analysis of Three Consumer Decision Strategies," *Journal of Consumer Research,* June 1975, pp. 29–37.

25. Raj Arora, "Consumer Involvement—What It Offers to Advertising Strategy," *International Journal of Advertising* 4, no. 2 (1985), pp. 119–30; Don R. Rahtz and David L. Moore, "Product Class Involvement and Purchase Intent," *Psychology and Marketing,* Summer 1989, pp. 113–28; Banwari Mittal, "Measuring Purchase Decision Involvement," *Psychology and Marketing,* Summer 1989, pp. 147–62; James D. Gill, Sanford Grossbart, and Russell N. Laczniak, "Influence of Involvement, Commitment, and Familiarity on Brand Beliefs and Attitudes of Viewers Exposed to Alternative Ad Claims," *Journal of Advertising* 17, no. 2 (1988), pp. 33–43; Marsha L. Richins and Peter H. Bloch, "After the New Wears Off: The Temporal Context of Product Involvement," *Journal of Consumer Research,* September 1986, pp. 280–85.

26. Adapted from E. M. Rogers with F. Shoemaker, *Communication of Innovation: A Cross Cultural Approach* (New York: Free Press, 1968).

27. "3M's Aggressive New Consumer Drive," *Business Week,* July 16, 1984, pp. 114–22.

28. William Cunnings and Mark Venkatesan, "Cognitive Dissonance and Consumer Behavior: A Review of the Evidence," *Journal of Marketing Research,* August 1976, pp. 303–8.

Chapter 7

1. "Japanese Auto Makers Help U.S. Suppliers Become More Efficient," *The Wall Street Journal,* September 9, 1991, p. A1ff.; *1990 Annual Report,* Toyota; David L. Blenkhorn and A. Hamid Noori, "What It Takes to Supply Japanese OEMs," *Industrial Marketing Management,* February, 1990, pp. 21–30.

2. A. Ben Oumlil and Alvin J. Williams, "Market-Driven Procurement," *Industrial Marketing Management* 18, no. 4 (1989), pp. 289–92; Vithala R. Rao and Edward W. McLaughlin, "Modeling the Decision to Add New Products by Channel Intermediaries," *Journal of Marketing,* January, 1989, pp. 80–88; Peter Banting et al., "Similarities in Industrial Procurement Across Four Countries," *Industrial Marketing Management,* May 1985, pp. 133–44; John Seminerio, "What Buyers Like from Salesmen," *Industrial Marketing Management,* May 1985, pp. 75–78; Edward F. Fern and James R. Brown, "The Industrial/Consumer Marketing Dichotomy: A Case of Insufficient Justification," *Journal of Marketing,* Spring 1984, pp. 68–77.

3. John R. G. Jenkins, "Consumer Media as an Information Source for Industrial Products: A Study," *Industrial Marketing Management,* February 1990, pp. 81–86; H. Michael Hayes and Steven W. Hartley, "How Buyers View Industrial Salespeople," *Industrial Marketing Management* 18, no. 2 (1989), pp. 73–80; Barbara C. Perdue, "The Size and Composition of the Buying Firm's Negotiation Team in Rebuys of Component Parts," *Journal of the Academy of Marketing Science,* Spring 1989, pp. 121–28; Erin Anderson, Wujin Chu, and Barton Weitz, "Industrial Purchasing: An Empirical Exploration of the Buy-Class Framework," *Journal of Marketing,* July 1987, pp. 71–86; Rowland T. Moriarty, Jr. and Robert E. Spekman, "An Empirical Investigation of the Information Sources Used During the Industrial Buying Process," *Journal of Marketing Research,* May 1984, pp. 137–47; Joseph A.

Bellizzi and Phillip McVey, "How Valid Is the Buy-Grid Model?" *Industrial Marketing Management,* February 1983, pp. 57−62.

4. M. Bixby Cooper, Cornelia Droge, and Patricia J. Daugherty, "How Buyers and Operations Personnel Evaluate Service," *Industrial Marketing Management* 20, no. 1 (1991), pp. 81−90; Richard Germain and Cornelia Dröge, "Wholesale Operations and Vendor Evaluation," *Journal of Business Research,* September 1990, pp. 119−30; James F. Wolter, Frank R. Bacon, Dale F. Duhan, R. Dale Wilson, "How Designers and Buyers Evaluate Products," *Industrial Marketing Management* 18, no. 2 (1989), pp. 81−90; Jim Shaw, Joe Giglierano, and Jeff Kallis, "Marketing Complex Technical Products: The Importance of Intangible Attributes," *Industrial Marketing Management* 18, no. 1 (1989), pp. 45−54; "Shaping Up Your Suppliers," *Fortune,* April 10, 1989, pp. 116−22; Vincent G. Reuter, "What Good Are Value Analysis Programs?" *Business Horizons,* March/April 1986, pp. 73−79.

5. Richard F. Beltramini, "Exploring the Effectiveness of Business Gifts: A Controlled Field Experiment," *Journal of the Academy of Marketing Science,* Winter 1992, pp. 87−92; I. Fredrick Trawick, John E. Swan, Gail W. McGee, and David R. Rink, "Influence of Buyer Ethics and Salesperson Behavior on Intention to Choose a Supplier," *Journal of the Academy of Marketing Science,* Winter 1991, pp. 17−24; Scott W. Kelley and Michael J. Dorsch, "Ethical Climate, Organizational Commitment, and Indebtedness among Purchasing Executives," *Journal of Personal Selling and Sales Management,* Fall 1991, pp. 55−66; Laura B. Forker, "Purchasing Professionals in State Government: How Ethical Are They?" *Journal of Business Ethics,* November 1990, pp. 903−10; "New Jolt for Nynex: Bawdy 'Conventions' of Buyers, Suppliers," *The Wall Street Journal,* July 12, 1990, p. A1ff.; I. Frederick Trawick, John E. Swan, and David Rink, "Industrial Buyer Evaluation of the Ethics of Salesperson Gift Giving: Value of the Gift and Customer vs. Prospect Status," *Journal of Personal Selling and Sales Management,* Summer 1989, pp. 31−38; "Vendors' Gifts Pose Problems for Purchasers," *The Wall Street Journal,* June 26, 1989, p. B1ff.; Monroe Murphy Bird, "Gift-Giving and Gift-Taking in Industrial Companies," *Industrial Marketing Management* 18, no. 2 (1989), pp. 91−94.

6. Robert D. McWilliams, Earl Naumann, and Stan Scott, "Determining Buying Center Size," *Industrial Marketing Management,* February 1992, pp. 43−50; Herbert E. Brown and Roger W. Brucker, "Charting the Industrial Buying Stream," *Industrial Marketing Management,* February 1990, pp. 55−62; Robert J. Thomas, "Industrial Market Segmentation on Buying Center Purchase Responsibilities," *Journal of the Academy of Marketing Science,* Summer 1989, pp. 243−52; Ajay Kohli, "Determinants of Influence in Organizational Buying: A Contingency Approach," *Journal of Marketing,* July 1989, pp. 50−65; Melvin R. Mattson, "How to Determine the Composition and Influence of a Buying Center," *Industrial Marketing Management,* August 1988, pp. 205−14; Donald L. McCabe, "Buying Group Structure: Constriction at the Top," *Journal of Marketing,* October 1987, pp. 89−98; W. E. Patton III, Christopher P. Puto, and Ronald H. King, "Which Buying Decisions Are Made by Individuals and Not by Groups?" *Industrial Marketing Management,* May 1986, pp. 129−38; Lowell E. Crow and Jay D. Lindquist, "Impact of Organizational and Buyer Characteristics on the Buying Center," *Industrial Marketing Management,* February 1985, pp. 49−58; Donald W. Jackson, Jr., Janet E. Keith, and Richard K. Burdick, "Purchasing Agents' Perceptions of Industrial Buying Center Influence: A Situational Approach," *Journal of Marketing,* Fall 1984, pp. 75−83; Michael H. Morris and Stanley M. Freedman, "Coalitions in Organizational Buying," *Industrial Marketing Management,* May 1984, pp. 123−32; Wesley J. Johnston and Thomas V. Bonoma, "The Buying Center: Structure and Interaction Patterns," *Journal of Marketing,* Summer 1981, pp. 143−56.

7. "Relationships: Six Steps to Success," *Sales and Marketing Management,* April 1992, pp. 50−58; "Suppliers Struggle to Improve Quality as Big Firms Slash Their Vendor Rolls," *The Wall Street Journal,* August 16, 1991, p. B1ff.; "Broken Promises," *Inc.,* July 1991, pp. 25−27; "Close Ties with Suppliers Can Pay for Small Firms," *The Wall Street Journal,* April 3, 1991, p. B1; "Service Enables Nuts-and-Bolts Supplier to Be More than the Sum of Its Parts," *The Wall Street Journal,* November 16, 1990, p. B1ff.; Randy Myer, "Suppliers—Manage Your Customers," *Harvard Business Review,* November/December 1989, pp. 160−72; Peter W. Turnbull and David T. Wilson, "Developing and Protecting Profitable Customer Relationships,"

Industrial Marketing Management 18, no. 3 (1989), pp. 233−40; David N. Burt, "Managing Suppliers Up to Speed," *Harvard Business Review,* July/August 1989, pp. 127−35; "With Customers, the Closer the Better," *Business Marketing,* July, 1989, pp. 68−70; "Machine-Tool Makers Lose Out to Imports Due to Price, Quality," *The Wall Street Journal,* August 17, 1987, p. 1ff.; "Detroit Raises the Ante for Parts Suppliers," *Business Week,* October 14, 1985, pp. 94−97.

8. Madhav N. Segal, "Implications of Single vs. Multiple Buying Sources," *Industrial Marketing Management,* August 1989, pp. 163−78; Peter Kraljic, "Purchasing Must Become Supply Management," *Harvard Business Review,* September/October 1983, pp. 109−17; Christopher P. Puto, Wesley E. Patton III, and Ronald H. King, "Risk Handling Strategies in Industrial Vendor Selection Decisions," *Journal of Marketing,* Winter 1985, pp. 89−98; John L. Graham, "The Problem-Solving Approach to Negotiations in Industrial Marketing," *Journal of Business Research,* December 1986, pp. 549−66.

9. *1991 Annual Report,* Clorox.

10. John W. Henke, Jr., A. Richard Krachenberg, and Thomas F. Lyons, "Competing Against an In-House Supplier," *Industrial Marketing Management* 18, no. 3 (1989), pp. 147−54; Ralph W. Jackson and William M. Pride, "The Use of Approved Vendor Lists," *Industrial Marketing Management,* August 1986, pp. 165−70.

11. For more on JIT, see Paul A. Dion, Peter M. Banting, and Loretta M. Hasey, "The Impact of JIT on Industrial Marketers," *Industrial Marketing Management,* February 1990, pp. 41−46. For more on reciprocity, see "You Buy My Widgets, I'll Buy Your Debt," *Business Week,* August 1, 1988, p. 85. See also Robert E. Weigand, "The Problems of Managing Reciprocity," *California Management Review,* Fall 1973, pp. 40−48.

12. U.S. Bureau of the Census, *County Business Patterns 1989, United States* (Washington, D.C.: U.S. Government Printing Office, 1991); *Information Please Almanac 1992* (Boston, Mass.: Houghton-Mifflin, 1991); U.S. Bureau of the Census, *1987 Census of Manufacturers, Subject Series, Establishment and Firm Size* (Washington, D.C.: U.S. Government Printing Office, 1991); "Looking to Lure Suppliers, USX Plays Up a Town," *The Wall Street Journal,* August 17, 1989, p. B1; "Migratory Habits of the 500," *Fortune,* April 24, 1989, pp. 400−401.

13. For more detail, see "SIC: The System Explained," *Sales and Marketing Management,* April 22, 1985, pp. 52−113; "Enhancement of SIC System Being Developed," *Marketing News Collegiate Edition,* May 1988, p. 4.

14. U.S. Bureau of the Census, *County Business Patterns 1989, United States* (Washington, D.C.: U.S. Government Printing Office, 1991); *1990 Annual Report,* Canon; "Can Anyone Duplicate Canon's Personal Copiers' Success?" *Marketing and Media Decisions,* Special Issue, Spring 1985, pp. 97−101.

15. *1990 Annual Report,* McKesson; "For Drug Distributors, Information Is the Rx for Survival," *Business Week,* October 14, 1985, p. 116; Robert E. Spekman and Wesley J. Johnston, "Relationship Management: Managing the Selling and the Buying Interface," *Journal of Business Research,* December 1986, pp. 519−32.

16. "Create Open-to-Buy Plans the Easy Way," *Retail Control,* December 1984, pp. 21−31.

17. *1990 Annual Report,* Safeway; *1990 Annual Report,* Food Lion; *1990 Annual Report,* Winn-Dixie; Daulatram B. Lund, "Retail Scanner Checkout System: How Buying Committees Functioned," *Industrial Marketing Management* 18, no. 3 (1989), pp. 179−86; Janet Wagner, Richard Ettenson, and Jean Parrish, "Vendor Selection Among Retail Buyers: An Analysis by Merchandise Division," *Journal of Retailing,* Spring 1989, pp. 58−79; "Supermarkets Demand Food Firms' Payments Just to Get on the Shelf," *The Wall Street Journal,* November 1, 1988, p. A1ff. For a historical perspective on supermarket chain buying, see J. F. Grashof, *Information Management for Supermarket Chain Product Mix Decisions,* unpublished doctoral dissertation, Michigan State University, 1968. For more on wholesaler overload, see Dan Hicks, "MEGA Means Superior Service and Super Selection," *Boise Cascade Quarterly,* August 1985, p. 9.

18. Based on U.S. Census data and "How Do You Chase a $17 Billion Market? With Everything You've Got," *Business Week,* November 23, 1987, pp. 120−22; M. Edward Goretsky, "Market Planning for Government Procurement," *Industrial Marketing Management,*

November, 1986, pp. 287–92; Warren H. Suss, "How to Sell to Uncle Sam," *Harvard Business Review,* November/December, 1984, pp. 136–44; M. Edward Goretsky, "When to Bid for Government Contracts," *Industrial Marketing Management,* February 1987, pp. 25–34.

19. Michael G. Harvey and James T. Rothe, "The Foreign Corrupt Practices Act: The Good, the Bad and the Future," in *1983 American Marketing Association Educators' Proceedings,* ed. P. E. Murphy et al. (Chicago: American Marketing Association, 1983), pp. 374–79. See also Massoud M. Saghafi, Fanis Varvoglis, and Tomas Vega, "Why U.S. Firms Don't Buy from Latin American Companies," *Industrial Marketing Management* 20, no. 3 (1991), pp. 207–14; Peter Banting, Jozsef Beracs, and Andrew Gross, "The Industrial Buying Process in Capitalist and Socialist Countries," *Industrial Marketing Management* 20, no. 2 (1991), pp. 105–14.

Chapter 8

1. "P&G Plans All-Family Pert," *Adweek's Marketing Week,* April 20, 1992, p. 6; "How Innovation at P&G Restored Luster to Washed-Up Pert and Made It No. 1," *The Wall Street Journal,* December 6, 1990, p. B1ff.; "Pert Plus' New Rivals," *Advertising Age,* November 12, 1990, p. 4; "Pert Plus Pops to No. 1," *Advertising Age,* March 19, 1990, p. 3ff.; *1990 Annual Report,* Procter & Gamble.

2. "Gurus of Quality Are Gaining Clout," *The Wall Street Journal,* November 27, 1990, p. B1ff.; Ross Johnson and William O. Winchell, *Marketing and Quality* (Milwaukee, WI: American Society for Quality Control, 1989); Joseph J. Belonax, Jr. and Rajshekhar G. Javalgi, "The Influence of Involvement and Product Class Quality on Consumer Choice Sets," *Journal of the Academy of Marketing Science,* Summer 1989, pp. 209–16; Robert Jacobson and David A. Aaker, "The Strategic Role of Product Quality," *Journal of Marketing,* October 1987, pp. 31–44; "Victories in the Quality Crusade," *Fortune,* October 10, 1988, pp. 80–88; John R. Hauser and Don Clausing, "The House of Quality," *Harvard Business Review,* May/June 1988, pp. 63–73; V. K. Shetty, "Product Quality and Competitive Strategy," *Business Horizons,* May/June, 1987, pp. 46–52; Jack Reddy and Abe Berger, "Three Essentials of Product Quality," *Harvard Business Review,* July/August 1983, pp. 153–59; Henry J. Kohoutek, "Coupling Quality Assurance Programs to Marketing," *Industrial Marketing Management,* August 1988, pp. 177–88.

3. *1990 Annual Report,* MCI; *1990 Annual Report,* Merrill Lynch; John Bowen, "Development of a Taxonomy of Services to Gain Strategic Marketing Insights," *Journal of the Academy of Marketing Science,* Winter 1990, pp. 43–50; "America Still Reigns in Services," *Fortune,* June 5, 1989, pp. 64–68; Sak Onkvisit and John J. Shaw, "Service Marketing: Image, Branding, and Competition," *Business Horizons,* January/February 1989, pp. 13–18; "How to Handle Customers' Gripes," *Fortune,* October 24, 1988, pp. 88–100; Leonard L. Berry, A. Parasuraman, and Valarie A. Zeithaml, "The Service-Quality Puzzle," *Business Horizons,* September/October 1988, pp. 35–43; James R. Stock and Paul H. Zinszer, "The Industrial Purchase Decision for Professional Services," *Journal of Business Research,* February 1987, pp. 1–16; Leonard L. Berry, "Services Marketing Is Different," in Christopher H. Lovelock, *Services Marketing* (Englewood Cliffs, N.J.: Prentice Hall, 1984), pp. 29–37; G. Lynn Shostack, "Designing Services That Deliver," *Harvard Business Review,* January/February 1984, pp. 133–39.

4. *1990 Annual Report,* Sara Lee; *1990 Annual Report,* Avis; J. B. Mason and M. L. Mayer, "Empirical Observations of Consumer Behavior as Related to Goods Classification and Retail Strategy," *Journal of Retailing,* Fall 1972, pp. 17–31; Edward M. Tauber, "Why Do People Shop?" *Journal of Marketing,* October 1972, pp. 46–49; Christopher H. Lovelock, "Classifying Services to Gain Strategic Marketing Insights," *Journal of Marketing,* Summer 1983, pp. 9–20.

5. Danny N. Bellenger, Dan H. Robertson, and Elizabeth C. Hirschman, "Impulse Buying Varies by Product," *Journal of Advertising Research,* December 1978, pp. 15–18; Dennis W. Rook, "The Buying Impulse," *Journal of Consumer Research,* September 1987, pp. 189–99; Cathy J. Cobb and Wayne D. Hoyer, "Planned versus Impulse Purchase Behavior," *Journal of Retailing,* Winter 1986, pp. 384–409.

6. William S. Bishop, John L. Graham, and Michael H. Jones, "Volatility of Derived Demand in Industrial Markets and Its Management Implications," *Journal of Marketing,* Fall 1984, pp. 95–103.

7. P. Matthyssens and W. Faes, "OEM Buying Process for New Components: Purchasing and Marketing Implications," *Industrial Marketing Management,* August 1985, pp. 145–57; Ralph W. Jackson and Philip D. Cooper, "Unique Aspects of Marketing Industrial Services," *Industrial Marketing Management,* May 1988, pp. 111–18.

8. Ruth H. Krieger and Jack R. Meredith, "Emergency and Routine MRO Part Buying," *Industrial Marketing Management,* November 1985, pp. 277–82; Warren A. French et al., "MRO Parts Service in the Machine Tool Industry," *Industrial Marketing Management,* November 1985, pp. 283–88.

9. "In Pursuit of the Elusive Euroconsumer," *The Wall Street Journal,* April 23, 1992, p. B1ff.

10. "Picking Pithy Names Is Getting Trickier as Trademark Applications Proliferate," *The Wall Street Journal,* January 14, 1992, p. B1ff.; "Sweeping Trademark Revisions Now in Effect," *Marketing News,* December 18, 1989, p. 2; "Name That Brand," *Fortune,* July 4, 1988, pp. 9–10; "Putting Muscle into Trademark Protection," *Advertising Age,* June 9, 1986, p. S13; Dorothy Cohen, "Trademark Strategy," *Journal of Marketing,* January, 1986, pp. 61–74; George Miaoulis and Nancy D'Amato, "Consumer Confusion and Trademark Infringement," *Journal of Marketing,* April 1978, pp. 48–55; Sak Onkvisit and John J. Shaw, "Service Marketing: Image, Branding, and Competition," *Business Horizons,* January/February 1989, pp. 13–18.

11. "Levi Tries to Round Up Counterfeiters," *The Wall Street Journal,* February 19, 1992, p. B1ff.; "The Patent Pirates Are Finally Walking the Plank," *Business Week,* February 17, 1992, pp. 125–27; "Companies Join Police in Pursuing T-Shirt Bootleggers," *The Wall Street Journal,* September 4, 1991, p. B2; "Whose Bright Idea?" *Time,* June 10, 1991, pp. 44–46; "Trademark Piracy at Home and Abroad," *The Wall Street Journal,* May 7, 1991, p. A22; "How Copycats Steal Billions," *Fortune,* April 22, 1991, pp. 157–64; "Where Trademarks Are Up for Grabs," *The Wall Street Journal,* December 5, 1989, p. B1ff.; Ronald F. Bush, Peter H. Bloch, and Scott Dawson, "Remedies for Product Counterfeiting," *Business Horizons,* January/February 1989, pp. 59–65.

12. "Alien New Product Strategy Lands on Mars," *Adweek's Marketing Week,* December 10, 1990, pp. 22–23. For more on brand extensions, see "Building on Brand Names: Companies Freshen Old Product Lines," *USA Today,* March 20, 1992, p. 1Bff.; "Multiple Varieties of Established Brands Muddle Consumers, Make Retailers Mad," *The Wall Street Journal,* January 24, 1992, p. B1ff.; "Ultimate Brand Extension: In-Store Bank," *The Wall Street Journal,* November 25, 1991, p. B1ff.; "A New Game of Catch for Rawlings," *Adweek's Marketing Week,* July 15, 1991, p. 24; "Spreading Betty's Name Around," *Adweek's Marketing Week,* March 25, 1991, p. 6; "Elmer's Breaks Out of Its Mold with Color," *Adweek's Marketing Week,* March 11, 1991, p. 8; "Häagen-Dazs Adds Frozen-Yogurt Line," *Adweek's Marketing Week,* February 11, 1991, p. 9; "Swiss Army Swells Ranks," *Adweek's Marketing Week,* June 4, 1990, p. 24; "A Tea in Mr. Coffee's Future," *Adweek's Marketing Week,* May 28, 1990, p. 17. For more on the importance of branding, see "A Lock That's Loaded: Kwikset Keys into a Branded Future," *Adweek's Marketing Week,* May 11, 1992; "Brand Loyalty Steady," *Advertising Age,* March 2, 1992, p. 19; "Brands in Trouble," *Advertising Age,* December 2, 1991, pp. 16–18ff.; "What's in a Name? Less and Less," *Business Week,* July 8, 1991, pp. 66–67; Chip Walker, "What's in a Name?" *American Demographics,* February 1991, pp. 54–56; "Name of the Game: Brand Awareness," *The Wall Street Journal,* January 14, 1991, p. B1ff.; "Brand Names Have Cachet in East Bloc," *The Wall Street Journal,* June 27, 1990, p. B1ff.; Leslie de Chernatony and Gil McWilliam, "The Varying Nature of Brands as Assets: Theory and Practice Compared," *International Journal of Advertising* 8, no. 4 (1989), pp. 339–50.

13. "Sunkist, a Pioneer in New Product Promotions," *Advertising Age,* November 9, 1988, p. 22ff. For more on licensing, see "Corporate Licensing Grows as Firms Seek 'Risk-Free' Products," *Marketing News,* April 29, 1991, p. 1ff.; "The 1990 Advertising Age Marketer's Resource to Licensing," (special supplement) *Advertising Age,* May 28, 1990; "Nestlé, Disney Team Abroad," *Advertising Age,* January 15, 1990, p. 1ff.; "Special Report: Licensing," *Advertising Age,* June 6, 1988, pp. S1–S6; "What's in a Name? Millions, if It's Licensed," *Business Week,* April 8, 1985, pp. 97–98.

14. "Brand Managers: '90s Dinosaurs?" *Advertising Age,* December 19, 1988, p. 19; "The Marketing Revolution at Procter & Gamble," *Business Week,* July 25, 1988, pp. 72–76; "P&G Widens Power Base—Adds Category Managers," *Advertising Age,* October 12, 1987, p. 1ff.; "P&G Creates New Posts in Latest Step to Alter How Firm Manages Its Brands," *The Wall Street Journal,* October 12, 1987, p. 6; "P&G Makes Changes in the Way It Develops and Sells Its Products," *The Wall Street Journal,* August 11, 1987, p. 1ff.; "Brand Managers Shelved?" *Advertising Age,* July 13, 1987, p. 81.

15. "Drugs: What's in a Name Brand? Less and Less," *Business Week,* December 5, 1988, pp. 172–76; "Ten Years May Be Generic Lifetime," *Advertising Age,* March 23, 1987, p. 76; Brian F. Harris and Roger A. Strang, "Marketing Strategies in the Age of Generics," *Journal of Marketing,* Fall 1985, pp. 70–81; "No-Frills Products: 'An Idea Whose Time Has Gone,' " *Business Week,* June 17, 1985, pp. 64–65; Martha R. McEnally and Jon M. Hawes, "The Market for Generic Brand Grocery Products: A Review and Extension," *Journal of Marketing,* Winter 1984, pp. 75–83.

16. "Supermarkets Push Private-Label Lines," *The Wall Street Journal,* November 15, 1988, p. B1; "Clothing Retailers Stress Private Labels," *The Wall Street Journal,* June 9, 1988, p. 33; "Fighting the Goliaths," *Advertising Age,* August 3, 1987, p. 24ff.; J. A. Bellizzi et al., "Consumer Perceptions of National, Private, and Generic Brands," *Journal of Retailing* 57 (1981), pp. 56–70; Walter J. Salmon and Karen A. Cmar, "Private Labels Are Back in Fashion," *Harvard Business Review,* May/June 1987, pp. 99–106.

17. "Beyond the Pump: A New Crest Dispenser," *The Wall Street Journal,* May 8, 1991, p. B1; "Romancing the Package," *Adweek's Marketing Week,* January 21, 1991, pp. 10–14; "Folgers Puts Coffee in the Bag," *Advertising Age,* January 21, 1991, p. 3ff.; "Pop-Open Packages for a Hurried Populace," *The Wall Street Journal,* April 2, 1990, p. B1; "Special Report: Packaging," *Advertising Age,* December 12, 1988, p. S1–S4; "Why the Heat-and-Eat Market Is Really Cooking," *Business Week,* June 27, 1988, pp. 90–91.

18. "UPC Registers Retailing Impact," *Advertising Age,* April 7, 1986, p. 3ff.; "Bar Codes: Beyond the Checkout Counter," *Business Week,* April 8, 1985, p. 90; "Bar Codes are Black-and-White Stripes and Soon They Will Be Read All Over," *The Wall Street Journal,* January 8, 1985, p. 39; "Firms Line Up to Check Out Bar Codes," *USA Today,* December 4, 1985, pp. B1–2.

19. For a discussion of one effort toward social responsibility, see "CD Marketers Will Eliminate Paper Packaging," *The Wall Street Journal,* February 28, 1992, p. B1ff.; "New CD Packages Cut Down on Trash," *The Wall Street Journal,* October 10, 1990, p. B1. For discussion of another effort, see "Shed the Egg, Spare the Image," *Adweek's Marketing Week,* July 15, 1991, p. 9; "L'eggs Egg Cracks," *Advertising Age,* July 15, 1991, p. 16. For additional discussion, see " 'Green' Packaging that Works," *Adweek's Marketing Week,* December 2, 1991, pp. 28–29; "Downy Refill Makes a Splash on Shelves," *Advertising Age,* July 8, 1991, p. 16; "Toiletries to Strip Excess Packaging," *Advertising Age,* May 13, 1991, p. 3; "States Debate Solid Waste Bills," *Food Business,* May 6, 1991, pp. 22–23; James H. Barnes, Jr., "Recycling: A Problem in Reverse Logistics," *Journal of Macromarketing* 2, no. 2 (1982), pp. 31–37.

20. For more on downsizing, see "State AGs Attack Downsized Brands," *Advertising Age,* February 18, 1991, p. 1ff.; "Incredible Shrinking Products," *USA Today,* February 7, 1991, p. 8B; "Critics Call Cuts in Package Size Deceptive Move," *The Wall Street Journal,* February 5, 1991, p. B1ff.; " 'Shrinking' the Brand to Fit the Hard Times," *Adweek's Marketing Week,* November 26, 1990, p. 6. For more discussion on disposable products, see "Disposing of the Green Myth," *Adweek's Marketing Week,* April 13, 1992, pp. 20–21; "The Waste Land," *Adweek,* November 11, 1991, p. 26; "Ridding the Nation of Polystyrene Peanuts," *Adweek's Marketing Week,* October 22, 1990, p. 17; "Convenience Packaging Continues to Pile Up," *The Wall Street Journal,* August 7, 1990, p. B1; "Package Firms Find It's Hard Being 'Green,' " *The Wall Street Journal,* May 25, 1990, p. B1ff. For more on product labeling, see " 'Adjectival' Food Label Gets High Marks," *USA Today,* June 24, 1991, p. 1D; "Group Criticizes FDA Approach on Food Labels," *The Wall Street Journal,* June 7, 1991, p. B3; "Shoppers Value Food's Nutrition Label over Price," *USA Today,* April 11, 1991, p. 1D; "Warning Labels on Alcohol: Just What Is 'Prominent?' " *The Wall Street Journal,* May 4, 1989, p. B1; Dennis L. McNeill and William L. Wilkie, "Public Policy and Consumer Information: Impact of the New Energy Labels," *Journal of Consumer Research,* June 1979, pp. 1–11.

21. J. E. Russo, "The Value of Unit Price Information," *Journal of Marketing Research,* May 1977, pp. 193–201; David A. Aaker and Gary T. Ford, "Unit Pricing Ten Years Later: A Replication," *Journal of Marketing,* Winter 1983, pp. 118–22.

22. Scott W. Kelley, "Developing Customer Orientation among Service Employees," *Journal of the Academy of Marketing Science,* Winter 1992, pp. 27–36; "More Firms Pledge Guaranteed Service," *The Wall Street Journal,* July 17, 1991, p. B1ff.; "Satisfaction Guaranteed for Customers and Crew," *The Wall Street Journal,* January 28, 1991, p. A10; Timothy W. Firnstahl, "My Employees Are My Service Guarantee," *Harvard Business Review,* July/August 1989, pp. 28–37.

23. "Volkswagen Offers Consumer Protection," *Adweek's Marketing Week,* February 3, 1992, p. 5; "Service Dealers Complain about Warranty Business," *The Wall Street Journal,* February 20, 1992, p. B2; "Sears Offers KidVantage," *Advertising Age,* July 22, 1991, p. 30; "Fine Print Can Make a Guarantee Not So Fine," *The Wall Street Journal,* July 17, 1991, p. B1; Craig A. Kelley and Jeffrey S. Conant, "Extended Warranties: Consumer and Manufacturer Perceptions," *The Journal of Consumer Affairs,* Summer 1991, pp. 68–83; Joshua Lyle Wiener, "Are Warranties Accurate Signals of Product Reliability?" *Journal of Consumer Research,* September 1985, p. 245ff.; Laurence P. Feldman, "New Legislation and the Prospects for Real Warranty Reform," *Journal of Marketing,* July 1976, pp. 41–47; F. K. Shuptrine and Ellen Moore, "Even after the Magnuson-Moss Act of 1975, Warranties Are Not Easy to Understand," *Journal of Consumer Affairs,* Winter 1980, pp. 394–404; C. L. Kendall and Frederick A. Russ, "Warranty and Complaint Policies: An Opportunity for Marketing Management," *Journal of Marketing,* April 1975, pp. 36–43; Craig A. Kelley, "An Investigation of Consumer Product Warranties as Market Signals of Product Reliability," *Journal of the Academy of Marketing Science,* Summer 1988, p. 72ff.

Chapter 9

1. "Toward a Better 'Peanut,' " *Adweek's Marketing Week,* August 5, 1991, p. 26; "100% Biodegradable Interior Cushioning Material: Storopack Introduces Renature," news release (Cincinnati, Ohio: Storopack U.S.A., July 8, 1991); "Camcorder Makers, with Growth Easing, Try to Bring New Markets into the Picture," *The Wall Street Journal,* December 26, 1991, p. B1ff.; "Telephone Companies Hope 'Voice Mail' Will Make Answering Machines Obsolete," *The Wall Street Journal,* July 23, 1991, p. B1ff.; "Pen-based Notebooks Find Their Niche," *Datamation,* October 1, 1991, pp. 44–46; "Pen PCs Are Making Big Mark," *USA Today,* June 21, 1991, pp. 1B–2B; "Hot New PCs that Read Your Writing," *Fortune,* February 11, 1991, pp. 113–18ff.; "Disc, DAT and D'Other Things," *Time,* January 14, 1991, p. 44.

2. George Day, "The Product Life Cycle: Analysis and Applications Issues," *Journal of Marketing,* Fall 1981, pp. 60–67; John E. Swan and David R. Rink, "Fitting Marketing Strategy to Varying Product Life Cycles," *Business Horizons,* January/February 1982, pp. 72–76; Igal Ayal, "International Product Life Cycle: A Reassessment and Product Policy Implications," *Journal of Marketing,* Fall 1981, pp. 91–96; George W. Potts, "Exploit Your Product's Service Life Cycle," *Harvard Business Review,* September/October, 1988, pp. 32–39; Roger C. Bennett and Robert G. Cooper, "The Product Life Cycle Trap," *Business Horizons,* September/October 1984, pp. 7–16; Sak Onkvisit and John J. Shaw, "Competition and Product Management: Can the Product Life Cycle Help?" *Business Horizons,* July/August 1986, pp. 51–62; Mary Lambkin and George S. Day, "Evolutionary Processes in Competitive Markets: Beyond the Product Life Cycle," *Journal of Marketing,* July 1989, pp. 4–20.

3. Jorge Alberto Sousa De Vasconcellos, "Key Success Factors in Marketing Mature Products," *Industrial Marketing Management* 20, no. 4 (1991), pp. 263–78; Paul C. N. Michell, Peter Quinn, and Edward Percival, "Marketing Strategies for Mature Industrial Products," *Industrial Marketing Management* 20, no. 3 (1991), pp. 201–6; "Computers Become a Kind of Commodity, to Dismay of Makers," *The Wall Street Journal,* September 5, 1991, p. A1ff.; "Sales of Major Appliances, TV

Sets Gain but Profits Fail to Keep Up: Gap May Widen," *The Wall Street Journal,* August 21, 1972, p. 22; "What Do You Do When Snowmobiles Go on a Steep Slide?" *The Wall Street Journal,* March 8, 1978, p. 1ff; "After Their Slow Year, Fast-Food Chains Use Ploys to Speed Up Sales," *The Wall Street Journal,* April 4, 1980, p. 1ff.; "Home Smoke Detectors Fall on Hard Times as Sales Apparently Peaked," *The Wall Street Journal,* April 3, 1980, p. 1; "As Once Bright Market for CAT Scanners Dims, Smaller Makers of the X-Ray Devices Fade Out," *The Wall Street Journal,* May 6, 1980, p. 40.

4. U.S. Bureau of the Census, *Statistical Abstract of the United States 1991* (Washington, D.C.: U.S. Government Printing Office, 1991), p. 844.

5. "A Sweet Case of the 'Blahs,' " *Advertising Age,* May 27, 1991, p. 3; "NutraSweet Launches New Ads," *Adweek's Marketing Week,* May 20, 1991, p. 6; "NutraSweet Tries Being More of a Sweetie," *Business Week,* April 8, 1991, p. 88; "NutraSweet Rivals Stirring," *Advertising Age,* June 26, 1989, p. 3ff.; "Calories and Cash: Sugar and Its Substitutes Fight for an $8 Billion Market," *Newsweek,* August 26, 1985, p. 54ff; "Searle Fights to Keep Red-Hot Aspartame Hot for a Long Time," *The Wall Street Journal,* September 18, 1984, p. 1ff.

6. "The Patent Pirates Are Finally Walking the Plank," *Business Week,* February 17, 1992, pp. 125–27; "Is It Time to Reinvent the Patent System?" *Business Week,* December 2, 1991, pp. 110–15; "Software Makers Are Pursuing 'Pirates' around the Globe with Fleets of Lawyers," *The Wall Street Journal,* December 13, 1990, p. B1ff.; Karen Bronikowski, "Speeding New Products to Market," *The Journal of Business Strategy,* September/October 1990, pp. 34–37; "How Managers Can Succeed through Speed," *Fortune,* February 13, 1989, pp. 54–59; "Going on the Offense: U.S. Manufacturers Belatedly Take Steps to Protect Product Lines from Imitators," *The Wall Street Journal,* November 14, 1988, p. R37ff.; "How Xerox Speeds Up the Birth of New Products," *Business Week,* March 19, 1984, pp. 58–59.

7. "Sony Isn't Mourning the 'Death' of Betamax," *Business Week,* January 25, 1988, p. 37; "Sony to Begin Selling VCRs in VHS Format," *The Wall Street Journal,* January 12, 1988, p. 39; Steven P. Schnaars, "When Entering Growth Markets, Are Pioneers Better than Poachers?" *Business Horizons,* March/April 1986, pp. 27–36.

8. "The Winning Organization," *Fortune,* September 26, 1988, pp. 50–58.

9. "Inside Nabisco's Cookie Machine," *Adweek's Marketing Week,* March 18, 1991, pp. 22–23; "Nabisco Unleashes a New Batch of Teddies," *Adweek's Marketing Week,* September 24, 1990, p. 18; *1990 Annual Report,* RJR Nabisco; "Making Breakfast Bear-Able," *Advertising Age,* October 16, 1989, p. 3ff.

10. Geoffrey L. Gordon, Roger J. Calantone, and C. Anthony di Benedetto, "Mature Markets and Revitalization Strategies: An American Fable," *Business Horizons,* May/June 1991, pp. 39–50; "Teflon Is 50 Years Old, but Du Pont Is Still Finding New Uses for Invention," *The Wall Street Journal,* April 7, 1988, p. 34; William Lazer, Mushtaq Luqmani, and Zahir Quraeshi, "Product Rejuvenation Strategies," *Business Horizons,* November/December 1984, pp. 21–28; "Ten Ways to Restore Vitality to Old, Worn-Out Products," *The Wall Street Journal,* February 18, 1982, p. 25; Patrick M. Dunne, "What Really Are New Products," *Journal of Business,* December, 1974, pp. 20–25.

11. "Smart Toothbrush," *Fortune,* November 4, 1991, p. 168; "Toothbrush Makers Hope to Clean Up with Array of 'New, Improved' Products," *The Wall Street Journal,* October 22, 1991, p. B1ff; "From Making Hearts to Winning Them," *Business Week,* November 16, 1987, pp. 153–56; "Alza Finally Finds a Cure for Losses," *Fortune,* April 28, 1986, p. 80.

12. "Multiple Varieties of Established Brands Muddle Consumers, Make Retailers Mad," *The Wall Street Journal,* January 24, 1992, p. B1ff.; "Do Americans Have Too Many Brands?" *Adweek's Marketing Week,* December 9, 1991, pp. 14–15; "Kimberly-Clark Bets, Wins on Innovation," *The Wall Street Journal,* November 22, 1991, p. A5; "Diaper Derby Heats Up as Firms Add Color, Frills," *The Wall Street Journal,* May 9, 1989, p. B1; "Burroughs Wellcome Reaps Profits, Outrage from Its AIDS Drug," *The Wall Street Journal,* September 15, 1989, p. A1ff.

13. "New-Product Troubles Have Firms Cutting Back," *The Wall Street Journal,* January 13, 1992, p. B1; "It Costs a Bundle to Get New Items Out," *Insight,* November 19, 1990, p. 45; G. Dean Kortge and Patrick A. Okonkwo, "Simultaneous New Product Development: Reducing the New Product Failure Rate," *Industrial Marketing Management* 18, no. 4 (1989), pp. 301–6; "Firms Grow More Cautious About New-Product Plans," *The Wall Street Journal,* March 9, 1989, p. B1.

14. "The 'Bloodbath' in Market Research," *Business Week,* February 11, 1991, pp. 72–74; "Why New Products Fail," *Adweek's Marketing Week,* November 5, 1990, pp. 20–25; Sharad Sarin and Gour M. Kapur, "Lessons From New Product Failures: Five Case Studies," *Industrial Marketing Management,* November 1990, pp. 301–14; "Diaper's Failure Shows How Poor Plans, Unexpected Woes Can Kill New Products," *The Wall Street Journal,* October 9, 1990, p. B1ff. See also Albert V. Bruno and Joel K. Leidecker, "Causes of New Venture Failure: 1960s vs. 1980s," *Business Horizons,* November/December 1988, pp. 51–56; Peter L. Link, "Keys to New Product Success and Failure," *Industrial Marketing Management,* May 1987, pp. 109–18.

15. "Suddenly, Hewlett-Packard Is Doing Everything Right," *Business Week,* March 23, 1992, pp. 88–89; "Closing the Innovation Gap," *Fortune,* December 2, 1991, pp. 56–62; "The Racy Viper Is Already a Winner for Chrysler," *Business Week,* November 4, 1991, pp. 36–38; "Deliberately Crude, Models Roar Appeal," *USA Today,* November 1, 1991, pp. 1B–2B; "IBM Bends Its Rules to Make a Laptop," *The Wall Street Journal,* April 15, 1991, p. A9B; "Turning R&D into Real Products," *Fortune,* July 2, 1990, pp. 72–77; "Manufacturers Strive and Slice Time Needed to Develop Products," *The Wall Street Journal,* February 23, 1988, p. 1ff.

16. Adapted from Frank R. Bacon, Jr., and Thomas W. Butler, Jr., *Planned Innovation,* rev. ed. (Ann Arbor: Institute of Science and Technology, University of Michigan, 1980). See also Linda Rochford, "Generating and Screening New Product Ideas," *Industrial Marketing Management* 20, no. 4 (1991), pp. 287–96; "Task Force for New Products," *Business Marketing,* July 1991, pp. 34–36; Robert G. Cooper and Elko J. Kleinschmidt, "New Product Processes at Leading Industrial Firms," *Industrial Marketing Management* 20, no. 2 (1991), pp. 137–48; "Product Development: Where Planning and Marketing Meet," *The Journal of Business Strategy,* September/October 1990, pp. 13–17; Massoud M. Saghafi, Ashok Gupta, and Jagdish N. Sheth, "R & D/Marketing Interfaces in the Telecommunications Industry," *Industrial Marketing Management,* February 1990, pp. 87–95; F. Axel Johne and Patricia A. Snelson, "Product Development Approaches in Established Firms," *Industrial Marketing Management,* May 1989, pp. 113–24; Gordon R. Foxall, "User Initiated Product Innovations," *Industrial Marketing Management,* May 1989, pp. 95–104; David T. Wilson and Morry Ghingold, "Linking R&D to Market Needs," *Industrial Marketing Management,* August 1987, pp. 207–14; G. Urban and J. Hauser, *Design and Marketing of New Products* (Englewood Cliffs, N.J.: Prentice Hall, 1990); "Listening to the Voice of the Marketplace," *Business Week,* February 21, 1983, p. 90ff.

17. "How to Let Innovation Happen," *Industry Week,* March 16, 1992, p. 43; "Striking Gold with the Explorer," *Adweek's Marketing Week,* January 14, 1991, pp. 20–21; Eric von Hippel, *The Sources of Innovation* (New York: Oxford University Press, 1988); Shelby H. McIntyre, "Obstacles to Corporate Innovation," *Business Horizons,* January/February 1982, pp. 23–28; "Cutting Costs without Killing the Business," *Fortune,* October 13, 1986, pp. 70–78.

18. "U.S. Companies Shop Abroad for Product Ideas," *The Wall Street Journal,* March 14, 1990, p. B1ff.

19. "Consumers Start Telling It to the Judge: They're Challenging Japan's Legal Shields," *Business Week,* March 9, 1992, p. 50; "Product Suits Yield Few Punitive Awards," *The Wall Street Journal,* January 6, 1992, p. B1; "The Class Action against Product-Liability Laws," *Business Week,* July 29, 1991, pp. 74–76; Frances E. Zollers and Ronald G. Cook, "Product Liability Reform: What Happened to the Crisis?" *Business Horizons,* September/October 1990, pp. 47–52; Marisa Manley, "Product Liability: You're More Exposed than You Think," *Harvard Business Review,* September/October, 1987, pp. 28–41; Phillip E. Downs and Douglas N. Behrman, "The Products Liability Coordinator: A Partial Solution," *Journal of the Academy of Marketing Science,* Fall 1990, p. 66ff.; T. M. Dworkin and M. J. Sheffet, "Product Liability in the 80s," *Journal of Public Policy and Marketing* 4 (1985), pp. 69–79; "When Products Turn Liabilities," *Fortune,* March 3, 1986, pp. 20–24; Fred W. Morgan, "Marketing and Product Liability: A Review and Update," *Journal of Marketing,* Summer 1982, pp. 69–78; Ronald J.

Adams and John M. Browning, "Product Liability in Industrial Markets," *Industrial Marketing Management,* November 1986, pp. 265–72.

20. "Want Shelf Space at the Supermarket? Ante Up," *Business Week,* August 7, 1989, pp. 60–61; "Grocer 'Fee' Hampers New-Product Launches," *Advertising Age,* August 3, 1987, p. 1ff.

21. Adapted from Frank R. Bacon, Jr., and Thomas W. Butler, Jr., *Planned Innovation,* rev. ed. (Ann Arbor: Institute of Science and Technology, University of Michigan, 1980).

22. "A Smarter Way to Manufacture," *Business Week,* April 30, 1990, pp. 110–17; "Oops! Marketers Blunder Their Way Through the 'Herb Decade,' " *Advertising Age,* February 13, 1989, p. 3ff.

23. "The Cutting Edge," *The Wall Street Journal,* April 6, 1992, p. R6; "How the King Maintains His Edge," *The Wall Street Journal,* April 23, 1990, p. A14; "It's One Sharp Ad Campaign, But Where's the Blade?" *Business Week,* March 5, 1990, p. 30; "How a $4 Razor Ends Up Costing $300 Million," *Business Week,* January 29, 1990, pp. 62–63; "International Ad Effort to Back Gillette Sensor," *Advertising Age,* October 16, 1989, p. 34; "Gillette Readies Sensor," *Advertising Age,* September 18, 1989, p. 1ff.; "At Gillette, Disposable Is a Dirty Word," *Business Week,* May 29, 1989, pp. 54–58; "A Recovering Gillette Hopes for Vindication in a High-Tech Razor," *The Wall Street Journal,* September 29, 1989, p. A1ff.

24. "Oops! Marketers Blunder Their Way through the 'Herb Decade,' " *Advertising Age,* February 13, 1989, p. 3ff.

25. "The Company Store: How to Test Market for Fun and Profit," *Inc.,* November 1989, pp. 153–55; "Test Marketing—The Next Generation," *Nielsen Researcher,* no. 3 (1984), pp. 21–23; "Test Marketing Enters a New Era," *Dun's Business Month,* October 1985, p. 86ff.; Steven H. Star and Glen L. Urban, "The Case of the Test Market Toss-Up," *Harvard Business Review,* September/October, 1988, pp. 10–27.

26. "3M Run Scared? Forget about It," *Business Week,* September 16, 1991, p. 59ff.; "How 3M, by Tiptoeing into Foreign Markets, Became a Big Exporter," *The Wall Street Journal,* March 29, 1991, p. A1ff.; "The 'Scotch Tape Company' Embraces Home Repair," *Adweek's Marketing Week,* February 5, 1990, pp. 20–21; *1990 Annual Report,* 3M; "Masters of Innovation," *Business Week,* April 10, 1989, pp. 58–67.

27. Peter F. Drucker, "A Prescription for Entrepreneurial Management," *Industry Week,* April 29, 1985, p. 33ff.; E. F. McDonough III and F. C. Spital, "Quick-Response New Product Development," *Harvard Business Review,* September/October 1984, pp. 52–61.

28. Gloria Barczak and David Wilemon, "Successful New Product Team Leaders," *Industrial Marketing Management,* February 1992, pp. 61–68; Don Frey, "Learning the Ropes: My Life as a Product Champion," *Harvard Business Review,* September/October 1991, pp. 46–57; "Brand Managers: The Buck Stops Here," *Food Business,* May 6, 1991, pp. 33–34; "Brand Managing's New Accent," *Adweek's Marketing Week,* April 15, 1991, pp. 18–22; "P&G Keen Again on Ad Managers," *Advertising Age,* September 25, 1989, p. 6; "RJR Trying Brand 'Teams,' " *Advertising Age,* August 14, 1989, p. 1ff.; Robert W. Eckles and Timothy J. Novotny, "Industrial Product Managers: Authority and Responsibility," *Industrial Marketing Management,* May 1984, pp. 71–76; William Theodore Cummings, Donald W. Jackson, Jr., and Lonnie L. Ostrom, "Differences between Industrial and Consumer Product Managers," *Industrial Marketing Management,* August 1984, pp. 171–80; Thomas J. Cosse and John E. Swan, "Strategic Marketing Planning by Product Managers—Room for Improvement?" *Journal of Marketing,* Summer 1983, pp. 92–102; P. L. Dawes and P. G. Patterson, "The Performance of Industrial and Consumer Product Managers," *Industrial Marketing Management,* February 1988, pp. 73–84.

Chapter 10

1. "Goodyear Is Gunning Its Marketing Engine," *Business Week,* March 16, 1992, p. 42; "Gault Turns Goodyear's Debt to Profit," *USA Today,* March 16, 1992, pp. 1B–2B; "Goodyear Plans to Sell Its Tires at Sears Stores," *The Wall Street Journal,* March 3, 1992, p. B1ff.; "Goodyear's Go-Getting Gault Just Never Seems to Tire," *The Wall Street Journal,* January 28, 1992, p. B4; "Tire Makers Are Traveling Bumpy Road as Car Sales Fall, Foreign Firms Expand," *The Wall Street Journal,* September 19, 1990, p. B1ff.; "After a Year of Spinning Its Wheels, Goodyear Gets a Retread," *Business Week,* March 26, 1990,

pp. 56–58; "Goodyear's Race with Michelin: Burning Rubber to Be No. 1," *Insight,* May 7, 1990, pp. 36–39; *1990 Annual Report,* Goodyear; "Goodyear Squares Off to Protect Its Turf from Foreign Rivals," *The Wall Street Journal,* December 29, 1989, p. A1ff.

2. For a discussion of the advantages and disadvantages of direct-channel systems, see Bert Rosenbloom, *Marketing Channels: A Managerial View* (Chicago: Dryden Press, 1987); Kenneth G. Hardy and Allan J. McGrath, *Marketing Channel Management* (Glenview, Ill.: Scott, Foresman, 1988). See also David Shipley, Colin Egan, and Scott Edgett, "Meeting Source Selection Criteria: Direct versus Distributor Channels," *Industrial Marketing Management* 20, no. 4 (1991), pp. 297–304; Thomas L. Powers, "Industrial Distribution Options: Trade-Offs to Consider," *Industrial Marketing Management* 18, no. 3 (1989), pp. 155–62.

3. Edward L. Nash, *Direct Marketing* (New York: McGraw-Hill, 1986).

4. For a discussion of indirect-channel systems, see Louis W. Stern, Adel I. El-Ansary, and James R. Brown, *Management in Marketing Channels* (Englewood Cliffs, NJ: Prentice Hall, 1989). See also Neil S. Novich, "Leading-Edge Distribution Strategies," *The Journal of Business Strategy,* November/December 1990, pp. 48–53; Donald B. Rosenfield, "Storefront Distribution for Industrial Products," *Harvard Business Review,* July/August 1989, pp. 44–49.

5. For a classic discussion of the discrepancy concepts, see Wroe Alderson, "Factors Governing the Development of Marketing Channels," in *Marketing Channels for Manufactured Goods,* ed. Richard M. Clewett (Homewood, Ill.: Richard D. Irwin, 1954), pp. 7–9. See also "Distributors: No Endangered Species," *Industry Week,* January 24, 1983, pp. 47–52; "Coke in the Cooler? Fountain Device Targets Small Offices," *Advertising Age,* November 28, 1988, p. B1; "Coke Unveils Compact Dispenser, Hoping to Sell More Soft Drinks in Small Offices," *The Wall Street Journal,* November 17, 1988, p. B1; Louis W. Stern and Frederick D. Sturdivant, "Customer-Driven Distribution Systems," *Harvard Business Review,* July/August 1987, pp. 34–41.

6. "PC Slump? What PC Slump?" *Business Week,* July 1, 1991, pp. 66–67; "Mail-Order Computers Can Be Bargains, but Some Firms Don't Deliver on Claims," *The Wall Street Journal,* October 4, 1990, p. B1ff.; "A Golden Age for Entrepreneurs," *Fortune,* February 12, 1990, pp. 120–25.

7. Arun Sharma and Luis V. Dominguez, "Channel Evolution: A Framework for Analysis," *Journal of the Academy of Marketing Science,* Winter 1992, pp. 1–16; Teresa Jaworska, "Channel Members' Behavior in Industrial Markets in Poland," *Journal of Business Research,* January 1992, pp. 51–56; B. Ramaseshan and Leyland F. Pitt, "Major Industrial Distribution Issues Facing Managers in Australia," *Industrial Marketing Management,* August 1990, pp. 225–34; *1990 Annual Report,* Wal-Mart; N. Mohan Reddy and Michael P. Marvin, "Developing a Manufacturer-Distributor Information Partnership," *Industrial Marketing Management,* May 1986, pp. 157–64; Gul Butaney and Lawrence H. Wortzel, "Distributor Power versus Manufacturer Power: The Customer Role," *Journal of Marketing,* January 1988, pp. 52–63; Bruce J. Walker, Janet E. Keith, and Donald W. Jackson, Jr., "The Channels Manager: Now, Soon or Never?" *Academy of Marketing Science,* Summer 1985, pp. 82–96; Patrick L. Schul, William M. Pride, and Taylor L. Little, "The Impact of Channel Leadership Behavior on Intrachannel Conflict," *Journal of Marketing,* Summer 1983, pp. 21–34; Bert Rosenbloom and Rolph Anderson, "Channel Management and Sales Management: Some Key Interfaces," *Academy of Marketing Science,* Summer 1985, pp. 97–106; Roy D. Howell et al., "Unauthorized Channels of Distribution: Gray Markets," *Industrial Marketing Management,* November, 1986, pp. 257–64.

8. "Pet-Food Makers Are Trying to Entice Dog, Cat Owners with Healthier Fare," *The Wall Street Journal,* August 16, 1991, p. B4B; "New Pet Food Scrap in Supermarkets," *Advertising Age,* January 28, 1991, p. 3ff.; *1990 Annual Report,* Colgate-Palmolive; "Pet Food Moves Upscale—and Profits Fatten," *Business Week,* June 15, 1987, pp. 80–82.

9. Saul Klein, "A Transaction Cost Explanation of Vertical Control in International Markets," *Journal of the Academy of Marketing Science,* Summer 1989, pp. 253–60; "Beer and Antitrust," *Fortune,* December 9, 1985, pp. 135–36; "Car Megadealers Loosen Detroit's Tight Rein," *The Wall Street Journal,* July 1, 1985, p. 6; Wilke D. English and Donald A. Michie, "The Impact of Electronic Technology upon the Marketing

Channel," *Academy of Marketing Science,* Summer 1985, pp. 57–71; Robert D. Buzzell, "Is Vertical Integration Profitable?" *Harvard Business Review,* January/February 1983, pp. 92–102; Michael Etgar and Aharon Valency, "Determinants of the Use of Contracts in Conventional Marketing Channels," *Journal of Retailing,* Winter 1983, pp. 81–92; "Why Manufacturers Are Doubling as Distributors," *Business Week,* January 17, 1983, p. 41; Louis W. Stern and Torger Reve, "Distribution Channels as Political Economies: A Framework for Comparative Analysis," *Journal of Marketing,* Summer 1980, pp. 52–64.

10. "Esprit's Spirited Style Is Hot Seller," *USA Today,* March 25, 1986, p. B5; "Apparel Firm Makes Profits, Takes Risks by Flouting Tradition," *The Wall Street Journal,* June 11, 1985, p. 1ff.; "Is Häagen-Dazs Trying to Freeze Out Ben & Jerry's?" *Business Week,* December 7, 1987, p. 65; "Card Rivals Deal Ads: Convenience vs. New Lines," *Advertising Age,* July 27, 1987, p. 28; "Little Publisher Has Big Ideas on Where to Sell His Books," *The Wall Street Journal,* March 19, 1987, p. 1ff.

11. "Antitrust Issues and Marketing Channel Strategy" and "Case 1—Continental T.V., Inc., et al. v. GTE Sylvania, Inc.," in Louis W. Stern and Thomas L. Eovaldi, *Legal Aspects of Marketing Strategy* (Englewood Cliffs, N.J.: Prentice Hall, 1984), pp. 300–61.

12. "Reebok's Direct Sales Spark a Retail Revolt," *Adweek's Marketing Week,* December 2, 1991, p. 7; *1990 Annual Report,* Reebok. See also James R. Burley, "Territorial Restriction and Distribution Systems: Current Legal Developments," *Journal of Marketing,* October 1975, pp. 52–56; "Justice Takes Aim at Dual Distribution," *Business Week,* July 7, 1980, pp. 24–25; Saul Sands and Robert J. Posch, Jr., "A Checklist of Questions for Firms Considering a Vertical Territorial Distribution Plan," *Journal of Marketing,* Summer 1982, pp. 38–43; Debra L. Scammon and Mary Jane Sheffet, "Legal Issues in Channels Modification Decisions: The Question of Refusals to Deal," *Journal of Public Policy and Marketing* 5 (1986), pp. 82–96.

13. Gary L. Frazier, James D. Gill, and Sudhir H. Kale, "Dealer Dependence Levels and Reciprocal Actions in a Channel of Distribution in a Developing Country," *Journal of Marketing,* January 1989, pp. 50–69; Allan J. Magrath and Kenneth G. Hardy, "Avoiding the Pitfalls in Managing Distribution Channels," *Business Horizons,* September/October 1987, pp. 29–33; Shelby D. Hunt, Nina M. Ray, and Van R. Wood, "Behavioral Dimensions of Channels of Distribution: Review and Synthesis," *Academy of Marketing Science,* Summer 1985, pp. 1–24; John F. Gaski, "The Theory of Power and Conflict in Channels of Distribution," *Journal of Marketing,* Summer 1984, pp. 9–29; John E. Robbins, Thomas W. Speh, and Morris L. Mayer, "Retailers' Perceptions of Channel Conflict Issues," *Journal of Retailing,* Winter 1982, pp. 46–67; James R. Brown, "A Cross-Channel Comparison of Supplier-Retailer Relations," *Journal of Retailing,* Winter 1981, pp. 3–18; Louis P. Bucklin, "A Theory of Channel Control," *Journal of Marketing,* January 1973, pp. 39–47.

14. See, for example, James H. Barnes, Jr., "Recycling: A Problem in Reverse Logistics," *Journal of Macromarketing* 2, no. 2 (1982), pp. 31–37.

15. Brian F. O'Neil and Jon L. Iveson, "Strategically Managing the Logistics Function," *The Logistics and Transportation Review,* December 1991, pp. 359–78; Lloyd M. Rinehart, M. Bixby Cooper, and George D. Wagenheim, "Furthering the Integration of Marketing and Logistics Through Customer Service in the Channel," *Journal of the Academy of Marketing Science,* Winter 1989, pp. 63–72; Ernest B. Uhr, Ernest C. Houck, and John C. Rogers, "Physical Distribution Service," *Journal of Business Logistics* 2, no. 2 (1981), pp. 158–69; Martin Christopher, "Creating Effective Policies for Customer Service," *International Journal of Physical Distribution and Materials Management* 13, no. 2 (1983), pp. 3–24; William D. Perreault, Jr., and Frederick A. Russ, "Physical Distribution Service in Industrial Purchase Decisions," *Journal of Marketing,* April 1976, pp. 3–10; Gary L. Frazier, Robert E. Spekman, and Charles R. O'Neal, "Just-in-Time Exchange Relationships in Industrial Markets," *Journal of Marketing,* October 1988, pp. 52–67.

16. Roy D. Shapiro, "Get Leverage from Logistics," *Harvard Business Review,* May/June 1984, pp. 119–26; James E. Morehouse, "Operating in the New Logistics Era," *Harvard Business Review,* September/October 1983 pp. 18–19; Graham Sharman, "The Rediscovery of Logistics," *Harvard Business Review,* September/October 1984, pp. 71–79.

17. A. Coskun Samli, Laurence W. Jacobs, and James Wills, "What Presale and Postsale Services Do You Need to be Competitive," *Industrial Marketing Management,* February 1992, pp. 33–42; Richard Germain and M. Bixby Cooper, "How a Customer Mission Statement Affects Company Performance," *Industrial Marketing Management,* February 1990, pp. 47–54; John T. Mentzer, Roger Gomes, and Robert E. Krapfel, Jr., "Physical Distribution Service: A Fundamental Marketing Concept?" *Journal of the Academy of Marketing Science,* Winter 1989, pp. 53–62; Frances G. Tucker, "Creative Customer Service Management," *International Journal of Physical Distribution and Materials Management* 13, no. 3 (1983), pp. 34–50; William D. Perreault, Jr., and Frederick R. Russ, "Physical Distribution Service: A Neglected Aspect of Marketing Management," *MSU Business Topics,* Summer 1974, pp. 37–46.

18. Bernard J. LaLonde and P. H. Zinszer, *Customer Service: Meaning and Measurement* (Chicago: National Council of Distribution Management, 1976).

19. For a more detailed comparison of mode characteristics, see Roger Dale Abshire and Shane R. Premeaux, "Motor Carriers' and Shippers' Perceptions of the Carrier Choice Decision," *The Logistics and Transportation Review,* December 1991, pp. 351–58; Ronald L. Coulter et al., "Freight Transportation Carrier Selection Criteria: Identification of Service Dimensions for Competitive Positioning," *Journal of Business Research,* August 1989, pp. 51–66; Donald J. Bowersox, David L. Closs, and Omar K. Helferich, *Logistical Management* (New York: Macmillan, 1986); Edward R. Bruning and Peter M. Lynagh, "Carrier Evaluation in Physical Distribution Management," *Journal of Business Logistics,* September 1984, pp. 30–47. See also Paul R. Murphy, Jonathan E. Smith, and James M. Daley, "Ethical Behavior of U.S. General Freight Carriers: An Empirical Assessment," *The Logistics and Transportation Review,* March 1991, pp. 55–72; Edward L. Fitzsimmons, "Factors Associated with Intramodal Competition Reported by Small Railroads," *The Logistics and Transportation Review,* March 1991, pp. 73–90; Phil Ramsdale and Steve Harvey, "Make Freight Cost Control Part of Planning," *The Journal of Business Strategy,* March/April 1990, pp. 42–45.

20. "Railroads Getting in Better Shape for the Long Haul," *The Wall Street Journal,* February 26, 1992, p. B4; "Big Rail Is Finally Rounding the Bend," *Business Week,* November 11, 1991, pp. 128–29; "Comeback Ahead for Railroads," *Fortune,* June 17, 1991, pp. 107–13; "The Road Ahead for Railroads," *Fortune,* May 20, 1991, pp. 13–14; "Trains Double Up to Get Truck Business," *The Wall Street Journal,* July 28, 1989, p. B3; "Railroad Brings Far-Flung Dispatchers Together in Huge Computerized Bunker," *The Wall Street Journal,* May 9, 1989, p. B9; "New Train Control Systems Pass Big Tests," *The Wall Street Journal,* October 26, 1988, p. B6.

21. George L. Stern, "Surface Transportation: Middle-of-the-Road Solution," *Harvard Business Review,* December 1975, p. 82.

22. "Federal Express Finds Its Pioneering Formula Falls Flat Overseas," *The Wall Street Journal,* April 15, 1991, p. A1ff.; "UPS Challenges Leaders in Air Express," *The Wall Street Journal,* December 20, 1990, p. A5; "Federal Express's Battle Overseas," *Fortune,* December 3, 1990, pp. 137–40; "Can UPS Deliver the Goods in a New World?" *Business Week,* June 4, 1990, pp. 80–82; Gunna K. Sletmo and Jacques Picard, "International Distribution Policies and the Role of Air Freight," *Journal of Business Logistics* 6, no. 1 (1985), pp. 35–53.

23. *1990 Annual Report,* CSX.

24. Paul A. Dion, Loretta M. Hasey, Patrick C. Dorin, and Jean Lundin, "Consequences of Inventory Stockouts," *Industrial Marketing Management* 20, no. 1 (1991), pp. 23–28; R. Douglas White, "Streamline Inventory to Better Serve Customers," *The Journal of Business Strategy,* March/April 1989, pp. 43–47; David J. Armstrong, "Sharpening Inventory Management," *Harvard Business Review,* November/December 1985, pp. 42–59.

25. Wade Ferguson, "Buying an Industrial Service Warehouse Space," *Industrial Marketing Management,* February 1983, pp. 63–66; "Warehousing: Should You Go Public?" *Sales & Marketing Management,* June 14, 1976, p. 52.; G. O. Pattino, "Public Warehousing: Supermarket for Distribution Services," *Handling and Shipping,* March 1977, p. 59.

26. Kenneth B. Ackerman and Bernard J. LaLonde, "Making Warehousing More Efficient," *Harvard Business Review,* April 1980, p. 94–102.

27. Shirley J. Daniel and Wolf D. Reitsperger, "Management Control Systems for J.I.T.: An Empirical Comparison of Japan and the U.S.," *Journal of International Business Studies,* Winter 1991, pp. 603–18; "How to Keep Truckin' in the Age of Just-in-Time Delivery," *Business Week,* December 10, 1990, p. 181; "Firms' Newfound Skill in Managing Inventory May Soften Downturn," *The Wall Street Journal,* November 19, 1990, p. A1ff.; Brian Dearing, "The Strategic Benefits of EDI," *The Journal of Business Strategy,* January/February 1990, pp. 4–6; Charles R. O'Neal, "JIT Procurement and Relationship Marketing," *Industrial Marketing Management* 18, no. 1 (1989), pp. 55–64; Prabir K. Bagchi, T. S. Raghumathan, and Edward J. Bardi, "The Implications of Just-in-Time Inventory Policies on Carrier Selection," *The Logistics and Transportation Review,* December 1987, pp. 373–84; "How Just-in-Time Inventories Combat Foreign Competition," *Business Week,* May 14, 1984, pp. 176D–76G.

28. "Circuit City's Wires Are Sizzling," *Business Week,* April 27, 1992, p. 76; "Earning More by Moving Faster," *Fortune,* October 7, 1991, pp. 89–94; "An Electronic Pipeline That's Changing the Way America Does Business," *Business Week,* August 3, 1987, p. 80ff.; "Computer Finds a Role in Buying and Selling, Reshaping Businesses," *The Wall Street Journal,* March 18, 1987, p. 1ff.; "Computers Bringing Changes to Basic Business Documents," *The Wall Street Journal,* March 6, 1987, p. 33.

29. "A Smart Cookie at Pepperidge," *Fortune,* December 22, 1986, pp. 67–74.

30. "As Stores Scrimp More and Order Less, Suppliers Take on Greater Risks, Costs," *The Wall Street Journal,* December 10, 1991, p. B1ff.

31. " 'Green Cars' Are Still Far in the Future," *The Wall Street Journal,* January 13, 1992, p. B1ff.; "Conservation Power," *Business Week,* September 16, 1991, pp. 86–91; "On the Road Again and Again and Again: Auto Makers Try to Build Recyclable Car," *The Wall Street Journal,* April 30, 1991, p. B1; "Clean-Air Proposal Eventually May Add as Much as $600 to Car Sticker Prices," *The Wall Street Journal,* October 11, 1990, p. B1ff.; "Shell Pumps Cleaner Gas in 'Dirtiest' Cities in U.S.," *The Wall Street Journal,* April 12, 1990, p. B1ff.; "Clean-Air Legislation Will Cost Americans $21.5 Billion a Year," *The Wall Street Journal,* March 28, 1990, p. A1ff.; *1990 Annual Report,* Du Pont; *1990 Annual Report,* Matlack; *1990 Annual Report,* Shell.

32. R. F. Lusch, J. G. Udell, and G. R. Laczniak, "The Future of Marketing Strategy," *Business Horizons,* December 1976, pp. 65–74. See also Jonathan R. Copulsky and Michael J. Wolf, "Relationship Marketing: Positioning for the Future," *The Journal of Business Strategy,* July/August 1990, pp. 16–21; John J. Burbridge, Jr., "Strategic Implications of Logistics Information Systems," *The Logistics and Transportation Review,* December 1988, pp. 368–83.

Chapter 11

1. "Toys 'R' Us Seeks Global Growth," *Advertising Age,* March 30, 1992, p. 33; "The World 'S' Ours," *Newsweek,* March 23, 1992, pp. 46–47; "Breaking into European Markets by Breaking the Rules," *Business Week,* January 20, 1992, pp. 88–89; "Toy Chains Learn to Play a New Game," *Adweek,* December 16, 1991, p. 9; "Guess Who's Selling Barbies in Japan Now?" *Business Week,* December 9, 1991, pp. 72–76; "Toys 'R' Us Learns Give-and-Take Game in Japan, Sets the Debut for First Store," *The Wall Street Journal,* October 8, 1991, p. A18; "How Toys 'R' Us Controls the Game Board," *Business Week,* December 19, 1988, pp. 58–60; "Toys 'R' Us, Big Kid on the Block, Won't Stop Growing," *The Wall Street Journal,* August 11, 1988, p. 6; "Germans 'R' Us," *Advertising Age,* November 9, 1987, p. 56; "Toys 'R' Us Goes Overseas—And Finds that Toys 'R' Them, Too," *Business Week,* January 26, 1987, pp. 71–72.

2. U.S. Bureau of the Census, *Statistical Abstract of the United States 1991* (Washington, D.C.: U.S. Government Printing Office, 1991) pp. 767–75; U.S. Bureau of the Census, *County Business Patterns 1989, United States* (Washington, D.C.: U.S. Government Printing Office, 1991); U.S. Bureau of the Census, *Current Business Reports:*

Monthly Retail Trade, Sales and Inventories, October, 1991 (Washington, D.C.: U.S. Government Printing Office, 1991).

3. For additional examples, see John P. Dickson and Douglas L. MacLachlan, "Social Distance and Shopping Behavior," *Journal of the Academy of Marketing Science,* Spring 1990, pp. 153–62; "Penney Moves Upscale in Merchandise but Still Has to Convince Public," *The Wall Street Journal,* June 7, 1990, p. A1ff.; "Can J. C. Penney Change Its Image without Losing Customers?" *Adweek's Marketing Week,* February 26, 1990, pp. 20–24; "Upscale Look for Limited Puts Retailer Back on Track," *The Wall Street Journal,* February 24, 1989, p. B1; "Selling to the Poor: Retailers That Target Low-Income Shoppers Are Rapidly Growing," *The Wall Street Journal,* June 24, 1985, p. 1ff.; "The Green in Blue-Collar Retailing," *Fortune,* May 27, 1985, pp. 74–77.

4. "Specialty Retailing, a Hot Market, Attracts New Players," *The Wall Street Journal,* April 2, 1987, p. 1.

5. U.S. Bureau of the Census, *County Business Patterns 1989, United States,* p. 54; U.S. Bureau of the Census, *Current Business Reports,* p. 5.

6. "Remaking a Dinosaur," *Newsweek,* February 10, 1992, pp. 38–43; Richard A. Rauch, "Retailing's Dinosaurs: Department Stores and Supermarkets," *Business Horizons,* September/October 1991, pp. 21–25; "Fighting the Tide, Owner Tries to Revive Big Department Store," *The Wall Street Journal,* August 14, 1991, p. A1ff.; Joe Schwartz, "Dump Department Stores?" *American Demographics,* December 1990, pp. 42–43; "Retailing in the '90s: How It Got Here from There," *Marketing News,* June 25, 1990, p. 14ff.; "If May Stores Are Plain Janes, Who Needs Flash?" *Business Week,* January 22, 1990, p. 32; "A Quiet Superstar Rises in Retailing," *Fortune,* October 23, 1989, pp. 167–74; "Why Big-Name Stores Are Losing Out," *Fortune,* January 16, 1989, pp. 31–32; "Stores See Loyal Customers Slip Away," *Advertising Age,* July 11, 1988, p. 12; "How Three Master Merchants Fell from Grace," *Business Week,* March 16, 1987, pp. 38–40; "Department Stores Shape Up," *Fortune,* September 1, 1986, pp. 50–52; "How Department Stores Plan to Get the Registers Ringing Again," *Business Week,* November 18, 1985, pp. 66–67.

7. David Appel, "The Supermarket: Early Development of an Institutional Innovation," *Journal of Retailing,* Spring 1972, pp. 39–53.

8. "Special Report: Grocery Marketing," *Advertising Age,* May 8, 1989, pp. S1–S22; Janice McCormick, "The Case of the Not-So-Supermarket," *Harvard Business Review,* March/April 1989, pp. 14–31; "The Transformation of the Nation's Supermarkets," *New York Times,* September 2, 1984, p. 1ff.

9. "Grocery-Cart Wars," *Time,* March 30, 1992, p. 49; "Selling in the Stores of the Future," *Adweek,* January 20, 1992, pp. 12–13; "How a Terrific Idea for Grocery Marketing Missed the Target," *The Wall Street Journal,* April 3, 1991, p. A1ff.; "Electronic Marketing Enters Supermarket Aisle," *Marketing News,* April 1, 1991, pp. 14–15; " 'Smart Card,' Coupon Eater Targeted to Grocery Retailers," *Marketing News,* June 6, 1988, pp. 1–2; "At Today's Supermarket, the Computer Is Doing It All," *Business Week,* August 11, 1986, pp. 64–65; "Bigger, Shrewder, and Cheaper Cub Leads Food Stores into the Future," *The Wall Street Journal,* August 26, 1985, p. 19.

10. "Catalog Showrooms Revamp to Keep Their Identity," *Business Week,* Industrial/Technology Edition, June 10, 1985, pp. 117–20; Pradeep K. Korgaonkar, "Consumer Preferences for Catalog Showrooms and Discount Stores," *Journal of Retailing,* Fall 1982, pp. 76–88; "Best Products: Too Much Too Soon at the No. 1 Catalog Showroom," *Business Week,* July 23, 1984, pp. 136–38.

11. *1991 Annual Report,* Wal-Mart; "Podunk Is Beckoning," *Business Week,* December 23, 1991, p. 76; "Wal-Mart Prepares for Urban Assault," *Adweek,* November 11, 1991, p. 10; "Merchants Mobilize to Battle Wal-Mart in a Small Community," *The Wall Street Journal,* June 5, 1991, p. A1ff.; "Is Wal-Mart Unstoppable?" *Fortune,* May 6, 1991, pp. 50–59; "Wal-Mart Finds New Rivals on Main Street," *Adweek's Marketing Week,* November 19, 1990, p. 5.

12. "Wal-Mart Gets Lost in the Vegetable Aisle," *Business Week,* May 28, 1990, p. 48; "Wal-Mart Pulls Back on Hypermarket Plans," *Advertising Age,* February 19, 1990, p. 49; "Retailers Fly into Hyperspace," *Fortune,* October 24, 1988, pp. 48–52.

13. "Warehouse Clubs Have Big Impact on Grocers," *The Wall Street Journal,* April 6, 1992, p. B1; "Shopping Clubs Ready for Battle in Texas Market," *The Wall Street Journal,* October 24, 1991, p. B1ff.; "You Have to Join to Pay," *Newsweek,* August 5, 1991, p. 65; "Bargains by the Forklift," *Business Week,* July 15, 1991, p. 152; "Campbell, Kellogg 'Bulk' Their Brands for Wholesale Clubs," *Adweek's Marketing Week,* April 29, 1991, p. 26; "Corn Flakes, Aisle 1. Cadillacs, Aisle 12," *Business Week,* April 29, 1991, pp. 68–70; Jack G. Kaikati, "The Boom in Warehouse Clubs," *Business Horizons,* March/April 1987, pp. 68–73.

14. "Tandy Bets Big with New Giant Stores," *The Wall Street Journal,* April 16, 1992, p. B1ff.; "There's No Place Like Home Depot," *Nation's Business,* February 1992, pp. 30–35; "This Is a Job for Superstores," *USA Today,* October 8, 1991, p. 4B; "Will Home Depot Be 'The Wal-Mart of the '90s?'" *Business Week,* March 19, 1990, pp. 124–26; "Office Supply Superstores Reshape the Industry," *Marketing News,* January 22, 1990, p. 2; "Born to Be Big," *Inc.,* June 1989, pp. 94–101; "Bookshop 'Super-Store' Reflects the Latest Word in Retailing," *The Wall Street Journal,* February 23, 1987, p. 29; "Hechinger's: Nobody Does It Better in Do-it-Yourself," *Business Week,* May 5, 1986, p. 96; "Electronics Superstores Are Devouring Their Rivals," *Business Week,* June 24, 1985, pp. 84–85.

15. "Some 7-Elevens Try Selling a New Image," *The Wall Street Journal,* October 25, 1991, p. B1ff.; "Stop N Go's Van Horn Wants to Reinvent the Convenience Store," *The Wall Street Journal,* February 6, 1991, pp. A1ff.; "In Japan, Conveniences Converge at 7-Eleven," *The Wall Street Journal,* April 6, 1990, p. B1; "Troubled Circle K Is Turning This Way and That," *Business Week,* November 20, 1989, pp. 78–80.

16. "Push-Button Lover," *The Economist,* November 16, 1991, p. 88; "Machines Start New Fast-Food Era," *USA Today,* July 19, 1991, pp. 1B–2B; "High-Tech Vending Machines Cook Up a New Menu of Hot Fast-Food Entrees," *The Wall Street Journal,* May 13, 1991, p. B1ff.; "The World's Most Valuable Company," *Fortune,* October 10, 1988, pp. 92–104.

17. "Extend Your Reach By Catalog Sales," *Nation's Business,* March 1992, pp. 33–37; "Catalogs Help Avon Get a Foot in the Door," *The Wall Street Journal,* February 28, 1992, p. B1ff.; "Postmark: Tokyo," *Adweek's Marketing Week,* February 24, 1992, p. 29; "Sears Roebuck to Streamline Catalog Business," *The Wall Street Journal,* January 8, 1992, p. B1ff.; "Catalog Firms Place an Order: Creativity," *USA Today,* November 12, 1991, p. 5B; "Catalog Houses that Once Boomed Find the Checks Are No Longer in the Mail," *The Wall Street Journal,* April 4, 1991, p. B1ff. "Lands' End Stumbles as Fashion Shifts Away from Retailer's Traditional Fare," *The Wall Street Journal,* April 27, 1990, p. B1ff.; "Lands' End Looks a Bit Frayed at the Edges," *Business Week,* March 19, 1990, p. 42; " 'Up to the Chin' in Catalogs," *Newsweek,* November 20, 1989, pp. 57–58; "Retailing Clips Wings of High Flying Mail-Order Firms," *The Wall Street Journal,* January 6, 1989, p. B2.

18. "It Helps to Be Cool and Klutzy if You Are Selling on TV," *The Wall Street Journal,* December 31, 1990, p. 1ff.; "Home Shoppers Keep Tuning In—But Investors Are Turned Off," *Business Week,* October 22, 1990, pp. 70–72; "From the Mall to Catalogs to Cable," *Insight,* May 7, 1990, p. 51; "Home Shopping Tries a Tonic for Its Sickly Stock," *Business Week,* April 25, 1988, p. 110; "Home Shopping," *Business Week,* December 15, 1986, pp. 62–69; Joel E. Urbany and W. Wayne Talarzyk, "Videotex: Implications for Retailing," *Journal of Retailing,* Fall 1983, pp. 76–92; George P. Moschis, Jac L. Goldstucker, and Thomas J. Stanley, "At-Home Shopping: Will Consumers Let Their Computers Do the Walking?" *Business Horizons,* March/April 1985, pp. 22–29.

19. "Computer-Ordering Method Helps Newcomer Blossom," *The Wall Street Journal,* January 22, 1991, p. B2; "Electronic Retailing Filling Niche Needs," *Discount Store News,* December 19, 1988, p. 111.

20. "Nabisco Plots Strategy to Sell Oreos with Videos," *Advertising Age,* May 4, 1992, p. 3ff.; "Stores Find Photo Minilabs Quick Way to Process Profit," *Supermarket News,* June 10, 1991, pp. 22–25; "Products No Longer Determine the Selection of Retail Outlet," *Marketing News,* April 1, 1991, p. 9; "Supermarketing Can Be Super Marketing," *ABA Banking Journal,* September 1989, pp. 49–61; Ruth Hamel, "Food Fight," *American Demographics,* March, 1989, pp. 36–39ff.; "No Holds Barred," *Time,* August 11, 1988, pp. 46–48; "Special Report: Stores Juggle Space, Specialties," *Advertising Age,* October 12, 1987, p. S1ff.

21. "Ikea Furniture Chain Pleases with Its Prices, Not with Its Service," *The Wall Street Journal,* September 17, 1991, p. A1ff.; "Furniture that Fits the Market," *Adweek,* July 29, 1991, pp. 18–19; "Ikea's Got 'Em Lining Up," *Fortune,* March 11, 1991, p. 72; "Ikea Building a Loyal Following with Style, Price," *Advertising Age,* January 28, 1991, p. 23; "Ikea, Swedish Home-Furnishing Chain, Prepares for a Major Expansion in U.S.," *The Wall Street Journal,* February 23, 1990, p. B7A; "Why Competitors Shop for Ideas at Ikea," *Business Week,* October 9, 1989, p. 88; "Ikea Furnishing Its U.S. Identity," *Advertising Age,* September 18, 1989, p. 79.

22. For more on Kmart seeking new markets, see "The Rebirth of Kmart," *Advertising Age,* October 7, 1991, p. 16; "Attention, Shoppers: Kmart Is Fighting Back," *Business Week,* October 7, 1991, pp. 118–20; "Will Kmart Ever Be a Silk Purse?" *Business Week,* January 22, 1990, p. 46. For more on how product-life cycles apply to retailers, see "Rewriting the Rules of Retailing," *The New York Times,* October 15, 1990, Sect. 3, p. 1ff.; "Video Chain Aims to Star as Industry Leader," *USA Today,* July 22, 1988, pp. B1–2; "What Ails Retailing," *Fortune,* January 30, 1989, pp. 61–64; "Don't Discount Off-Price Retailers," *Harvard Business Review,* May/June 1985, pp. 85–92; Ronald Savitt, "The 'Wheel of Retailing' and Retail Product Management," *European Journal of Marketing* 18, no. 6/7 (1984), pp. 43–54; Jack G. Kaikati, Rom J. Markin, and Calvin P. Duncan, "The Transformation of Retailing Institutions: Beyond the Wheel of Retailing and Life Cycle Theories," *Journal of Macromarketing* 1, no. 1 (1981), pp. 58–66.

23. "How Did Sears Blow This Gasket?" *Business Week,* June 29, 1992, p. 38; "An Open Letter to Sears Customers," *USA Today,* June 25, 1992, p. 8A.

24. "Variety Stores Struggle to Keep the Dimes Rolling In," *The Wall Street Journal,* May 7, 1991, p. B2; "Retailers Grab Power, Control Marketplace," *Marketing News,* January 16, 1989, pp. 1–2; Dale D. Achabal, John M. Heineke, and Shelby H. McIntyre, "Issues and Perspectives on Retail Productivity," *Journal of Retailing,* Fall 1984, p. 107ff.; Charles A. Ingene, "Scale Economies in American Retailing: A Cross-Industry Comparison," *Journal of Macromarketing* 4, no. 2 (1984), pp. 49–63; "Mom-and-Pop Videotape Shops Are Fading Out," *Business Week,* September 2, 1985, pp. 34–35; Vijay Mahajan, Subhash Sharma, and Roger Kerin, "Assessing Market Penetration Opportunities and Saturation Potential for Multi-Store, Multi-Market Retailers," *Journal of Retailing,* Fall 1988, pp. 315–34.

25. "Look Who Likes Franchising Now," *Fortune,* September 23, 1991, pp. 125–30; "New Rules for Franchising," *USA Today,* May 6, 1991, p. 11E; "Franchisers and Franchisees Make Some Concessions," *The Wall Street Journal,* February 7, 1991, p. B2; "For U.S. Firms, Franchising in Mexico Gets More Appetizing, Thanks to Reform," *The Wall Street Journal,* January 3, 1991, p. A6; "More Concerns Are Franchising Existing Outlets," *The Wall Street Journal,* December 17, 1990, p. B1ff.; "Flaring Tempers at the Frozen-Yogurt King," *Business Week,* September 10, 1990, pp. 88–90; "Foreign Franchisers Entering U.S. in Greater Numbers," *The Wall Street Journal,* June 11, 1990, p. B2; "Franchisers See a Future in East Bloc," *The Wall Street Journal,* June 5, 1990, p. B1ff.; "Avis Hit by Almost Every Obstacle in Franchise Book," *The Wall Street Journal,* May 3, 1990, p. B2.

26. For more on shopping malls, see "Special Report: Mega Malls," *Advertising Age,* January 27, 1992, pp. S1–S8; "The Shopping Mall of Dreams," *Newsweek,* December 23, 1991, p. 44; Chip Walker, "Strip Malls: Plain but Powerful," *American Demographics,* October 1991, pp. 48–51; "Developers of Big Shopping Malls Tutor Faltering Tenants in Retail Techniques," *The Wall Street Journal,* April 24, 1991, p. B1; "Japan Becomes Land of the Rising Mall," *The Wall Street Journal,* February 11, 1991, p. B1ff.; "Largest of All Malls in the U.S. Is a Gamble in Bloomington, Minn.," *The Wall Street Journal,* October 30, 1990, p. A1ff.; "When a Mall's Biggest Retailers Fall, Surviving Shops Get an Unpleasant Jolt," *The Wall Street Journal,* October 25, 1990, p. B1ff.; "Going Without: Gap Drops Anchors in Its Plan to Develop Upscale Malls," *The Wall Street Journal,* October 25, 1990, p. B1ff.; Eugene H. Fram and Joel Axelrod, "The Distressed Shopper," *American Demographics,* October 1990, pp. 44–45; "Retailers Use Bans, Guards, and Ploys to Curb Teen Sport of Mall-Mauling," *The Wall Street Journal,* August 7, 1990, p. B1ff.; "New Retailers Face Struggle Getting in Malls," *The Wall Street Journal,* July 24, 1990, p. B1ff.; "Rodeo Drive Mini-Mall Is Looking Smart," *The Wall Street Journal,* June 14, 1990, p. B1; Francesca Turchiano, "The (Un)Malling of America," *American*

Demographics, April 1990, pp. 37–39; "Too Many Malls Are Chasing a Shrinking Supply of Shoppers," *Adweek's Marketing Week,* February 5, 1990, pp. 2–3. For more on discount malls, see "Shopper Sightings Reported," *Business Week,* January 13, 1992, p. 81; " 'They're Here to Shop' at Mall Mecca," *USA Today,* December 23, 1991, p. 1A–2A; "Thriving Factory Outlets Anger Retailers as Store Suppliers Turn into Competitors," *The Wall Street Journal,* October 8, 1991, p. B1ff.; "The Price Is Always Right," *Time,* December 17, 1990, pp. 66–68; John Ozment and Greg Martin, "Changes in the Competitive Environments of Rural Trade Areas: Effects of Discount Retail Chains," *Journal of Business Research,* November 1990, pp. 277–88; "Discount Clothing Stores, Facing Squeeze, Aim to Fashion a More Rounded Image," *The Wall Street Journal,* March 15, 1990, p. B1; "The Wholesale Success of Factory Outlet Malls," *Business Week,* February 3, 1986, pp. 92–94.

27. "Europe Chains in Power Play with Manufacturers," *Supermarket News,* June 3, 1991, pp. 18–19; "Retailing Around the World: Endless Possibilities or Endless Problems?" *Discount Store News,* May 6, 1991, pp. 69–115; "International Intriguing," *Advertising Age,* January 29, 1990, pp. S1–S2; Philip R. Cateora, *International Marketing* (Homewood, Ill.: Richard D. Irwin, 1990), pp. 586–93.

28. "Ringing in the Future by Changing the Past," *Insight,* January 8, 1990, pp. 9–17; "Home Banking Gets Another Chance," *The Wall Street Journal,* December 7, 1989, p. B1; "IBM, Sears—Their Gamble May Set Pace for Videotex," *USA Today,* September 20, 1988, p. B1; "Are IBM and Sears Crazy? Or Canny?" *Fortune,* September 28, 1987, pp. 74–79; "Electronic Retailing Goes to the Supermarket," *Business Week,* March 25, 1985, pp. 78–79; "Computer Users Shop at Home over the Phone," *The Wall Street Journal,* February 20, 1985, p. 35.

29. "21st Century Supermarket Shopping," *Adweek's Marketing Week,* March 9, 1992, p. 9; "What Selling Will Be Like in the '90s," *Fortune,* January 13, 1992, pp. 63–65; "The New Stars of Retailing," *Business Week,* December 16, 1991, pp. 120–22; "Retailers with a Cause," *Newsweek,* December 16, 1991, p. 51; "Shop Talk: What's in Store for Retailers," *The Wall Street Journal,* April 9, 1991, p. B1ff.; "The Little Stores That Could," *Adweek's Marketing Week,* February 4, 1991, pp. 16–17; "Retailing: Who Will Survive," *Business Week,* November 26, 1990, pp. 134–44; "Retailing's Winners & Losers," *Fortune,* December 18, 1989, pp. 69–78; Leslie de Chernatony, "Branding in an Era of Retailer Dominance," *International Journal of Advertising* 8, no. 3 (1989), pp. 245–60; "Special Report: A Crash Course in Surviving '90s," *Advertising Age,* April 24, 1989, pp. S1–S18; Dale D. Achabal and Shelby H. McIntyre, "Guest Editorial: Information Technology Is Reshaping Retailing," *Journal of Retailing,* Winter 1987, pp. 321–25; Leonard L. Berry and Larry G. Greshan, "Relationship Retailing: Transforming Customers into Clients," *Business Horizons,* November/December 1986, pp. 43–47; Jon M. Hawes and James R. Lumpkin, "Perceived Risk and the Selection of a Retail Patronage Mode," *Journal of the Academy of Marketing Science,* Winter 1986, pp. 37–42; Terry R. Hiller, "Going Shopping in the 1990s," *The Futurist,* December 1983, pp. 63–68; Patrick J. Kelly and William R. George, "Strategic Management Issues for the Retailing of Services," *Journal of Retailing,* Summer 1982, pp. 26–43; Larry J. Rosenberg and Elizabeth C. Hirschman, "Retailing without Stores," *Harvard Business Review,* July/August 1980, pp. 103–12.

Chapter 12

1. "Strange Fruits," *Inc.,* November 1989, pp. 80–90; "The Produce Marketer," *Savvy,* June 1988, pp. 26–28.

2. James D. Hlavacek and Tommy J. McCuistion, "Industrial Distributors—When, Who, and How?" *Harvard Business Review,* January/February 1983, pp. 96–101; Steven Flax, "Wholesalers," *Forbes,* January 4, 1982. See also Roger J. Calantone and Jule B. Gassenheimer, "Overcoming Basic Problems between Manufacturers and Distributors," *Industrial Marketing Management* 20, no. 3 (1991), pp. 215–22; Geoff Gordon, Roger Calantone, and C. A. diBenedetto, "How Electrical Contractors Choose Distributors," *Industrial Marketing Management* 20, no. 1 (1991), pp. 29–42; Nicholas Nickolaus, "Marketing New Products With Industrial Distributors," *Industrial Marketing Management,* November 1990, pp. 287–300; Allan J. Magrath and Kenneth G. Hardy, "Gearing Manufacturer Support Programs to Distributors," *Industrial Marketing Management* 18, no. 4 (1989), pp. 239–44; Donald M. Jackson and Michael F. d'Amico,

"Products and Markets Served by Distributors and Agents," *Industrial Marketing Management,* February 1989, pp. 27–34; Thomas L. Powers, "Switching from Reps to Direct Salespeople," *Industrial Marketing Management,* August 1987, pp. 169–72; N. Mohan Reddy and Michael P. Marvin, "Developing a Manufacturer-Distributor Information Partnership," *Industrial Marketing Management,* May 1986, pp. 157–64; Michael Levy and Michael Van Breda, "How to Determine Whether to Buy Direct or through a Wholesaler," *Retail Control,* June/July 1985, pp. 35–55.

3. Richard Greene, "Wholesaling," *Forbes,* January 2, 1984, pp. 226–28; Lyn S. Amine, S. Tamer Cavusgil, and Robert I. Weinstein, "Japanese Sogo Shosha and the U.S. Export Trading Companies," *Journal of the Academy of Marketing Science,* Fall 1986, pp. 21–32.

4. "Sysco Corp.'s Bill of Fare Is Inviting," *USA Today,* August 11, 1989, p. B3; "Dean Foods Thrives among the Giants," *The Wall Street Journal,* September 17, 1987, p. 6; "Food Distribution: The Leaders Are Getting Hungry for More," *Business Week,* March 24, 1986, pp. 106–8.

5. Robert F. Lusch, Deborah S. Coykendall, and James M. Kenderdine, *Wholesaling in Transition: An Executive Chart Book* (Norman, Okla.: Distribution Research Program, University of Oklahoma, 1990).

6. *1990 Annual Report,* McKesson; "Computer Finds a Role in Buying and Selling, Reshaping Businesses," *The Wall Street Journal,* March 18, 1987, p. 1ff.

7. "Direct Marketing: A Modern Marketing Solution," *Directions* (New York: Direct Marketing Association, 1990); "Special Report: Direct Marketing," *Advertising Age,* September 25, 1990, pp. S1–S16.

8. Robert F. Lusch, Deborah S. Coykendall, and James M. Kenderdine, *Wholesaling in Transition: An Executive Chart Book* (Norman, Okla.: Distribution Research Program, University of Oklahoma, 1990).

9. "Fruit Fight: Independent Growers Challenge Agribusiness Giants," *Insight,* July 29, 1991, pp. 13–19; "Why Farm Cooperatives Need Extra Seed Money," *Business Week,* March 21, 1988, p. 96; "Independent Farmers Oppose Rules Letting Cartels Decide Output," *The Wall Street Journal,* June 17, 1987, p. 1ff.

10. For more on manufacturers' agents being squeezed, see "Wal-Mart Draws Fire: Reps, Brokers Protest Being Shut Out by New Policy," *Advertising Age,* January 13, 1992, p. 3ff.; "Independent Sales Reps Are Squeezed by the Recession," *The Wall Street Journal,* December 27, 1991, p. B1. For more discussion on wholesaling abroad, see "Japan Rises to P&G's No. 3 Market," *Advertising Age,* December 10, 1990, p. 42; "P&G Rewrites the Marketing Rules," *Fortune,* November 6, 1989, pp. 34–48; " 'Papa-Mama' Stores in Japan Wield Power to Hold Back Imports," *The Wall Street Journal,* November 14, 1988, p. 1ff.; "Campbell's Taste of the Japanese Market Is Mm-Mm Good," *Business Week,* March 28, 1988, p. 42; "Brazil Captures a Big Share of the U.S. Shoe Market," *The Wall Street Journal,* August 27, 1985, p. 35; Jim Gibbons, "Selling Abroad with Manufacturers' Agents," *Sales & Marketing Management,* September 9, 1985, pp. 67–69; Evelyn A. Thomchick and Lisa Rosenbaum, "The Role of U.S. Export Trading Companies in International Logistics," *Journal of Business Logistics,* September 1984, pp. 85–105.

11. "Why Manufacturers Are Doubling as Distributors," *Business Week,* January 17, 1983, p. 41.

12. "Sanyo Sales Strategy Illustrates Problems of Little Distributors," *The Wall Street Journal,* September 10, 1984, p. 33.

13. "It's 'Like Somebody Had Shot the Postman,' " *Business Week,* January 13, 1992, p. 82; "Steel Service Centers: No More Warehouses," *Industry Week,* February 3, 1992, pp. 36–43; Joseph G. Ormsby and Dillard B. Tinsley, "The Role of Marketing in Material Requirements Planning Systems," *Industrial Marketing Management* 20, no. 1 (1991), pp. 67–72; Bert Rosenbloom, "Motivating Your International Channel Partners," *Business Horizons,* March/April 1990, pp. 53–57; Allan J. Magrath, "The Hidden Clout of Marketing Middlemen," *Journal of Business Strategy,* March/April 1990, pp. 38–41; S. Tamer Cavusgil, "The Importance of Distributor Training at Caterpillar," *Industrial Marketing Management,* February, 1990, pp. 1–10; "Getting Cozy with Their Customers," *Business Week,* January 8, 1990, p. 86; J. A. Narus and J. C. Anderson, "Turn Your Industrial Distributors into Partners," *Harvard Business Review,* March/April 1986, pp. 66–71; J. J. Withey, "Realities of Channel Dynamics: A Wholesaling Example," *Academy of*

Marketing Science, Summer 1985, pp. 72–81; J. A. Narus, N. M. Reddy, and G. L. Pinchak, "Key Problems Facing Industrial Distributors," *Industrial Marketing Management,* August 1984, pp. 139–48.

14. "Cold War: Amana Refrigeration Fights Tiny Distributor," *The Wall Street Journal,* February 26, 1992, p. B2; "Four Strategies Key to Success in Wholesale Distribution Industry," *Marketing News,* March 13, 1989, pp. 22–23. For another example, see "Quickie-Divorce Curbs Sought By Manufacturers' Distributors," *The Wall Street Journal,* July 13, 1987, p. 27; "Merger of Two Bakers Teaches Distributors a Costly Lesson," three-part article, *The Wall Street Journal,* September 14, 1987, p. 29; October 19, 1987, p. 35; November 11, 1987, p. 33. For yet another example, see "Independent TV Distributors Losing a Starring Role," *The Wall Street Journal,* April 14, 1989, p. B2.

Chapter 13

1. *1990 Annual Report,* Ryder System; *Mover's Advantage: The Complete Home Moving Guide & Planning Kit,* (Ryder System, October 1990); "At the Echo Awards, It's Not Just Junk Mail Anymore," *Adweek's Marketing Week,* October 29, 1990, pp. 20–21.

2. "Cabbage Patch Campaigner Tells Secret," *The Chapel Hill Newspaper,* December 1, 1985, p. D1.

3. "PR Shouldn't Mean 'Poor Relations,' " *Industry Week,* February 3, 1992, p. 51; "The Great Escape from Kuwait—Pepsi-Style," *Adweek's Marketing Week,* August 13, 1990, p. 7; "Ads Convert Rejection into Free Publicity," *The Wall Street Journal,* July 30, 1990, p. B5; "Wooing Press and Public at Auto Shows," *The Wall Street Journal,* January 8, 1990, p. B1; "Free Association," *Advertising Age,* October 23, 1989, p. 36ff.; Len Kessler, "Get the Most Bang for Your PR Dollars," *The Journal of Business Strategy,* May/June 1989, pp. 13–17; "PR on the Offensive," *Advertising Age,* March 13, 1989, p. 20; Thomas H. Bivins, "Ethical Implications of the Relationship of Purpose to Role and Function in Public Relations," *Journal of Business Ethics,* January, 1989, pp. 65–74; E. Cameron Williams, "Product Publicity: Low Cost and High Credibility," *Industrial Marketing Management,* November 1988, pp. 355–60; "Despite Ban, Liquor Marketers Finding New Ways to Get Products on Television," *The Wall Street Journal,* March 14, 1988, p. 31; "More Prime-Time TV Shows Plug Airlines, Hotels in Scripts," *The Wall Street Journal,* May 28, 1987, p. 33; "Small Firms Push Their Own Stock on Cable TV's New 'Infomercials,' " *The Wall Street Journal,* October 3, 1986, p. 31.

4. "Eye-Catching Logos All Too Often Leave Fuzzy Images in Minds of Consumers," *The Wall Street Journal,* December 5, 1991, p. B1ff.; Ronald E. Dulek, John S. Fielden, and John S. Hill, "International Communication: An Executive Primer," *Business Horizons,* January/February 1991, pp. 20–25; Tony Meenaghan, "The Role of Sponsorship in the Marketing Communications Mix," *International Journal of Advertising* 10, no. 1 (1991), pp. 35–48; Kaylene C. Williams, Rosann L. Spiro, and Leslie M. Fine, "The Customer-Salesperson Dyad: An Interaction/Communication Model and Review," *Journal of Personal Selling and Sales Management,* Summer 1990, pp. 29–44; Susan M. Petroshius and Kenneth E. Crocker, "An Empirical Analysis of Spokesperson Characteristics on Advertisement and Product Evaluations," *Journal of the Academy of Marketing Science,* Summer 1989, pp. 217–26; Samuel Rabino and Thomas E. Moore, "Managing New-Product Announcements in the Computer Industry," *Industrial Marketing Management* 18, no. 1 (1989), pp. 35–44; Marc G. Weinberger and Jean B. Romeo, "The Impact of Negative Product News," *Business Horizons,* January/February 1989, pp. 44–50; "High-Tech Hype Reaches New Heights," *The Wall Street Journal,* January 12, 1989, p. B1; "Car Ads Turn to High-Tech Talk—But Does Anybody Understand It?" *The Wall Street Journal,* March 7, 1988, p. 23. For interesting perspectives on this issue, see Jacob Jacoby and Wayne D. Hoyer, "The Comprehension/Miscomprehension of Print Communication: Selected Findings," *Journal of Consumer Research,* March 1989, pp. 434–43. See also Reed Sanderlin, "Information Is Not Communication," *Business Horizons,* March/April 1982, pp. 40–42.

5. "When Slogans Go Wrong," *American Demographics,* February 1992, p. 14; "How Does Slogan Translate?" *Advertising Age,* October 12, 1987, p. 84; "More Firms Turn to Translation Experts to Avoid Costly Embarrassing Mistakes," *The Wall Street Journal,* January 13, 1977, p. 32.

6. "Totally Hidden Video," *Inside PR,* August 1990, pp. 11–13; " 'News' Videos That Pitch Drugs Provoke Outcry for Regulations," *The Wall Street Journal,* February 8, 1990, p. B6; "Public Relations Firms Offer 'News' to TV," *The Wall Street Journal,* April 2, 1985, p. 6.

7. "Reaching Influential Buyers," *Inc.,* May 1991, p. 86–88; Jagdip Singh, "Voice, Exit, and Negative Word-of-Mouth Behaviors: An Investigation Across Three Service Categories," *Journal of the Academy of Marketing Science,* Winter 1990, pp. 1–16; "Selling Software That's Hard to Describe," *The Wall Street Journal,* July 11, 1988, p. 23; Jacqueline Johnson Brown and Peter H. Reingen, "Social Ties and Word-of-Mouth Referral Behavior," *Journal of Consumer Research,* December 1987, pp. 350–62; Robin A. Higie, Lawrence F. Feick, and Linda L. Price, "Types and Amount of Word-of-Mouth Communications about Retailers," *Journal of Retailing,* Fall 1987, pp. 260–78; Marsha L. Richins, "Negative Word-of-Mouth by Dissatisfied Consumers: A Pilot Study," *Journal of Marketing,* Winter 1983, pp. 68–78; John A. Czepiel, "Word-of-Mouth Processes in the Diffusion of a Major Technological Innovation," *Journal of Marketing Research,* May 1974, pp. 172–80; Leon G. Schiffman and Vincent Gaccione, "Opinion Leaders in Institutional Markets," *Journal of Marketing,* April 1974, pp. 49–53.

8. Meera P. Venkatraman, "Opinion Leaders, Adopters, and Communicative Adopters: A Role Analysis," *Psychology and Marketing,* Spring 1989, pp. 51–68; Mary Dee Dickerson and James W. Gentry, "Characteristics of Adopters and Non-Adopters of Home Computers," *Journal of Consumer Research,* September 1983, pp. 225–35; Everett M. Rogers and F. Floyd Shoemaker, *Communication of Innovations: A Cross-Cultural Approach* (New York: Free Press, 1971), pp. 203–9; Kenneth Uhl, Roman Andrus, and Lance Poulsen, "How Are Laggards Different? An Empirical Inquiry," *Journal of Marketing Research,* February 1970, pp. 43–50; Thomas S. Robertson, "The Process of Innovation and the Diffusion of Innovation," *Journal of Marketing,* January 1967, pp. 14–19.

9. See, for example, "Drug Firms Pitching Consumers Directly," *The Wall Street Journal,* September 4, 1990, p. B9; "Kellogg Shifts Strategy to Pull Consumers In," *The Wall Street Journal,* January 22, 1990, p. B1ff.; "Small Drug Maker Breaks Taboo with Ads Targeted at Consumers," *The Wall Street Journal,* April 20, 1989, p. B1ff.; Alvin A. Achenbaum and F. Kent Mitchel, "Pulling Away from Push Marketing," *Harvard Business Review,* May/June 1987, pp. 38–42; Michael Levy, John Webster, and Roger Kerin, "Formulating Push Marketing Strategies: A Method and Application," *Journal of Marketing,* Winter 1983, pp. 25–34.

10. "Cereal Namesake Slips into Schools," *The Wall Street Journal,* February 14, 1992, p. B1; "Book-Cover Ads Enter Grade School," *Adweek's Marketing Week,* July 29, 1991, p. 9; "Firms Learn that Subtle Aid to Schools Can Polish Their Images, Sell Products," *The Wall Street Journal,* March 25, 1991, p. B1ff.; "The Classroom as a Marketing Tool," *Insight,* September 24, 1990, pp. 40–41; "Consumer-Products Firms Hit the Books, Trying to Teach Brand Loyalty in School," *The Wall Street Journal,* July 17, 1990, p. B1ff.; "Why Channel One May Be Here to Stay," *Adweek's Marketing Week,* June 3, 1991, pp. 22–23.

11. "The Cost of Selling Is Going Up," *Boardroom Reports,* December 15, 1991, p. 15; "An In-House Sales School," *Inc.,* May 1991, pp. 85–86; "Average Business-to-Business Sales Call Increases by 9.5%," *Marketing News,* September 12, 1988, p. 5; "Personal Touch Costs More," *USA Today,* July 27, 1988, p. B1.

12. "What's New in Joint Promotions," *The New York Times,* March 10, 1985; Henry H. Beam, "Preparing for Promotion Pays Off," *Business Horizons,* January/February 1984, pp. 6–13; P. Rajan Varadarajan, "Horizontal Cooperative Sales Promotion: A Framework for Classification and Additional Perspectives," *Journal of Marketing,* April, 1986 pp. 61–73.

13. J. F. Engel, M. R. Warshaw, and T. C. Kinnear, *Promotional Strategy* (Homewood, Ill.: Richard D. Irwin, 1988).

14. "Special Report: Sales Promotion," *Advertising Age,* May 4, 1992, pp. 29–36; " 'Recession-Proof' Industry Feels Pinch," *Advertising Age,* April 29, 1991, pp. 31–38; "Special Report: Marketing's Rising Star, Sales Promotion 1989," *Advertising Age,* May 1, 1989, pp. S1–S20; "Special Report: Premiums, Incentives," *Advertising Age,* May 2, 1988, pp. S1–S12.

15. For some examples of successful sales promotions, see "Solutions: Hit by the Pitch," *Adweek,* November 11, 1991, pp. 44–45; "The Selling of the Green," *Time,* September 16, 1991, p. 48; "Beyond the Plastic Swizzle Stick," *Adweek's Marketing Week,* May 13, 1991, p. 20; "Helene Curtis' Degree Makes Competitors Sweat," *Advertising Age,* October 29, 1990, p. 20; "Hallmark Gives Away Its Best Cards in an Unusual Promotion," *Adweek's Marketing Week,* July 9, 1990, p. 10; "Audubon Society Hopes Music Videos and Movies Get Its 'Green' Message Out," *The Wall Street Journal,* April 10, 1990, p. B1ff.

16. "The Party's Over: Food Giants Pull Back on Marketing, but Boost Promotion," *Advertising Age,* February 27, 1989, p. 1ff.; "Sales-Promo Surge Has Shops Scrambling," *Advertising Age,* April 14, 1986, p. 114.

17. "Couponing Reaches Record Clip," *Advertising Age,* February 3, 1992, p. 1ff.; "Coupons Maintain Redeeming Qualities," *Direct Marketing,* December 1991, pp. 25–27; "Coupon Vehicles Proliferate," *Adweek's Marketing Week,* November 11, 1991, p. 30; "Get Ready for Global Coupon Wars," *Adweek's Marketing Week,* July 8, 1991, pp. 20–22; Jamie Howell, "Potential Profitability and Decreased Consumer Welfare through Manufacturers' Cents-Off Coupons," *The Journal of Consumer Affairs,* Summer 1991, pp. 164–84; "Clutter Anyone? Marketers Dropped More than 300 Billion Coupons in the Past Year," *Adweek's Marketing Week,* April 8, 1991, pp. 22–25; "ActMedia Rolls Out Coupons," *Adweek's Marketing Week,* February 11, 1991, p. 42.

18. "Marketers Swap More than Goodwill at Trade Show," *Business Marketing,* September 1990, pp. 48–51; "Latest in Corporate Freebies Try to Be Classy instead of Trashy," *The Wall Street Journal,* August 7, 1989, p. B4; Rockney G. Walters, "An Empirical Investigation into Retailer Response to Manufacturer Trade Promotions," *Journal of Retailing,* Summer 1989, pp. 253–72; "Don't Just Exhibit—Do Something," *Business Marketing,* May 1989, pp. 78–79; "Trade Shows Can Pay Off for New Firms," *The Wall Street Journal,* January 1, 1989, pp. B1–2; Ronald C. Curhan and Robert J. Kopp, "Obtaining Retailer Support for Trade Deals: Key Success Factors," *Journal of Advertising Research,* December 1987–January 1988, pp. 51–60; Donald W. Jackson, Janet E. Keith, and Richard K. Burdick, "The Relative Importance of Various Promotional Elements in Different Industrial Purchase Situations," *Journal of Advertising* 16, no. 4 (1987), pp. 25–33; Daniel C. Bello and Hiram C. Barksdale, Jr., "Exporting at Industrial Trade Shows," *Industrial Marketing Management,* August 1986, pp. 197–206; Kenneth G. Hardy, "Key Success Factors for Manufacturers' Sales Promotions in Package Goods," *Journal of Marketing,* July 1986, pp. 13–23.

19. "Trade Promos Devour Half of All Marketing $," *Advertising Age,* April 13, 1992, p. 3ff.; Sunil Gupta, "Impact of Sales Promotions on When, What, and How Much to Buy," *Journal of Marketing Research,* November 1988, pp. 342–55; John A. Quelch, "It's Time to Make Trade Promotion More Productive," *Harvard Business Review,* May/June 1983, pp. 130–36.

20. "IBM Is Offering Workers Prizes to Hawk OS/2," *The Wall Street Journal,* March 27, 1992, p. B1ff.; "3M Distributors Go for the Gold," *Business Marketing,* May 1991, p. 49; "Chain Finds Incentives a Hard Sell," *The Wall Street Journal,* July 5, 1990, p. B1ff.; "Rewards for Good Work," *USA Today,* April 8, 1988, p. B1; Joanne Y. Cleaver, "Employee Incentives Rising to Top of Industry," *Advertising Age,* May 5, 1986, p. S1ff.

21. Donald R. Glover, "Distributor Attitudes Toward Manufacturer-Sponsored Promotions," *Industrial Marketing Management* 20, no. 3 (1991), pp. 241–50; Jean J. Boddewyn and Monica Leardi, "Sales Promotions: Practice, Regulation and Self-Regulation Around the World," *International Journal of Advertising* 8, no. 4 (1989), pp. 363–74; Thomas L. Powers, "Should You Increase Sales Promotion or Add Salespeople?" *Industrial Marketing Management* 18, no. 4 (1989), pp. 259–64; "Promotion 'Carnival' Gets Serious," *Advertising Age,* May 2, 1988, p. S1ff.

Chapter 14

1. *1990 Annual Report,* Alcoa; *1990 Annual Report,* Boeing; "A New Way to Wake Up a Giant," *Fortune,* October 22, 1990, pp. 90–103; "Alcoa Tries to Tap Entrepreneurial Spirit," *The Wall Street Journal,*

August 1, 1990, p. B2; "O'Neill Recasts Alcoa with His Eyes Fixed on a Decade Ahead," *The Wall Street Journal,* April 9, 1990, p. A1ff.

2. Philip R. Cateora, *International Marketing* (Homewood, Ill.: Richard D. Irwin, 1990), p. 113; Carl R. Ruthstrom and Ken Matejka, "The Meanings of 'YES' in the Far East," *Industrial Marketing Management,* August 1990, pp. 191–92; John S. Hill and Richard R. Still, "Organizing the Overseas Sales Force—How Multinationals Do It," *Journal of Personal Selling and Sales Management,* Spring 1990, pp. 57–66; Lennie Copeland and Lewis Griggs, *Going International* (New York: Random House, 1985), pp. 111–12; Phyllis A. Harrison, *Behaving Brazilian* (Rowley, Mass.: Newbury House Publishers, 1983), pp. 23–24.

3. Tom Richman, "Seducing the Customer: Dale Ballard's Perfect Selling Machine," *Inc.,* April, 1988, pp. 96–104; *1987 Annual Report,* Ballard Medical Products.

4. Thomas R. Wotruba, "The Evolution of Personal Selling," *Journal of Personal Selling and Sales Management,* Summer 1991, pp. 1–12; "Sizing Up Your Sales Force," *Business Marketing,* May, 1990; Douglas M. Lambert, Howard Marmorstein, and Arun Sharma, "Industrial Salespeople as a Source of Market Information," *Industrial Marketing Management,* May 1990, pp. 141–48; Michael J. Morden, "The Salesperson: Clerk, Con Man, or Professional?" *Business and Professional Ethics Journal,* 8, no. 1 (1989), pp. 3–24; George J. Avlonitis, Kevin A. Boyle, and Athanasios G. Kouremenos, "Matching the Salesmen to the Selling Job," *Industrial Marketing Management,* February 1986, pp. 45–54; Kenneth R. Evans and John L. Schlacter, "The Role of Sales Managers and Salespeople in a Marketing Information System," *Journal of Personal Selling and Sales Management,* November 1985, pp. 49–58; "Reach Out and Sell Something," *Fortune,* November 26, 1984, p. 127ff.; James H. Fouss and Elaine Solomon, "Salespeople as Researchers: Help or Hazard?" *Journal of Marketing,* Summer 1980, pp. 36–39; P. Ronald Stephenson, William L. Cron, and Gary L. Frazier, "Delegating Pricing Authority to the Sales Force: The Effects on Sales and Profit Performance," *Journal of Marketing,* Spring 1979, pp. 21–24.

5. "Pushing Doctors to Buy High Tech for the Office," *Business Week,* September 2, 1985, pp. 84–85.

6. "Truck-driving 'Sales Force' Hauls in Extra Customers," *Marketing News,* May 8, 1989, p. 2.

7. S. Joe Puri and Pradeep Korgaonkar, "Couple the Buying and Selling Teams," *Industrial Marketing Management* 20, no. 4 (1991), pp. 311–18; "P&G Rolls Out Retailer Sales Teams," *Advertising Age,* May 21, 1990, p. 18; Frank C. Cespedes, Stephen X. Doyle, and Robert J. Freedman, "Teamwork for Today's Selling," *Harvard Business Review,* March/April 1989, pp. 44–59.

8. John Barrett, "Why Major Account Selling Works," *Industrial Marketing Management,* February 1986, pp. 63–74; Jerome A. Colletti and Gary S. Tubridy, "Effective Major Account Sales Management," *Journal of Personal Selling and Sales Management,* August 1987, pp. 1–10.

9. "Telemarketers Take Root in the Country," *The Wall Street Journal,* February 2, 1989, p. B1.

10. "What Flexible Workers Can Do," *Fortune,* February 13, 1989, pp. 62–64; "Apparel Makers Play Bigger Part on Sales Floor," *The Wall Street Journal,* March 2, 1988, p. 31; David W. Cravens and Raymond W. LaForge, "Salesforce Deployment Analysis," *Industrial Marketing Management,* July 1983, pp. 179–92; Michael S. Herschel, "Effective Sales Territory Development," *Journal of Marketing,* April 1977, pp. 39–43.

11. "Salespeople on Road Use Laptops to Keep in Touch," *The Wall Street Journal,* April 25, 1991, p. B1; "If Only Willy Loman Had Used a Laptop," *Business Week,* October 12, 1987, p. 137.

12. "Systematizing Salesperson Selection," *Sales and Marketing Management,* February 1992, pp. 65–68; "The Fear Factor: Why Traditional Sales Training Doesn't Always Work," *Sales and Marketing Management,* February 1992, pp. 60–64; Robert C. Erffmeyer, K. Randall Russ, and Joseph F. Hair, Jr., "Needs Assessment and Evaluation in Sales-Training Programs," *Journal of Personal Selling and Sales Management,* Winter 1991, pp. 17–30; Warren S. Martin and Ben H. Collins, "Sales Technology Applications: Interactive Video Technology in Sales Training: A Case Study," *Journal of Personal Selling and Sales*

Management, Summer 1991, pp. 61–66; Jeffrey K. Sager, "Recruiting and Retaining Committed Salespeople," *Industrial Marketing Management* 20, no. 2 (1991), pp. 99–104; "The New Deal in Cars," *Adweek's Marketing Week,* August 13, 1990, pp. 18–20; "Two Days in Boot Camp—Learning to Love Lexus," *Business Week,* September 4, 1989; Earl D. Honeycutt and Thomas H. Stevenson, "Evaluating Sales Training Programs," *Industrial Marketing Management* 18, no. 3 (1989), pp. 215–22; Donald B. Guest and Havva J. Meric, "The Fortune 500 Companies Selection Criteria for Promotion to First Level Sales Management: An Empirical Study," *Journal of Personal Selling and Sales Management,* Fall 1989, pp. 47–58; Thomas R. Wotruba, Edwin K. Simpson, and Jennifer L. Reed-Draznick, "The Recruiting Interview as Perceived by College Student Applicants for Sales Positions," *Journal of Personal Selling and Sales Management,* Fall 1989, pp. 13–24; Richard Nelson, "Maybe It's Time to Take Another Look at Tests as a Sales Selection Tool?" *Journal of Personal Selling and Sales Management,* August 1987, pp. 33–38; Thomas W. Leigh, "Cognitive Selling Scripts and Sales Training," *Journal of Personal Selling and Sales Management,* August 1987, pp. 49–56; Barry J. B. Robinson, "Role Playing as a Sales Training Tool," *Harvard Business Review,* May/June, 1987, pp. 34–37; Robert H. Collins, "Sales Training: A Microcomputer-based Approach," *Journal of Personal Selling and Sales Management,* May 1986, p. 71; Wesley J. Johnston and Martha Cooper, "Analyzing the Industrial Salesforce Selection Process," *Industrial Marketing Management,* April 1981, pp. 139–47.

13. Bradley S. O'Hara, James S. Boles, and Mark W. Johnston, "The Influence of Personal Variables on Salesperson Selling Orientation," *Journal of Personal Selling and Sales Management,* Winter 1991, pp. 61–68; "Fire Up Your Sales Force," *Business Marketing,* July 1990, pp. 52–55; Richard F. Beltramini and Kenneth R. Evans, "Salesperson Motivation to Perform and Job Satisfaction: A Sales Contest Participant Perspective," *Journal of Personal Selling and Sales Management,* August 1988, pp. 35–42; William L. Cron, Alan J. Dubinsky, and Ronald E. Michaels, "The Influence of Career Stages on Components of Salesperson Motivation," *Journal of Marketing,* January 1988, pp. 78–92.

14. Russell Abratt and Michael R. Smythe, "A Survey of Sales Incentive Programs," *Industrial Marketing Management,* August 1989, pp. 209–14; "Now Salespeople Really Must Sell for Their Supper," *Business Week,* July 31, 1989, pp. 50–52; Thomas R. Wotruba, "The Effect of Goal-Setting on the Performance of Independent Sales Agents in Direct Selling," *Journal of Personal Selling and Sales Management,* Spring 1989, pp. 22–29; William Strahle and Rosann L. Spiro, "Linking Market Share Strategies to Salesforce Objectives, Activities, and Compensation Policies," *Journal of Personal Selling and Sales Management,* August 1986, pp. 11–18; Pradeep K. Tyagi and Carl E. Block, "Monetary Incentives and Salesmen Performance," *Industrial Marketing Management,* October 1983, pp. 263–70; John P. Steinbrink, "How to Pay Your Sales Force," *Harvard Business Review,* July/August 1978, pp. 111–22.

15. David J. Good and Robert W. Stone, "How Sales Quotas Are Developed," *Industrial Marketing Management* 20, no. 1 (1991), pp. 51–56; James W. Gentry, John C. Mowen, and Lori Tasaki, "Salesperson Evaluation: A Systematic Structure for Reducing Judgmental Biases," *Journal of Personal Selling and Sales Management,* Spring 1991, pp. 27–38; William A. Weeks and Lynn R. Kahle, "Salespeople's Time Use and Performance," *Journal of Personal Selling and Sales Management,* Winter 1990, pp. 29–38; Daniel A. Sauers, James B. Hunt, and Ken Bass, "Behavioral Self-Management as a Supplement to External Sales Force Controls," *Journal of Personal Selling and Sales Management,* Summer 1990, pp. 17–28; "Manage Your Sales Force," *Inc.,* January 1990, pp. 120–22; Jan P. Muczyk and Myron Gable, "Managing Sales Performance Through a Comprehensive Performance Appraisal System," *Journal of Personal Selling and Sales Management,* May 1987, pp. 41–52; "High-Tech Sales: Now You See Them, Now You Don't?" *Business Week,* November 18, 1985, pp. 106–7; Douglas N. Behrman and William D. Perreault, Jr., "A Role Stress Model of the Performance and Satisfaction of Industrial Salespersons," *Journal of Marketing,* Fall 1984, pp. 9–21; J. S. Schiff, "Evaluate the Sales Force as a Business," *Industrial Marketing Management,* April 1983, pp. 131–38; Douglas N. Behrman and William D. Perreault, Jr., "Measuring the Performance of Industrial Salespersons," *Journal of Business Research,* September 1982, pp. 350–70.

16. "Chief Executives Are Increasingly Chief Salesmen," *The Wall Street Journal,* August 6, 1991, p. B1ff.; John E. Swan and Richard L. Oliver, "An Applied Analysis of Buyer Equity Perceptions and Satisfaction with Automobile Salespeople," *Journal of Personal Selling and Sales Management,* Spring 1991, pp. 15–26; Joe F. Alexander, Patrick L. Schul, and Emin Babakus, "Analyzing Interpersonal Communications in Industrial Marketing Negotiations," *Journal of the Academy of Marketing Science,* Spring 1991, pp. 129–40.

17. William C. Moncrief et al., "Examining the Roles of Telemarketing in Selling Strategy," *Journal of Personal Selling and Sales Management,* Fall 1989, pp. 1–12; J. David Lichtenthal, Saameer Sikri, and Karl Folk, "Teleprospecting: An Approach for Qualifying Accounts," *Industrial Marketing Management,* February 1989, pp. 11–18; Judith J. Marshall and Harrie Vredenburg, "Successfully Using Telemarketing in Industrial Sales," *Industrial Marketing Management,* February 1988, pp. 15–22; Eugene M. Johnson and William J. Meiners, "Selling & Sales Management in Action: Telemarketing—Trends, Issues, and Opportunities," *Journal of Personal Selling and Sales Management,* November 1987, pp. 65–68; Herbert E. Brown and Roger W. Brucker, "Telephone Qualifications of Sales Leads," *Industrial Marketing Management,* August 1987, pp. 185–90.

18. "The New Wave of Sales Automation," *Business Marketing,* June 1991, pp. 12–16; L. Brent Manssen, "Using PCs to Automate and Innovate Marketing Activities," *Industrial Marketing Management,* August 1990, pp. 209–14; Doris C. Van Doren and Thomas A. Stickney, "How to Develop a Database for Sales Leads," *Industrial Marketing Management,* August 1990, pp. 201–8; Michael H. Morris, Alvin C. Burns, and Ramon A. Avila, "Computer Awareness and Usage by Industrial Marketers," *Industrial Marketing Management,* August 1989, pp. 223–32; Al Wedell and Dale Hempeck, "Sales Force Automation: Here and Now," *Journal of Personal Selling and Sales Management,* August 1987, pp. 11–16; Robert H. Collins, "Microcomputer Applications in Selling and Sales Management: Portable Computers—Applications to Increase Salesforce Productivity," *Journal of Personal Selling and Sales Management,* November 1984, p. 75ff.

19. For more on sales presentation approaches, see C. A. Pederson, M. D. Wright, and B. A. Weitz, *Selling: Principles and Methods* (Homewood, Ill.: Richard D. Irwin, 1986), pp. 224–356; Morgan P. Miles, Danny R. Arnold, and Henry W. Nash, "Adaptive Communication: The Adaption of the Seller's Interpersonal Style to the Stage of the Dyad's Relationship and the Buyer's Communication Style," *Journal of Personal Selling and Sales Management,* Winter 1990, pp. 21–28; "Presentations That Spell Pizzazz," *Business Marketing,* February 1989, pp. 86–88; Marvin A. Jolson, "Canned Adaptiveness: A New Direction for Modern Salesmanship," *Business Horizons,* January/February, 1989, pp. 7–12.

20. "Did Sears Take Other Customers for a Ride?" *Business Week,* August 3, 1992, pp. 24–25; "An Open Letter to Sears Customers," *USA Today,* June 25, 1992, p. 8A; Joseph A. Bellizzi and D. Wayne Norvell, "Personal Characteristics and Salesperson's Justifications as Moderators of Supervisory Discipline in Cases Involving Unethical Salesforce Behavior," *Journal of the Academy of Marketing Science,* Winter 1991, pp. 11–16; Alan J. Dubinsky, Marvin A. Jolson, Masaaki Kotabe, and Chae Un Lim, "A Cross-National Investigation of Industrial Salespeople's Ethical Perceptions," *Journal of International Business Studies,* Winter 1991, pp. 651–70; K. Douglas Hoffman, Vince Howe, and Donald W. Hardigree, "Ethical Dilemmas Faced in the Selling of Complex Services: Significant Others and Competitive Pressures," *Journal of Personal Selling and Sales Management,* Fall 1991, pp. 13–26; Anusorn Singhapakdi and Scott J. Vitell, "Analyzing the Ethical Decision Making of Sales Professionals," *Journal of Personal Selling and Sales Management,* Fall 1991, pp. 1–12; Rosemary R. Lagace, Robert Dahlstrom, and Jule B. Gassenheimer, "The Relevance of Ethical Salesperson Behavior on Relationship Quality: The Pharmaceutical Industry," *Journal of Personal Selling and Sales Management,* Fall 1991, pp. 39–48; Joseph A. Bellizzi and Robert E. Hite, "Supervising Unethical Salesforce Behavior," *Journal of Marketing,* April 1989, pp. 36–47.

Chapter 15

1. "Lighten Up, Energizer—Accept the Flattery," *Adweek's Marketing Week,* May 27, 1991, p. 37; "How the Bunny Charged Eveready," *Advertising Age,* April 8, 1991, p. 20ff.; "America's Favorite Campaigns,"

Adweek's Marketing Week, March 11, 1991, pp. 27–37; "Energizer's E.B. Parades into Ad History," *USA Today,* January 26, 1990, pp. 1B–2B; "Energizer's Parody Campaign Is One Bunny of a Concept," *Advertising Age,* October 23, 1989, p. 120.

2. Philip R. Cateora, *International Marketing* (Homewood, Ill.: Richard D. Irwin, 1990); Subhash C. Jain, *International Marketing Management* (Boston: PWS-Kent Publishing, 1990); Lee D. Dahringer and Hans Muhlbacher, *International Marketing: A Global Perspective* (Reading, Mass.: Addison-Wesley Publishing, 1991); Courtland L. Bovee and William F. Arens, *Contemporary Advertising* (Homewood, Ill.: Richard D. Irwin, 1992), pp. 670–97.

3. "Media Suffer Worst Year Since WWII," *USA Today,* December 10, 1991, pp. 1B–2B; "Coen Expects '92 Recovery, 9% Ad $ Hike," *Advertising Age,* October 28, 1991, p. 1ff.; "Media Outlook 1992," *Adweek's Marketing Week,* October 7, 1991; "Ad, Promotion Spending Expected to Grow 6.8%," *Marketing News,* July 22, 1991, p. 2; "Ad Spending Forecast Cut," *USA Today,* June 5, 1991, p. 1B; Lee D. Dahringer and Hans Muhlbacher, *International Marketing: A Global Perspective,* p. 481; Gary Levin and Jon Lafayette, "Ad Spending Hikes May Lag Inflation," *Advertising Age,* December 17, 1990, pp. 3, 34; Subhash C. Jain, *International Marketing Management,* pp. 528–30; Andrew Green, "International Advertising Expenditure Trends," *International Journal of Advertising* 8, no. 1 (1989), pp. 89–92; "Strong Spending: Foreign Ad Budgets Again Beat U.S.," *Advertising Age,* March 28, 1988, p. 6; "U.S. Outspends the World in Ads," *Marketing News,* February 2, 1988, p. 15.

4. "The 100 Leading National Advertisers," *Advertising Age,* September 25, 1991, pp. S1–S72; "Ad Ratio Gains Posted for '91," *Advertising Age,* September 16, 1991, p. 32; "Global Marketing & Media," *Advertising Age International,* November 19, 1990, pp. S1, S4, S10; Charles F. Keown et al., "Transnational Advertising-to-Sales Ratios: Do They Follow the Rules?" *International Journal of Advertising* 8, no. 4 (1989), pp. 375–90.

5. "How Bad a Year for Ads Was '91? Almost the Worst," *Advertising Age,* May 4, 1992, p. 3ff.

6. Exact data on this industry are elusive, but see U.S. Bureau of the Census, *Statistical Abstract of the United States 1991* (Washington, D.C.: U.S. Government Printing Office, 1991), p. 395; "Number of Jobs in Advertising Declines 3.7%," *The Wall Street Journal,* August 5, 1991, p. B1ff.; "A Blizzard of Pink Slips Chills Adland," *Business Week,* December 10, 1990, pp. 210–12.

7. For some examples of comparative advertising, see "Comparative TV Ad Reviews Criticized," *The Wall Street Journal,* October 23, 1990, p. B6; "Ford Accuses Chevy of Telling Whoppers in Pickup Truck Ads," *The Wall Street Journal,* October 17, 1990, p. B10; "Chemical Firms Press Campaigns to Dispel Their 'Bad Guy' Image," *The Wall Street Journal,* September 20, 1988, p. 1ff.; "Spiffing up the Corporate Image," *Fortune,* July 21, 1986, pp. 68–72; Lewis C. Winters, "The Effect of Brand Advertising on Company Image: Implications for Corporate Advertising," *Journal of Advertising Research,* April/May, 1986, p. 54ff. See also "A Comeback May Be Ahead for Brand X," *Business Week,* December 4, 1989, p. 35; "New Law Adds Risk to Comparative Ads," *The Wall Street Journal,* June 1, 1989, p. B6; Steven A. Meyerowitz, "The Developing Law of Comparative Advertising," *Business Marketing,* August 1985, pp. 81–86.

8. John K. Ross III, Larry T. Patterson, and Mary Ann Stutts, "Consumer Perceptions of Organizations That Use Cause-Related Marketing," *Journal of the Academy of Marketing Science,* Winter 1992, pp. 93–98; "Conscience Raising," *Advertising Age,* August 26, 1991, p. 19; "Whales, Human Rights, Rain Forests—And the Heady Smell of Profits," *Business Week,* July 15, 1991, pp. 114–15; "Charity Doesn't Begin at Home Anymore," *Business Week,* February 25, 1991, p. 91; "More Charities Reach Out for Corporate Sponsorship," *The Wall Street Journal,* October 1, 1990, p. B1ff.; "Ads That Work Against the Market," *Insight,* November 27, 1989, pp. 40–41.

9. For more on co-op ads, see "Hard Times Mean Growth for Co-op Ads," *Advertising Age,* November 12, 1990, p. 24; "Co-op Ads Attempt to Look More Like Brand-Name Commercials," *The Wall Street Journal,* July 21, 1989, p. B7; "Co-op: A Coup for Greater Profits," *Marketing Communications,* September 1985, pp. 66–73; "Ad Agencies Press Franchisees to Join National Campaigns," *The Wall Street Journal,* January 17, 1985, p. 29. For more on joint promotions see "Joint

Promotions Spawn Data Swap," *Advertising Age,* October 7, 1991, p. 44; "H&R Block, Excedrin Discover Joint Promotions Can Be Painless," *The Wall Street Journal,* February 28, 1991, p. B3; "Marketers Team in Time of Trouble," *Advertising Age,* February 18, 1991, p. 36.

10. "How Bad a Year for Ads Was '91? Almost the Worst," *Advertising Age,* May 4, 1992, pp. 51ff.; *Standard Rate and Data,* April 1992; "What's Right, What's Wrong with Each Medium," *Business Marketing,* April 1990, pp. 40–47; Richard W. Pollay, "The Subsiding Sizzle: A Descriptive History of Print Advertising, 1900–1980," *Journal of Marketing,* Summer 1985, pp. 24–37; Murphy A. Sewall and Dan Sarel, "Characteristics of Radio Commercials and Their Recall Effectiveness," *Journal of Marketing,* January 1986, pp. 52–60; "Special Report: Outdoor Marketing," *Advertising Age,* October 9, 1989, p. 1ff.; "Confused Advertisers Bemoan Proliferation of Yellow Pages," *The Wall Street Journal,* February 27, 1986, p. 23.

11. "No Sexy Sales Ads, Please—We're Brits and Swedes," *Fortune,* October 21, 1991, p. 13; "It's Hot! It's Sexy! It's Drop-Dead Calvin Klein," *Advertising Age,* September 23, 1991, p. 46; "Why Jockey Switched Its Ads from TV to Print," *Business Week,* July 26, 1976, pp. 140–42.

12. "Weighing the Worth of the Super Bowl," *Adweek,* January 14, 1991, p. 16; "Cost of TV Sports Commercials Prompts Cutbacks by Advertisers," *The Wall Street Journal,* January 15, 1985, p. 37; "Study of Olympics Ads Casts Doubts on Value of Campaigns," *The Wall Street Journal,* December 6, 1984, p. 33.

13. "Ads Head for Bathroom," *Advertising Age,* May 18, 1992, p. 24; "Product Placement Can Be Free Lunch," *The Wall Street Journal,* November 25, 1991, p. B6; "Consumers Seek Escape from Captive-Ad Gimmicks," *The Wall Street Journal,* September 13, 1991, p. B1ff.; "Turner Aims to Line Up Captive Audience," *The Wall Street Journal,* June 21, 1991, p. B1ff.; "Where Should Advertising Be?" *Adweek's Marketing Week,* May 6, 1991, pp. 26–27; "TV Takes on Tabloids at Checkout Line," *American Demographics,* April 1991, p. 9; "In-Store Ads Are Getting Harder to Ignore," *The Wall Street Journal,* October 16, 1990, p. B6; "Turning PCs into Salesmen," *Newsweek,* March 12, 1990, p. 69; "Video Renters Watch the Ads, Zapping Conventional Wisdom," *The Wall Street Journal,* April 28, 1989, p. B1.

14. "How to Spend $1 Million a Minute," *Business Week,* February 3, 1992, p. 34; "An Expensive 30 Seconds," *USA Today,* October 3, 1991, p. 1D; "Prime-Time Rates Take a Tumble," *Advertising Age,* September 16, 1991, p. 6; Darrel D. Muehling and Carl S. Bozman, "An Examination of Factors Influencing Effectiveness of 15-Second Advertisements," *International Journal of Advertising* 9, no. 4 (1990), pp. 331–44.

15. "Now, They're Selling BMWs Door-to-Door—Almost," *Business Week,* May 14, 1990, p. 65; Keith Fletcher, Colin Wheeler, and Julia Wright, "Database Marketing: a Channel, a Medium or a Strategic Approach?" *International Journal of Advertising* 10, no. 2 (1991), pp. 117–28; "Devising Mailing Lists for Every Marketer," *The Wall Street Journal,* May 7, 1991, p. B1; "Warner Tries Target Marketing to Sell Film Lacking Typical Box-Office Appeal," *The Wall Street Journal,* October 3, 1990, p. B1ff.; "Direct Marketing Agency Report," *Advertising Age,* May 21, 1990, pp. S1–S10; "Direct Marketing: A Modern Marketing Solution," *Directions* (New York: Direct Marketing Association, 1990); "Special Report: Direct Marketing," *Advertising Age,* September 25, 1990, pp. S1–S16; "Breakthrough Direct Marketing," *Business Marketing,* August 1990, pp. 20–29; Robert L. Sherman, *Mailing Lists, Information and Privacy* (New York: Prepared for DMA, June 1989); Lindsay Meredith, "Developing and Using a Data Base Marketing System," *Industrial Marketing Management* 18, no. 4 (1989), pp. 245–58; Gordon Storholm and Hershey Friedman, "Perceived Common Myths and Unethical Practices among Direct Marketing Professionals," *Journal of Business Ethics,* December 1989, pp. 975–80; Steven Miller, "Mine the Direct Marketing Riches in Your Database," *The Journal of Business Strategy,* November/December 1989, pp. 33–36; Frank K. Sonnenberg, "Marketing: Direct Mail—The Right Audience and the Right Message," *The Journal of Business Strategy,* January/February 1989, pp. 60–68; "Special Report: Direct Marketing," *Advertising Age,* January 18, 1988, pp. S1–S20; Roger Craver, "Direct Marketing in the Political Process," *Fundraising Management,* October 1987; Rose Harper, *Mailing List Strategies* (New York: McGraw-Hill, 1986); Bob Stone and John Wyman, *Successful Telemarketing* (Lincolnshire, Ill.: NTC Books, 1986); Pierre

Passavant, "Direct Marketing Strategy," *The Direct Marketing Handbook,* ed. by Edward L. Nash (New York: McGraw-Hill, 1984). For more on the privacy issue, see "As Phone Technology Swiftly Advances, Fears Grow They'll Have Your Number," *The Wall Street Journal,* December 13, 1991, p. B1ff.; "Firms Peddle Information from Driver's Licenses," *The Wall Street Journal,* November 25, 1991, p. B1; "Equifax to Stop Selling Its Data to Junk-Mailers," *The Wall Street Journal,* August 9, 1991, p. B1ff.; "How Did They Get My Name?" *Newsweek,* June 3, 1991, pp. 40–42; "Amid Privacy Furor, Lotus Kills a Disk," *Adweek's Marketing Week,* January 28, 1991, p. 9.

16. "Benetton Brouhaha," *Advertising Age,* February 17, 1992, p. 62; "Mixing Politics and Separates," *Adweek,* February 17, 1992, p. 30; "Debate Brews over Selling Beer with Sex," *USA Today,* November 15, 1991, pp. 1B–2B; "Controversial Adman Bares His Concept," *USA Today,* July 25, 1991, p. 8B; Prema Nakra, "Zapping Nonsense: Should Television Media Planners Lose Sleep over It?" *International Journal of Advertising* 10, no. 3 (1991), pp. 217–22; Gary L. Clark, Peter F. Kaminski, and Gene Brown, "The Readability of Advertisements and Articles in Trade Journals," *Industrial Marketing Management,* August 1990, pp. 251–60; "Advertisers See Big Gains in Odd Layouts: Page Position Can Make Ads More Prominent," *The Wall Street Journal,* June 29, 1988, p. 25; Joel Saegert, "Why Marketing Should Quit Giving Subliminal Advertising the Benefit of the Doubt," *Psychology and Marketing,* Summer 1987, pp. 107–20; "And Now, a Wittier Word From Our Sponsors," *Business Week,* March 24, 1986, pp. 90–94.

17. "Smooth Talk Wins Gillette Ad Space in Iran," *Advertising Age International,* April 27, 1992, p. I–40; Courtland L. Bovee and William F. Arens, *Contemporary Advertising,* pp. 671–72; Joshua Levine, "Global Lather," *Forbes,* February 5, 1990, pp. 146, 148; Alison Fahey, "International Ad Effort to Back Gillette Sensor," *Advertising Age,* October 16, 1989, p. 34.

18. Theodore Levitt, "The Globalization of Markets," *Harvard Business Review,* May/June 1983, pp. 92–102. See also Kamran Kashani, "Beware the Pitfalls of Global Marketing," *Harvard Business Review,* September/October 1989, pp. 91–98; Donald R. Glover, Steven W. Hartley, and Charles H. Patti, "How Advertising Message Strategies Are Set," *Industrial Marketing Management* 18, no. 1 (1989), pp. 19–26.

19. "Special Issue: Agency Report," *Advertising Age,* April 13, 1992, pp. S1–S44; "Special Issue: Agency Report Card," *Adweek,* March 23, 1992; "International: World Brands," *Advertising Age,* September 2, 1991, pp. 25–36.

20. "Blame-the-Messenger Mentality Leaves Scars on Madison Avenue," *The Wall Street Journal,* November 20, 1991, p. B4; Brian Jacobs, "Trends in Media Buying and Selling in Europe and the Effect on the Advertising Agency Business," *International Journal of Advertising* 10, no. 4 (1991), pp. 283–92; "Feeling a Little Jumpy," *Time,* July 8, 1991, pp. 42–43; "More Agencies Seek Payment in Advance," *The Wall Street Journal,* May 6, 1991, p. B6; "Big Agency, Small Agency: Which One Is Right for Your Business?" *Business Marketing,* May 1991, pp. 13–15; "DDB Needham 'Results' Plan Draws Yawns," *Advertising Age,* April 1, 1991, p. 3ff.; Ali Kanso, "The Use of Advertising Agencies for Foreign Markets: Decentralized Decisions and Localized Approaches?" *International Journal of Advertising* 10, no. 2 (1991), pp. 129–36; Richard Beltramini and Dennis A. Pitta, "Underlying Dimensions and Communications Strategies of the Advertising Agency–Client Relationship," *International Journal of Advertising* 10, no. 2 (1991), pp. 151–60; "Pursuing Results in the Age of Accountability," *Adweek's Marketing Week,* November 19, 1990, pp. 20–22; "As Ad Research Gains Followers, Agencies Point Out Its Failures," *The Wall Street Journal,* April 5, 1989, p. B11; "Carnation Links Pay, Research," *Advertising Age,* March 6, 1989, p. 1ff.; "More Companies Offer Their Ad Agencies Bonus Plans that Reward Superior Work," *The Wall Street Journal,* July 26, 1988, p. 37; "A Word from the Sponsor: Get Results—or Else," *Business Week,* July 4, 1988, p. 66; Michael G. Harvey and J. Paul Rupert, "Selecting an Industrial Advertising Agency," *Industrial Marketing Management,* May 1988, pp. 119–28; Daniel B. Wackman, Charles T. Salmon, and Caryn C. Salmon, "Developing an Advertising Agency–Client Relationship," *Journal of Advertising Research,* December 1986–January 1987, pp. 21–28.

21. Lee D. Dahringer and Hans Muhlbacher, *International Marketing: A Global Perspective,* p. 483; *International Werburg,* December 1, 1986, p. 9.

22. "Behind the Scenes at an American Express Commercial," *Business Week,* May 20, 1985, pp. 84–88.

23. "Ads Aimed at Older Americans May Be Too Old for Audience," *The Wall Street Journal,* December 31, 1991, p. B4; "Research Tactic Misses the Big Question: Why?" *The Wall Street Journal,* November 4, 1991, p. B1ff.; "Ads on TV: Out of Sight, Out of Mind?" *The Wall Street Journal,* May 14, 1991, p. B1ff.; "Magazines Helping Advertisers Measure Response to Their Ads," *The Wall Street Journal,* January 16, 1991, p. B5; "TvB Rebuts Prof: Adds Its Voice to Defense of Ads," *Advertising Age,* May 1, 1989, p. 26; "Television Ads Ring Up No Sale in Study," *The Wall Street Journal,* February 15, 1989, p. B6; George M. Zinkhan, "Rating Industrial Advertisements," *Industrial Marketing Management,* February 1984, pp. 43–48; Lawrence C. Soley, "Copy Length and Industrial Advertising Readership," *Industrial Marketing Management,* August 1986, pp. 245–52; David W. Stewart, "Measures, Methods, and Models in Advertising Research," *Journal of Advertising Research,* June/July 1989, p. 54ff.

24. "Pepsi Challenges Japanese Taboo as It Ribs Coke," *The Wall Street Journal,* March 6, 1991, p. B1ff. For additional examples, see Courtland L. Bovee and William R. Arens, *Contemporary Advertising,* pp. 694–96; Subhash C. Jain, *International Marketing Management,* pp. 559–63; Philip R. Cateora, *International Marketing,* pp. 492–93; Lee D. Dahringer and Hans Muhlbacher, *International Marketing: A Global Perspective,* p. 479; Albert Schofield, "International Differences in Advertising Practices: Britain Compared with Other Countries," *International Journal of Advertising* 10, no. 4 (1991), pp. 299–308; Philip Circus, "Alcohol Advertising—The Rules," *International Journal of Advertising* 8, no. 2 (1989), pp. 159–66; Marc G. Weinberger and Harlan E. Spotts, "A Situational View of Information Content in TV Advertising in the U.S. and U.K.," *Journal of Marketing,* January 1989, pp. 89–94; Jean Boddewyn, "The One and Many Worlds of Advertising: Regulatory Obstacles and Opportunities," *International Journal of Advertising* 7, no. 1 (1988); "Advertisers Find the Climate Less Hostile Outside the U.S.," *The Wall Street Journal,* December 10, 1987, p. 29; Rein Riijkens and Gordon E. Miracle, *European Regulation of Advertising* (New York: Elsevier Science Publishing, 1986); "EEC Media Experts Push for New Limits on Pan-Europe Ads," *Advertising Age,* January 30, 1984, p. 52.

25. "FTC under Industry Pressure, Shows New Life in Backing Deceptive Ad Laws," *The Wall Street Journal,* April 17, 1989, p. B4; "Lowest-Price Claims in Ads Stir Dispute," *The Wall Street Journal,* August 12, 1988, p. 17.

26. Gary T. Ford and John E. Calfee, "Recent Developments in FTC Policy on Deception," *Journal of Marketing,* July 1986, pp. 82–103; Dorothy Cohen, "Unfairness in Advertising Revisited," *Journal of Marketing,* Winter 1982, pp. 73–80; "Lysol's Maker Keeps Fighting FTC over Advertising Claims," *The Wall Street Journal,* February 24, 1983, p. 29; John S. Healey and Harold H. Kassarjian, "Advertising Substantiation and Advertiser Response: A Content Analysis of Magazine Advertisements," *Journal of Marketing,* Winter 1983, pp. 107–17; Michael A. Kamins and Lawrence J. Marks, "Advertising Puffery: The Impact of Using Two-Sided Claims on Product Attitude and Purchase," *Journal of Advertising* 16, no. 4 (1987), pp. 6–15.

27. S. K. List, "The Right Place to Find Children," *American Demographics,* February 1992, pp. 44–47; "Pediatric Academy Prescribes Ban on Food Ads Aimed at Children," *The Wall Street Journal,* July 24, 1991, p. B8; "Is TV Ruining Our Children?" *Time,* October 15, 1990, pp. 75–76; "Kids' Advertisers Play Hide-and-Seek, Concealing Commercials in Every Cranny," *The Wall Street Journal,* April 30, 1990, p. B1ff.; "NAD Tackles Kids' 900-Number Ads," *Advertising Age,* February 20, 1989, p. 64; "Double Standard for Kids' TV Ads," *The Wall Street Journal,* June 10, 1988, p. 25; "Watchdogs Zealously Censor Advertising Targeted to Kids," *The Wall Street Journal,* September 5, 1985, p. 35; Priscilla A. LaBarbera, "The Diffusion of Trade Association Advertising Self-Regulation," *Journal of Marketing,* Winter 1983, pp. 58–67.

Chapter 16

1. "After the Miata, Mazda Isn't Just Idling," *Business Week,* September 2, 1991, p. 35; "Mazda's Bold New Global Strategy," *Fortune,* December 17, 1990, pp. 109–13; *1990 Annual Report,* Mazda;

"Miatific Bliss in Five Gears," *Time,* October 2, 1989, p. 91; "Sexy Ragtop Puts Buyers in Scramble," *USA Today,* August 11–13, 1989, pp. A1–A2; "Miata Success Story Has Curious Twists," *The Wall Street Journal,* August 3, 1989, p. B1; "Romancing the Roadster," *Time,* July 24, 1989, p. 39; "Mazda Rolls Out a Poor Man's Maserati," *Business Week,* June 26, 1989, p. 66.

2. "Car Makers Seek to Mask Price Increases," *The Wall Street Journal,* August 16, 1989, p. B1.

3. Alfred Rappaport, "Executive Incentives versus Corporate Growth," *Harvard Business Review,* July/August 1978, pp. 81–88.

4. Pricing "in the public interest" is often an issue in pricing government services; for an interesting example, see "Price Policy on Space Shuttle's Commercial Use Could Launch—or Ground—NASA's Rockets," *The Wall Street Journal,* March 21, 1985, p. 64.

5. "Computer Price Cuts Seem Likely Despite Efforts to Hold the Line," *The Wall Street Journal,* September 5, 1985, p. 25.

6. "Harvester Sells Many Trucks below Cost, Citing Need to Maintain Dealer Network," *The Wall Street Journal,* April 19, 1983, p. 8.

7. "Why the Price Wars Never End," *Fortune,* March 23, 1992, pp. 68–78; "Middle-Price Brands Come Under Siege," *The Wall Street Journal,* April 2, 1990, p. B1ff.; "Avis, Sidestepping Price Wars, Focuses on the Drive Itself," *Adweek's Marketing Week,* February 12, 1990, p. 24; "Leave the Herd and Leap off the Old Price Treadmill," *Chicago Tribune,* November 11, 1985, Sec. 4, p. 21ff.

8. "Aluminum Firms Offer Wider Discounts but Price Cuts Stop at Some Distributors," *The Wall Street Journal,* November 16, 1984, p. 50.

9. Elliot B. Ross, "Making Money with Proactive Pricing," *Harvard Business Review,* November/December 1984, pp. 145–55; Thomas Nagle, "Pricing as Creative Marketing," *Business Horizons,* July/August 1983, pp. 14–19. See also Subhash C. Jain and Michael B. Laric, "A Framework for Strategic Industrial Pricing," *Industrial Marketing Management* 8 (1979), pp. 75–80; Mary Karr, "The Case of the Pricing Predicament," *Harvard Business Review,* March/April 1988, pp. 10–23; Saeed Samiee, "Pricing in Marketing Strategies of U.S. and Foreign-Based Companies," *Journal of Business Research,* February 1987, pp. 17–30; Gerard J. Tellis, "Beyond the Many Faces of Price: An Integration of Pricing Strategies," *Journal of Marketing,* October 1986, pp. 146–60.

10. "Ford Expands 'One-Price' Plan for Its Escorts," *The Wall Street Journal,* March 12, 1992, p. B1ff.; "18-Month-Old Saturn Walking Tall," *USA Today,* February 24, 1992, p. 1B. For an interesting discussion of the many variations from a one-price system in retailing, see Stanley C. Hollander, "The 'One-Price' System—Fact or Fiction?" *Journal of Marketing Research,* February 1972, pp. 35–40. See also Michael J. Houston, "Minimum Markup Laws: An Empirical Assessment," *Journal of Retailing,* Winter 1981, pp. 98–113; "Flexible Pricing," *Business Week,* December 12, 1977, pp. 78–88; Michael H. Morris, "Separate Prices as a Marketing Tool," *Industrial Marketing Management,* May 1987, pp. 79–86.

11. "Squeezin' the Charmin," *Fortune,* January 16, 1989, pp. 11–12; "Grocers Join Winn-Dixie," *Advertising Age,* November 7, 1988, p. 3; "Grocery Chains Pressure Suppliers for Uniform Prices," *The Wall Street Journal,* October 21, 1988, p. B1; "Grocery Chain Dumps Major Package Goods," *Advertising Age,* October 10, 1988, p. 1ff.

12. Alan Reynolds, "A Kind Word for 'Cream Skimming,'" *Harvard Business Review,* November/December 1974, pp. 113–20.

13. "Breakthrough in Birth Control May Elude Poor," *The Wall Street Journal,* March 4, 1991, p. B1ff; "Burroughs Wellcome Reaps Profits, Outrage from Its AIDS Drug," *The Wall Street Journal,* September 15, 1989, p. A1ff.

14. Stuart U. Rich, "Price Leadership in the Paper Industry," *Industrial Marketing Management,* April 1983, pp. 101–4; "OPEC Member Offers Discounts to Some Amid Downward Pressure on Oil Prices," *The Wall Street Journal,* November 16, 1984, p. 4.

15. *1990 Annual Report,* Campbell; "Campbell's Taste of the Japanese Market is Mm-Mm Good," *Business Week,* March 28, 1988, p. 42; "Most U.S. Firms Seek Extra Profits in Japan, at the Expense of Sales," *The Wall Street Journal,* May 15, 1987, p. 1ff.

16. Exchange rates are from the July 17, 1992 issue of *The Wall Street Journal,* but they are available on a daily basis. David N. Hyman, *Economics,* 2nd edition (Homewood, Ill.: Richard D. Irwin, 1992), pp. 82–83; Timothy A. Luehrman, "Exchange Rate Changes and the Distribution of Industry Value," *Journal of International Business Studies,* Winter 1991, pp. 619–50.

17. "Fast-Food Chains Hope Diners Swallow New 'Value' Menu of Higher-Priced Items," *The Wall Street Journal,* March 13, 1992, p. B1ff.; "Value Marketing," *Business Week,* November 11, 1991, pp. 132–40; "Why Chic Is Now Cheaper," *Time,* November 11, 1991, pp. 68–70; "Ford Motor Ventures into 'Value' Pricing," *The Wall Street Journal,* September 18, 1991, p. B1; "Fashion Designers Snip Prices," *Fortune,* May 6, 1991, p. 9; "'Value Pricing' Is Hot as Shrewd Consumers Seek Low-Cost Quality," *The Wall Street Journal,* March 12, 1991, p. A1ff.; Louis J. De Rose, "Meet Today's Buying Influences With Value Selling," *Industrial Marketing Management* 20, no. 2 (1991), pp. 87–90; "A Buyer's Market Has Shoppers Demanding and Getting Discounts," *The Wall Street Journal,* February 8, 1991, p. A1ff.; "'Value' Strategy to Battle Recession," *Advertising Age,* January 7, 1991, p. 1ff.; "'Value' Brands Head for Shelves," *Adweek's Marketing Week,* October 29, 1990, p. 6.

18. For more on quantity discounts, see George S. Day and Adrian B. Ryans, "Using Price Discounts for a Competitive Advantage," *Industrial Marketing Management,* February 1988, pp. 1–14; James B. Wilcox et al., "Price Quantity Discounts: Some Implications for Buyers and Sellers," *Journal of Marketing,* July 1987, pp. 60–70. For more on frequent flier programs, see "Air Miles Program Takes Off," *Direct Marketing,* March 1992, pp. 40–43; "Forget the Green Stamps—Give Me a Ticket to Miami," *Business Week,* February 24, 1992, pp. 70–71; "Frequent Fliers Get New Perks from Airlines," *The Wall Street Journal,* January 5, 1990, p. B1. For more on other frequent buyer programs, see "Frequent Shopper Programs Ripen," *Advertising Age,* August 6, 1990, p. 21; "Clubs Reward Buyers at Bookstore Chains," *Insight,* March 26, 1990, p. 43; "Frequent-Stay Plans Are Best Checked Out," *The Wall Street Journal,* March 20, 1990, p. B1; "Frequent Reader Clubs: A New Book Battleground," *Adweek's Marketing Week,* March 12, 1990, p. 28; "Waldenbooks' Big-Buyer Lure May Mean War," *The Wall Street Journal,* February 27, 1990, p. B1ff. For more on cash discounts, see "Cash Discounts," *Electrical Wholesaling,* May 1989, pp. 90–96.

19. "P&G Plays Pied Piper on Pricing," *Advertising Age,* March 9, 1992, p. 6; "P&G Tries to Build Brand Loyalty with Lower Prices," *The Wall Street Journal,* November 7, 1991, p. B1; "Grocery Price Wars Squeeze Marketers," *The Wall Street Journal,* November 7, 1991, p. B1; "Addiction to Cost Cutting Feeds Slump," *USA Today,* June 5, 1991, pp. 1B–2B; "Store's Concept of 'Sale' Pricing Gets Court Test," *The Wall Street Journal,* May 15, 1990, p. B1ff.; "As Retailers' Sales Crop Up Everywhere, Regulators Wonder if the Price Is Right," *The Wall Street Journal,* February 13, 1990, p. B1ff.; "The 'Sale' Is Fading as a Retailing Tactic," *The Wall Street Journal,* March 1, 1989, p. B1ff.

20. "Getting Around Slotting Fees," *Food Business,* June 17, 1991, p. 12; "Slotting Fees May Get FTC OK," *Advertising Age,* June 18, 1990, p. 4; "P&G 'Teams' Serve Retailers' Needs: To Reduce Role of Slotting Fees," *Advertising Age,* August 14, 1989, p. 21; "Want Shelf Space at the Supermarket? Ante Up," *Business Week,* August 7, 1989, pp. 60–61; "Supermarkets Demand Food Firms' Payments Just to Get on the Shelf," *The Wall Street Journal,* November 1, 1988, p. A1ff.

21. For more on coupons, see "Coupon Scams Are Clipping Companies," *Business Week,* June 15, 1992, pp. 110–11; "Pious Town Finds Mighty Temptation in Coupon Clipping," *The Wall Street Journal,* February 21, 1992, p. A1ff.; "Recession Feeds the Coupon Habit," *The Wall Street Journal,* February 20, 1991, p. B1; "Redeeming Feature: Special Printing May Cut Coupon Counterfeits," *Advertising Age,* February 4, 1991, p. 35; "ActMedia Puts the Coupon on the Shelf," *Adweek's Marketing Week,* January 21, 1991, p. 8. For more on rebates, see "Rebate Program Rings Wright Bell," *Advertising Age,* May 21, 1990, p. 44; "Marketers Tighten Rules on Rebate Offers in Effort to Reduce Large Fraud Losses, *The Wall Street Journal,* March 18, 1987, p. 33.

22. For an excellent discussion of laws related to pricing, see Louis W. Stern and Thomas L. Eovaldi, *Legal Aspects of Marketing Strategy: Antitrust and Consumer Protection Issues* (Englewood Cliffs, N.J.: Prentice Hall, 1984).

23. Donald R. Lichtenstein and William O. Bearden, "Contextual Influences on Perceptions of Merchant-Supplied Reference Prices," *Journal of Consumer Research,* June 1989, pp. 55–66; John Liefeld and Louise A. Heslop, "Reference Prices and Deception in Newspaper Advertising," *Journal of Consumer Research,* March 1985, pp. 868–76. Individual states often have their own laws; see, for example, "States Crack Down on Phony Price-cutting 'Sales,' " *The Wall Street Journal,* January 30, 1986, p. 1; Willard F. Mueller and Thomas W. Paterson, "Effectiveness of State Sales-below-Cost Laws: Evidence from the Grocery Trade," *Journal of Retailing,* Summer 1986, pp. 166–85.

24. "How Three Companies Allegedly Conspired to Fix Matzo Prices," *The Wall Street Journal,* March 11, 1991, p. A1ff.; "Anti-Discount Policies of Manufacturers Are Penalizing Certain Cut-Price Stores," *The Wall Street Journal,* February 27, 1991, p. B1ff.; "State Attorneys General Battle for Direction of Antitrust Law," *Insight,* February 25, 1991, pp. 40–42; "Relaxing the Antitrust Laws to Allow Firms to Join Hands," *Insight,* June 25, 1990, pp. 42–43; "Court Says Indirect Buyers Can Sue Violators of State Antitrust Laws," *The Wall Street Journal,* April 19, 1989, p. B7; "Panasonic to Pay Rebates to Avoid Antitrust Charges," *The Wall Street Journal,* January 19, 1989, p. B1ff. See also Mary Jane Sheffet and Debra L. Scammon, "Resale Price Maintenance: Is It Safe to Suggest Retail Prices?" *Journal of Marketing,* Fall 1985, pp. 82–91.

25. Morris L. Mayer, Joseph B. Mason, and E. A. Orbeck, "The Borden Case—A Legal Basis for Private Brand Price Discrimination," *MSU Business Topics,* Winter 1970, pp. 56–63; T. F. Schutte, V. J. Cook, Jr., and R. Hemsley, "What Management Can Learn from the Borden Case," *Business Horizons,* Winter 1966, pp. 23–30.

26. "Is the Cost Defense Workable?" *Journal of Marketing,* January 1965, pp. 37–42; B. J. Linder and Allan H. Savage, "Price Discrimination and Cost Defense—Change Ahead?" *MSU Business Topics,* Summer 1971, pp. 21–26; "Firms Must Prove Injury from Price Bias to Qualify for Damages, High Court Says," *The Wall Street Journal,* May 19, 1981, p. 8.

27. "FTC Accuses Six Large Book Publishers of Price Bias Against Independent Stores," *The Wall Street Journal,* December 23, 1988, p. B4; Lawrence X. Tarpey, Sr., "Who Is a Competing Customer?" *Journal of Retailing,* Spring 1969, pp. 46–58; John R. Davidson, "FTC, Robinson-Patman and Cooperative Promotion Activities," *Journal of Marketing,* January 1968, pp. 14–18; L. X. Tarpey, Sr., "Buyer Liability under the Robinson-Patman Act: A Current Appraisal," *Journal of Marketing,* January 1972, pp. 38–42.

Appendix B

1. Checking the accuracy of forecasts is a difficult subject. See "Don't Be Trapped By Past Success," *Nation's Business,* March 1992, pp. 52–54; David L. Kendall and Michael T. French, "Forecasting the Potential for New Industrial Products," *Industrial Marketing Management* 20, no. 3 (1991), pp. 177–84; John T. Mentzer and Roger Gomes, "Evaluating a Decision Support Forecasting System," *Industrial Marketing Management* 18, no. 4 (1989), pp. 313–24; James E. Cox, Jr., "Approaches for Improving Salespersons' Forecasts," *Industrial Marketing Management* 18, no. 4 (1989), pp. 307–12; Ronald D. Michman, "Why Forecast for the Long Term?" *The Journal of Business Strategy,* September/October 1989, pp. 36–41; F. William Barnett, "Four Steps to Forecast Total Market Demand," *Harvard Business Review,* July/August 1988, pp. 28–40; Anthony D. Cox and John O. Summers, "Heuristics and Biases in the Intuitive Projection of Retail Sales," *Journal of Marketing Research,* August 1987, pp. 290–97; Robert H. Collins and Rebecca J. Mauritson, "Microcomputer Applications: Artificial Intelligence in Sales Forecasting Applications," *Journal of Personal Selling and Sales Management,* May 1987, pp. 77–80; Arthur J. Adams, "Procedures for Revising Management Judgment Forecasts," *Journal of the Academy of Marketing Science,* Fall 1986, pp. 52–57; D. M. Georgoff and R. G. Murdick, "Manager's Guide to Forecasting," *Harvard Business Review,* January/February 1986, pp. 110–20.

Chapter 17

1. "Wal-Mart Expands Sam's Choice Line," *Advertising Age,* April 27, 1992, p. 4; "Pioneer Changed Face of Retailing," *USA Today,* April 6, 1992, pp. 1B–2B; "O.K., So He's Not Sam Walton," *Business Week,* March 16, 1992, pp. 56–58; "Wal-Mart Puts Its Own Spin on Private Label," *Advertising Age,* December 16, 1991, p. 26; "The Sam's Generation?" *Business Week,* November 25, 1991, pp. 36–38; "America's Most Successful Merchant," *Fortune,* September 23, 1991, pp. 46–59; "Is Wal-Mart Unstoppable?" *Fortune,* May 6, 1991, pp. 50–59; "Mr. Sam Stuns Goliath," *Time,* February 25, 1991, pp. 62–63; *1991 Annual Report,* Wal-Mart; *1991 Annual Report,* Kmart.

2. Marvin A. Jolson, "A Diagrammatic Model for Merchandising Calculations," *Journal of Retailing,* Summer 1975, pp. 3–9.

3. "Blouse-Cleaning Rates Are Unfair, Woman Charges," *The Raleigh News & Observer,* July 7, 1992, p. 3B.

4. Mary L. Hatten, "Don't Get Caught with Your Prices Down: Pricing in Inflationary Times," *Business Horizons,* March 1982, pp. 23–28; "Why Detroit Can't Cut Prices," *Business Week,* March 1, 1982, p. 110; Douglas G. Brooks, "Cost-Oriented Pricing: A Realistic Solution to a Complicated Problem," *Journal of Marketing,* April 1975, pp. 72–74.

5. Approaches for estimating price-quantity relationships are reviewed in Kent B. Monroe, *Pricing: Making Profitable Decisions* (New York: McGraw-Hill, 1979). For a specific example see Frank D. Jones, "A Survey Technique to Measure Demand under Various Pricing Strategies," *Journal of Marketing,* July 1975, pp. 75–77; or Gordon A. Wyner, Lois H. Benedetti, and Bart M. Trapp, "Measuring the Quantity and Mix of Product Demand," *Journal of Marketing,* Winter 1984, pp. 101–9. See also Michael H. Morris and Mary L. Joyce, "How Marketers Evaluate Price Sensitivity," *Industrial Marketing Management,* May 1988, pp. 169–76.

6. Benson P. Shapiro and Barbara P. Jackson, "Industrial Pricing to Meet Customer Needs," *Harvard Business Review,* November/December 1978, pp. 119–27; "The Race to the $10 Light Bulb," *Business Week,* May 19, 1980, p. 124; see also Michael H. Morris and Donald A. Fuller, "Pricing an Industrial Service," *Industrial Marketing Management,* May 1989, pp. 139–46.

7. Thomas T. Nagle, *The Strategy and Tactics of Pricing* (Englewood Cliffs, N.J.: Prentice Hall, 1987), pp. 249–55.

8. For an example applied to a high-price item, see "Sale of Mink Coats Strays a Fur Piece from the Expected," *The Wall Street Journal,* March 21, 1980, p. 30.

9. B. P. Shapiro, "The Psychology of Pricing," *Harvard Business Review,* July/August 1968, pp. 14–24; C. Davis Fogg and Kent H. Kohnken, "Price-Cost Planning," *Journal of Marketing,* April 1978, pp. 97–106.

10. Robert M. Schindler and Alan R. Wiman, "Effects of Odd Pricing on Price Recall," *Journal of Business Research,* November 1989, pp. 165–78; "Strategic Mix of Odd, Even Prices Can Lead to Increased Retail Profits," *Marketing News,* March 7, 1980, p. 24.

11. "Special Report: Marketing to the Affluent," *Advertising Age,* October 19, 1987, pp. S1–S32; Peter C. Riesz, "Price versus Quality in the Marketplace," *Journal of Retailing,* Winter 1978, pp. 15–28; John J. Wheatly and John S. Y. Chiu, "The Effects of Price, Store Image, and Product and Respondent Characteristics on Perceptions of Quality," *Journal of Marketing Research,* May 1977, pp. 181–86; N. D. French, J. J. Williams, and W. A. Chance, "A Shopping Experiment on Price-Quality Relationships," *Journal of Retailing,* Fall 1972, pp. 3–16; J. Douglas McConnell, "Comment on 'A Major Price-Perceived Quality Study Reexamined,' " *Journal of Marketing Research,* May 1980, pp. 263–64; K. M. Monroe and S. Petroshius, "Buyers' Subjective Perceptions of Price: An Update of the Evidence," in *Perspectives in Consumer Behavior,* ed. T. Robertson and H. Kassarjian (Glenview, Ill.: Scott Foresman, 1981), pp. 43–55; Valarie A. Zeithaml, "Consumer Perceptions of Price, Quality, And Value: A Means-End Model and Synthesis of Evidence," *Journal of Marketing,* July 1988, pp. 2–22.

12. Thomas T. Nagle, *The Strategy and Tactics of Pricing,* pp. 170–72.

13. Daniel T. Ostas, "Ethics of Contract Pricing," *Journal of Business Ethics,* February 1992, pp. 137–46; J. Steve Davis, "Ethical Problems in Competitive Bidding: The Paradyne Case," *Business and Professional Ethics Journal,* 7, no. 2 (1988), pp. 3–26; Wayne J. Morse, "Probabilistic Bidding Models: A Synthesis," *Business Horizons,* April 1975, pp. 67–74; Stephen Paranka, "Competitive Bidding Strategy," *Business Horizons,* June 1971, pp. 39–43.

14. For references to additional readings in the pricing area, see Michael H. Morris and Roger J. Calantone, "Four Components of Effective Pricing," *Industrial Marketing Management,* November 1990, pp. 321–30; Valerie Kijewski and Eunsang Yoon, "Market-Based Pricing: Beyond Price-Performance Curves," *Industrial Marketing Management,* February 1990, pp. 11–20; Kent B. Monroe, D. Lund, and P. Choudhury, *Pricing Policies and Strategies: An Annotated Bibliography* (Chicago: American Marketing Association, 1983); "Pricing of Products Is Still an Art, Often Having Little Link to Costs," *The Wall Street Journal,* November 25, 1981, p. 29ff.

Chapter 18

1. "Little Is Common beyond Gender?" *Insight,* December 10, 1990, pp. 48–49.

2. "Push-Button Age," *Newsweek,* July 9, 1990, pp. 56–57; "After the Beep: The Message Is Convenience Matters Most," *The Wall Street Journal,* September 19, 1989, pp. B1–2; "Design Is Hot in the Cold Business," *Insight,* September 18, 1989, pp. 44–45; "Will U.S. Warm to Refrigerated Dishes?" *The Wall Street Journal,* August 18, 1989, p. B1; "As 'Fresh Refrigerated' Foods Gain Favor, Concerns about Safety Rise," *The Wall Street Journal,* March 11, 1988, p. 27; "Life in the Express Lane," *Time,* June 16, 1986, p. 64.

3. John P. Robinson, "Your Money or Your Time," *American Demographics,* November 1991, pp. 22–26; "Flood of Information Swamps Managers, but Some Are Finding Ways to Bail Out," *The Wall Street Journal,* August 12, 1991, p. B1ff.; "Fast-Track Kids Exhaust Their Parents," *The Wall Street Journal,* August 7, 1991, p. B1ff.; John P. Robinson, "The Time Squeeze," *American Demographics,* February 1990, pp. 30–33; "Smart Cards: Pocket Power," *Newsweek,* July 31, 1989, pp. 54–55; "How America Has Run Out of Time," *Time,* April 24, 1989, pp. 58–67; Cheryl Russell, "What's Your Hurry," *American Demographics,* April 1989, p. 2; Ruth Hamel, "Living in Traffic," *American Demographics,* March 1989, pp. 49–51.

4. Glenn DeSouza, "Designing a Customer Retention Plan," *The Journal of Business Strategy,* March/April 1992, pp. 24–28; Frank V. Cespedes, "Once More: How Do You Improve Customer Service?" *Business Horizons,* March/April 1992, pp. 58–67; Mary C. Gilly, William B. Stevenson, and Laura J. Yale, "Dynamics of Complaint Management in the Service Organization," *The Journal of Consumer Affairs,* Winter 1991, pp. 295–322; C. Dröge and D. Halstead, "Postpurchase Hierarchies of Effects: The Antecedents and Consequences of Satisfaction for Complainers versus Non-Complainers," *International Journal of Research in Marketing,* November 1991, pp. 315–28; Jagdip Singh, "Industry Characteristics and Consumer Dissatisfaction," *The Journal of Consumer Affairs,* Summer 1991, pp. 19–56; Jerry Plymire, "Complaints as Opportunities," *Business Horizons,* March/April 1991, pp. 79–81; Barbara C. Garland and Robert A. Westbrook, "An Exploration of Client Satisfaction in a Nonprofit Context," *Journal of the Academy of Marketing Science,* Fall 1989, pp. 297–304; A. Parasuraman, Valarie A. Zeithaml, and Leonard L. Berry, "SERVQUAL: A Multiple-Item Scale for Measuring Consumer Perceptions of Service Quality," *Journal of Retailing,* Spring 1988, pp. 12–40; "Banks Stress Resolving Complaints to Win Small Customers' Favor," *The Wall Street Journal,* December 8, 1986, p. 31; John F. Gaski and Michael J. Etzel, "The Index of Consumer Sentiment toward Marketing," *Journal of Marketing,* July 1986, pp. 71–81; Robert B. Woodruff, Ernest R. Cadotte, and Roger L. Jenkins, "Modeling Consumer Satisfaction Processes Using Experience-Based Norms," *Journal of Marketing Research,* August 1983, pp. 296–304.

5. "Prof: TV Ads Not as Effective as Price and Promotions," *Marketing News,* March 27, 1989, p. 7; "IRI Research Bolsters Value of Advertising," *Advertising Age,* March 6, 1989, p. 71; "Don't Blame Television, Irate Readers Say," *The Wall Street Journal,* March 1, 1989, p. B6; "Television Ads Ring Up No Sale in Study," *The Wall Street Journal,* February 15, 1989, p. B6. For classic discussions of the problem and mechanics of measuring the efficiency of marketing, see Stanley C. Hollander, "Measuring the Cost and Value of Marketing," *Business Topics,* Summer 1961, pp. 17–26; Reavis Cox, *Distribution in a High-Level Economy* (Englewood Cliffs, N.J.: Prentice Hall, 1965).

6. The restaurant case is adapted from Marie Gaudard, Roland Coates and Liz Freeman, "Accelerating Improvement," *Quality Progress,*

October 1991, pp. 81–88. For more on quality management and control, see "Total Quality By Satellite," *Nation's Business,* March 1992, pp. 49–51; "Quality Control from Mars," *The Wall Street Journal,* January 27, 1992, p. A12; "Can American Steel Find Quality?" *Industry Week,* January 20, 1992, pp. 36–39; "The Quality Imperative," *Business Week,* (special issue) October 25, 1991; "Motorola's Baldrige Award-Winning Ways," *Business Marketing,* September 1991, pp. 14–15; " 'Q' Tips," *CIO,* August 1991, pp. 26–31; "The Fabric of Quality," *CIO,* August 1991, pp. 34–41.

7. Harvey N. Shycon, "Improved Customer Service: Measuring the Payoff," *The Journal of Business Strategy,* January/February 1992, pp. 13–17; A. Lynn Daniel, "Overcome the Barriers to Superior Customer Service," *The Journal of Business Strategy,* January/February 1992, pp. 18–24; Leonard A. Schlesinger and James L. Heskett, "The Service-Driven Service Company," *Harvard Business Review,* September/October 1991, pp. 71–81; David A. Collier, "New Marketing Mix Stresses Service," *The Journal of Business Strategy,* March/April 1991, pp. 42–45; M. P. Singh, "Service as a Marketing Strategy: A Case Study at Reliance Electric," *Industrial Marketing Management,* August 1990, pp. 193–200; "For Computer Makers, Service Is the Soul of the New Machine," *Adweek's Marketing Week,* May 21, 1990, pp. 20–26; James S. Hensel, "Service Quality Improvement and Control: A Customer-Based Approach," *Journal of Business Research,* January 1990, pp. 43–54; William George, "Internal Marketing and Organizational Behavior: A Partnership in Developing Customer-Conscious Employees at Every Level," *Journal of Business Research,* January 1990, pp. 63–70; Frank K. Sonnenberg, "Marketing: Service Quality: Forethought, Not Afterthought," *The Journal of Business Strategy,* September/October 1989, pp. 54–58; Glenn DeSouza, "Now Service Businesses Must Manage Quality," *The Journal of Business Strategy,* May/June 1989, pp. 21–25; Stephen W. Brown and Teresa A. Swartz, "A Gap Analysis of Professional Service Quality," *Journal of Marketing,* April 1989, pp. 92–98.

8. For more on this point, see Robert L. Steiner, "Does Advertising Lower Consumer Prices?" *Journal of Marketing,* October 1973, pp. 19–26; Robert L. Steiner, "Marketing Productivity in Consumer Goods Industries—A Vertical Perspective," *Journal of Marketing,* January 1978, pp. 60–70; see also Robert B. Archibald, Clyde A. Haulman, and Carlisle E. Moody, Jr., "Quality, Price, Advertising, and Published Quality Ratings," *Journal of Consumer Research,* March 1983, pp. 347–56.

9. Arnold J. Toynbee, *America and World Revolution* (New York: Oxford University Press, 1966), pp. 144–45; see also John Kenneth Galbraith, *Economics and the Public Purpose* (Boston: Houghton Mifflin, 1973), pp. 144–45.

10. Russell J. Tomsen, "Take It Away," *Newsweek,* October 7, 1974, p. 21.

11. J. L. Engledow, "Was Consumer Satisfaction a Pig in a Poke?" *MSU Business Topics,* April 1977, p. 92.

12. "Deregulating America," *Business Week,* November 28, 1983, pp. 80–82; E. T. Grether, "Marketing and Public Policy: A Contemporary View," *Journal of Marketing,* July 1974, pp. 2–7; "Intellectuals Should Re-Examine the Marketplace: It Supports Them, Helps Keep Them Free," *Advertising Age,* January 28, 1963; David A. Heenan, "Congress Rethinks America's Competitiveness," *Business Horizons,* May/June 1989, pp. 11–16; Irvin Grossack and David A. Heenan, "Cooperation, Competition, and Antitrust: Two Views," *Business Horizons,* September/October 1986, pp. 24–28; Donald P. Robin and R. Eric Reidenbach, "Identifying Critical Problems for Mutual Cooperation between the Public and Private Sectors: A Marketing Perspective," *Journal of the Academy of Marketing Science,* Fall 1986, pp. 1–12; Frederick Webster, *Social Aspects of Marketing* (Englewood Cliffs, N.J.: Prentice Hall, 1974), p. 32.

13. " 'Greens' Add to Junk Mail Mountain," *The Wall Street Journal,* May 13, 1991, p. B1; "Direct Mailer Leads Fight against Too Much Junk," *Marketing News,* December 10, 1990, pp. 6–7.

14. Robert F. Lusch and Gene R. Laczniak, "Macroenvironmental Forces, Marketing Strategy and Business Performance: A Futures Research Approach," *Journal of the Academy of Marketing Science,* Fall 1989, pp. 283–96; "The Community's Persuasive Power," *Insight,* December 12, 1988, pp. 58–59; "Companies as Citizens: Should They

Have a Conscience?" *The Wall Street Journal,* February 19, 1987, p. 29; John H. Antil, "Socially Responsible Consumers: Profile and Implications for Public Policy," *Journal of Macromarketing* 4, no. 2 (1984), pp. 18–39; James T. Roth and Lissa Benson, "Intelligent Consumption: An Attractive Alternative to the Marketing Concept," *MSU Business Topics,* Winter 1974, pp. 30–34. For more on privacy, see "The $3 Billion Question: Whose Info Is It, Anyway?" *Business Week,* July 4, 1988, pp. 106–7; "Federal Agencies Press Data-Base Firms to Curb Access to 'Sensitive' Information," *The Wall Street Journal,* February 5, 1987, p. 23. For more on shoplifting, see "Marketing Solution Can Cure Shoplifting Problems," *Marketing News,* June 25, 1990, p. 8; "Indelible Color Guard against Shoplifting," *Insight,* June 25, 1990, p. 46; "Chicago Retailers' 'Sting' Aims to Put Shoplifting Professionals Out of Business," *The Wall Street Journal,* June 5, 1990, p. B1ff.; "Retailers Use Hidden Gadgets, High Alertness to Battle Theft," *Insight,* December 18, 1989, pp. 42–43; Warren A. French, Melvin R. Crask, and Fred H. Mader, "Retailers' Assessment of the Shoplifting Problem," *Journal of Retailing,* Winter 1984, pp. 108–15; Robert E. Wilkes, "Fraudulent Behavior by Consumers," *Journal of Marketing,* October 1978, pp. 67–75. For more on ethics, see Joel J. Davis, "Ethics and Environmental Marketing," *Journal of Business Ethics,* February 1992, pp. 81–88; Scott J. Vitell, James R. Lumpkin, and Mohammed Y. A. Rawwas, "Consumer Ethics: An Investigation of the Ethical Beliefs of Elderly Consumers," *Journal of Business Ethics,* May 1991, pp. 365–76; Gene R. Laczniak and Patrick E. Murphy, "Fostering Ethical Marketing Decisions," *Journal of Business Ethics,* April 1991, pp. 259–72; Robert E. Pitts and Robert Allan Cooke, "A Realist View of Marketing Ethics," *Journal of Business Ethics,* April 1991, pp. 243–4; R.

Eric Reidenbach, Donald P. Robin, and Lyndon Dawson, "An Application and Extension of a Multidimensional Ethics Scale to Selected Marketing Practices and Marketing Groups," *Journal of the Academy of Marketing Science,* Spring 1991, pp. 83–92; Shelby D. Hunt, Van R. Wood, and Lawrence B. Chonko, "Corporate Ethical Values and Organizational Commitment in Marketing," *Journal of Marketing,* July 1989, pp. 79–90; Dennis E. Garrett et al., "Issues Management and Organizational Accounts: An Analysis of Corporate Responses to Accusations of Unethical Business Practices," *Journal of Business Ethics,* July 1989, pp. 507–20; Donald P. Robin and R. Eric Reidenbach, "Social Responsibility, Ethics, and Marketing Strategy: Closing the Gap between Concept and Application," *Journal of Marketing,* January 1987, pp. 44–58.

15. "Environmental Price Tags," *Nation's Business,* April 1992, pp. 36–41; "It Doesn't Pay to Go Green When Consumers Are Seeing Red," *Adweek,* March 23, 1992, pp. 32–33; "Pollution Prevention Picks Up Steam," *Industry Week,* February 17, 1992, pp. 36–42; "Reach Out and Prod Someone," *Newsweek,* October 14, 1991, p. 50; "Herman Miller: How Green Is My Factory," *Business Week,* September 16, 1991, pp. 54–56; "The Big Muddle in Green Marketing," *Fortune,* June 3, 1991, pp. 91–100; "The Greening of Detroit," *Business Week,* April 8, 1991, pp. 54–60; "Exxon's Army Scrubs Beaches, but Many Don't Stay Cleaned," *The Wall Street Journal,* July 27, 1989, p. 1ff.; "CFC Curb to Save Ozone Will Be Costly," *The Wall Street Journal,* March 28, 1988, p. 6; "Du Pont Plans to Phase Out CFC Output," *The Wall Street Journal,* March 25, 1988, p. 2.

Illustration Credits

Chapter 1

Exhibits: *p. 13,* 1–2, adapted from Wroe Alderson, "Factors Governing the Development of Marketing Channels," in *Marketing Channels for Manufactured Products,* ed. Richard M. Clewett (Homewood, Ill.: Richard D. Irwin, 1954), p. 7. *p. 17,* 1–3, adapted from William McInnes, "A Conceptual Approach to Marketing," in *Theory in Marketing,* 2d ser., ed. Reavis Cox, Wroe Alderson, and Stanley J. Shapiro (Homewood, Ill.: Richard D. Irwin, 1964), pp. 51–67. *p. 18,* 1–4, model suggested by Professor A. A. Brogowicz, Western Michigan University.

Photos/ads: *p. 3,* Vickers & Beechler. *p. 4,* (left) Courtesy Dunlop Slazenger Corporation; (right) Courtesy Mendelsohn/Zien Advertising, Los Angeles. *p. 7,* Courtesy Sony Corporation of America. *p. 8,* (left) Paul Fusco/Magnum Photos; (right) Courtesy The Hertz Corporation. *p. 9,* (left) P. LeSegretain/Sygma; (right) Courtesy Chiquita Bananas International. *p. 11,* (left) © John Madere 1990 for International Paper annual report; (right) © 1992 by Marianne Barcellona. *p. 12,* Louis Villotai/The Stock Market. *p. 15,* © 1989 Mary Beth Camp/Matrix. *p. 19,* (left) Courtesy United Parcel Service of America, Inc.; (right) Courtesy Canadian Yellow Pages/McKim Advertising.

Chapter 2

Exhibits: *p. 30,* 2–2, adapted from R. F. Vizza, T. E. Chambers, and E. J. Cook, *Adoption of the Marketing Concept—Fact or Fiction* (New York: Sales Executive Club, Inc., 1967), pp. 13–15. *p. 34,* 2–3, adapted from discussion of an American Marketing Association Strategic Planning Committee.

Photos/ads: *p. 25,* Courtesy The Black & Decker Corporation. *p. 29,* Courtesy Lowe Howard-Spink. *p. 31,* The Zoological Society of San Diego. *p. 36,* (left) Courtesy L. L. Bean, Inc.; (right) Warren Morgan/Westlight. *p. 39,* (left) Hitoshi Fugo; (right) Courtesy Promus Companies. *p. 42,* (left) Reprint permission granted by Timex Corporation; (right) Courtesy Tissot.

Appendix A

Photos/ads: *p. 56,* Martin Rogers/Tony Stone Worldwide.

Chapter 3

Exhibits: *p. 64,* 3–2, Igor Ansoff, *Corporate Strategy* (New York: McGraw-Hill, 1965). *p. 80,* 3–12, Russell I. Haley, "Benefit Segmentation: A Decision-Oriented Research Tool," *Journal of Marketing,* July 1968, p. 33.

Photos/ads: *p. 61,* William D. Perreault, Jr. *p. 63,* Reprinted courtesy Eastman Kodak Company. *p. 65,* Courtesy Philip Morris Companies. *p. 68,* (left) Courtesy Samsung Electronics; (right) Courtesy Young & Rubicam Inc. *p. 70,* (left) Courtesy Yashica, Inc./Michael Meyers & Associates, Inc.; (right) Courtesy Sony Corporation of America. *p. 72,* Both ads courtesy Heinz U.S.A. *p. 78,* Copyright 1991 Mazda Motor of America, Inc. Used by permission. *p. 79,* (left) Courtesy Den-Mat Corporation; (right) Courtesy Colgate-Palmolive Company.

Chapter 4

Exhibits: *p. 96,* 4–3, "Europe: Special Report," *Fortune,* December 2, 1991, pp. 136–72. *p. 99,* 4–5, table developed by the authors based on U.S. Census data, United Nations statistical data, and PCGLOBE software (Tempe, Arizona: PC Globe, Inc., 1990). *p. 100,* 4–6, *Statistical Abstract of the United States, 1991,* p. 16. *p. 101,* 4–7, map developed by the authors based on data from *Statistical Abstract of the United States, 1991,* p. 20 and *Statistical Abstract of the United States, 1988,* p. 23. *p. 106,* 4–10, adapted from M. G. Allen, "Strategic Problems Facing Today's Corporate Planner," speech given at the Academy of Management, 36th Annual Meeting, Kansas City, Missouri, 1976.

Photos/ads: *p. 85,* Courtesy Giant Food Inc. *p. 86,* (left) Courtesy Little Tykes Company; (right) © John S. Abbot. *p. 89,* (left) Photo courtesy Ball Corporation; (right) Arthur Meyerson Photography. *p. 90,* Both ads courtesy Hammermill Papers. *p. 93,* Courtesy Singapore Airlines, Ltd. *p. 98,* (left) Courtesy Allstate Insurance Company; (right) Courtesy Basel Pharmaceuticals. *p. 102,* (left) R. Ian Lloyd/Westlight; (right) H. Wong/Westlight. *p. 107,* Courtesy Philip Morris Companies. *p. 108,* (left) Courtesy Ricoh Electronics Inc./Gigante Vaz & Partners; (right) Courtesy Nissin Foods.

Chapter 5

Exhibits: *p. 127,* 5–4, adapted from Paul E. Green, Frank J. Carmone, and David P. Wachpress, "On the Analysis of Qualitative Data in Marketing Research," *Journal of Marketing Research,* February 1977, pp. 52–59.

Photos/ads: *p. 113,* © 1989 Jay Brousseau. *p. 114,* (left) Courtesy Urban Decision Systems, Inc.; (right) Courtesy Norand Corporation. *p. 122,* Steve Smith/Onyx. *p. 123,* Courtesy Colgate-Palmolive Company. *p. 125,* Courtesy Vons Companies. *p. 126,* (left) Courtesy Carewell Industries Inc.; (right) Courtesy Nice-Pak Products Inc. *p. 128,* (left) Courtesy SAS Institute Inc.; (right) Courtesy STSC, Inc. *p. 129,* (left) Courtesy Survey Sampling, Inc.; (right) Courtesy Donnelly Marketing Information Services.

Chapter 6

Exhibits: *p. 135,* 6–1, *Current Population Reports, Series P-60, No. 174,* p. 216 and unpublished data from the National Center for Income Statistics. *p. 136,* 6–2, *Consumer Expenditure Survey, 1988–89,* U.S. Department of Labor, 1991, pp. 15–17. *p. 138,* 6–4, adapted from C. Glenn Walters, *Consumer Behavior,* 3rd ed. (Homewood, Ill.: Richard D. Irwin, 1979). *p. 144,* 6–7, Joseph T. Plummer, "The Concept and Application of Life-Style Segmentation," *Journal of Marketing,* January 1974, pp. 33–37. *p. 145,* 6–8, Patrick E. Murphy and William A. Staples, "A Modernized Family Life Cycle," *Journal of Consumer Research,* June 1979, p. 17. *p. 147,* 6–9, adapted from Steven L. Diamond, Thomas S. Robertson, and F. Kent Mitchel, "Consumer Motivation and Behavior," in *Marketing Manager's Handbook,* ed. S. H. Britt and N. F. Guess (Chicago: Dartnell, 1983), p. 239; Richard P. Coleman, "The Continuing Significance of Social Class to Marketing," *Journal of Consumer Research,* December 1983, pp. 265–80; "What Is Happening to the Middle Class?" *American Demographics,* January 1985, pp. 18–25; Donald W. Hendon,

Emelda L. Williams, and Douglas E. Huffman, "Social Class System Revisited," *Journal of Business Research,* November 1988, pp. 259–70.

Photos/ads: *p. 133,* Zephyr Pictures. *p. 134,* © 1991 The Gillette Company. *p. 140,* Courtesy MGTB Ayer. *p. 141,* Courtesy 3M. *p. 142,* Courtesy Forsman & Bodenfors. *p. 148,* (left) Courtesy United Airlines; (right) Courtesy Texas Department of Commerce, Tourism Division. *p. 153,* (left) Courtesy PPG Industries, Inc.; (right) Frederick Charles/Time Magazine.

Chapter 7

Exhibits: *p. 158,* 7–1, *County Business Patterns—United States, 1989; Statistical Abstract of the United States, 1991; Information Please Almanac, 1992* (Boston: Houghton-Miflin, 1991). *p. 161,* 7–3, Rowland T. Moriarty, Jr., and Robert E. Spekman, "An Empirical Investigation of the Information Sources Used During the Industrial Buying Process, *Journal of Marketing Research,* May 1984, pp. 137–47. *p. 169,* 7–5, data adapted from *County Business Patterns—United States, 1989,* p. 8 and *1987 Census of Manufacturers, Subject Series, General Summary,* p. 99. *p. 170,* 7–6, adapted from *Standard Industrial Classification Manual, 1987.*

Photos/ads: *p. 157,* Courtesy Toyota Motor Corporation. *p. 159,* Courtesy Hercules Food & Functional Products Company. *p. 162,* (left) Courtesy Univex; (right) Courtesy Spring Air. *p. 164,* Courtesy Texaco Inc. *p. 165,* (left) Courtesy Super Valu Stores, Inc.; (right) Steve Smith/Onyx. *p. 166,* (left) Courtesy Hanaqua International Corporation; (right) Courtesy Treats Ice Cream. *p. 168,* Courtesy Ryder System, Inc. *p. 171,* Courtesy Walgreen Co. *p. 173,* (left) Courtesy Big Toys; (right) Courtesy Edmont.

Chapter 8

Exhibits: *p. 192,* 8–6, NESTLE and the NESTLE NEST DEVICE are registered trademarks of Société des Produits Nestlé S.A.

Photos/ads: *p. 179,* Sharon Hoogstraten. *p. 181,* (left) Courtesy Toyota Industrial Equipment; (right) Courtesy The Hertz Corporation. *p. 183,* (left) Courtesy Inland Steel Industries, photo by Archie Lieberman; (right) Courtesy United Parcel Service of America, Inc. *p. 184,* Courtesy Quaker Oats/Bayer, Bess, Vanderwarker. *p. 187,* Courtesy Quaker State Corporation. *p. 191,* Courtesy International Business Machines Corporation. *p. 194,* Courtesy CPC International. *p. 196,* Louis Psihoyos/Matrix. *p. 197,* Courtesy Lever Brothers Company. *p. 199,* (left) Reprinted courtesy Eastman Kodak company; (right) Courtesy Deere & Company.

Chapter 9

Exhibits: *p. 216,* 9–4, adapted from Frank R. Bacon, Jr., and Thomas W. Butler, *Planned Innovation* (Ann Arbor: University of Michigan Institute of Science and Technology, 1980). *p. 217,* 9–5, adapted from Philip Kotler, "What Consumerism Means for Marketers," *Harvard Business Review,* May–June 1972, pp. 55–56.

Photos/ads: *p. 205,* Courtesy Storopack, Inc. *p. 207,* (left) Gerry Gropp/Sipa Press; (right) Courtesy Tandy Corporation. *p. 208,* Courtesy Motorola Inc. *p. 210,* Courtesy CLM/BDO, Paris. *p. 212,* (left) Grant Peterson; (right) Frank Veronsky. *p. 213,* Courtesy Du Pont Company. *p. 215,* Mark Joseph. *p. 217,* Courtesy 3M. *p. 219,* Courtesy Ford Motor Company.

Chapter 10

Photos/ads: *p. 225,* Reproduced with permission from The Goodyear Tire & Rubber Company, Akron, Ohio. *p. 227,* Courtesy Archer Daniels Midland Co. *p. 229,* Richard Pasley/Stock Boston. *p. 230,* Courtesy The Southland Corporation. *p. 231,* Courtesy Sunbrella/Glen Raven Mills, Inc. *p. 235,* (left) © 1991 Leaf, Inc.; (right) Courtesy Godiva Chocolatier, Inc. *p. 238,* (left) Shigeru Kunita; (right) Paul Chesley/Photographers Aspen. *p. 239,* (left) Courtesy Intralox, Inc.; (right) Courtesy Americold. *p. 244,* (left) Photo courtesy Hewlett-Packard Company; (right) Courtesy Air France. *p. 246,* All photos used with permission of Mattel, Inc.

p. 247, Courtesy CSX Corporation. *p. 249,* (left) Courtesy Du Pont; (right) Courtesy Matlack, Inc.

Chapter 11

Exhibits: *p. 254,* 11–2, adapted from Louis Bucklin, "Retail Strategy and the Classification of Consumer Goods," *Journal of Marketing,* January 1963, pp. 50–55. *p. 266,* 11–6, based on data from *1987 Census of Retail Trade, Subject Series, Establishment and Firm Size.*

Photos/ads: *p. 253,* Courtesy Toys "R" Us, Inc. *p. 257,* (left) Robert Wallis/JB Pictures; (right) Burt Glinn/Magnum Photos, Inc. *p. 259,* Reprinted from "Marketing News," published by the American Marketing Association, January 2, 1989. *p. 260,* © Steve Niedorf. *p. 261,* (top) © Jeff Zaruba; (bottom) Scott Wanner/Nawrocki Stock Photos. *p. 263,* (left) Courtesy Kayser-Roth Hosiery, Inc.; (right) Courtesy Golden Valley Microwave Foods, Inc. *p. 268,* (left) © Bruce Zake 1990; (right) Courtesy Home Shopping Network, Inc. *p. 269,* (left) © Reinhold Spiegler; (right) © John McGrail 1992. *p. 270,* Courtesy The Great Atlantic & Pacific Tea Co., photo by Steven Begleiter.

Chapter 12

Exhibits: *p. 278,* 12–1, based on data from *1987 Census of Wholesale Trade, Geographic Area Series, United States.*

Photos/ads: *p. 275,* © Robert Holmgren. *p. 280,* (top) David Barnes/The Stock Market; (bottom) © Steve Niedorf. *p. 283,* (left) Courtesy Cutter's Exchange, Inc.; (right) Courtesy R. C. Steele. *p. 284,* Courtesy ARA Services. *p. 286,* © John Madere. *p. 288,* (left) © Michael Abramson; (right) Courtesy Vons Companies. *p. 289,* (left) Courtesy T. L. Ashford & Associates; (right) Courtesy Weber Marking Systems.

Chapter 13

Photos/ads: *p. 293,* Courtesy Ryder System Inc. *p. 296,* (left) © Seth Resnick; (right) Courtesy Kellogg Company. *p. 298,* (top) © 1991 FTD; (bottom) Courtesy Good Housekeeping. *p. 301,* Courtesy United Parcel Service of America, Inc. *p. 302,* (left) Courtesy Polaroid Corporation; (right) Courtesy Creighton Younnel Advertising, Inc. *p. 303,* (left) Courtesy Marion Merrell Dow U.S.A.; (right) Courtesy Merck & Co., Inc., photo by Bruce Davidson. *p. 306,* (left) Courtesy Aerostar International, Inc.; (center) Vince Streano/Tony Stone Worldwide; (right) Courtesy Wave Promotions. *p. 307,* (left) Courtesy VideOcart Inc.; (right) Courtesy Catalina Marketing.

Chapter 14

Exhibits: *p. 326,* 14–2, exhibit suggested by Professor A. A. Brogowicz, Western Michigan University.

Photos/ads: *p. 313,* Courtesy Alcoa; photo by Robert Feldman. *p. 315,* (left) Caroline Parsons/Aria Pictures; (right) Courtesy Toyota Motor Corporation. *p. 317,* Courtesy Circuit City Stores; photos by Jeff Zaruba. *p. 319,* (left) Courtesy of AT&T Archives; (right) © Terry Husebye. *p. 321,* (left) © Joe Stewartson; (right) Courtesy Alcoa; photo by Robert Feldman. *p. 323,* Courtesy Ross Roy Advertising Agency. *p. 325,* (left) Courtesy Lance; (right) Courtesy Merck & Co. *p. 328,* (left) Courtesy Giltspur, Inc.; (right) Courtesy Software Publishing Company.

Chapter 15

Exhibits: *p. 337,* 15–2, "Advertising Ratio Gains Posted for '91," *Advertising Age,* September 16, 1991, p. 32. *p. 339,* 15–3, adapted from R. J. Lavidge and G. A. Steiner, "A Model for Predictive Measurements of Advertising Effectiveness," *Journal of Marketing,* October 1961, p. 61. *p. 343,* 15–4, cost data from Standard Rate and Data Service, April 1992, and sales estimates from "How Bad a Year Was '91? Almost the Worst," *Advertising Age,* May 4, 1992, p. 3ff.

Photos/ads: *p. 335,* © Rob Brown. *p. 338,* (left) Courtesy Richmond Public Schools; Agency: Earle Palmer Browne/Richmond, VA; (right) Courtesy Leo Burnett USA. *p. 340,* (left) Courtesy National Dairy Board; Agency: Stricevic O'Connell Advertising Marketing Inc.; (right) Courtesy

Hotel Bar Foods, Inc. *p. 341,* Courtesy Michelin Tire Corporation. *p. 342,* Reprinted courtesy Eastman Kodak Company. *p. 345,* Courtesy Yellow Pages Publishers Association. *p. 346,* Courtesy Lawner Reingold Britton & Partners, Boston. *p. 347,* (left) Courtesy Wm. Wrigley Jr. Company; (right) Courtesy General Mills, Inc. *p. 351,* Agency: TBWA Hamburg; Photos Account Manager: Joachim Schadewaldt; Managing Director: Lutz Kuikuck; Creative Director: Gunther Heinrich; Copy: Stephan Chrzeschinski; Art Director: Sven Hillie; Producer: Dorit Bahlburg; Film Producer: What Else; Regisseur and Camera: David McDonald.

Chapter 16

Photos/ads: *p. 357,* © Rob Gage. *p. 361,* (left) Courtesy Malt-O-Meal Company; (right) Courtesy Pagano, Schenck & Kay, Inc. *p. 364,* Courtesy United Parcel Service of America, Inc. *p. 369,* Courtesy Cargill, Inc., Seed Division. *p. 370,* Andy Freeberg Photography. *p. 372,* (left) Courtesy Broder Brothers; (right) Courtesy Veryfine. *p. 374,* Michael J. Hruby.

Appendix B

Exhibits: *p. 391,* B–4, *Sales & Marketing Management,* August 19, 1991.

Chapter 17

Photos/ads: *p. 395,* Courtesy Wal-Mart Stores, Inc. *p. 397,* © Will Van Overbeek. *p. 398,* Don Smetzer/Tony Stone Worldwide. *p. 399,* Courtesy Vons Companies. *p. 402,* (left) Courtesy Geo. Hormel & Company; (right) © Kim Steele. *p. 407,* Courtesy Philips Lighting. *p. 410,* (left) Courtesy Severin Montres AG; (right) Courtesy Tiffany & Co. *p. 411,* Courtesy Affordable Furniture ®.

Chapter 18

Exhibits: *p. 423,* 18–1, Marie Gaudard, Roland Coates, and Liz Freeman, "Accelerating Improvement," *Quality Progress,* October 1991, pp. 81–88. *p. 424,* 18–2, Marie Gaudard, Roland Coates, and Liz Freeman, "Accelerating Improvement," *Quality Progress,* October 1991, pp. 81–88. *p. 432,* 18–3, adapted from discussions of an American Marketing Association Strategic Planning Committee.

Photos/ads: *p. 417,* John Chiasson/Gamma-Liaison. *p. 418,* (left) © Ed Kashi; (right) Melanie Carr/Zephyr Pictures. *p. 421,* Courtesy Du Pont. *p. 425,* Courtesy Columbia Sportswear. *p. 427,* (left) © 1991 Binney & Smith Inc.; (right) Courtesy Grid Systems Corporation. *p. 428,* Courtesy Rollerblade, Inc. *p. 429,* Todd Stoddart/Woodfin Camp & Associates. *p. 430,* (right) Courtesy Sears Roebuck & Co. *p. 431,* Peter Turnley/Black Star. *p. 435,* (left) Courtesy McDaniels, Henry & Sproul, San Francisco; (right) Courtesy the North Carolina Governor's Highway Safety Program.

Appendix C

Exhibits: *p. 440,* C–1, adapted and updated from Charles G. Burck, "A Group Profile of the Fortune 500 Chief Executive," *Fortune,* May 1976, p. 172. *p. 444,* C–3, adapted and updated from Lila B. Stair, *Careers in Business: Selecting and Planning Your Career Path* (Homewood, Ill.: Richard D. Irwin, 1980) and *Northwestern Lindquist-Endicott Report, 1988* (Evanston, Ill.: Northwestern University, The Placement Center).

Photos/ads: *p. 443,* (left) KRAFT, GENERAL FOODS, and OSCAR MAYER are registered trademarks of Kraft General Foods, Inc. Reproduced with permission.; (right) Courtesy Colgate-Palmolive Company.

Author Index

Subject Index

Glossary

Accessories short-lived capital items—tools and equipment used in production or office activities.

Accumulating collecting products from many small producers.

Administered channel systems various channel members informally agree to cooperate with each other.

Administered prices consciously set prices aimed at reaching the firm's objectives.

Adoption curve shows when different groups accept ideas.

Adoption process the steps individuals go through on the way to accepting or rejecting a new idea.

Advertising any *paid* form of nonpersonal presentation of ideas, goods, or services by an identified sponsor.

Advertising agencies specialists in planning and handling mass selling details for advertisers.

Advertising allowances price reductions to firms further along in the channel to encourage them to advertise or otherwise promote the firm's products locally.

Advertising managers managers of their company's mass selling effort in television, newspapers, magazines, and other media.

Agent middlemen wholesalers who do not own (take title to) the products they sell.

AIDA model consists of four promotion jobs—(1) to get *Attention*, (2) to hold *Interest*, (3) to arouse *Desire*, and (4) to obtain *Action*.

Allowance (accounting term) occurs when a customer is not satisfied with a purchase for some reason and the seller gives a price reduction on the original invoice (bill), but the customer keeps the goods or services.

Allowances reductions in price given to final consumers, customers, or channel members for doing "something" or accepting less of "something."

Assorting putting together a variety of products to give a target market what it wants.

Attitude a person's point of view toward something.

Auction companies agent middlemen who provide a place where buyers and sellers can come together and complete a transaction.

Automatic vending selling and delivering products through vending machines.

Average cost (per unit) the total cost divided by the related quantity.

Average-cost pricing adding a "reasonable" markup to the average cost of a product.

Average fixed cost (per unit) the total fixed cost divided by the related quantity.

Average variable cost (per unit) the total variable cost divided by the related quantity.

Bait pricing setting some very low prices to attract customers but trying to sell more expensive models or brands once the customer is in the store.

Balance sheet an accounting statement that shows the assets, liabilities, and net worth of a company.

Basic list prices the prices that final customers or users are normally asked to pay for products.

Basic sales tasks *order getting, order taking*, and *supporting*.

Battle of the brands the competition between dealer brands and manufacturer brands.

Belief a person's opinion about something.

Bid pricing offering a specific price for each possible job rather than setting a price that applies for all customers.

Brand equity the value of a brand's overall strength in the market.

Brand familiarity how well customers recognize and accept a company's brand.

Brand insistence customers insist on a firm's branded product and are willing to search for it.

Brand managers manage specific products, often taking over the jobs formerly handled by an advertising manager—sometimes called product managers.

Brand name a word, letter, or a group of words or letters.

Brand nonrecognition a brand is not recognized by final customers at all—even though middlemen may use the brand name for identification and inventory control.

Brand preference target customers will usually choose the brand over other brands, perhaps because of habit or past experience.

Brand recognition customers remember the brand.

Brand rejection   the potential customers won't buy a brand—unless its image is changed.

Branding   the use of a name, term, symbol, or design—or a combination of these—to identify a product.

Breakthrough opportunities   opportunities that help innovators develop hard-to-copy marketing strategies that will be very profitable for a long time.

Brokers   agent middlemen who specialize in bringing buyers and sellers together.

Bulk-breaking   dividing larger quantities into smaller quantities as products get closer to the final market.

Business and organizational customers   any buyers who buy for resale or to produce other goods and services.

Business products   products meant for use in producing other products.

Buying center   all the people who participate in or influence a purchase.

Buying function   looking for and evaluating goods and services.

Capital item   a long-lasting product that can be used and depreciated for many years.

Cash-and-carry wholesalers   like service wholesalers, except that the customer must pay cash.

Cash discounts   reductions in the price to encourage buyers to pay their bills quickly.

Catalog showroom retailers   stores that sell several lines out of a catalog and display showroom with backup inventories.

Central markets   convenient places where buyers and sellers can meet face-to-face to exchange goods and services.

Chain store   one of several stores owned and managed by the same firm.

Channel captain   a manager who helps direct the activities of a whole channel and tries to avoid—or solve—channel conflicts.

Channel of distribution   any series of firms or individuals who participate in the flow of goods and services from producer to final user or consumer.

Close   the salesperson's request for an order.

Clustering techniques   approaches used to try to find similar patterns within sets of data.

Combination export manager   a blend of manufacturers' agent and selling agent—handling the entire export function for several producers of similar but noncompeting lines.

Combined target market approach   combining two or more submarkets into one larger target market as a basis for one strategy.

Combiners   firms that try to increase the size of their target markets by combining two or more segments.

Commission merchants   agent middlemen who handle products shipped to them by sellers, complete the sale, and send the money (minus their commission) to each seller.

Communication process   a source trying to reach a receiver with a message.

Community shopping centers   planned shopping centers that offer some shopping stores as well as convenience stores.

Comparative advertising   advertising that makes specific brand comparisons using actual product names.

Competitive advantage   means that a firm has a marketing mix that the target market sees as better than a competitor's mix.

Competitive advertising   advertising that tries to develop demand for a specific brand rather than a product category.

Competitive barriers   the conditions that may make it difficult, or even impossible, for a firm to compete in a market.

Competitive bids   the terms of sale offered by different suppliers in response to the buyer's purchase specifications.

Competitive environment   the number and types of competitors the marketing manager must face, and how they may behave.

Competitor analysis   an organized approach for evaluating the strengths and weaknesses of current or potential competitors' marketing strategies.

Complementary product pricing   setting prices on several related products as a group.

Components   processed expense items that become part of a finished product.

Concept testing   getting reactions from customers about how well a new product idea fits their needs.

Consultative selling approach   a type of sales presentation in which the salesperson develops a good understanding of the individual customer's needs before trying to close the sale.

Consumer panel   a group of consumers who provide information on a continuing basis.

Consumer Product Safety Act   a 1972 law that set up the Consumer Product Safety Commission to encourage more awareness of safety in product design—and better quality control.

Consumer products   products meant for the final consumer.

Consumer surplus   the difference to consumers between the value of a purchase and the price they pay.

Consumerism   a social movement that seeks to increase the rights and powers of consumers.

Containerization   grouping individual items into an economical shipping quantity and sealing them in protective containers for transit to the final destination.

Continuous improvement   a commitment to constantly make things better one step at a time.

Contractual channel systems   channel members agree by contract to cooperate with each other.

Convenience (food) stores   a convenience-oriented variation of the conventional limited-line food stores.

Convenience products   products a consumer needs but isn't willing to spend much time or effort shopping for.

Convenience store a convenient place to shop—either centrally located near other shopping or "in the neighborhood."

Cooperative advertising middlemen and producers sharing in the cost of ads.

Cooperative chains retailer-sponsored groups, formed by independent retailers, to run their own buying organizations and conduct joint promotion efforts.

Copy thrust what the words and illustrations of an ad should communicate.

Corporate chain store one of several stores owned and managed by the same firm.

Corporate channel systems corporate ownership all along the channel.

Corrective advertising ads to correct deceptive advertising.

Cost of sales total value (at cost) of the sales during the period.

Countertrade a special type of bartering in which products from one country are traded for products from another country.

Cues products, signs, ads, and other stimuli in the environment.

Cultural and social environment affects how and why people live and behave as they do.

Culture the whole set of beliefs, attitudes, and ways of doing things of a reasonably homogeneous set of people.

Cumulative quantity discounts reductions in price for larger purchases over a given period, such as a year.

Customer service level how rapidly and dependably a firm can deliver what customers want.

Dealer brands brands created by middlemen.

Decision support system (DSS) a computer program that makes it easy for marketing managers to get and use information *as they are making decisions*.

Decoding the receiver in the communication process translating the message.

Demand-backward pricing setting an acceptable final consumer price and working backward to what a producer can charge.

Demand curve a graph of the relationship between price and quantity demanded in a market—assuming that all other things stay the same.

Department stores larger stores that are organized into many separate departments and offer many product lines.

Derived demand demand for business products derived from the demand for final consumer products.

Description (specification) buying buying from a written (or verbal) description of the product.

Determining dimensions the dimensions that actually affect the customer's purchase of a *specific* product or brand in a *product-market*.

Direct marketing direct communication between a seller and an individual customer using a promotion method other than face-to-face personal selling.

Direct type advertising competitive advertising that aims for immediate buying action.

Discount houses stores that sell "hard goods" (cameras, TVs, appliances) at substantial price cuts.

Discounts reductions from list price that are given by a seller to a buyer who either gives up some marketing function or provides the function himself.

Discrepancy of assortment the difference between the lines a typical producer makes and the assortment wanted by final consumers or users.

Discrepancy of quantity the difference between the quantity of products it is economical for a producer to make and the quantity normally wanted by final users or consumers.

Discretionary income what is left of income after paying taxes and paying for necessities.

Dissonance tension caused by uncertainty about the rightness of a decision.

Distribution center a special kind of warehouse designed to speed the flow of goods and avoid unnecessary storing costs.

Diversification moving into totally different lines of business—which may include entirely unfamiliar products, markets, or even levels in the production-marketing system.

Diversion in transit redirection of railroad carloads already in transit.

Door-to-door selling going directly to the consumer's home.

Drive a strong stimulus that encourages action to reduce a need.

Drop-shippers wholesalers who take title to the products they sell—but do not actually handle, stock, or deliver them.

Dual distribution when a producer uses several competing channels to reach the same target market.

Dumping pricing a product sold in a foreign market below the cost of producing it or at a price lower than in its domestic market.

Early adopters the second group in the adoption curve to adopt a new product, these people are usually well respected by their peers and often are opinion leaders.

Early majority a group in the adoption curve that avoids risk and waits to consider a new idea after many early adopters have tried it—and liked it.

Economic and technological environment affects the way firms and the whole economy use resources.

Economic buyers people who know the facts and logically compare choices in terms of cost and value received—to get the greatest satisfaction from spending their time and money.

Economic needs needs concerned with making the best use of a consumer's time and money—as the consumer sees it.

Economic system the way an economy organizes to use scarce resources to produce goods and services and distribute them for consumption by various people and groups in the society.

Economies of scale as a company produces larger numbers of a particular product, the cost for each of these products goes down.

Elastic demand if prices are dropped, the quantity demanded will stretch enough to increase total revenue.

Elastic supply the quantity supplied does stretch more if the price is raised.

Electronic data interchange (EDI) an approach which puts information in a standardized format that can be easily shared between different computer systems.

Emergency products products that are purchased immediately when the need is great.

Empowerment giving employees the authority to correct a problem without first checking with management.

Empty nesters people whose children are grown and who are now able to spend their money in other ways.

Encoding the source in the communication process deciding what it wants to say and translating it into words or symbols that will have the same meaning to the receiver.

Equilibrium point the quantity and the price sellers are willing to offer are equal to the quantity and price that buyers are willing to accept.

Everyday low pricing setting a low list price rather than relying on frequent discounts or allowances from a high list price.

Exclusive distribution selling through only one middleman in a particular geographic area.

Expense item a product whose total cost is treated as a business expense in the period when it is purchased.

Expenses all the remaining costs that are subtracted from the gross margin to get the net profit.

Experimental method a research approach in which researchers compare the responses of groups that are similar, except on the characteristic being tested.

Export agents manufacturers' agents who specialize in export trade.

Export brokers brokers in international marketing.

Export commission houses brokers in international trade.

Extensive problem solving the type of problem solving involved when a need is completely new or important to a consumer and much effort is taken to decide how to satisfy the need.

Facilitators firms that provide one or more of the marketing functions other than buying or selling.

Factor a variable that shows the relation of some other variable to the item being forecast.

Factor method an approach to forecast sales by finding a relation between the company's sales and some other factor (or factors).

Family brand a brand name that is used for several products.

Farm products products grown by farmers, such as oranges, wheat, sugar cane, cattle, poultry, eggs, and milk.

Fashion currently accepted or popular style.

Federal Fair Packaging and Labeling Act a 1966 law requiring that consumer goods be clearly labeled in easy-to-understand terms.

Federal Trade Commission (FTC) federal government agency that polices antimonopoly laws.

Financing provides the necessary cash and credit to produce, transport, store, promote, sell, and buy products.

Fishbone diagram a visual aid that helps to organize cause and effect relationships for "things gone wrong."

Flexible-price policy offering the same product and quantities to different customers at different prices.

F.O.B. a transportation term that means "free on board" some vehicle at some point.

Focus group interview an interview of 6 to 10 people in an informal group setting.

Foreign Corrupt Practices Act a law passed by the U.S. Congress in 1977 that prohibits U.S. firms from paying bribes to foreign officials.

Form utility provided when someone produces something tangible.

Franchise operation a franchisor develops a good marketing strategy, and the retail franchise holders carry out the strategy in their own units.

Freight absorption pricing absorbing freight cost so that a firm's delivered price meets the price of the nearest competitor's.

Full-line pricing setting prices for a whole line of products.

General merchandise wholesalers service wholesalers who carry a wide variety of nonperishable items such as hardware, electrical supplies, plumbing supplies, furniture, drugs, cosmetics, and automobile equipment.

General stores early retailers who carried anything they could sell in reasonable volume.

Generic market a market with *broadly* similar needs—and sellers offering various and *often diverse* ways of satisfying those needs.

Generic products have no brand at all other than identification of their contents and the manufacturer or middleman.

Gross margin (gross profit) the money left to cover the expenses of selling the products and operating the business.

Gross national product (GNP) the total market value of goods and services produced in a year.

Gross sales the total amount charged to all customers during some time period.

Heterogeneous shopping products shopping products that the customer sees as different—and wants to inspect for quality and suitability.

Homogeneous shopping products shopping products that the customer sees as basically the same—and wants at the lowest price.

Hypermarket very large store that tries to carry, not only foods, but all goods and services the consumer purchases *routinely* (also called superstore).

Hypotheses educated guesses about the relationships between things or what will happen in the future.

Ideal market exposure when a product is widely enough available to satisfy target customers' needs—but not to exceed them.

Implementation putting marketing plans into operation.

Import agents manufacturers' agents who specialize in import trade.

Import brokers brokers in international marketing.

Import commission houses brokers in international trade.

Impulse products products that are bought quickly as *unplanned* purchases because of a strongly felt need.

Indirect type advertising competitive advertising that points out product advantages—to affect future buying decisions.

Individual brands separate brand names used for each product.

Inelastic demand the quantity demanded would increase if the price were decreased, but the quantity demanded would not "stretch" enough to avoid a decrease in total revenue.

Inelastic supply the quantity supplied does not stretch much (if at all) if the price is raised.

Innovation the development and spread of new ideas and products.

Innovators the first group to adopt new products.

Inspection buying looking at every item.

Installations important capital items such as buildings, land rights, and major equipment.

Institutional advertising advertising that tries to promote an organization's image, reputation or ideas—rather than a specific product.

Intensive distribution selling a product through all responsible and suitable wholesalers or retailers who will stock and/or sell the product.

Introductory price dealing temporary price cuts to speed new products into a market.

Inventory the amount of goods being stored.

Job description a written statement of what a salesperson is expected to do.

Jury of executive opinion forecasting by combining the opinions of experienced executives—perhaps from marketing, production, finance, purchasing, and top management.

Just-in-time delivery reliably getting products to the customer *just* before the customer needs them.

Laggards prefer to do things the way they have been done in the past and are very suspicious of new ideas—sometimes called nonadopters—see *adoption curve*.

Late majority a group of adopters who are cautious about new ideas—see *adoption curve*.

Law of diminishing demand if the price of a product is raised, a smaller quantity will be demanded—and if the price of a product is lowered, a greater quantity will be demanded.

Leader pricing setting very low prices on some products to get customers into retail stores.

Learning a change in a person's thought processes caused by prior experience.

Licensed brand well-known brand that sellers pay a fee to use.

Life-style analysis the analysis of a person's day-to-day pattern of living as expressed in his or her *A*ctivities, *I*nterests, and *O*pinions—sometimes referred to as AIOs or psychographics.

Limited-function wholesalers merchant wholesalers who provide only *some* wholesaling functions.

Limited-line stores stores that specialize in certain lines of related products rather than a wide assortment—sometimes called single-line stores.

Limited problem solving when a consumer is willing to put *some* effort into deciding the best way to satisfy a need.

Logistics the transporting and storing of goods so as to match target customers' needs with a firm's marketing mix—within individual firms and along a channel of distribution (i.e., another name for physical distribution).

Low-involvement purchases purchases that do not have high personal importance or relevance for the customer.

Macro-marketing a social process that directs an economy's flow of goods and services from producers to consumers in a way that effectively matches supply and demand and accomplishes the objectives of society.

Magnuson-Moss Act a 1975 law requiring that producers provide a clearly written warranty if they choose to offer any warranty.

Mail-order wholesalers sell out of catalogs that may be distributed widely to smaller industrial customers or retailers.

Major accounts sales force salespeople who sell directly to large accounts such as major retail chain stores.

Manufacturer brands brands created by manufacturers.

Manufacturers' agents agent middlemen who sell similar products for several noncompeting producers for a commission on what is actually sold.

Manufacturers' sales branches separate businesses that producers set up away from their factories.

Markdown a retail price reduction that is required because customers won't buy some item at the originally marked-up price.

Markdown ratio a tool used by many retailers to measure the efficiency of various departments and their whole business.

Market a group of potential customers with similar needs and sellers offering various products—that is, ways of satisfying those needs *or* a group of sellers and buyers who are willing to exchange goods and/or services for something of value.

Market development trying to increase sales by selling present products in new markets.

Market-directed economic system the individual decisions of the many producers and consumers make the macro-level decisions for the whole economy.

Market growth a stage of the product life cycle when industry sales are growing fast—but industry profits rise and then start falling.

Market information function the collection, analysis, and distribution of all the information needed to plan, carry out, and control marketing activities.

Market introduction a stage of the product life cycle when sales are low as a new idea is first introduced to a market.

Market maturity a stage of the product life cycle when industry sales level off—and competition gets tougher.

Market penetration trying to increase sales of a firm's present products in its present markets—usually through a more aggressive marketing mix.

Market potential what a whole market segment might buy.

Market segment a relatively homogeneous group of customers who will respond to a marketing mix in a similar way.

Market segmentation a two-step process of (1) *naming* broad product-markets and (2) *segmenting* these broad product-markets in order to select target markets and develop suitable marketing mixes.

Marketing company era a time when, in addition to short-run marketing planning, marketing people develop long-range plans—sometimes 10 or more years ahead—and the whole company effort is guided by the marketing concept.

Marketing concept the idea that an organization should aim *all* its efforts at satisfying its *customers*—at a *profit.*

Marketing department era a time when all marketing activities are brought under the control of one department to improve short-run policy planning and to try to integrate the firm's activities.

Marketing ethics the moral standards that guide marketing decisions and actions.

Marketing information system (MIS) an organized way of continually gathering and analyzing data to provide marketing managers with information they need to make decisions.

Marketing management process the process of (1) *planning* marketing activities, (2) directing the *implementation* of the plans, and (3) *controlling* these plans.

Marketing mix the controllable variables that the company puts together to satisfy a target group.

Marketing model a statement of relationships among marketing variables.

Marketing orientation trying to carry out the marketing concept.

Marketing plan a written statement of a marketing strategy *and* the time-related details for carrying out the strategy.

Marketing program blends all of the firm's marketing plans into one "big" plan.

Marketing research procedures to develop and analyze new information to help marketing managers make decisions.

Marketing research process a five-step application of the scientific method that includes (1) defining the problem, (2) analyzing the situation, (3) getting problem-specific information, (4) interpreting the data, and (5) solving the problem.

Marketing strategy specifies a target market and a related marketing mix.

Markup a dollar amount added to the cost of products to get the selling price.

Markup chain the sequence of markups used by firms at different levels in a channel—determining the price structure in the whole channel.

Markup (percent) the percentage of selling price that is added to the cost to get the selling price.

Mass marketing the typical production-oriented approach that vaguely aims at "everyone" with the same marketing mix.

Mass-merchandisers large, self-service stores with many departments that emphasize "soft goods" (housewares, clothing, and fabrics) and selling on lower margins to get faster turnover.

Mass-merchandising concept the idea that retailers can get faster turnover and greater sales volume by charging lower prices that will appeal to larger markets.

Mass selling communicating with large numbers of potential customers at the same time.

Merchant wholesalers wholesalers who own (take title to) the products they sell.

Message channel the carrier of the message.

Metropolitan Statistical Area (MSA) an integrated economic and social unit with a large population nucleus.

Micro-macro dilemma what is "good" for some producers and consumers may not be good for society as a whole.

Micro-marketing the performance of activities that seek to accomplish an organization's objectives by anticipating customer or client needs and directing a flow of need-satisfying goods and services from producer to customer or client.

Middleman someone who specializes in trade rather than production.

Missionary salespeople supporting salespeople who work for producers by calling on their middlemen and their customers.

Modified rebuy the in-between process where some review of the buying situation is done—though not as much as in new-task buying or as little as in straight rebuys.

Monopolistic competition a market situation that develops when a market has (1) different products and (2) sellers who feel they do have some competition in this market.

Multiple buying influence the buyer shares the purchasing decision with several people—perhaps even top management.

Multiple target market approach segmenting the market and choosing two or more segments, each of which will be treated as a separate target market needing a different marketing mix.

Nationalism an emphasis on a country's interests before everything else.

Natural products products that occur in nature—such as fish and game, timber and maple syrup, and copper, zinc, iron ore, oil, and coal.

Needs the basic forces that motivate a person to do something.

Negotiated contract buying agreeing to a contract that allows for changing the purchase arrangements.

Negotiated price a price set based on bargaining between the buyer and seller.

Neighborhood shopping centers planned shopping centers that consist of several convenience stores.

Net an invoice term that means that payment for the face value of the invoice is due immediately—also see *cash discounts*.

Net profit what the company has earned from its operations during a particular period.

Net sales sales dollars the company will receive.

New product a product that is new *in any way* for the company concerned.

New-task buying when a firm has a new need and the buyer wants a great deal of information.

New unsought products products offering really new ideas that potential customers don't know about yet.

Noise any distraction that reduces the effectiveness of the communication process.

Nonadopters prefer to do things the way they have been done in the past and are very suspicious of new ideas—sometimes called laggards—see *adoption curve.*

Noncumulative quantity discounts reductions in price when a customer purchases a larger quantity on an *individual order*.

Nonprice competition aggressive action on one or more of the Ps other than Price.

Odd-even pricing setting prices that end in certain numbers.

Oligopoly a special market situation that develops when a market has (1) essentially homogeneous products, (2) relatively few sellers, and (3) fairly inelastic industry demand curves.

One-price policy offering the same price to all customers who purchase products under essentially the same conditions and in the same quantities.

Open to buy a buyer has budgeted funds that he can spend during the current time period.

Operating ratios ratios of items on the operating statement to net sales.

Operating statement a simple summary of the financial results of the operations of a company over a specified period of time.

Opinion leader a person who influences others.

Order getters salespeople concerned with getting new business.

Order getting seeking possible buyers with a well-organized sales presentation designed to sell a product, service, or idea.

Order takers salespeople who sell the regular or typical customers.

Order taking the routine completion of sales made regularly to the target customers.

Packaging promoting and protecting the product.

Pareto chart a graph that shows the number of times a cause of a problem occurs, with problem causes ordered from most frequent to least frequent.

Penetration pricing policy trying to sell the whole market at one low price.

Perception how we gather and interpret information from the world around us.

Personal needs an individual's need for personal satisfaction unrelated to what others think or do.

Personal selling direct communication between a seller and a potential customer, usually in person but sometimes over the telephone.

Phony list prices misleading prices that customers are shown to suggest that the price they are to pay has been discounted from "list."

Physical distribution (PD) the transporting and storing of goods so as to match target customers' needs with a firm's marketing mix—within individual firms and along a channel of distribution.

Physical distribution (PD) concept all transporting and storing activities of a business and a channel system should be coordinated as one system—which should seek to minimize the cost of distribution for a given customer service level.

Physiological needs biological needs such as the need for food, drink, rest, and sex.

Pioneering advertising advertising that tries to develop primary demand for a product category rather than a specific brand.

Place making products available in the right quantities and locations—when customers want them.

Place utility having the product available *where* the customer wants it.

Planned economic system government planners decide what and how much is to be produced and distributed by whom, when, and to whom.

Planned shopping center a set of stores planned as a unit to satisfy some market needs.

Population in marketing research, the total group you are interested in.

Positioning shows where customers locate proposed and/or present brands in a market.

Possession utility obtaining a product and having the right to use or consume it.

Prepared sales presentation a memorized presentation that is not adapted to each individual customer.

Prestige pricing setting a rather high price to suggest high quality or high status.

Price what is charged for "something."

Price discrimination injuring competition by selling the same products to different buyers at different prices.

Price fixing sellers illegally getting together to raise, lower, or stabilize prices.

Price lining setting a few price levels for a product line and then marking all items at these prices.

Primary data information specifically collected to solve a current problem.

Primary demand demand for the general product idea, not just the company's own brand.

Private brands brands created by middlemen.

Private warehouses storing facilities owned or leased by companies for their own use.

Producers' cooperatives operate almost as full-service wholesalers—with the "profits" going to the cooperative's customer-members.

Product the need-satisfying offering of a firm.

Product advertising advertising that tries to sell a specific product.

Product-bundle pricing setting one price for a set of products.

Product development offering new or improved products for present markets.

Product liability the legal obligation of sellers to pay damages to individuals who are injured by defective or unsafe products.

Product life cycle the stages a new product idea goes through from beginning to end.

Product managers manage specific products, often taking over the jobs formerly handled by an advertising manager—sometimes called brand managers.

Product-market a market with *very* similar needs—and sellers offering various *close substitute* ways of satisfying those needs.

Production actually *making* goods or *performing* services.

Production era a time when a company focuses on production of a few specific products—perhaps because few of these products are available in the market.

Production orientation making whatever products are easy to produce and *then* trying to sell them.

Professional services specialized services that support the operations of a firm.

Profit maximization objective an objective to get as much profit as possible.

Promotion communicating information between seller and potential buyer to influence attitudes and behavior.

Prospecting following down all the "leads" in the target market to identify potential customers.

Psychographics the analysis of a person's day-to-day pattern of living as expressed in his *A*ctivities, *I*nterests,

and *O*pinions—sometimes referred to as AIOs or life-style analysis.

Psychological pricing setting prices that have special appeal to target customers.

Public relations communication with noncustomers—including labor, public interest groups, stockholders, and the government.

Public warehouses independent storing facilities.

Publicity any *unpaid* form of nonpersonal presentation of ideas, goods, or services.

Pulling using promotion to get consumers to ask middlemen for the product.

Purchase discount a reduction of the original invoice amount for some business reason.

Purchasing agents buying specialists for their employers.

Pure competition a market situation that develops when a market has (1) homogeneous products, (2) many buyers and sellers who have full knowledge of the market, and (3) ease of entry for buyers and sellers.

Pure subsistence economy each family unit produces everything it consumes.

Push money (or prize money) allowances allowances (sometimes called "PMs" or "spiffs") given to retailers by manufacturers or wholesalers to pass on to the retailers' sales-clerks for aggressively selling certain items.

Pushing using normal promotion effort—personal selling, advertising, and sales promotion—to help sell the whole marketing mix to possible channel members.

Qualifying dimensions the dimensions that are relevant to including a customer type in a product-market.

Qualitative research seeks in-depth, open-ended responses.

Quality the ability of a product to satisfy a customer's needs or requirements.

Quantitative research seeks structured responses that can be summarized in numbers—like percentages, averages, or other statistics.

Quantity discounts discounts offered to encourage customers to buy in larger amounts.

Quotas the specific quantities of products that can move in or out of a country.

Rack jobbers merchant wholesalers who specialize in non-food products that are sold through grocery stores and supermarkets—and they often display them on their own wire racks.

Raw materials unprocessed expense items—such as logs, iron ore, wheat, and cotton—that are handled as little as needed to move them to the next production process.

Rebates refunds to consumers after a purchase has been made.

Receiver the target of a message in the communication process, usually a customer.

Reciprocity   trading sales for sales—that is, "if you buy from me, I'll buy from you."

Reference group   the people to whom an individual looks when forming attitudes about a particular topic.

Reference price   the price that a consumer expects to pay.

Regional shopping centers   large, planned shopping centers that emphasize shopping stores and shopping products.

Regrouping activities   adjusting the quantities and/or assortments of products handled at each level in a channel of distribution.

Regularly unsought products   products that stay unsought but not unbought forever.

Reinforcement   occurs in the learning process when the consumer's response is followed by satisfaction—that is, reducing the drive.

Reminder advertising   advertising to keep the product's name before the public.

Requisition   a request to buy something.

Research proposal   a plan that specifies what marketing research information will be obtained and how.

Resident buyers   independent buying agents who work in central markets for several retailer or wholesaler customers from outlying areas.

Response   an effort to satisfy a drive.

Response rate   the percent of people contacted in a research sample who complete the questionnaire.

Retailing   all of the activities involved in the sale of products to final consumers.

Return   when a customer sends back purchased products.

Return on assets (ROA)   the ratio of net profit (after taxes) to the assets used to make the net profit—multiplied by 100 to get rid of decimals.

Return on investment (ROI)   ratio of net profit (after taxes) to the investment used to make the net profit—multiplied by 100 to get rid of decimals.

Reverse channels   channels used to retrieve products that customers no longer want.

Risk taking   bearing the uncertainties that are part of the marketing process.

Robinson-Patman Act   a 1936 law that makes illegal any price discrimination—i.e., selling the same products to different buyers at different prices—if it injures competition.

Routinized response behavior   regularly selecting a particular way of satisfying a need when it occurs.

Safety needs   needs concerned with protection and physical well-being.

Sale price   a temporary discount from the list price.

Sales decline   a stage of the product life cycle when new products replace the old.

Sales era   a time when a company emphasizes selling because of increased competition.

Sales forecast   an estimate of how much an industry or firm hopes to sell to a market segment.

Sales managers   managers concerned with managing personal selling.

Sales-oriented objective   an objective to get some level of unit sales, dollar sales, or share of market—without referring to profit.

Sales presentation   a salesperson's effort to make a sale.

Sales promotion   promotion activities—other than advertising, publicity, and personal selling—that stimulate interest, trial, or purchase by final customers or others in the channel.

Sales promotion managers   managers of their company's sales promotion effort.

Sales quota   the specific sales or profit objective a salesperson is expected to achieve.

Sales territory   a geographic area that is the responsibility of one salesperson or several working together.

Sample   a part of the relevant population.

Sampling buying   looking at only part of a potential purchase.

Scientific method   a decision-making approach that focuses on being objective and orderly in *testing* ideas before accepting them.

Scrambled merchandising   retailers carrying any product lines that they think they can sell profitably.

Seasonal discounts   discounts offered to encourage buyers to stock earlier than present demand requires.

Secondary data   information that has been collected or published already.

Segmenters   aim at one or more homogeneous segments and try to develop a different marketing mix for each segment.

Segmenting   an aggregating process that clusters together people with similar needs into a market segment.

Selective demand   demand for a specific brand rather than a product category.

Selective distribution   selling through only those middlemen who will give the product special attention.

Selective exposure   our eyes and minds seek out and notice only information that interests us.

Selective perception   people screen out or modify ideas, messages, and information that conflict with previously learned attitudes and beliefs.

Selective retention   people remember only what they want to remember.

Selling agents   agent middlemen who take over the whole marketing job of producers—not just the selling function.

Selling formula approach   a sales presentation that starts with a prepared presentation outline, gets customers to discuss needs, and then leads the customer through some logical steps to a final close.

Selling function   promoting the product.

Service   a deed performed by one party for another.

Service mark   those words, symbols, or marks that are legally registered for use by a single company to refer to a service offering.

Service wholesalers   merchant wholesalers who provide all the wholesaling functions.

Shopping products   products that a customer feels are worth the time and effort to compare with competing products.

Shopping stores   stores that attract customers from greater distances because of the width and depth of their assortments.

Single-line (or general-line) wholesalers   service wholesalers who carry a narrower line of merchandise than general merchandise wholesalers.

Single-line stores   stores that specialize in certain lines of related products rather than a wide assortment—sometimes called limited-line stores.

Single target market approach   segmenting the market and picking one of the homogeneous segments as the firm's target market.

Situation analysis   an informal study of what information is already available in the problem area.

Skimming price policy   trying to sell the top of the demand curve at a high price before aiming at more price-sensitive customers.

Social class   a group of people who have approximately equal social position as viewed by others in the society.

Social needs   needs concerned with love, friendship, status, and esteem—things that involve a person's interaction with others.

Social responsibility   a firm's obligation to improve its positive effects on society and reduce its negative effects.

Sorting   separating products into grades and qualities desired by different target markets.

Source   the sender of a message.

Specialty products   consumer products that the customer really wants and is willing to make a special effort to find.

Specialty shop   a type of limited-line store—usually small and with a distinct "personality."

Specialty stores   stores for which customers have developed a strong attraction.

Specialty wholesalers   service wholesalers who carry a very narrow range of products and offer more information and service than other service wholesalers.

Standard Industrial Classification (SIC) codes   codes used to identify groups of firms in similar lines of business.

Standardization and grading   sorting products according to size and quality.

Staples   products that are bought often and routinely—without much thought.

Statistical packages   easy-to-use computer programs that analyze data.

Status quo objectives   "don't-rock-the-*pricing*-boat" objectives.

Stocking allowances   allowances given to middlemen to get shelf space for a product—sometimes called slotting allowances.

Stockturn rate   the number of times the average inventory is sold in a year.

Storing   the marketing function of holding goods.

Storing function   holding goods until customers need them.

Straight rebuy   a routine repurchase that may have been made many times before.

Strategic (management) planning   the managerial process of developing and maintaining a match between the resources of an organization and its market opportunities.

Substitutes   products that offer the buyer a choice.

Supermarket   a large store specializing in groceries—with self-service and wide assortments.

Superstore   very large store that tries to carry, not only foods, but all goods and services the consumer purchases *routinely* (also called hypermarket).

Supplies   expense items that do not become a part of a finished product.

Supply curve   the quantity of products that will be supplied at various possible prices.

Supporting salespeople   salespeople who support the order-oriented salespeople—but don't try to get orders themselves.

Target market   a fairly homogeneous (similar) group of customers to whom a company wishes to appeal.

Target marketing   a marketing mix is tailored to fit some specific target customers.

Target return objective   a specific level of profit as an objective.

Tariffs   taxes on imported products.

Task utility   provided when someone performs a task for someone else—for instance, when a bank handles financial transactions.

Team selling   different sales reps working together on a specific account.

Technical specialists   supporting salespeople who provide technical assistance to order-oriented salespeople.

Technological base   the technical skills and equipment that affect the way the resources of an economy are converted to output.

Telemarketing   using the telephone to "call" on customers or prospects.

Telephone and direct-mail retailing   allows consumers to shop at home—usually placing orders by mail or a toll-free long distance telephone call and charging the purchase to a credit card.

Time utility   having the product available *when* the customer wants it.

Total cost   the sum of total fixed and total variable costs.

Total cost approach evaluating each possible PD system and identifying *all* of the costs of each alternative.

Total fixed cost the sum of those costs that are fixed in total—no matter how much is produced.

Total quality management (TQM) a management approach in which everyone in the organization is concerned about quality, throughout all of the firm's activities, to better serve customer needs.

Total variable cost the sum of those changing expenses that are closely related to output—such as expenses for parts, wages, packaging materials, outgoing freight, and sales commissions.

Trade (functional) discount a list price reduction given to channel members for the job they're going to do.

Trade-in allowance a price reduction given for used products when similar new products are bought.

Trademark those words, symbols, or marks that are legally registered for use by a single company.

Traditional channel systems a channel in which the various channel members make little or no effort to cooperate with each other.

Transporting the marketing function of moving goods.

Transporting function the movement of goods from one place to another.

Trend extension extends past experience to predict the future.

Truck wholesalers wholesalers who specialize in delivering products that they stock in their own trucks.

2/10, net 30 means that a 2 percent discount off the face value of the invoice is allowed if the invoice is paid within 10 days.

Unfair trade practice acts set a lower limit on prices, especially at the wholesale and retail levels.

Uniform delivered pricing making an average freight charge to all buyers.

Unit-pricing placing the price per ounce (or some other standard measure) on or near the product.

Universal functions of marketing buying, selling, transporting, storing, standardizing and grading, financing, risk taking, and market information.

Universal product code (UPC) special identifying marks for each product that can be "read" by electronic scanners.

Unsought products products that potential customers don't yet want or know they can buy.

Utility the power to satisfy human needs.

Validity the extent to which data measures what it is intended to measure.

Value in use pricing setting prices that will capture some of what customers will save by substituting the firm's product for the one currently being used.

Value pricing setting a fair price level for a marketing mix that really gives customers what they need.

Vendor analysis formal rating of suppliers on all relevant areas of performance.

Vertical integration acquiring firms at different levels of channel activity.

Vertical marketing systems a whole channel focuses on the same target market at the end of the channel.

Voluntary chains wholesaler-sponsored groups that work with "independent" retailers.

Wants "needs" that are learned during a person's life.

Warranty what the seller promises about its product.

Wheel of retailing theory new types of retailers enter the market as low-status, low-margin, low-price operators and then—if they are successful—evolve into more-conventional retailers offering more services—with higher operating costs and higher prices.

Wheeler Lea Amendment law that bans unfair or deceptive acts in commerce.

Wholesalers firms whose main function is providing *wholesaling activities*.

Wholesaling the *activities* of those persons or establishments that sell to retailers and other merchants, and/or to industrial, institutional, and commercial users, but who do not sell in large amounts to final consumers.

Zone pricing making an average freight charge to all buyers within specific geographic areas.